Advanced Glassworking Techniques
An Enlightened Manuscript

Edward T. Schmid

Glass Mountain Press
Bellingham Washington

Y'know... there's not much preventing you from photocopying any or all parts of this book, despite our copywrite laws... except a guilty conscience and well... um... THE CURSE

THE CURSE

May all your glass check. May you suffer from inexplicable minor burns and cuts, and may all of your creative juices dry up like the Mojave Desert should you copy this book or reproduce it in any fashion without the written consent of the author.

ACKNOWLEDGEMENTS:

I would like to thank all the folks who have helped me each step of the way of this neverending odyssey. And especially ELENA ENOS for assistance, patience and support with this project and helping me see it to completion. Thank you everybody, thank ya' very much!

ADVANCED GLASSWORKING TECHNIQUES ©1997

I.S.B.N. 0-9638728-1-8

Library of Congress Catalog Card Number: 97-94639

Suggested Retail Price $32.95

GLASS MOUNTAIN PRESS*
BELLINGHAM, WASHINGTON

* Where we write books the old fashioned way - by hand!

Contact me @ Glass Mtn. Press*
927 Yew Street
Bellingham, WA.
98226
U.S.A.

(* This address is guaranteed for at least one year.)

Table of Contents

- Forward 4
- Introduction 5
- Back-2-Basics 7
- Teamwork 59
- Punties 83
- Color 94
- Venetian-Style Techniques 133
- Intro to Solidworking 212
- Moldblowing 227
- Special Techniques 241
- Resourceful Info 271
- Glossary 301
- Index 314

FORWARD

I MUST BE INSANE. WHAT WAS I THINKING? I MEAN, THIS BOOK IS A MONSTER. IT ENCOMPASSES FAR MORE THAN I EVER ANTICIPATED IT WOULD, WHICH TRANSLATES → MORE WORK FOR ME AND MORE INFO FOR YOU. IT TOOK ME THREE YEARS, WORKING ON & OFF, TO GET THIS THING TO THE STATE THAT YOU FIND IT IN NOW. (TIME THAT I WOULD'VE LOVED TO HAVE SPENT BLOWING GLASS...) IN ANY CASE...

THIS IS NOT A GOSPEL. NOR IS IT INTENDED TO BE. THERE MAY BE SOME INFORMATION PRESENTED THAT MAY BE DIFFERENT THAN WHAT YOU KNOW OR DO. SHOULD YOU COME ACCROSS PASSAGES WHICH ARE INACCURATE OR NOT EXPLAINED WELL ENOUGH, LET ME KNOW!

THIS IS YOUR BOOK. YOU MUST HELP ME, SO THAT I MAY IN TURN HELP YOU AND OTHERS. ALMOST ALL OF THIS INFORMATION IS FROM ME - THROUGH MY EYES - AND WHAT I HAVE EXPERIENCED IN THE PAST THIRTEEN YEARS OF GLASSWORKING, AND GLASS-RELATED RESEARCH. SOME OF THE TECHNIQUES COME FROM PERSONAL EXPERIENCE, OTHERS FROM DEMOS AND WATCHING THE MAESTROS, AND SOME FROM BOOTLEGGED VIDEOS TAKEN A FEW YEARS BACK BY WHO KNOWS WHO. **PLEASE CONTACT ME** AT THE ADDRESS IN THE FRONT OF THE BOOK WITH COMMENTS, CRITICISMS AND ANY ADDITIONS YOU'D LIKE TO SEE IN THE NEXT EDITION. I'LL REVIEW IT ALL AND UPDATE IT IN THE NEXT BOOK (SOMETIME IN THE NEXT MILLENNIUM).

Q. WHY DIDN'T I DO THIS ON A COMPUTER? I MEAN, LIKE, IT WOULD'VE, COULD'VE SAVED ME HOURS AND HOURS OF TIME AND BEEN SO MUCH EASIER... ...

A. WHY DON'T YOU JUST HAVE SOMEONE ELSE BLOW THE OBJECTS YOU WANT, SIGN YOUR NAME ON IT AND SAVE YOURSELF AN IMMENSE AMOUNT OF TIME N' FRUSTRATION?

IT'S ABOUT STYLE. IT'S ABOUT SUBTLETIES. IT'S ABOUT BEING HUMAN - AN INDIVIDUAL AND THE SELF-SERVING DESIRE (CALL IT PRIDE) TO DO THINGS YOUR WAY (OR "MY WAY"...). I MEAN, **YOU KNOW YOU'RE IN TROUBLE WHEN YOU NEED A MACHINE TO DRAW...** BESIDES, MOST COMPUTER-GENERATED IMAGES THAT I'VE SEEN ARE STERILE AND BORING (SURE, I COULD'VE SCANNED THE IMAGES/ILLUSTRATIONS IN... BUT... I DON'T HAVE A COMPUTER). I, FOR ONE, LIKE THE HANDMADE TOUCH, AND HOPE THAT YOU DO TOO.

FINALLY, I PITY THE FOOL THAT HAS TO DO EVERYTHING "BY-THE-BOOK", IN OTHER WORDS... LET THIS SERVE AS A REFERENCE, A STARTING POINT. COMBINE IT WITH YOUR OWN EXPERIENCE IN THE HOT SHOP. MIX OR MATCH TECHNIQUES TO SUIT YOUR OWN STYLE OR APPROACH. ABOVE ALL, HAVE THE GUTS TO DO IT YOUR WAY - THE WAY YOU LIKE IT. YOUR ARTISTIC VISION IS JUST THAT: YOURS, TO DO WITH WHICH EVER WAY YOU SEE FIT. LEARN THE LANGUAGE AND EXPRESS YOURSELF. PRACTICE, PERSEVERE, AND CONTINUE TO GROW - FURTHUR....

ASSORTED THOUGHTS FOR THE HOPELESSLY AFFLICTED:

GLASSBLOWING... 4 TIMES MORE ADDICTIVE THAN HEROIN OR CRACK COCAINE

INTRODUCTION

What have I gotten myself into? I'm not certain but it sure is a sticky mess!... ...Glassblowing is an incredible process. It's fun to watch and even more spectacular to do. You love it when it works, and be hatin' it when it doesn't. There are so many variables in glassblowing that you'd swear the stuff has a mind of its own. But it doesn't... you have to convince this amorphous molten goo to render a specific shape and stay that way for all eternity. But how do you go about doing that? Glad you asked...

This book begins with a review of the basics. Then it moves on to activities like teamwork, color applications, Venetian-style techniques and more advanced forms of glassblowing. I've tried to include as much information about the various techniques I know in such a format.

I'll show you how to make glass objects, not what to make. That's your part. And again, I can't stress enough the importance of drawing and research. Many of the techniques are hundreds of years old. Learn from them. 'Master' them as well as you can. Then, you can break with tradition and strive for something truly unique or contemporary.

It is up to you, the artist, to decide what it is that you want to make — via what technique, style, vocabulary and dialog you wish to address. You have to decide what it is that you want to say with your glass, how you need to present it and what type of audience will be viewing it.

Hot glass as an art material is demanding in the time and skill it takes in order to achieve predictable and desireable results. Some of you may delight in the ability to reproduce 15th century cristallo-ware, while others of you might like to try solid-sculpting a torso. I myself want more. I am more interested in applying these techniques to create a personal form of expression. In many ways, how people view your work is how they view you. Pull out all of the stops. Now's your chance to blow 'em away! Draw every day, and best of luck with the 'lava'.

Edward T. Schmid
August 11th 1997

> Glass is a liquid
> You must be fluid.
> Remember that...
> And you'll go far.

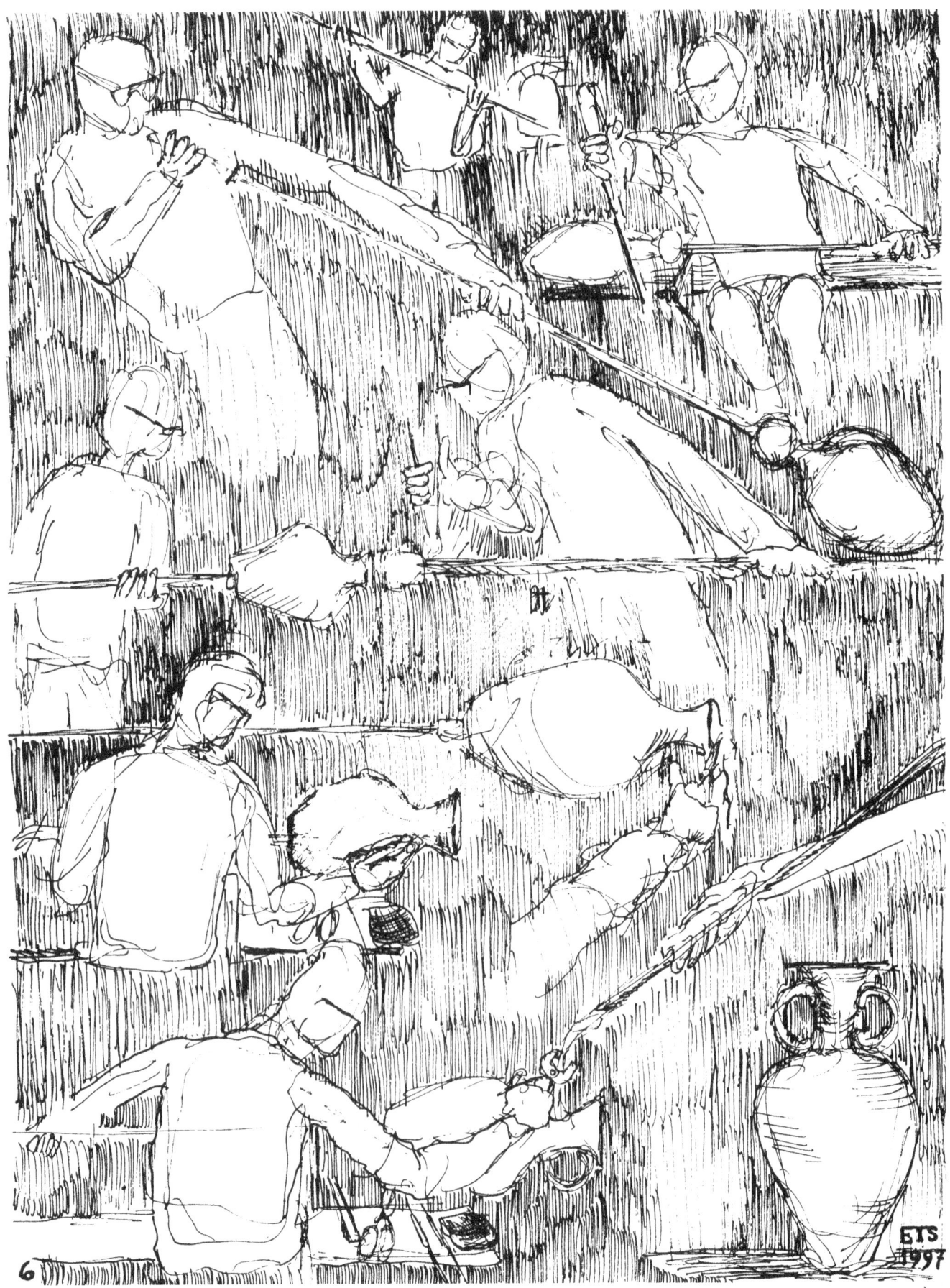

BACK-2-BASICS

- Intro, Directory of Forms ... 8
- Getting Started 11
- Design 13
- Gathering 14
- The Start 16
- Blow 'n Cap 18
- Blocking 19
- Marvering 21
- Papering 23
- Necking 25
- The Transfer 27
- Trimming 30
- Vases 34
- Bowls 36
- Feet 38
- Rondels 42
- Handles 44

BACK-2-BASICS

As good as anyplace to start → a review of techniques which should be second-nature to you as you embark into more advanced methods of working. My own observations of most beginning and intermediate glassblowers reveal that most work too cold and too slow, or better put → too slow thereby everything is too cool.   Economy of motion and maintaining fluidity & plasticity in your blown glass is essential to easier, swifter glassblowing.   Many students of glass become so engrossed in the PERFECT BUBBLE or executing absolutely perfect pieces that they sacrifice time better spent developing different or innovative approaches to working the glass.   I would rather see people 'PUSH THE ENVELOPE' of their blowing skills to work hotter and faster than struggle with cold, overworked pieces.

Review the following pages for information which might help you in executing your pieces with greater ease and swifter motions. Become versed in the tools, techniques and forms which are the fundamental building blocks to becoming a better glassblower. Train yourself like an ATHLETE trains for a sport: only through practice and repetition will your mind and body develop the skills and muscles to achieve your goal.   Remember also: **GRAVITY IS YOUR FRIEND, HOT GOOD - COLD BAD, AND YOU'RE DEALING WITH A LIQUID → YOU MUST BE FLUID.**

DIRECTORY OF BASIC BLOWN FORMS:

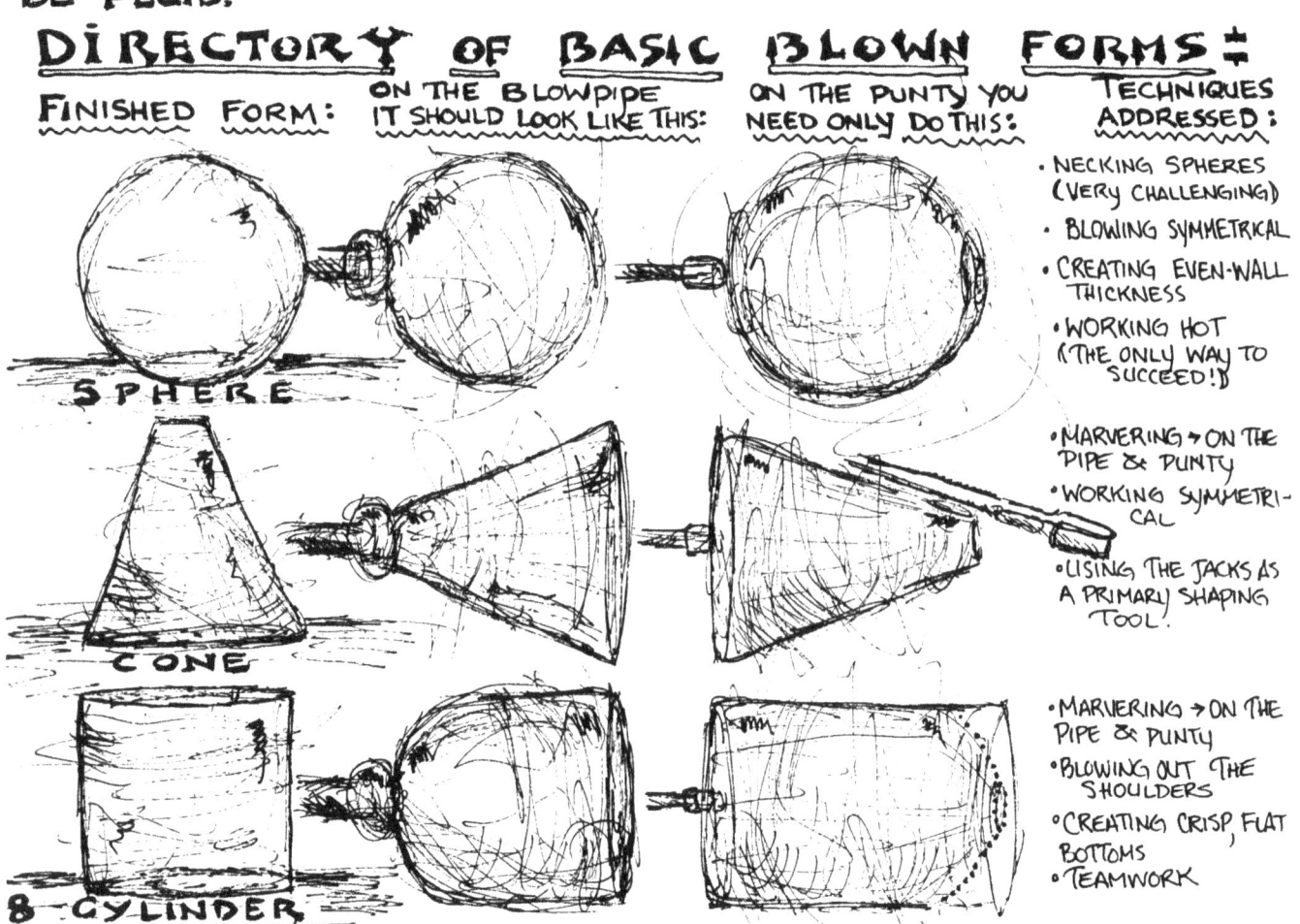

Finished Form: | **On the blowpipe it should look like this:** | **On the punty you need only do this:** | **Techniques Addressed:**

SPHERE
- Necking spheres (very challenging)
- Blowing symmetrical
- Creating even-wall thickness
- Working hot (the only way to succeed!)

CONE
- Marvering → on the pipe & punty
- Working symmetrical
- Using the jacks as a primary shaping tool

CYLINDER
- Marvering → on the pipe & punty
- Blowing out the shoulders
- Creating crisp, flat bottoms
- Teamwork

8

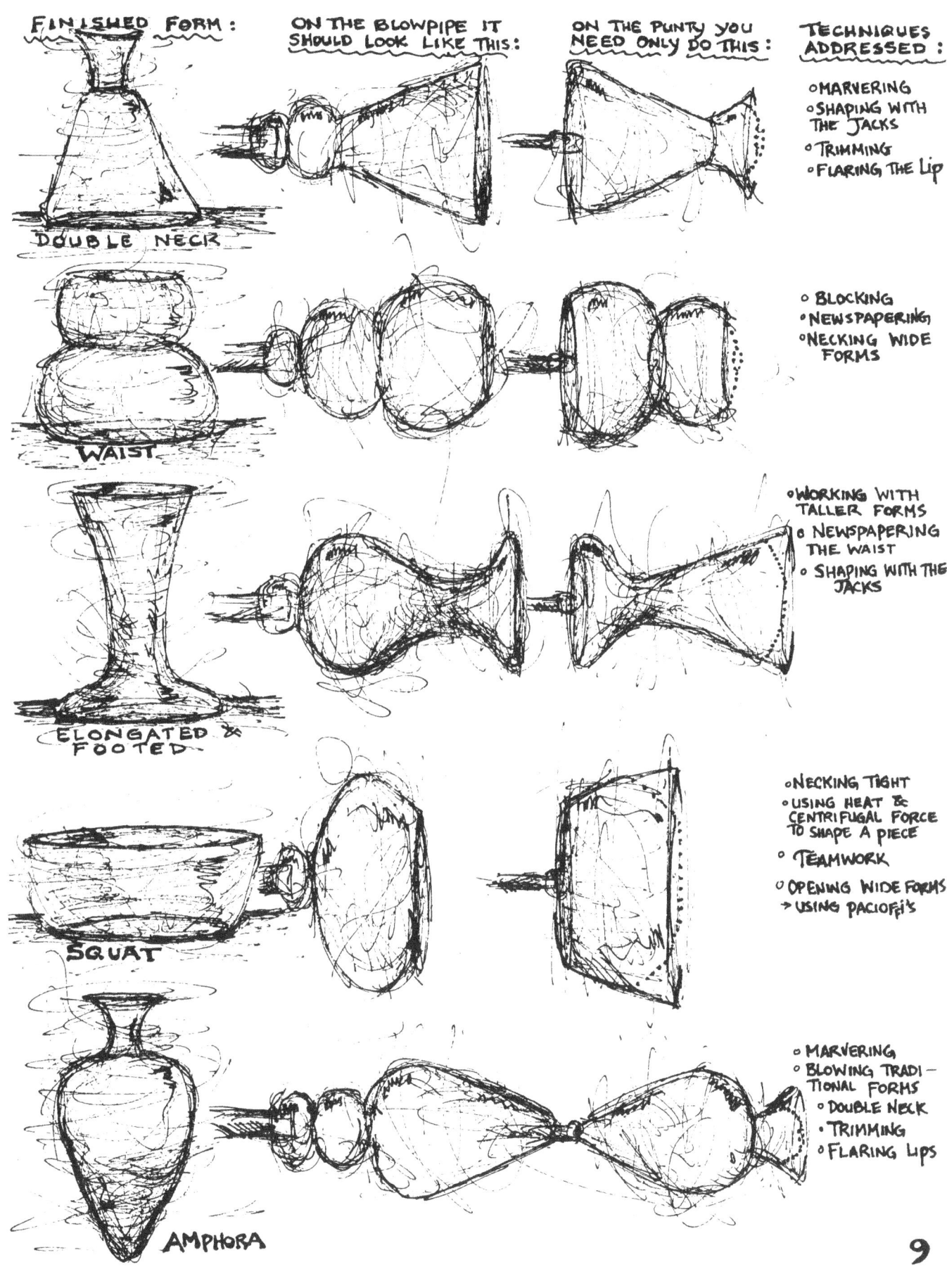

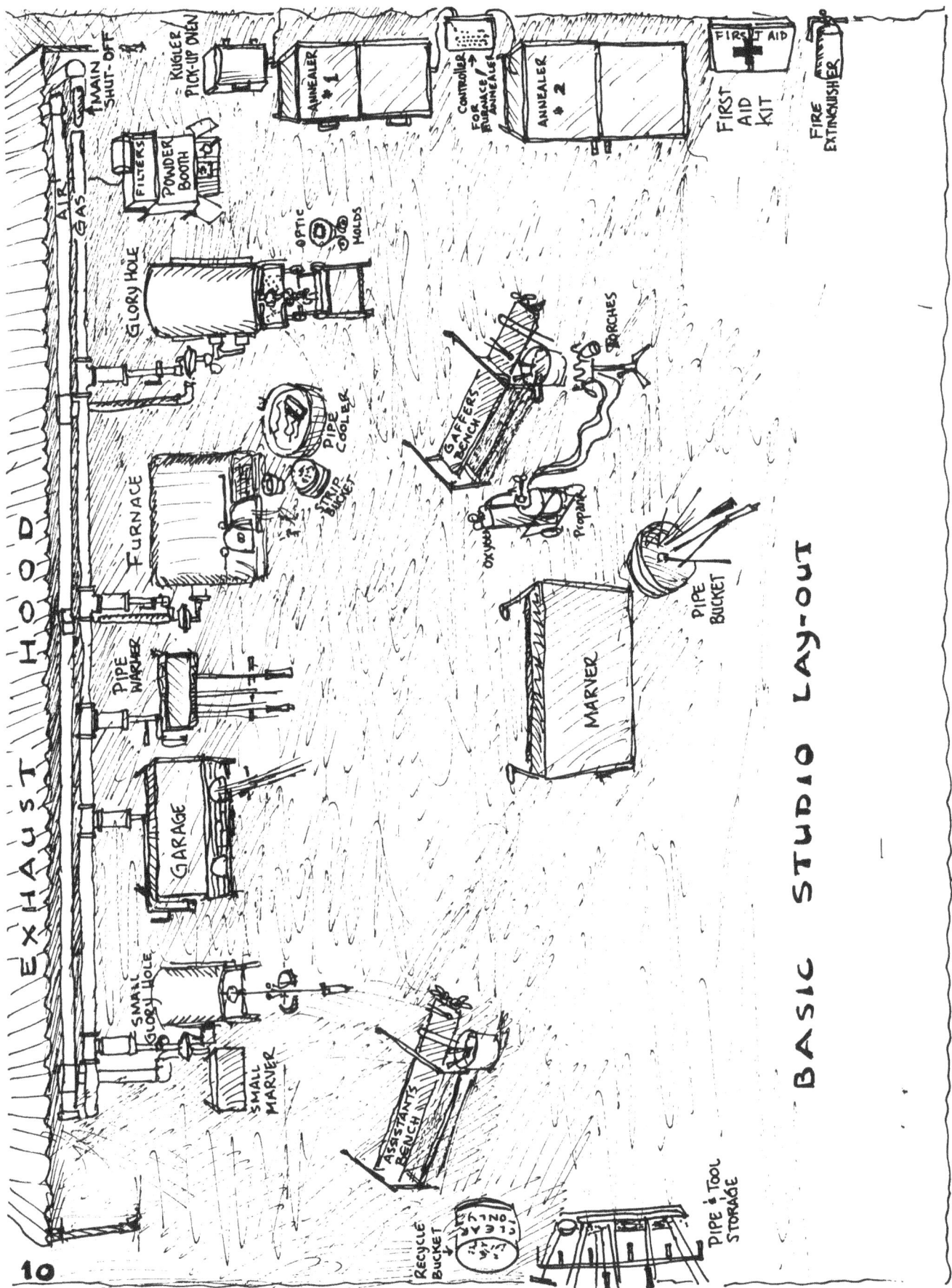

GETTING STARTED
THE SET-UP

When you first walk into the studio in the morning (afternoon or night or whatever) there are some procedures you should do to insure a healthy, happy, **STRESS-FREE** day of blowing. Some of these should be familiar to you, others may not. In any case, these activities may be performed by the gaffer or more likely, the assistant (in need of some brownie points? → DO IT!).

First order of business is to get the glory hole lit and heating up. Unload the annealers and get them fired-up and ready. Check the condition of the glass in the furnace → make sure it has melted correctly and rake the bubbles back if necessary. Adjust the temperature if necessary, to the style of glass you're blowing. **NOTE:** If you are not trained and checked-out on the operation of any equipment → DO **NOT** ATTEMPT TO ADJUST ANYTHING! Damage to equipment, serious injury or even death may result in improper use of certain glass equipment. Perform only those tasks which you're familiar with → or make the extra effort to inform yourself via shop & equipment manuals and instruction from the shop technician or gaffer. BE SAFE!

Let's see... got the glory hole lit, annealers ramping-up, furnace checked out — next, prepare the workspace and tools. First, empty out the pipe buckets [**RECYCLE YOUR CLEAR GLASS!** ↻] ← Wear a respirator and dump the glass in a well-ventilated area (outside) away from other people. Watch out for glass which is still hot (from previous blowers) → it can easily catch other garbage on fire. And, of course, it's potentially sharp as well — so handle with care! Check the pipe cooler (if you have one) — change the water if necessary. Then empty and clean-out the block buckets (at least once-a-week, unless you're fond of the rotting wood stench and mosquito farm potential!) Replace the blocks and fill with clean water.

Next, direct your attention to the bench. Sweep up any mess on the bench and around the floor (it should have been left clean by the previous blowers). Depending on the gaffers wish you may lay-out a fresh sheet (or two) of newspaper on the tool area to cover up wax and unwanted stuff from former blowers, and to make identifying the tools easier. Or you might use a 'hot glass mop' to burn off the excess wax on the tool area → To make one take a two gather blob on a punty — marver the glass off the end and allow it to flatten a little bit → then head over to the bench and 'mop' the surface of the tool area to burn off excess unwanted wax. (fig. 1).

Every gaffer has their own way of setting-up the bench → from how they fold their newspaper (now you just gotta ask yourself one question: was it five sheets or six?) → to the direction which the points

fig. 1. HOT GLASS MOP

of their tweezers and jacks lay. Make sure you know how the gaffer likes it arranged if you are doing it for them — and keep it that way the entire time they are working. There should never be any time lost searching or fumbling around for tools.

You can clean your tools: First by removing the cats and dogs off with steel wool and then by burning off the remaining wax with hot glass. Simply gather-up a healthy one to two dip blob on a punty — head over to the bench and make many small crimps on the glass to burn the wax off. (fig 2 below) The tweezers may get hot and start sticking to the glass → indicating they're pretty much clean. Quench them in cool water or wipe 'em clean with a cloth and they're pretty much ready to go. You may do a similar process with the trimming and straight shears as well. Clean tools are important. There's nothing that'll piss-off a gaffer more than having wax on their tweezers or shears! You just can't grip or cut anything with them in that state.

On the otherhand, it's good to have a nice layer of wax on the jacks. Blast the tips with the torch or preheat them by the glory hole door and lubricate liberally with some beeswax. Make sure there's an adequete supply of wax where the gaffer wants it (eg. on the corner of the bench or at the end of the rails).

If you need to clean-off the marver — some steel wool, denatured alcohol and lots of elbow grease can remove stains, residue etc. and leave you with a nice surface to marver on.

Next, light the pipe warmer. Check to make sure the pipes are unclogged and that they roll straight.(see page 279 for information on on how to clean and straighten clogged and bent pipes.)

Make sure you have an adequete supply of the right kind of pipes and punties for the 'days' activities set up and preheating in the pipe warmer.

Lastly, make ready any special items or equipment which you or the gaffer may require. This may involve cleaning and organizing the powdering booth (wear a respirator whenever dealing with powders!) lighting torches or the garage → make sure there is enough propane or oxygen in the bottles, cutting and preheating color bar, locating special paddles, blocks or making a paper marver, or even selecting CD's. Essentially taking care of those things ahead of time which may cost you valuable time while on the stick later. Anticipate, prepare, and be ready for everything! *Let's Blow some Glass!*

fig 2. CLEANING TOOLS WITH HOT GLASS

OPEN THE PAPER 5-8 SHEETS FOR THICKNESS FOLD IN 3d's ON DOTTED LINE

FOLD THAT SECTION IN 3ds

TUCK ONE SIDE IN THE CENTER OF THE OTHER TO HOLD YOUR PAPER TOGETHER

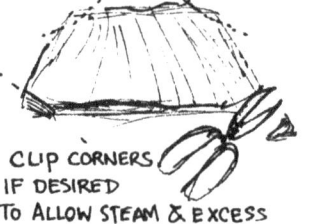
CLIP CORNERS IF DESIRED TO ALLOW STEAM & EXCESS WATER AN ESCAPE ROUTE

fig 3. A POPULAR METHOD FOR FOLDING NEWSPAPER

HOLD THE PHONE!
LET'S TAKE SOME TIME OUT TO THINK ABOUT
GLASS DESIGN
Steps to Elightenment

Well before you reach for that blowpipe to take your next gather you should know WHAT it is you're trying to make. First off, think of WHY you're trying to make that particular object. Consider the material, why do it in glass? 'Cause it sells? Because it looks nice? Or are you trying to learn a new technique? Or is it a challenging form to make, and you enjoy punishing yourself trying to pull it off? Here's a brief list of:

QUALITIES + **REFERENCES** & **SOURCES** **QUESTIONS**
TO THINK ABOUT / TO CONSIDER AND / TO LOOK AT & WORK ON / TO ANSWER:
OR ADDRESS / UTILIZE

- FORM
- TEXTURE
- FLUIDITY
- WEIGHT
- TRANSPARENCY / OPAQUENESS
- OPTICS
- LIGHT

- HISTORICAL
- PEOPLE / ANIMALS
- ART
- CONCEPTS
- NATURE
- ABSTRACTION

- FORM
- FUNCTION
- AUDIANCE
- NEEDS
- SCULPTURE

- WHY MAKE IT LOOK THE WAY IT DOES?
- WHAT'S THE PURPOSE OF THIS OBJECT?
- WHO IS IT FOR?
- WHO NEEDS IT? OR WHAT NEEDS ARE MET BY ITS CREATION?
- ARE YOU REINVENTING THE WHEEL OR BREAKING NEW GROUND?

Eliminate the guesswork and circumvent chaos in the hot shop. Make the best use of your limited and expensive bench time. **HAVE A PLAN! HEY! MAKE A DRAWING FIRST!** ← It's the easiest way to communicate your ideas to you and your (or 100) assistants. It will serve as a reference as to what you're shooting for and what you expect of your assistants. It can also aid in problem-solving, and troubleshooting those tough-to-make pieces.

Perhaps you're motivated by becoming a technically proficient glassblower. Don't be discouraged by the fact that it takes usually decades of hard, full-time work to become a **MAESTRA** or **MAESTRO**. Unless you're a "natural" who picks up techniques quickly and exhibits a keen sensitivity to this material; **to gain the skills you gotta pay your dues.** Repetition is the best way. Make 100 attempts before moving on. There aren't too many short cuts in becoming a skilled glassblower, unfortunately. It took me two years of hard work and countless floor models before I had acquired the basic skills to execute my semi-simple designs and drawings in glass. Even now, after thirteen years of working with this material, I continue to learn and devolop my skills as a glassblower. Woe is me when I feel that I've stopped learning or can no longer think of something new or exciting to make. **ENDEAVOR TO PERSEVERE, AND MAKE GOOD GLASS!**

13

GATHERING

The process of gathering is **MOLTO IMPORTANTE!** You should already be familiar with this most fundamental step of the glassmaking process. Some subtle variations on how you "DIP-UP" can greatly effect the shape, size, and 'quality' of your gather. Seldom does anyone explain it. If you are like me the T.A. handed you a pipe, opened the door to the furnace and said: "GATHER", and "KEEP IT TURNING". I kinda figgered it out from there....

Basically there are two methods or styles of gather. #1 "THE DIP" or "COAT" → where the rod is plunged below the surface of the glass, turned and withdrawn. Simply put, you are merely coating the surface of the rod or previous gather. (fig 4)

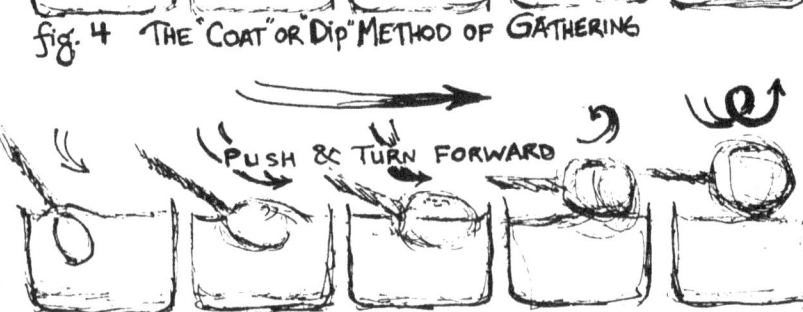

#2. "THE COLLECTIVE GATHER." This is where you want to gather as much glass as possible. The rod is plunged into the glass and turned slowly at first. You want to drive the pipe forward as you begin to increase your speed turning. Keep pushing forward, bringing the pipe upwards to 'collect' as much glass as you can. Turning the pipe faster will prevent excess glass from trailing off back into the furnace. On the otherhand, you may opt to strip-off in the furnace to reduce the amount of glass collected. You need to stop or slow the rotation significantly to allow the glass an opportunity to trail-off. This is the best method for guaging the size or quantity of your gather. Knowing what you're up against can help you when the time comes to take that next dip. (fig.5)

FACTORS EFFECTING THE GATHERING PROCESS:

TEMPERATURE OF THE GLASS: If the furnace is running **HOT**, it will be hard to amass a quantity of glass all at once. You'll probably have to make many more gathers to increase the size of your piece. Conversely, if the furnace is on the cold side, you'll have no choice but to **GATHER HEAVY**. It will be very difficult to blow & work Venetian-style without having to reheat the gathers first. The dynamics change so much that it's almost not worth it! Ideally the furnace will be at the working temperature suitable for the style of glass you're blowing. It's amazing what an extra 50°-100° F can do for you!

YOUR HEAT EXPOSURE WHILE GATHERING: It's too easy to get cooked while gathering. Anything from having the door open too much to the furnace's design and location of it's burner will effect you during the gathering process. I've worked out of some furnaces where you barely perceive the heat while gathering, and others where there's so much heat blasting you, your nosehairs sizzle and your hands fry. It's a wonder that anyone can gather glass in that kind of situation. Nobody needs unnecessary pain while blowing glass! Have an assistant close-down the door while you gather to limit your exposure.

YOUR ABILITY TO CLEARLY SEE: IF YOU HAVE TROUBLE SEEING THE LEVEL OF THE GLASS, YOU'LL PROBABLY EXPERIENCE SOME DIFFICULTY IN GATHERING. PERHAPS THE POSITION OF THE GATHERING PORT IS TOO HIGH → FIND A STEP, PLATFORM OR BRICK YOU CAN STAND ON WHILE GATHERING SO YOU CAN BETTER SEE WHAT YOU'RE TRYING TO DO. MAYBE THE FURNACE IS TOO BRIGHT TO SEE CLEARLY WHERE THE LEVEL OF THE GLASS IS. YOU MIGHT NEED BETTER SAFETY GLASSES CAPABLE OF FILTERING OUT THE EXCESSIVE RADIATION IMPAIRING YOUR EYESIGHT.

THE SIZE OF THE GATHER: THE AMOUNT OF GLASS WHICH YOU'RE CAPABLE OF GATHERING IS CONTINGENT UPON THE VISCOSITY OF THE GLASS IN THE FURNACE (SEE "TEMPERATURE OF THE GLASS" ON THE PREVIOUS PAGE). YOUR MOILE AND THE ACTUAL SIZE OF THE PIECE YOU'RE GATHERING OVER PLAYS AN IMPORTANT ROLE IN HOW MUCH GLASS YOU CAN GATHER. THE LARGER THE PIECE IS, THE MORE EFFORT AND MOLTEN GLASS IT WILL TAKE TO COVER THE PREVIOUS GATHER. SOMETIMES THE GATHERING PORT WILL BE THE LIMITING FACTOR ON THE SIZE OF YOUR GATHER. OTHER TIMES, IT MIGHT BE THE LEVEL OF THE GLASS WHICH DICTATES HOW LARGE YOU CAN WORK. IT CAN BE DISHEARTENING TO 'SCRAPE BOTTOM' WHEN TRYING TO COMPLETE A LARGE GATHER OR MAX-OUT THE DOOR SIZE WHEN TRYING TO EXIT THE FURNACE!

SIZE ISN'T EVERYTHING: **SHAPE MATTERS TOO!** SOME SHAPES ARE EASIER TO GATHER OVER THAN OTHERS. BLOCKS ARE GREAT TOOLS TO USE TO MAINTAIN YOUR BUBBLE IN THE IDEAL SHAPE FOR SUBSEQUENT GATHERS. THE TEAR DROP SHAPE IS THE EASIEST FORM TO GATHER OVER. SQUAT OR ELONGATED FORMS MAKE THE GATHERING PROCESS MUCH MORE DIFFICULT AND SHOULD BE AVOIDED. **SPEED** OF THE PIPE ROTATION CAN ALSO EFFECT YOUR ABILITY TO GATHER MORE GLASS. IF YOU DIDN'T TURN THE PIPE AT ALL DURING THE GATHERING PROCESS — YOU'D PROBABLY WIND UP WITH THE LEAST AMOUNT OF GLASS. ON THE OTHER HAND, THE MORE YOU SPEED-UP DURING THE GATHER, THE MORE SURFACE AREA (OF THE PIECE) IS EXPOSED AND HAS THE POTENTIAL FOR ACCUMULATING MORE GLASS. YOU CAN, HOWEVER, TURN THE PIPE SO FAST AS TO TRAIL OFF THE SKIN OR EXCESS GLASS, THUS REDUCING THE AMOUNT OF GLASS YOU CAN GATHER UP.

THE TEMPERATURE OF YOUR PIECE: YOU'LL BE ABLE TO MAKE BETTER AND LARGER GATHERS OVER PIECES WHICH YOU ALLOW TO COOL SUFFICIENTLY BEFORE ATTEMPTING TO GATHER OVER THEM. IT IS ALSO MUCH EASIER TO HANDLE YOUR PIECE WHEN IT'S NOT FLOPPING ALL OVER THE PLACE AND ON THE VERGE OF TOTAL COLLAPSE! MUCH OF IT HAS TO DO WITH THE TYPE OF PIECE YOU'RE MAKING. SOMETIMES YOU DON'T WANT YOUR BUBBLE COMPLETELY **STONE COLD** BEFORE GATHERING OVER. → IF THE INTERIOR'S STILL WARM, IT WILL FORCE YOU TO RESPOND FASTER AND BLOW IT OUT QUICKER → WHICH IN THE LONG RUN SAVES YOU VALUABLE TIME AND FORCES YOU TO WORK MORE FLUIDLY → CONSEQUENTLY MAKING YOU A BETTER GLASSBLOWER! AND SOMETIMES YOU HAVE TO GET THE PIECE STONE COLD BEFORE ATTEMPTING TO GATHER OVER THEM. SUCH IS THE CASE FOR **GRAALS** AND **PAINTED PIECES** WHERE YOU DON'T WANT YOUR IMAGERY 'MOVING' WHILE YOU'RE GATHERING OVER THEM. ALSO, IN PIECES WHERE THE MOILE SIZE IS SMALL OR WHERE THE WALL THICKNESS IS DANGEROUSLY THIN → YOU'LL WANT TO ALLOW THOSE ITEMS TO GET AS COLD AS YOU DARE BEFORE EXPOSING THEM TO THE RIGORS OF THE MOLTEN GLASS.

EXPERIENCE: AS WITH MOST PHASES OF HOT GLASS WORKING, EXPERIENCE IS ONE OF THE BEST GUIDES TO IMPROVING YOUR SKILLS. TAKE SOME TIME OUT AND SEE WHAT CHANGING ONE ELEMENT OF YOUR GATHERING TECHNIQUE CAN DO FOR YOU. THIS MAY BE THE ACTUAL ANGLE YOU GATHER AT, TO THE SPEED OR TEMPERATURE AT WHICH YOU ATTEMPT TO GATHER OVER. AND TRY TO REMEMBER WHAT DOES WHAT!

The Start

The start of your bubble is a crucial step to establishing even wall thickness and getting your piece on-center. With a good foundation, blowing the rest of your piece can be a whole lot easier!

Most gaffers will do a double dip when starting a piece. The first gather just coats the tip of the pipe. It is allowed to chill briefly (creating a 'skin') and then a second gather is taken on top of that one to accumulate more glass. The exceptions to this 'rule' include: using Kugler, making very small pieces and special occasions.

WHOA PAL! After you take your initial gather, it is up to you where you go from there. Most beginners tend to be hasty and run to the marver or bench to shape-up the piece as quick as possible. **It's not necessary to immediately chill the hot glass!** *relax!*

Rather, take some time out to chill the pipe at the pipe cooler. Maintain your piece on-center, as you do so. Do not underestimate the power and value of the 'air marver.' In fact, the more you can shape your piece without the aid of tools, the more skill you'll develop in handling the glass altogether.

Molten glass can teach you how to be more fluid. The effects of gravity will become more obvious. Understanding how your gathers can work for you - how they hold the heat and how they cool naturally versus chilling their surface, is fundamental to all glassworking.

For Practice: An exercise to train yourself about handling hot glass is to take two gathers and see how much you can blow them out without reheating or any physical shaping, save minimal amounts of marvering to set-up the form. Take an hour out of your day to try and blow as many shapes as you can: bulbous spheres, long-neck tear drops and bottle forms, and short squat oval shapes. Play with the glass. Swing it out. Blow it while pointing the pipe at the ceiling. Understand what we mean when we say **GRAVITY IS YOUR FRIEND!**

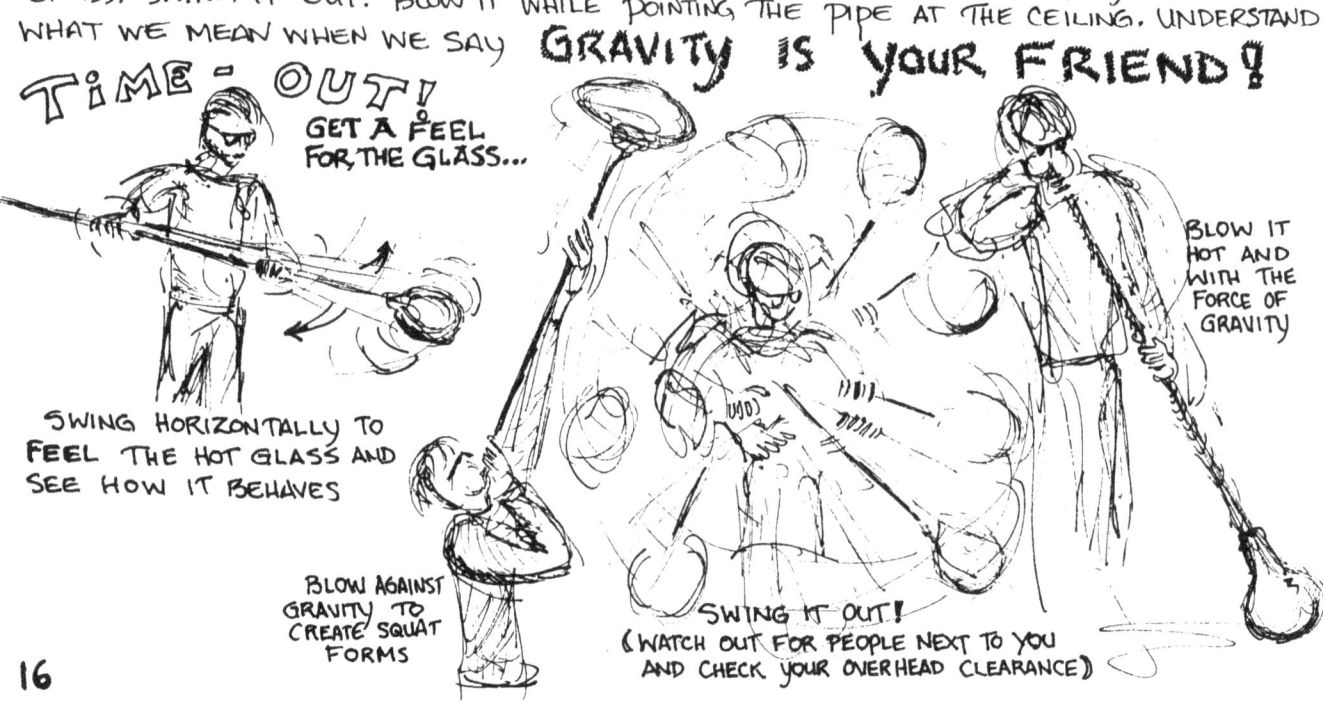

TIME-OUT! Get a feel for the glass...

Swing horizontally to feel the hot glass and see how it behaves

Blow against gravity to create squat forms

Swing it out! (Watch out for people next to you and check your overhead clearance)

Blow it hot and with the force of gravity

16

The first order of business is to get the glass off the end of the pipe where you can use it. Essentially you need to squeeze the glass outwards by pressing and rolling the blowpipes sides against a firm surface. There are several different ways of accomplishing this. Some gaffers will use the edge of the marver (**fig. 6** at the right →) while others prefer doing it at the bench with the back of their jacks (**fig. 8**), or by using a block (**Fig. 9**) or wet newspaper. Whichever method you choose, the principle is the same — you must make the glass on the neck of the blowpipe (A.K.A. the Moile) as even and as thin as you can. If the glass is not marvered completely with full revolutions, you may end up with a lop-sided moile. A lop-sided moile will contribute to subsequent uneven gathers and uneven bubbles → and nobody wants that to happen!

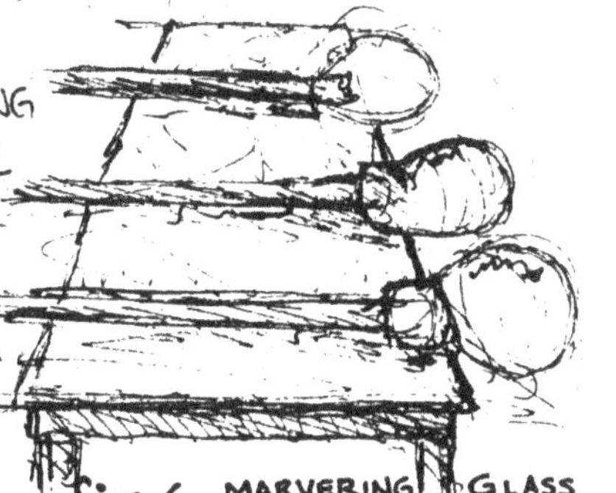

fig. 6 MARVERING GLASS OFF THE END.

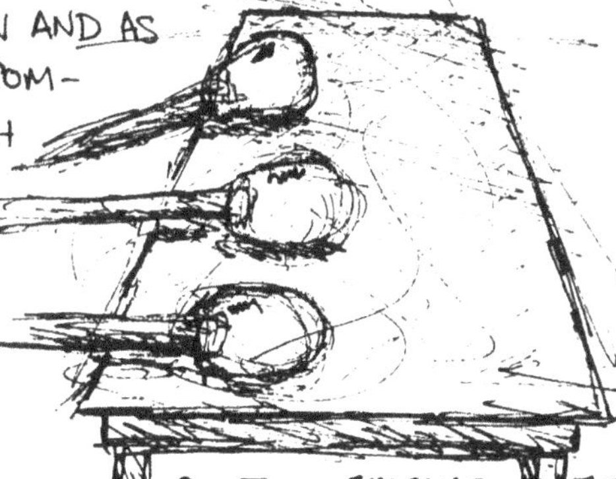

Once the glass is off the end of the pipe, it needs to be shaped quickly and then blown. If you're at the marver, you can start down low, (with your hands below the surface of the marver) and shape-up the back area of the glass first. Then a couple passes with your hands level with the surface of the marver to shape the side walls nice-and-even. If you lift your pipe up and off the surface of the marver between rolls → you can "AIR MARVER" the skin of the glass. This will help you maintain your glass in a compact form rather than cause it to elongate into an unusable weenie.

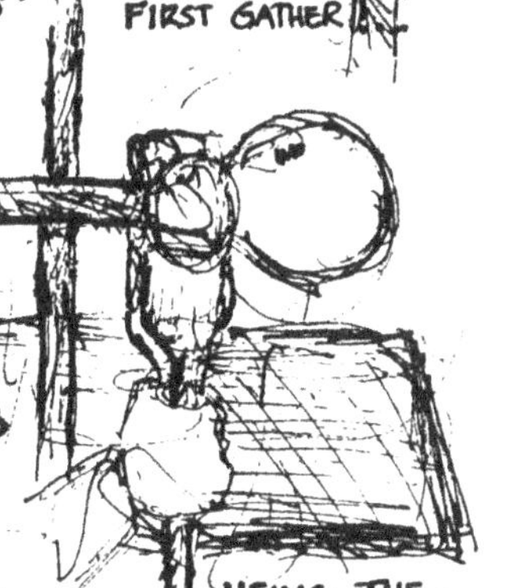

fig. 7 SHAPING THE FIRST GATHER.

The air marver is a valuable technique in glassblowing. It offers you an opportunity to shape your bubble naturally while examining it for flaws and anticipating your next maneuver. Or it may give you a chance to re-wet your block or newspaper. Simply by tilting the pipe off the horizontal plane, it will cause your glass to flow with gravity, either compacting your form or elongating it. Remember: gravity is your friend!

fig. 8 USING THE BACK OF THE JACKS FOR THE FIRST GATHER.

Just prior to blowing your starter bubble you may need to marver or shape the tip a bit. Just "**POINT UP**" the tip either by marvering at a steep angle or by adjusting the angle of the pipe as you block or newspaper the glass. Once the glass is in the bullet shape you can go ahead and blow n' cap. Some gaffers do this at the marver or at the bench, it is entirely up to you. If the blow and cap method is still a challenge for you — then **HERE'S** what you need to do:

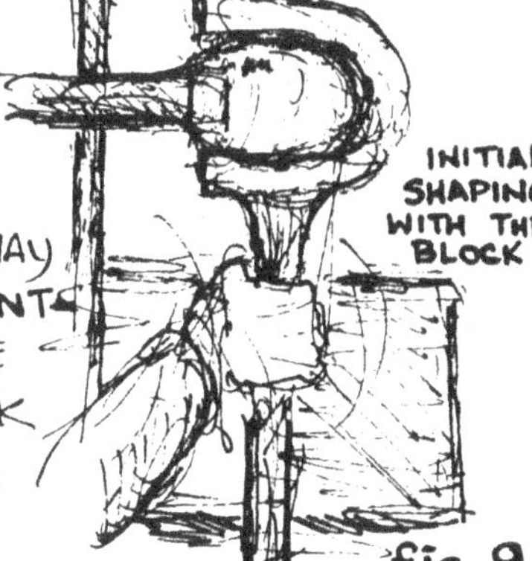

fig. 9 INITIAL SHAPING WITH THE BLOCK

BLOW 'N' CAP EXPLAINED

This technique is for some people a tricky one to learn. Perhaps because thumb-sucking is so heavily frowned-upon in our society that the mere thought of inserting your opposing digit in your mouth is repulsive. Whatever the case may be, that's what you must do in order to make it work.

The idea is this: your blowpipe is a tube. Hot glass covers one end of the tube. The laws of physics state that gases will expand when heated. If you pressurize the air in the tube (with your breath) and seal it with your thumb, the glass on the end of the pipe will heat the gas inside the tube, causing it to expand. This expanding gas seeks the path of least resistance to escape. If the glass is hot enough, it will expand there to inflate and make a bubble. If your thumb slips off, the pressurized air will escape, and your bubble will cease to expand. period!

To make it work for you, have your hot glass marvered/shaped as described on the previous page. Slip your thumb in the side of your mouth with the blowpipe next to it in the center. Begin blowing &/or give a forceful puff into the pipe and slip your thumb over the end while doing so - to trap your air in the pipe. KEEP YOUR THUMB ON THE END to get the bubble to EXPAND! Try and not let it slip off!.. Keep your pipe turning as well. As soon as the bubble inflates to the optimal size, remove your thumb from the end to halt the expansion. A final shaping on the marver (or blocks or newspaper - whatever) may be needed and/or an extra puff to get everything looking right, as in figure 10.

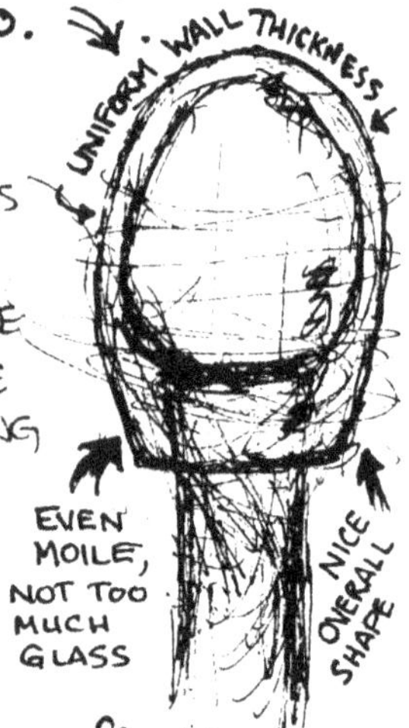

The Successive Gather

With every extra gather you take on top of the previous one, there comes with it the added mass and increase in surface area. Heat is also introduced into the piece as well. There are times when you want to gather on a fairly hot bubble and there are times when the piece should be pretty cold before 'dipping up,' as stated earlier. Again, experience will be your guide.

Things to look for in your bubble prior to making the next gather: COLOR, → if the orange glow has disappeared and the glass is pretty clear → you may gather over it.

MOVEMENT → if the bubble doesn't show much movement when you stop rotating the pipe → you may gather over it. With some movement showing, you might 'hang-out' and wait for it to stiffen-up some more or go ahead and gather over it and go with the flow!

WALL THICKNESS → if you blow the walls of your bubble on the thin-side, you might want to allow the piece to get stone cold before gathering over. Otherwise the heat from the furnace and successive gather may penetrate your bubble quickly - setting you on the brink of total collapse.

fig. 10
ANATOMY OF A STARTER BUBBLE

UNIFORM WALL THICKNESS
EVEN MOILE, NOT TOO MUCH GLASS
NICE OVERALL SHAPE

Other things to consider when taking the next dip: How much glass do you want? Should you merely try to coat the next layer or try a collective-style gather to amass as much quantity as possible? Or do you want to let the glass trail off in the furnace, or even go as far as a dip n' strip approach (see page 64 for details)? The answer to these questions lie in what it is you're trying to make, or in the event you are assisting someone → what the gaffer wants. Rarely is it a problem to gather too much glass (except for mold blowing). There are many avenues by which you may deal with excess glass at a later point in time.

Perhaps more important than the quantity of glass that you can gather, is the resulting shape of the gathering process. It's important that you do full revolutions in the glass to obtain an even gather. Allowing the glass a moment to trail off any excess into the furnace before you exit prevents stringers from happening and unnecessary glass from being wasted.

Q. "I get these mysterious 'dog ears' forming on my bubble right after I take a gather and before I get a chance to block the piece. What's up with that?"

A. This ailment is somewhat common to many glassblowers. It comes from a **change in the direction** in which you rotate the pipe, and the centrifugal force which you establish by turning the pipe. I had this problem for years - probably stemming from the fact that I'm a switch-hitter → a lefty who blows righty → and the shift in axis rotation I used to do in order to gather in a right-handed dominated world. It wasn't until a woman trained at Orrefors in Sweden pointed out what I was doing wrong, that I was able to adapt and do it right. The cure is: **Once you start turning the pipe in one direction → do not reverse the direction until you begin blocking or shaping the glass.** If you start with clockwise rotations - finish with clockwise rotations. Another cure is to strip the piece after you exit the furnace (page 64), but that tends to be a waste of glass.

Once you get your gather, you have several options on how to shape it. Blocking the glass is the method preferred by most gaffers, while some prefer newspaper, or marvering, or a combo of both. You probably have a method which is tried and true for you - and maybe you should stick with it, but in the interest of filling-in-the-blanks, I'll review some of those processes in hope of shedding new light on them.

BLOCKING

If you examine the blocking process closely, you'll notice how the block seems to cover 50% of the hot glass bubble. Indeed, with that type of coverage you're shaping a full one-half of your bubble at a time. That's pretty good contact with the glass! You'll notice too, how

GAFFERS REPEATEDLY WET THEIR BLOCKS DURING THE SHAPING PROCESS AND 'AIR MARVER' IN BETWEEN. THIS SAVES THEIR BLOCKS FROM BURNING AND ALLOWS THEM A CHANCE TO ASSESS THE BEHAVIOR OF THE BUBBLE/GLASS.

It's very easy to start with blocks and continue to use them during the whole process of making your glass — up to a point. After you take your last gather → you block and shape the piece as usual — and that's it. Once you reach a certain point, your blocks can no longer shape the piece the way you want, or need.

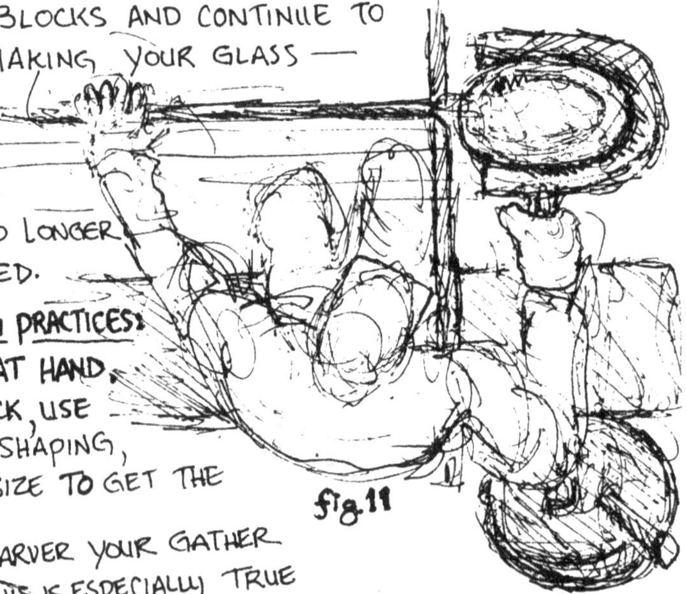

SOME TIPS ON SUCCESSFUL BLOCKING PRACTICES:

⇒ USE THE RIGHT SIZED BLOCK FOR THE JOB AT HAND.
⇒ IF YOUR GATHER DOESN'T FIT IN YOUR BLOCK, USE A LARGER BLOCK FIRST TO DO SOME INITIAL SHAPING, AND THEN CHANGE TO A MORE APPROPRIATE SIZE TO GET THE FULL EFFECT, OR...
⇒ SOMETIMES YOU MIGHT HAVE TO PAPER OR MARVER YOUR GATHER FIRST TO GET IT TO FIT IN YOUR BLOCK — THIS IS ESPECIALLY TRUE IF YOUR GATHER ISN'T TOO EVEN, & IS GETTING 'WONKY.'
⇒ CHOKE-UP ON THE HANDLE OF THE BLOCK TO GAIN MORE STABILITY AND TO HAVE A BETTER FEEL FOR THE GLASS. THIS ALSO HELPS BALANCE THE BLOCK BETTER IN YOUR HAND. SOME GAFFERS WILL ALSO BRACE THE HANDLE OF THE BLOCK AGAINST THEIR ARM FOR INCREASED SUPPORT. (fig 11).
⇒ KEEP THE BLOCK WET! THAT WAY IT WON'T BURN OUT TOO QUICKLY, AND WON'T LEAVE ANY RESIDUE ON YOUR HOT GLASS. IF YOU NOTICE ANY STICKING, GET IT WET!
⇒ USE THE WHOLE BENCH TO BLOCK. AVOID INCOMPLETE ROTATIONS. THE MORE FULL REVOLUTIONS YOU CAN MAKE, THE MORE UNIFORM YOUR BUBBLE WILL BE.
⇒ USE AIR MARVERING AS A TECHNIQUE TO ASSESS YOUR BUBBLES PROGRESS AND AS AN OPPORTUNITY TO WET YOUR BLOCK. ALSO, AVOID BLOCKING GATHERS IMMEDIATELY AFTER COMING OUT OF THE FURNACE. ALLOW THE GLASS SOME TIME TO 'SKIN-UP' — OTHERWISE IT IS VERY LIKELY TO STICK TO YOUR BLOCK AND MAKE A MESS OF THINGS. TAKE THE TIME OUT TO CHILL THE PIPE. THE CLOSER YOUR LEFT HAND CAN GET TO THE GLASS, THE EASIER IT IS TO TURN THE PIPE.
⇒ ANGLE THE PIPE INTO THE BLOCK TO SHAPE THE TIP. (fig 12 above). THIS ALSO ALLOWS GRAVITY TO DO ITS THING AS WELL.
⇒ CHANGE THE ANGLE AT WHICH YOU HOLD THE BLOCK AS YOU GO BACK AND FORTH DOWN THE RAILS. IT NEED ONLY BE A SLIGHT CHANGE. THIS WAY YOU INSURE THAT YOU FULLY COVER THE WHOLE SURFACE AREA.
⇒ NEVER TAKE OR USE SOMEONE ELSES BLOCKS WITHOUT THEIR PERMISSION FIRST. A SET OF BLOCKS CAN BE AN EXPENSIVE INVESTMENT, AND SOME PEOPLE ARE VERY PICKY

fig. 11

fig. 12

about who uses their tools and how they use them. Respect other peoples tools, and **ASK FIRST!**

⇒ **NEW BLOCKS REQUIRE A BREAK-IN PERIOD.** Oftentimes they'll leave scum or scudge on your glass until a sufficient layer of carbon builds up on them.

⇒ **MAKE SURE YOUR BLOCKS ARE EASILY IDENTIFIABLE.** Carve some notches in the handle, drill a hole and use a colored shoelace to mark it, or number the handle — whatever. You don't want to waste valuable time fumbling around for the right block. Also, your assistant can help you by pre-selecting the block for you while you gather.

⇒ **ALWAYS STORE YOUR BLOCKS IN WATER.** Otherwise they may dry out and crack. Change your water fairly frequently unless you like the smell of old block water — I know dogs love the taste — go figure...

⇒ **AVOID BLOWING AND BLOCKING AT THE SAME TIME.** It seems to make the bubble stick more and it's hard to control the expansion. About the only time you might want to do that is when the bubble's on the verge of collapsing (from gathering over it too hot, or it's too thin). A quick puff and cap may maintain your bubble's interior long enough to get the exterior a little cooler and back in shape.

⇒ And finally, **ALLOW THE BLOCK TO DO THE JOB IT IS DESIGNED TO DO.** Do not try to force the glass into shape. Allow the glass to be cradled by the block — shaping it gently with full revolutions. Be fluid with your movements and work hot ⇒ it's much easier. See the next chapter for more information on blocking large style glass pieces.

MARVERING

Don't let the simplicity of this tool fool you. The marver can be the most useful device for shaping your glass with in the whole studio. That is, of course, if you know how to use it to your advantage. In the past the marver was made of marble, and it is from the french language that we have adapted or adopted this word into our vocabulary. Indeed, using a marble surface instead of steel has certain advantages. Marble doesn't suck the heat out of your glass quite as quickly as the steel can. But finding the right size, thickness, and composition of marble suitable for a marver can be alot more complicated than heading down to your local scrap yard for a slab of steel. Therefore, most of the studios you work at or visit are equipped with the steel type of marver in various sizes and heights.

Learning how to marver hot objects is extremely important to advancing your skills as a glassblower. It is one of the best ways to teach yourself about the "feel" for the glass, and how it behaves. There are a few things to keep in mind while you

fig. 13

MARVER, THE FIRST AND FOREMOST BEING: WHAT AM I TRYING TO ACHIEVE BY MARVERING THE PIECE IN THIS MANNER? FOR EXAMPLE, IF YOU NEED TO GET YOUR GLASS UNDER CONTROL, THE BEST METHOD IS TO SHAPE-UP THE NECK AND SHOULDER AREA FIRST. (see fig.14). THIS HELPS ESTABLISH SYMMETRY IN YOUR PIECE AS WELL AS HELPS GET THE GLASS OFF THE END OF THE PIPE WHERE YOU CAN USE IT.

fig. 14
SHAPING-UP THE NECK AREA ON THE MARVER

IF YOU NEED TO SHAPE THE SIDEWALLS YOU CAN MARVER THE PIECE HORIZONTALLY OR AT A SLIGHT ANGLE TO CREATE MORE OF A CONE SHAPE (see fig. 15 BELOW). YOU CAN EASILY BLOW THE PIECE WHILE AT THE MARVER - SIMPLY BY HANGING IT OVER THE EDGE AND KEEPING IT TURNING AS YOU INFLATE THE BUBBLE.

IF YOU NEED TO SHAPE THE TIP, YOU HAVE TO BRING THE PIPE UP ALMOST PERPENDICULAR TO THE MARVER AND SIMULTANEOUSLY SUPPORT THE WEIGHT OF THE GLASS AND TURN THE PIPE. THIS IS A VITAL STEP IN BEING ABLE TO BLOW OUT THE SHOULDERS ON YOUR PIECE.

MARVERING TECHNIQUES

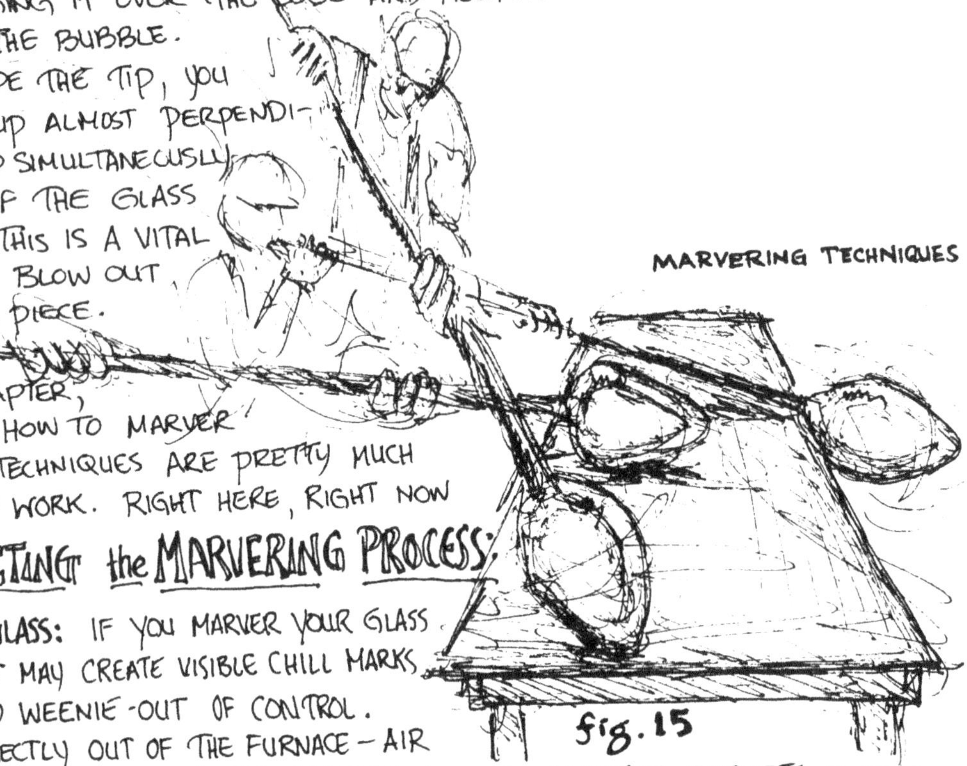

IN THE NEXT CHAPTER, THERE ARE MORE TIPS ON HOW TO MARVER LARGE PIECES, AND THE TECHNIQUES ARE PRETTY MUCH THE SAME FOR ANY SIZE OF WORK. RIGHT HERE, RIGHT NOW ARE **FACTORS EFFECTING the MARVERING PROCESS:**

⇒ **TEMPERATURE OF YOUR GLASS:** IF YOU MARVER YOUR GLASS WHEN IT'S SCREAMIN' HOT, IT MAY CREATE VISIBLE CHILL MARKS, AND IT HAS A TENDENCY TO WEENIE-OUT OF CONTROL. AVOID MARVERING GLASS DIRECTLY OUT OF THE FURNACE - AIR MARVER IT FIRST TO ALLOW IT TO 'SKIN-UP'. THIS PRACTICE HELPS YOU MAINTAIN COMPLETE CONTROL OVER YOUR AMORPHOUS BLOB. LIKEWISE, **AIR MARVER BETWEEN PASSES DOWN THE STEEL SURFACE.** **LIFT THE GLASS OFF THE SURFACE OF THE MARVER** - IT'S A GREAT WAY TO KEEP YOUR FORM AND IT ALLOWS YOU TO STUDY AND ASSESS THE BEHAVIOR OF YOUR BUBBLE. ON THE OTHERHAND, IF YOU ATTEMPT TO MARVER GLASS WHICH IS TOO COLD, NOT MUCH IS GOING TO HAPPEN EXCEPT PUTTING CHILL MARKS ALL OVER THE SURFACE OF YOUR PIECE. HOT GOOD - COLD BAD!

fig. 15

⇒ **COMPLETE REVOLUTIONS ARE A MUST!** IT'S IMPORTANT TO MAKE FULL REVOLUTIONS WHILE MARVERING. IT'S THE ONLY WAY YOU CAN SHAPE YOUR PIECE SYMMETRICALLY. IF FOR SOME REASON YOU OBTAIN A PIECE THAT IS LOP-SIDED → YOU CAN CORRECT IT BY MARVERING BACK N' FORTH TO TRY AND SQUEEZE THE GLASS BACK INTO SHAPE. ALSO, A SHORT PUFF OF AIR CAN HELP SOMETIMES GET YOUR FORM BACK IN-THE-ROUND, IN ORDER TO MARVER IT MORE SYMMETRICALLY.

⇒ **HEIGHT AND SIZE OF THE MARVER:** IF THE MARVER IS TOO HIGH, IT WILL BE MORE OF A STRUGGLE TO SHAPE YOUR PIECE ON. MAINTAINING DECENT LEVERAGE OVER YOUR

PIECE MAKES IT ALOT EASIER TO SHAPE AND SEE WHAT IT IS YOU ARE DOING. RARELY ARE MARVERS SET TOO-LOW, AND SELDOM DOES THAT PRESENT AS BIG AS A PROBLEM IF THEY ARE TOO HIGH. ALSO, IF THE MARVER IS TOO SMALL, YOU MAY NOT BE ABLE TO COMPLETE FULL ROTATIONS ON IT. & IF THAT IS THE CASE, YOU MAY OPT FOR OTHER METHODS OF SHAPING IN ORDER TO MAINTAIN SYMMETRY. TOO BIG A MARVER? NEVER!

⇒ **BALANCE & SUPPORT ARE VITAL!** YOU MUST BE ABLE TO SUPPORT THE WEIGHT OF YOUR PIECE IN YOUR ARMS AND WRISTS AND KEEP THE PIPE TURNING. WHEN YOU WATCH 'THE PROS' BLOW GLASS, PAY SPECIAL ATTENTION TO THEIR HANDS AS THEY MARVER. YOU'LL NOTICE HOW, WHEN GOING IN ONE DIRECTION, THEIR RIGHT HAND IS DOING THE TURNING WHILE THE LEFT SUPPORTS THE WEIGHT OF THE GLASS AND PIPE. AS SOON AS THEY GET TO THE END, THE ROLES ARE REVERSED AND THEIR LEFT HAND TURNS WHILE THE RIGHT HAND ACTS AS SUPPORT. TRY IT FOR YOURSELF. WITH EXPERIENCE, THIS SKILL BECOMES 'NATURAL' AND YOU DON'T EVEN HAVE THINK ABOUT IT.

⇒ **SCALE OF THE PIECE**: MAINTAINING YOUR PIECE ON CENTER REQUIRES BALANCE AS STATED ABOVE. THE LARGER THE PIECE, THE MORE YOU FEEL THIS EFFECT. THE BEST ADVICE I CAN GIVE YOU IS TO **CHILL THE PIPE** SO THAT YOU CAN CHOKE UP ON THE PIPE. MORE MASS ON THE PIPE MEANS MORE EFFORT YOU NEED TO EXERT TO GET THE GLASS TO DO WHAT YOU WANT IT TO DO. MUCH OF THE MARVERING PROCESS IS ALLOWING THE WEIGHT OF THE GLASS, COMBINED WITH THE ROTATION OVER THE SURFACE OF THE STEEL, TO DO THE SHAPING. THE CLOSER YOU CAN GET TO HANDLING THE GLASS THE MORE CONTROL YOU WILL HAVE OVER HOW THE BUBBLE WILL BEHAVE. REALLY LARGE AND TALL PIECES REQUIRE MORE SKILL AND EFFORT TO MARVER — OFTENTIMES IN AWKWARD POSITIONS — BUT SUCH IS THE NATURE OF INCREASING THE SCALE OF YOUR WORK. SEE THE NEXT CHAPTER FOR ADDITIONAL HINTS ON MARVERING LARGE GLASS.

PAPERING

FOR SEVERAL REASONS I PREFER THIS METHOD OF SHAPING ABOVE ALL OTHERS. IT ALLOWS ME THE CLOSEST PHYSICAL CONTACT AND FEEL FOR THE GLASS THAT I CAN GET. I DON'T HAVE MY OWN SET OF BLOCKS, SO NEWSPAPER USUALLY HAS TO DO THE TRICK IN ITS STEAD. NEWSPAPER IS ALSO AVAILABLE IN ALMOST ANY STUDIO IN THE WORLD AND TAKES NO TIME AT ALL TO MAKE, IS COMPLETELY DISPOSABLE, AND RELATIVELY EASY TO USE. PLUS, IT'S FREE!

YOU HAVE TO PAY ATTENTION WHILE PAPERING. IF YOU DON'T KEEP YOUR PAPER WET, THE BURNING PAPER (ASH) WILL STICK TO YOUR GLASS AND LEAVE A PERMANENT RESIDUE BEHIND. IF THE GLASS IS REALLY **HOT, PAPER IN ONE DIRECTION** ONLY OR PAY THE STICKY PRICE! CHILL AND SHAPE THE NECK AREA FIRST, AND THEN PAPER THOSE AREAS WHICH YOU NEED TO. YOU CAN COVER ALOT OF AREA, PARTICULARLY IF YOU HAVE HANDS AS LARGE AS MINE! WITH TEAMWORK, YOU CAN ACCURATELY SEE AND SHAPE THE BUBBLE IN A WIDE VARIETY OF FORMS.

BY HAVING YOUR ASSISTANT BLOW WHILE YOU PAPER THE BUBBLE,

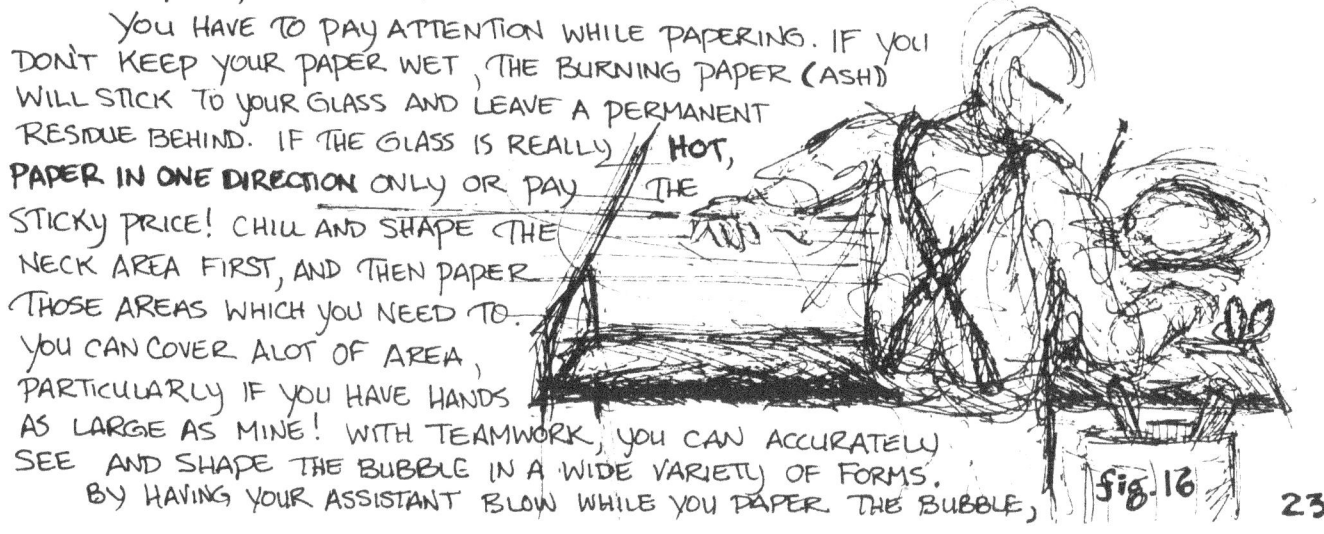

fig. 16

You can get the bubble to expand in areas where you need it to, and to prevent it from blowing out in those places where you don't want it to. This can be especially useful when trying to blow out the shoulders ⇒ you paper the bottom while your partner blows to expand the bubble and shoulder area (fig 17)

Like blocking, you can paper your piece while turning the pipe on an angle with your left hand. This technique is useful in papering the tip and allowing gravity to do its thing. It also helps the neck area to stretch somewhat, making the necking process a little easier to perform later on down the road. In the next chapter, additional information on papering will be presented. Here are points to consider in the meantime:

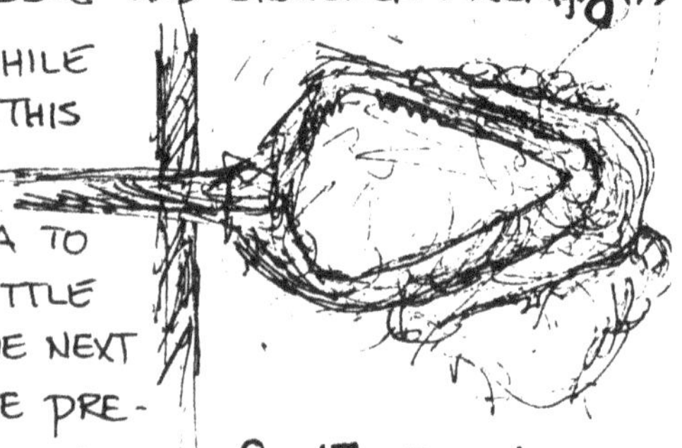

Factors Effecting Papering:

⇒ Temperature of the Glass
If your glass is too hot it will severly burn-up your newspaper, possibly causing the ensuing ash to adhere permanently to it's surface. Keep the paper wet (not too wet-[with puddles in it] or you may end-up quenching, not cooling, your glass). If you get tons of smoke pouring outta your paper, wet it down! New paper blocks are especially prone to this, and require a re-wetting at nearly every pass down the rails.
If your glass is too cold, you can paper it 'til you're blue in the face and nothing will happen. Hot good....

⇒ Not all newspaper is created equal.
The various compositions of newspapers these days vary so much that it's becoming more difficult to find ones that burn well. I still prefer the N.Y. Times and Wall St. Journal when I can get 'em. Avoid using colored newspaper, (the inks are not healthy to breathe when they are burned), the comics, advertisement supplements or the "Thrifty N'ickle" for your source of newspaper pad. As stated earlier new paper blocks burn and smoke severly at first. They require a burn-in period until a layer of carbon builds up on 'em — so keep them sufficiently wet at first. Some gaffers will store their newspaper in a plastic bag overnight so they can re-use it the next time they blow, instead of having to remake one everyday, and having to break it in each time.

⇒ Thickness of the Paper
Keep your paper thick enough so you don't burn your hand!...duh... but don't have it so thick that you can't feel what it is that you're doing!

⇒ Don't Force the Glass
Allow the glass to do it's thing - coax it along with the movements of your newspaper coinciding with full, complete revolutions down the bench. Basically your hand and paper act as a trough (very similar to the idea behind your block(s)) in which the glass is rotated and shaped. As with blocking and marvering, taking a few moments out to 'air marver' between shaping procedures (also a good

fig 17 BLOWING-OUT THE SHOULDERS WHILE PAPERING THE BOTTOM

fig. 18 PAPERING ON AN ANGLE

time to re-wet your paper) can help assess the behavior and heat of your bubble, and allow you some time to think of what to do next.

⇒ **CHOKE-UP ON THE PIPE**
Like blocking and marvering, the closer you can get to your hot glass the more intimate you'll be with it, and the more control you'll have in turning the pipe.

Perhaps the biggest disadvantage to papering is that it is very difficult to get crisp flat surfaces/sidewalls. Most everything comes out curvilinear. If you need straighter walls, marvering is a better technique for achieving them. On the other hand, papering doesn't leave any tool marks behind (except residue if your paper sticks!), and papering does allow you to get a **REAL FEEL** for the glass over most other tools.

SHAPING WITH THE JACKS / NECKING

Another handy method for shaping your glass is with your jacks. It is very direct and straightforward. You can easily see what is happening. It does, however, take some getting used-to. Essentially the blades of the jacks perform the role of the marver while you remain seated at the bench.

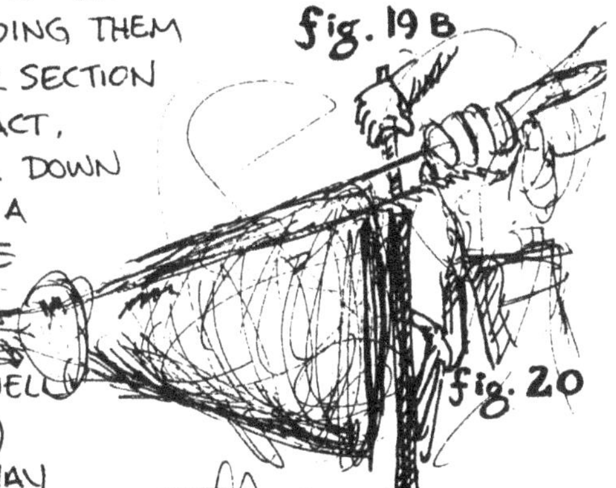

Figure 19 at the right shows the jacks being used to shape the bottom of a piece into a tapered point. The assistant may blow and/or cap the pipe when indicated to further expand the shoulders or maintain internal pressure, if so desired.

fig. 19A
BLOWING OUT THE SHOULDERS WHILE SHAPING.

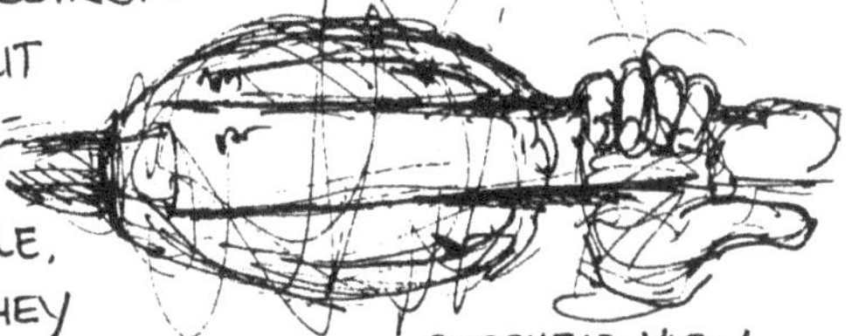

Like the marver, the jacks will suck the heat out of your glass, but not as quickly. In order for this technique to work for you - you must begin shaping with the tips of the blades on the most stable point on your bubble. The blades should be spread far apart enough that they touch the piece equidistantly. Use the cool portion of the bubble as a guide. By angling your jacks and riding them on the cool section, you can begin to shape the hotter section slowly increasing your surface area / point of contact. As you gain increased stability you may move further down the piece to shape the rest of the glass. If it gets a little wonky → you can always move back up the piece to chill and re-establish the piece on center.

OVERHEAD VIEW
fig. 19B

fig. 20

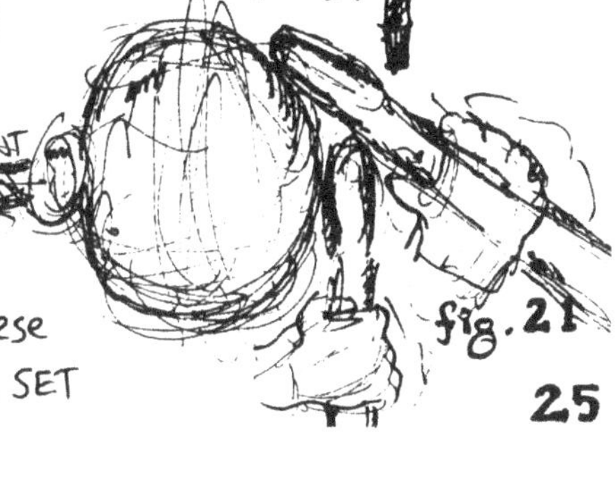

Keep your jacks well lubricated! In order for this technique to work, you should have your jacks well coated with beeswax. If your jacks 'dry-out' they may screech in pain and leave tool marks behind. They may also skip on the surface instead of **GLIDING** smoothly.

You can make really crisp bottoms on your pieces by shaping with the jacks and having one assistant blowing while another paddles the bottom flat as in figure 20.

You may also use the back of your jacks to smooth or 'paddle' the bottoms of your pieces. Are these tools versatile or what? No wonder a good pair will set

fig. 21

you back $200.00 or more! A word of caution: when shaping the hot glass with the jacks be aware that the metal will get HOT TOO! Almost every glassblower has received the tell-tale jack scars on their arm from touching-up against the blades of smokin' hot jacks. They're akin to track marks on a junkies arm — part of the price you pay for using the tool. It's even more pronounced when the jacks are ladden with hot wax! TIP→ Wear a long sleeve shirt while blowing to offer yourself added protection against such accidents. It'll also help your arm from getting cooked while necking.

Of course, the primary function of the jacks lies in cutting-in a neckline. The neckline can be established anywhere on your bubble, but usually is reserved for the area closest to the neck. You may also shape your bubble dramatically by necking-in lines elsewhere on the bubble. Or you can angle your jacks to stretch and shape the piece in a more complicated fashion (see fig. 2.2 below). The neckline method of shaping can also be done fairly severly to create a Roman-Ring (see page 264 for more info). In the following chapter you'll find techniques illustrated on how to neck more effectively in a teamwork situation. **The bottom line to shaping with the jacks is: the glass must be hot. Hot hot in order for it to work efficiently!** Other tips for successful shaping with the jacks:

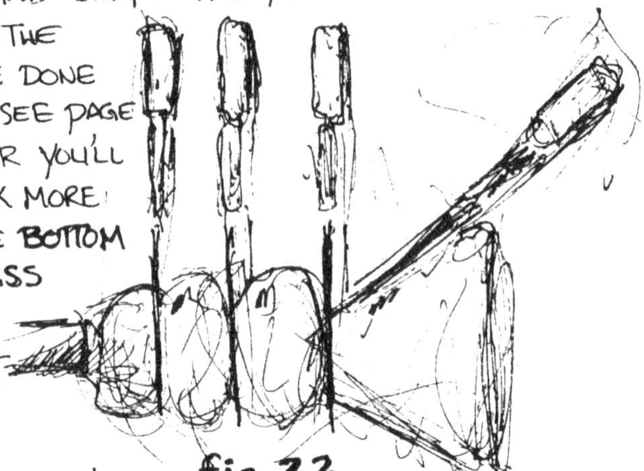

fig. 2.2 SHAPING WITH THE JACKS

⇒ **Full Revolutions are a must!**
Use the whole bench not just four inches of it!

⇒ **High Revolutions help too!**
This means → turn the pipe faster! That way you make more contact with the glass in a shorter period of time. This helps maintain your piece on center and keeps things symmetrical.

⇒ **Your piece should be symmetrical to begin with.**
Its very difficult to shape a piece with the jacks if it's flopping about all over the place. Be sure to use one of the more tried and true methods of shaping to set-up the piece first. Once it's on-center, you can use the jacks in a variety of ways to shape it further to completion. Indeed, the more experienced you become in all phases of the shaping process, the more techniques you have at your disposal and the more intuition you'll have on when and where to use them. Very few pieces are made with only one style of shaping.

⇒ **Use the right tool for the job at hand**
You don't need jumbo jacks to shape two-gather bubbles and it's not recommended to shape eight-gathered vessels with goblet jacks (you'll fry from the excess heat!). Try to find the appropriate sized jacks for each piece that you're making.

THE TRANSFER

It's Easy! *It's Fun!* *It's Death Defying!*

One of the most anxiety ridden moments in all of glassblowing comes when it's time to transfer. Given the life or death nature of the situation, it's no wonder people can get a little tense during this maneuver. In an effort to dispell some of those fears and boost your confidence level, here's a brief review:

① Inspect & Attach Punty

The Dry Method

The simple steps outlined to the right → illustrate one method of transferring a piece without the use of water. **It's important that the neckline is clean and well-defined.** The neck area should be sufficiently chilled with the cooler portion of your jacks (the upper part of the blades work well for this). A few passes up n' down the rails should do the trick. A quick tap with the back of the jacks → next to the moile and perpendicular to the axis of the pipe → should release the piece. →

If it doesn't, chill the neck further with the jacks and try again. If it still doesn't release, you might try a drop of water on the neckline and 'bonk' it again. See below for the sure-fire method.

② Chill the Neck

BONK ③ Tap Free.

fig. 23
THE DRY TRANSFER TECHNIQUE

The Wet Look

This technique works well for most pieces, small or large, and seems to be the most popular of the assisted transfer methods. While your partner is preparing the correct style of punty for the piece you're making (see the Punty section for more information, pages 83-93), you may chill the neckline by rolling and necking the piece at the same time (as in fig. 23 above).

The punty is brought over and stuck-up by the gaffer using the tweezers to guide it on center. It's important that the assistant remains loose → just barely supporting the weight of the punty and keeping it evenly balanced. Even though the assistant has a better perspective on where the center of the bottom is — the gaffer takes control and has a better 'feel' for where it is → or he/she will as soon as it's attached.

Give the piece a few full revolutions down the bench and back, to check and center the punty's position. If the punty seems way-too-hot (by obvious movement up & down on the punty rod) your assistant may

Either blow on the punty area with a soffietta or the gaffer might blast it with some compressed air to chill and stiffen it up. Another way is to crimp or chill that area with the tweezers or back of the jacks.

Communication is helpful. The gaffer should check with the assistant prior to knocking the piece free. The assistant should have their hands spread out, balancing the weight of the punty and getting ready to deal with the weight of the soon-to-be transferred piece.

Once the punty exhibits signs of stiffening up, the gaffer dunks their whole hand in the water with the tweezers and carefully applies one good drop of water on the neckline → right on top-dead center.

This small amount of water should be all you need to thermal-shock the neckline and to release the piece. With really thick necks → some gaffers will trail a consistent flow of water all the way around the neck - being careful not to accidently splash the piece in the process (**fig. 25**).

The gaffer stands up. They lift the pipe off the rails of the bench and 'bonk' the pipe next to the moile with the back of the tweezers. It should break free with just a firm tap. If not...

USE MORE WATER! DON'T <u>CONTINUE</u> TO HAMMER **WHAM! WHAM! WHAM!** IT'S ONLY A SIGN OF IMPATIENCE AND A DEMON-*CRASH!*-STRATION THAT YOU'RE NOT *relaxed!* WATER WILL CURE THE PROBLEM BETTER THAN BRUTE FORCE.

The reason you lift the pipe off the bench prior to striking it is that the **rails** tend to absorb some of the shock & vibration which you're using to release the piece from the blowpipe. The situation is, that the piece is gonna "give" somewhere. Usually it'll "give" at the point where it's the coldest and least attached. If your punty cools too much before you try tapping the piece free → it will more-than-likely pop-off before the neck will. And then you have to do it all over again.. Sigh ☹ Or worse, both the punty and the piece will release, and you'll watch in seemingly slow-motion, the piece cascading to crash n' burn on the floor – (even a bigger SIGH ☹)! The lesson here is to have the punty ready and hot when it's needed, and to be swift in the transfer process. Unnecessary delays or improper punties may cost you your piece.

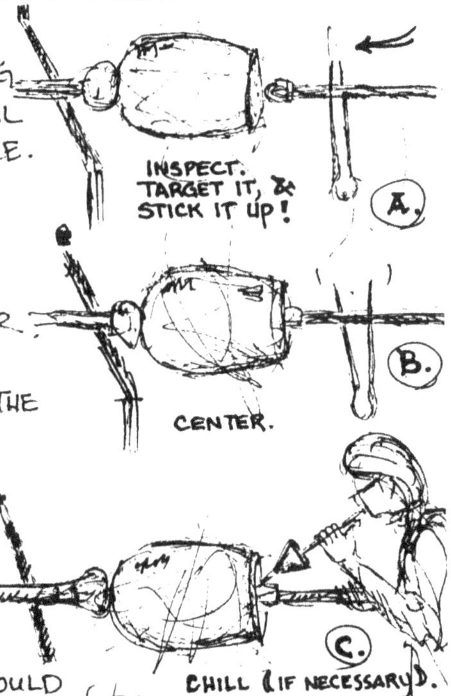

A. INSPECT, TARGET IT, & STICK IT UP!

B. CENTER.

C. CHILL (IF NECESSARY).

fig. 24

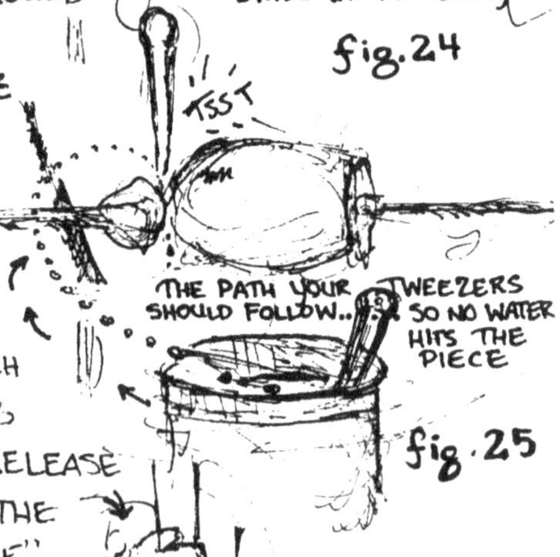

THE PATH YOUR TWEEZERS SHOULD FOLLOW.. SO NO WATER HITS THE PIECE

fig. 25

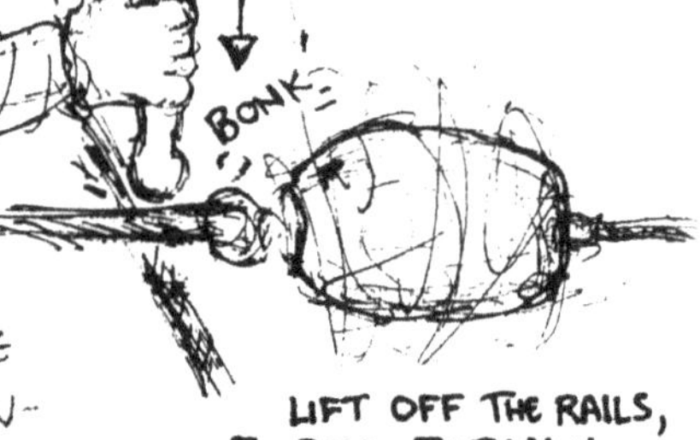

LIFT OFF THE RAILS, & BONK FIRMLY

fig. 26
THE WET-TRANSFER TECHNIQUE

28

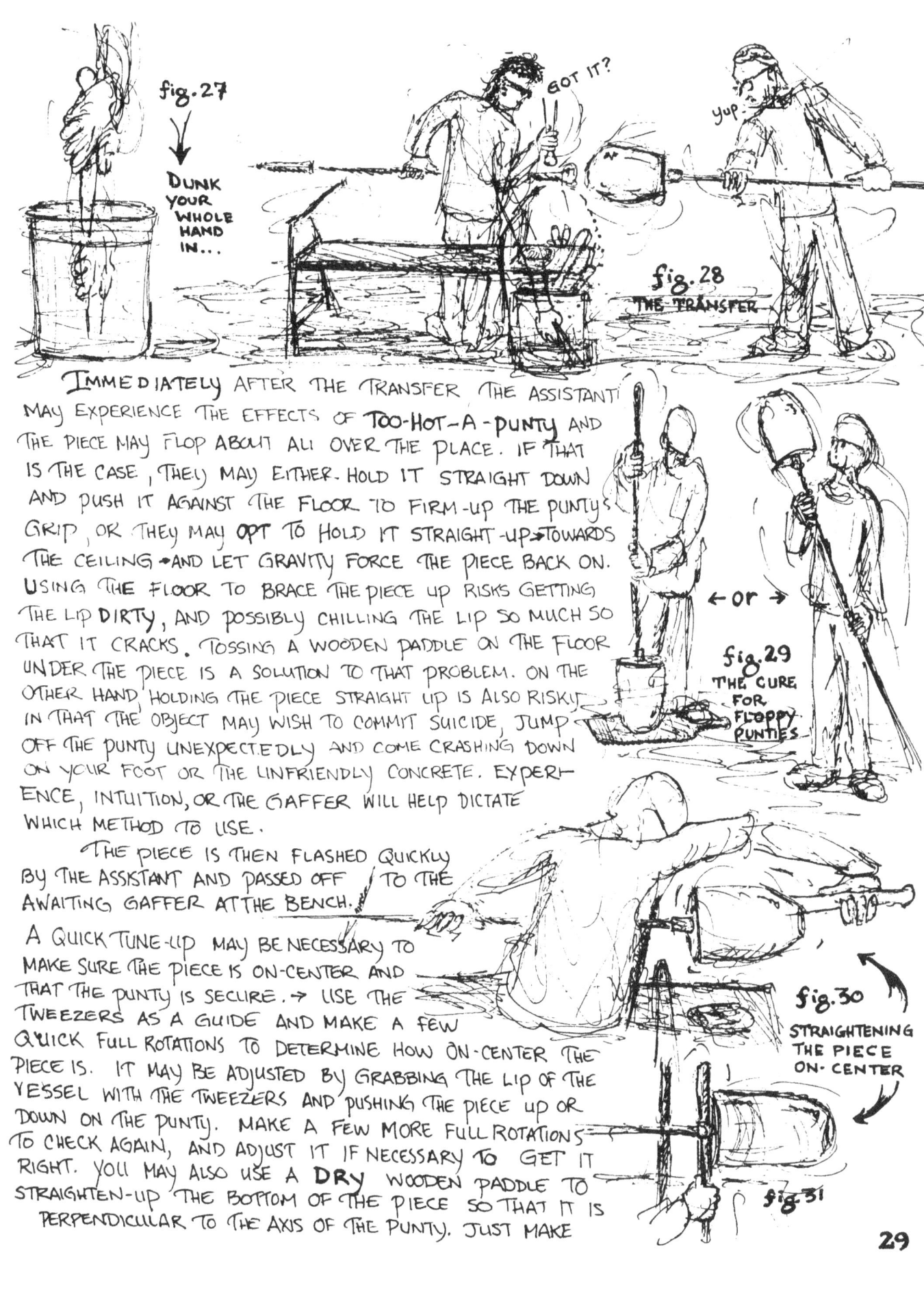

fig. 27 — Dunk your whole hand in...

"GOT IT?" "yup."

fig. 28 THE TRANSFER

IMMEDIATELY AFTER THE TRANSFER THE ASSISTANT MAY EXPERIENCE THE EFFECTS OF **TOO-HOT-A-PUNTY** AND THE PIECE MAY FLOP ABOUT ALL OVER THE PLACE. IF THAT IS THE CASE, THEY MAY EITHER HOLD IT STRAIGHT DOWN AND PUSH IT AGAINST THE FLOOR TO FIRM-UP THE PUNTY'S GRIP, OR THEY MAY **OPT** TO HOLD IT STRAIGHT-UP→TOWARDS THE CEILING →AND LET GRAVITY FORCE THE PIECE BACK ON. USING THE FLOOR TO BRACE THE PIECE UP RISKS GETTING THE LIP **DIRTY**, AND POSSIBLY CHILLING THE LIP SO MUCH SO THAT IT CRACKS. TOSSING A WOODEN PADDLE ON THE FLOOR UNDER THE PIECE IS A SOLUTION TO THAT PROBLEM. ON THE OTHER HAND, HOLDING THE PIECE STRAIGHT UP IS ALSO RISKY IN THAT THE OBJECT MAY WISH TO COMMIT SUICIDE, JUMP OFF THE PUNTY UNEXPECTEDLY AND COME CRASHING DOWN ON YOUR FOOT OR THE UNFRIENDLY CONCRETE. EXPERIENCE, INTUITION, OR THE GAFFER WILL HELP DICTATE WHICH METHOD TO USE.

←or→

fig. 29 THE CURE FOR FLOPPY PUNTIES

THE PIECE IS THEN FLASHED QUICKLY BY THE ASSISTANT AND PASSED OFF TO THE AWAITING GAFFER AT THE BENCH.

A QUICK TUNE-UP MAY BE NECESSARY TO MAKE SURE THE PIECE IS ON-CENTER AND THAT THE PUNTY IS SECURE. → USE THE TWEEZERS AS A GUIDE AND MAKE A FEW QUICK FULL ROTATIONS TO DETERMINE HOW ON-CENTER THE PIECE IS. IT MAY BE ADJUSTED BY GRABBING THE LIP OF THE VESSEL WITH THE TWEEZERS AND PUSHING THE PIECE UP OR DOWN ON THE PUNTY. MAKE A FEW MORE FULL ROTATIONS TO CHECK AGAIN, AND ADJUST IT IF NECESSARY TO GET IT RIGHT. YOU MAY ALSO USE A **DRY** WOODEN PADDLE TO STRAIGHTEN-UP THE BOTTOM OF THE PIECE SO THAT IT IS PERPENDICULAR TO THE AXIS OF THE PUNTY. JUST MAKE

fig. 30 STRAIGHTENING THE PIECE ON-CENTER

fig. 31

A FEW FULL ROTATIONS WHILE GENTLY PADDLING THE BOTTOM OF THE PIECE. THIS LITTLE BIT OF TWEAKING WILL HOPEFULLY GET YOUR PIECE FULLY ON CENTER AND ALLOW THE PUNTY AN OPPORTUNITY TO COOL OFF AND SET UP. YOU MAY THEN PROCEED TO TRIM AND/OR OPEN UP THE PIECE TO FINISH IT OFF.

TRIMMING

THE FIRST QUESTION YOU NEED TO ASK YOURSELF IS: "DO I NEED TO TRIM THIS PIECE?" NOT ALL VESSELS NEED TO BE TRIMMED AFTER THE TRANSFER - ESPECIALLY THOSE WHICH ARE BLOWN WELL TO BEGIN WITH. TRIMMING THE LIP CAN BE ONE OF THE MORE CHALLENGING HOT GLASS SKILLS TO ACQUIRE. THERE ARE NUMEROUS VARIABLES WHICH EFFECT THE OUTCOME OF THE TRIMMING PROCESS, AS REVIEWED BELOW.

TRIMMING CAN HELP THIN THE LIPS ON YOUR BLOWN OBJECTS. TRIMMING CAN HELP "CLEAN-UP" THE JAGGED EDGE LEFT FROM THE TRANSFER PROCESS. YOU MAY ALSO WISH TO KILL TWO BIRDS WITH ONE STONE BY ELONGATING THE NECK AND TRIMMING AT THE SAME TIME.

OVERHEAD VIEW

METHOD ONE:

THERE ARE BASICALLY TWO METHODS WHICH WORK WELL FOR TRIMMING. IN METHOD ONE (PICTURED AT THE RIGHT), YOU CRIMP AND SIMULTANEOUSLY PULL THE LIP WITH THE TWEEZERS, REHEAT AND CUT THE EXCESS OFF WITH THE TRIMMING SHEARS. IN METHOD TWO (ON THE NEXT PAGE), THE LIP IS INITIALLY CRIMPED AND PULLED WITH THE TWEEZERS, THEN NECKED AND DRAWN OUT FURTHER WITH THE JACKS - REHEATED AND THE EXCESS NECKED AND TAPPED OFF.

PULLING THE LIP FIRST...

METHOD ONE WORKS WELL FOR EVERYTHING, FROM GOBLETS TO WIDE-MOUTHED VESSELS, WHERE YOU NEED ONLY TO 'TRUE-UP' THE LIP AND THIN ACCORDINGLY. IT DOES NOT NECESSARILY ALTER THE FORM AS MUCH AS METHOD TWO CAN.

WORKING ON THE TOP SIDE

METHOD ONE: BEGIN BY MAKING CERTAIN THAT YOUR PIECE IS ON CENTER (AS DESCRIBED IN THE PREVIOUS SECTION). NEXT, THE LIP MUST BE HEATED WELL ENOUGH TO PULL AND CRIMP WITHOUT USING TOO MUCH FORCE → HOT GOOD, COLD BAD! IF THE LIP IS HEATED WELL ENOUGH YOU MAY CRIMP, PULL AND CUT THE LIP ALL IN ONE FELL SWOOP. OR YOU MAY END UP TAKING AN EXTRA REHEAT TO FINISH THE TRIM.

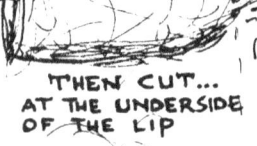
THEN CUT... AT THE UNDERSIDE OF THE LIP

IN ANY CASE, START ON THE TOP OF THE LIP, CRIMP AND PULL THE LIP OUTWARDS, MAKING MANY SMALL RAPID 'NIPS'. CONTINUE TO FEED MORE LIP INTO THE PATH OF THE TWEEZERS' TIPS KEEPING YOUR HAND STATIONARY. USUALLY TWO FULL ROTATIONS OF 'NIPPEN AT THE LIPPEN' SHOULD EVEN-OUT THE TOP PORTION OF THE VESSEL.

WITH YOUR TRIMMING SHEARS IN HAND, CUT FIRST IN DIAGONALLY TO THE LIP. THIS IS DONE ON THE BOTTOM SECTION OF THE LIP SO THAT THE TRAILINGS WILL FALL DOWN TOWARDS THE FLOOR VERSUS BACK ON TO YOUR PIECE. ALSO, IT WON'T BLOCK YOUR VIEW! ONCE YOU'VE CUT-IN DEEP ENOUGH, RE-ANGLE THE DIRECTION OF YOUR SHEARS PERPENDICULAR TO THE PIECE AND CONTINUE TO TRIM THE WHOLE LIP. SMALL SHORT SNIPS WORK BETTER FOR TRIMMING THAN ATTEMPTING LARGE SWEEPING CUTS.

SO THE TRAILINGS FALL DOWN.

HAVE AN ASSISTANT STANDING BY TO SHIELD YOUR

fig. 32 SMOOTHING IT OUT...

HAND FROM THE EXCESSIVE HEAT (especially the THUMB!). THIS IS PARTICULARLY IMPORTANT WHEN WORKING ON LARGE PIECES. THE ASSISTANT SHOULD ALSO HAVE A PAIR OF TWEEZERS OR SOME TOOL TO GUIDE THE CUTTINGS TO THE FLOOR AND NOT BACK ON YOUR PIECE. THEY ARE NOT TO GRAB OR PULL ON THE CUTTINGS AS IT WILL **DISTORT** THE **LIP** AND DISRUPT YOUR TRIMMING PROCEDURE.

IF THERE'S SUFFICIENT HEAT LEFT IN THE LIP AFTER CRIMPING AND PULLING → YOU MIGHT BE ABLE TO TRIM THE WHOLE THING CLEAN. IF NOT YOU MAY END UP HAVING TO BAIL-OUT HALFWAY OR SO TO REHEAT IN ORDER TO FINISH THE JOB. IF THAT'S THE CASE, BE SURE TO SNIP OFF WHATEVER TRAILINGS YOU'VE CREATED BEFORE REHEATING. ← THEY MAY WANT TO FALL BACK ON THE PIECE → REQUIRING YOU TO **RE-DO** THE WHOLE TRIMMING PROCESS ALL OVER AGAIN!

METHOD TWO: PULL THE LIP...

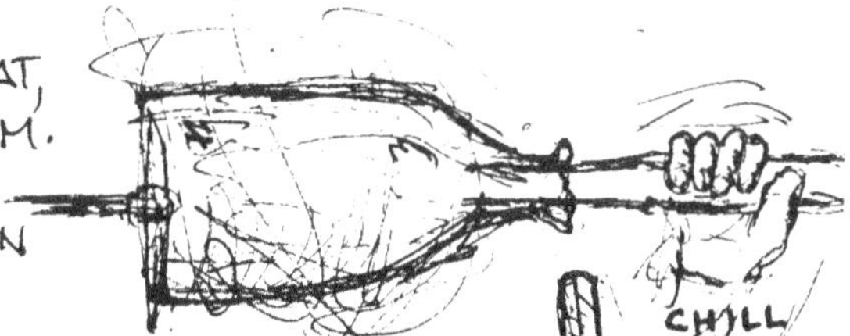

ONCE THE LIP IS FULLY TRIMMED, YOU MAY REHEAT, OPEN, AND PADDLE THE LIP SMOOTH TO IT'S FINAL FORM. OR YOU MAY OPT TO PUFF-OUT THE SHOULDERS OF THE FORM WITH THE SOFFIETTA OR STEAM STICK, AND THEN OPEN UP THE PIECE.

METHOD TWO: THIS METHOD MAY BE EMPLOYED TO ELONGATE THE SHOULDERS AND NECK AREA AS WELL AS A TECHNIQUE TO THIN THE UPPER PART OF YOUR VESSEL. BEGIN BY CRIMPING AND PULLING THE LIP AND NECK OUT AS IN METHOD ONE. REHEAT AGAIN, CONCENTRATING ON THE SHOULDERS AND NECK AREA (DON'T FORGET TO FLASH THAT PUNTY) - RETURN TO THE BENCH WHEN HOT.

CHILL THE INSIDE...

BEGIN TO CHILL THE INSIDE OF THE NECK WITH THE BLADES OF THE JACKS. → THIS HELPS SET-IT-UP AND MAINTAIN THINGS ON-CENTER. THEN MOVE THE JACKS TO THE OUTSIDE AND INITIATE A NECKLINE SQUEEZING LIGHTLY. YOU'RE MOSTLY CHILLING THE NECK AND ESTABLISHING A DEFINED LINE, NOT SO MUCH TIGHTENING OR CLOSING-DOWN THE OPENING WITH THIS PROCEDURE. AFTER A COUPLE OF SWIFT REVOLUTIONS BACK N' FORTH, BEGIN TO PULL THE NECK OUTWARDS AWAY FROM THE BOTTOM OF THE PIECE (CONTINUING THOSE QUICK REVOLUTIONS AS YOU DO SO).

NECK & PULL...

IT MAY TAKE YOU ONE OR TWO MORE REHEATS AND PULLS TO OBTAIN THE LENGTH AND WALL-THICKNESS YOU DESIRE.

ONCE THE PIECE IS STRETCHED TO YOUR SATISFACTION, YOU CAN KNOCK-OFF THE EXCESS. FIRST, CHILL THE NECK WITH THE JACKS; CRIMP IT THEN WITH THE DIAMOND SHEARS. AS YOU'RE DOING THAT, HAVE YOUR ASSISTANT TAP OFF THE EXCESS WITH THE BACK END OF THE TWEEZERS OR SIMILAR TOOL, WHEN YOU FEEL THAT IT IS COLD ENOUGH TO DO SO. THEY MAY ALSO BLOW ON THE NECK AREA WITH THE SOFFIETTA TO CHILL IT FASTER AND INSURE THAT IT BREAKS OFF CLEAN.

TAP OFF EXCESS

THE PIECE MAY THEN BE REHEATED, FIRE-POLISHED OR OPENED FURTHER TO YOUR SATISFACTION.

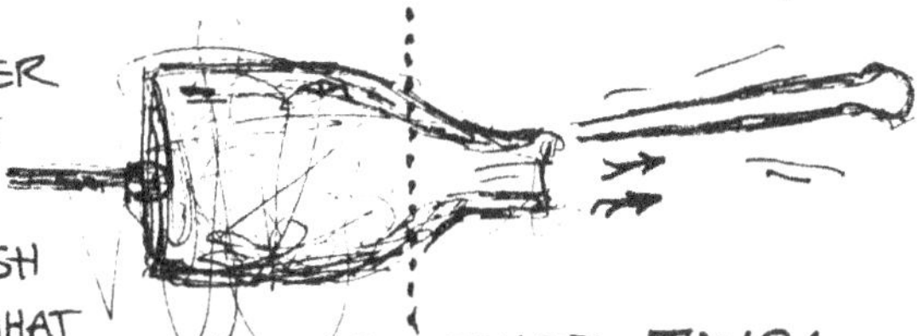

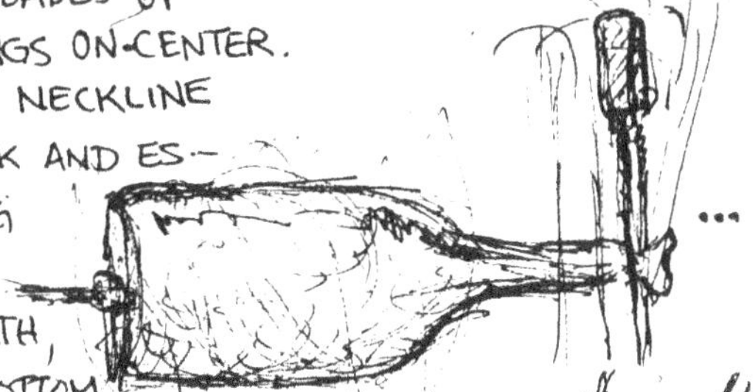

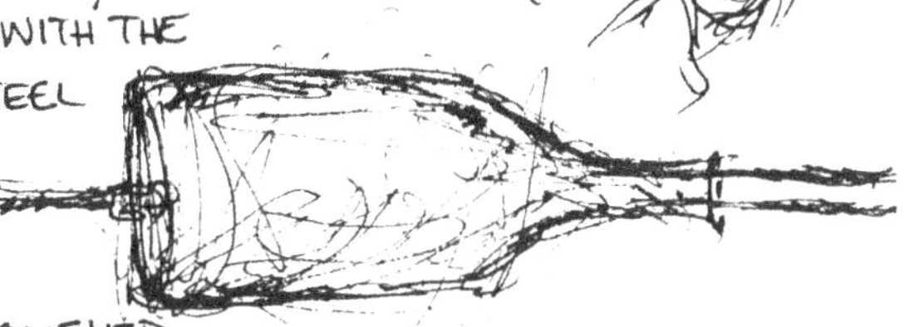

fig 33   SMOOTH IT OUT.

The same effect may be achieved if you're working by yourself. You may set the piece on the rail of the bench, right on the pre-chilled neckline. This helps brace the piece as you tap off the excess with the back of the jacks (see fig. 34 to the right→). The piece then may be reheated and finished-off as you wish.

FACTORS EFFECTING THE TRIMMING PROCESS:

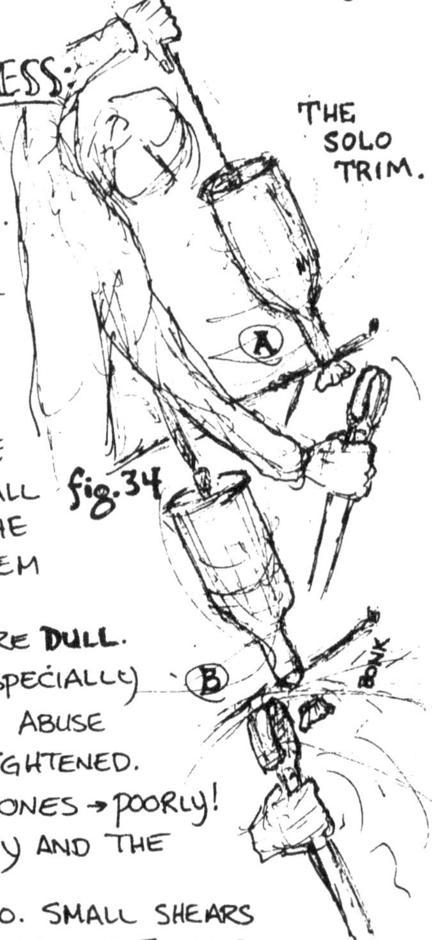

TOOLS Maybe your **TWEEZERS** won't grip the glass. If they seem to slip off the hot glass instead of grab it, there's a good chance they have some wax on them. Have your assistant clean them for you (see page 12) while you go for a reheat. Or to prevent it from happening in the first place, make sure they're clean to begin with and avoid setting them down near any wax source.

Maybe your **SHEARS** won't cut either because there's wax on them too! (Where does this stuff come from?!) For some reason wax seems to creep-up on all tools except your jacks! Clean your shears in the same manner as your tweezers and try to steer them away from the wax.

Perhaps your shears don't work because they're **DULL**. They probably need to be sharpened (see page 286), especially if they're 'shop shears' which endure a MYRIAD of abuse and neglect. Or perhaps they may need only to be tightened. Loose trimming shears work about as well as dull ones→poorly! Tighten up the nut so the handles still move freely and the blades meet snugly.

Having the right shears for the job helps too. Small shears work great for trimming. Many gaffers have a special pair of these solely for the purpose of trimming. Large shears are too bulky and don't allow you complete access. Small ones can get-in to tight spaces and are easier to maneuver.

THE SOLO TRIM.

fig. 34

TEMPERATURE & TIMING
Vital to nearly all hot glass processes, timing is everything! (well... almost). Having the correct heat to perform all the steps you wish to accomplish is also critical. This is especially true with trimming. If the lip ain't hot enough, you'll end up chewing and crunching it. Not only does it send particles of glass everywhere, it is a particularly unkind of thing to do to your shears, and it makes a jagged mess on the top of your vessel. Yuk! HOT GOOD - COLD BAD.

On the other hand, if you heat your piece too deeply in the glory hole, it can make trimming your glass a really difficult task. Without the stability of the cooled shoulder area - the activity of trimming may distort the whole upper area of your piece and ruin the tight form you were diligently trying to attain. In other words, heat only those areas which you wish to work on, and do your best to avoid overheating it. Likewise, if the punty gets too hot, the whole piece might start moving around on you as you try to trim your piece ~ making it very difficult to keep things symmetrical.

SPEED & SKILL
If you trim too slowly, the lip area may cool off too much, making it very difficult to complete the trim. Hint: work faster. If you have to fumble around to find your tools you may lose valuable seconds which will also cause the lip to cool off.

This technique takes practice to perfect (imagine that!) One exercise to improve your skills is to make small tumblers quickly and trim them several times. This means pulling out the lip, trimming, and reshaping the lip area to do it all over again. Do it as many times as you can until you wind-up with an ashtray. Repeat as often as necessary.

SIZE OF WORK
The scale of your piece can effect the outcome of the trimming process, both in terms of the thickness of the lip and it's diameter. Thicker lips are easier to trim because they hold the heat longer than their thinner counterparts. Smaller openings are easier to trim because there's less distance to cut through.

Radiant heat can make it physically punishing to trim larger pieces, especially if there is no protection available. More than once I've dropped my smokin' hot shears during the trimming process 'cause my hand couldn't take the heat. Find someone to block the heat (not your vision!) while you trim. (See page 246 for tips on shielding). Some gaffers I've seen will dunk their hand in cold water prior to trimming as an effort to keep cool. Another trick is to have a damp cool washcloth to cover your hand as you trim. It may protect you long enough to get all the way through those tough trim jobs, or it'll start steaming like crazy and fry you even worse!

Also, really long pieces may require you to work off the end of the bench if you max-out your reach while sitting. This completely changes your perspective on trimming, as well as how you go about doing it. See page 80 in the teamworking section for more information.

BITING OFF MORE THAN YOU CAN CHEW
This is related to speed and skill. Sometimes you may end up cutting too much too fast and everything gets all outta wack. Do not be hasty! A delay is better than a disaster.

WHEN IT'S TIME TO BOX IT...
For Pete's sake be CAREFUL! Try to avoid hitting your punty or bumping into things en route to the annealer. Angle the punty so no water hits the piece. Use the tweezers to apply a drop or five on the joint where the piece meets the punty. Allow the assistant to lift gently on the piece and bonk it free!

VASES

IF ALL YOUR BOWLS LOOK LIKE UPSIDEDOWN FLOPPY HATS AND ALL YOUR VASES END UP AS CYLINDERS WITH FUNKY LIPS, THEN THESE NEXT TWO SECTIONS ARE FOR YOU. BEYOND THE SKILLS YOU NEED TO EXECUTE THEM, IT HELPS TO KNOW SOMETHING ABOUT DESIGN. BECOME INFORMED, TAKE A COURSE IN 3-D DESIGN. STUDY OTHER OBJECTS AND DESIGNS. LEARN THE BASIC ELEMENTS WHICH MAKE A BOWL A BOWL — OR A VASE A VASE. ALSO, **IT'S IMPORTANT THAT YOU DRAW THE FORMS YOU WANT TO MAKE.** DRAWING HELPS YOU **VISUALIZE** IN YOUR **MINDS EYE** EXACTLY WHAT IT IS THAT YOU'RE SHOOTING FOR. VISUALIZING THE PIECE BEFOREHAND, PLUS HAVING A DRAWING TO GUIDE YOU, CAN SAVE TREMENDOUS AMOUNTS OF TIME AND EFFORT, PLUS MAKE YOU ALL AROUND A BETTER GLASS BLOWER!

MY RECOMMENDATION IS TO FIRST ATTEMPT TO BLOW THESE FORMS IN CLEAR GLASS — NO COLOR. KEEP THEM ON THE SMALL SIDE → 3 to 4 GATHERS. THIS WILL HELP YOU UNDERSTAND THE STEPS NECESSARY TO COMPLETING THE SHAPES WITHOUT THE EXTRA TIME AND RESOURCES THAT LARGER OR COLORED PIECES REQUIRE.

BASIC CYLINDER — MARVERED MAIN FORM — PAPERED & PADDLED FOOT, FLARED LIP

4 TIERED BUBBLE — PAPERED OR BLOCKED — NECKED SECTIONS PADDLED FOOT FLARED LIP

JACK-IN-THE PULPIT — BLOCKED, NECKED AND STRETCHED (LOWER HALF) PADDLED BOTTOM FLARED AND PULLED LIP

AMPHORA — BLOCKED, DOUBLE-NECKED. PAPERED WAIST, COOKIE FOOT FLARED LIP

CONE — MARVERED FORM USE JACKS TO SHAPE BLOW & PADDLE FOOT FLARED UP & HANDLES

MOST VASES WILL HAVE MORE OR LESS THE FOLLOWING ELEMENTS — STARTING FROM THE GROUND ON UP: A FOOT, A WAIST, SHOULDERS, A NECK AND A LIP. SOMETIMES A WAIST OR SHOULDER AREA MAY BE VISUALLY ABSENT — THAT IS, NOT IMMEDIATELY IDENTIFIABLE, WHEREAS OTHER TIMES IT MAY BE THE MOST IMPORTANT PART.

CERTAIN SIZE RATIOS OF EACH ELEMENT ARE VITAL TO THE FUNCTION AND FORM OF EACH VESSEL. SOME VASES ARE VERY FUNCTIONAL — WITH RESPECT TO DOMESTIC PURPOSES. THEY ARE VERY STABLE, THEY HOLD WATER AND CAN CONTAIN AN ASSORTMENT OF

FLOWERS OR OTHER THINGS. CONVERSELY, SOME 'VASES' ARE STYLISTICLY INTERESTING BUT NEVER HAVE THE POSSIBILITY OF HOLDING WATER, ARE UNSTABLE AND HIGHLY UNLIKELY TO EVER SPORT FLOWERS. VASES FALLING UNDER (OR OVER) IN THIS CATAGORY ARE AESTHETIC OBJECTS WHOSE FUNCTION IS BEAUTY AND WHOSE ROOTS MAY LIE IN HISTORY, OR OUTER SPACE.

THE FIVE THINGS PEOPLE LOOK FOR IN A VASE ARE: ① MATERIAL → "IS THAT GLASS?" ② COLOR ③ SIZE OF THE PIECE ④ WILL IT HOLD FLOWERS? ⑤ PRICE. ALL OF THESE FACTORS ARE AT YOUR DISPOSAL. FEEL FREE TO CHANGE ANY OF THEM, ANYTIME. REALISTICALLY SPEAKING, THERE'S ONLY SO MANY FORMS A GLASS BUBBLE MIGHT YIELD TO BECOMING A FLOWER RECEPTICAL, BUT WITH STYLISTIC VARIATIONS SUCH AS BITS, HANDLES, FEET AND COLOR, AN INFINITE VARIETY ABOUND.

☠ A WORD OF CAUTION: BE EXTRA CAREFUL WHEN DESIGNING, BLOWING AND MARKETING YOUR 'WARES'. YOU MAY HIT UPON A VASE DESIGN WHICH EVERYBODY WANTS; AND YOU MAY GET STUCK MAKING THEM FOR THE REST OF YOUR LIFE! FOR SOME GLASSBLOWERS I KNOW THIS HAS BECOME ONE OF THOSE FATES-WORSE-THAN-DEATH. REALLY, IF YOU HAVEN'T FIGURED IT OUT ALREADY, GLASS SELLS (esp. COBALT BLUE). IT'S VERY EASY TO BECOME LOCKED-IN TO THE LUCRATIVE 'CRAFT MARKET' TO FINANCE YOUR GLASS HABIT, BUT IT CAN BE A DOUBLE-EDGED SWORD. SOON YOUR "FREE TIME" TO PLAY AND EXPLORE EXCITING AVENUES OF GLASSMAKING WILL DISOLVE INTO 'FILLING MORE ORDERS' - AND GLASSBLOWING MAY BECOME A CHORE INSTEAD OF THE CREATIVE OUTLET THAT IT USED TO BE.

BACK-2-THE-BASICS → REFER TO THE DIRECTORY OF BASIC BLOWN FORMS THAT STARTED OUT THIS CHAPTER FOR IDEAS ON HOW TO BLOW A VARIETY OF SHAPES SUITABLE FOR VASES. WITH THE PIECE ON THE PUNTY YOU CAN EASILY AUGMENT YOUR VESSELS APPEARANCE TEN-FOLD MERELY BY STRETCHING THE NECK, FLARING OR TRIMMING THE LIP, PUFFING OUT THE SHOULDERS, OR NECKING IN ADDITIONAL LINES.

ONCE YOU CONQUER THE SKILLS IT TAKES TO MAKE THE TRADITIONAL FORMS MAKING. YOU MAY EMBARK ON MORE ELABORATE TECHNIQUES SUITABLE FOR ALL STYLES OF VESSEL YOUR PIECES. YOU MAY CHOOSE TO USE **CANEWORK** OR **INCALMO** METHODS FOR COLORING CAGEWORK OR DECORATIVE TRAILS N' BITS. THERE IS A WHOLE VARIETY OF SURFACE DECORATIONS AND TREATMENTS TO CONSIDER AS WELL. **MOLDBLOWING** OR EXPLORING ASYMMETRICAL FORMS MAY BE OF INTEREST TO YOU. AND WHY STOP THERE? CONSIDERING THE TECHNOLOGICAL BREAK-THROUGHS IN THE ADHESIVE INDUSTRY TODAY - YOU MAY INDULGE YOURSELF IN GLUING MULTIPLE PARTS TO CREATE SOME REALLY LARGE FORMS WHICH MAY OTHERWISE BE IMPOSSIBLE TO MAKE HOT. AND THAT TOUCHES ON YET ANOTHER OUTLET FOR VISUAL ENHANCEMENT → **COLDWORKING**. THINK ABOUT HOW YOUR PIECES WILL BE FINISHED. THEY MAY BE PAINTED, ENAMELED, SANDBLASTED, BATUTOED, CUT, GROUND, POLISHED, DRILLED, SAWED, - YOU NAME IT. YOU'RE THE BUS DRIVER. IN THE NEXT CHAPTER I'LL COVER HOW TO GO ABOUT BLOWING LARGE VESSELS IN A TEAMWORK SITUATION - CHECK IT OUT FOR ADDITIONAL INFORMATION.

BOWLS

Since the advent of glassblowing some two thousand years ago, gaffers have been making one of the most functional forms of vessels → the bowl. With the domestication of goldfish, there has always been at least one thing to put in them...

Bowls can be relatively easy to execute and can be made in a variety of sizes and shapes. They may sport an extra foot or simply lay flat. They can be intensely colorful and loose in form or remain pure & simple in clear glass, in a nice traditional style. The Swedes tend to excell in making the most precise off-hand versions of this form, to the point of being very particular (anal) about each and every element. The results of their labors are nevertheless flawless. And it all begins on the drawing board. Where else?

You can teach yourself a number of useful techniques by practicing the **BOWL FORM**. It's crucial to have a symmetrical start and to maintain uniform wall-thickness throughout the process. Any deviation will wreak havoc with your ability to open the form evenly when it's on the punty.

Begin by blowing a squat form, (as in fig.35(A) above). You then have the option of: applying a button (see page 71 for more info), adding a foot (or feet), or paddling the form flat and sticking it up. ← You can use the jacks to shape the sides of your bowl as your assistant paddles the bottom in.

Once the piece has been transferred, you can either trim the lip, puff out the shoulders or open up the form with the jacks, or a combo of all three. To open the piece, you can use the metal jacks to get it

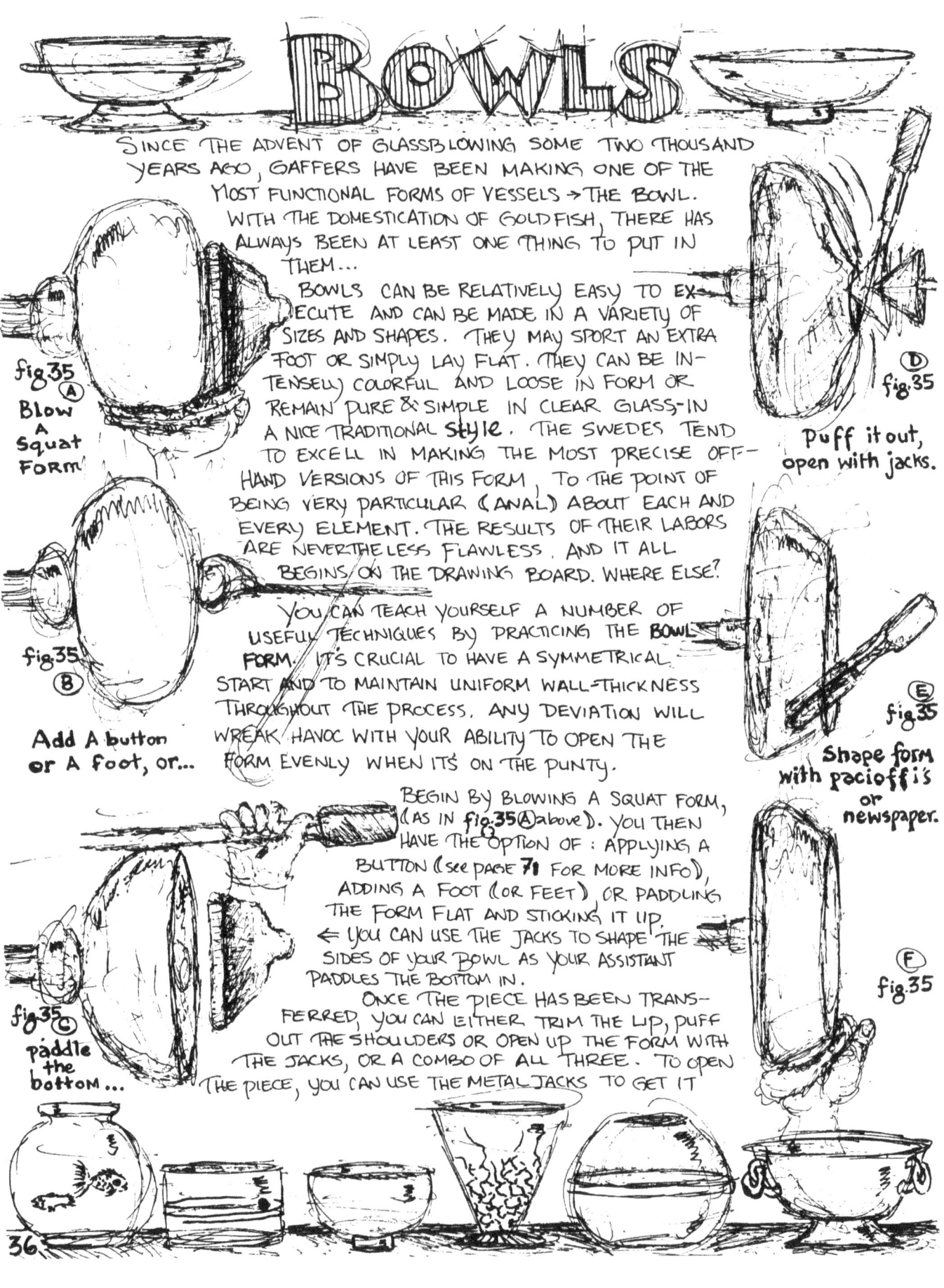

fig.35 (A) Blow a squat form

fig.35 (B) Add a button or a foot, or...

fig.35 (C) Paddle the bottom...

fig.35 (D) Puff it out, open with jacks.

fig.35 (E) Shape form with pacioffi's or newspaper.

fig.35 (F)

36

ABOUT HALFWAY THERE. BE SURE YOUR JACKS ARE WELL-LUBED WITH BEESWAX OR SUFFER THE CONSEQUENCES (UNSIGHTLY SCRATCH MARKS). THEN SWITCH TO THE PACIOFFI'S TO FINISH OPENING THE BOWL (SEE fig. 35E). YOU MAY ALSO KEEP YOUR FORM CONTAINED BY NEWSPAPERING IT TO PREVENT IT FROM FLARING-OUT PREMATURELY. AT ANY POINT DURING THE OPENING PROCESS YOU MAY HAVE YOUR ASSISTANT STANDING BY WITH THE PADDLE TO SMOOTH THE LIP NICE N' EVEN.

TIPS FOR SUCCESSFUL BOWL MAKING:

⇒ **PRACTICE SMALL CLEAR PIECES FIRST.** LEARN ALL THE STEPS INVOLVED IN MAKING THESE FORMS BEFORE EMBARKING ON MORE ELABORATE CREATIONS. GET TO THE POINT WHERE YOU CAN DUPLICATE THE FORMS WITHOUT TOO MUCH EFFORT. UNDERSTAND HOW TO CORRECT YOUR MISTAKES SHOULD THEY HAPPEN, OR TRY TO PREVENT THEM IN THE FIRST PLACE. LET EXPERIENCE AND SKILL BE YOUR GUIDE.

⇒ **WATCH YOUR SIZE CAREFULLY.** EAT A DIET RICH IN VEGETABLES AND FRESH FRUIT, WITH PLENTY OF FIBER AND CUT-OUT SWEETS AND FOODS HIGH IN FAT. NO... ACTUALLY, BE CAREFUL WHEN SHAPING AND BLOWING YOUR BOWL THAT YOU DON'T MAX-OUT THE DIAMETER OF THE GLORY HOLE. WHEN BOWLS GET LARGE AND WIDE THEY TEND TO DEVELOP AN AFFINITY WITH THE INSIDE OF YOUR GLORY HOLE OR IT'S DOORS AND VERY MUCH WANT TO STICK THERE! PLAY IT SAFE AND LEAVE YOURSELF SOME CLEARANCE. IT'S ALOT EASIER TO CONCENTRATE ON YOUR GLASSBLOWING IF YOU DON'T HAVE TO WORRY ABOUT WHETHER OR NOT YOUR PIECE IS GONNA FIT OR GET STUCK IN THE GLORY HOLE.

⇒ **USE THE RIGHT DIAMETER PUNTY.** DON'T ACCEPT THOSE SKINNY GOBLET PUNTIES IF SOMEONE BRINGS ONE TO YOU TO STICK-UP YOUR BOWL WITH. FOR OPENING BOWLS YOU WILL WANT A LARGER DIAMETER PUNTY ROD WHICH REQUIRES LESS TURNING THAN THEIR THINNER COUNTERPARTS. THIS WAY YOU'LL ENJOY THE STABILITY AND ADDITIONAL TORQUE PROVIDED BY A STURDIER, MORE SUBSTANSIAL STYLE OF PUNTY.

⇒ **TAKE NUMEROUS REHEATS.** PROCEDE WITH CAUTION. OPEN THE BOWL A LITTLE AT A TIME VERSUS JUST SPINNING IT OUT. YOU WILL GAIN MORE CONTROL OVER YOUR FORM. IT WILL ALSO ALLOW YOU MORE LEE-WAY IN HOW THE FINISHED PIECE WILL LOOK BY CHANGING THE SLIGHT VARIATIONS POSSIBLE IN THE LIP OF THE PIECE.

⇒ **DO NOT HEAT TOO DEEPLY IN THE GLORY HOLE.** IT'S VERY EASY TO GET THE BOTTOM TOO HOT AND PULL IT OUT WITH THE PUNTY, THUS DESTROYING ANY HOPE OF THE PIECE SITTING FLAT. TAKE IT EASY, AND REHEAT WITH CARE.

⇒ **WATCH YOUR SPEED.** AVOID TURNING THE PIPE TOO FAST. CENTRIFUGAL FORCE WILL WANT TO OPEN UP YOUR PIECE FOR YOU. THE FASTER YOU TURN IT, THE MORE PRONOUNCED THIS EFFECT WILL BE.

⇒ **LET NATURE BE YOUR GUIDE.** BUT YOU SHOULD BE THE GLASS'ES MASTER. THE LESS TOOLS YOU USE THE BETTER. YOU CAN ALLOW THE NATURAL TURNING MOTION HELP YOU OPEN UP YOUR FORM WITHOUT GETTING TOOL MARKS IN THE GLASS, BUT ULTIMATELY THE FINAL SHAPING SHOULD COME FROM YOU. THIS MIGHT MEAN: A SLIGHT TUNE-UP IN THE FORM WITH THE JACKS AND PADDLES JUST BEFORE YOU BOX IT, OR POSSIBLY PAPERING-IN THE SIDEWALLS TO ACHIEVE A CURVED SURFACE WHICH YOU DESIRE, OR MAYBE, CREATING AN UNDULATION IN THE LIP WITH THE TWEEZERS - WHATEVER.

FEET

The foot has the ability to significantly change the overall impression of your vessel. It may reflect or accent the main body's form. It may serve as a means to up-lift the piece ⇒ to showcase the **REALLY IMPORTANT STUFF**. Or it may act as structural support to aid in balancing the vessel.

Stylistic variations on feet are numerous. The cookie foot is one which you may have already picked up on. The dropped foot (Swedish-style) is another which is appropriate for many styles of vessels. The blown foot can lift your vessels to new heights without the weight that their solid counterparts add. You can also make feet or "landing pads" with bits of glass. Handle-style bits can also double as legs for your vessels as well. —NOTE: Three legs are easier to deal with than four or more. The tripod-method is the most stable of leg supports — whereas with four legs you almost always end up with one leg being shorter than another and the piece may rock when set on a flat surface.

COOKIE FOOT REVIEW
2-3 GATHERS

The cookie foot is a simple way to apply a stable base to your piece. Have your assistant get 2 or 3 gathers on a punty — allowing it to ball-up on the way over to the marver. Simply by maintaining the punty horizontal and keeping the rotation even, the gathers will round themselves out with little-to-no extra effort. This extra bit of air marvering will insure your cookie is round instead of oval. The bit is then allowed to drop onto the marver and is cut-off with the diamond shears.

The piece is centered over the cookie (use your diamond shears to guide your pipe) lightly touched down and then rotated side-to-side to determine if it's on-center. Any adjustments can be made by slightly angling or pushing the pipe to make further contact and line the cookie up. Then the piece may be reheated. Get the foot hot enough that the chill marks disappear. Then you can take it back to the bench and paddle it flat-n-smooth or you may elect to create a kicked-foot by angling the jacks against the inside part of the foot and having your assistant paddle the bottom smooth and uniform. Use quick full rotations to insure a nice even taper to the foot. Punty as usual.

SIMPLE BLOWN FOOT

THIS IS AN ALTERNATIVE TO THE ITALIAN METHOD OF BLOWN FEET (SEE PAGE 142). HERE A TWO OR THREE-GATHER BUBBLE IS BLOWN AND NECKED BY THE ASSISTANT. THE BOTTOM OF THEIR BUBBLE IS HEATED FAIRLY HOT AND THEN PRESENTED TO THE GAFFER AT THE BENCH LIKE A PUNTY. THE GAFFER THEN CENTERS AND ATTACHES IT TO THE BOTTOM. A FEW ROTATIONS ARE MADE TO CENTER THINGS UP. THE NECK OF THE FOOT BUBBLE IS CHILLED WITH THE JACKS AND THEN TAPPED FREE BY THE ASSISTANT WITH THE BACK OF THEIR TWEEZERS.

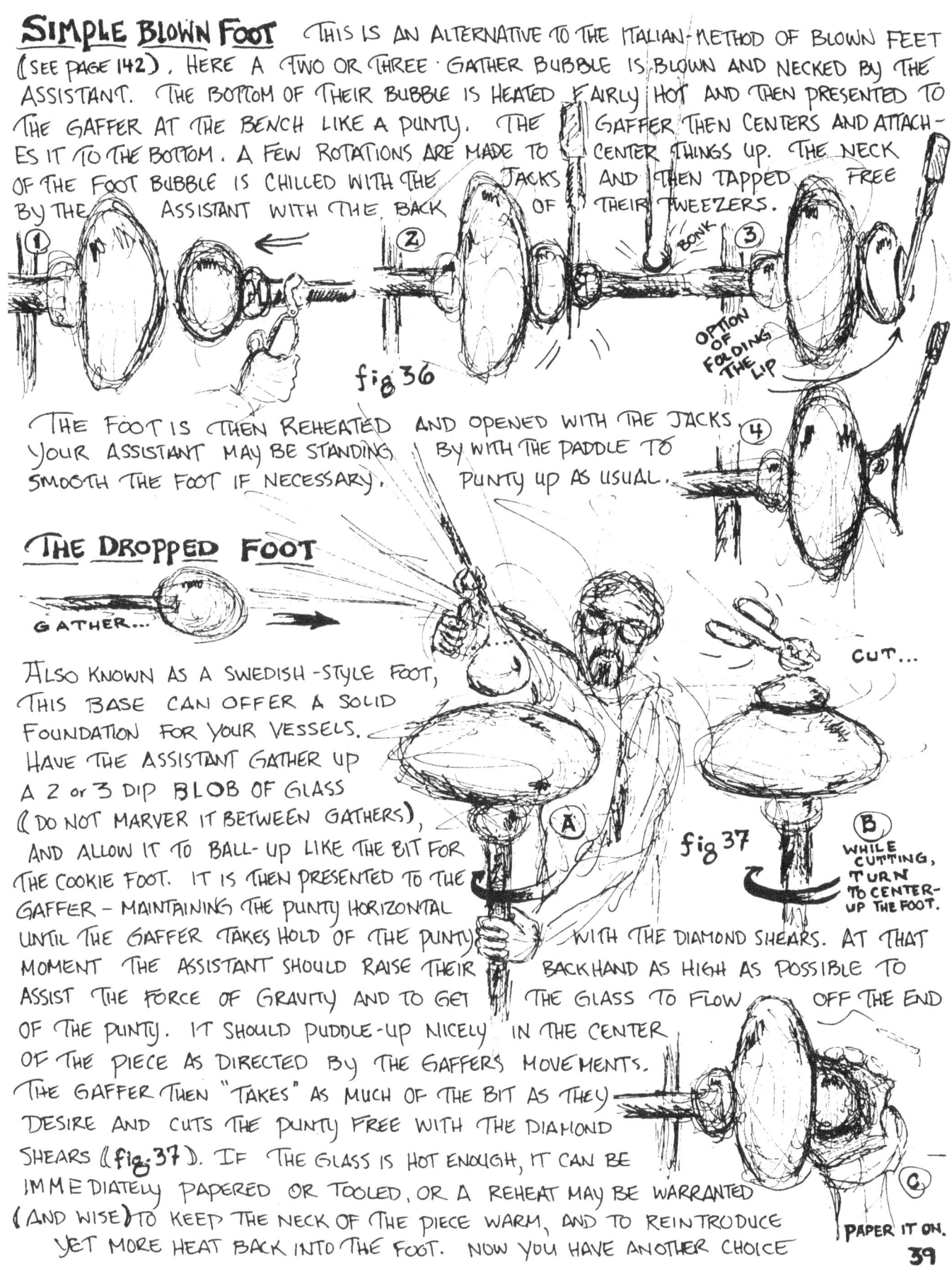

fig 36

THE FOOT IS THEN REHEATED AND OPENED WITH THE JACKS. YOUR ASSISTANT MAY BE STANDING BY WITH THE PADDLE TO SMOOTH THE FOOT IF NECESSARY. PUNTY UP AS USUAL.

THE DROPPED FOOT

ALSO KNOWN AS A SWEDISH-STYLE FOOT, THIS BASE CAN OFFER A SOLID FOUNDATION FOR YOUR VESSELS. HAVE THE ASSISTANT GATHER UP A 2 OR 3 DIP BLOB OF GLASS (DO NOT MARVER IT BETWEEN GATHERS), AND ALLOW IT TO BALL-UP LIKE THE BIT FOR THE COOKIE FOOT. IT IS THEN PRESENTED TO THE GAFFER — MAINTAINING THE PUNTY HORIZONTAL UNTIL THE GAFFER TAKES HOLD OF THE PUNTY WITH THE DIAMOND SHEARS. AT THAT MOMENT THE ASSISTANT SHOULD RAISE THEIR BACKHAND AS HIGH AS POSSIBLE TO ASSIST THE FORCE OF GRAVITY AND TO GET THE GLASS TO FLOW OFF THE END OF THE PUNTY. IT SHOULD PUDDLE-UP NICELY IN THE CENTER OF THE PIECE AS DIRECTED BY THE GAFFER'S MOVEMENTS. THE GAFFER THEN "TAKES" AS MUCH OF THE BIT AS THEY DESIRE AND CUTS THE PUNTY FREE WITH THE DIAMOND SHEARS (fig. 37). IF THE GLASS IS HOT ENOUGH, IT CAN BE IMMEDIATELY PAPERED OR TOOLED, OR A REHEAT MAY BE WARRANTED (AND WISE) TO KEEP THE NECK OF THE PIECE WARM, AND TO REINTRODUCE YET MORE HEAT BACK INTO THE FOOT. NOW YOU HAVE ANOTHER CHOICE to make. You can use either the newspaper or the back of the jacks (or a Tagliol or similar styled tool) to shape the foot with, (as in figures 38 & 39). Your assistant can slip a paddle in to flatten the bottom as you make quick full rotations and straighten-up the sides of the foot. If everything goes well you'll end up with a nice crisp clear hockey-puck shape on the bottom of your vessel. It should be ready then to punty in the usual fashion.

FACTORS EFFECTING THE DROPPED FOOT:

⇒ THICKNESS OF YOUR VESSEL. Don't allow the bottom of your vessel to get too thin - otherwise when you drop a hot gather on it, it may heat up the bottom so much that collapses inside the piece.

⇒ THE DROPPED FOOT MUST BE HOT. If the bit comes off clumpy or is irregularly shaped, it will be difficult to control. It may be even harder to get on center.

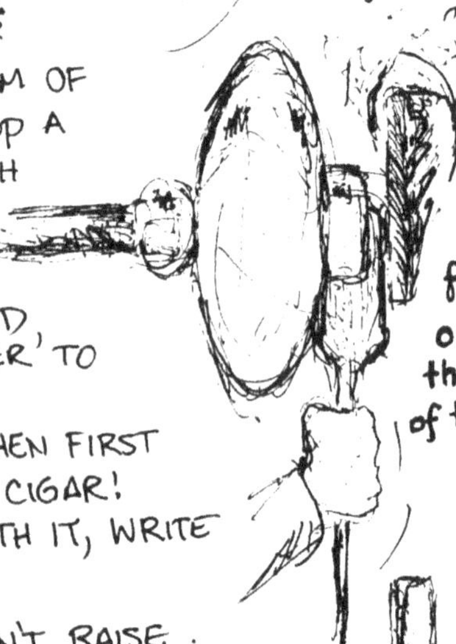

⇒ HITTING DEAD CENTER TAKES PRACTICE. Oftentimes when first attempting this style foot you'll get close - but no cigar! Your foot may end up a tad bit off-center. Deal with it, write it off to experience and try better next time.

⇒ YOUR ASSISTANT IS TOO SHORT. If your assistant can't raise their backhand high enough while dropping the foot on, the glass will fail to flow properly. Have them jump up on a box (or something) to get the height that you need. It is also possible that you are too short or the piece itself is too big. If that is the case you may have to arrange a box or step system to gain more altitude or apply the foot at the bench like a punty or making an avolio.

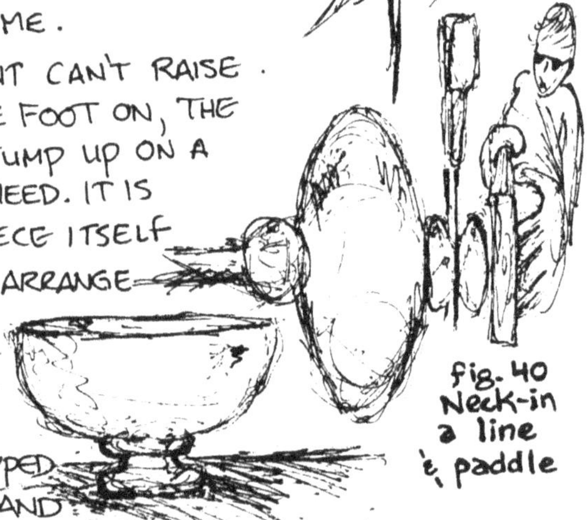

A few stylistic variations on the dropped foot are available for your further enjoyment and exploration. You can cut in a line with the jacks (as in fig. 40 to the right) making a jumbo avolio out of your foot.

You might also desire a wider base. In that case you can shape the dropped foot into a sphere, or hockey-puck, or spool shape, and then add either a blown foot or cookie-foot on top of that, as in fig. 41 to the right. Of course you can feel free to add color to any one of these elements at any time during the foot making process. And there's yet more →...!

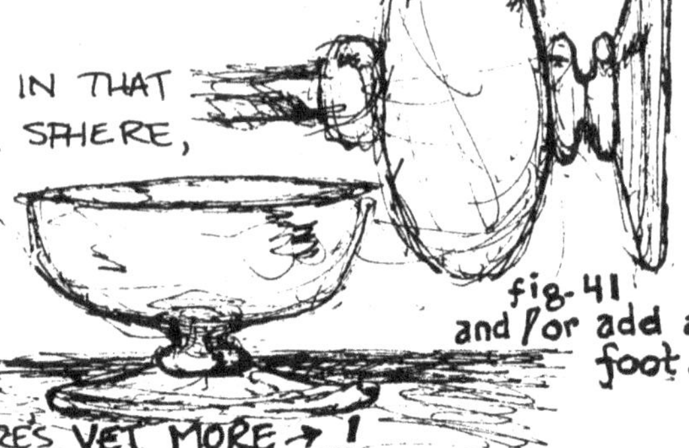

fig. 38 paper it in...

fig. 39 or use the back of the jacks

fig. 40 Neck-in a line & paddle

fig. 41 and/or add a foot.

FOOT WRAP

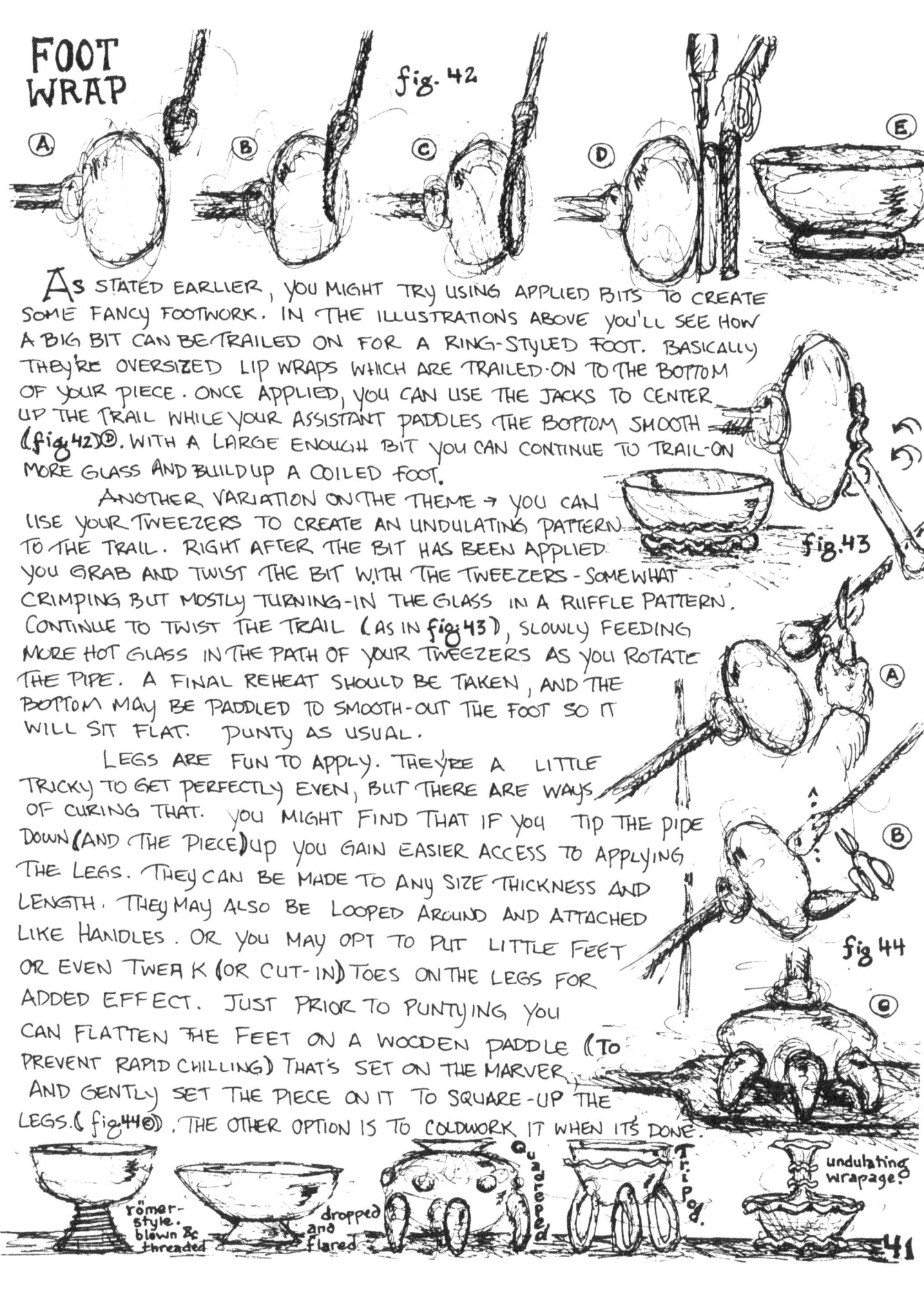

fig. 42 Ⓐ Ⓑ Ⓒ Ⓓ Ⓔ

As stated earlier, you might try using applied bits to create some fancy footwork. In the illustrations above you'll see how a big bit can be trailed on for a ring-styled foot. Basically they're oversized lip wraps which are trailed-on to the bottom of your piece. Once applied, you can use the jacks to center up the trail while your assistant paddles the bottom smooth (fig. 42 Ⓓ). With a large enough bit you can continue to trail-on more glass and build up a coiled foot.

Another variation on the theme → You can use your tweezers to create an undulating pattern to the trail. Right after the bit has been applied you grab and twist the bit with the tweezers - somewhat crimping but mostly turning-in the glass in a ruffle pattern. Continue to twist the trail (as in fig. 43), slowly feeding more hot glass in the path of your tweezers as you rotate the pipe. A final reheat should be taken, and the bottom may be paddled to smooth-out the foot so it will sit flat. Punty as usual.

fig. 43

Legs are fun to apply. They're a little tricky to get perfectly even, but there are ways of curing that. You might find that if you tip the pipe down (and the piece) up you gain easier access to applying the legs. They can be made to any size thickness and length. They may also be looped around and attached like handles. Or you may opt to put little feet or even tweak (or cut-in) toes on the legs for added effect. Just prior to puntying you can flatten the feet on a wooden paddle (to prevent rapid chilling) that's set on the marver, and gently set the piece on it to square-up the legs (fig. 44 Ⓒ). The other option is to coldwork it when it's done.

fig. 44 Ⓐ Ⓑ Ⓒ

römer-style. blown & threaded — dropped and flared — Quadropeded — Tri Pod. — undulating wrapage.

RONDELS (SPIN TO WIN)

KNOWN THROUGHOUT THE AGES AS: **BULLSEYES, CROWN GLASS OR WINDOW PANES**, AND IN RECENT YEARS THE UNGLAMOUROUS AND SLIGHTLY INACCURATE TITLE "**PLATTER**" OR **PLATE**, THE **RONDEL** HAS A RICH HISTORY AND LONG-STANDING TRADITION IN GLASS HOUSES ALL OVER THE GLOBE. ORIGINALLY MADE FOR THE STAINED-GLASS INDUSTRY, RONDELS ARE ESSENTIALLY FLAT, UNIFORMLY THICK 'SHEETS' OF GLASS MADE BY SPINNING OUT A CAREFULLY BLOWN BUBBLE.

THE RONDEL IS A CHALLENGING FORM TO MAKE. EVERY STEP LEADING UP TO THE FINAL SPIN-OUT IS CRUCIAL TO IT'S SUCCESS. AS ALWAYS, PRACTICE WILL HELP YOU UNDERSTAND THE SMALL BUT IMPORTANT CHARACTERISTICS NECESSARY TO EXECUTE THIS SEEMINGLY ELUSIVE FLAT FORM.

BEGIN BY BLOWING A SHAPE SIMILAR TO A LOW BOWL (AS IN figs. 45 (A)-(D) TO THE LEFT). IT'S MUCH EASIER TO GET THE FEEL FOR THIS PROCESS IF YOU MAKE THE PIECES ON THE THICK SIDE. THEY TEND TO HOLD THE HEAT MORE EFFECTIVELY AND HAVE A HIGHER RATE OF SUCCESS THAN THEIR THINNER COUNTERPARTS.

AS WITH MOST FORMS IN GLASS, YOU'LL WANT TO SHAPE YOUR BUBBLE AS CLOSE TO THE COMPLETED FORM AS POSSIBLE WHILE IT'S STILL ON THE BLOWPIPE. THIS MEANS MAKING YOUR FORM AS WIDE AND SQUAT AS YOU DESIRE. IT IS NOT COMPLETELY NECESSARY TO FLATTEN THE BOTTOM OF THE PIECE IF YOU ARE SHOOTING FOR A TRUE RONDEL.* IF ON THE OTHER HAND YOU WANT TO MAKE A PLATE OR PLATTER, A WELL-ESTABLISHED → SLIGHTLY THICK BOTTOM IS A GOOD IDEA.

ONCE YOU ACHIEVE YOUR FORM, YOU MAY USE A **CROWN-STYLE** PUNTY TO TRANSFER THE PIECE. BE SURE TO MATCH THE DIAMETER OF THE BLOWPIPE WITH AN EQUIVALENT DIAMETER OF PUNTY — TO MAINTAIN CONTINUITY AND AID IN TURNING THE PUNTY WHEN THE TIME COMES TO SPIN IT OUT. IT'S ALSO IMPORTANT THAT YOU STICK UP THE PUNTY AS CLOSE TO THE CENTER AS HUMANLY POSSIBLE. IT HELPS INSURE THAT THE RONDEL WILL SPIN-OUT EVENLY, AND NOT LOPSIDED OR ASYMMETRICAL. TRANSFER IN THE USUAL FASHION. AFTER TRANSFERRING, YOU MAY

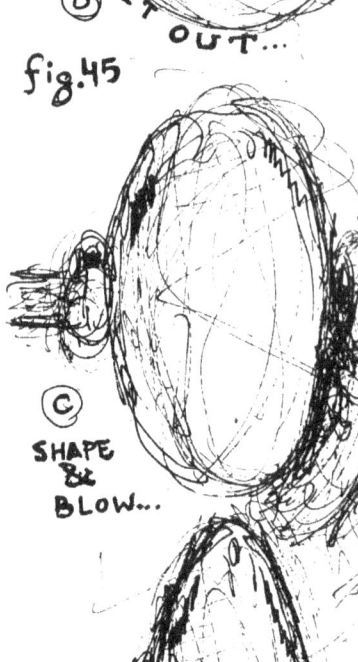

fig. 45
(A) GATHER...
(B) BLOW IT OUT...
(C) SHAPE & BLOW...
(D) TRANSFER
(E) OPEN IT.
(F) HEAT WITH CARE...
(G)

* DURING THE SPIN-OUT PROCESS, CENTRIFUGAL FORCE WILL CAUSE IT TO GO FLAT.

NEED TO TRIM THE LIP TO EVEN THINGS OUT (SEE PAGE 30). AFTER THIS POINT, YOU NEEDN'T DO ALOT OF SHAPING WITH THE TOOLS OTHER THAN OPENING THE LIP A LITTLE WITH THE JACKS, OR PACIOFFS. YOU MAY ALSO USE THE NEWSPAPER TO KEEP THE SHOULDERS IN-CHECK AND PREVENT PRE-MATURE FLARING. MOST OF THE SHAPING IS DONE BY CAREFUL REHEATING AT THE GLORY HOLE, AND THE SPEED AT WHICH YOU ROTATE THE PIPE. TAKE IT EASY. IF YOU SPIN IT TOO FAST TOO EARLY, YOU'LL END UP FLARING ONLY THE LIPS, LEAVING THE SHOULDERS BEHIND — AND YOU ARE STUCK WITH A WONKY NOT-SO-FLAT BOWL THINGAMAGIG.

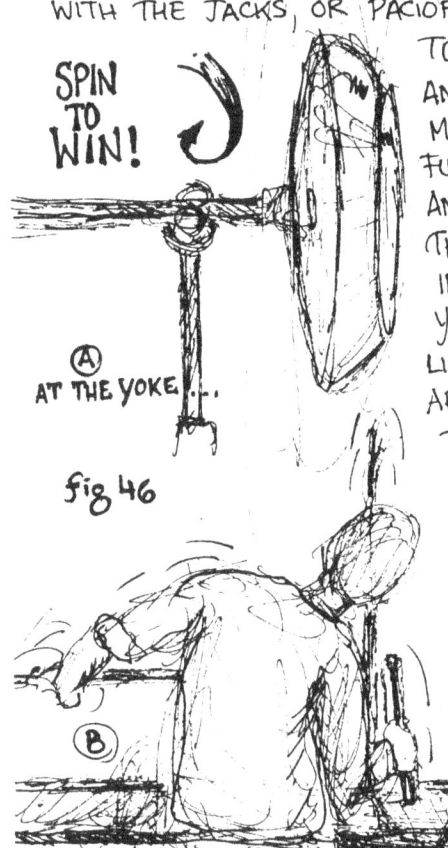

fig 46

WHEN YOUR 'BOWL' IS WIDENING UP AND SHAPED LIKE THE ONE ILLUSTRATED IN FIGURE 46Ⓐ ABOVE, YOU CAN TAKE YOUR FINAL HEAT AND THEN SPIN IT OUT. SOME GAFFERS MAY SPIN IT OUT AT THE YOKE — JUST OUTSIDE OF THE GLORY HOLE DOORS, WHILE OTHERS PREFER TAKING IT TO THE BENCH AND SPINNING IT OUT THERE. AT THE BENCH WORKS NICE 'CAUSE YOU HAVE TOOLS LIKE PADDLES TO COAX THE FORM NICE N' FLAT IF NECESSARY. YOU JUST HAVE TO MAKE CERTAIN YOU HAVE ENOUGH CLEARANCE BETWEEN THE TOOL BENCH AND THE PIECE OR YOU MAY RUN INTO TROUBLE.

BE CAREFUL NOT TO SPIN TOO FAST-TOO SOON! THE EDGES OF THE RONDEL MAY FLY AWAY FROM YOU, DASHING ALL HOPES OF A NICE EVEN ROUND FLAT FORM. YOU SHOULD ALLOW THE FORM TO SET-UP A BIT BEFORE BOXING IT. YOU CAN SAVE SPACE BY STACKING THE RONDELS ON TOP OF EACH OTHER WITH PRE-HEATED FIBREFRAX IN BETWEEN OR BY USING A RONDEL RACK AS IN FIGS. 47 Ⓐ&Ⓑ SET INSIDE OF THE ANNEALER BEFOREHAND.

FACTORS EFFECTING THE RONDEL PROCESS:

→ **THICKNESS OF THE BUBBLE:** CONTRARY TO MOST BLOWN OBJECTS, A THICK LIP AND NECK AREA ARE DESIREABLE. THE GREATER MASS THERE CONTRIBUTES MORE HEAT RETENTION AND HAS MORE ROOM TO STRETCH VIA CENTRIFUGAL FORCE DURING THE SPIN-OUT.

→ **SHAPE AND HEAT OF THE PIECE:** IF YOUR BUBBLE ISN'T AS SQUAT AS YOU CAN GET IT — YOU MAY END-UP WITH A BELL-SHAPED PLATTER INSTEAD OF A FLAT RONDEL. THIS CAN ALSO HAPPEN IF YOU DON'T HAVE THE RIGHT HEAT IN YOUR PIECE AND TRY TO OPEN IT WHEN IT'S TOO COLD.

→ **COLOR:** COLOR CAN REALLY SCREW THINGS UP SOMETIMES AND WITH RONDELS IT'S NO EXCEPTION. YOU NEED TO GET YOUR COLOR ON AS EVEN AS POSSIBLE, AND BLOW IT OUT CAREFULLY AS WELL.

→ **GLORY HOLE SIZE:** WATCH IT! LIKE MAKING BOWLS, IT'S VERY EASY TO 'MAX-OUT' YOUR GLORY HOLE. OR WORSE → TAG A DOOR OR THE WALL OR SOMETHING ELSE. PLUS IT CAN BE **VERY HOT** WHEN YOU HAVE "FOUR-IN-THE-FACE" (ALL DOORS OPEN) IN ORDER TO GET THE HEAT RIGHT IN ORDER FOR THE LAST OF YOUR RONDEL TO OPEN-UP. → GET SOME PROTECTION! AND HAVE SOMEONE STANDING BY TO OPEN THE DOORS etc.

→ **ON-CENTERNESS:** IT'S GOTTA BE RIGHT-ON or else... practice PRACTICE PRACTICE!

GETTING A HAND ON... HANDLES

At one point or another in your glassblowing career you'll probably find the need to apply a handle or two to some of the objects you make. Handles can greatly enhance your piece's function and overall appearance. They tend to be tricky to make if you don't practice them. **HINT:** Repetition is the key to making good handles. For practice, put 4, 8, or 64 handles on a single object. This will help train you and your assistant the subtleties involved in this process.

BITS FOR HANDLES

The four basic shapes drawn above are examples of bits suitable for handle making. Each has its own design/structure based on the style of handle being made. Important considerations should be taken into account before you start making them, such as: contact points (those areas where the handle is actually attached to the piece), size and thickness of the handle, function and/or aesthetic concerns, and the selection of tools used to apply the handle (e.g. using the diamond shears vs. the straight shears to cut the bit with).

STEAL YOUR HANDLE IDEAS!!

Hey, there's no need to reinvent the wheel here! Considering that most types of handles have been done before, why make it hard on yourself? Visit the **Corning Museum of Glass** (in Corning, New York) for hundreds of approaches to handle making. For more examples closer to home, visit any store selling functional vessels to feel how handles operate → look at how they are constructed. Examine how placement of the handle affects the physical and visual balance of the piece. Take a gander at the ceramics field. There's a host of handles which are innovative and stylish → and very applicable to hot glass working.

For a basic handle such as might be put on a beer mug, the technique is relatively simple to apply, yet rather challenging to perfect. Again, my suggestion is to practice placing many handles on one single piece. This process of trial & error will boost your skill in cutting, pulling/drawing out the glass, and final attachments. Your assistant will also become trained in preparing the bits to your own taste.

Handles are almost always applied to the piece last, just prior to 'boxing' it. That way they are not subjected to the rigors of reheating, shaping or the transfer process → and maintain their own

SHAPE AND DESIGN.   ## BASIC HANDLE REVIEW:
FOR THE ASSISTANT: LISTEN TO YOUR GAFFER!

EVEN IF YOU "KNOW BETTER" – BRING THE HANDLE THE WAY THE GAFFER WANTS IT. ALWAYS KEEP THE BIT PIPE/PUNTY HORIZONTAL TO MAINTAIN THE GLASS'ES POSITION ON THE PUNTY SO THAT IT DOESN'T DRIP OFF, OR PREMATURELY ELONGATE, PRIOR TO ATTACHMENT. APPROACH THE ANXIOUSLY AWAITING GAFFER FROM THE DIRECTION WHICH THEY INDICATE ～ IN FRONT OR FROM THE SIDE OF THE BENCH. ASK FIRST 'HOW THEY LIKE IT' AND ELIMINATE THE GUESSWORK. THIS INCLUDES THE SIZE AND SHAPE OF THE BIT FOR THE HANDLE. TAKE A LITTLE TIME OUT BEFOREHAND AND HAVE THE GAFFER 'DEMO' THE PROCESS FOR YOU.

TARGET & APPLY...

WHEN INDICATED, THE HANDS AND PUNTY ARE SHIFTED PERPENDICULAR TO THE GAFFER'S PUNTY (AND PIECE). (THUS BEGINS THE FLOW OF GLASS DOWNWARD. THE GAFFER GRABS HOLD OF THE PUNTY WITH THE SHEARS → CLOSE TO THE BIT OF GLASS, AND DIRECTS THE BIT WHERE SHE/HE WANTS IT.

AS AN ASSISTANT, IT'S IMPORTANT TO BECOME ALMOST 'LIMP' AT THIS POINT ～ SO AS NOT TO INTERFERE WITH THE MOVEMENTS OF THE GAFFER. USE **TWO** HANDS (VS. ONE) → IT OFFERS GREATER STABILITY AND PREVENTS ACCIDENTS FROM HAPPENING, PARTICULARLY **AFTER** THE BIT HAS BEEN CUT FREE. THE THING TO KEEP IN MIND IS TO REMAIN AS STABLE AS POSSIBLE. TUCKING YOUR ELBOW AGAINST YOUR BODY LESSENS THE LIKELIHOOD OF INADVERTENT AND UNDESIRABLE SWAY.

AS GAFFER, IT'S UP TO YOU AS TO WHETHER OR NOT YOU ACCEPT THE BIT.

WITH PRACTICE, THE BEHAVIOR OF THE GLASS BECOMES MORE APPARENT ～ ITS MOVEMENT (HEAT), HOW MUCH GLASS IS ON & OR OFF THE PUNTY etc. THERE'S NO HARM IN REJECTING A BIT FOR WHATEVER REASON, OR REQUESTING THAT IT BE HEATED OR RESHAPED SOME MORE.

TARGET AND APPLY THE BIT WHERE YOU WANT IT. THE FURTHER YOU PUSH THE BIT DOWN, THE GREATER CONTACT AND SURFACE AREA THE HANDLE

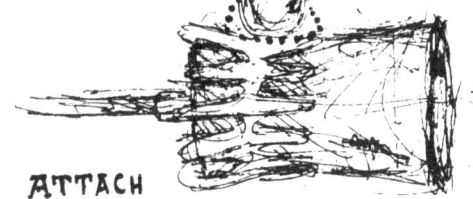

ATTACH   PULL UP...   AND CUT...

45

will have. It's an aesthetic choice as well as a functional one. Handles with small contact areas are physically more fragile, but visually appear more delicate. Beer mugs of the **HEFTY** variety are appropriate with thick, 'chunky' handles. Of course, you can go overboard and apply a handle so thick as to cause your mug to topple over from it's excessive weight!

After attaching the bit, begin to pull the punty upwards ⇝ slowly thinning the diameter of the bit as you do so. The faster you pull, the thinner it gets. If you pull too quickly, you run the risk of having some hot spaghetti on your hands and the bit will noodle itself uncontrollably all over your piece! Conversely, the slower you draw out the bit, the greater stability you gain. However, the bit may cool so rapidly that it may become very difficult to cut free.

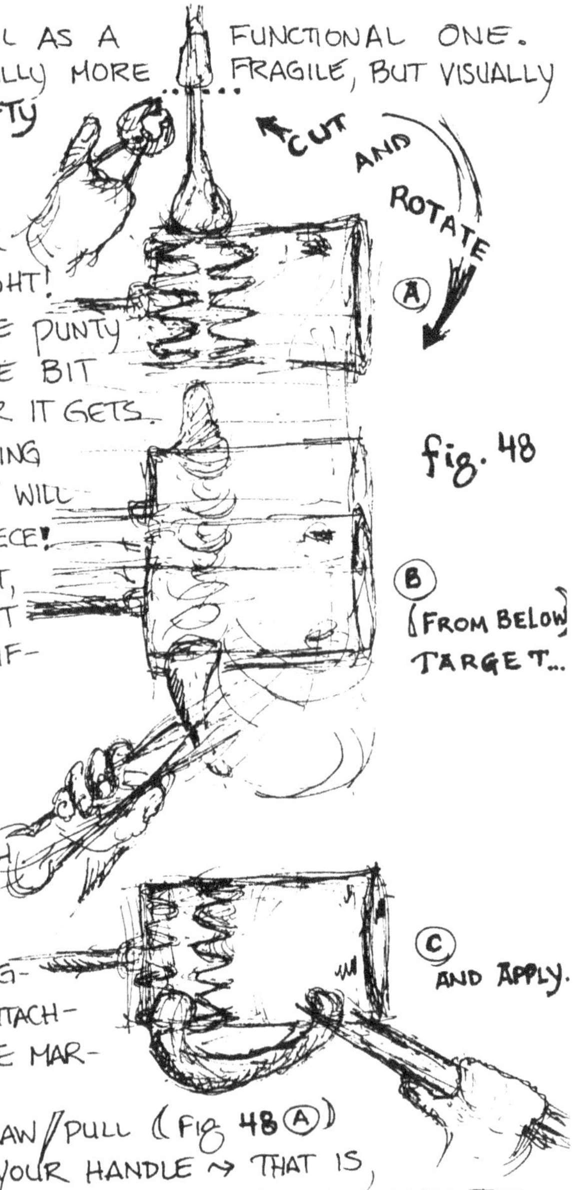

Much of the success in this operation, depends on the temperature of the bit. Hot is always good. Too hot is NOT! Overly-hot bits can be difficult to deal with. They lose their shape quickly and squirm way-to-much! Sometimes, if you notice it beforehand, you may have your assistant "hang-out" and let the bit chill somewhat before attaching to your piece ⇝ or take another pass on the marver to set it up.

fig. 48

Ⓐ CUT AND ROTATE

Ⓑ (FROM BELOW) TARGET...

Ⓒ AND APPLY.

Now, after you've begun the upward draw/pull (fig. 48 Ⓐ) it's time to determine the size & length of your handle ⇝ that is, where you're going to cut it free. You don't always have to stick with the length that you draw the bit out to. Oftentimes you'll 'overpull' the bit to get the diameter of the handle right and cut somewhere below the punty itself to obtain the length that you want.

It's important that you be ready to rotate the piece ½ turn <u>immediately</u> after you cut it (esp. if its really hot!) It's your choice as to which shears to use (see page 49 for more visual clues). Cut the bit free and flip it towards the floor with a quick turn of your left hand, simultaneously visualizing the contact point where and how you want the handle to be attached (fig 48 Ⓑ).

Allow gravity (your friend) to work for you, i.e. the handle should continue to slowly flow downwards, thinning & stretching while giving you a few seconds to grab your tweezers and stick the end up right where you want it. A twist of the wrist one way curls the

TIP OF THE BIT INWARD WHILE A FLIP OF THE WRIST IN THE OPPOSITE DIRECTION TURNS IT OUTWARD ~ IF YOU SO DESIRE, OR YOU MAY ELECT TO SQUASH THE TIP OF THE HANDLE BUTT-END IN. NOTE 👉 THE MORE YOU **MAN·HANDLE** THE TIP OF THE BIT, THE MORE IRREVERSIBLE MARKS AND INDENTATIONS YOU'LL MAKE IN YOUR HANDLE. SQUEEZE GENTLY (IF YOU MUST) AND AVOID GRIPPING THE BIT ANY MORE THAN NECESSARY.

ONCE THE HANDLE'S ATTACHED, IT'S TIME TO GO FOR A REHEAT. AVOID TURNING THE PIECE **ANY** FASTER THAN NECESSARY. CENTRIFUGAL FORCE CAN STRETCH YOUR HANDLE FURTHER THAN YOU MIGHT LIKE IT ~ SO PROCEDE WITH CAUTION. ALSO, MAKE SURE THE GLORY HOLE DOOR IS OPENED ENOUGH FOR YOU TO GET INSIDE.

IF YOUR HANDLE IS TOO HOT, IT'S VERY EASY FOR IT TO WANT TO FLOP BACK DOWN ON THE PIECE AND LAY THERE FOR ALL ETERNITY (OR UNTIL YOU CUT IT **FREE!**), OR IT MAY STRETCH OUT TOO THIN AS MENTIONED ABOVE.

<u>KEEP YOUR EYE ON IT AT ALL TIMES!</u> THIS WAY YOU MAY ASSESS THE MOVEMENTS NECESSARY TO KEEP IT IN LINE AND FROM PREMATURELY FLOPPING ALL OVER THE PLACE OR STICKING TO THE GLORY HOLE DOOR (THIS IS THE VOICE OF EXPERIENCE SPEAKING!). TRY TO TURN THE PUNTY SLOWLY - 180° BACK N' FORTH VS. THE CONTINUAL ROTATION TO MAINTAIN THE HANDLE'S INTEGRITY. (fig 50).

AFTER THE PIECE HAS BEEN FLASHED SATISFACTORILY, EXIT THE GLORY HOLE WITH CARE, POINTING THE HANDLE DOWN OR UP, ALLOWING GRAVITY TO DO ITS THING, AND ENABLE YOU TO SLIP THROUGH A MORE NARROW SPACE.

NOW YOU MAY 'FINE-TUNE' THE HANDLE BACK AT THE BENCH. (THIS MAY MEAN STRETCHING THE HANDLE BACK AND FORTH TO GIVE YOU A LITTLE MORE LENGTH, OR PULLING IT UPWARDS FOR A LITTLE MORE SPACE OR BOTH. TWEEZERS WORK O.K FOR THIS, BUT I KNOW SOME GLASSBLOWERS WHO PREFER USING A PIECE OF PIPE, ROD OF GRAPHITE, OR STICK OF CHARRED WOOD ~ WHICH REDUCES THE MARKS LEFT IN THE HANDLE. FINALLY YOU MAY STRAIGHTEN AND ALIGN THE HANDLE USING THE TWEEZERS TO COMPRESS IT INTO SHAPE (fig. 51 →). IF EVERYTHING LOOKS IN ORDER GIVE THE PIECE A FINAL FLASH AND BOX IT! (MAKE SURE THAT THE HANDLE ISN'T STILL MOVING.)

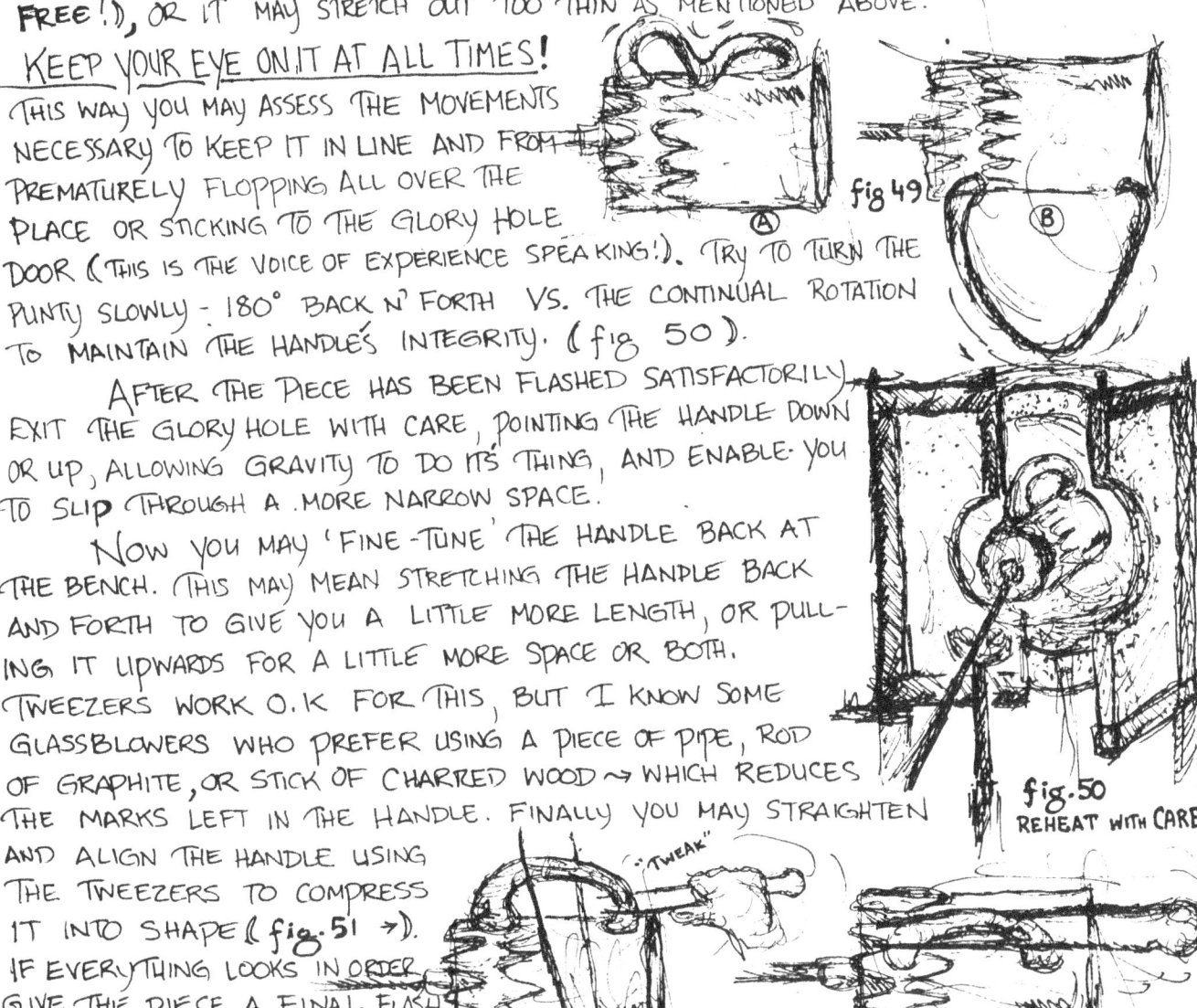

fig 49 Ⓐ Ⓑ

fig. 50 REHEAT WITH CARE!

"TWEAK"

fig. 51 Ⓐ Ⓑ

The basic handle review on the previous pages is just the starting point. There are some subtle variations on the process which may make your life a little easier and your handles looking a tad bit cleaner. Since we're only human beings (and not machines... yet) it's hard to expect getting the exact same handle every time your assistant brings one to you. No matter how hard you try to train them (your assistants - that is), the types of bits you receive will be ever-so-slightly different. There are ways to correct this, and it won't really become important or apparent until you begin doing sets or multiples of handles. Making a matched set of handles is one of the more challenging hot glass techniques to master. So much of it depends on the bits brought to you. As gaffer, one of the best ways of reproducing a handle happens immediately after you make initial contact with the handle-bit. It is the process of thinning the handle that will allow you to guage its eventual outcome.

Guaging & Thinning Handles

One way to thin and elongate the handle is to to stretch the bit (as outlined on the previous pages). Another method is to attach the bit and **use the diamond shears** to pull up on the glass, stretching and thinning it as you go. The excess glass is 'gathered-up' by the assistant's punty. Once the desired thickness is achieved, the handle is cut free from the punty and touched-up where desired. This is one method of dealing with bits that are excessively hot and squirrelly, and in danger of noodling all over you piece.

Another opportunity to thin and guage your handle comes right after you cut the initial bit free. Once you flip the piece around and the handle bit is pointing down towards the floor, you may use your diamond shears to draw the glass thinner. As soon as you obtain the desired thickness in the handle, you can cut it with the shears to the desired length and attach it where you want it.

fig.52 Thinning a Handle Anti-Grav. Approach

And then there's the old world way. It's slightly less predictable, unless of course you perform the technique a hundred times-a-day in some production facility — but it looks really slick and leaves little-to-no tool marks on your handle. Begin by applying your handle bit in the normal fashion, drawing it out ½ to ¾'s

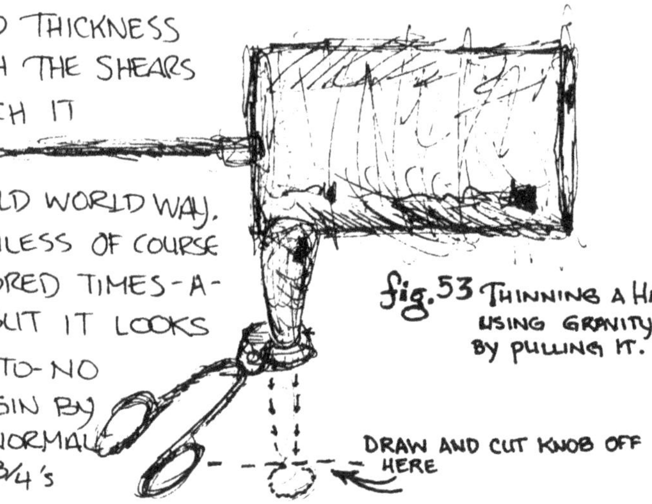

fig.53 Thinning a Handle using gravity and by pulling it.

DRAW AND CUT KNOB OFF HERE

48

THE WAY AND CUTTING IT THERE, LEAVING ENOUGH GLASS TO STRETCH OUT THE REST OF THE WAY. A QUICK REHEAT MAY BE TAKEN IF NECESSARY. THE PIECE IS THEN SPUN RAPIDLY USING CENTRIFUGAL FORCE TO DRAW THE HANDLE OUT NATURALLY. KNOWING WHEN TO STOP IS WHERE THE PRACTICE PART COMES IN. IT'S VERY EASY TO SPIN THE PIECE TOO FAST AND WIND-UP WITH A MUCH LONGER HANDLE THAN DESIRED. **REMEMBER:** <u>KEEP YOUR EYE ON IT AT ALL TIMES</u>! WITH THE RIGHT TIMING & HEAT YOU CAN DRAW THE HANDLE OUT - AND THEN, WITH THE PUNTY TILTING DOWN TOWARDS THE FLOOR, YOU STOP THE ROTATION. THE TOP OF THE HANDLE WILL FALL RIGHT INTO PLACE - GUIDED BY A WOODEN DOWEL OR GRAPHITE STICK - AND GET ATTACHED WHERE YOU WANT IT. I REMEMBER SEEING THE GLASSBLOWERS IN JAMESTOWN VA MAKE HANDLES THIS WAY WHEN I WAS 8 YEARS OLD (WHEN I FIRST GOT BITTEN BY "THE BUG") - AND EVEN THEN IT LOOKED COOL! TRY IT, YOU MIGHT LIKE IT. IT MAKES A VERY NATURAL, COMFORTABLE HANDLE, FREE OF TOOL MARKS AND IS AESTHETICALLY PLEASING!

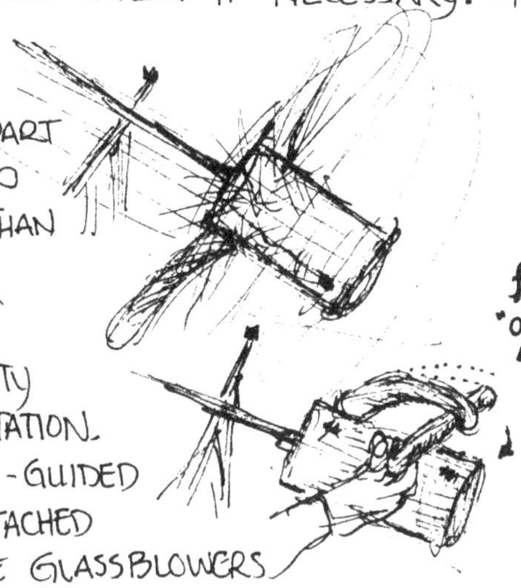

fig. 54 "OLD-WORLD" APPROACH

¿ <u>STRAIGHT VS. DIAMOND SHEARS</u> ?

ONE MORE OPTION YOU HAVE WHEN MAKING HANDLES IS THE TYPE OF SHEARS TO USE TO CUT THE BITS WITH. EACH LEAVES IT'S OWN FORM OF TOOL MARK AFTER CUTTING. THE DIAMOND SHEARS USUALLY CREATE A SEMI-BLUNT SURFACE, WHEREAS THE STRAIGHT SHEARS WILL

fig. 55 THE STRAIGHT-SHEAR APPROACH

CREATE EITHER A FLAT 'TAB' OR A SHARP POINT - DEPENDING ON HOW YOU CUT IT. STYLISTIC VARIATIONS ABOUND! WITH A QUICK FLIP OF THE WRIST, YOU CAN USE THE TWEEZERS TO CURL THE POINT (OF A STRAIGHT SHEAR CUT) IN OR OUT - CHANGING THE WHOLE DYNAMIC OF THE HANDLE (SEE FIG. 55 ABOVE).

? Q ? WHAT DO I DO ABOUT THE JAGGED EDGES LEFT BEHIND FROM THE CUTTING PROCESS?

A. #1. SHARPEN YOUR SHEARS (SEE PAGE 286). #2. TURN THE HANDLE POINT 90 DEGREES (OR 180°) AND SET THAT POINT AGAINST THE PIECE TO HIDE IT.

#3. WORK HOTTER SO NO JAGGED EDGE IS CREATED FROM CUTTING THE BIT TOO COLD. **#4.** FIRE POLISH IT IN THE GLORY HOLE OR WITH THE AID OF A TORCH. **#5.** ALL, OR MANY OF THE ABOVE...

?? Q ?: "WHAT DO I DO IF THE HANDLE COOLS OFF SO FAST AFTER I CUT IT THAT IT DOESN'T WANT TO STICK TO THE PIECE?"

A. **#1** FIRE YOUR ASSISTANT FOR BRINGING SUCH A COLD BIT. **#2.** WORK HOTTER AND FASTER SO THAT IT DOESN'T COOL OFF SO FAST. **#3.** LAY-UP THE HANDLE AS CLOSE TO THE CONTACT POINT AS YOU CAN — DON'T ROTATE THE PIECE AND REHEAT IT IN THE GLORY HOLE TO GET SOME HEAT ON THE SITUATION. THEN USE THE TWEEZERS TO ATTACH IT MORE FIRMLY AFTER EXITING THE GLORY HOLE. **#4.** USE A TORCH AND HEAT THE HANDLE WHERE YOU NEED IT AND STICK IT UP.

MULTIPLE HANDLES

IN THE EVENT YOU WANT MULTIPLE HANDLES OR SETS WHICH LOOK IDENTICAL, IT'S IMPORTANT THAT YOU DUPLICATE THE STEPS THAT YOU USE TO MAKE THEM IN THE FIRST PLACE. EVEN THOUGH IT'S POSSIBLE TO REGATHER THE SECOND HANDLE ON THE SAME PUNTY WITH HOPES OF SAVING TIME → IT IS NOT ALWAYS THE BEST OPTION. OFTEN, THE CORE LEFT FROM THE PREVIOUS HANDLE IS COLD AND MAY INTERFERE WITH THE DYNAMICS OF MAKING AN IDENTICAL MATCH FOR THE FIRST. ALSO, THE MASS AND SURFACE AREA OF THE PUNTY IS CHANGED → THE MOILE MAKES IT OBVIOUSLY LARGER → AND MAY CAUSE YOU TO GATHER MUCH MORE GLASS THAN DESIRED. IN LESS WORDS, IT'S BETTER TO USE A FRESH PUNTY EVERY TIME, (USING THE SAME DIAMETER PUNTY RODS AS WELL.).

A SIMPLE TRICK FOR TARGETING YOUR HANDLES IN A SYMETRICAL FASHION IS TO USE A PIECE OF CHALK TO MAKE MARKS/LINES ON YOUR PIECE WHERE YOU WANT THE BITS TO LAND. THE CHALK IS HELD BY A WOODEN HANDLE SO YOU DON'T ROAST YOUR FINGERS. THE CHALK IS EASILY 'ERASED' BUT WON'T DISAPPEAR TOO QUICKLY (EVEN DURING REHEATS) AND LEAVES VIRTUALLY NO RESIDUE (SEE fig. 56Ⓐ). →

CHALK IT UP! Ⓐ

AGAIN, TRY TO MIMIC THE MOVEMENTS AS BEST AS YOU CAN TO REPRODUCE LIKE-STYLED HANDLES → FROM CUTTING THE CORRECT LENGTH TO THE CURL OR MANNER IN WHICH THE HANDLE IS ATTACHED.

CUT & PASTE... Ⓑ

SHOULD THE HANDLES NOT GO ON QUITE AS PERFECT AS YOU'D LIKE, YOU MAY: A.→ TRASH THE WHOLE SHEBANG IN AN ACT OF FRUSTRATION OR TRY PLAN "B".

B.→ "PLAN B": HIDE THE IMPERFECTIONS WITH MORE GLASS. GO AHEAD AND ADD TWO MORE HANDLES LIKE THE FIRST. THAT WAY THE FOCUS IS SHIFTED AND MORE CONVOLUTED, MAKING THE IMPERFECTIONS LESS IMPORTANT OR NOTICEABLE. YOU ALSO HAVE THE OPTION OF TRAILING-ON MORE DECORATIVE BIT-WORK TO ACHIEVE A SIMILAR EFFECT AND ENHANCE YOUR OVERALL DESIGN.

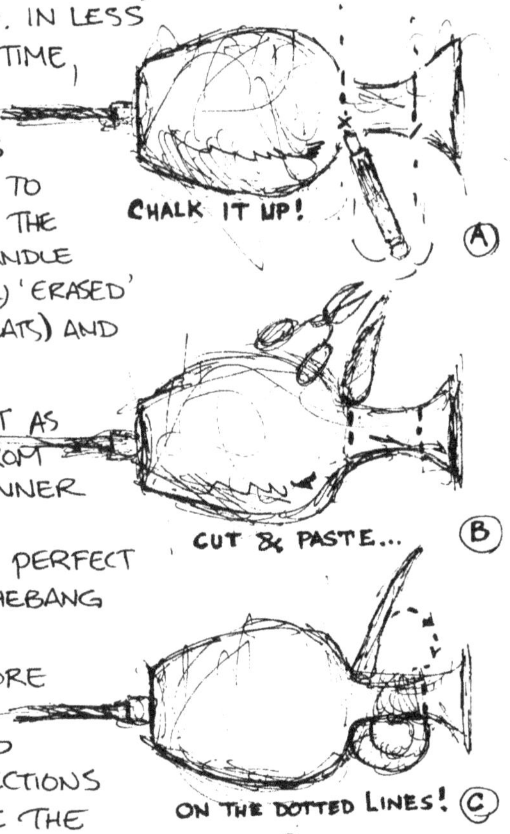

ON THE DOTTED LINES! Ⓒ

fig. 56

BITWORK DECORATIONS CAN TAKE A SIMPLE HANDLE AND MAKE THEM LOOK ELEGANT. PLUS THEY CAN COVER-UP SLIGHT 'DEFECTS' SUCH AS TOOL MARKS OR CHUNKS OF GLORY HOLE DOORS ((THAT MIGHT GET ACCIDENTLY STUCK-ON THERE)) OR WHATEVER.

FIGURES 57 Ⓐ TO Ⓒ AT THE RIGHT SHOW ONE POPULAR 'VENETIAN-STYLE' DECORATIVE MOTIF. A HOT BIT (NO MARVE) IS LAID DOWN ON THE BACK OF THE HANDLE AND CRIMPED BY THE TIPS OF THE TWEEZERS. IF YOU WORK FAST ENOUGH YOU SHOULD BE ABLE TO CRIMP THE WHOLE THING BEFORE THE BIT FREEZES UP. GLASS MAKERS HAVE BEEN HIDING 'HAPPY ACCIDENTS' LIKE THIS FOR CENTURIES!

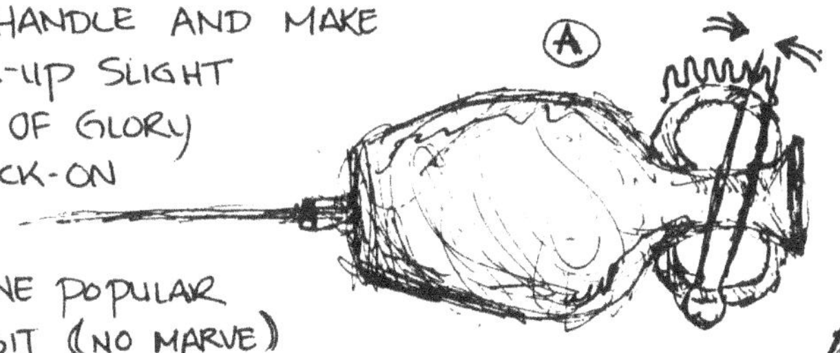

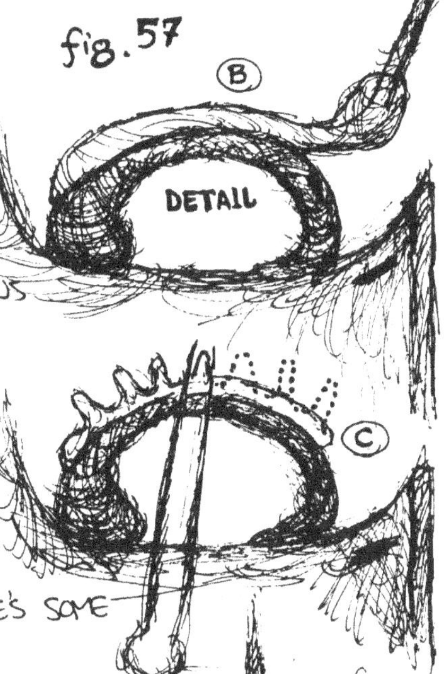

OTHER STYLISTIC CHOICES EXIST SUCH AS: OPTIC HANDLES, SPLIT HANDLES, COILED, BLOWN OR COMBINATIONS OF EACH. AND OF COURSE, THERE'S COLOR! READ ON...

fig. 57

⊛PTIC HANDLES

OPTIC HANDLES ARE APPLIED IN A SIMILAR FASHION TO MOST TYPES OF HANDLES. THE BIG DIFFERENCE HERE IS THAT THE ASSISTANT STUFFS A VERY HOT GATHER INTO THE OPTIC MOLD TO OBTAIN THE RIBBED PATTERN OF CHOICE. HERE'S SOME TIPS FOR ENHANCED SUCCESS:

YOU'LL NOTICE AFTER TRYING A NUMBER OF OPTIC HANDLES THAT EITHER THE MOLD CHILLS THE GLASS SO MUCH THAT IT BECOMES DIFFICULT TO CUT, OR, THAT IN AN EFFORT TO GET THE BIT HOT ENOUGH AFTER MOLDING IT, THAT THE RIBBED EFFECT MYSTERIOUSLY DISAPPEARS! YES, IT IS A FINE LINE BETWEEN CRISPY SEMI-COLD OPTIC HANDLES AND HOT, BARELY PERCEPTIBLE OPTIC PATTERNS WHICH ARE EASIER TO CUT. THE SOLUTION BEING THAT TIMING AND SPEED ARE CRITICAL TO IT'S SUCCESS.

IT'S IMPORTANT THAT THE GLASS IS INTRODUCED INTO THE OPTIC MOLD AS HOT AS POSSIBLE. USUALLY IT WILL GO STRAIGHT INTO THE MOLD FROM THE FURNACE WITH LITTLE-TO-NO SHAPING IN BETWEEN. THE GLASS IS THEN ALLOWED TO 'SET-UP' IN THE MOLD TO OBTAIN THE OPTIC PATTERN, BUT NOT SO LONG AS TO CHILL IT TOO MUCH. THE BIT THEN MAY BE FLASHED IN THE GLORY HOLE AND APPLIED IN THE USUAL MANNER.

YOU MAY ALSO HAVE YOUR ASSISTANT TWIST/TURN THE PUNTY IMMEDIATELY AFTER MAKING INITIAL CONTACT TO CREATE A COIL-TYPE PATTERN. YOU MAY THEN DRAW OUT THE DESIRED LENGTH (WHILE STILL TWISTING) CUT AND APPLY AS NORMAL. (SEE FIG. 58 ⇢). AVOID EXTENDED REHEATS AFTER PUTTING ON OPTIC HANDLES AS THE HEAT CAN ADVERSELY SOFTEN THE OPTIC PATTERN AND CAUSE THEM TO DISAPPEAR. AN ADDITIONAL BLAST FROM A TORCH MAY BE NECESSARY TO FIRE-POLISH ANY SHARP POINTS LEFT FROM THE SHEARS.

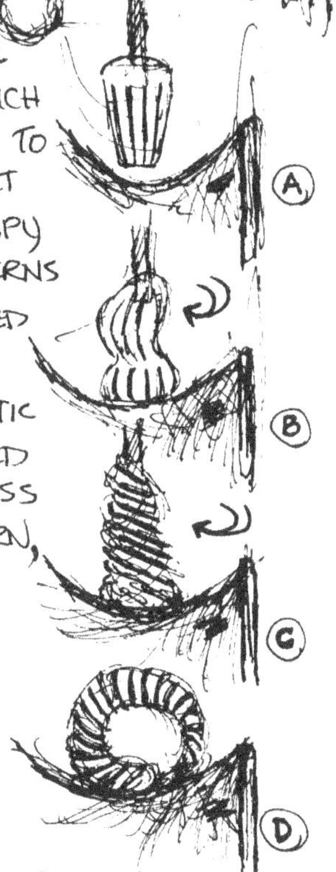

fig. 58

FLAT HANDLES

Another option available for your 'bag of tricks' is the flat handle. Simply stated, the handle bit is flattened either before or after it's attached to your piece, with slightly different results. In the first method, the assistant may flatten the bit on the marver prior to presenting it to the gaffer (fig. 59→). Basically you marver off the glass into a cylinder shape, then lift it off the marver → stop the punty rotation and lay the bit on the marver causing it to flatten. Lift off the marver again → flip the bit 180° and flatten the other side. You might even go the extra step and squash the bit with a flattening tool, TAGLIOL or paddle. The bit is reheated and presented to the gaffer. NOTE 👉 To maintain the handle's integrity — that is, to keep it flat → avoid rotating the punty quickly. The slower you turn the bit, the better. In fact - use the 180° method of reheating → i.e. flip the punty back and forth 180 degrees versus a continual rotation.

In the second method, the bit is dropped-on and then squashed flat with flat-bladed tweezers (as in fig. 60). Or you might split the bit in half with your pointed tweezers, and then use the same tweezers to pull, elongate and apply the handle.

Yet another way is to split the bit in half before bringing it to the gaffer — very similar to the flattening method above, except that you score a line in the middle with the tweezers or similar tool. This same bit may be applied straight or given a twist as it's being put on to create a **COIL** or **ROPE-STYLE HANDLE** (see fig 62 Ⓐ - Ⓒ below).

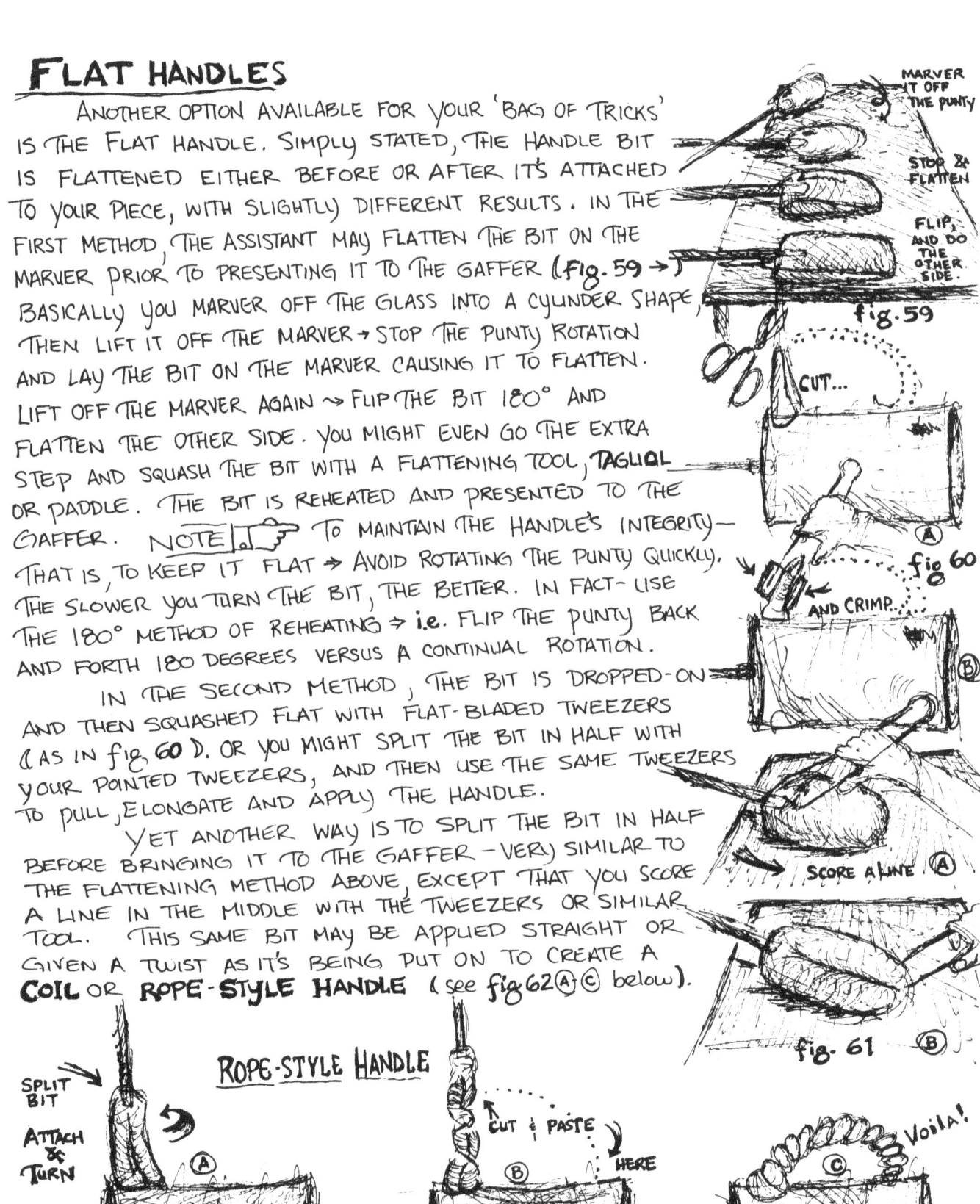

fig. 59

fig. 60

fig. 61

ROPE-STYLE HANDLE

fig. 62

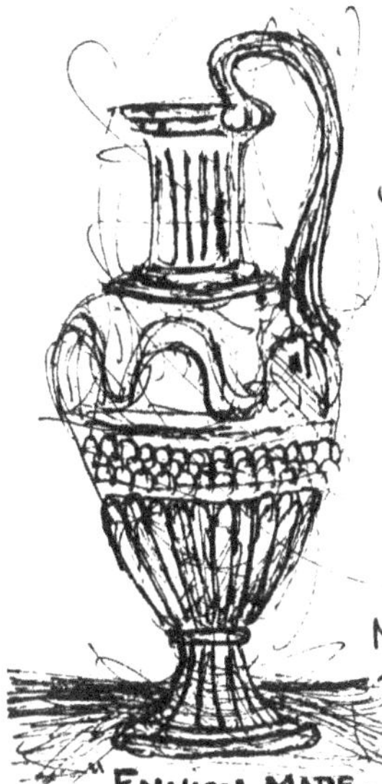

The "Roman" Handle

For bonus "style-points" there's the 'Roman' handle. It is prepared in a very similar fashion to the previous handle, except that two lines are scored into the bit instead of just one. You then end-up with a bit that has three equal rows of glass in one. This is then quickly reheated - again using the 180° method (a back n' forth motion vs. continual rotation) to prevent the bit from twisting. The tip of the bit may be also trimmed flat if desired - reheated and then presented to the gaffer.

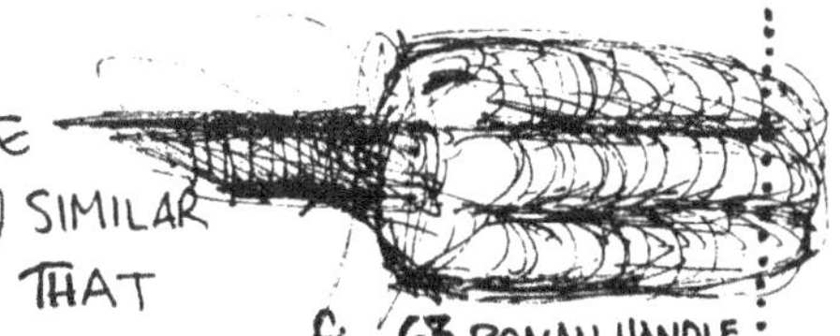

You might also have a torch handy to fire-polish, and additionally heat-up, the cut marks and tip of the handle before making the final attachment.

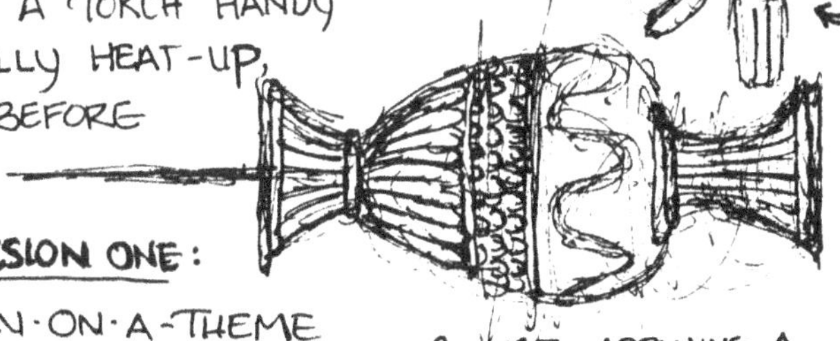

"Ennion Made Me" 1st C. A.D. Roman

fig. 63 Roman Handle Bit — trim if necessary

fig. 64 Scoring the bit — turn to align

fig. 65 Applying a Roman Handle

Split Handles - Version One:

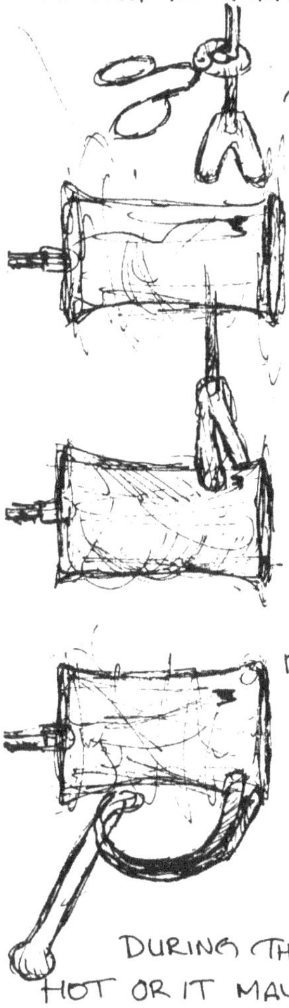

There's another variation-on-a-theme worthy of mention here. In this first version, the bit is cut in two and applied, pulled and cut again, touched-up ↝ leaving you with a stylish V-cut-handle.

To prepare this puppy, begin by marvering your gather of glass off the punty into a cylindrical form (as usual). Then use the straight shears to cut into the bit halfway or so (more-or-less to your desire). You may spread the two resulting points apart using the shears or tweezers and then go for a reheat. The faster you turn the punty → the more centrifugal force will cause them (the points) to spread apart, so keep your eyes on the bit and turn with care. Once the bit is sufficiently hot → present it to the gaffer and apply in the usual manner.

Listen for clues given by the gaffer to aid in the placement process such as "turn faster" - to cause the points to spread apart further, or "turn to the right (or left) a little" to get the bit to line-up correctly. The bit may then be drawn, cut and applied in the normal fashion. It's important during the reheating process that you don't get the handle too hot or it may collapse back in on itself or stretch-out too far. Take your time - "a stitch in time, saves nine" or something to that effect.

53

SPLIT HANDLE - VERSION TWO

IN THIS VERSION - TWO SEPERATE HANDLES ARE APPLIED SIDE-BY-SIDE → REHEATED, AND THEN CRIMPED TOGETHER TO FORM A SINGLE ELEGANT HANDLE.

BEGIN AS YOU WOULD TO APPLY A SINGLE HANDLE - BUT TRY TO LEAVE THE BIT A LITTLE ON THE THICK SIDE. YOU'LL BE THINNING IT LATER. NEXT, LAY ANOTHER HANDLE CLOSE TO THE FIRST ONE → DRAWING IT OUT TO THE EXACT SIZE AND SHAPE AS THE FIRST BIT. NEXT, REHEAT AND TORCH IF NECESSARY THE ENDS OF THE TWO BITS. USE THE TWEEZERS TO GUIDE THE ENDS TOGETHER. OR IF YOU CAN, THE DIAMOND SHEARS → TO CRIMP THEM TOGETHER.

THEN, YOU CAN SLOWLY DRAW THE HANDLE OUT FURTHER TO THE DESIRED THICKNESS AND LENGTH, AND CUT OFF THE EXCESS KNOB/GLASS. THE TIP OF THE HANDLE MAY BE TORCHED OR REHEATED TO FIRE POLISH IT. THEN, FINAL ADJUSTMENTS MAY BE MADE TO ALIGN OR FINE-TUNE THE HANDLE PRIOR TO BOXING IT. OR YOU MIGHT GO THE EXTRA STEP AND BALANCE THE PIECE OUT BY ADDING ANOTHER SET OF HANDLES ON THE OTHER SIDE OF THE PIECE. REMEMBER TO KEEP THAT PUNTY HOT!

THE BLOWN HANDLE

IN SOME SITUATIONS, A BLOWN HANDLE MAY BETTER SUIT YOUR NEEDS OR AESTHETIC DESIRES. THEY CAN OFFER YOU A LARGER SIZED HANDLE WITHOUT THE EXCESSIVE WEIGHT BROUGHT-ON BY A SOLID ONE. IT'S SOMEWHAT MORE DIFFICULT TO MAKE - SIMPLY BY THE FEW EXTRA STEPS INVOLVED. ALSO, **GETTING THE HEAT RIGHT IS CRITICAL TO EXECUTING A CLEAN AND SMOOTH HANDLE VERSUS A CRINKLY DISTORTED MANGY THANG.**

BEGIN WITH A 1, 2, or 3* GATHER/DIP ON A GOBLET PIPE (* DEPENDING ON THE SIZE DESIRED). FORM A STARTER BUBBLE MARVERING IT SUCH THAT THE BUBBLE TRAVELS ALL THE WAY DOWN TO THE END → LEAVING YOU WITH A UNIFORM WALL THICKNESS THROUGHOUT. A NECKLINE MAY BE INITIATED CLOSE TO THE PIPE TO AID IN CUTTING THE HANDLE FREE WHEN THAT TIME COMES. CHECK WITH THE GAFFER FIRST TO SEE HOW THEY LIKE IT.

THE BUBBLE IS THEN HEATED AS HOT AS POSSIBLE, PARTICULARLY NEAR THE NECK WHERE IT WILL BE CUT, AND THEN PRESENTED TO THE GAFFER. IT MAY BE TOUCHED-UP IN THE USUAL MANNER, HOWEVER A GENTLE CURVE OR SLOPE TO THE HANDLE MAY BE INITIATED AT THE SAME TIME BY HAVING THE ASSISTANT ADJUST THE ANGLE OF THE PIPE ACCORDINGLY. HAVE THEM ALSO **CAP THE PIPE** SIMULTANEOUSLY TO PREVENT THE BUBBLE FROM COLLAPSING.

The handle is then drawn to length and cut free. Once the handle/bubble's been snipped free, it is no longer possible to inflate it further. Therefore, if a larger handle is warranted → be sure to do it beforehand. Also, **the more you have to manipulate the handle after this point, the more marks, indentations or distortions you may leave imprinted on it, so HANDLE WITH CARE** (pun intended)!

Try to get the bubble in position as close to it's final form as possible before cutting it free. This will also help prevent 'defects', dents and such from happening - from trying to get the handle into the correct shape.

The tip of the handle may be brought around and touched-up on the piece with the tweezers. Some reheating or torching may be necessary to smooth out the connection.

Colored Handles

Colored handles are made and applied in the same way as the "colorless" or clear variety → the exception being that color is introduced at some point along the way. The most popular method to pick-up color is by rolling a hot gather directly out of the furnace into some powdered glass or frit. A number of studio artists will place their powders in stainless steel or wooden bowls, pie pans or baking tins for easy access and mobility. The activity of applying color in this manner (vs. sifting it on) aids in shaping the bit making it ready for the handle-making process. Using Kugler rod often takes too much time to prepare and is seldom used.

The bit(s) should be **reheated**, shaped further, and either applied as usual, or, more color is rolled on → should a denser value be desired. It's also possible to **case** the color in clear or with another color for added effect. Casing the color in clear prevents the color from reducing and somewhat insures that the handle will stick well.

It should be noted that adding color will change the dynamics of how the bit will behave. It can make it **'stiffer'** or **'softer'** or cause it to stick better or worse - depending on the color chosen.

The Garaged Handle

With **garage** techniques becoming increasing popular and more accessible these days, no handle section would complete without mention of them. The garage enables you to create individually elaborate handles prior to blowing the piece to which they will be applied. These handles may have complex curves, additional bitwork or hot sculpting done to them. They are then set or 'parked' in the garage or pick-up

OVEN UNTIL NEEDED. A HOT BIT OR TWO IS THEN APPLIED TO THE PIECE AND THE HANDLE CAREFULLY SET IN PLACE (REMEMBER TO PREHEAT YOUR TWEEZERS BEFORE HANDLING ANY GARAGED PIECE - TO PREVENT THERMAL SHOCK!). SEE THE VENETIAN TECHNIQUES SECTION NEAR THE MIDDLE OF THIS BOOK FOR MORE RELATED INFORMATION.

PRO's & CON's OF VARIOUS TYPES OF HANDLES:

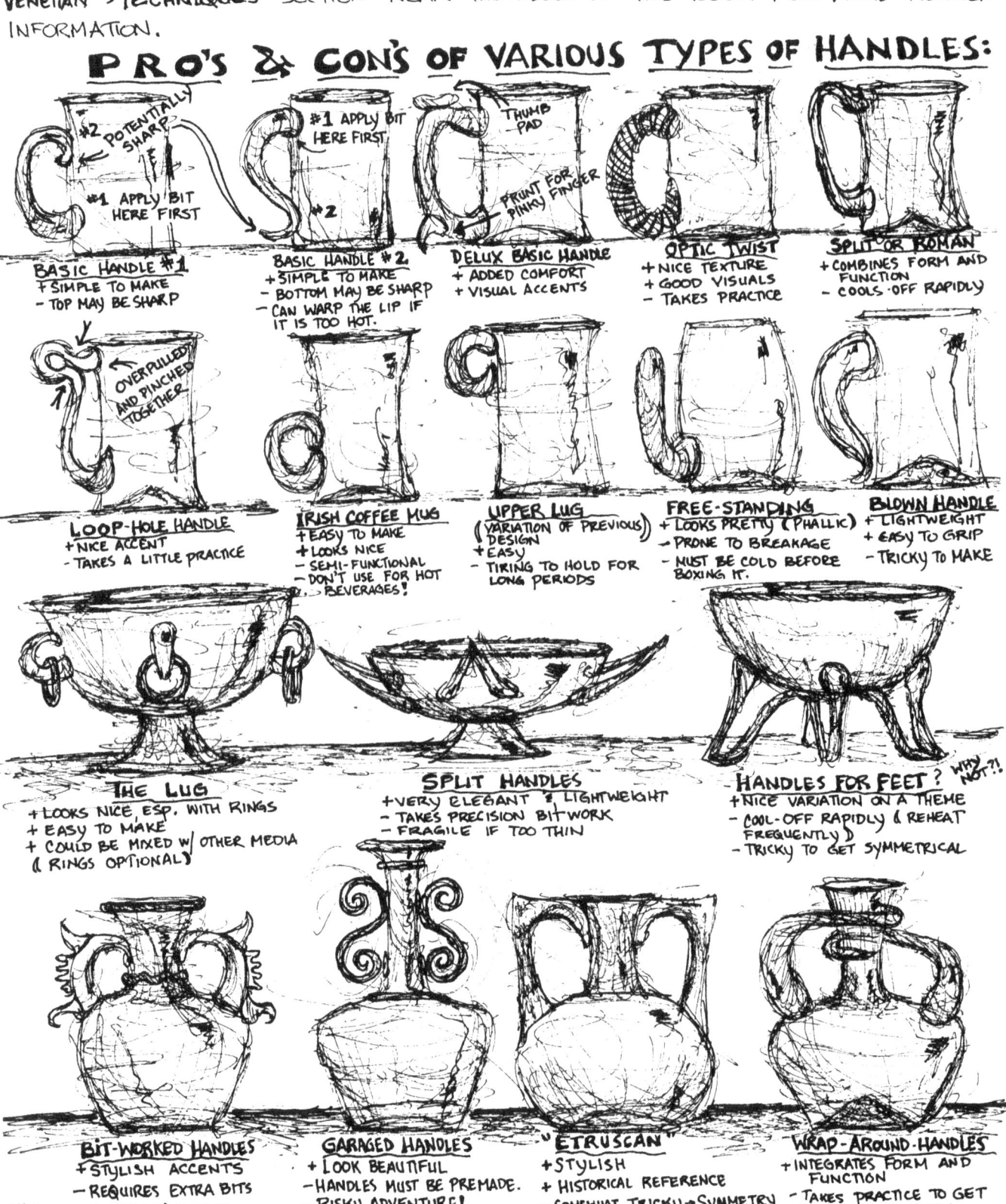

Auxiliary Information: Factors Effecting the Quality of Handles

As simple as handles appear, there's a whole lot more to making them than meets the eye! Sometimes it can be hard to pin down exactly what makes them work and what doesn't. Being gaffer you can always blame your assistant for the failures, but unfortunately that isn't always the case. Presented here are some of the more common factors and ailments in the handle making process.

Symptom	Cause	Cure
Bit is stiff - hard to cut	Too cold. Maybe marvered too much.	Work faster, hotter and marver less.
Bit just puddles on piece	Too hot.	Marver and shape the bit more.
Handles are too thin	Too hot. Overly stretched. Prematurely elongated.	Marver the bit more. Avoid pointing the punty down - keep it horizontal.
Irregular shaped handles	Core of bit is cold, exterior is hot.	Do not marver the bit between gathers.
Punty gets cold. Piece dies the end.	Failure to reheat punty	Reheat more frequently. Use a torch to introduce more heat in the punty.
Top of handle doesn't stick	Time lost fumbling for tools. Bit gets too cold.	Set up your bench so you know exactly where each tool is - beforehand
Inconsistent handles - mismatched set	Assistant brings a different handle every time. Failure to compensate on gaffer's part	Train your assistant (or find a new one) Pay attention & thin the bits to match.
Sharp points on handles	Dull shears or glass is too cold to cut.	Sharpen you shears. Work hotter, faster Use a torch to fire polish.
Handle-bit comes off in a big clump	Improper marvering & shaping techniques	Retrain your assistant. Ask them to work hotter, faster and read this section.
Handle warps the shape of the piece	Piece is too thin or hot when handle is applied. Handle too heavy. Excessive reheating.	Make sure your piece is stone cold before applying handles. Make smaller, thinner handles. Don't reheat too much.
Handle(s) looks stupid	Bad design. Inexperience. Failure to practice.	Fire the designer. Make more drawings and practice, practice, P R A C T I C E !
Piece topples over when I set it down.	Handle is too heavy. Bad design.	Make thinner handle or try blown ones.
Handle snaps off piece when I pick it up.	Handle too thin. Attached too cold, or not enough to hold weight	Beef-up your handle. Work hotter.

ADDITIONAL FACTORS EFFECTING THE HANDLEMAKING PROCESS:

SIZE OF THE PIECE — Larger pieces make it more challenging to apply handles to. The radiant heat alone can sizzle your fingers (especially your thumb!) if they're not protected. It really helps to have a trained assistant standing by with some paddles to shield you from the excess heat. Also, larger pieces often command larger handles → thus compounding the factors you're up against with the additional size and weight.

MOVEMENT — If your piece is still moving about on your punty → it greatly increases the already challenging task of handle making. Chill the punty with a blast of compressed air, a puff from a soffietta or adjust your timing to allow the piece to set-up. Also, if your piece itself is too hot → it will be difficult to apply handles to it without warping it all to hell.

SHAPE OF THE HANDLE — Does the bottom of the handle curve in or out? Does the bit start at the bottom or top of the piece? How does it feel when you pick it up? These questions on design and function are very valid ones. Answer them for yourself. Try making a couple different styles of handles on a cylinder and compare/contrast the dynamics and attributes of each.

PLACEMENT OF THE HANDLE → As important as the shape of the handle; where you plop that handle down greatly effects the aesthetics and function of the piece. In terms of function → every piece of glass has it's own balancing point. This is effected by the volume, shape and density of the glass object. It is compounded by whether the vessel is empty or full (of liquids or solids).

EXPERIENCE — Last but not least → There's no substitute for experience and skill in any glassmaking process except DUMB LUCK! Seriously practice making handles until you and your assistant fully comprehend the subtleties involved in this highly challenging activity. Also watch how other glassblowers make their handles. Pay close attention to their hands → how they hold their tools and how they cut and manipulate the glass.

TIMING — You and your assistant need to coordinate your movements, reheats and gathers — so on, so forth... so that no time is lost in putting on handles. Bits may cool off so rapidly as to make them difficult to cut and reattach. Conversely, if you try to rush it all, you may end up messing everything up, with hot noodles going ka-splooey all over. Take your time, but work swiftly and above all → CONCENTRATE! Anticipate. Visualize your movements. And PRACTICE. PRACTICE. PRACTICE.

TEAMWORK

- TEAMWORK DEFINED 60
- LIST OF ESSENTIALS 63
- BLOWING THE JUMBO DIXIE-CUP
- DIP 'N' STRIP 64
- HANDLING HEAVY GLASS . . . 65
- BLOCKING / PAPERING . . . 66
- NECKING 67
- MARVERING 68
- ADDING A BUTTON 70
- FLATTENING THE BOTTOM . . 71
- THE TRANSFER 72
- OPENING THE VESSEL 73
- LARGE AMPHORA THING . . . 75
- TORCHES 76
- SHAPING THE AMPHORA . . . 78
- PUNTY / MOILE WRAP 80
- OPENING THE AMPHORA . . . 81
- PASSING THE PIPE 82

TEAMWORK

So.... you wanna make it **BIGGER** 'cause it's better....

Tip from **DANTE**: Never name a piece "A WHOPPER" - it's a difficult title to live with, and even a harder one to get rid of...

TEAMWORK IS THE METHOD OF CHOICE BY TODAY'S BEST GLASSBLOWERS. IT IS THROUGH TEAMWORK THE LARGEST AND/OR MOST COMPLEX FORMS CAN BE ACCOMPLISHED. TO BE SUCCESSFUL IT REQUIRES THAT EACH MEMBER OF THE TEAM IS FULLY AWARE OF THE TASK THAT THEY ARE TO PERFORM.

IN THE BEGINNING IT INVOLVES A PLAN. THIS IS NOT JUST A DRAWING ON THE WALL OR AN OBJECT ON A TABLE TO COPY. IT INVOLVES TIMING, CHOREOGRAPHY, AND PRACTICE. A WELL-HONED TEAM UNDERSTANDS WHAT EACH MEMBER IS DOING, AND WHAT THEY ARE ABOUT TO DO. THERE'S NOT MUCH DISCUSSION, MOSTLY ACTION. RARELY IS TIME WASTED, AND EVEN MORE SELDOM ARE PIECES LOST. BY THE TIME ONE MEMBER OF TEAM IS SUITING-UP TO BOX A PIECE, ANOTHER MEMBER IS BEGINNING THE NEXT STARTER BUBBLE. THE GAFFER REMAINS SEATED. LIKE A CONDUCTOR FOR AN ORCHESTRA — THE GAFFER SETS THE TIME, TEMPO AND MOVEMENT FOR ALL THE PLAYERS. IT IS AN HONORED POSITION TO HAVE. IT SHOULD BE RESPECTED.

REGARDLESS OF WHETHER YOU ARE WORKING ON A 2, 3, 4 or 10 MEMBER TEAM — **THE PERSON WHO IS DEEMED GAFFER CALLS THE SHOTS**. THEIR WISHES SHOULD BE OBEYED AND CARRIED-OUT TO THE BEST OF EVERYONE'S ABILITY. THIS, HOWEVER, PLACES A NUMBER OF RESPONSIBILITIES ON THE GAFFER. THE GAFFER MUST RECOGNIZE EACH MEMBERS STRENGTHS (AND WEAKNESSES) AND DELEGATE THE TASKS ACCORDINGLY. WHICH BRINGS US TO THE NEXT STAGE ⇒ ASSEMBLING A TEAM.

THERE ARE TWO BASIC WAYS IN WHICH I'VE SEEN TEAMS PUT TOGETHER: BY CHOICE, AND 'LUCK-OF-THE-DRAW'. **THE MOST PREFERABLE WAY IS TO WORK WITH YOUR FRIENDS** ⇒ WHO YOU **CAN** AND **CHOOSE** TO WORK WITH. NOW JUST BECAUSE THEY'RE YOUR FRIEND(S) DOESN'T MEAN THAT THEY WILL MAKE GOOD ASSISTANTS. SOMETIMES A BIT OF **FRICTION** MAY ARISE, AND FRIENDS DEVELOP INTO **GO ENEMIES** AND EVERYTHING GETS SHOT-TO-HELL. I KNOW SOME MARRIED

COUPLES, WHERE BOTH PARTNERS BLOW GLASS BUT CANNOT WORK WITH EACH OTHER. AND WISELY CHOOSE NOT TO. WHY? DON'T ASK. JUST KNOW THAT **IF YOUR TEAM ISN'T WORKING FOR YOU → THEN IT'S TIME TO CHANGE.** SOME GLASSBLOWERS ARE GREAT IN THE GAFFER'S SEAT, BUT WHEN THE SHOE IS ON THE OTHER FOOT, AND THEY'RE ASKED TO HELP OUT, THEY BECOME TERRIBLE ASSISTANTS. THEY FAIL TO PAY ATTENTION. THEY'RE NOT DRIVEN OR FOCUSED ON THE PIECE AT HAND, AND IN ALL FRANKNESS - COULD CARE LESS. IT'S EVIL. AND NOT FAIR. WHICH BRINGS US TO THE NEXT METHOD OF ASSEMBLING A TEAM - LUCK OF THE DRAW.

LUCK OF THE DRAW IS JUST THAT. LUCK. IN MOST SCHOOL PROGRAMS, YOU NEVER KNOW WHO YOU'RE GONNA GET PAIRED-UP WITH. OR YOU DON'T KNOW THE SKILL LEVEL OF YOUR PARTNER OR WHAT THEIR INTERESTS ARE. SOMETIMES YOU GET STUCK WITH SOME REAL LOSERS. AND OTHER TIMES → IT CAN BE THE BEGINNING OF A BEAUTIFUL RELATIONSHIP. MAKE THE BEST OF WHAT EVER HAND YOU'RE DEALT. IF YOU GET "STUCK" WITH SOMEONE WHO WORKS MUCH DIFFERENTLY THAN YOU, OR YOU KNOW YOU CAN'T WORK WITH BECAUSE OF SOME OTHER REASON - TRY TO SWITCH SLOTS WITH SOMEONE ELSE. IF THAT IS NOT POSSIBLE, DO TRY TO MAKE THE BEST OF IT. IT WON'T LAST FOREVER.

Q: WHY WORK ON A TEAM? WHY NOT JUST BLOW IT ALL BY YOURSELF?

A: → THERE ARE MANY BENEFITS TO WORKING ON A TEAM. LET'S TAKE A STEP BACK AND LOOK FOR A MOMENT AT THE STUDIO GLASS MOVEMENT IN THE UNITED STATES TO SHED A LITTLE LIGHT ON THE SUBJECT. THIS IS THE WAY I UNDERSTAND IT TO BE.

IN THE 1960'S, GLASS WAS DISCOVERED BY SOME 'COLLEGE KIDS' TO BE A FUN, INTERESTING AND PROFITABLE MATERIAL TO WORK WITH. LIKE THE ADDICTIVE SENSATION IT IS, THE ART OF GLASSBLOWING WAS PASSED FROM HAND-TO-HAND THROUGH WORKSHOPS AND SCHOOLS ALL OVER THE COUNTRY.

IT SPREAD LIKE **WILDFIRE!** STUDIOS POPPED UP ALL OVER THE PLACE. THE INTERESTING THING ABOUT IT WAS ALL THESE GUYS - AND A HANDFUL OF WOMEN, WORKED BY THEMSELVES (JUST LIKE IN CERAMICS). THAT WAS **THE WAY.** THAT IS UNTIL **THE WAY** GOT CHANGED BY THE **NEW WAY. THE WAY**, OR WHAT MIGHT NOW BE REFERRED TO AS 'THE OLD SCHOOL', WAS TO DO EVERYTHING SOLO (A NOBLE EFFORT INDEED). IT MADE SENSE. HOW ELSE COULD YOU CLAIM THAT THE PIECE WAS TRULY YOURS?

SOME OF THE SOLO BLOWERS CAME UP WITH INGENIOUS DEVICES AND INNOVATIVE TECHNIQUES TO HELP THEMSELVES WORK ALONE. ELABORATE FOOT-ACTIVATED PIPE COOLERS, SELF-TURNING YOKES AND PIPE WARMERS, AND PNEUMATIC DOORS ON THE FURNACE AND GLORY HOLES MADE IT SO YOU DIDN'T NEED ASSISTANTS. IT NEVERTHEless was a lonely and exhausting way to work. Some "old dogs" continue to blow in this manner today.

Glass was a hot new item 'back then'. It didn't have to be blown symmetrical. It didn't really matter what the piece looked like, as long as it was blue, fumed or mirrored → IT SOLD!

Things change. And like all good things → for the better. Some of the more influential glassblowers returned from Italy/Murano and brought with them the wisdom, techniques and tradition of working in teams as had been done in the factories there for centuries.

The teamwork approach made sense. You could have two people turn the pipe to handle larger quantities of glass. It was easier to make things symmetrical if one person was blowing while another was shaping the piece. It was faster and more fun to have extra hands working on the team making pieces. And so much more became possible.

Summer schools like Pilchuck, Penland and Haystack helped foster the teamwork and collaborative approach. Especially influential was (is) the Italian Maestro Lino Tagliapietra. No single glassblower has changed the way Americans blow glass as significantly as Lino has. This master from Murano graciously shares his 'secrets' with young and hungry audiances of maestro wanna-bes. Watching him work is a joy. The fluidity, dexterity and skill he exhibits while working with this material is incredible. And an education. It is no wonder that the Venetian virus hit and infected a large number of college students and professionals alike. Teamwork became the NEW WAY to work and continues to be. It's not such a struggle or juggling act as blowing solo. And working on a team always allows you to blame someone else for your mistakes.

Teamwork is also the fastest way to learn how to blow glass. By working on a team you become immersed in the process. Not only that, you become involved. And it always feels good to be needed! Since the traditional apprentice-type program fails to exist in this country in any great numbers, or in an established circut (I think it should be revived) - you have to do whatever it takes to get involved. You may have to do some traveling.

One of the easiest ways to become involved in a team of your choice, or to work in a studio which looks "cool" to you is: **OFFER TO WORK FOR FREE.** Really! I can't tell you how effective this approach is! It is an excellent educational opportunity. **Offer to open doors, sweep floors, do chores** - wash cullet or whatever in exchange for the chance to 'hang-out'. Once you get your foot in the door and your smiling face becomes famaliar - you may become assimilated into the team and put on the payroll. It is these type of open-minded (and obedient) assistants that in-turn become great glassblowers. Of course, you might inadvertently volunteer at a studio where the owner is hot-head (an asshole who blows his/her top at the drop of a hat). If that's the case ⇒ exit-stage right and bail. You have nothing to lose, and nobody needs to put-up with abusive (usually money-hungry) buttheads. I digress... Back to the issue at hand. Most people work in a team so that they can blow bigger pieces - easier. Here's the list of essential items to do just that.

THE LIST OF ESSENTIAL ITEMS FOR WORKING LARGE:

1. A PLAN OF WHAT YOU'RE DOING → e.g. A SKETCH/DESIGN
2. A LARGE GLORY HOLE
3. AN ADEQUETE SELECTION OF BLOCKS (INCLUDING LARGE ONES)
4. A MOBILE YOKE AT THE GLORY HOLE
5. A TORCH
6. LARGE PIPES AND PUNTIES
7. STRIPPING BUCKET
8. MUSCLES (TRAINED ASSISTANTS)
9. HEAT SHIELDS - PADDLES (FOR PROTECTION)
10. WRIST AND/OR BACK SUPPORTS
11. LOTS OF GLASS
12. GOOD MUSIC AND/OR A POSITIVE ATTITUDE.

THE LIST ABOVE COMPRISES **THE BASICS** NECESSARY TO BLOW LARGE GLASS WITH GREATER EASE AND LESS FRICTION. THERE MAY ARISE THE NEED FOR ADDITIONAL DEVICES, TOOLS OR TECHNIQUES FOR THE SPECIFIC OBJECT(S) WHICH YOU ARE ATTEMPTING TO MAKE - BUT THAT'LL COME LATER. ALL GOOD THINGS IN ALL GOOD TIME.

FOR THE MAJORITY OF GLASS ARTISTS WISHING TO INCREASE THE SCALE OF THEIR WORK — THEY NEED TO BECOME FAMALIAR WITH HANDLING LARGE QUANTIES OF HOT GLASS. THE **JUMBO DIXIE-CUP** IS JUST THE FORM TO DO THAT. IT IS A CHALLENGING FORM TO STRIVE FOR AND WILL BE THE FIRST OF OUR FORMS INTRODUCING YOU TO **LARGE GLASS**.

ONCE YOUR TEAM IS ASSEMBLED AND THE SHOP IS SET-UP FOR WORKING LARGE, IT'S TIME TO BEGIN. HAVE YOUR ASSISTANT MAKE ALL THE GATHERS FOR YOU. SOMETIMES THE PIPE WILL BE PASSED OFF TO THE GAFFER FOR THE LAST DIP → TO INSURE HE/SHE GETS IT "JUST RIGHT" - BUT THAT IS A MATTER OF PERSONAL PREFERENCE AND ENTIRELY UP TO THE GAFFER.

Fig. 66 Jumbo Dixie-Cup

DEPENDING ON HOW HOT THE FURNACE IS YOU'LL NEED ANYWHERE FROM FIVE TO NINE GATHERS OF GLASS TO BUILD UP ENOUGH MASS TO BLOW THIS STYLE OF PIECE. USE THE BLOCKS TO SHAPE THE BUBBLE WITH, AND BLOW N' PAPER THE FORM TO END-UP WITH A NICE UNIFORM EVEN-WALLED Q-TIP SHAPE. KEEP THE WALLS OF THE BUBBLE JUST THICK ENOUGH TO WITHSTAND THE NEXT GATHER. IT WILL MAKE BLOWING OUT AND SHAPING THE FORM MUCH EASIER FURTHER DOWN THE ROAD. CONTINUE TO GATHER AS USUAL - MAKING SURE YOU DO FULL ROTATIONS WHILE IN THE FURNACE

KEEP YOURSELF FROM COOKING! HAVE SOMEONE CLOSE THE DOOR WHILE YOU GATHER, AND OPEN IT BACK UP WHEN YOU NEED OUT.

AND YOU COMPLETELY COVER THE PREVIOUS GATHER. ON THE LAST GATHER(S) YOU MAY WISH TO POSITION A YOKE IN FRONT OF THE FURNACE TO ASSIST IN THE TURNING OF THE PIPE WHILE GATHERING. WITH THOSE LAST GATHERS YOU MAY WISH TO DIP N' STRIP THE GATHER TO MAKE IT NICE 'N' UNIFORM:

Dip 'n' Strip:

NO, IT'S NOT A LAS VEGAS SEQUEL TO "DUMB AND AND DUMBER". IT IS A TECHNIQUE WHICH YOU CAN USE TO EVEN-OUT YOUR GATHER AND/OR TO OBTAIN JUST THE RIGHT AMOUNT OF GLASS WHICH YOU NEED. (IT CAN BE A POTENTIALLY WASTEFUL TECHNIQUE - PARTICULARLY IF YOU DON'T 'RECYCLE' THE GLASS YOU STRIP OFF. SO, WHY NOT PUT SOME OF THAT GLASS BACK INTO USE FOR YOU?...)

HAVE A MEDIUM-SIZED "CLEAR GLASS ONLY" BUCKET CLOSE TO THE FURNACE - ONE WHICH IS CAPABLE OF HANDLING MOLTEN GLASS.
⇒ BEWARE OF PAINTED STEEL DRUMS - THEY SMELL REALLY BAD AS THE HOT GLASS BURNS OR MELTS IT. (STAINLESS STEEL WORKS GREAT BUT IS EXPENSIVE AND SOMETIMES HARDER TO FIND.)

[THIS MIGHT ALSO BE A WONDERFUL OPPORTUNITY FOR YOU TO MAKE SOME FRIT FOR CASTING OR SURFACE DECORATION. YOU CAN FILL THE AFOREMENTIONED RECEPTACLE WITH WATER AND STRIP INTO THAT.]

WHATEVER SIZED GATHER YOU TAKE, THE PROCESS IS THE SAME. COMING STRAIGHT OUTTA THE FURNACE - YOU HEAD OVER TO THE BUCKET. KEEP THE PIPE TURNING AND HORIZONTAL TO THE FLOOR. AS SOON AS YOU'VE CLEARED THE LIP OF THE STRIPPING BUCKET - HOLD THE PIPE STRAIGHT UP N' DOWN. ALLOW GRAVITY TO PULL THE EXCESS SKIN OFF. IT IS NOT NECESSARY TO TURN THE PIPE WHILE YOU'RE IN THE VERTICAL POSITION.

AS SOON AS THE BULK OF THE UNWANTED GLASS PUDDLES OFF, START TURNING THE PIPE AGAIN AND BRING IT BACK TO THE HORIZONTAL POSITION.

A QUICK JERK UP AND DOWN JUST AS YOU LEVEL-OUT SHOULD RELEASE THAT LAST TAIL OF GLASS FROM THE BOTTOM OF THE PIECE. (SEE fig 67Ⓑ ⇒) YOU MAY THEN PROCEED TO CHILL THE PIPE AND CONTINUE TO WORK AS USUAL!

fig. 67Ⓐ

fig 67Ⓑ

fig 67Ⓒ STRIPPING ON THE MARVER.
SCOOP IT UP & RECYCLE!

ANOTHER MORE-IMMEDIATE WAY TO RECYCLE IS WHERE THE HOT STRIP-OFF IS PUDDLED ON THE MARVER - AND THEN SCOOPED-UP ON A TAGLIOL OR LONG SPATULA, AND TOSSED BACK INTO THE BACK OF THE FURNACE FOR IMMEDIATE REMELT AND CONSERVATION OF ENERGY. Ⓒ THE ONLY DRAWBACK TO THIS METHOD IS HAVING TO LIFT THE PIECE UP N' OVER THE MARVER. IT MIGHT BE UNCOMFORTABLE - BOTH IN THE **HEFT** NECESSARY TO CLEAR THE MARVER AND THE RESULTING RADIANT HEAT LIKELY TO BAKE YOUR UNPROTECTED MID-SECTION. YOU COULD PLACE A PLATE ON THE FLOOR DEDICATED SOLELY FOR THIS PURPOSE. CONSIDERING HOW MUCH FUEL YOU SPENT ON HEATing up the stuff, why not?

Your next step is to chill the pipe at the pipe cooler. This is an important step in being able to handle large n' heavy pieces. **The closer you can grip to the mass of glass, the better your ability to turn the pipe will be.** This also helps you balance and distribute the weight of the glass more evenly and with less physical effort. Turning "bowling balls on broomsticks" can toast your wrists quicker than you can say "lickety-split", which explains why gaffers give you they evil eye **if** you hand them a pipe "on the hot-side." It throws all of their body english off, and turning the pipe, or simple manuvers, becomes a chore. Which brings us to the next point:

Handling Heavy Glass

Rotating large pipes with massive blobs of hot glass on them requires skill and some muscle. Many gaffers will protect their wrists with flexible wrist supports. It is pretty easy to over-extend yourself when you're focused on manuvering something which seems as bright and heavy as the SUN on the end of your blowpipe.

Try to integrate as much of your whole body into the process as you can. Move your upper body with the glass. Use your legs to help you lift anytime you need to. Spread your hands apart as much as you can to **gain greater stability and balance. Your legs too. Use a yoke or other support as often as you can to help you turn the pipe.**

Keep the glass as close to your body as you can — without burning of course! This will improve your body english and prevent you from unnecessary and possibly painful overextension.

Try your best to keep the form on-center and as compact as possible. It is when the shapes get wonky and long that they become increasingly more difficult to handle.

Pass the pipe off and allow someone else to "turn pole" for a while. This is especially important if your arms are beginning to cramp-up. Take a break. Moving heavy glass can be physically demanding. It's not a bad idea to get 'in-shape' for it by training with weights and building-up your muscles and endurance, particularly if you anticipate working on a large-scale consistently.

Try to move as fluidly as you can. Avoid abrupt starts and stops. Try to make each movement *flow* into the next. Your body works better that way, and the glass responds more favorably when it's treated like the liquid it is! The next order of business is to shape the glass. Blocks are the preferred tool to do just that.

fig. 68 Chilling The Pipe

fig. 69 Anatomy of a Heavy-Duty Glassblower

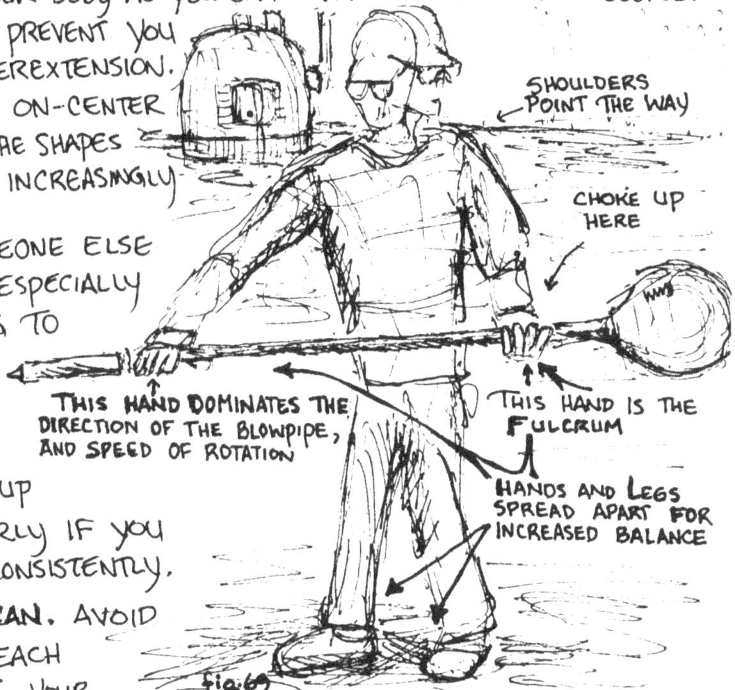

- SHOULDERS POINT THE WAY
- CHOKE UP HERE
- THIS HAND DOMINATES THE DIRECTION OF THE BLOWPIPE, AND SPEED OF ROTATION
- THIS HAND IS THE FULCRUM
- HANDS AND LEGS SPREAD APART FOR INCREASED BALANCE

65

BLOCKING LARGE GLASS

MANY GAFFERS SET THEIR BLOCKS ON THE RAILS OF THE BENCH WHILE BLOCKING IN THE LAST GATHER(S). THE WEIGHT OF WATER-LOGGED CHERRY WOOD BLOCKS THE SIZE OF STUMPS ARE HEAVY ENOUGH WITHOUT THE ADDED WEIGHT OF THE HOT GLASS IN THEM — SO THE BLOCKS ARE SUPPORTED ON THE BENCH. THE HOT GATHER IS BROUGHT OVER AND ROTATED IN THE BLOCK. THE ANGLE OF THE PIPE IS ADJUSTED DURING THE TURNING MOTION TO INSURE ALL AREAS OF THE BUBBLE GET 'MOLDED' INTO SHAPE.

USE TWO HANDS TO STABILIZE THE BLOCK ON THE RAIL. ALSO — HAVE AN ASSISTANT STAND BY TO SHIELD THE HANDS (HOLDING THE BLOCK) WITH A PADDLE. (THOSE JUMBO GATHERS GET PRETTY HOT!

KEEP THE BLOCK WET TOO! IF YOU NOTICE ANY STICKING — SET THE PIPE ON THE RAILS AND REWET THE BLOCK.

ONCE YOU'VE GOT THE FORM BLOCKED-IN — SET THE BLOCK AWAY AND HAVE THE ASSISTANT TAKE A DEEP REHEAT. THE PIECE SHOULD GET PRETTY HOT. IT'S TIME TO SHAPE AND BLOW-OUT THE BUBBLE.

fig. 70 BLOCKING A LARGE GATHER

fig 71

PAPERING

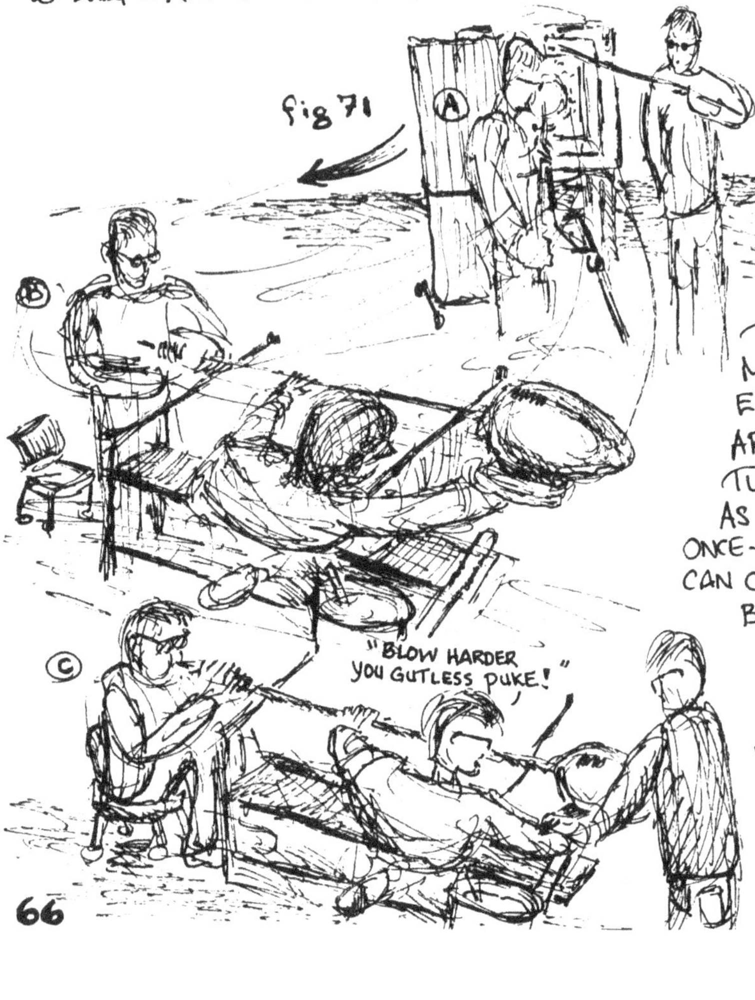

THE PIECE IS RETURNED TO THE BENCH! THE ASSISTANT MAY CONTINUE TO ROTATE THE PIPE AS THE GAFFER BEGINS TO PAPER THE PIECE. ANOTHER ASSISTANT SHOULD BE STATIONED BEHIND THE BENCH TO OFFER PROTECTION.

BEGIN PAPERING THE MOILE-NECK AREA FIRST AND WORK YOUR WAY DOWN TO THE BOTTOM OF THE PIECE. IT'S PRETTY MUCH THE SAME TECHNIQUE AS FOR SMALLER PIECES — ONLY YOU HAVE MORE SURFACE AREA TO COVER — AND SOMEONE HELPING YOU TURN THE PIPE.

AS SOON AS THE PIECE HAS BEEN GIVEN THE ONCE-OVER WITH THE PAPER (OR MORE) YOU CAN CONTINUE TO SHAPE IT AS YOUR ASSISTANT BEGINS TO BLOW.

AT FIRST — AUDIBLE CLUES ➔ LOUD AND CLEAR ONES AT THAT LIKE "BLOW please" AND "STOP" or "BLOW HARDER" or "BLOW SOFTER" please... SHOULD BE GIVEN BY THE GAFFER TO CONTROL THE EXPANSION OF THE BUBBLE. AFTER A PERIOD

OF TIME WORKING TOGETHER THE ORAL DIRECTIONS WILL GIVE WAY TO VISUAL CLUES. A NOD OR TILT OF THE HEAD INDICATES TO YOUR ASSISTANT TO BEGIN BLOWING. A QUICK TURN OF THE HEAD FROM SIDE-TO-SIDE TELLS THEM TO STOP BLOWING. AVOID SAYING "WHOA" WHEN YOU WANT THE ASSISTANT TO CEASE BLOWING → IT SOUNDS TOO MUCH LIKE "BLOW" AND THAT'S THE LAST THING YOU NEED!

ANOTHER METHOD TO GET YOUR ASSISTANT TO STOP BLOWING IS TO YANK THE PIPE OUT OF THEIR MOUTH. SIMPLY PULL OR SLIDE THE PIPE QUICKLY AWAY FROM YOUR ASSISTANT'S HEAD. IT SHOULD BE ENOUGH TO INDICATE THAT THEY SHOULD STOP TRYING TO BLOW — IF NOT COMPLETELY PREVENTING THEM FROM DOING SO (fig. 72 - above).

fig. 72 — PULL THE PIPE THIS WAY

AT THIS STAGE OF THE PIECE YOU WANT TO CONCENTRATE ON BLOWING OUT THE SHOULDERS AND SHAPING THE BOTTOM IN PREPARATION FOR THE NECKING PROCEDURE. SOME GAFFERS WILL DO ALL THE SHAPING AT THE BENCH WITH THE NEWSPAPER WHILE OTHERS MAY MARVER THE FORM. WHICHEVER METHOD YOU PREFER, IT'S VITAL THAT YOU KEEP THE NECK AREA HOT AND MOVING. AVOID OVER-CHILLING IT (WITH THE PAPER OR MARVER) AND TAKE A FEW SECONDS OUT TO TORCH THE NECK PRIOR TO REHEATING (fig. 73). THIS ADDITIONAL BLAST OF **BTU**'S WILL HELP INTRODUCE HEAT INTO THE NECK AREA MAKING IT MUCH EASIER TO NECK THE PIECE LATER. WHILE YOUR ASSISTANT IS HEATING UP THE PIECE IN THE GLORY HOLE, YOU CAN BLAST THE BLADES OF YOUR JACKS WITH THE TORCH AND LUBE THEM UP WITH SOME FRESH BEESWAX.

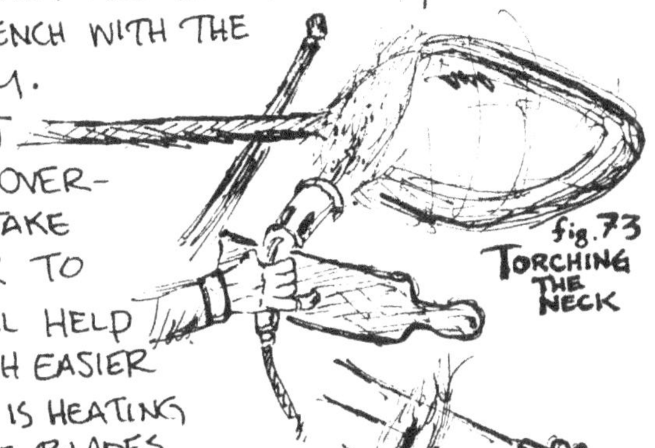

fig. 73 TORCHING THE NECK

(A) TORCH THE JACKS...

(B) LUBE WITH WAX!

NECKING

YOU CAN USE TWO HANDS TO HELP SQUEEZE THE JACKS AROUND THE NECK OF YOUR PIECE.

IF YOU SQUEEZE **TOO HARD-TOO FAST** YOU MAY PREVENT YOUR ASSISTANT FROM BEING ABLE TO TURN THE PIECE. SO, TAKE IT EASY!

IT OFTEN HELPS TO TILT THE PIPE DOWN ON AN ANGLE AND NECK IN THAT POSITION. THIS HELPS STRETCH THE NECK AND GIVES YOU EASIER ACCESS FOR THE JACKSES.

HOPEFULLY YOU'LL HAVE AN ASSISTANT STANDING-BY WITH A PADDLE TO PROTECT YOUR ARMS, WRISTS AND HANDS FROM COOKING FROM THE RADIANT HEAT.

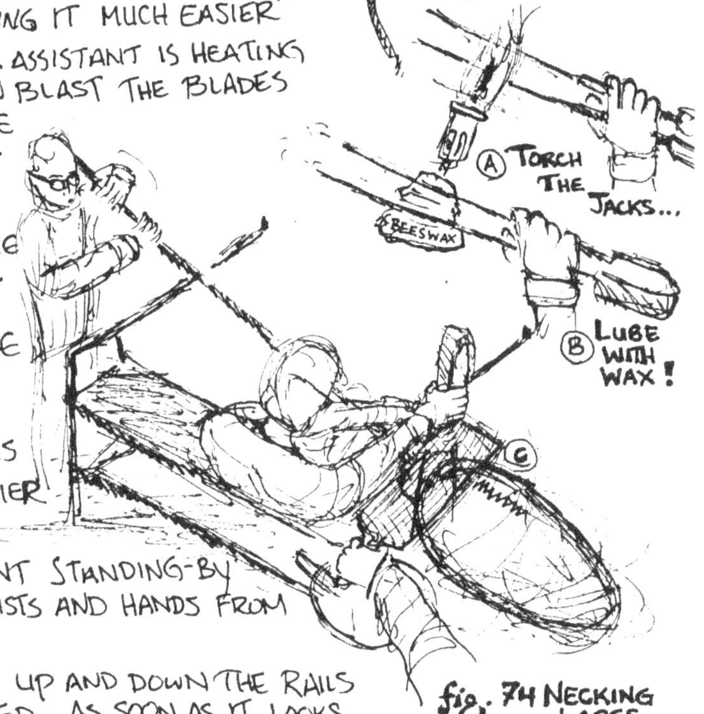

IT SHOULD TAKE A COUPLE PASSES UP AND DOWN THE RAILS TO GET THE NECK PRETTY-WELL ESTABLISHED. AS SOON AS IT LOOKS GOOD, THE PIPE MAY BE RESET ON BOTH RAILS AND TURNED AS USUAL. SOME ADDITIONAL PAPERING AND BLOWING MAY BE POSSIBLE BEFORE RETURNING TO THE GLORY HOLE FOR ANOTHER REHEAT.

fig. 74 NECKING LARGE GLASS

MARVERING

If marvering is more your cup of tea, then the Jumbo Dixie Cup is a great piece to hone your skills on. (The whole piece can be practically made entirely using the marver. The process is pretty much the same as marvering smaller pieces except the added mass makes turning the piece a little more trickier. Again, choke up on the pipe as much as you dare. **Marver the tip and the sidewalls first in order to blow the shoulders out.**

The added weight of extra gathers puts a little more strain on your wrists - particularly when you have to support the entire weight of the piece and blowpipe while marvering the tip. (Need I say it takes practice to develop a feel for this technique?...)...

Remember to lift off the marver's surface completely and air marver between occasional passes. You can also rest and roll the pipe on the back end of the marver (as in fig. 76 →) It also creates an opportunity to blow out the shoulders as well.

fig. 75 MARVIN' THE TIP

When working with large pieces you may be surprised how much more working time you have. That's because the larger mass holds and insulates the heat longer than smaller ones. That is until you blow the walls of the piece pretty thin. When the wall thickness diminishes so does it's ability to hold the heat, and it becomes just as vulnerable to thermal shock and stress as any piece of blown glass - perhaps more so.

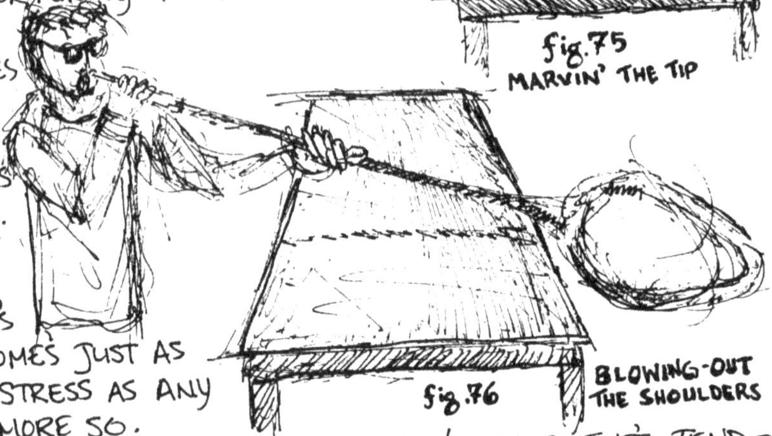

fig. 76 BLOWING-OUT THE SHOULDERS

When you get the piece inflated fairly large, you'll notice it's tendency to collapse-in on itself when you attempt to marver it nice-'n'-hot like. The poor piece can't even support it's own weight! If that happens to you, just have your assistant "cap" the blowpipe with the palm of their hand while you marver to maintain the internal pressure. →

As with small pieces, try to use as much of the marver as you can. Make sure it's been dusted off prior to using it, or that "stuff" that accumulates on there will be transferred to the surface of your piece. Yuk!

fig. 77 CAPPING & MARVERING

Try to use as much of your upper body as you can to marver and heft the glass around with. Direct the motion of the rolling and turning by pointing your shoulders where you want the piece to go. **STAY PUT!** Keep your feet

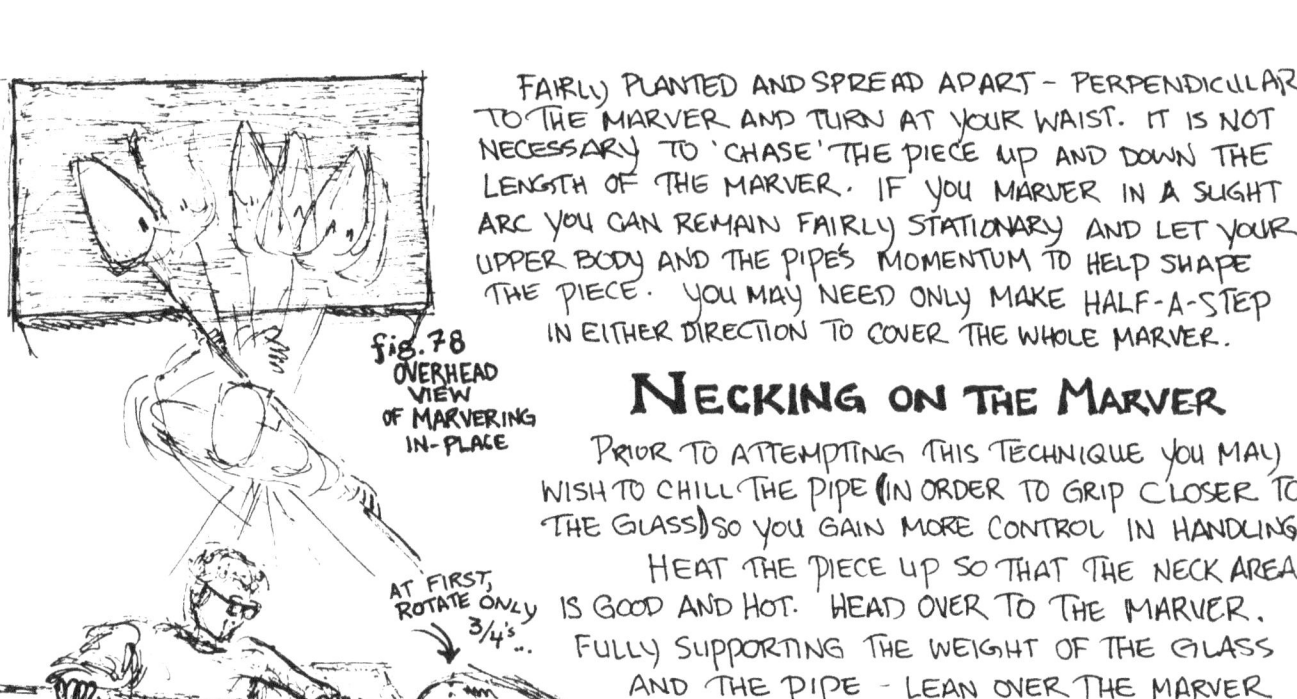

fig. 78 OVERHEAD VIEW OF MARVERING IN-PLACE

AT FIRST, ROTATE ONLY 3/4's..

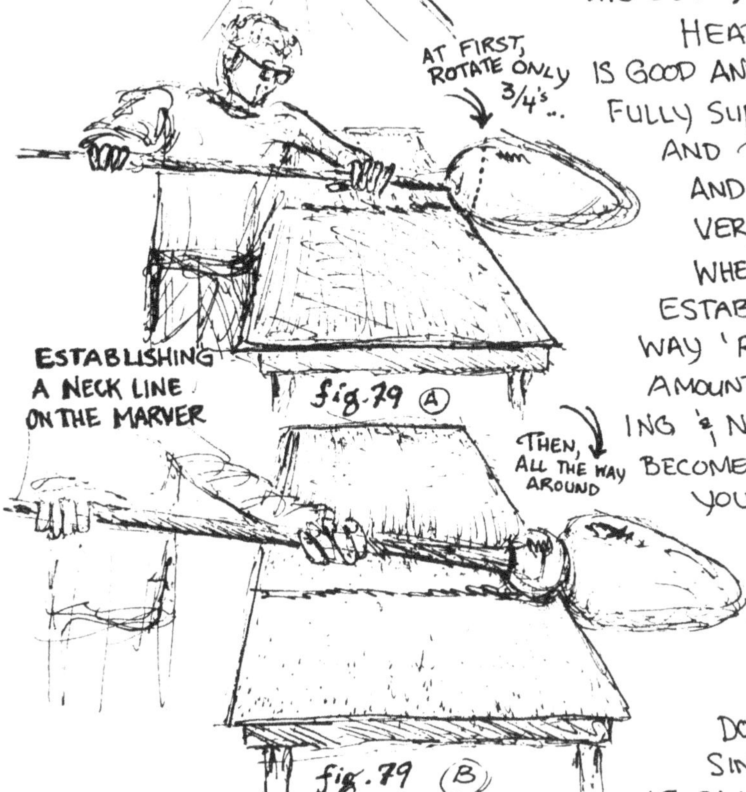

ESTABLISHING A NECK LINE ON THE MARVER

fig. 79 Ⓐ

THEN, ALL THE WAY AROUND

fig. 79 Ⓑ

FAIRLY PLANTED AND SPREAD APART - PERPENDICULAR TO THE MARVER AND TURN AT YOUR WAIST. IT IS NOT NECESSARY TO 'CHASE' THE PIECE UP AND DOWN THE LENGTH OF THE MARVER. IF YOU MARVER IN A SLIGHT ARC YOU CAN REMAIN FAIRLY STATIONARY AND LET YOUR UPPER BODY AND THE PIPE'S MOMENTUM TO HELP SHAPE THE PIECE. YOU MAY NEED ONLY MAKE HALF-A-STEP IN EITHER DIRECTION TO COVER THE WHOLE MARVER.

NECKING ON THE MARVER

PRIOR TO ATTEMPTING THIS TECHNIQUE YOU MAY WISH TO CHILL THE PIPE (IN ORDER TO GRIP CLOSER TO THE GLASS) SO YOU GAIN MORE CONTROL IN HANDLING.

HEAT THE PIECE UP SO THAT THE NECK AREA IS GOOD AND HOT. HEAD OVER TO THE MARVER. FULLY SUPPORTING THE WEIGHT OF THE GLASS AND THE PIPE - LEAN OVER THE MARVER AND GENTLY SET THE PIECE DOWN ON THE VERY BACK EDGE OF THE MARVER - EXACTLY WHERE YOU WANT THE NECKLINE TO BE ESTABLISHED. TURN THE PIPE 3/4's THE WAY 'ROUND AND ROTATE BACKWARDS THE SAME AMOUNT. THEN REPEAT OR CONTINUE ON ROLLING & NECKING THE PIECE UNTIL THE NECKLINE BECOMES FULLY ESTABLISHED. THE REASON YOU ONLY PARTIALLY NECK AT FIRST IS TO CREATE A SINGLE NECKLINE VS. A SPIRAL MISHAP. OFTENTIMES WHEN YOU FIRST ATTEMPT THIS TECHNIQUE YOU END-UP ROLLING IN ONE DIRECTION AND CORKSCREWING DOWN THE NECK INSTEAD OF MAKING A SINGLE NECKLINE. IT'S TRICKY! BUT IT CAN BE A USEFUL TECHNIQUE TO KNOW IN THE EVENT CONVENTIONAL NECKING PROCEDURES WON'T WORK FOR YOU - e.g. YOU'RE WORKING ALONE OR UNDER-STAFFED, OR IF YOU'RE IN A BIG HURRY etc...

ANOTHER BONUS OF NECKING ON THE MARVER IS THAT ONCE YOU HAVE THE NECKLINE ESTABLISHED - YOU CAN GO AHEAD AND SHAPE AND BLOW THE PIECE FURTHER WHILE AT THE MARVER. THIS SAVES YOU ALOT OF RUNNING AROUND.

AS SOON AS YOU HAVE THE NECKLINE CUT-IN, YOU CAN FINISH BLOWING OUT THE SHOULDERS AND CONCENTRATE ON COMPLETING THE BOTTOM HALF OF THE VESSEL. THE BEST WAY TO EXPAND YOUR BUBBLE, AND MAKE USE OF ALL THE GLASS DOWN THERE, IS TO NEWSPAPER WHILE YOUR ASSISTANT BLOWS. THIS WAY YOU CAN EASILY OBSERVE, CONTROL, AND CORRECT THE RATE OF EXPANSION UP AND DOWN THE LENGTH OF THE BUBBLE. SEE FIGURE 80 ON THE FOLLOWING PAGE.

ANOTHER ASSISTANT MAY ASSIST IN TURNING THE PIPE WHILE STANDING BETWEEN the rails ↙. And another can protect the gaffer's arm from frying ↘.

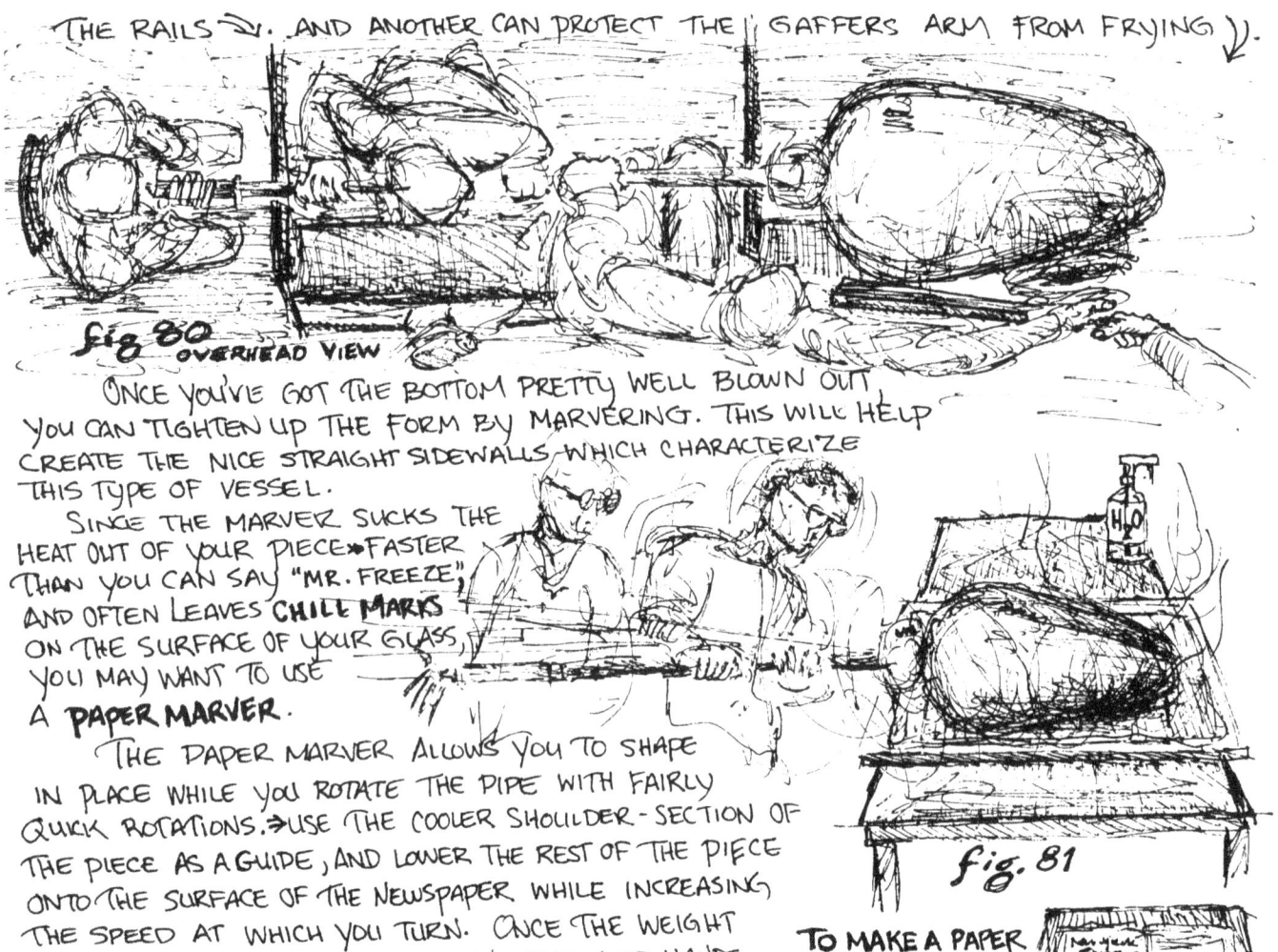

fig 80 OVERHEAD VIEW

Once you've got the bottom pretty well blown out, you can tighten up the form by marvering. This will help create the nice straight sidewalls which characterize this type of vessel.

Since the marver sucks the heat out of your piece→faster than you can say "Mr. Freeze", and often leaves **CHILL MARKS** on the surface of your glass, you may want to use a **PAPER MARVER**.

The paper marver allows you to shape in place while you rotate the pipe with fairly quick rotations. → Use the cooler shoulder-section of the piece as a guide, and lower the rest of the piece onto the surface of the newspaper while increasing the speed at which you turn. Once the weight of the piece is balanced you can move your hands closer together to help you turn faster.

Have an assistant cap the pipe with their hand (as necessary) to maintain the internal pressure. I've even seen some people blow while at this stage to further inflate the bubble and prevent it from collapsing. Whatever it takes....

If you notice your bubble beginning to stick - lift up and off the paper marver - and have an assistant re-mist the surface. Watch out for water

fig. 81

TO MAKE A PAPER MARVER:
1. Soak several sections of newspaper until they are saturated w/water.
2. Lay-out the newspaper flat on a large piece of plywood. This may then be moved around as needed and slapped on the marver when the time comes.
3. Have a squirt-bottle handy to re-soak the paper as necessary.
4. Make sure all excess water (puddles) is squeezed-off before using, or you may end-up quenching the surface of your glass.

that may form into puddles as they may quench your glass — Not what you want to have happen at this stage of the game.

When the sidewalls are blown-out and shaped to your satisfaction, you need to focus on shaping the bottom of your piece. The decision to make here is: **BUTTON OR NO BUTTON?** The main reason you'd want to apply a button is because the bottom of your piece is dangerously thin. The button can give you additional support for your punty to attach to and insure that you won't take the bottom of your piece out when boxing it.

If, on the other hand, you've left yourself a decent thickness on the bottom of your piece, a button is totally unnecessary, and only serves to compound the coldworking process later.

Applying the button is almost **IDENTICAL** to doing an avolio (see page 139). On a medium sized punty, have an assistant gather-up a healthy blob of glass. **NO MARVERING IS NECESSARY!** You want the glass as hot as you can get it. You also need it off the end of the punty where you can use it, so the assistant should tilt the punty slightly down on the way over to the bench.

It is presented horizontally to the gaffer - who inspects it first before applying it to the bottom. (They always have the right of refusal and may reject a bit if it doesn't look right or if it isn't big enough for the job at hand.)

Using either the jacks or tweezers you can lightly grab the punty and target the center of the bottom. The bit is lightly touched-up. The punty is lifted up a little so the glass will trail off - like winding a thread on a spool. Once a sufficient amount of glass has been coiled up (fig 82 B to the right) the punty is yanked back behind the bench in one fell swoop to wick-off the excess (82 C).

The back of the jacks are used to smooth and center the button as in figure 82 D to the right. The piece is then reheated (flashed-first) - concentrating on getting just the bottom hot enough so that it may be paddled smooth.

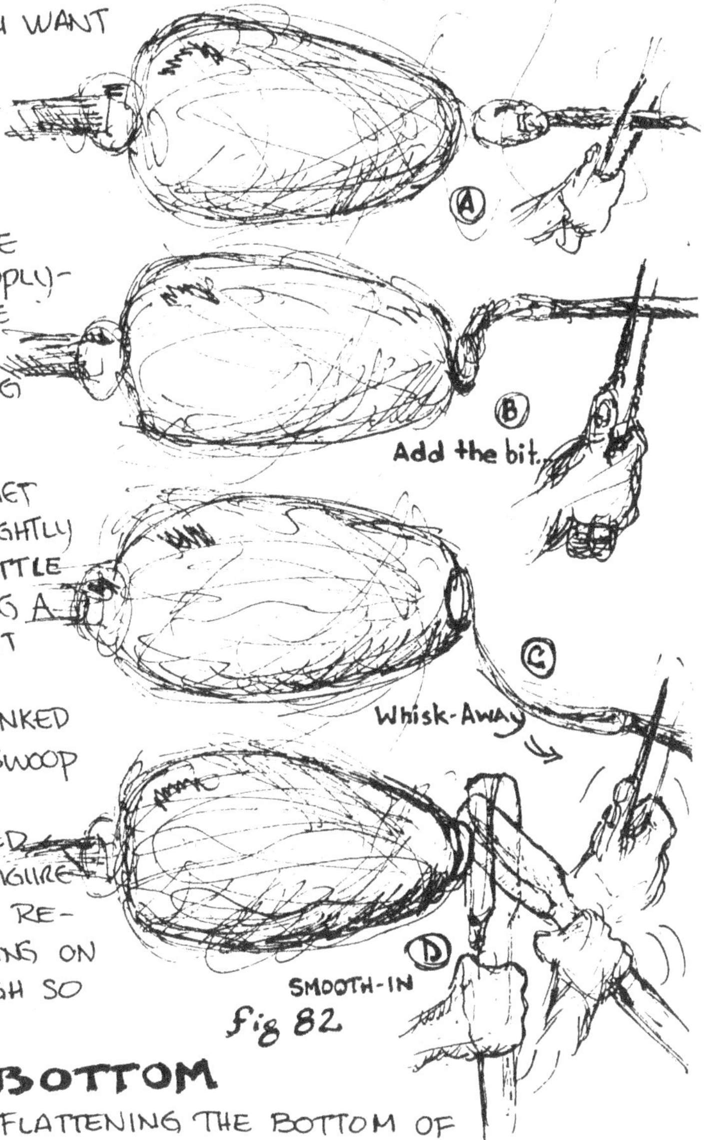

(A)

Add the bit. (B)

Whisk-Away (C)

SMOOTH-IN (D)

fig 82

FLATTENING THE BOTTOM

One of the best methods for flattening the bottom of your vessel is to have one assistant blow while you paper and another assistant paddles the foot flat simultaneously. Communication is important so that everyone involved knows just how far to blow or paddle; so make yourself heard! "**PADDLE HARDER**" - "**BLOW SOFTER**" or "**CAP THE PIPE**" are a few clues that might help you achieve a nice crisp bottom on your piece. As usual, make complete rotations to insure that you're getting everything even and on-center. It may take an additional reheat or two to achieve the type of bottom that

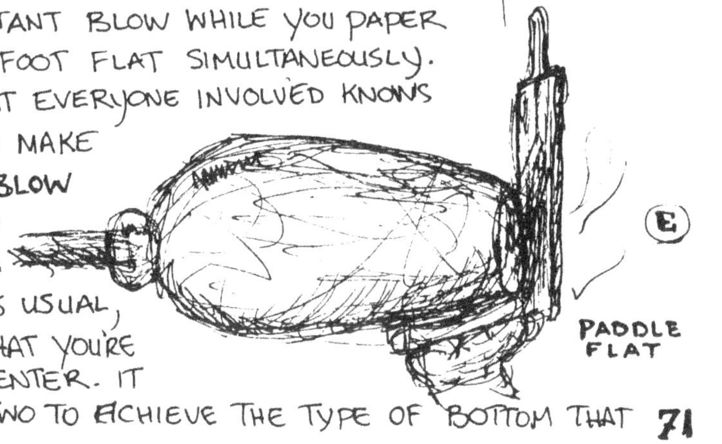

(E)

PADDLE FLAT

YOU'RE LOOKING FOR. YOU MAY WISH TO KICK THE FOOT IN A TAD (BY PADDLING IT IN) SO YOU WIND UP WITH A SLIGHTLY CONCAVE BOTTOM, (IT MAKES IT EASIER TO GRIND THE PUNTY).

WHILE YOUR ASSISTANT IS PREPARING THE PUNTY YOU CAN TORCH THE NECK OF THE PIECE IN PREPARATION FOR THE TRANSFER. THIS LITTLE BIT OF HEAT CAN HELP STABALIZE THE TEMPERATURE IN THE PIECE MORE DIRECTLY AND FASTER THAN TRYING TO DO IT IN THE GLORY HOLE. YOU DO, HOWEVER, WANT TO GIVE THE PIECE ONE FINAL FLASH IN THE GLORY HOLE PRIOR TO STICKING-UP THE PUNTY.

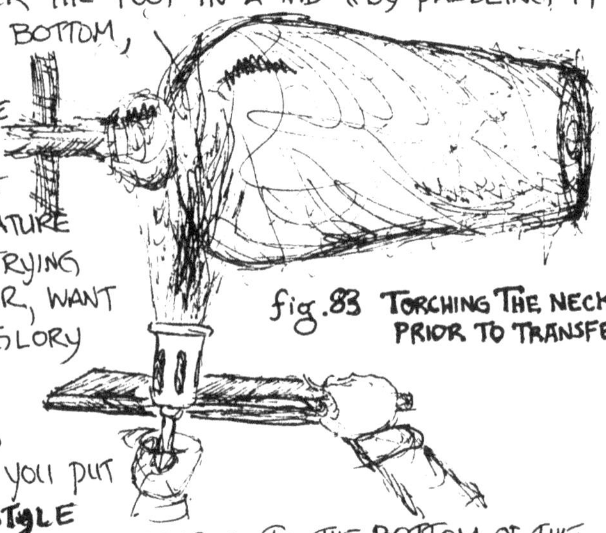

fig. 83 TORCHING THE NECK PRIOR TO TRANSFER

THE TRANSFER PROCESS FOR LARGE GLASS IS THE SAME AS FOR MOST EVERYTHING ELSE. IF YOU PUT A BUTTON ON THE BOTTOM, A LARGE-SCALE **DOME-STYLE** PUNTY IS PREFERRED, WHEREAS IF YOU ARE PUNTYING DIRECTLY TO THE BOTTOM OF THE PIECE - A **CROWN** OR **SCULPTURE** PUNTY MIGHT DO THE TRICK. (SEE THE PUNTY CHAPTER, PAGES 83-93 FOR MORE INFORMATION.) THE CHALLENGE HERE IS GETTING THE PIECE STUCK-UP AND ON-CENTER. SOMETIMES IT TAKES A BIT OF LEANING OVER TO SEE WHAT YOU'RE DOING. WHATEVER IT TAKES!

fig. 84 Ⓐ

ONCE YOU ATTACH THE PUNTY, YOU CAN MAKE A FEW EXTRA ROLLS UP AND DOWN THE BENCH AND CENTER THE PUNTY UP BY SPREADING THE TWEEZERS AND GUIDING THE PUNTY (fig 84 A).

THE ASSISTANT MAY PUFF ON THE PUNTY WITH A 'SOFFIE' TO STIFFEN IT UP QUICKER IF NECESSARY. A TOUCH OF WATER, A LIFT OF THE PIPE, AND A BONK WITH THE BACK OF THE TWEEZERS—AND THE PIECE SHOULD COME FREE.

BONK

Ⓑ

THE GAFFER REMAINS SEATED. THE PIPE IS TAKEN BY ONE ASSISTANT AND TOSSED IN THE PIPE BUCKET WHILE ANOTHER HEATS UP THE PIECE ON THE PUNTY IN THE GLORY HOLE. AFTER A GOOD LONG FLASH, THE PIECE IS RETURNED TO THE GAFFER FOR INSPECTION. **TO TRIM OR NOT TO TRIM? THAT IS THE QUESTION....**

IF THE LIP LOOKS FINE - WHY MESS WITH IT? IF IT DOESN'T, AND APPEARS JAGGED OR MANGLED OR LOOKS OUTRIGHT TOO **FAT** ⇒ SOME TRIMMING MAY BE IN ORDER. FOLLOW THE SAME STEPS AS YOU WOULD FOR TRIMMING SMALLER PIECES (AS ILLUSTRATED IN THE PREVIOUS CHAPTER) - TWEEZE N' CRIMP, CUT - HEAT AND SMOOTH UNTIL YOU WIND UP WITH A NICE CLEAN SYMMETRICAL LIP. YOUR ASSISTANT THEN MAY HEAT UP THE LIP AREA AGAIN, AND ALSO CONCENTRATE ON HEATING-UP PART OF THE

SHOULDERS AS WELL. AT THE BENCH THE SHOULDERS CAN BE PAPERED-IN A TAD TO PREVENT THEM FROM OPENING UP TOO MUCH TOO SOON. IT ALSO HELPS KEEP YOUR PIECE IN-CHECK AND HELPS MAINTAIN SYMMETRY.

YOU MAY AT THIS POINT BLOW THE SHOULDERS OUT WITH A PUFF FROM YOUR ASSISTANT WITH THE SOFFIETTA. YOU CAN USE THE JACKS TO GUIDE THE SOFFIETTA, GENTLY PRESS IT AGAINST THE LIPS AND HAVE YOUR ASSISTANT BLOW. IF YOU'VE GOT A COMPLETE SEAL THE SHOULDERS SHOULD PUFF OUT A LITTLE.

NOW YOU CAN TAKE ANOTHER REHEAT AND PROCEED TO OPEN UP THE REST OF THE WAY, OR NOW WOULD BE A GOOD TIME TO ADD A **LIP WRAP**, IF YOU SO DESIRE!

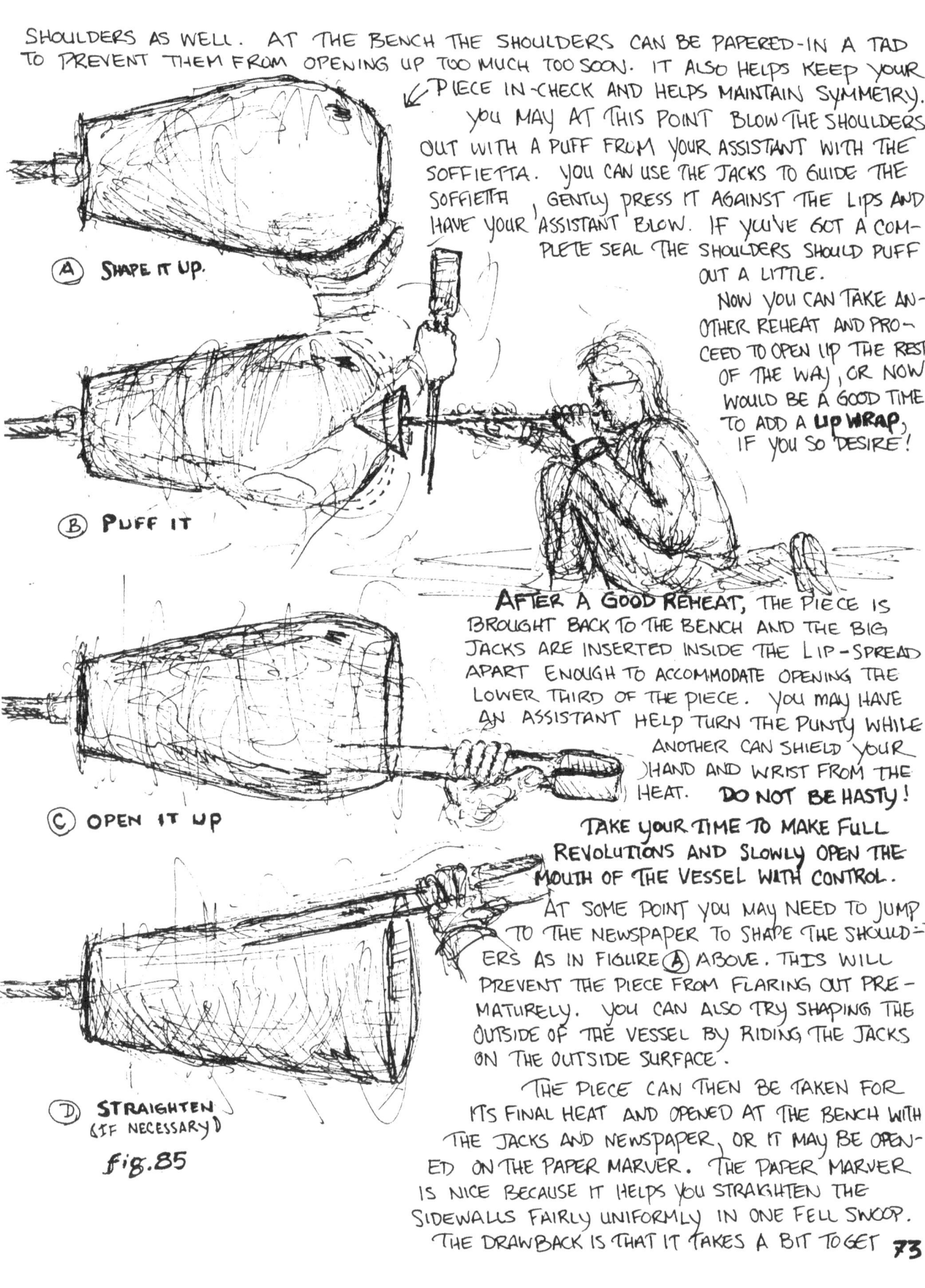

(A) SHAPE IT UP.
(B) PUFF IT
(C) OPEN IT UP
(D) STRAIGHTEN (IF NECESSARY)
fig. 85

AFTER A GOOD REHEAT, THE PIECE IS BROUGHT BACK TO THE BENCH AND THE BIG JACKS ARE INSERTED INSIDE THE LIP-SPREAD APART ENOUGH TO ACCOMMODATE OPENING THE LOWER THIRD OF THE PIECE. YOU MAY HAVE AN ASSISTANT HELP TURN THE PUNTY WHILE ANOTHER CAN SHIELD YOUR HAND AND WRIST FROM THE HEAT. **DO NOT BE HASTY!** TAKE YOUR TIME TO MAKE FULL REVOLUTIONS AND SLOWLY OPEN THE MOUTH OF THE VESSEL WITH CONTROL.

AT SOME POINT YOU MAY NEED TO JUMP TO THE NEWSPAPER TO SHAPE THE SHOULDERS AS IN FIGURE (A) ABOVE. THIS WILL PREVENT THE PIECE FROM FLARING OUT PREMATURELY. YOU CAN ALSO TRY SHAPING THE OUTSIDE OF THE VESSEL BY RIDING THE JACKS ON THE OUTSIDE SURFACE.

THE PIECE CAN THEN BE TAKEN FOR ITS FINAL HEAT AND OPENED AT THE BENCH WITH THE JACKS AND NEWSPAPER, OR IT MAY BE OPENED ON THE PAPER MARVER. THE PAPER MARVER IS NICE BECAUSE IT HELPS YOU STRAIGHTEN THE SIDEWALLS FAIRLY UNIFORMLY IN ONE FELL SWOOP. THE DRAWBACK IS THAT IT TAKES A BIT TO GET

USED TO! ESSENTIALLY THE BOTTOM OF THE PIECE IS GLIDED INTO POSITION ON THE PAPER MARVER, GENTLY RESTING IT THERE, AND USING IT AS A GUIDE TO TURN THE REST OF THE PIECE ON. THE REVOLUTIONS ARE INCREASED TO AID IN FLARING THE LIP AND CREATING A UNIFORM WALL. THE GAFFER, STANDING AT THE OPPOSITE END OF THE MARVER CAN INSERT THE JACKS INSIDE THE LIP OF THE PIECE AND GENTLY RIDE THEM THERE TO SMOOTH OUT THE REST OF TOP OF THE PIECE. A THIRD ASSISTANT MAY STAND-BY WITH A PADDLE TO SHIELD THE GAFFER AND/OR SMOOTH THE LIP WITH IT - TO GET EVERYTHING NICE AND SYMMETRICAL. IF THE FORM IS IN PRETTY GOOD SHAPE IT MAY NOT BE NECESSARY TO USE THE JACKS OR THE PADDLE → AN' SIMPLY TUNE EVERYTHING UP WITH A QUICK SPIN ON THE PAPER MARVE'.

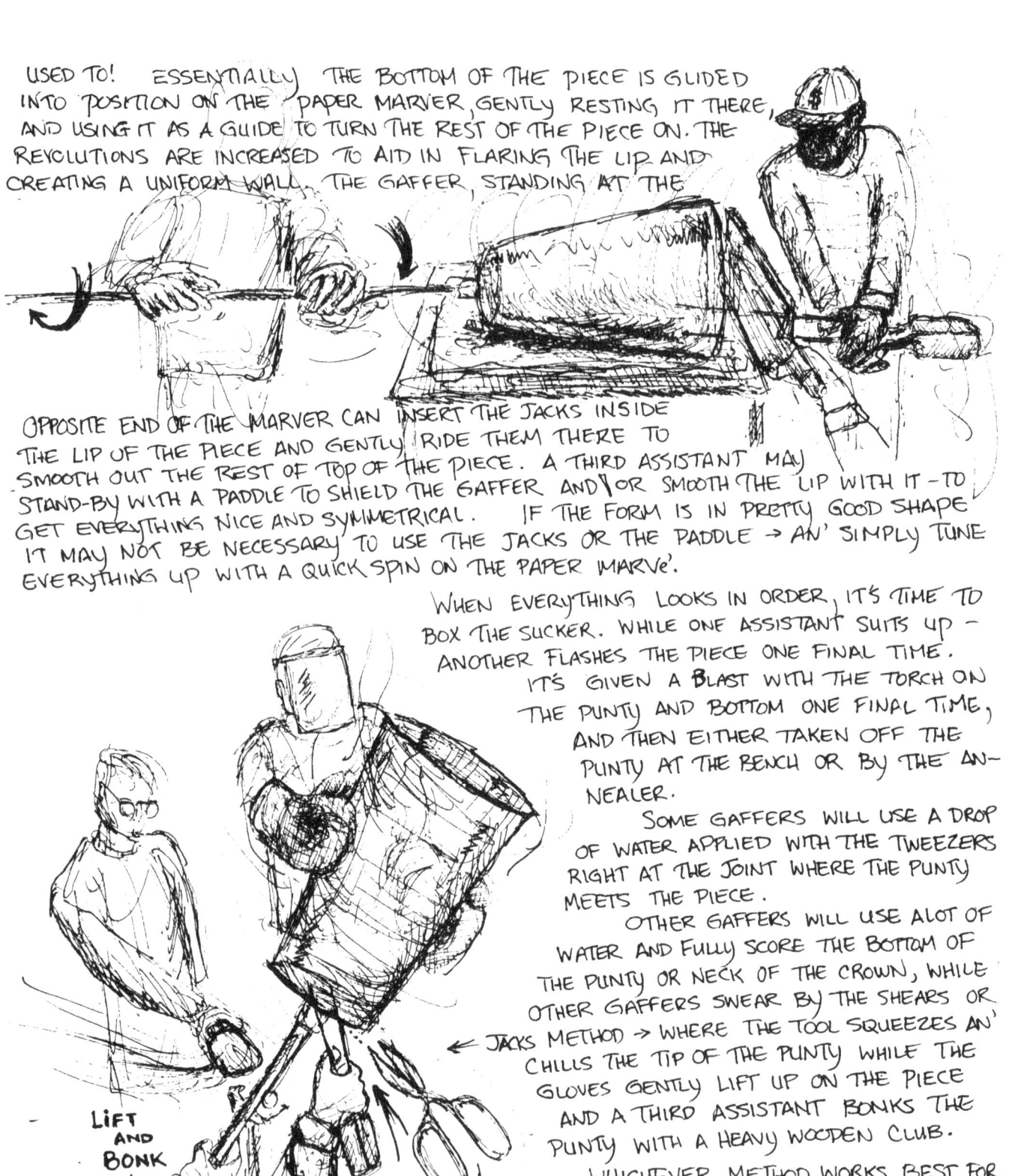

LIFT AND BONK

JACKS OR SHEARS

WHEN EVERYTHING LOOKS IN ORDER, IT'S TIME TO BOX THE SUCKER. WHILE ONE ASSISTANT SUITS UP - ANOTHER FLASHES THE PIECE ONE FINAL TIME.

IT'S GIVEN A BLAST WITH THE TORCH ON THE PUNTY AND BOTTOM ONE FINAL TIME, AND THEN EITHER TAKEN OFF THE PUNTY AT THE BENCH OR BY THE ANNEALER.

SOME GAFFERS WILL USE A DROP OF WATER APPLIED WITH THE TWEEZERS RIGHT AT THE JOINT WHERE THE PUNTY MEETS THE PIECE.

OTHER GAFFERS WILL USE ALOT OF WATER AND FULLY SCORE THE BOTTOM OF THE PUNTY OR NECK OF THE CROWN, WHILE OTHER GAFFERS SWEAR BY THE SHEARS OR JACKS METHOD → WHERE THE TOOL SQUEEZES AN' CHILLS THE TIP OF THE PUNTY WHILE THE GLOVES GENTLY LIFT UP ON THE PIECE AND A THIRD ASSISTANT BONKS THE PUNTY WITH A HEAVY WOODEN CLUB.

WHICHEVER METHOD WORKS BEST FOR YOU - JUST MAKE SURE YOUR ASSISTANT BOXING THE PIECE DOESN'T SQUEEZE IT TOO HARD! IT MAY INADVERTENTLY BE TOO MUCH PRESSURE AND SQUASH YOUR FORM OVAL - AND EVERYBODY KNOWS HOW HARD IT IS TO GET THEM BACK 'ROUND AFTER THEY'RE ANNEALED!

LARGE AMPHORA VASE-THING

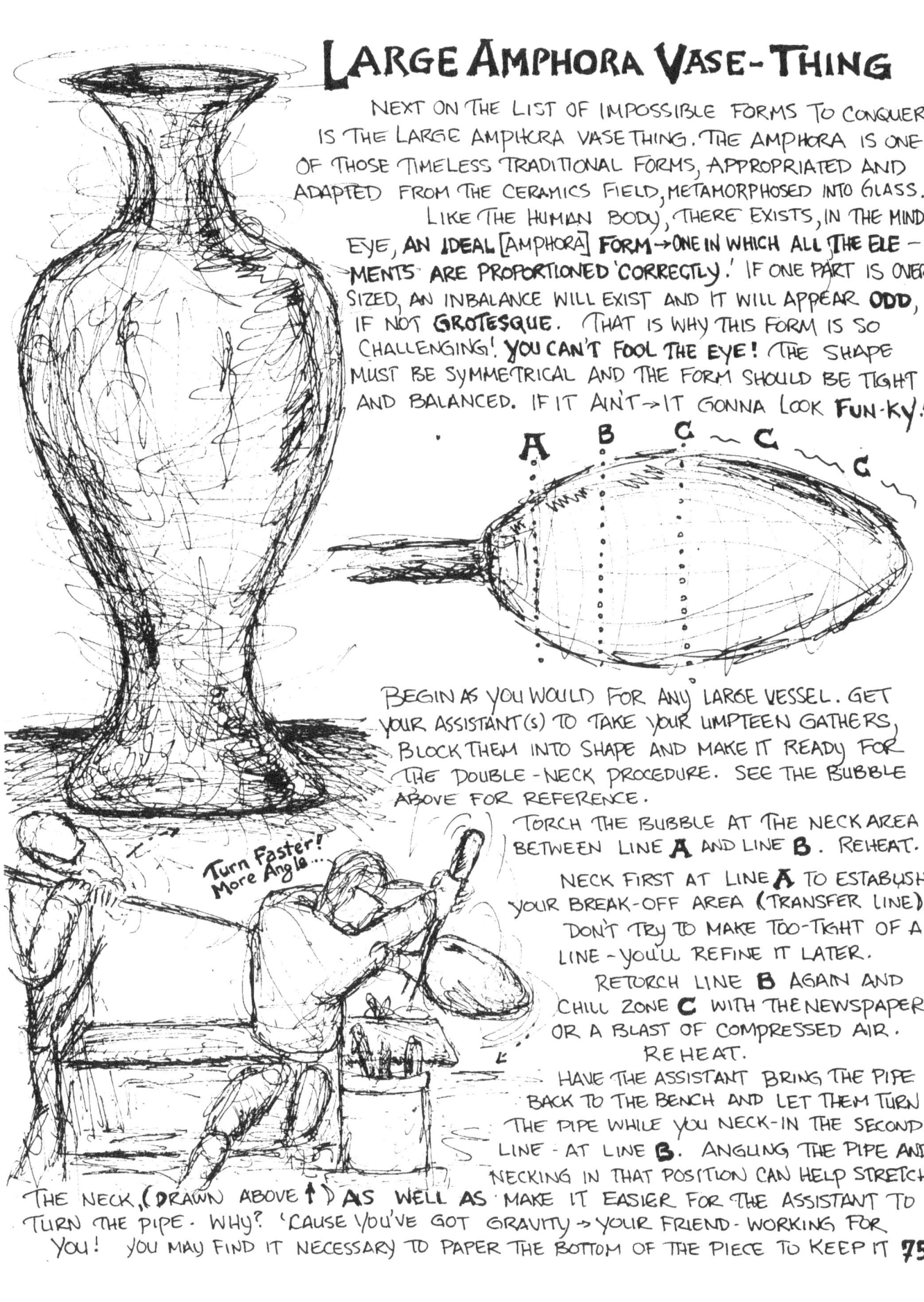

Next on the list of impossible forms to conquer is the Large Amphora Vase Thing. The Amphora is one of those timeless traditional forms, appropriated and adapted from the ceramics field, metamorphosed into glass.

Like the human body, there exists, in the mind's eye, an IDEAL [AMPHORA] FORM → ONE IN WHICH ALL THE ELEMENTS ARE PROPORTIONED 'CORRECTLY.' IF ONE PART IS OVERSIZED, AN INBALANCE WILL EXIST AND IT WILL APPEAR **ODD**, IF NOT **GROTESQUE**. THAT IS WHY THIS FORM IS SO CHALLENGING! **YOU CAN'T FOOL THE EYE!** THE SHAPE MUST BE SYMMETRICAL AND THE FORM SHOULD BE TIGHT AND BALANCED. IF IT AIN'T → IT GONNA LOOK **FUN-KY**!

Begin as you would for any large vessel. Get your assistant(s) to take your umpteen gathers, block them into shape and make it ready for the double-neck procedure. See the bubble above for reference.

Torch the bubble at the neck area between line **A** and line **B**. Reheat.

Neck first at line **A** to establish your break-off area (transfer line). Don't try to make too-tight of a line - you'll refine it later.

Retorch line **B** again and chill zone **C** with the newspaper or a blast of compressed air. Reheat.

Have the assistant bring the pipe back to the bench and let them turn the pipe while you neck-in the second line - at line **B**. Angling the pipe and necking in that position can help stretch the neck, (drawn above ↑) as well as make it easier for the assistant to turn the pipe. Why? 'Cause you've got gravity → your friend - working for you! You may find it necessary to paper the bottom of the piece to keep it

IN-CHECK, AND NOT RUNNING AWAY FROM YOU. NEXT RETURN TO TORCHING THE NECK AGAIN, CONCENTRATING ON LINE **A**. YOU'RE GONNA NEED TO REESTABLISH A NICE CRISP NECKLINE WHERE THE PIECE WILL CRACK-OFF AT.

TIPS ON TORCHING:

THE TORCH IS A RELATIVELY NEW TOOL TO THE REALM OF GLASSBLOWING. IT CAN MAKE YOUR LIFE AND EXPERIENCE WITH WORKING THE GLASS A WHOLE LOT EASIER - AND... IT CAN ALSO BLOW YOU UP! (AND TAKE EVERYTHING ELSE WITH YOU!)

THEREFORE, **YOU MUST TAKE RESPONSIBILITY AND CARE WHENEVER HANDLING PROPANE CYLINDERS.** WATCH WHERE YOU SET IT. DON'T STICK IT ANYWHERE NEAR THE FURNACE OR GLORY HOLE OR OTHER HEAT SOURCE. THERE ARE MANY DIFFERENT TYPES OF TORCHES AND FUELS WHICH THEY BURN. SOME ARE MORE APPROPIATE THAN OTHERS FOR EACH GIVEN SITUATION.

THE POCKET TORCH: A.K.A. THE LIGHTER.

PERHAPS ONE OF THE MOST POPULAR OF ALL SELF-CONTAINED TORCHES. THE ONLY REASON TO MENTION IT HERE IS TO WARN YOU: IT'S A BAD IDEA TO BLOW GLASS WITH ONE OF THESE (POTENTIALLY) EXPLOSIVE DEVICES IN YOUR POCKET. WHO KNOWS WHAT IT WILL DO TO YOU IF IT DOES BLOW-UP? COULD RUIN YOUR FRIDAY AND SATURDAY NITES FOR THE REST OF YOUR LIFE.

THE PLUMBERS TORCH:

THESE SELF-CONTAINED HAND HELD UNITS CAN BE SOMEWHAT USEFUL IN THE GLASS STUDIO. THEY'RE HANDY TO LITE EQUIPMENT WITH, AND WITH THE RIGHT TIP, THEY CAN BE USED FOR SPOT-HEATING AND **CANE DRAWING**. THEY'RE ALSO CONVENIENT FOR FIRE-POLISHING POTENTIALLY SHARP POINTS LIKE HANDLES (WHERE THEY'RE CUT) AND THE LOOPS ON CHRISTMAS ORNAMENTS. BEYOND THAT, THEY DON'T PRODUCE ENOUGH HEAT OR WIDE ENOUGH FLAME FOR MUCH MORE. THE ELECTRONIC IGNITING ONES, ALTHOUGH EXPENSIVE, ARE A BREEZE TO USE AND ELIMINATES THE NEED TO SEARCH FOR THE ELUSIVE STRIKER.

THE HAND TORCH:

THIS IS ONE OF THE MOST VALUABLE TYPES OF TORCHES FOR WORKING GLASS ON A MEDIUM-TO-LARGE SCALE, AND ESPECIALLY FOR SOLID-WORKING. THEY RANGE IN SIZE AND PRICES, ANYWHERE FROM 50,000 BTU's - to 250,000 BTU's, FROM $50.00 to $150.00 or MORE. THE THERMAL OUT-PUT ON SOME OF THE LARGER ONES MAY EXCEED WHAT YOUR GLORY HOLE PRODUCES! INDEED, IT'S KIND OF LIKE HAVING A MINI-GLORY HOLE IN THE PALM OF YOUR HAND!

ALMOST ALWAYS THEY ARE FUELED WITH PROPANE. PROPANE IS A DANGEROUS GAS IN THE GLASS SHOP AND MUST BE HANDLED WITH CARE. I STRONGLY RECOMMEND THE USE OF

CHECK VALVES IN YOUR PROPANE LINE. THESE VALVES, AVAILABLE FROM ANY WELDING SUPPLY FOR UNDER $10.00, ARE AN ADDED INSURANCE POLICY AGAINST **FLAME** FROM FLOWING BACK INTO THE LINE & CYLINDER AND POSSIBLE **BACK BURN** (a potentially explosive situation). THEY ARE AVAILABLE FOR BOTH OXYGEN AND PROPANE AND ARE EASILY PLUMBED-IN NEXT TO THE REGULATOR.

THESE TORCHES TAKE A LITTLE GETTING USED-TO, BUT ONCE YOU DO, YOU'LL WONDER HOW YOU EVER BLEW WITHOUT ONE! THE HOTTEST REGION OF THE FLAME IS NEAR THE CENTER PORTION - AFTER THE GAS HAS BEEN FULLY COMBUSTED. STICKING THE TORCH RIGHT AGAINST THE GLASS IS NOT VERY EFFECTIVE IN HEATING IT, AS THE GAS HASN'T HAD AN OPPORTUNITY TO FULLY MIX WITH THE AIR AND BURN COMPLETELY.

THERE IS OFTEN A SET-KNOB WHICH WILL ALLOW YOU TO CANDLE A FLAME WHEN IT'S NOT BEING USED. THIS ELIMINATES THE NEED TO KEEP RE-LIGHTING IT EVERY TIME. **Tip:** IT'S NOT A BAD IDEA TO HAVE 2 OR 3 STRIKERS AROUND WHEN USING THESE TYPES OF TORCHES. THEY ARE NOTORIOUS FOR BLOWING THEMSELVES OUT WHEN YOU'RE TOO AGGRESSIVE WITH THEM, AND IT'S A DRAG TO STOP AND SEARCH FOR A STRIKER WHEN YOU'RE TRYING TO HEAT SOME GLASS.

DO USE A STRIKER TO LIGHT THESE TORCHES AND NOT A LIGHTER. IT'S MUCH SAFER AND YOU DON'T RISK FRYING YOUR HAND.

IT'S ALSO A GOOD IDEA TO USE A HAND-CART TO MOVE YOUR PROPANE TANKS ABOUT. JUST MAKE SURE THAT THE PROPANE BOTTLE IS SECURED (WITH CHAIN for example) AND STABLE. A TORCH STAND SHOULD ALSO BE SET UP BEHIND THE GAFFER AND EASILY ACCESSIBLE. ALSO - REMEMBER THAT THE GAFFER'S HAND MAY NEED SHIELDING WHILE TORCHING. THE RADIANT HEAT FROM THE GLASS AND TORCH CAN MAKE THINGS PRETTY DARN HOT!

Oxy-Pro. & Oxy-Acetylene

OXYGEN-PROPANE AND OXYGEN-ACETYLENE TORCHES CAN ALSO BE USED FOR TORCHING THE GLASS. THE **OXY-ACETYLENE** MIX-COMMON TO CUTTING TORCHES AND WELDING/SOLDERING PROCEDURES IN METAL WORKING FIELDS PRODUCES THE HOTTEST FLAME AVAILABLE. IT CAN LITERALLY MELT HOLES IN YOUR GLASS - WHICH MAY BE APPROPRIATE FOR SOME ACTIVITIES. **IT CAN ALSO EASILY BURN OR DISCOLOR YOUR GLASS, SO BE CAREFUL IN HOW YOU USE IT.** PURE ACETYLENE IS ALSO USED TO CARBONIZE SAND MOLDS. THE CARBON ACTS AS A RELEASING AGENT AND IS EASY TO APPLY - BUT VERY BAD TO BREATHE ⇒ WEAR A MASK TO PROTECT YOUR LUNGS FROM THOSE NASTY BLACK FLOATIES WHEN CARBONIZING MOLDS IN THAT MANNER.

THE **OXYGEN-PROPANE** TORCH IS MOST USED BY LAMPWORKERS AND A NUMBER OF PAPERWEIGHT MAKERS. IT CAN PROVIDE A TREMENDOUS AMOUNT OF HEAT WITHOUT FRYING THE GLASS AS MUCH AS THE OXY-ACETYLENE CAN. A WIDE RANGE OF TORCH HEADS EXIST FOR THIS TYPE OF SET UP. YOU CAN HAVE WIDE, BUSHY FLAMES AND PIN-POINT SPOT-HEAT FLAMES, DEPENDING ON YOUR TORCH TIP. THEY'RE AVAILABLE IN **PRE-MIX** AND **SURFACE-MIX** STYLES, THE SURFACE MIX BEING MORE EXPENSIVE. THE PRE-MIX TORCHES ARE LIKE THE ONES COMMON TO WELDING TORCHES WHERE THE GASES ARE MIXED INSIDE THE TORCH AND ARE BURNED AT THE TIP.

The surface mix torch, most common to lampworking, mix and burn the gases right at the tip. Whichever type of torch you may end-up using - be sure to handle them with care. Check valves should be plumbed-in to prevent flashback (flames traveling up the hoses back towards the tank(s).). Make sure all fuel-bottles are safely secured. Make certain you are fully trained on how to use and operate these torches **BEFOREHAND**.

There's also an additional device which is convenient to use if you're frequently torching pieces. It's a torch stand which has a pilot-light and a self-actuating valve built into it. When you lift the torch piece off the hanger, a valve opens up the flow of gases to the torch and you can easily light it off the pilot light without the need for a striker. When you hang it back up, the valve shuts off, and cuts the supply of gas going to the torch.

Regardless of which torch you use - **you must handle them with care and pay attention to all safety issues.** Bleed the lines when you're done, store the cylinders in safe locations when they are not in use, and above all, get the training necessary to inform you about how to operate them safely. **period.**

Picking up where we left off → have the assistant reheat the piece in the glory hole, bring it back after it's nice n' hot - and finish necking in your transfer line at line **A**. You may also neck at line **B** once more to make it a little more defined and help stabilize the piece. Now it's time to blow out the shoulders and finish up the bottom half of the piece.

After a good heat (on zones **C** & **D** below), paper the waist and bottom while your assistant blows out the shoulder area. When you get the wall-thickness and size where you want it, you can then concentrate on stretching and blowing out the waist and bottom of the vessel.

There are two ways of elongating the form. Both require that you have an adequate amount of glass on the bottom and that the glass is pretty hot.

In **METHOD ONE** you use the shears to grip the point on the very bottom and pull the tip out - thus elongating the form. The tip may then be necked into a knob with the jacks - which will also help to center up the bottom section, and the resulting knob can get cut off with the diamond shears. The form then may be papered and blown some before another reheat is necessary.

In **METHOD TWO**, the form is elongated by swinging-it-out. The trick here is to get the heat just right to obtain the length you need,

AND KNOWING HOW FAR TO SWING IT AND WHEN TO STOP!
IF YOU HEAT THE FORM TOO DEEPLY, THE SHOULDERS MIGHT GET TOO
HOT AND ALSO BE STRETCHED WITH THE REST OF THE PIECE — THUS CHANGING
YOUR OVERALL FORM, SO BE CAREFUL ON HOW YOU HEAT IT. GET
THE AREA JUST BELOW THE SHOULDERS HOT — A TORCH IS AN EXCELLENT
WAY TO INTRODUCE THE HEAT THAT WAY TOO! AND SWING OUT
THE BOTTOM — TAKING CARE TO ADJUST THE HEIGHT OF THE
PIPE SO YOUR PIECE DOESN'T HIT THE GROUND (OR ANY-
THING ELSE FOR THAT MATTER!).

HEAT & STRETCH

AS SOON AS YOU'VE GOT YOUR PIECE TO
THE DESIRED LENGTH, HEAD BACK TO THE BENCH AND
PAPER THE FORM, AND BEGIN TO BLOW IT SOME MORE.

TAKE ANOTHER REHEAT AND FOCUS ON GETTING
THE WAIST PAPERED IN TO A NICE TAPER. YOU MAY **ALSO**
USE THE **PACIOFFIS** TO TIGHTEN UP THE FORM (fig 86).

BLOW OUT THE BOTTOM AT THIS TIME AS
WELL. YOU NEED TO OVERBLOW IT INTO
A BALL SHAPE FIRST AND THEN WITH
CAREFUL HEATING, PAPERING AND
PADDLING YOU CAN FLATTEN THE
FOOT BACK IN. (fig. 87).

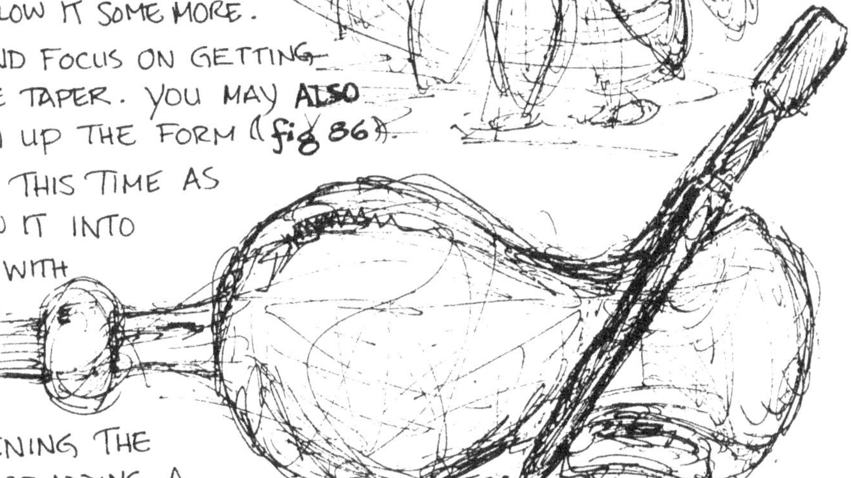

PRIOR TO COMPLETELY FLATTENING THE
BOTTOM, YOU HAVE THE OPTION OF ADDING A
BUTTON IF THE BOTTOM APPEARS THIN, OR IF YOU PREFER
THAT METHOD OF PUNTYING.

fig. 86 CUT OR PAPER THE WAIST IN

IT MAY TAKE SEVERAL REHEATS TO GET THE SHAPE LOOKING RIGHT. TAKE YOUR
TIME TO DO IT RIGHT IN THE FIRST PLACE. **BE PATIENT**. ONE STEP AT A TIME. REMEM-
BER TO TORCH THE NECK. WHEN PIECES GET LONG (OR TALL) IT'S SOMETIMES DIFFICULT
TO KEEP THE NECK WARM AND THE MOILE FROM CHECKING. YOU MAY NEED TO DO
A MOILE WRAP (SEE THE NEXT PAGE) IF YOU DO NOTICE CRACKS APPEARING.

BE CAREFUL REHEATING THESE LONG FORMS. IT'S VERY EASY TO MAX-OUT THE
GLORY HOLE AND HIT THE BACK — CAUSING SOME REFRACTORY TO MAYBE ADHERE THERE.
AND SOME OF THAT STUFF DOESN'T WIPE OFF — YUK! ☹

WHEN THE FORM LOOKS ACCEPTABLE,
GO AHEAD AND TRANSFER AS USUAL.

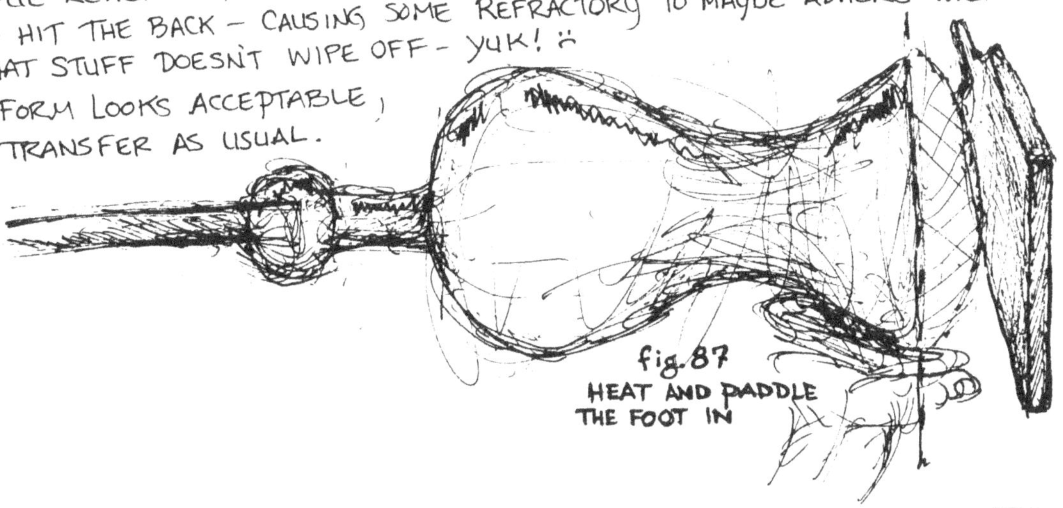

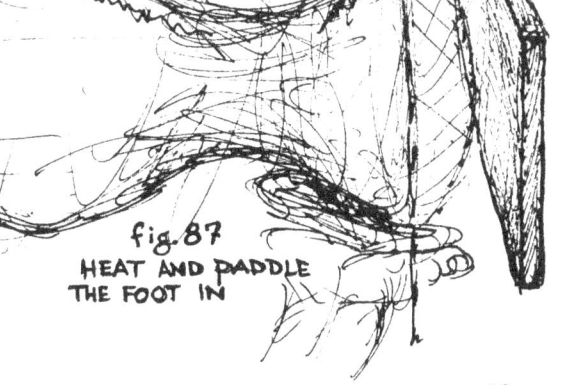

fig. 87 HEAT AND PADDLE THE FOOT IN

The next order of business, after a successful transfer is to elongate and trim the neck/lip area. It may take as many as four or five reheats to pull it off. You can torch the neck to get it hotter, softer, & faster.

Chill the lower neckline by shaping it up with the jacks. Then crimp and tweak the lip, and draw the neck out longer as you do so.

It is altogether possible when making large forms like these that you max-out your reach, or it becomes very difficult to see and do things on the top of the vessel. The standard way of working becomes awkward and inappropriate. If that is the case, you may elect to work off the end of the bench instead.

This takes some getting used-to (no big surprise there!). It completely changes your perspective on everything and forces you to totally trust your team and their skills to help you through these tricky tasks.

Your timing has to be down-pat. You'll have to access the glass from the angle which is most comfortable for you. Some gaffers will work from the front side while others prefer to lean over the backside of the bench. Some angles work better for tweaking and pulling, while other angles make it easier to neck the piece at.

Once you get the neck pulled out to the correct length, you can go ahead and trim the lip — either by cutting it with the straight (trimming) shears or by the necking-a-knob-tapping-it-off technique.

During all this, you have to keep that punty warm! Blast it with the torch (or have your assistant do that) when you can; just before reheating, for example. If you notice your punty cracking or see pieces of it jumping off — a punty wrap may be in order:

The Punty/Moile Wrap

This technique is an insurance policy of sorts. It can help heat the moile/punty without jeopardizing the form of the piece from deep extended heats. It also prevents premature cracking (of the punty) due to stress in handling and thermal loss (from lack of heat).

Simply get 1 to 2 gathers on a punty → straight outta the furnace or give it a quick marve' to set it up. Directly set the tip of the bit/blob on the punty (or moile) and allow the rotation of the pipe to pull the gather off. It should evenly coat the whole moile, and not the piece! The excess should be yanked backwards to wick it away without trailing glass behind. The wrap may then be smoothed out with the back of the jacks. The piece should be reheated, and then it's back to business as usual.

At this point you may wish to slap a **LIP-WRAP** on the piece or just go with it—as is. Then it's time to open up the lip. After your assistant heats up the neck of the piece, ride the jacks on the outside of the neck to set-up the exterior's skin. Set the tips of the jacks as close to the shoulders as you can and guide the glass on-center using swift full rotations provided by your trusty assistant. It may take quite a lean on your part to gain full access, but do what you must to make it happen—even if you have to work off the end of the bench (see below).

Insert the jacks inside the lip and let them mimic the interior's surface as closely as you can. Gently ride the blades on the inside and slowly work the tips out to the lip area as you gradually open the blades and bring them up on an angle.

② FLARE & PADDLE SMOOTH

① STRAIGHTEN

This, with quick full rotations, should flare the lip in a matter of a couple passes up and down the bench. You might want to ride the jacks back up on the outside of the lip to straighten-out or tune-up the angle of the flare.

An assistant with a paddle may be standing by to flatten or smooth the lip, if so requested by the gaffer. An additional tightening of the neck at the shoulders with the jacks and/or newspaper may be warranted, followed-up by tuning-up the rest of the form.

WORKING OFF THE BENCH.

When all of it looks in order—box it in the usual fashion.

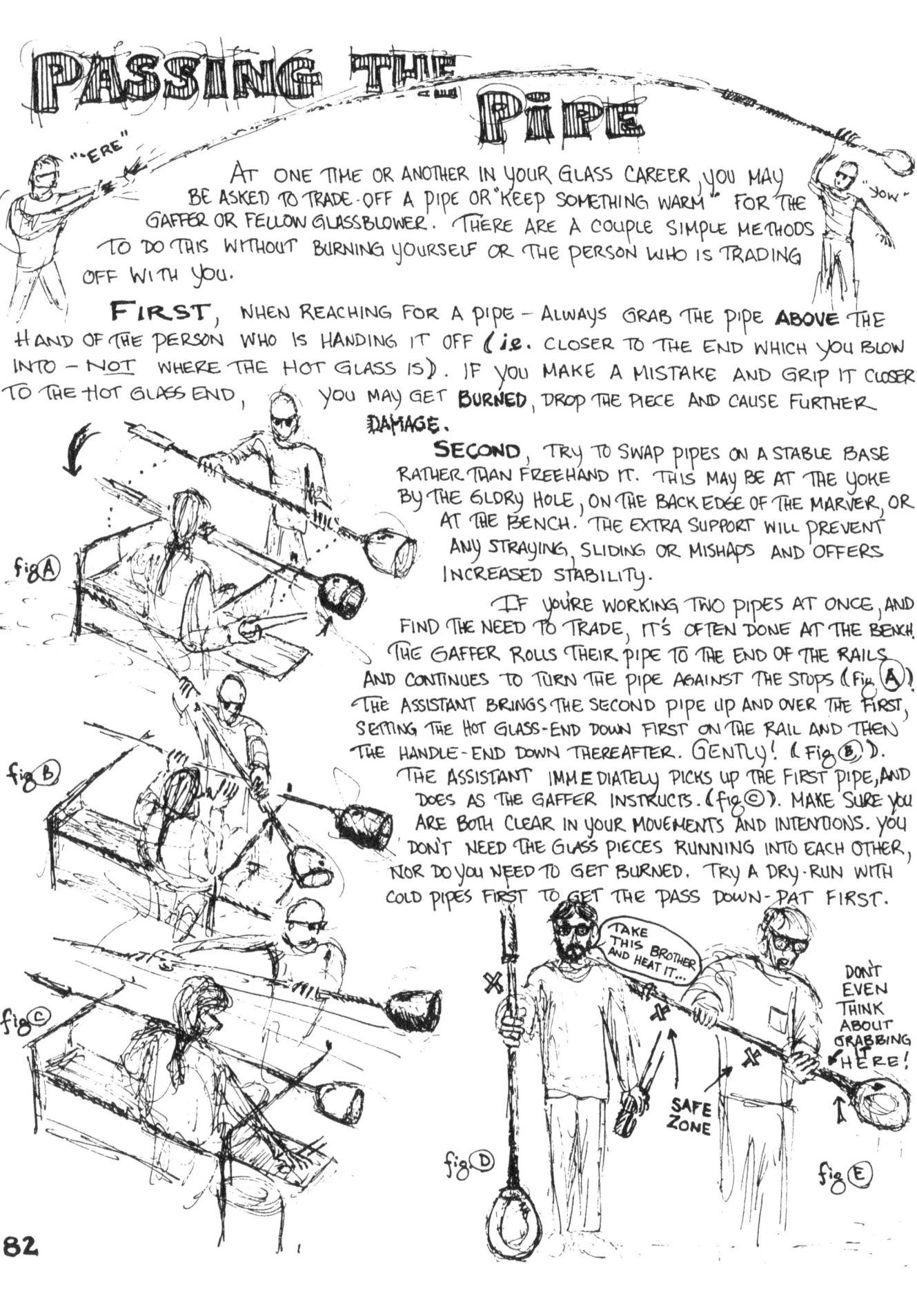

PUNTIES

Intro 84
Goblet version 1 . . 84
Goblet version 2 . . 85
Dome 85
Sand 86
Doughnut / Ring . . . 87
Crown 88
Sculpture / Cheater . . 90
2 & 3 Prong / Claw . . 91
Blowpipes as Punties . 92

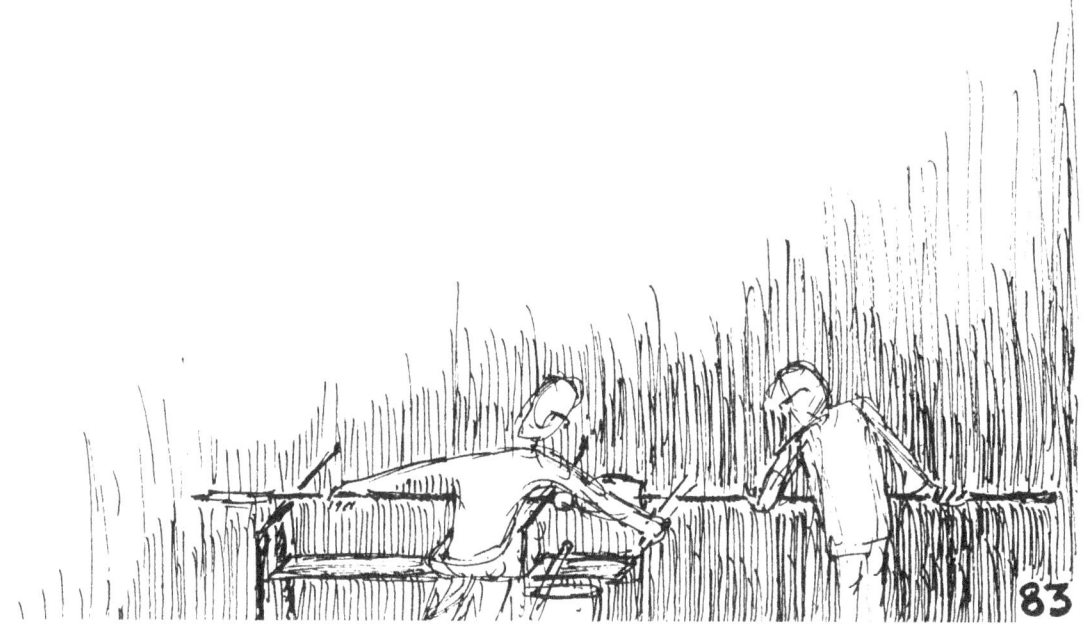

PUNTIES

For every work executed in hot glass that is to be transferred from one 'stick' to another → there exists an appropriate punty style for that piece. The actual rod (or blowpipe) you select to punty with is as important as the shape and temperature of the glass on it's end. If you're making Venetian-style goblets, you'll want light-weight (preferably hollow) punty rods with some flex in the shaft → and as 'true' as possible. On the other hand if you're working large, **LARGER** or **ELEPHANTINE** in scale or mass, you'll want heftier pipes, possibly counter-weighted (to balance out the weight and aid in turning) — ideally the same diameter rod as the one that the piece is being transferred from.

Nothing's worse (well almost) than trying to torque a small diameter punty with a big **FAT** object on it — particularly if you're trying to spin out a rondel or open a large bowl. Conversely, opening goblets with a thick or heavy punty won't give you the light responsive **FEEL** you need to do the delicate work at hand.

The lesson here to be learned is that having the correct punty for the job can make or break the final touches to your phenomenal glass piece. Make sure there's the '**RIGHT ONE**' in the pipe warmer <u>BEFORE</u> you start blowing, and that your assistant knows how to shape the punty you desire.

There are so many schools of thought on how to make a punty that it can be difficult to choose the 'right one'. If it works for you and comes off the way you like it — then continue to do it that way. If it doesn't work, then you may have to revise the method by which you prepare your punty. Listed below are a variety of punty styles that I have encountered over the years that seem to work well for the type of work being created.

Goblet / Small Stuff Punty #1. (could also be used as a "Punteto")

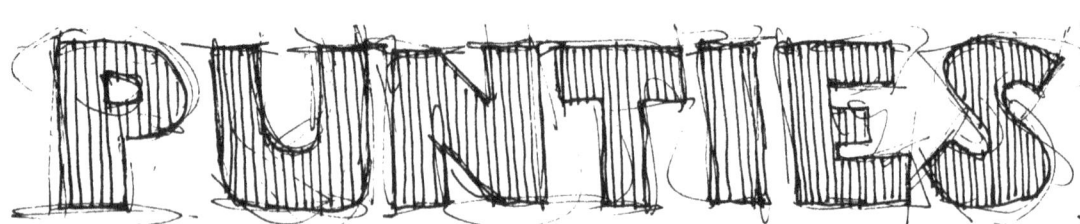

fig. 88 — GRAVITY & FLOW OF GLASS

fig. 89 MARVERING THE POINT — THE STEEPER THE ANGLE HERE / THE LESS GLASS YOU TRAP HERE.

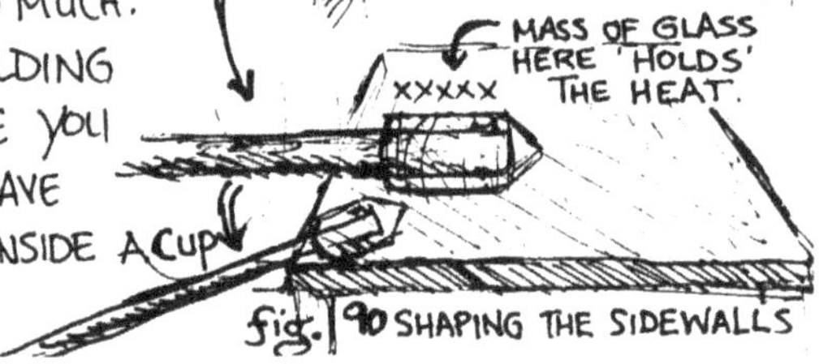

fig. 90 SHAPING THE SIDEWALLS — MASS OF GLASS HERE 'HOLDS' THE HEAT. xxxxx

On a lightweight punty gather a small bit of glass. Immediately upon exiting the furnace, hold the glass end straight up (fig 88) → allowing gravity to pull the glass back on to the punty where you want it. Head over to the marver and **point-up** the punty. Start with a fairly high angle (fig. 89) — almost perpendicular to the marver — and push the glass back onto the punty as you quickly rotate it. Continue to marver, lowering your hands as you do so, until you are level with the surface of the marver — and shaping the side walls of the punty, and back end.

The punty's ready-to-go if you're quick enough, or a quick flash may be advised if you've chilled the tip too much. (Better safe than sorry!) These punties do well in holding most styles of goblets, tumblers, small vases etc. where you have easy access to the bottom of the piece. If you have a severe kick-foot, limited access, or are puntying-up inside a cup you may wish to use style #2....

GOBLET/SMALL STUFF PUNTY #2

VERSION ONE.

"LESS IS MORE" - annonymous. WITH THIS PUNTY, YOU WANT AS LITTLE GLASS ON THE END AS POSSIBLE. GATHER A SMALL BIT OF GLASS ON THE END OF A LIGHTWEIGHT PUNTY - HEAD OVER TO THE MARVER AND BEGIN BY ROLLING THE GLASS HORIZONTALLY (fig. 91) - LEVEL WITH THE MARVER - ALMOST PULLING THE PUNTY TOWARDS YOU AS YOU DO SO. ESSENTIALLY YOU'RE SQUEEZING THE GLASS BETWEEN THE MARVER AND THE PUNTY, FORCING IT TO 'FLOW' TO THE TIP OF THE PUNTY.* NEXT, GRAB YOUR HANDY DANDY DIAMOND SHEARS AND CUT-OFF ALL THE EXCESS GLASS - AS CLOSE TO THE PUNTY AS YOU CAN. (fig. 92) MARVER THE TIP AND SIDEWALLS (fig. 93) - GO FOR A QUICK REHEAT AND PRESENT IT TO THE GAFFER.

* SOME GLASSWORKERS WILL PERFORM THIS MARVERING TECHNIQUE WHILE AT THE BENCH USING THE BACK OF THEIR JACKS.

VERSION TWO.

INSTEAD OF MARVERING THE GLASS OFF THE END, SIMPLY STRIP ALL EXCESS GLASS OFF OF THE END OF THE PUNTY WITH YOUR DIAMOND SHEARS AS SOON AS YOU COME OUT OF THE FURNACE. JUST CLOSE THE DIAMOND SHEARS AROUND THE PUNTY AND PULL WITH YOUR LEFT HAND, ALMOST SCRAPING THE GLASS OFF THE END, IT MAY TAKE TWO OR THREE PASSES TO GET MOST OF THE GLASS OFF. CUT ANY EXCESS OFF AS CLOSE TO THE PUNTY AS YOU CAN AND REHEAT. FINISH BY MARVERING IT SMOOTH N' EVEN AS IN fig. 93. REHEAT A FINAL TIME AND PRESENT TO THE GAFFER.

BOTH STYLES OF GOBLET PUNTIES MAY BE PRE-MADE AND 'PARKED' IN THE PIPEWARMER TO SAVE TIME. MANY GOBLET MAKERS RE-USE THESE PUNTIES ALL DAY LONG!

THE DOME-STYLE PUNTY FOR SMALL-TO-LARGE PIECES

ESSENTIALLY IT'S THE SAME PROCEDURE AS THE GOBLET PUNTY STYLE #1, EXCEPT THAT IT'S DONE ON A SLIGHTLY LARGER OR THICKER PUNTY - OR ON A STEP-DOWN PUNTY ROD. AGAIN, AS YOU EXIT THE FURNACE, POINT THE PUNTY TIP TOWARDS THE CEILING SO THE GLASS FLOWS BACK ONTO THE ROD. TAKE IT TO THE MARVER AND FURTHER PUSH BACK THE GLASS BY ROLLING IT PERPENDICULAR TO THE SURFACE FIRST, THEN WORK YOUR WAY DOWN TO MARVER THE SIDES SMOOTH AND EVEN (fig. 93). YOU SHOULD END UP WITH A NICE DOME SHAPE ON THE END (NOT TOO MUCH GLASS OFF THE END) WITH FAIRLY UNIFORM WALL THICKNESS ON ITS SIDES. IF YOU'RE FAST ENOUGH, YOU MAY BE ABLE TO STICK-IT-UP WITHOUT ANY ADDITIONAL REHEATS.

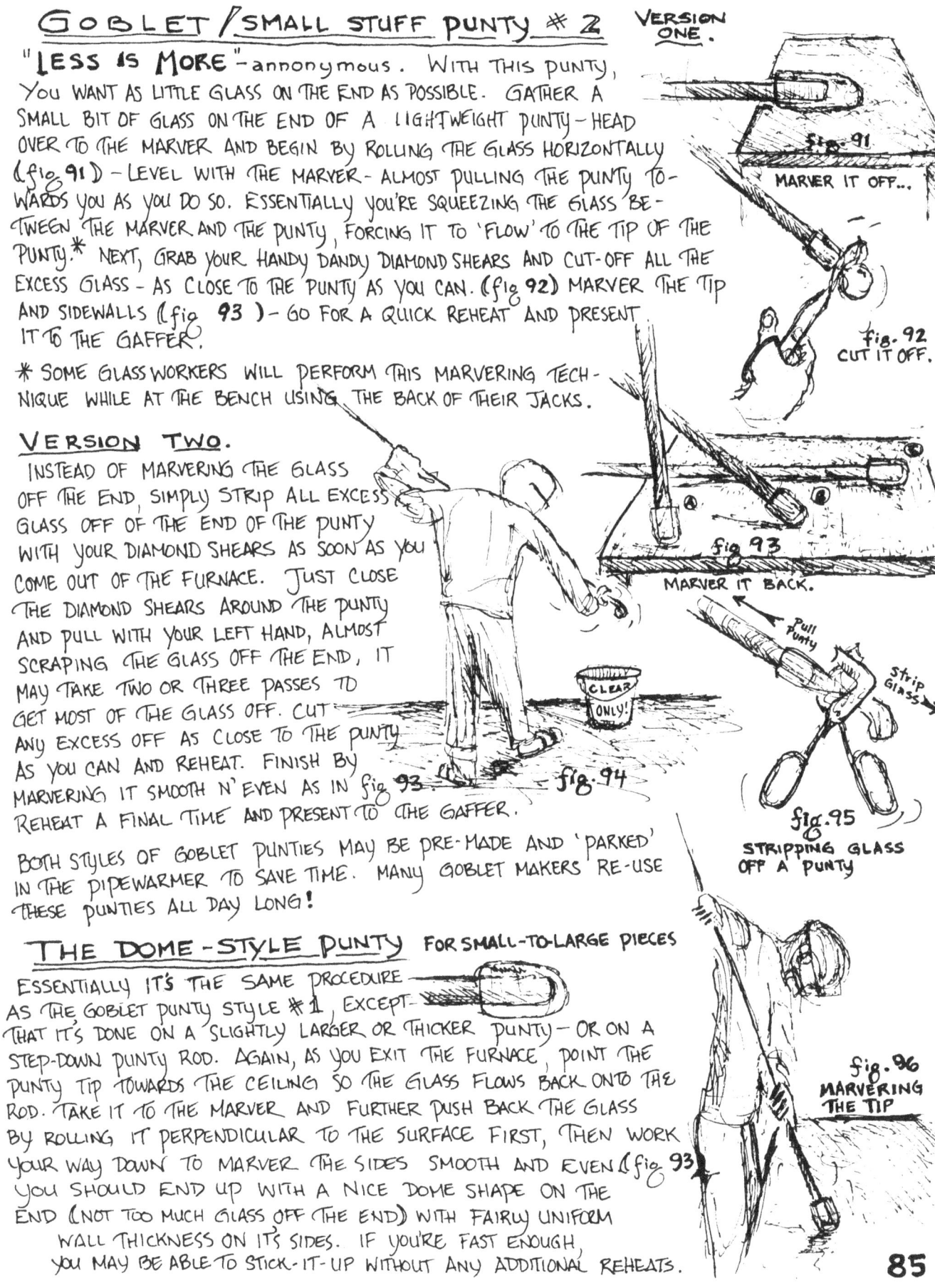

fig. 91 MARVER IT OFF...

fig. 92 CUT IT OFF.

fig. 93 MARVER IT BACK.

fig. 95 STRIPPING GLASS OFF A PUNTY

fig. 94

fig. 96 MARVERING THE TIP

The Sand Punty — for light-to-medium sized pieces

I call it a "Swedish Sand Punty" 'cause the first person I saw make it was from Sweden and she was very fond of these punties. Maybe coldworking isn't your bag or you don't like the look of diamond engraved punty rings on the bottom of your pieces, then maybe this may be your punty of choice.

The sandpunty is made virtually the same way as the dome punty — you may, however, prefer the tip to be a little more pointed. The difference here is that **AFTER** you do an initial shape-up → very quickly → you'll roll the punty in a thin layer of sand. It's a good idea to have the sand on a seperate surface to prevent contaminating the marver with unwanted silica — maybe set a mini-marver off to the side dedicated solely for this purpose.

fig 97 Picking up sand

A quick pass over the sand is all that's needed. Too much sand will prevent the punty from sticking, and too little will cause it to stick too well and potentially leave a sharp scar instead of a sandy disc impression. Yes, it's a fine line between too much and too little, and I can almost guarantee a fair share of **FLOOR MODELS** as you discover the subtleties of this style of punty!

fig. 98 The point is pushed-in.. thus, creating more surface area

This type of punty seems to be popular with Mexican production glassblowers. It's evident on the bottom of those inexpensive cobalt blue lipped tumblers & goblets common to import shops accross America — and it seems to work well! To remove your piece, you only have to use a butterknife and successively chill the joint area as you rotate the punty (fig 99). A half dozen taps or so should be all that's needed, and one final bonk should release the piece.

fig 99 Chill & Tap Method

Some glassblowers will do a variation on this style of punty by rolling on an old softbrick instead of sand to pick-up smaller particles. This is particularly helpful if you're puntying-up inside of deep tapered cups where you're in jeopardy of sticking to the sides accidently.

The Cross or "X" Punty — for medium-to-large pieces

The popularity of this style of punty seems to have waned in recent years as the American studio glass movement becomes increasingly influenced by European masters and their techniques. I'm a firm believer in the "variety is the spice of life" theory, and there may be some of you out there that find this punty works well for you → or in case an 'old dog' calls on you to "make me a cross punty" you'll know what he means.

On a medium-sized punty (ca. 3/4" or so) gather a blob of glass. On the way over to the marver you may tilt the rod upwards to allow the glass to flow back on the punty. Proceed to marver the glass horizontally (level with the marver) chilling and shaping the side walls. DON'T marver the tip as you'll want that area to remain hot. Once the sides have been shaped, grab a butterknife or pair of tweezers, set the handle end of the punty on the

FLOOR (FOR STABILITY) AND PRESS A LINE IN THE CENTER OF THE HOT GLASS. ROTATE THE PUNTY 90° AND PRESS ANOTHER LINE IN THE GLASS, THUS CREATING THE DESIRED "CROSS" OR "X" DESIGN (fig 100). THIS ESSENTIALLY GIVES YOU FOUR SMALL PUNTIES IN ONE! YOU MAY END UP WITH FOUR SMALL POINTS OR DIVOTS IN THE BOTTOM OF YOUR PIECE WHEN YOU'RE DONE, BUT IT SELDOMLY TAKES OUT A HUGE CHUNK LIKE CERTAIN ROUND-STYLE PUNTIES SEEM TO. TO TAKE THE PIECE OFF YOU MAY CHILL THE JOINT BETWEEN THE PUNTY AND YOUR WORK WITH A KNIFE OR THE TWEEZERS (AS IN THE PREVIOUS fig 99) AND/OR ADD A DROP OF WATER TO INDUCE THE THERMAL SHOCK POTENTIAL, AND BONK IT OFF WITH A WOODEN PADDLE.

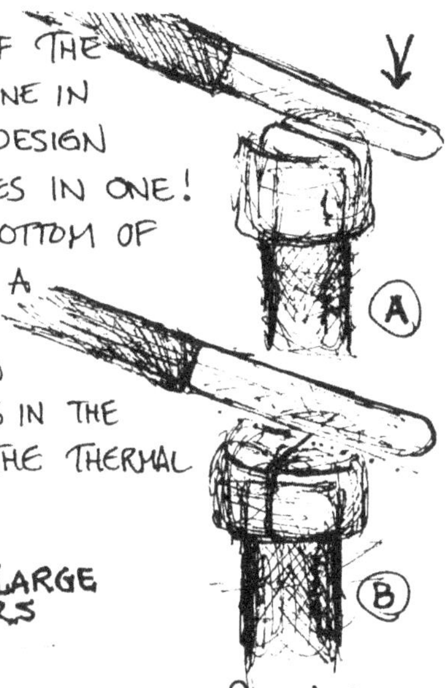

THE DOUGHNUT OR RING PUNTY — FOR MEDIUM-TO-LARGE CLUNKERS

THIS PREDECESSOR TO THE CROWN PUNTY GIVES YOU GREATER SURFACE AREA AND LONGER GRIPPING POWER. PLUS IT'LL LEAVE YOU WITH A SMALL RING OF GLASS ON THE BOTTOM OF YOUR PIECE, OR IT MAY COME OFF CLEAN. OR (WORST CASE SCENARIO) IT MAY PULL THE WHOLE BOTTOM OUT OF YOUR PIECE — ESPECIALLY IF IT'S TOO THIN! THIS STYLE OF PUNTY ALSO SEEMS TO BE FADING IN POPULARITY AS MORE PEOPLE ARE BITTEN BY THE **VENETIAN VIRUS** AND FOREGO THE QUICK N' EASY APPROACH FOR MORE ELABORATE METHODS. THERE ARE TWO WAYS OF MAKING THIS PUNTY:

VERSION #1: TAKE A DECENT-SIZED GATHER OF GLASS ON A MEDIUM-TO-LARGE PUNTY (e.g. 3/4" STRAIGHT OR STEP-DOWN) AND MARVER THE SIDE WALLS FIRST. THIS SHOULD PUSH THE GLASS OFF THE END. NEXT, BRING THE PUNTY UP AND PERPENDICULAR TO THE MARVER SURFACE AND SQUASH IT FLAT AGAINST THE MARVER (fig 101 → STEP Ⓑ) — THEN QUICKLY BRING IT BACK LEVEL WITH THE MARVER AND RESHAPE THE SIDEWALLS AGAIN ↪ THIS SHOULD PUSH THE GLASS BACK OFF THE END AGAIN AND CREATE A RING OR DOUGHNUT SHAPE. FINISH SHAPING THE SIDEWALLS SMOOTH AND REHEAT JUST THE TIP INSIDE THE GLORY HOLE (IF NECESSARY) AND PRESENT TO THE GAFFER.

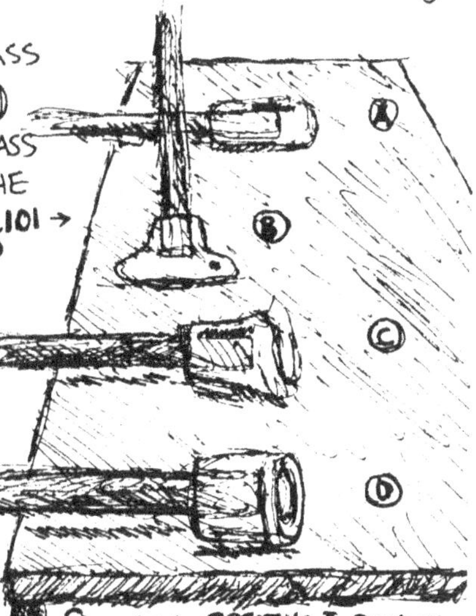

VERSION #2: TAKE A DIP ON A MEDIUM TO LARGE PUNTY. MARVER THE SIDEWALLS FIRST → PUSHING A FAIR QUANTITY OF GLASS OFF THE END — SIMILAR TO VERSION #1 ABOVE.

NOW INSTEAD OF SQUASHING IT FLAT AGAINST THE MARVER, YOU HOLD THE PUNTY UP (SETTING THE HANDLE END DOWN AGAINST THE FLOOR) AND POKE A HOLE DEAD CENTER IN THE GLASS WITH THE POINT OF A FILE OR YOUR TWEEZERS. THE RESULTING DONUT SHOULD STILL BE HOT ENOUGH TO TAKE TO THE GAFFER AND STICK UP. THIS VERSION WILL HAVE A SOMEWHAT SMALLER HOLE THAN THE FIRST, WITH GREATER CONTACT AREA — POSSIBLY INCREASING THE HOLDING POWER. BOTH PUNTIES MAY BE RELEASED BY THE CHILL N' TAP MANUVER, BUT A DROP OR TWO OF WATER SHOULD HELP IT RELEASE EASIER (SEE PAGE 33 FOR DETAILS).

fig 100

fig. 101 CREATING A DONUT PUNTY

Assorted Thoughts on...

The Use of the File
(or misuse)

for score and twenty years ago...

fig. 102 - A beat-up blowpipe

The bastard file was a tool commonly found on the benches of glassblowers all across the U.S. a few years back. It seemed to work well as any implement for puntying pieces and getting through those **ANXIETY-RIDDEN MOMENTS** of the transfer process. All too often I witnessed students abusing the pipes and punties and glass as well → they would be sawing their thick necks and moiles with the wet file like their glass was a piece of wood. — And then hammering away on the blowpipe with the file to break the piece free. This banging motion often left permanent teeth scars and dents on the pipe, thus reducing its lifespan and effectiveness to roll smooth. Activities such as this would peeve the instructors to no end, and is a practice which is frowned upon by those who know better.

The physical structure of the glass is perhaps the most influencial factor in terms of the transfer and subsequent release from the punty. By physical structure I mean the thickness of the glass (at the neckline &/or bottom), the piece's weight, and internal temperature (sure, it looks cold on the outside, but the piece's interior may still be HOT!). The object sketched below (**fig. 103**) is a classic example of the poorly necked vessel common to impatient and uninformed glass-blowers. Forget the file man, break out the diamond chainsaw! In addition to the anatomy of the object being transferred, **IT IS THERMAL SHOCK AND SHARP VIBRATION WHICH RELEASE GLASSWARE FROM PIPES AND PUNTIES.**

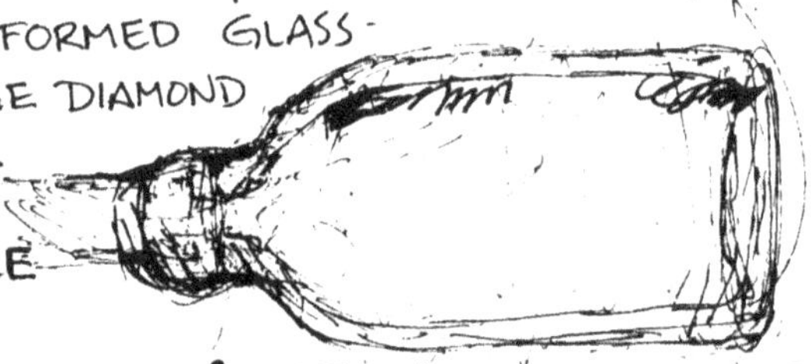

fig. 103 A poorly necked vessel

WATER is an excellent vehicle to induce thermal shock to hot glass. It helps disrupt surface tension by quenching and cracking the skin of the glass. It has, however, little effect on cooling the interior of your piece. Patience, understanding, and the ability to let the glass cool sufficiently before transfer will guarentee you success in this task. **COLD METAL** is another tool by which you may chill the glass with to aid in the transfer. The upper area of your jacks work well for this method. (A **TAGLIOL** is often used in lieu of this by solid-workers.) A combination of both is often used by most glassworkers today, and the file will hopefully disappear and rust away by the roadside.... See page 27 for more helpful information on the transfer process.

The Crown Punty — for heavy &/or large pieces

This **HIGHFALUTIN'** relative of the donut punty seems to be popular with many of the professional gaffers I know. As a coldworker, I find them a little annoying to grind and polish — they often take longer to work out than a **CHEATER** punty would, with little added benefit — except "they look cooler" (the crown punty marks) when they come out of the annealer. The reality is that

They do work well. The crown punty offers you a larger surface area & contact point to grip your piece with, longer working time and a cute little bottlecap-shaped ring on the bottom of your piece when you are done. They do, however, take more time and effort to make than most types of punties. **HERE'S HOW:**

Gather a quantity of glass on a large, heavy-weight punty — one which is ideally the same diameter as the blowpipe, so as to maintain continuity (or, if you're in a pinch → use another blowpipe as the punty and worry about unclogging it later). A large diameter punty is also much easier to turn. Hold the punty up as you exit the furnace to get the glass to flow back onto the punty. Marver the glass back onto the punty as though you were make a **DOME-STYLE** punty (page 85). The sidewalls are smoothed-out (fig. 104) and the glass is allowed to get **STONE COLD**.

fig. 104 Marving the first dip back

Take another gather, covering the first one almost entirely. Quickly roll the glass level with the surface of the marver, shaping the sidewalls smooth and symmetrical — keeping the tip very hot. Next, squash the tip flat against the marver by holding the punty verticle and letting the weight of the punty squeeze the glass on the end (fig B). Then remarver the sidewalls — thus creating the base structure of the crown — it's the same procedure as the **DOUGHNUT** punty version #1 (page 87).

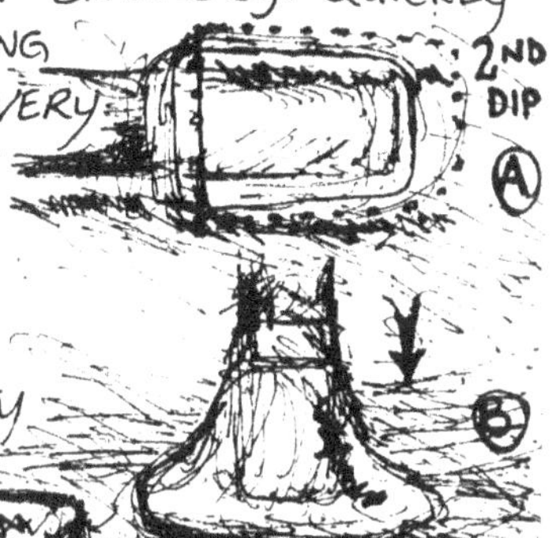

2nd dip Ⓐ Ⓑ

Take the punty to the bench, and using the tweezers → begin to crimp and pull small points or fingers outward. Lots of little points are preferred over fewer larger ones as they offer you more contact points and greater surface area (fig Ⓓ).

Continue to rotate the punty and crimp until you obtain an uniform bottlecap shape (fig Ⓔ). Next, use the back of the jacks to marver smooth n' even the sidewalls of the punty.

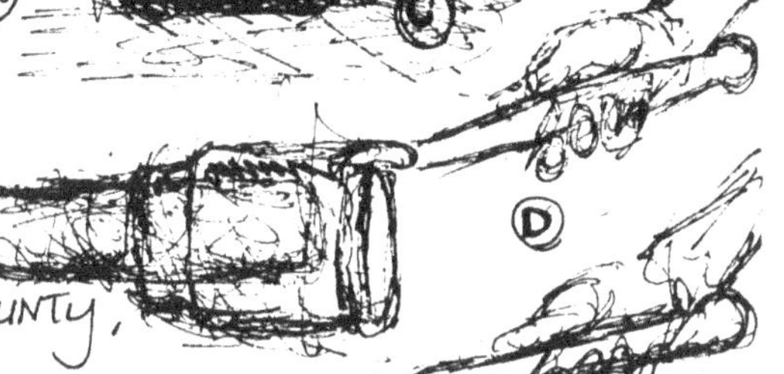

Ⓒ Ⓓ

The punty should then be reheated before presenting it to the gaffer. Now don't get it so hot as to lose all those neat little crimps! Just get it warm enough to stick well to the bottom of the piece.

The punty is brought over to the gaffer who targets it (hopefully) dead-on-center and gently attaches it to the bottom. A few full rotations and adjustments are made to make certain the punty is on-center. The jacks are then used to neck the crown until a defined line is established. Do not

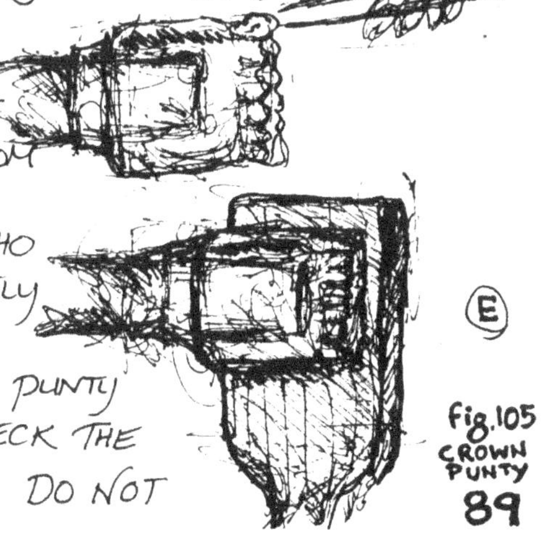

Ⓔ

fig. 105 Crown Punty

NECK IT TOO TIGHT OR YOU'LL LOSE SOME OF THE STRUCTURAL INTEGRITY OF THIS TYPE OF PUNTY, (fig 106). IF THE GLASS IS STILL VERY HOT, YOU CAN CHILL IT BY MARVERING THAT AREA WITH THE BACK OF THE JACKS OR BY BLOWING ON IT WITH A SOFFIETTA. THEN TRANSFER AS NORMAL.

WHEN THE PIECE IS FINISHED, YOU MAY TAKE IT OFF THE PUNTY BY PUTTING WATER ON THE NECKLINE AREA, IN SEVERAL SPOTS → THEN HAVE ONE ASSISTANT LIFT UP ON THE PIECE WITH PRE-HEATED GLOVES WHILE YOU CRIMP THE CROWN'S NECKLINE WITH THE JACKS OR STRAIGHT SHEARS, AS A THIRD ASSISTANT BONKS THE PUNTY WITH A HEAVY WOODEN PADDLE OR BONKER TOOL (SEE PAGE 74 FOR ADDITIONAL VISUAL CLUES).

fig 106 NECKING THE CROWN-PUNTY

THE "CHEATER" \ SCULPTURE PUNTY — FOR ALL OCCASIONS, PARTICULARLY LARGE/HEAVY WORK

"*Cheating*" REPLIED THE CHEATER, "*is a matter of perspective. I prefer to call it 'acknowledging an advantage' and making use of it...*"

WHOEVER FIRST NAMED THIS PUNTY MUST'VE HAD A SENSE OF HUMOR. I'M NOT SURE WHAT OR WHO IS BEING CHEATED BY MAKING THIS TYPE OF PUNTY, BUT UNDER THE "WHATEVER WORKS FOR YOU" CATAGORY — THIS ONE RANKS PRETTY HIGH IN MY BOOK.

ESSENTIALLY THIS PUNTY CREATES IT'S OWN **BUTTON** AND PUNTY IN ONE SHOT. THIS IS ESPECIALLY USEFUL IF YOU'RE BLOWING SOLO OR ARE WORKING WITH AN INEXPERIENCED HELPER. **IT'S FAST, EASY-TO-LEARN, AND RARELY TAKES DIVOTS OR THE BOTTOM OUT OF YOUR PIECE.** IT DOES HOWEVER LEAVE YOU WITH A BUTTON ON THE BOTTOM WHICH YOU MAY WISH TO GRIND AWAY AT A LATER DATE.

BEGIN WITH A DIP OR TWO ON A SIZEABLE PUNTY (i.e. the correct size for the job!) AND MARVER JUST THE SIDES OF THE PUNTY. THIS SHOULD PUSH ½" – 1" OF GLASS OFF THE END OF THE PUNTY → WHERE YOU WANT IT. DON'T TOUCH OR CHILL THE TIP, 'CAUSE YOU NEED IT TO STAY NICE N' HOT SO THAT IT STICKS WELL TO THE BOTTOM OF YOUR PIECE (fig. 107). AFTER A COUPLE OF QUICK PASSES ON THE MARVER, HEAD OVER AND STICK-UP THE PIECE AS CLOSE TO THE CENTER AS POSSIBLE.

fig 107

fig 108 Ⓐ

LIKE THE CROWN PUNTY, A NECKLINE IS CUT-IN WITH THE JACKS. YOU MAY PUSH AND PULL THE PUNTY SOMEWHAT TO CLOSE THE GAP (NECKLINE) OR INCREASE IT. LESS GAP WILL INCREASE YOUR SURFACE AREA AND GIVE YOU BETTER HOLDING POWER. A TIGHTER NECKLINE IS EASIER TO TAKE OFF, BUT IS MORE VULNERABLE TO CHILLING AND BREAKING. LET EXPERIENCE BE YOUR GUIDE. THE PIECE MAY BE

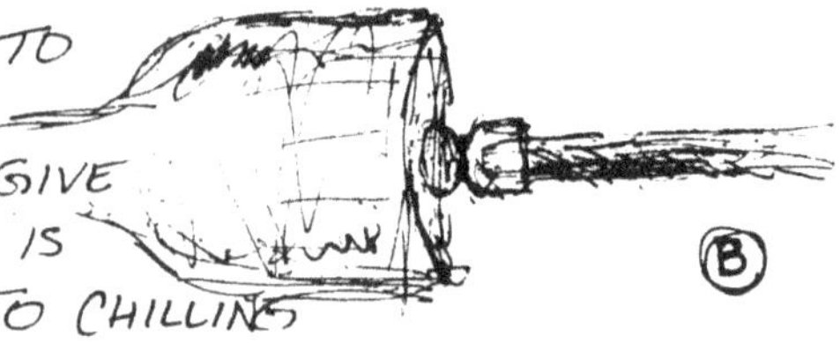

Ⓑ

TRANSFERRED AS NORMAL ONCE THE PUNTY HAS SET UP AND BEEN ADJUSTED "ON CENTER".

THESE PUNTIES CAN BE MADE IN ANY SIZE, FROM VERY SMALL TO JUMBO, AND FOR BLOWN WORK OR SOLID PIECES. JUST A DROP OR TWO (OR MORE IF NECESSARY) OF WATER — PLUS PRE-CHILLING WITH THE JACKS OR SHEARS SHOULD GIVE YOU A CLEAN AND WORRY-FREE BREAK OFF.

THE 2 & 3 PRONG PUNTY A.K.A. "THE CLAW"
FOR SPECIFIC APPLICATIONS AND THE STRANGE & UNUSUAL

THESE SPECIAL FORCES PUNTIES MAY BE USED TO TRANSFER HOLLOW OBJECTS, ASYMMETRICAL THINGUMAJIGS AND OTHER ITEMS WHERE CONVENTIONAL PUNTIES WON'T DO THE TRICK. THEY TOO ARE MADE IN A VARIETY OF SIZES AS NEEDED.

THE **THREE PRONG PUNTY** IS MADE LIKE A **COOKIE FOOT**, EXCEPT THAT YOU KEEP THE COOKIE ON YOUR PUNTY AND TWEEZE IT SO YOU HAVE 3 (OR IT COULD BE MORE) PRONG-SHAPED FINGERS WHICH WILL ACT AS YOUR PUNTY.

GATHER UP THE DESIRED AMOUNT OF GLASS ON A SUBSTANSIAL PUNTY ROD AND SHAPE/MARVER IT OFF THE END OF THE PUNTY. THEN SQUASH IT FLAT ON THE MARVER (fig. 109 Ⓐ). THIS MAY ALSO BE DONE AT THE BENCH USING THE BACK OF YOUR JACKS AS A MINI-MOBILE-MARVER (IF THE CLAW IS TO BE ON THE SMALL SIDE. (fig. 109 Ⓑ).) ONCE THE TIP HAS BEEN FLATTENED USE YOUR TWEEZERS TO PULL THREE POINTS APPROXIMATELY EQUA-DISTANT FROM EACH OTHER.

IF THE GLASS IS REALLY HOT AND MOVING AROUND QUITE A BIT, YOU CAN CHILL IT BY MARVERING THE BACK AREA OF THE PUNTY WITH THE BLADES OR BACK OF YOUR JACKS — TO SHAPE AND CENTER THE PUNTY AS WELL.

THE PUNTY IS CHECKED BY THE GAFFER, MAKING SURE THE POINTS OF THE PUNTY MATCH-UP WITH THE BOTTOM (OR WHEREVER.) OF THE PIECE TO BE TRANSFERRED. IT MAY BE NECESSARY TO EXPAND THE DISTANCE BETWEEN POINTS. REHEAT THE PUNTY AND PULL THE PRONGS FURTHER APART WITH THE TWEEZERS OR DIAMOND SHEARS. IF, ON THE OTHER HAND, THE CLAWS ARE TOO LARGE, YOU CAN SHRINK THEM DOWN BY REHEATING AND MARVERING THE FORM DOWN, OR BY USING THE TWEEZERS TO TAP OR PUSH THEM TOGETHER.

ONCE EVERYTHING MATCHES UP, JUST THE POINTS GET REHEATED AT THE GLORY HOLE AND THE PUNTY IS PRESENTED TO THE GAFFER. THE PUNTY IS LIGHTLY APPLIED AND CHECKED THOROUGHLY FOR ADEQUATE CONTACT. THE PUNTY MAY BE TILTED UP N' DOWN — PUSHED N' PULLED **TO** INCREASE CONTACT AREA AND ALIGN THINGS **ON-CENTER**. THE PIECE THEN MAY BE TRANSFERRED IN THE USUAL FASHION — AND PERHAPS WITH A LITTLE MORE CARE DUE TO THE

FRAGILE NATURE OF OBJECTS BEING PUNTIED IN THIS FASHION.

A **TWO-PRONG PUNTY** MIGHT WORK WELL FOR YOU IN CERTAIN SITUATIONS. LET'S SAY, FOR EXAMPLE, YOU HAD A FISH YOU WANTED TO PUNTY UP ON IT'S TAIL SECTION. TAKE ONE OR TWO (OR MORE, IF NECESSARY) GATHERS ON A PUNTY. MARVER IT OFF THE END. NOW YOU CAN EITHER FLATTEN THE GLASS BEFORE OR AFTER YOU SNIP THE GLASS IN HALF TO CREATE THE SPLIT OR TWO PRONGS. TO FLATTEN, SIMPLY STOP ROTATION OF THE PUNTY AND ALLOW THE GLASS TO SAG FLAT, FLIP IT OVER TO FLATTEN AND EVEN-OUT THE OTHER SIDE. YOU MAY SPREAD THE WIDTH OF THE PRONGS BY REHEATING IN THE GLORY HOLE AND SPINNING IT RAPIDLY TO ALLOW CENTRIFUGAL FORCE TO PULL THEM APART. YOU MAY ALSO ADJUST THEM WITH THE TWEEZERS OR DIAMOND SHEARS. RECHECK THE SHAPE AND CONFIGURATION WITH THE GAFFER TO MAKE CERTAIN IT WILL WORK BEFORE THE FINAL HEAT TO PUNTY IT UP.

WHEN IT COMES TIME TO BOX THE PIECE, AND THIS GOES FOR THE THREE PRONG PUNTY AS WELL, SIMPLY APPLY A DROP OF WATER AT EACH CONTACT POINT THAT THE PUNTY MAKES. LIFT UP ON THE PIECE WITH PREHEATED GLOVES AND BONK THE PUNTY ROD WITH A HEAVY WOODEN TOOL (OR BONKER).

DUE TO THEIR UNUSUAL CONFIGURATION, BOTH OF THESE STYLES OF PUNTIES REQUIRE EXTRA ATTENTION IN TERMS OF REHEATS AND CARE IN HANDLING. THEY TEND TO BE MORE PRONE TO THERMAL SHOCK, THEREFORE HAVING A TORCH HANDY TO REHEAT AT THE BENCH OR KEEP THE PUNTY 'WARM' IS A GOOD IDEA. ALSO BE EXTRA CAREFUL WHEN SETTING THE PUNTY DOWN ON THE BENCH OR YOKE — UNINTENTIONAL JARRING OR VIBRATION MAY CAUSE YOUR PIECE TO JUMP OFF THE END — AND YOU-KNOW-WHAT.

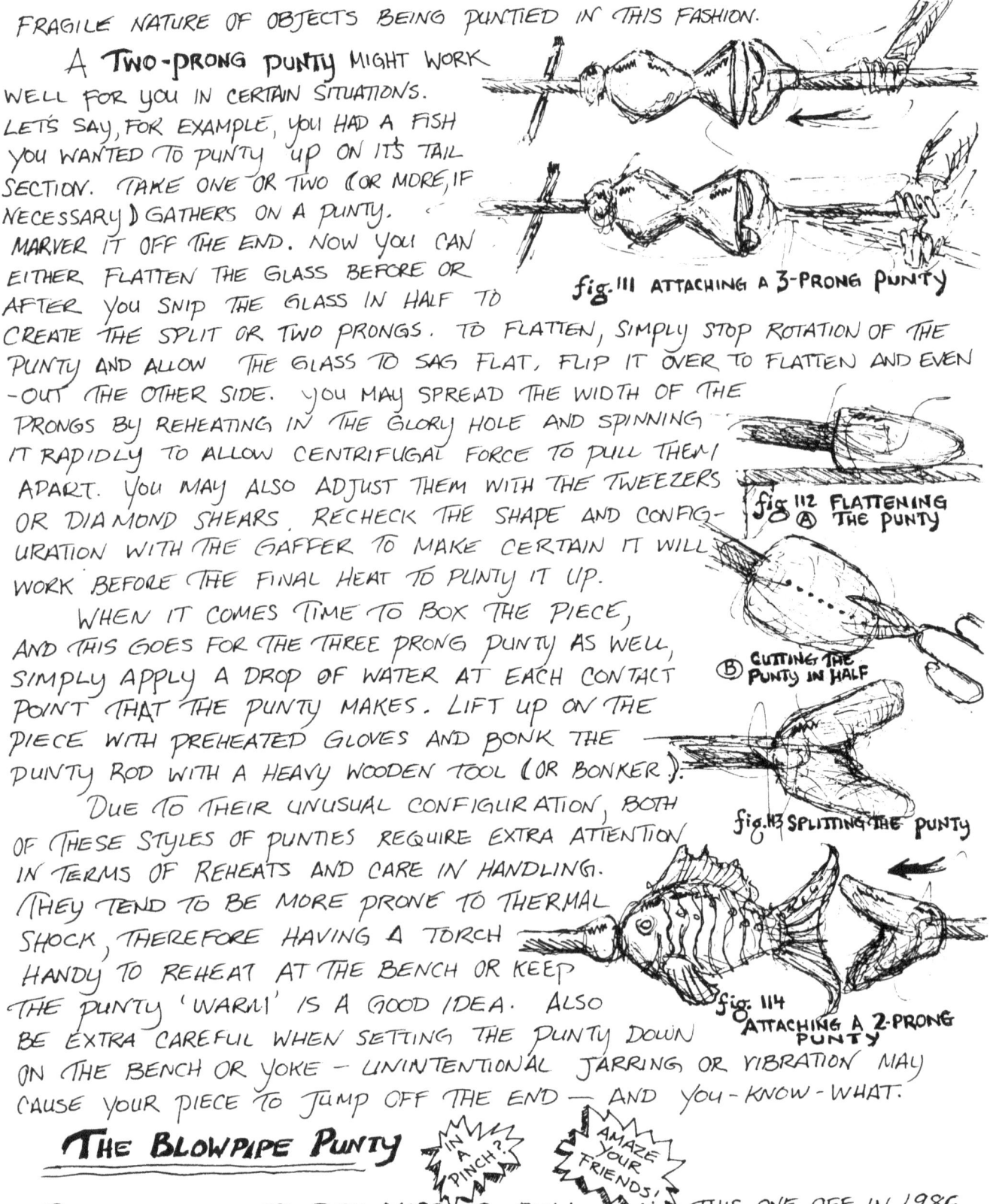

fig. 111 ATTACHING A 3-PRONG PUNTY

fig. 112 (A) FLATTENING THE PUNTY

(B) CUTTING THE PUNTY IN HALF

fig. 113 SPLITTING THE PUNTY

fig. 114 ATTACHING A 2-PRONG PUNTY

THE BLOWPIPE PUNTY

IN A PINCH? AMAZE YOUR FRIENDS!

I FIRST WITNESSED **DICK MARQUIS** PULL THIS ONE OFF IN 1986 DURING A WORKSHOP HE GAVE AT THE UNIVERSITY OF ILLINOIS-CHAMPAIGN/URBANA. IT BLEW ME AWAY! (I WAS EASILY IMPRESSED BY ALL FORMS OF GLASS WIZARDRY BACK THEN.) IT WAS SO **QUICK 'N' E-Z**! OR SO IT APPEARED...

It looks cool - but isn't the most reliable method for puntying a piece - although I suspect it has been used by glassblowers since the dawn of the blowpipe. Try it, you might like it.

You blow an object as normal → making sure that you have a single, clean tight neckline which will release easily during the transfer.

Prior to the transfer, chill the neck with the jacks and go for your final flash/reheat. Flash the whole piece, then concentrate a little extra heat on the bottom of the piece. This extra bit of heat will insure the piece will stick to the blowpipe.

Return to the bench, chill the neck quickly with the jacks (or crimp it with the diamond shears) grab the piece further down its neck (or stem or wherever you can get a decent grip on it ✱) lift the piece and blowpipe off the bench somewhat (a couple of inches) and let it fall back down → hard enough to 'pop' or tap the piece off at the neckline. You then quickly flip the piece around and stick it on your blowpipe - guiding it as close to the center of the piece as you can manage. You might even have a little time (a second or three) to adjust the piece on center once it's attached.

This is, of course, a marginal style of punty, i.e. a short lifespan with marginal gripping power. You'll need to work swiftly to open up and finish the lip of your piece.

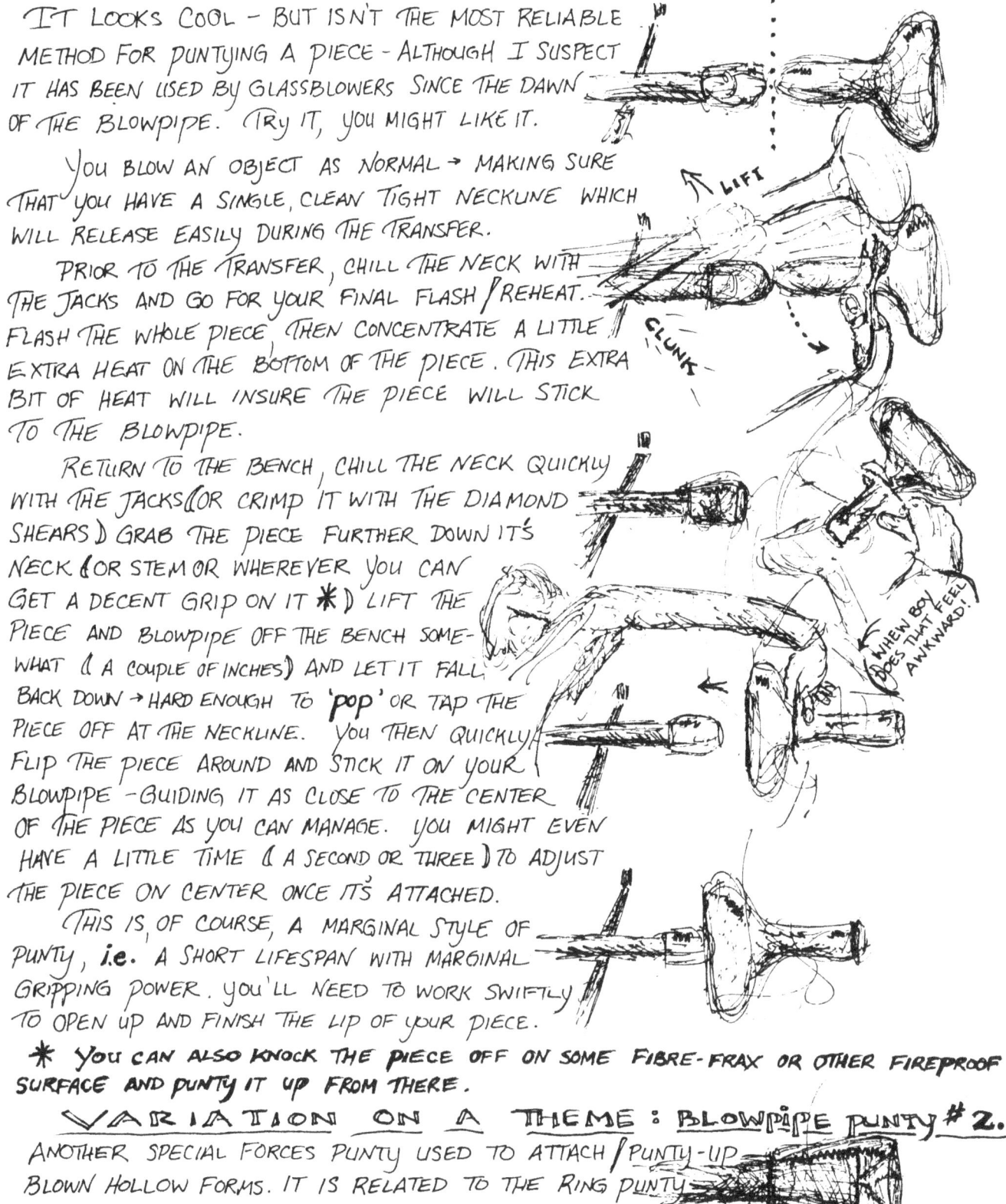

✱ You can also knock the piece off on some fibre-frax or other fireproof surface and punty it up from there.

VARIATION ON A THEME: BLOWPIPE PUNTY #2.

Another special forces punty used to attach/punty-up blown hollow forms. It is related to the ring punty but differs in that you can blow through it to inflate (if necessary) the object being transferred (e.g. Montage technique page 269). It's identical to making a collar (page 98) and may be sized-up if desired by either gathering more glass, or by simply flaring the end hole with the jacks.

COLOR

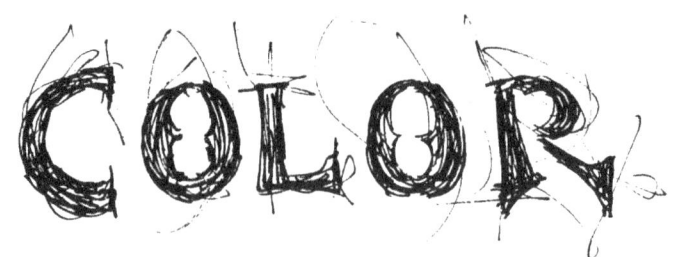

COLOR BAR	95
PREHEATING COLOR	96
MAKING A COLLAR	98
COLOR OVERLAY	99
GRADATIONS	102
CUP OVERLAY	102
BUBBLE OVERLAY	104
POWDERS	108
SCAVO	111
FRIT	112
SHARDS	113
THREADING	116
CANE DRAWING	120
INCALMO	121
GRAALS	125
PARADISE PAINTS	130

COLOR

"How do you get the color in the glass?" is perhaps one of the most common questions asked of glassblowers by the general public. "Magic" might be one response. Considering the complexity of designs that some artists create with colored glass, it indeed seems the result of magic, alchemy, or even sorcery! The truth of the matter is that certain metals/metallic oxides mixed into the glass batch formula will result in colored glass. The type of metal used, and it's quantity, will determine it's color and concentration.

For those artists not interested in glass chemistry, batching colors, and handling assorted chemicals — not to mention pull-tests, coefficients of expansion and compatibility, there is **KUGLER**. Like Kleenex or Xerox, Kugler is a specific manufacturers name that has become synonymous with the product that they produce. Thus, when glassblowers speak or write about Kugler, they are really referring to **COLOR** or colored glass. As with forms and shapes in glass, there are infinite varieties/methods to working with color.

RODS, **FRITS** and **POWDERS** are just some of the most common vehicles by which we introduce color into our crystal. Other methods such as painting on glass with cold enamels, fired-on enamels, or hot glass 'paints' exist. Using metals such as gold, silver and copper directly with hot glass offer other possibilities of decoration and visual enhancement. First, I'll present the basics of working with color and then proceed to more involved processes. Mix or match for the method which suits your style or needs.

Working with Colored Rod:

First, you must cut your Kugler into chunks so that they may be preheated prior to using them. One of the most common methods for doing this is with a hammer and chisel. An angle iron 'trough' may be constructed to hold the rod, with a cold chisel inset at one end perpendicular to the rod on top of which it rests. A flat bladed hammer is used to chop the Kugler by firmly striking the rod against the fulcrum of the chisel below. If the blade or chisel is dull, or the rod is particularly dense or thick, it may take several blows to get the piece to break free. I've seen some pretty sophisticated "guillotine-style" Kugler-cutters created by inventive glassblowing tech-heads which work fairly well. Whatever method you have available, try to cut the color as clean as you can. Sometimes the impact marks left by hammering can be seen as visible 'scars' when heated-up and blown out. Also, **be sure to wear safety glasses to protect your eyes when cutting color** → flakes and chips are common by-products of this process, and you never know where or how far they'll end up. Clean-up any excess debris as well.

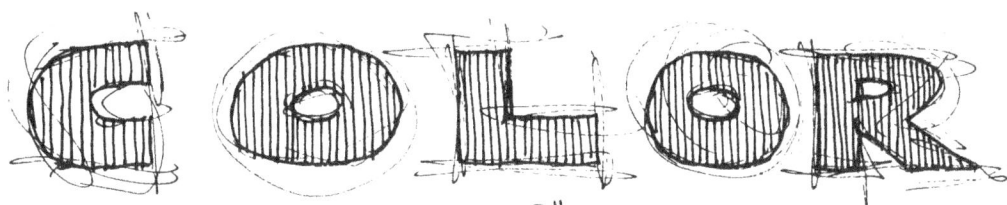

fig. 115 KUGLER CUTTER

fig. 116 CHOPPING COLOR BAR

Some people also resort to using a diamond or tile-cutting saw to slice their color. They end up loosing a little color to the sawing process, but can get nice tidy pieces to exactly the quantity they desire. The saw marks may also leave visible 'residue' when heated and blown out. It's a trade-off.

Q. How much color should I use?

As much as you can afford. ... No, really it depends on how big your piece will be and how dense you would like the color to appear. Some colors are denser than others.

For **OVERLAYS** and **GRAAL** work, you may wish to use more color than normal. This makes it easier to work with and simplifies the stretching-over technique, in addition to providing richer color with less chance of gradation or fading.

It's important that the glass is preheated to prevent thermal shock when picking-up color with a hot punty or pipe. You may use a small kiln designed specifically for this purpose. Some of the more popular ceramic kilns work well for preheating color. Or you may place your kugler in an available annealing oven prior to blowing. In any case, kugler should soak at least 15 minutes to ½ hour at annealing temperature prior to using it. That way your color won't explode and decorate the interior of your glory hole when you try to heat it up! Also when placing your color into an already hot oven, it is recommended to set your color on a cold firebrick, piece of kilnshelf - etc. and then put it into the oven. This, too, reduces thermal shock and prevents your kugler from blowing up into little bits.

fig. 117
A KUGLER OVEN

Make a diagram in chalk on the annealer or floor or on a seperate piece of paper, of what color's what. This will eliminate any guesswork or mistakes in identifying your color by you or your assistants. It's amazing how similar chunks of color appear when they get hot!

Keep an eye on the temperature of your color oven. They're notorious for exceeding annealing temp. and melting into nicely colored puddles in the bottom of the kiln → and are a real bear to clean out!

When picking up color, use a single gather of clear glass on a punty. Choose a punty which is appropriate for the amount of color that you'll be heating up. Marver most of the glass onto the punty itself, flatten the tip and marver & chill the sides smooth. Reheat just the tip in the glory hole to insure your color will stick to the punty. Pick-up the color out of the preheated kiln by sticking your punty on the desired color and pressing somewhat firmly. This gives you the largest surface area and a relatively stable base from which to work. Examine the bottom of the kugler for any pieces of kiln shelf or softbrick that might have stuck there during the preheating process. You may have to wipe them off with some damp newspaper to clean your color of unwanted **DEBRIS**. In some cases, bits of brick

MAY ACTUALLY FUSE THEMSELVES TO THE BOTTOM OF YOUR COLOR (TURN YOUR OVEN DOWN IF THIS HAPPENS OFTEN!) — YOU'LL HAVE TO HEAT THE COLOR UP AND CUT OFF ANY UNWANTED CONTAMINANTS.

HEAT THE COLOR JUST INSIDE OF THE GLORY HOLE DOOR. TURN THE PUNTY SLOWLY, BACK AND FORTH, AND ALLOW THE HEAT TO DO THE WORK. THE GLASS SHOULD SOFTEN AND BALL-UP ON THE END.

IF THE COLOR YOU'RE HEATING UP IS GOING TO BE DROPPED ON A BLOWPIPE, EITHER STRAIGHT OR AS AN OVERLAY, YOU'LL WANT TO SHAPE IT LIKE AN INVERTED TEAR DROP. SOME GAFFERS MAY PREFER A SHAPE MORE LIKE AN INVERTED CONE, SO ASK FIRST, FOR THE SHAPE THEY LIKE BEST. YOU MAY ACHIEVE SUCH A SHAPE BY MARVERING THE COLOR ON THE FRONT 2-3 INCHES OF THE MARVER WITH YOUR HANDS DOWN LOW (BELOW THE LEVEL OF THE MARVER). THIS HELPS SHAPE THE GLASS OFF THE END OF THE PUNTY AND ALLOWS GRAVITY TO WORK IT'S WONDERS BY COMPRESSING THE FORM TOGETHER. YOU MAY ALSO FLATTEN THE BOTTOM BY SQUASHING THE COLOR FLAT AGAINST THE MARVER. CONTINUE TO SHAPE THE SIDES AND TIP SMOOTH BY MARVERING BACK AND FORTH, REHEATING WHEN NECESSARY.

IDEAL SHAPE

PAY CLOSE ATTENTION WHILE HEATING COLOR IN THE GLORY HOLE. IT IS VERY EASY TO TAG THE DOOR AND CONTAMINATE YOUR PRECIOUS COLOR. ALSO, YOU WANT TO MAKE SURE THAT THE COLOR AND BIT OF CLEAR GLASS ON YOUR PUNTY DON'T BECOME INTERMIXED. THE RESULTING COLOR MAY HAVE UNDESIREABLE GRADATIONS OR EVEN CLEAR WINDOWS → **NOT** WHAT YOU WANT WHEN YOU'RE SHOOTING FOR NICE, EVEN COLOR DISTRIBUTION.

WHEN YOU OBTAIN THE DESIRED SHAPE, YOU'LL WANT TO COORDINATE WITH THE GAFFER SO THAT THEY ARE READY WHEN YOU ARE. TIMING IS EVERYTHING!

THE COLOR IS HEATED THOROUGHLY JUST INSIDE THE GLORYHOLE, THE PUNTY KEPT HORIZONTAL SO THAT COLOR STAYS PUT, AND THEN BROUGHT OVER TO THE ANXIOUSLY AWAITING GAFFER. AS SOON AS THE PUNTY IS GRIPPED BY THE GAFFERS DIAMOND SHEARS, RAISE THE BACK END OF THE PUNTY AS HIGH AS YOU CAN TO ENCOURAGE THE COLOR TO FLOW ONTO THE GAFFER'S BLOWPIPE. ALLOW THE GAFFER TO DO THE GUIDING OF THE PUNTY AND CUTTING THE COLOR FREE. YOUR JOB IS TO REMAIN LOOSE AND SUPPORTIVE.

LIFT

DETAIL

CUT FREE

MAKING A COLLAR:

WHEN WORKING WITH COLORED ROD, IT'S A GOOD IDEA TO START WITH A CLEAR COLLAR ON THE BLOWPIPE. THERE ARE SEVERAL REASONS FOR THIS, TWO OF THE BEST BEING THAT YOU'LL MAKE THE MOST OUT OF COLOR WITH LITTLE-TO-NO WASTE AND YOUR PIPES WON'T BE SUBJECT TO KUGLER CONTAMINATION.

THE CLEAR COLLAR HAS OTHER APPLICATIONS SUCH AS: PICKING-UP CANE, PICKING-UP GRAAL BLANKS, AS A MEANS TO TRANSFER BUBBLES (SEE MONTAGE pg. 269), OR AS A "SPECIAL FORCES" PUNTY (SEE pg. 93). IT'S A GOOD TECHNIQUE TO LEARN AND RELATIVELY EASY TO PERFORM.

BEGIN BY GATHERING A SMALL BLOB OF GLASS ON YOUR BLOWPIPE. IMMEDIATELY AFTER YOU EXIT THE FURNACE, HOLD THE GLASS END UP SO THE GLASS FLOWS BACK ONTO THE BLOWPIPE.

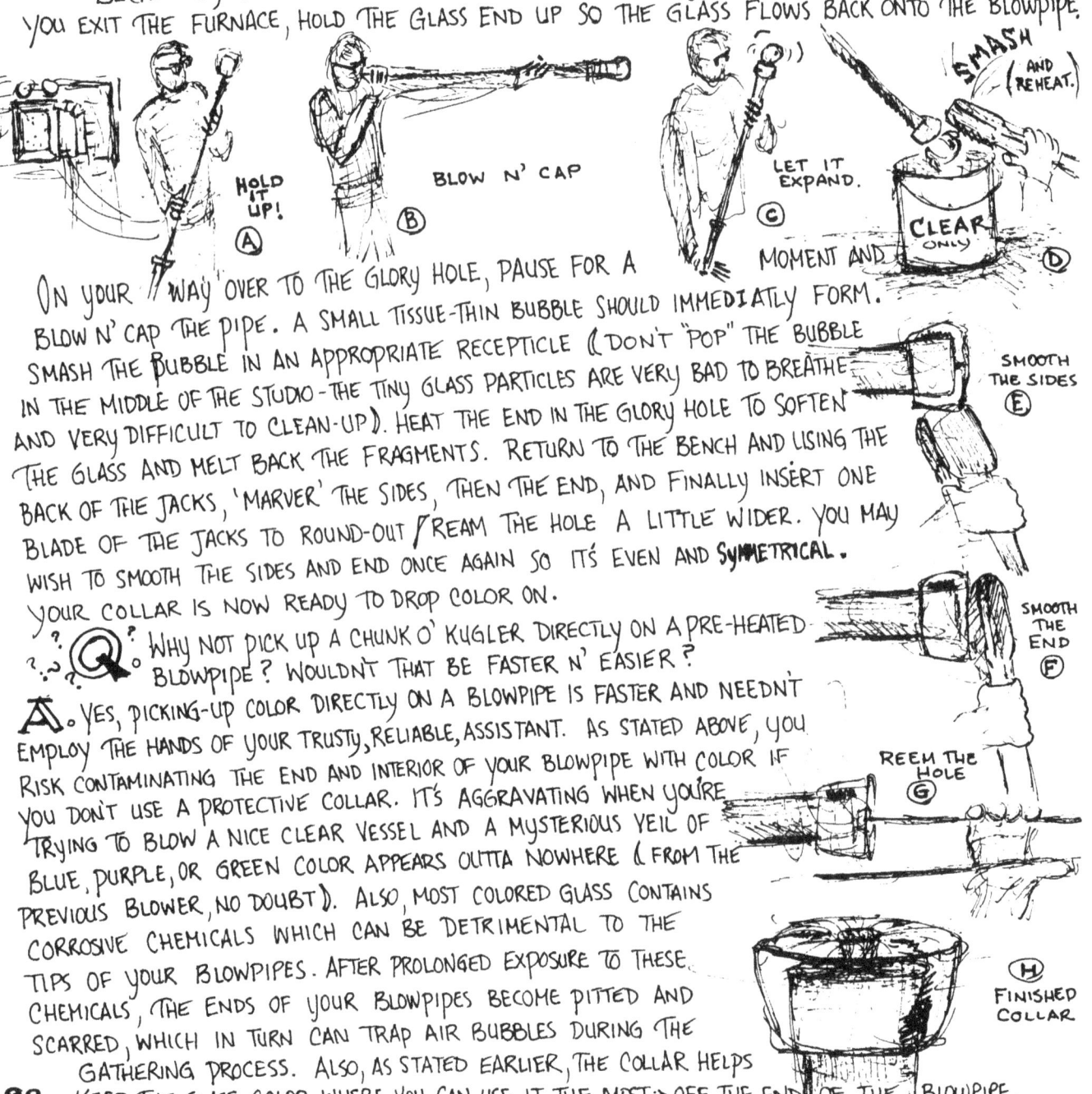

ON YOUR WAY OVER TO THE GLORY HOLE, PAUSE FOR A MOMENT AND BLOW N' CAP THE PIPE. A SMALL TISSUE-THIN BUBBLE SHOULD IMMEDIATELY FORM. SMASH THE BUBBLE IN AN APPROPRIATE RECEPTACLE (DON'T "POP" THE BUBBLE IN THE MIDDLE OF THE STUDIO — THE TINY GLASS PARTICLES ARE VERY BAD TO BREATHE AND VERY DIFFICULT TO CLEAN-UP). HEAT THE END IN THE GLORY HOLE TO SOFTEN THE GLASS AND MELT BACK THE FRAGMENTS. RETURN TO THE BENCH AND USING THE BACK OF THE JACKS, 'MARVER' THE SIDES, THEN THE END, AND FINALLY INSERT ONE BLADE OF THE JACKS TO ROUND-OUT/REAM THE HOLE A LITTLE WIDER. YOU MAY WISH TO SMOOTH THE SIDES AND END ONCE AGAIN SO IT'S EVEN AND **SYMMETRICAL**. YOUR COLLAR IS NOW READY TO DROP COLOR ON.

Q: WHY NOT PICK UP A CHUNK O' KUGLER DIRECTLY ON A PRE-HEATED BLOWPIPE? WOULDN'T THAT BE FASTER N' EASIER?

A: YES, PICKING-UP COLOR DIRECTLY ON A BLOWPIPE IS FASTER AND NEEDN'T EMPLOY THE HANDS OF YOUR TRUSTY, RELIABLE, ASSISTANT. AS STATED ABOVE, YOU RISK CONTAMINATING THE END AND INTERIOR OF YOUR BLOWPIPE WITH COLOR IF YOU DON'T USE A PROTECTIVE COLLAR. IT'S AGGRAVATING WHEN YOU'RE TRYING TO BLOW A NICE CLEAR VESSEL AND A MYSTERIOUS VEIL OF BLUE, PURPLE, OR GREEN COLOR APPEARS OUTTA NOWHERE (FROM THE PREVIOUS BLOWER, NO DOUBT). ALSO, MOST COLORED GLASS CONTAINS CORROSIVE CHEMICALS WHICH CAN BE DETRIMENTAL TO THE TIPS OF YOUR BLOWPIPES. AFTER PROLONGED EXPOSURE TO THESE CHEMICALS, THE ENDS OF YOUR BLOWPIPES BECOME PITTED AND SCARRED, WHICH IN TURN CAN TRAP AIR BUBBLES DURING THE GATHERING PROCESS. ALSO, AS STATED EARLIER, THE COLLAR HELPS KEEP THE GLASS COLOR WHERE YOU CAN USE IT THE MOST → OFF THE END OF THE BLOWPIPE.

It's important that the color is **VERY HOT** before you present it to the gaffer, especially for overlays. There's nothing worse than having to struggle with color that's too cold! Once the color has been cut free from the punty, the gaffer goes for a reheat and proceeds to marver and shape the color smooth n' even.

The next thing to do is to establish a starter bubble in the color. Once the color has been thoroughly heated, you'll want to marver the side walls very quickly to prevent the bubble from blowing out there prematurely.

CHILL THE SIDES

Then, holding the pipe horizontally or slightly pointed upwards, blow & cap the pipe and wait for your bubble to appear.

"If I'm using opaque glass and can't see through it, how do I know that I've got a bubble started?"

A. Look for a **BULGE** in your color. Usually the side walls will inflate first, indicating that your bubble is forming. Once it does, **take your thumb off the end of the pipe or else**... the bubble may completely blow through and pop a hole in the side, or it may make your bubble too thin and unmanageable.

BLOW N' CAP...

WATCH FOR SIGNS OF EXPANSION

Once your bubble is initially established, you'll want to marver the sides of the color; blow a little further to make certain the bubble has traveled all the way to the bottom, and that you have uniform wall thickness. It may take several reheats to achieve the 'perfect' starter bubble, but it's worth the effort.

If your bubble has a tendency to blow out on one side instead of uniformly inflating, you may have not heated the color thoroughly enough. Reheat the whole thing up again, marver the sides and tip again, and try again to inflate the color to a nice round bubble, again. It can be quite frustrating at times when your color doesn't seem to behave itself — and seems to have a will of it's own, but patience and practice will help you overcome this hurdle.

Once your bubble is fully established, you may gather over it and proceed as normal. Should you wish to do an overlay of another color, you may wish to point-up the tip somewhat while your assistant prepares the second color.

The Overlay

Simply stated: an overlay is the process of placing one color over a clear starter bubble or over another color. With color pot furnaces or day tanks, this technique is achieved simply by gathering one color over another. With Kugler, you're forced to try and stretch a blob of color over your initial bubble, somewhat similar to putting on a glove. It can be a tricky process. There are steps you can take to insure a successful overlay. Read further ➔

Q: Why would anyone wish to do an overlay over clear? Wouldn't it be simpler to just pick-up the color on the blowpipe or on a collar?

A: Placing a color over clear is primarily a 'safety' procedure. If you're making a vase, bowl or rondel and don't want the interior color to reduce, become discolored or get burned-up, the clear interior may offer you protection from over-exposure in the glory hole. The thin clear layer on the inside is also less likely to reveal accidental scratches than those of pure or straight color. This becomes more apparent to those of you who do large amounts of coldworking, particularly when you cut or grind through such surfaces. Color is less prone to chip or flake-off if it has the protective clear "underlay." It can also be an aesthetic decision as well. You may want a thin layer of clear within your phenomenal art object.

Overlays offer the glassblower an opportunity to create seemingly complexed colored pieces via a fairly simple process. You may wish to make a piece with an interior of one color and an exterior of a completely different one. Some interesting effects are possible by placing transparent colors over opaque ones - and vice-versa. e.g. an opaque red interior with a transparent blue overlay may yield a purple vessel with a bright red core. *AN OVERLAY BOWL*

NOTE: Not all colors are compatible with each other, nor do they always behave as you might expect. Some colors are "stiffer" than others and may blow out "funky" - almost possessing a mind of it's own. Likewise, some colors may appear denser than they actually are. They may bleed or thin-out quicker than you expect e.g. black with white, or white with black (on the outside) is always a tricky overlay combo to pull off. The colors melt and blow out at such different rates that it becomes very difficult to keep everything even and on-center. My suggestion is to: **1.** Make compatibility tests or blow small quick cups of what you plan to make - that way you don't waste time, glass and effort on something that might be doomed from the beginning. **2.** Ask around! Other glassblowers may be more familiar with successful combinations of colors and of those which don't work. **3.** Experiment. Break new ground. Boldly blow what noone has blown before.

To make an overlay, you pretty much duplicate the steps (as outlined in the previous pages) for dropping color on a blowpipe. You do want the interior bubble to be slightly pointed (it's easier to stretch color over) and stone cold. If the bubble's too hot, it won't provide you with a stable foundation to squeeze the next color over. Your bubble will probably then collapse while you attempt to marver the second color over the first, dashing all your dreams of beautiful overlays. Then it's back to square one.

The assistant will heat up the overlay color while the gaffer finishes preparing the underlying color (or clear) bubble. The color is brought over and presented to the gaffer as hot as possible. The gaffer aims for the center of the bubble and guides the flowing mass on the top. A quick snip with

THE DIAMOND SHEARS AND A SLIGHT PAT ON TOP TO FLATTEN THE COLOR A LITTLE, AND THEN A QUICK REHEAT. INSERT JUST THE COLOR INSIDE OF THE GLORY HOLE DOOR. YOU WANT ONLY THE COLOR TO GET HOT, NOT THE BUBBLE.

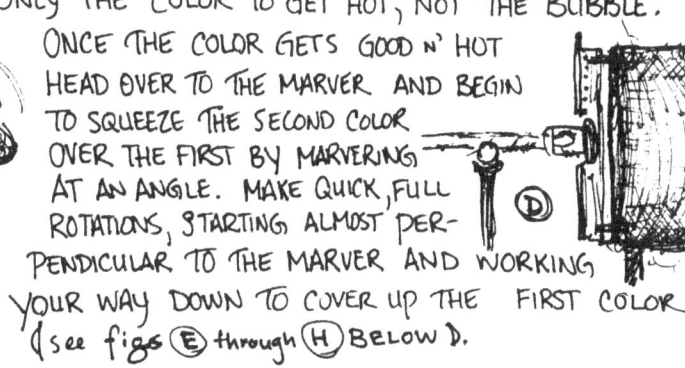

ONCE THE COLOR GETS GOOD N' HOT HEAD OVER TO THE MARVER AND BEGIN TO SQUEEZE THE SECOND COLOR OVER THE FIRST BY MARVERING AT AN ANGLE. MAKE QUICK, FULL ROTATIONS, STARTING ALMOST PERPENDICULAR TO THE MARVER AND WORKING YOUR WAY DOWN TO COVER UP THE FIRST COLOR. (see figs E through H BELOW D.

WITH A PROPER HEAT IN THE COLOR, THIS MANUVER SHOULD BE DONE IN ONE SHOT. STIFFER COLORS OR LARGER OVERLAYS MAY REQUIRE ADDITIONAL REHEATS.

NOTE: IF THE MARVER HAS ANY 'SCUDGE' ON IT, IT WILL MORE-THAN-LIKELY TRANSFER ITSELF TO YOUR HOT COLOR AND CREATE UNWANTED DEFECTS OR BLEMISHES. MAKE SURE YOUR MARVER IS CLEAN, FREE OF DUST & DEBRIS BEFORE YOU BEGIN THIS PROCESS.

fig 118 — IDEAL OVERLAY

fig 119. BUMMER! NOT ENOUGH COLOR! — INCOMPLETE OVERLAY

SHOULD YOU FINISH THE OVERLAY AND DISCOVER THAT YOUR COLOR DIDN'T COMPLETELY COVER THE BUBBLE - DON'T PANIC! YOU HAVE TWO OPTIONS: #1 YOU MAY LEAVE IT AS IS AND HOPE TO BLOW THE BUBBLE FURTHER INTO THE COLOR WITH SUCCESSIVE GATHERS. #2 YOU CAN HEAT THE WHOLE THING UP, TAKE IT TO THE BENCH AND USING YOUR TWEEZERS PULL THE COLOR UP & OVER THE BUBBLE TOWARDS THE PIPE. IT MAY TAKE SEVERAL REHEATS TO ACCOMPLISH THIS TASK. IT WILL ALSO DISTORT YOUR INTERIOR BUBBLE SOMEWHAT, BUT THAT MAY BE REMEDIED BY HEATING THE WHOLE THING UP AGAIN, MARVERING IT SMOOTH WITH THE BACK OF THE JACKS (OR ON THE MARVER ITSELF) AND GIVING IT A LIGHT PUFF TO REINFLATE YOUR BUBBLE ROUND AGAIN.

← Pull This Way

← Scooch This Way

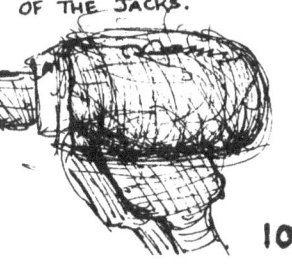

MARVER SMOOTH WITH THE BACK OF THE JACKS.

PRIOR TO THE NEXT GATHER OR OVERLAY, YOU'LL WANT TO MAKE SURE YOUR INTERIOR BUBBLE IS WELL-ESTABLISHED, AND THAT THE WALL-THICKNESS IS UNIFORM AND NOT-TOO-THIN. SIMPLY HEAT THE WHOLE BUBBLE UP, MARVER IT A TAD, AND BLOW N' CAP WHILE LOOKING FOR THE TELL-TALE BULGE. ONCE YOU SEE IT APPEAR, MARVER THE BUBBLE SMOOTH AND UNIFORM AND PROCEED TO THE NEXT STEP.

COLOR GRADATION

You may achieve an interesting color gradation in your blown work via a variation of the overlay process. If you wish the top of your piece to be the darkest/densest ⇒ start with a small clear bubble on your blowpipe. Marver and blow it so the bubble reaches the end with little excess or thickness on the tip.

If you repeatedly marver and chill the sides of the bubble while stopping to inflate the bubble in-between, the bubble should travel down to the hottest point, that is - the tip. The color is then dropped on from above as hot as possible, quickly squashed flat on top with the diamond shears, reheated and marvered back so the bulk of the color is on the sides rather than the tip. See fig. 120

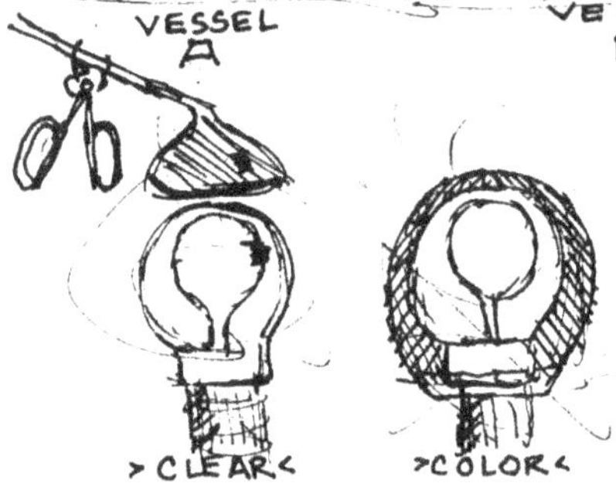

VESSEL A VESSEL B

>CLEAR<   >COLOR<
FOR VESSEL "A"
fig. 120

Just the opposite approach is utilized to achieve a vessel with thick or dense color on the bottom and almost clear near the top. (See 'Vessel "B"' above). This time you'll want a starter bubble with relatively thin side walls and somewhat thick glass on the tip. Drop the color on from above, again as hot as you can, and marver quickly the color back up and over the starter bubble. Press firmly, push aggressively and grimace slightly (for added effect!) as you marver the sides of the color and bubble so as to squeeze the color on as thin as you can get it - ending up with something like fig 121. As soon as it's cool, you may procede to gather over and finish the vessel as normal.

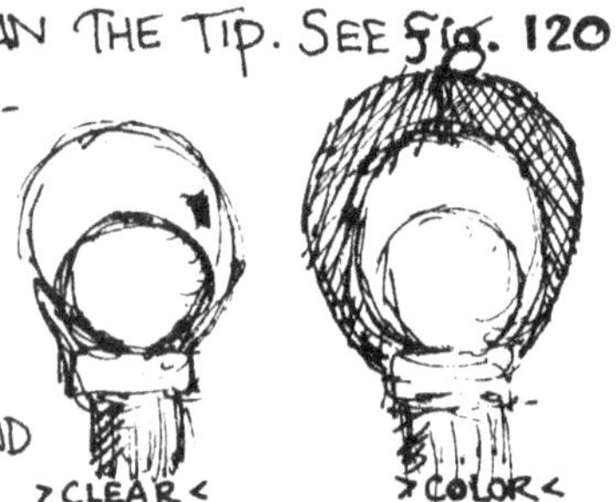

>CLEAR<   >COLOR<
FOR VESSEL "B"
fig. 121

THE CUP OVERLAY

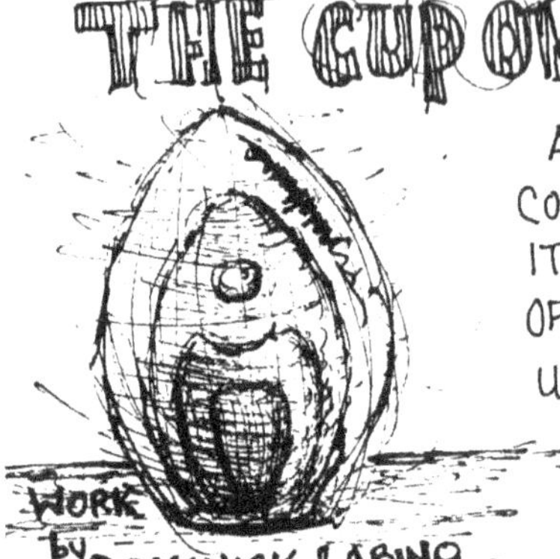

This color technique is useful in creating pieces which have an even wall of color with a clear interior or core. Often enhanced visually by various coldworking techniques, such as in the work of **HARVEY LITTLETON**, it can also be the mainstay of your art as well - as in the work of studio glass pioneer **DOMINICK LABINO**. This technique is also used by glassblowers for making colored cane with clear interiors. Although it's not the easiest technique in the world, it may be the best one to suit your needs. It does take a fair amount of time, and impeccable timing to pull off, so try to schedule your blowslot accordingly.

WORK by DOMINICK LABINO

Begin by picking up the color of your choice on the end of your blowpipe, get your starter bubble going and then **CASE** it with two-to-three (or more depending on the scale you're working) gathers of clear. Essentially, you are shooting for a **CUP SHAPE** with relatively thick walls, so continue to blow and shape your bubble as such.

Once you've obtained a cup shape with your desired thickness, you may punty it up and begin to open up the lips. You're aiming for a straight-walled cup with a slight taper and no undercuts or flared lips (see below). At the same time the cup is being opened a second pipe is started → creating the solid interior core. This may be made by the assistant or gaffer, trading off pipes if necessary. The core should be just large enough to fully fill the cup without much excess. Prior to the last hot gather of clear on the core, check its size in relation to the cup. It may be necessary to **DIP N' STRIP** in order to get the right quantity of glass on the core.

COLOR

CASED IN CLEAR

TRANSFER...

OPEN THE CUP...

SHAPE THE CORE...

TAP THE CUP FREE

AND DROP THE CORE INSIDE

Now is when your timing becomes critical. Once the cup is fully opened, it is allowed to set-up, i.e. get cold and stable, and the final clear gather is taken on the core pipe. The core is then briefly papered to shape it so it's symmetrical and will flow into the cup in a predictable fashion. If necessary, the cup may be given a quick flash in the glory hole. It is then tapped off into the assistants pre-heated gloves and set into an optic mold. NOTE: To prevent thermal shock to the cup, the lip of the optic mold may be pre-heated by exposing it to the heat coming from a nearby glory hole. Also, when transferring the cup, avoid squeezing it. It may still be very hot and can easily be compressed out-of-round by excessive force.

Once the cup is in place, the core is removed from its final reheat in the glory hole and slowly & carefully dropped into the center of the cup. Allow gravity to do it's thing → filling the cup with that very hot gather - slowly, as steadily as possible. Resist the urge to stuff the whole thing in in one shot → you're likely to trap air bubbles that way.

As soon as you've filled the cup halfway, you may lower the pipe further, filling the rest of the cup. You're then free to pick-up the cup and return to the glory hole, heating it's exterior so that you may marver and shape it uniform. It'll probably start flopping around due to the liquid state of the core → Don't panic! Try marvering it to get it under

103

CONTROL. BEGIN BY MARVERING THE NECK AREA TO GAIN STABILITY AND ALSO TO SMOOTH-OUT THE TRANSITION AREA OF THE CORE AND THE CUP.

IT'S POSSIBLE THAT THE INTERIOR CORE IS EITHER TOO SMALL OR TOO LARGE FOR THE CUP ITSELF. NO WORRIES. WITH REPEATED REHEATS AND SKILLFULL MARVERING PRACTICES, IT MAY BE POSSIBLE TO EVEN-OUT THE NECK AREA WITH NO ILL EFFECT. OF COURSE, IT IS VERY EASY TO TRAP SOME AIR BUBBLES DURING THIS PROCESS, IN WHICH CASE, YOU EITHER LIVE WITH 'EM, OR CREATE A NECKLINE BELOW THEM - AND ELIMINATE THEM THAT WAY.

CHILL HERE & MARVER SMOOTH

OVERLAY CUPS (CROSS SECTION) — TOO LITTLE / TOO MUCH

AT THIS JUNCTURE, WHEN YOU'VE GOT YOUR OVERLAY CUP MARVERED SMOOTH AND SYMMETRICAL, YOU MAY EITHER PICK-UP ANOTHER CUP, OR PULL IT INTO CANE, OR CONTINUE GATHERING MORE — WHATEVER. **YOU'RE THE BUS DRIVER. YOU DECIDE WHERE IT GOES & WHEN AND WHERE IT STOPS.**

SHOULD YOU FIND YOURSELF SHORTHANDED OR PREFER WORKING BY YOURSELF SOLO, IT IS POSSIBLE TO DO THE WHOLE PROCESS ALONE. A SOFT BRICK MAY BE HOLLOWED-OUT TO CREATE A RECEPTICLE FOR THE OVERLAY CUP. THIS MAY BE THEN SET INTO A PRE-HEATED KUGLER OVEN. THE CUP MAY BE BLOWN AND PLACED INSIDE ON THE BRICK AND HELD AT ANNEALING TEMPERATURE WHILE YOU GATHER-UP THE CORE. JUST PRIOR TO THE PICK-UP, THE ANNEALER IS RAMPED UP AN ADDITIONAL 50°-100°F FOR CA. 10 MINUTES TO REDUCE THE THERMAL SHOCK DURING THE PICK-UP PROCESS.

CARVED SOFT BRICK CUP HOLDER

IT IS ALSO POSSIBLE TO PRE-MAKE SEVERAL SETS OF OVERLAY CUPS AND "GARAGE" THEM IN THIS FASHION, MAKING BETTER USE OF YOUR TIME AND EFFORT. DON'T FORGET TO RESET THE KILN TO ANNEALING TEMP. AFTER YOU PICK-UP YOUR CUP, LESS YOU RISK SLUMPING WHATEVER ELSE IS IN THE KILN!

THE BUBBLE OVERLAY

THIS TECHNIQUE IS OFTEN USED TO CREATE "BLANKS" FOR **GRAAL** WORK OR PIECES WHICH MAY BE LATER ENGRAVED OR SANDBLASTED IN A **CAMEO**-STYLE OF SURFACE DECORATION. SIMPLY STATED: IT PUTS THE COLOR ON THE OUTSIDE OF THE PIECE BY TURNING YOUR BUBBLE INSIDE-OUT. ALTHOUGH NOT ESSENTIAL, IT HELPS TO HAVE TWO BENCHES, TWO GLORY HOLES, TWO PIPES AND AT LEAST ONE (TRAINED) ASSISTANT AT YOUR DISPOSAL. A PAIR OF PACIOFFIS ARE NECESSARY AS WELL, (PREFERABLY 'BROKEN-IN' ONES.)

LET'S SAY FOR EXAMPLE, YOU'D LIKE A GRAAL BLANK (OR FINISHED PIECE) WITH A WHITE INTERIOR (CORE) AND A BLACK-RED EXTERIOR, BLACK BEING ON THE OUTSIDE SURFACE. BEGIN BY HAVING ONE PIPE ⇒ **PIPE A** — PICK-UP A CHUNK O' WHITE ⇒ FORM A STARTER BUBBLE AND CASE IT WITH 2-to-3 (OR MORE AS NEEDED/DESIRED) GATHERS OF CLEAR. THIS WILL BE THE CORE BUBBLE

OVER WHICH THE SECOND BUBBLE IS STRETCHED. IT IS NOT RECOMMENDED THAT THE CORE BUBBLE BE BLOWN-OUT MUCH THINNER THAN YOUR STARTER BUBBLE DIAMETER, AS YOU WILL NEED THE STABILITY OF A NEAR-SOLID FORM TO SQUEEZE YOUR SECOND BUBBLE OVER. **PIPE B** WILL PICK-UP FIRST A CHUNK O' BLACK, THEN DO A RED OVERLAY ON TOP OF THAT. NOTE☞ IT'S A GOOD IDEA TO USE A 'HEALTHY' AMOUNT OF COLOR BAR FOR THIS PROCESS. IF YOU DESIRE TRULY OPAQUE OR DENSE COLORS, IT IS NECESSARY TO USE LARGER QUANTIES THAN NORMAL BECAUSE THE COLOR IS LITERALLY STRETCHED AND SUBSEQUENTLY BLOWN-OUT RELATIVELY THIN.

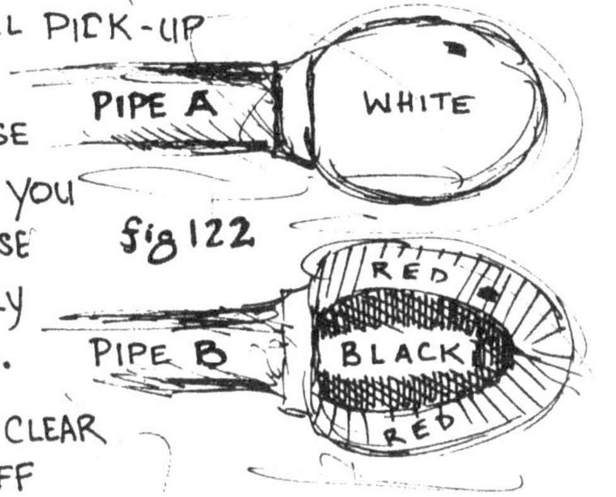

fig 122

PIPE B WILL ALSO GET CASED IN TWO OR THREE LAYERS OF CLEAR ON TOP OF ITS COLOR. THIS TECHNIQUE IS EASIER TO PULL-OFF IF THE BUBBLES REMAIN SOMEWHAT SMALL. **PIPE B** WILL ULTIMATELY BE THE ONE WHICH WILL GET STRETCHED OVER **PIPE A**'s CORE BUBBLE, THUS REVERSING THE COLOR IN **PIPE B**'s BUBBLE. THE BUBBLES MAY BE STARTED SIMULTANEOUSLY. **PIPE A** SHOULD BE GATHERED AND SHAPED TO A BASIC BULLET FORM (SEE fig. 123→). DO NOT NECK IT AS YOU'LL NEED THE STABILITY OF ITS FORM, AS WELL AS A UNIFORM SURFACE TO ACHIEVE A SUCCESSFUL OVERLAY.

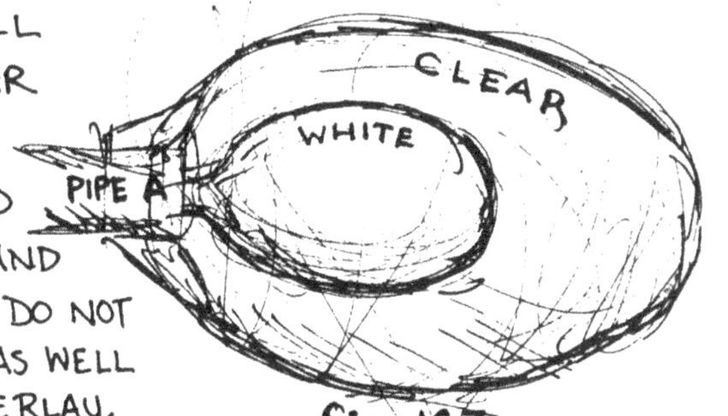

fig. 123

PIPE B's BUBBLE WILL BE BLOWN SOMEWHAT THINNER AND SLIGHTLY LARGER THAN **PIPE A**'s BUBBLE. THIS BUBBLE SHOULD BE UNIFORM IN WALL THICKNESS. IT SHOULD ALSO BE NECKED FAIRLY TIGHTLY, ENSURING A CLEAN AND TROUBLE-FREE TRANSFER (SEE fig. 124→). AFTER NECKING THE BUBBLE ON **PIPE B** IS COMPLETED, IT IS TIME TO **HEAT UP THE BOTTOM HALF** OF THE PIECE UNTIL IT IS VERY HOT → TAKING CARE **NOT** TO HEAT THE NECK. BY REHEATING JUST INSIDE THE OPENING OF THE GLORY HOLE DOOR, YOU CAN CONCENTRATE THE HEAT RIGHT WHERE YOU NEED IT. ONCE THE BOTTOM HALF APPEARS NICE N' HOT, IT IS BROUGHT OVER TO THE GAFFER AT THE BENCH AND PRESENTED AS YOU IF YOU WERE 'PUNTYING-UP'. AT THIS POINT THE GAFFER TAKES CONTROL – HE/SHE GRABS THE NECK OF **PIPE B** ⇒ CLOSE TO THE BUBBLE – WITH THE DIAMOND SHEARS AND GUIDES THE BUBBLE ON CENTER.

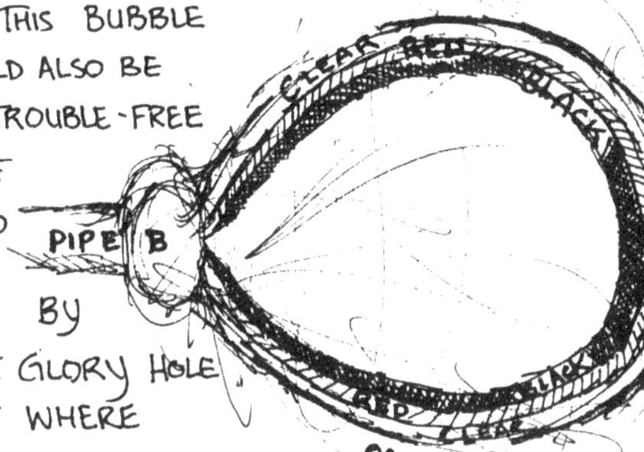

fig 124

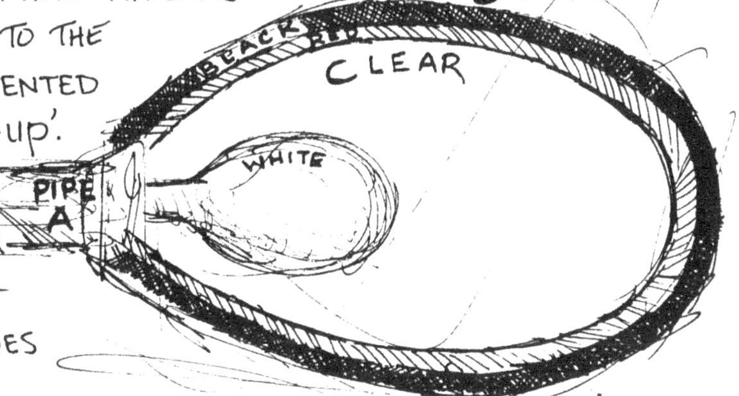

fig. 125 FINAL FORM (PRIOR TO NECKING)

THE ASSISTANT WITH **PIPE B** REMAINS LOOSE AND ALLOWS THE GAFFER TO MAKE ALL THE MOTIONS. THEY SHOULD ALSO BE PREPARED TO CAP THE PIPE IF REQUESTED BY THE GAFFER (TO MAINTAIN SOME PRESSURE IN THE BUBBLE AND KEEP IT FROM COLLAPSING). PIPE ROTATION IS ALSO HALTED MOMENTARILY, AS THE BUBBLES ARE JOINED.

ESSENTIALLY THE BUBBLE ON **PIPE B** IS PUSHED ON ABOUT HALFWAY. THE PIPES ARE ROTATED TO CHECK THAT THE BUBBLES ARE UNIFORMLY JOINED, AND THE **NECK** ON **PIPE B** IS CHILLED WITH THE JACKS. THE ASSISTANT MAY THEN TAP THEIR PIPE WITH THE BACK END OF SOME TWEEZERS TO FREE IT AND COMPLETE THE TRANSFER. NOW FOR THE TRICKY PART!

THE WHOLE PIECE IS GIVEN A QUICK FLASH, AND THEN BROUGHT OUT SO THAT JUST THE **LIP & SHOULDER** OF **BUBBLE B** GET REHEATED. TURN SLOWLY. YOU DO NOT WANT THE LIP TO FLARE OUT PREMATURELY. ONCE THE LIP OF PIECE SEEMS GOOD N' HOT AND ON THE VERGE OF TOTAL COLLAPSE → RETURN TO THE BENCH AND BEGIN TO PUSH THE REST OF THE BUBBLE ON. USING YOUR PACIOFFI'S, FIRST LIFT OFF THE SURFACE OF THE CORE BUBBLE SLIGHTLY BY INSERTING THE 'CIOF's (PRONOUNCED "CHOFE"s) ALL THE WAY INSIDE **BUBBLE B** AND ANGLING UPWARDS. SWIFT ROTATIONS HELP COVER MORE SURFACE AREA IN A SHORTER TIME - SO BE QUICK. ONCE YOU'VE GOT THE INITIAL LIFT-OFF → PROCEDE TO FURTHER PUSH DOWN THE LENGTH OF THE CORE BUBBLE. IF YOU'RE LUCKY (OR HIGHLY SKILLED) YOU CAN DO THIS ALL IN ONE HEAT. OFTENTIMES IT TAKES TWO OR THREE REHEATS TO WORK THE EXTERIOR BUBBLE ALL THE WAY DOWN FOR COMPLETE COVERAGE. AGAIN, DURING REHEATS, TURN SLOWLY TO PREVENT MAKING A **RONDEL** OUT OF YOUR OVERLAY BUBBLE. ALSO, HAVE YOUR ASSISTANT

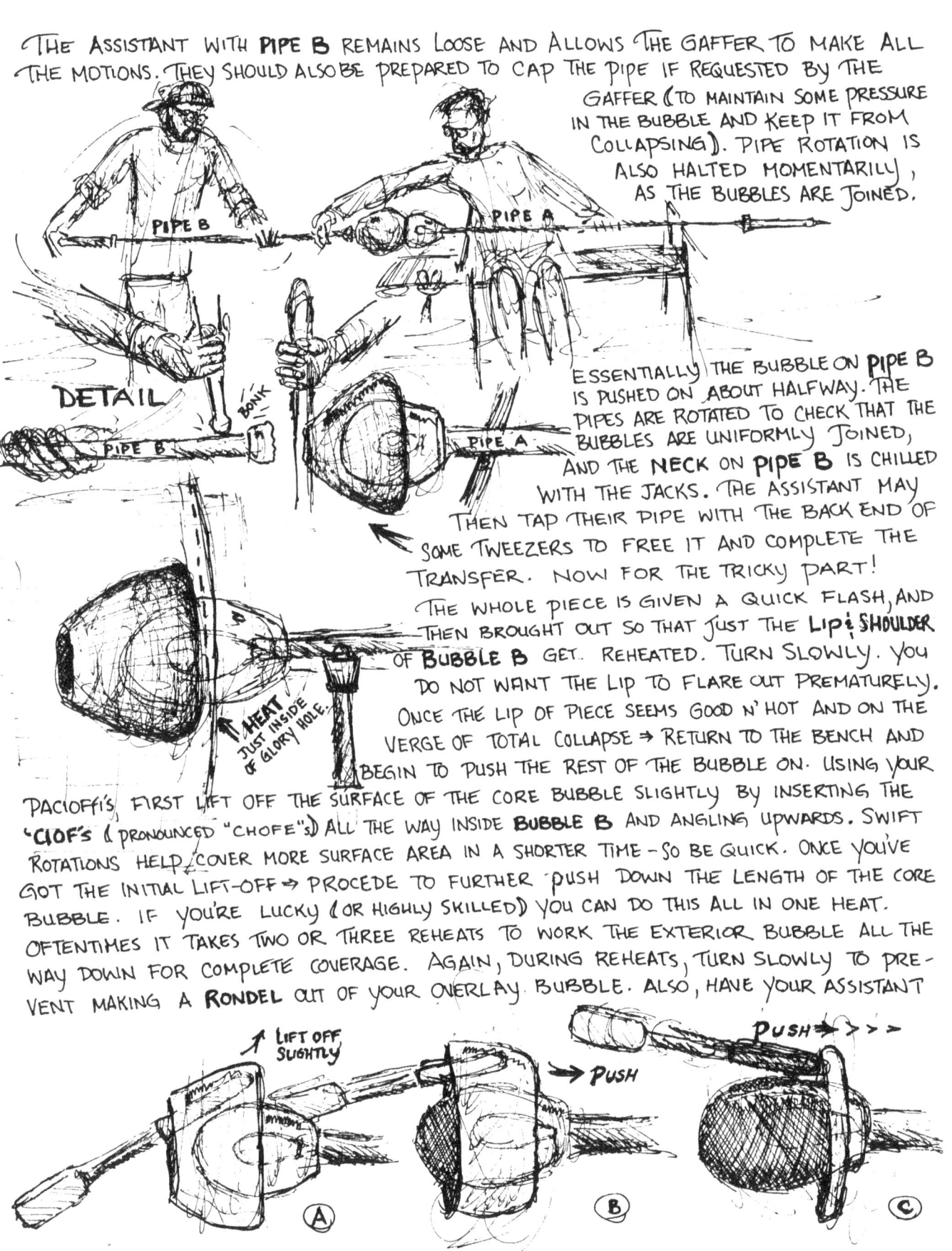

STANDING BY DOING DOORS SO THAT YOU DON'T GET IN A PINCH AND ACCIDENTLY TAG A DOOR OR WHATEVER. ALSO, SOME **PROTECTION** MAY BE REQUIRED TO KEEP THE GAFFERS HAND, WRIST, AND ARM FROM BURNING FROM THE EXCESSIVE RADIANT HEAT COMMONLY EXPERIENCED DURING THIS PROCESS. **KEEP YOUR EYE ON THE BUBBLE AT ALL TIMES!** IT'S VERY EASY TO COLLAPSE, FOLD AND CRINKLE THE LIP OF THE OVERLAY! CONTINUE TO 'RIDE' THE WOODEN JACKS ON THE TOP SURFACE OF THE BUBBLE (SEE fig.126 BELOW) AND PUSH THE LAST OF THE OVERLAY ON. ANY EXCESS MAY THEN BE TRIMMED OFF

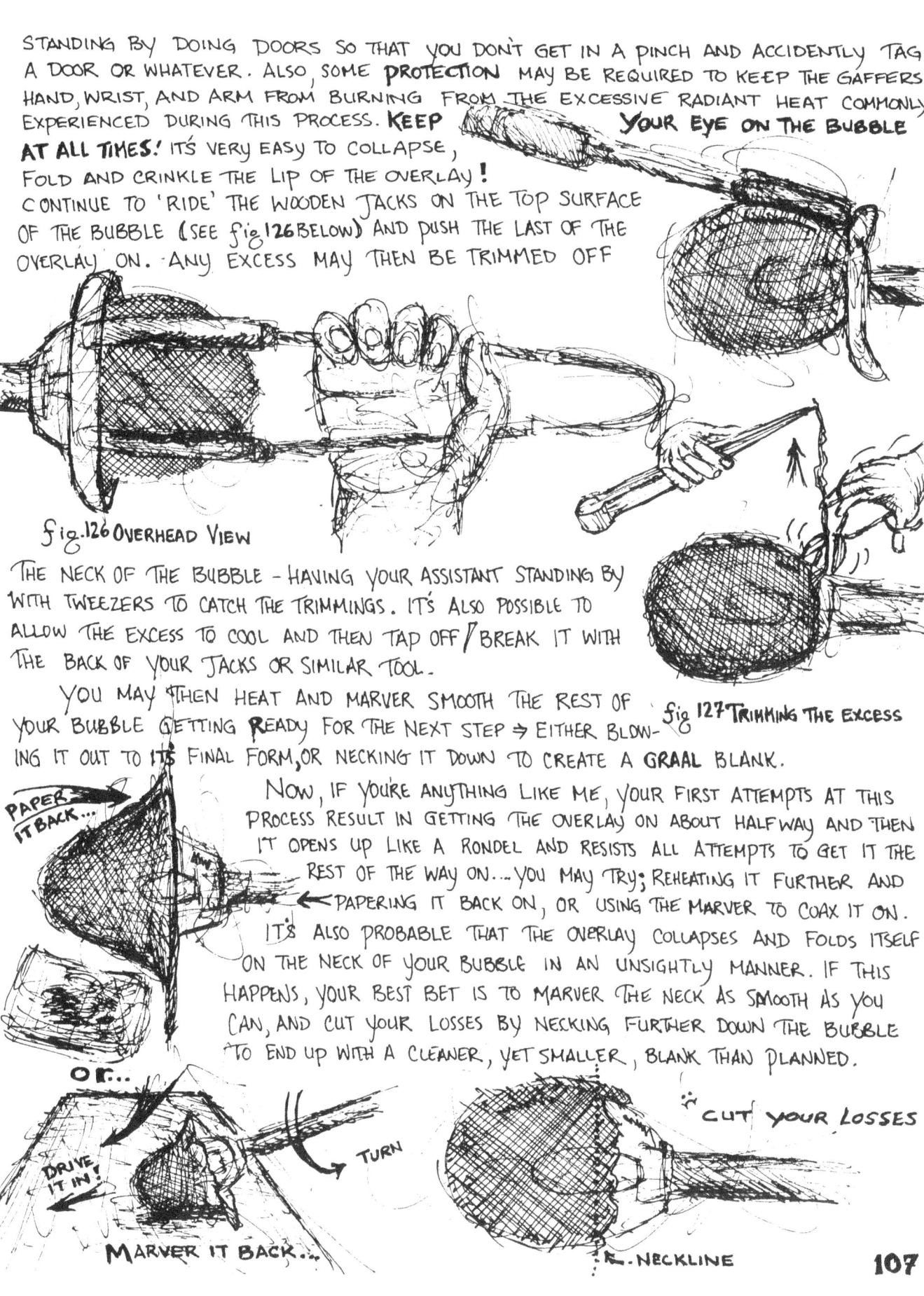

fig.126 OVERHEAD VIEW

THE NECK OF THE BUBBLE - HAVING YOUR ASSISTANT STANDING BY WITH TWEEZERS TO CATCH THE TRIMMINGS. IT'S ALSO POSSIBLE TO ALLOW THE EXCESS TO COOL AND THEN TAP OFF / BREAK IT WITH THE BACK OF YOUR JACKS OR SIMILAR TOOL.

YOU MAY THEN HEAT AND MARVER SMOOTH THE REST OF YOUR BUBBLE GETTING READY FOR THE NEXT STEP ⇒ EITHER BLOWING IT OUT TO ITS FINAL FORM, OR NECKING IT DOWN TO CREATE A **GRAAL BLANK**.

fig.127 TRIMMING THE EXCESS

NOW, IF YOU'RE ANYTHING LIKE ME, YOUR FIRST ATTEMPTS AT THIS PROCESS RESULT IN GETTING THE OVERLAY ON ABOUT HALFWAY AND THEN IT OPENS UP LIKE A RONDEL AND RESISTS ALL ATTEMPTS TO GET IT THE REST OF THE WAY ON... YOU MAY TRY; REHEATING IT FURTHER AND PAPERING IT BACK ON, OR USING THE MARVER TO COAX IT ON.

IT'S ALSO PROBABLE THAT THE OVERLAY COLLAPSES AND FOLDS ITSELF ON THE NECK OF YOUR BUBBLE IN AN UNSIGHTLY MANNER. IF THIS HAPPENS, YOUR BEST BET IS TO MARVER THE NECK AS SMOOTH AS YOU CAN, AND CUT YOUR LOSSES BY NECKING FURTHER DOWN THE BUBBLE TO END UP WITH A CLEANER, YET SMALLER, BLANK THAN PLANNED.

PAPER IT BACK...

or...

DRIVE IT IN!

TURN

MARVER IT BACK...

CUT YOUR LOSSES

R. NECKLINE

POWDERS

Unlike it's solid counterpart → the rod – **POWDERED COLORED** glass poses certain health risks in addition to the endless combinations and applications in which they may be incorporated. Care must be taken in handling, storing and applying this material. A respirator (with appropriate fresh (new) cartridges) is highly recommended to protect your lungs from breathing hazardous dusts common to working with powder.

¿Q?: When was the last time you changed those filters??? A paper dust mask, tho' underrated for this material, is still better than nothing. If you have any question about the toxicity of this stuff, request a M.S.D.S. (Material Data Safety Sheet) from your color supplier and become informed.

Many artists store their powders in re-sealable plastic food storage containers marked with the number of the color on the outside. This helps keep the powders dry and free of contaminates, as well as being easily stored and organized.

There are a variety of methods for applying powders to the surface of your glass. Each procedure will produce it's own effect. Much of the success in powdering glass lies in how hot the glass is. The hotter the glass, the more powder will adhere to it.

You may wish to roll a hot gather directly into an awaiting pile of powder on the marver to cover a 'bit' or the entire bubble or mass of glass on your blowpipe. This techniques kills two birds with one stone by coloring and shaping your glass at the same time! This technique is suitable for general color coating versus highly accurate placement of the 'pigment'. You may also create bands of color by laying out the powder in lines on the marver and rolling in them.

ROLL ROLL ROLL YOUR BUBBLE

fig A.

NOTE! → Many studios prohibit **THE USE OF POWDERS ON THE MARVER!** The powders present a health risk for the members of the studio and often can contaminate the workspace. One solution is to lay your powders in stainless steel mixing bowls and roll your glass in them. Baking pans and cookie sheets (steel, not aluminum!) seem to work as well, and are easy to come by at garage sales and thrift stores. You may then have a selection of colors at your disposal, and find the colors easier and cleaner to handle.

For more specific imagery, you may spread out a thin layer of powder(s) and draw designs into it, creating positive and negative spaces of color. This may be done on a steel plate (mini-marver) which is then laid over a hot plate or burner and pre-heated to ca. 900°F. This helps insure color adhesion and complete transfer. NOTE: Your imagery will be reversed via this technique ⇒ so if you'd like words to look right – spell them BACKWARDS to appear correct.

Another method involves the use of a template. If you wish to reproduce a pattern or design or some symbols, letters etc. – you may make a template out of card-stock, cardboard or similar easily-cuttable material – incise your

HOT PLATE

fig. B.

DESIRED IMAGERY, LAY IT ON THE MARVER (OR YOUR HOTPLATE FOR QUALITY TRANSFER), SIFT YOUR POWDERS OVER THE TEMPLATE - REMOVE THE STENCIL AND ROLL YOUR HOT PIECE OVER IT TO PICK UP THE DESIGN. ROLL SLOWLY TO MAKE SURE YOU HAVE COMPLETE SURFACE CONTACT,

SMALL SIFTER → ← STENCILED POWDERED PATTERN

HOT PIECE

AND DON'T FORGET ABOUT REVERSING THE IMAGE SO THAT IT APPEARS "RIGHT".

Q: IF I WANT MY DESIGN TO WRAP ALL THE WAY AROUND MY PIECE, HOW BIG SHOULD I MAKE IT? **A.** REMEMBER THE GEOMETRIC FORMULA → $C = 2\pi r$ — OR SIMPLY MULTIPLY THE DIAMETER OF YOUR BUBBLE BY 3.1416 AND YOU SHOULD END UP WITH THE LENGTH YOUR DESIGN SHOULD BE. FOR THE MATHEMATICALLY CHALLENGED AMONG US, THERE EXISTS A SET OF CALIPERS WITH THIS RATIO ALREADY CALCULATED FOR YOU - WHERE YOU MEASURE THE DIAMETER WITH ONE END AND THE CIRCUMFERENCE IS GIVEN AT THE OTHER END. THEN IT'S JUST A MATTER TO GET YOUR BUBBLE TO FIT THE DESIGN OR VICE VERSA - THE DESIGN TO FIT YOUR BUBBLE. THE TOOL IS CALLED A "**PI DIVIDER**".

circumference = two × pi × radius

IF YOU'RE REALLY FOND OF YOUR DESIGN AND WANT TO REPRODUCE HUNDREDS OF OBJECTS WITH IT ON IT, YOU MAY WISH TO USE A GRAPHITE BLOCK OR PLATE WITH THE DESIGN ENGRAVED, MACHINED OR SANDBLASTED INTO IT. THEN YOU SIMPLY DUST THE CAVITIES AND GROOVES WITH POWDERS, WIPE-OFF THE EXCESS AND ROLL-UP THE DESIGN. **NOTE:** GRAPHITE CAN BE VERY MESSY TO WORK WITH. WHEN CARVING/ENGRAVING THIS MATERIAL, ALWAYS WEAR A RESPIRATOR! THE DUST IS VERY BAD TO BREATHE. ALSO, HAVE AVAILABLE SOME MEANS OF REMOVING & DISPOSING THE EXCESS DUST (eg. A VACUUM CLEANER WITH APPROPRIATE FILTERS). A GUARANTEED WAY TO PISS-OFF YOUR STUDIO MATES IS TO CARVE OR MACHINE GRAPHITE AND NOT CLEAN IT UP! :-: THIS STUFF FINDS IT WAY INTO THE SMALLEST NOOKS AND CRANNIES AND CAN BE A NIGHTMARE TO CLEAN UP! HOWEVER, NOTHING WORKS QUITE LIKE IT, AND IT MAY BE YOUR BEST BET IN YIELDING THE RESULTS YOU DESIRE. THE RELIEF NEED NOT BE TOO DEEP, CA. 1/4" OR LESS - YOU WANT THE GLASS TO BE ABLE TO PICK-UP THE POWDERS IN THE CAVITIES, AND AGAIN - DON'T FORGET TO REVERSE THE IMAGE IF NECESSARY.

CARVED GRAPHITE POWDERED PICK-UP

SIFTING POWDERS

YET ANOTHER METHOD OF POWDER APPLICATION IS BY DUSTING THE POWDERED COLOR OVER THE SURFACE OF THE HOT GLASS. USING A METAL-MESH (KITCHEN-STYLE) STRAINER ATTACHED TO A LONGER WOODEN HANDLE (THOSE PLASTIC HANDLES ARE TOO SHORT AND TEND TO GET HOT & MELT NEAR THE HEAT!) - THE POWDER IS LOADED IN IT AND TAPPED REPEATEDLY OVER THE HOT PARISON TO RELEASE A DUSTING OF COLOR. THE GLASS MUST BE HOT TO INSURE THAT THE POWDER WILL STICK TO IT. IT MAY TAKE SEVERAL REHEATS TO ACHIEVE AN EVEN-COATING AND COMPLETE DISTRIBUTION OF COLOR.

A RESPIRATOR (OR AT LEAST A PAPER DUST MASK) SHOULD BE WORN BY THE ASSISTANT DUSTING THE PIECE. IT'S A GOOD IDEA TO DO THIS WORK UNDER THE EXHAUST HOOD (NEAREST THE EXITING VENTILATION AND AWAY FROM PEOPLE). IF YOU ANTICIPATE DOING POWDERED PIECES WITH GREAT REGULARITY, I SUGGEST YOU TAKE THE TIME AND EFFORT TO MAKE A **POWDERING BOOTH**. THIS STRUCTURE IS DESIGNED TO WITHSTAND THE HEAT OF HOT GLASS AND ALLOW SPACE FOR THE PIPE AND ASSISTANT TO WORK COMFORTABLY AND SAFELY. THE BOOTH SHOULD SUCK-UP THE AIRBORN EXCESS, FILTERING IT AWAY SAFELY.

A POWDER BOOTH

PIECES MAY BE POWDERED AT ANY STAGE OF THE GLASS MAKING PROCESS. SOME ARTISTS PREFER TO DUST THEIR PIECES JUST PRIOR TO BOXING THEM. A LIGHT-TO-HEAVY COAT OF COLOR MAY ACCENTUATE THE OVERALL SURFACE DESIGN - AND HIGHLIGHT THE SCULPTURAL EFFECT OF HOT-WORKED GLASS.

SOME POWDERS **REDUCE** REALLY WELL, AND MAY 'SILVER' OR 'IRIDIZE' WHEN GIVEN THE PROPER ENVIORNMENT TO DO SO → EITHER CRANK-UP THE GAS GOING INTO YOUR GLORY HOLE, OR CUT-BACK ON IT'S SUPPLY AIR — AND EXPOSE YOUR PIECE TO 5-10 SECOND BLASTS OF THE GAS JUST PRIOR TO BOXING IT. THIS SHOULD BRING THE METALS TO THE SURFACE AND TURN YOUR GLASS NICE n' SHINY — IT MAY HOWEVER TAKE 3 OR 4 REHEATS TO GET THE SURFACE YOU DESIRE.

GRADATIONS OF COLOR ARE FAIRLY EASY TO ACHIEVE VIA THE POWDERING PROCESS. SIMPLY ROLL INTO OR DUST-ON A BAND OF COLOR WHERE YOU WANT IT — PLACING HIGHER CONCENTRATIONS OF THE POWDER (BY REPEATED REHEATS & REDUSTS) WHERE YOU NEED IT.

BLENDING TWO OR MORE POWDERED COLORS MAY YIELD INTERESTING RESULTS AS WELL. IT DOESN'T NECESSARILY WORK THE SAME WAY THAT COLORED PIGMENTS IN PAINT WORK, AND COMPATIBILITY MAY BECOME AN ISSUE TO DEAL WITH AS A RESULT. FEEL FREE TO EXPERIMENT! TRY DIFFERENT COMBINATIONS, MAKE COLOR SAMPLES, BLOW SOME TEST PIECES AND FIND OUT WHAT YOUR COLORS CAN DO FOR YOU!

THREADING POWDERED GLASS PIECES WITH CLEAR OR OTHER COLORS CAN YIELD INTERESTING PATTERNS AND OPTICAL EFFECTS (SEE PAGE 116 FOR TIPS ON THREADING). **REDUCING** THE POWDER ON THE SURFACE OF THE PIECE AND THEN THREADING IT WITH CLEAR GLASS IS ONE WAY. THIS MAY THEN BE GATHERED OVER RESULTING IN A FORM WITH AN OVERALL COLOR OF ONE INTENSITY AND A SPIRALING THREAD OF ANOTHER. OR YOU MIGHT TRY THREADING A DUSTED PARISON WITH CLEAR AND THEN STUFFING IT IN AN OPTIC MOLD TO CREATE A **WAVY** OR **VARIGATED** PATTERN.

OH, THE POSSIBILITIES HERE ARE ENDLESS. ... O.K. I'LL SUGGEST A COUPLE MORE.

QUENCHING A FRESHLY POWDERED PIECE INTO A BUCKET OF COLD WATER CAN PRODUCE TACTILE VISUALS AS WELL. FIRST, START WITH A FAIRLY THICK BUBBLE. THE BUBBLE MAY BE CLEAR, OR HAVE AN INTERIOR COLOR IF YOU SO DESIRE — AND THEN IT GETS A FAIRLY

HEAVY COATING OF POWDER BY EITHER ROLLING OR DUSTING IT ON. NEXT, IT'S HEATED UNTIL IT'S VERY HOT N' FLOPPY IN THE GLORY HOLE AND THEN THE WHOLE BUBBLE IS PLUNGED INTO A BUCKET OF COOL, CLEAN WATER — ALL THE WAY UP TO THE NECK OF THE PIECE — AND QUENCHED FOR SEVERAL SECONDS. REMOVE IT FROM THE WATER AND IMMEDIATLY **BLOW 'N' CAP** THE PIPE. THE INTERIOR OF THE GLASS SHOULD STILL BE HOT AND MOLTEN, WHEREAS THE EXTERIOR IS COLD AND CRACKED ALL OVER ITS SURFACE. WHEN BLOWN, THE INTERIOR BEGINS TO EXPAND, AS DO THE CRACKS ON THE OUTSIDE AND FISSURES BEGIN TO APPEAR. BE READY TO LET YOUR THUMB OFF THE END OF THE PIPE ONCE YOU NOTICE THE BUBBLE EXPANDING. YOU RISK BLOWING OUT ONE SIDE OR COLLAPSING THE BUBBLE BECAUSE IT'S TOO THIN, IF **YOU'RE** NOT CAREFUL. IT MAY TAKE CONSIDERABLE BACK PRESSURE TO GET THE THING TO EXPAND, SO **PUFF HARD!** AVOID REHEATING THE BUBBLE TOO MUCH AS THE CRACKS **TEND** TO MELT BACK TOGETHER — THUS REDUCING YOUR CRACKLED-EFFECT. BUT ONCE THE FISSURES ARE APPARENT ENOUGH → THEY'RE THERE TO STAY! AND YOU MAY EITHER GATHER OVER THE PARISON TO **CASE** YOUR INTERESTING PATTERN OR SIMPLY BLOW IT OUT TO IT'S FINAL FORM.

fig. 128 A QUENCHED VASE

SCAVO, IS ANOTHER FORM OF SURFACE DECORATION WHICH CAN GIVE YOUR PIECES THAT INSTANT ANTIQUITY FEEL AND LOOK. IT IS APPLIED JUST PRIOR TO BOXING THE PIECE SINCE THE CORROSIVE NATURE OF THE SUBSTANCE WILL EAT YOUR PUNTY ALIVE. IN ORDER FOR SCAVO TO STICK, IT MUST BE 'FIRED-ON' IN THE GLORY HOLE. IT MAY TAKE TWO OR THREE (OR MORE) DUSTINGS AND REHEATS TO GET THE SURFACE TEXTURE AND DENSITY YOU DESIRE. **NOTE:** SCAVO IS A HAZARDOUS CHEMICAL COMPOUND. IT MUST BE HANDLED, MIXED, STORED AND APPLIED WITH CARE. ALWAYS WEAR A RESPIRATOR OR DUST MASK WHEN MIXING AND APPLYING SCAVO! DO NOT APPLY SCAVO TO ANY FOOD BEARING SURFACES. USE AT YOUR OWN RISK! THE CRUSTY CORROSIVE SURFACE THAT SCAVO PRODUCES CAN GIVE YOUR WORK THAT FRESH, DUG-UP LOOK ASSOCIATED WITH ANCIENT GLASSES WHICH HAVE UNDERGONE VARIOUS STAGES OF DECOMPOSITION DUE TO UNSTABLE GLASS CHEMISTRY OR REACTIONS TO THE SOIL OR ENVIORNMENT IN WHICH THEY WERE FOUND.

BASE FORMULA
3 PARTS ⇒ POTASSIUM NITRATE
1 PART ⇒ WHITING (Calcium Carbonate)
1 PART ⇒ WOOD ASH

"+"

ADDITIONS FOR COLOR SPOTS
ADD ONLY ONE AND IN SMALL QUANTIES
- TIN OXIDE (WHITE SPOTS)
- MANGANESE (PURPLE)
- POTASSIUM CARBONATE
- LEAD (COOL SPOTS & TOXIC TOO!)

ADDITIONAL CHEMICALS (FLAVORING AGENTS)
- BORAX
- LIME (WHITENER)
- POTASSIUM BICHROMATE (YELLOWERD)
- SODA ASH (FLUX & WHITENER)
- CHROME OXIDE (YELLOWER)
- STANNOUS CHLORIDE (BIG BITE — METALLIC)

= **SCAVO**

THANKS TO **RIK ALLEN** FOR HIS HELP AND RESEARCH INTO THE ABOVE FORMULA, AND PASSING IT ON TO YOU HERE.

FRITS

NO,... NOT YOU FRITZ!

Take a Kugler rod — smash it into a b'zillion pieces and you end up with **FRIT**. Frit is essentially a crushed form of color rod that looks suprisingly alot like aquarium gravel. It is sifted through various screens to yield particles of like-size, available from "0" to "4" (zero being the smallest) from your local color distributor. Or if you only need a small quantity of frit, you can smash-up any color rod with a **COLOR CRUSHER**. →
Crushing color in this manner is noisy, dusty and potentially **HAZARDOUS** → so do it outdoors or away from people. Wear safety glasses, a dust mask and ear protection to shield yourself from the nuisances produced by this process.

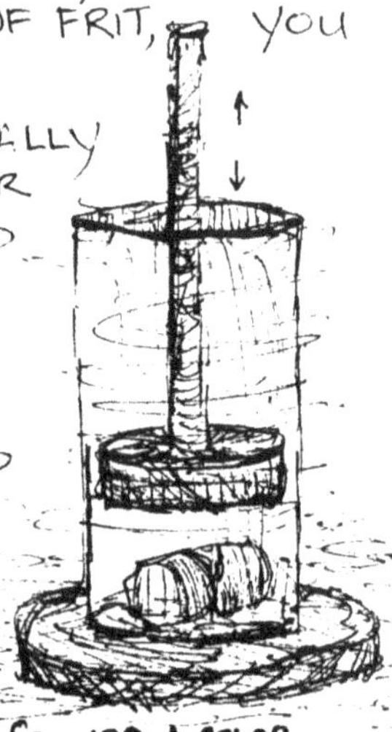

Another method of producing frit is to thermal shock the glass into small pieces. One way to do this is by preheating your Kugler to ca. 900°F and tossing it into a bucket of cold water. It should crack and chill the glass into small pieces. Should you wish clear frit (or if you have a colored glass furnace) you may simply ladle or gather right out of the furnace straight into a metal bucket (stainless steel is preferred) of cold water. After it has cooled, the glass may be strained and sifted through screens of various mesh sizes to obtain frit with consistent size.

fig. 129 A COLOR CRUSHER

You may lay-out the frit in rows, piles, or whatever arrangement suits your fancy, on the marver — and simply roll or lay your hot glass into it to pick it up. Again, the hotter the glass is — the more frit will adhere to it. So it may take several reheats to get the density and coverage you desire. Preheating the color by working-off a hot plate or steel plate over a gas burner (as in **fig. B. page 108**) will insure better adhesion and that you pick up more frit.

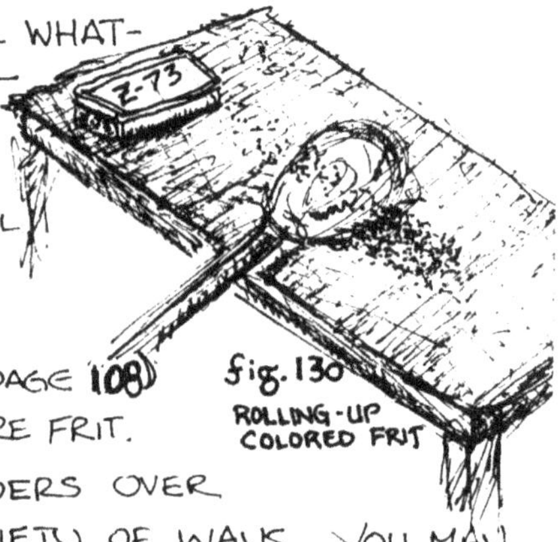

fig. 130 ROLLING-UP COLORED FRIT

Naturally you may combine frits and powders over and under layers of clear in an infinite variety of ways. You may apply the frit as colored bits, handles or thread it on — to produce interesting patterns and enhance your overall design. It's faster and easier to heat-up colored frit than colored rod which makes it more attractive to production-style work where timing is everything. It is, of course, not quite as dense as colored rod — and may have a mottled appearance if it is not laid-on too thick, or completely melted-in.

Feel free to experiment with transparent and opaque frits — **MIX OR MATCH** to a palette that pleases you. See what effect melting the color in has versus leaving it semi-cold and chunky. Maybe the **RAISED TEXTURE PLUS COLOR** is something your aesthetic sense **DESIRES**, and which works best with your design.

SHARDS

Another method of introducing color **ON** or **IN** a piece of blown glass is with shards. Shards may be simply broken chunks of glass from a previous **FLOOR MODEL** — or can be deliberate elements created for specific effects and color combinations. They can produce an organic feel to your work, or offer abstract color-fields which may then be combined with threads, murrines or any other color technique(s) to yield unique one-of-a-kind 'masterpieces'.

BEGIN FIRST BY HAVING A PLAN. Design and draw what it is you want to make, and how you propose to integrate the shards. Ask yourself these questions: Will they be the focus of the piece or exist as backround decoration? Are they to remain tactile and above the surface, or melted & marvered-in? Or should the shards get **CASED** below the surface of the glass? Will the colors accent or contrast the other colors within the piece?...Once you've determined what it is your piece should look like, you then need to figger-out how to pull it off.

fig-131 Picking up shards.

There are several methods to producing shards, as well as ways of applying them. The fastest and most immediate is to pick-up a chunk of color on a blowpipe ⇒ heat it up and blow it into a thin bubble — anywhere from a softball to basketball size. Allow the bubble to cool somewhat and then smash the bubble with the back of your jacks or a hammer or similar tool. The resulting thin shards may then be laid out on the marver (or preheated on a hot plate or in a pick-up oven) and picked-up on a hot bubble — the same as if you were picking-up frit or powder — i.e. **the hotter the bubble is, the more glass shards will stick to it.** In fact, a gather straight out of the furnace is your best bet for complete shard pick-up.

You may enhance the above technique by doing overlays of different colors and then blowing them out. You then end up with shards with interior and exterior colors which may yield some fascinating patterns when picked-up and blown out on your bubble.

As stated above, you may utilize old floor models for a source for your shards. Ever wonder what to do with those platters you made where the **PUNTY** broke out of? Here's a perfect opportunity to recycle them back into something new. If you find that the curvilinear nature of blown shards are trapping too many air bubbles when you try picking them up, you may wish to go

113

The extra step and **SLUMP** those pieces flat first. Simply lay the shards on a freshly washed kiln-shelf (washed with kiln wash that is!) in an available annealer. Ramp the kiln up to 1350°F and keep an eye on it every few minutes (once it's attained temperature). Allow the pieces to slump flat and then vent the kiln to annealing temperature and ramp it down. If the pieces are thin enough you can probably get by by just shutting the kiln off and allowing it to cool naturally. Or if the pieces are thicker, you may opt to send them through a short annealing cycle. It's also possible to **FUSE** your shards together in this fashion as well.

Yet another shard technique is to blow **RONDELS** with contrasting underlay/overlay colors. Once annealed, the rondels may be cut with a glass cutter or diamond saw into shapes of predetermined sizes. These shapes may then become the subject of your piece. Or you may go one step further and **SANDBLAST** or **ENGRAVE IMAGERY** on those shards. It's possible to enamel them and fire them on in the annealer or pick-up oven just before you apply them. You can also decorate your shards with **PARADISE PAINTS** and obtain some specific imagery via that process.

fig. 132 SHARDS PREHEATING; PICK-UP

Again, preheating your shards on a hot plate/burner or in a pick-up oven will insure you won't lose any to thermal shock from your hot bubble. Front-loading annealers work well for this process too. Just ramp the kiln up to annealing temp. (after carefully arranging them on a kiln shelf) and hold them there until you're ready with your bubble. Just prior to picking them up (ca. 10 minutes) crank the annealer up another 50°F → this also helps reduce the thermal shock and may prevent your shards from becoming even smaller shards! (Don't forget to turn the annealer back down after you're done!).

Other items such as murrines, cane, threads, stringers may be picked-up in a similar fashion. If you're skilled at **LAMPWORKING**, you can also pre-make objects on the torch (out of compatible furnace glass &/or colors) and pick 'em up as well. If you expect to be making many pieces via this process, an electric pick-up kiln may help facilitate the whole procedure and insure greater success.

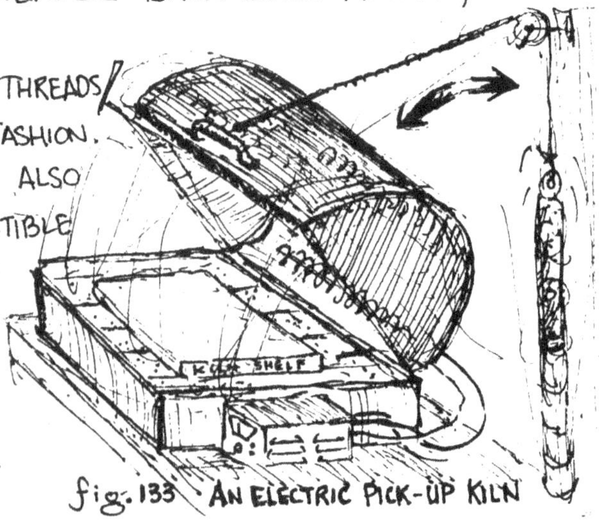

fig. 133 AN ELECTRIC PICK-UP KILN

Factors Effecting The Outcome of Pick-ups:

① **HEAT** ⇒ If your bubble is not hot enough, the pick-up may not adhere to it. *Solution* ↝ Get it hotter and maybe preheat your pick-up.

② **THERMAL SHOCK** ⇒ If your pick-up's are cracking when you go to apply them — the temperature difference between the bubble and pick-up maybe too great and thermal shock occurs. *Solution* ↝ Pre-heat the pick-up even more.

③ **BUBBLE AND SHARD THICKNESS** ⇒ The thicker the pick-up is, the more influence it will have on the behavior of your bubble and your ability to blow it out. Conversely, the thinner your bubble is, the more influence (and distortion) the pick-up may have on it. *Solution* ↝ Play it safe and try to keep your bubble on the thick side, unless you like the distortion(s) that the pick-up(s) generate.

④ **COLOR** ⇒ Certain colors blow-out at different rates. This effect is visible in shards and pick-ups where there are underlays and overlays sandwiching clear → the edge of the shard (or pick-up) seems almost to seperate as one color blows-out or expands faster than another. *Solution* ↝ This may be an effect you like. It can contribute an interesting design element to your work. Experiment with different color combinations as well as color applications to enhance or limit this effect. Also the density of the color can have an influence on your results → The more color you have in the pick-up, the more you'll be able to blow it out without losing detail and color saturation.

⑤ **SIZE** ⇒ Both the size of the bubble and size of the pick-up play important roles in the developent and execution of your work. The larger the pick-up-to-bubble size ratio is, the more influence and effect the pick-up will have on your bubble. The amount to which the bubble is blown-out and worked, have tremendous impact on the appearance of the pick-up → i.e. **The thinner and larger you expand your bubble the less detail and color density you'll retain.** Also, the natural effect of a rotating blowpipe and the forces of gravity and thermal dynamics can easily distort the imagery and form of your pick-up. *Solution* ↝ If you wish to retain the crispness and detail of your pick-up → limit the amount of work you do to your piece after you've applied it. The more you marver, paper or blow your piece, the more melted-in and possibly distorted your shard or pick-up will be.

Now, if your pick-up is larger than your bubble, and you wish for it to wrap around your piece, you can try the following:

① PICK-UP SHARD ② REHEAT & MELT-IN ③ USE A TORCH IF NECESSARY... ④ MARVER IT IN! (ROCK IT)

Preheat your pick-up. ① When you go to pick-up your pick-up → have your bubble fairly thick and pretty hot → lay it on the pick-up in the center and rock slightly the blowpipe to the right & left (to gain as much surface area as you can make contact with). ② Reheat immediatly in the glory hole. Do not rotate the pipe. Keep your pick-up on top so as to allow gravity and heat to start wrapping the pick-up around your bubble for you. ③ Either marver the rest of the pick-up on using the rocking motion back n' forth, or continue to coax the pick-up on by using a torch and tweezers → heating and guiding your design on. ④ Finish up by marvering your pick-up on smooth and re-establishing your bubble back on-center. Finish the piece as desired.

In conclusion, shards and pick-ups can offer the aspiring glass artist and designer a wide variety of potential surface decoration and visual vocabulary. The studio glass pioneer and educator JOEL PHILIP MEYERS has been successfully integrating shards into his sculptures for decades. Check out his work, and also the blown work of PAUL MARIONI for examples of this technique. In addition, DALE CHIHULY'S "BASKET" series exemplify the colors and textures that are possible utilizing this approach to color and surface application.

THREADING

From ancient core-formed vessels to the works of TIFFANY, CHIHULY and MOORE, the thread has been the subject of color decoration for centuries of glassmakers. This relatively simple technique can be used to generate a vast number of different color designs.

THREADED CORE-FORMED AMPHORISKOS 2nd-1st C. B.C.

Equipped with a set of rollers mounted on the bench or marver or other convienent accessible area you may create a 'machine-like' thread pattern on your parison. The rollers are often clamped (with "C" clamps or vice-grips) to the arms of the bench almost parallel to each other and perpendicular to the blowpipe. The set of rollers closest to the parison will be slightly off-set to create a tracking movement as the pipe is rotated. You'll notice if adjusted one way the pipe may track left-to-right → with the greater the angle adjustment, the larger the distance the pipe will track when rotated. Use a piece of chalk (held stationary) against the neck of the pipe to check the tracking and adjust as necessary to make tighter or wider threads. Notice also, that turning the pipe clockwise or counter-clockwise will make it track left-to-right or right-to-left, so adjust and turn in a manner that is most com-

TOUCH UP ON NECK FIRST

WITH CHALK CHECK AND ADJUST TRACKING

TURN

fortable for you and your assistant, and try to remember in which direction to turn it when it comes time to apply the thread!

Much of the success in getting 'good thread' depends on how hot the bit of color is, speed at which the pipe is turned and the hand-to-eye coordination of the gaffer AND assistant. Preparing the color bit is the first step and perhaps the most crucial one in the threading process. Whether you use rod, frit, powder, or just clear for your thread, the shape and temperature of the bit is the same. Figures 134-136 show the shape-up process for using colored rod as the source of the thread. The color is picked-up on a punty, heated just inside the glory hole door and then marvered horizontal first, (to chill and stabilize the back half of the bit) followed by a 'tip-up' manuver where you raise your hands and marver at an angle to shape the color into a cone form. This may take several reheats depending on the size of the bit and how hot your glory hole is. During this reheating and marvering process the gaffer may be preparing the bubble (or object) to be threaded.

fig. 134 CHILL HERE
fig. 135 SHAPE...
fig. 136 AND POINT IT UP! 

Its' important that the bit is heated thoroughly. Uneven heating and marvering will result in a bit which may come off in one big clump instead of one even thread. Take the extra minute or two to make sure the bit's hot-to-the core. Some gaffers also prefer that the bit is marv'ed back up on the punty somewhat — to provide a more stable bit, so check with the boss to see how they like it.

The parison should be warm, not too hot n' floppy as to be difficult to maintain on center, and not too cold → otherwise the thread won't stick ~ it needs to be JUST RIGHT (hint: practice practice practice). A yoke may be placed behind the bench to help stabilize the punty while threading.

The bit is touched-up on the moile first, and then pulled back several inches to initiate the threading process. As soon as the color makes contact the gaffer begins to turn the pipe. The open-palm technique of turning seems to work well in providing a consistent and (hopefully) uninterrupted rotation. For thicker threads turn slower, for thinner ones vice-versa. The distance between the bit and the piece also plays a crucial role in the results. The greater the distance, the more time and space the thread has to cool before hitting the piece. This distance also acts as a guage for the gaffer as to how fast to turn the pipe to get the thickness of thread he/she desires. Audible clues such as "pull back" or "turn faster" between the assistant and gaffer should be given to insure successful threading. If your pipe is tracking correctly, the color bit is touched-up, pulled back and held as stationary as possible while the parison spins by. In order to maintain a consistent thread it may be necessary to move closer or further back from the piece as the thread goes on, so pay atten-

fig 137 THREAD IT ON.

TION! ONCE THE PIECE IS COMPLETELY THREADED, THE BIT MAY BE YANKED QUICKLY BACKWARDS TO BREAK AWAY CLEAN, OR THE COLOR MAY BE SNIPPED WITH SOME STRAIGHT SHEARS CLOSE TO THE PIECE.

IMMEDIATELY AFTER APPLYING THE THREADS YOU'LL WANT TO REHEAT THE PARISON TO MELT THE THREADS ONTO THE SURFACE, WHICH WILL PREVENT THEM FROM POPPING OFF. YOU THEN HAVE SEVERAL OPTIONS ON HOW TO PROCEED. YOU MAY ELECT TO CONTINUE TO BLOW THE OBJECT OUT TO ITS FINAL FORM, OR ADD MORE THREADS, OR AUGMENT THE THREADED PATTERN VIA OTHER TECHNIQUES SUCH AS: **COMBING** (OR 'FEATHERING'), **OPTIC MOLDING**, OR **OFF-CENTER WRAPPING** AS OUTLINED BELOW.

fig. 138

COMBING GLASS THAT HAS BEEN THREADED IS A TECHNIQUE WHICH HAS BEEN FASCINATING GLASSMAKERS FOR THOUSANDS OF YEARS (AND BORING SOME TO TEARS!). ASSOCIATED WITH THE **ART NOUVEAU** MOVEMENT AND THE LIKES OF **TIFFANY** AND **GALLÉ**, THIS TECHNIQUE IS FAIRLY SIMPLE TO ACQUIRE AND RESULTS COME QUICKLY. EVEN IMPERFECT ONES LOOK GOOD! ONCE THE SKIN OF THE BUBBLE IS NICE N' HOT AFTER REHEATING IN THE GLORY HOLE (THE COLORED THREAD(S) WILL APPEAR BRIGHT ORANGE) HEAD OVER TO THE BENCH AND BEGIN COMBING. A SCRATCH AWL OR SIMILAR POINTED TOOL WITH A HOOK-SHAPE BENT AT THE TIP WORKS WELL FOR THIS PROCESS ⇒

YOU MAY START AT THE BOTTOM OF THE PIECE (OR THE TOP - IT'S A MATTER OF PERSONAL PREFERENCE) AND SCRATCH/PULL THE TOP LAYER OF GLASS ALL THE WAY UP TO THE NECK. FLIP THE PIECE OVER AND COMB THE OPPOSITE SIDE. IT MAY BE NECESSARY TO REHEAT BETWEEN EACH COMB MOVEMENT, WHICH MAY GIVE YOU AN OPPORTUNITY TO REALIGN THE BUBBLE BACK ON-CENTER.

YOU MAY ALSO COMB IN THE OPPOSITE DIRECTION AND/OR ALTERNATE TO CREATE EVEN MORE COMPLICATED PATTERNS (SEE THE NEXT PAGE). TRY THEM ALL!

fig. 139

fig. 140

fig. 141

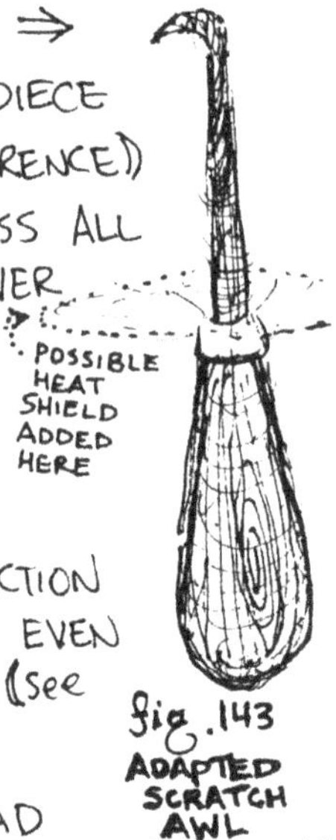

POSSIBLE HEAT SHIELD ADDED HERE

fig. 143 ADAPTED SCRATCH AWL FOR COMBING

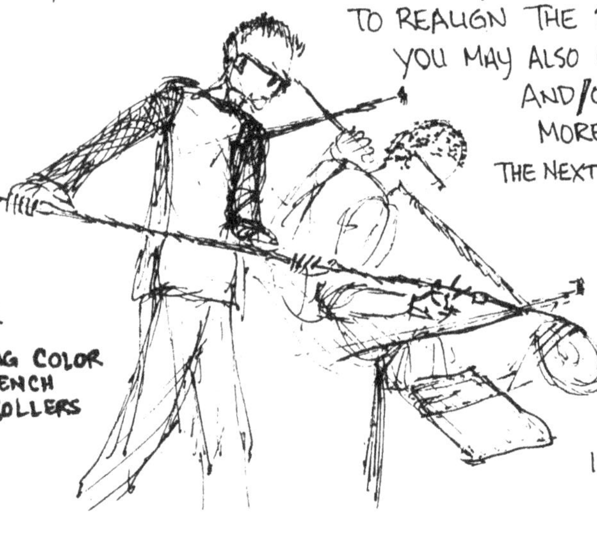

fig 142 THREADING COLOR AT THE BENCH WITHOUT ROLLERS

IT IS POSSIBLE TO THREAD YOUR PIECE AT THE BENCH WITHOUT THE AID OF ROLLERS. YOU ARE, HOWEVER, LIMITED BY THE LENGTH OF THE BENCH ARMS. YOU MAY END UP HITTING THE END OF THE RAILS BEFORE YOU GET THE WHOLE PIECE WRAPPED, IN WHICH CASE YOU DO YOUR BEST TO

CONTINUE ROTATING AGAINST THE RAIL-STOP AND FINISH UP THE THREAD (SEE FIG. 142 ON THE PREVIOUS PAGE). IT'S A LITTLE TRICKIER TO GET CONSISTENT THREADS THIS WAY, BUT NOT IMPOSSIBLE. TIMING, PRACTICE AND PERSEVERANCE WILL SEE YOU THROUGH.

VARIATIONS OF THE THREADED BUBBLE

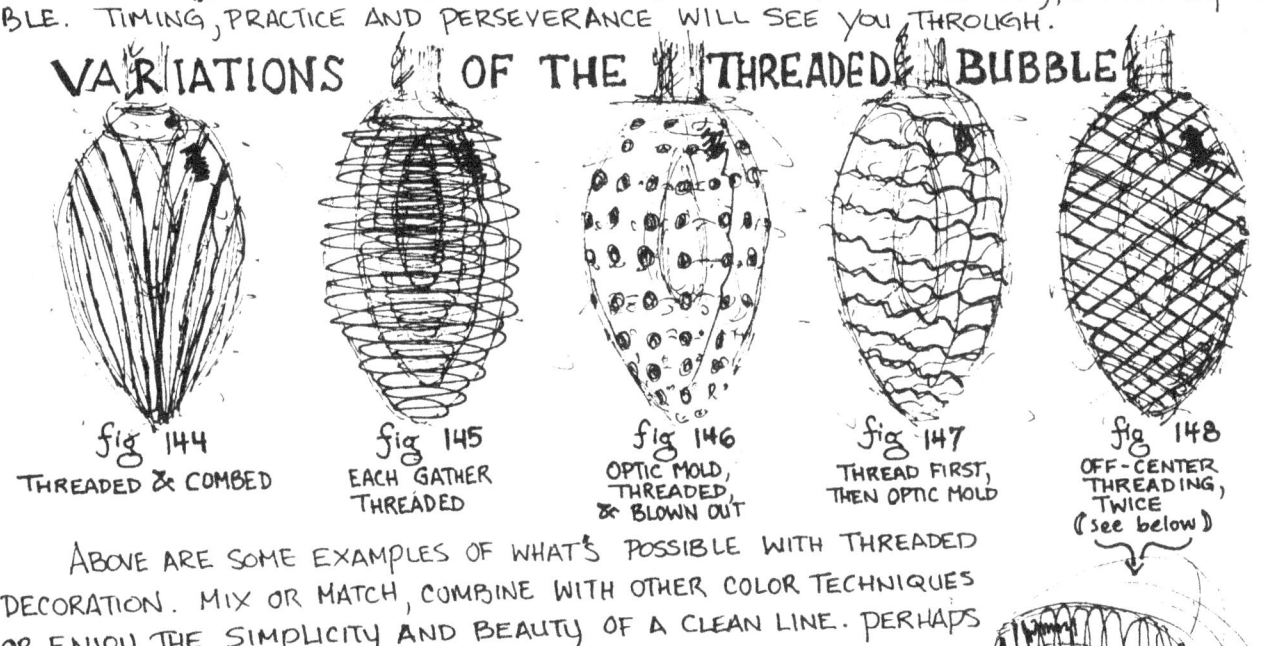

fig 144 — THREADED & COMBED
fig 145 — EACH GATHER THREADED
fig 146 — OPTIC MOLD, THREADED, & BLOWN OUT
fig 147 — THREAD FIRST, THEN OPTIC MOLD
fig 148 — OFF-CENTER THREADING, TWICE (see below)

ABOVE ARE SOME EXAMPLES OF WHAT'S POSSIBLE WITH THREADED DECORATION. MIX OR MATCH, COMBINE WITH OTHER COLOR TECHNIQUES OR ENJOY THE SIMPLICITY AND BEAUTY OF A CLEAN LINE. PERHAPS THE MOST CHALLENGING DESIGN IS THE **OFF-CENTER WRAP**, fig.s 149-151, WHERE YOU ALLOW YOUR BUBBLE TO DELIBERATELY FALL WAY OFF-CENTER AND THEN ATTEMPT TO THREAD A STRAIGHT LINE ON IT, (fig 149). TURNING AN OFF-CENTER BUBBLE FEELS AWKWARD AND UNNATURAL. YOU MAY TRY USING A YOKE TO STABILIZE THE COLOR BIT-PUNTY AND DO YOUR BEST TO THREAD THE COLOR ON EVENLY. AFTERWARDS, DURING YOUR NEXT REHEAT, YOU AGAIN STOP THE PIPE ROTATION AND ALLOW THE BUBBLE TO FALL OFF-CENTER IN THE OPPOSITE DIRECTION OF THE FIRST (fig 150). THIS THEN WILL GET A SECOND WRAP OF THE SAME COLOR (OR A DIFFERENT ONE IF YOU CHOOSE), (fig 151) WHICH SHOULD CREATE AN INTERESTING CRISS-CROSS PATTERN. THE BUBBLE THEN IS REHEATED, REALIGNED (BY FALLING BACK ON-CENTER) AND THEN BLOWN OUT.

fig 149 — 1ST: LET FALL OFF CENTER, THEN THREAD
fig 150 — NEXT: LET FALL OFF CENTER AGAIN OPPOSITE SIDE 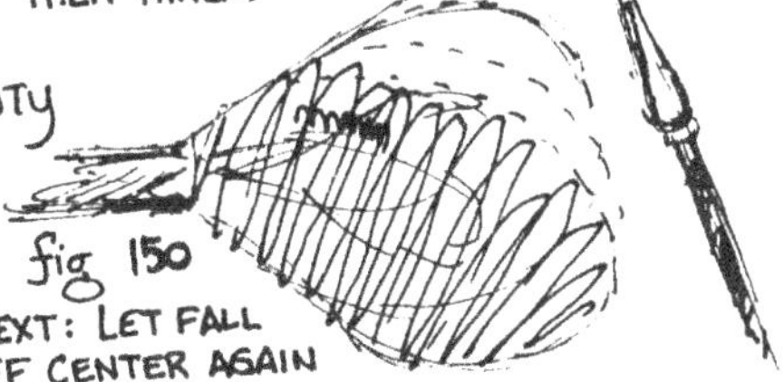
fig 151 — APPLY SECOND THREAD 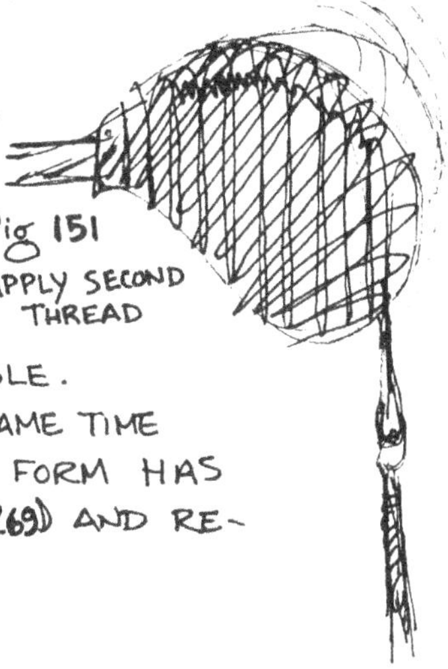

THE PREVIOUS EXAMPLES OF THE THREADED GLASS PARISON ARE JUST THE TIP OF THE ICEBURG OF WHAT'S POSSIBLE. EXPERIMENT. TRY WRAPPING TWO OR MORE COLORS AT THE SAME TIME WITH THE SAME BIT. SEE WHAT EFFECT FLATTENING YOUR FORM HAS ON THE DESIGN. OR TRY A MONTAGE TECHNIQUE (PAGE 269) AND REVERSE THE AXIS OF THE BUBBLE AFTER THREADING.

CANE DRAWING

This color technique offers the hot glassworker an opportunity to apply imagery and words directly to the surface of the glass. Essentially it is a form of **LAMPWORKING**. A torch is used to melt thin rods of color onto a hot piece of glass → blown or solid. You may use a simple hand held propane torch (available from most hardware stores → the kind with the electronic starter are really convenient and work well), or a more sophisticated oxy-propane set-up with a concentrated tip (small flame) if it's available. Cane approximately the thickness of spaghetti seem best suited for drawing — they heat up fast and are easy to make. You can pull oodles of cane suitable for drawing using the traditional **FILIGRANA** method (page 167), or create short pieces fairly quickly by heating small chunks of color on a punty and stretching them out with diamond shears → either with the help of a partner or all by yourself.

Once you have all your color ready, and an idea of what you want to draw on the piece, you can procede to make the piece. Thick pieces seem to hold up to the multiple reheats necessary in creating an image better than thin pieces, so you may start by making a fairly thick blank. The closer to the finished product you can blow it the less distortion or stretching of the imagery will occur. Pass it off to your assistant.

Begin by pre-heating the cane, moving the tip of the cane in and out of the path of the torch flame. As soon as it exhibits some movement (it may 'ball-up' a little bit) you can fire it on to the surface. The torch flame should be aimed first at the cane and then the piece. Adjust your angle of fire if it seems to be taking a long time to heat-up. The color should melt on fairly quickly if you're doing it correctly. You can continue to 'feed' the color on the surface in this manner until it's necessary to take a reheat or flash. If you're cane gets stuck on the surface, just blast the contact point with the torch and pull — the cane should come free. Also, it's nice to have pieces of cane in excess of 12 inches or more to keep your hands from bar-b-queing from the radiant heat. It's amazing how much thin cane you can draw on the surface — so pull lots of 'stock' if you plan on using this technique frequently. NOTE ⇒ If your cane goes on too thin, it may shrivel-up and disappear during your next reheat ∴. Also, if you overheat your bubble it may distort your imagery or text. Blowing the piece out or casing the design may also have an adverse or positive effect on the final product — depending on your viewpoint. Try a couple of small test pieces and see what it can do for you. Also you might look up the early colloborative works of **FLORA MACE** and **JOEY KIRKPATRICK** for excellent examples of this technique.

INCALMO

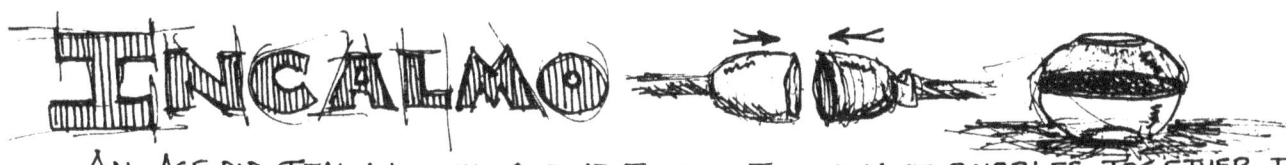

An age-old Italian technique of joining two or more bubbles together to form one piece. Some of the best known examples of this process are the vessels of **Sonja Blomdahl** and the goblets of **Lino Tagliapietra**. There are several slightly different approaches to achieving this form although the principle remains the same. Two benches, two glory holes, two blowpipes and at least two assistants are recommended. Also a set of calipers (or some type measuring device) are necessary to guage bubble diameters — so have those handy as well.

Transparent colors seem to work best for this technique. The transmitted light that you get, on top of the interplay of colors in the form are heightened visually by the clear seam that join the two bubbles together. Of course, opaque colors work well too, but the effect is different.

Let's say for example, you'd like a vessel with a **RED TOP** and **YELLOW BOTTOM**. Pipe #one can pick up a chunk o' red and pipe #two can pick-up a chunk of yellow. Each pipe will take 3 or 4 gathers of clear (or however many you'd like) on top of the color. They should be blocked and blown-out to achieve even wall thickness. Since pipe #1 has the red, it is not necessary to neck it at this point (but you can if you'd like!), however pipe #2 **WILL** require a break-away point — therefore a tight neckline is desireable.

In order to join the two bubbles together, you'll need to open the ends of them. There are two different methods of accomplishing this. One way (pictured at the left) is to tweeze open the end and the other (shown in the following pages) is to neck a small knob off the end, break it off and open it that way. Both methods work well, so choose the one you feel most comfortable with.

To tweeze open the end, heat just the very tip of your bubble in the glory hole. The glass must be very hot in order for this to work. Back at the bench, the tweezers are closed together, inserted into the center of the tip slightly, then immediately allowed to spring open an inch or so while momentarily stopping the rotation of the blowpipe (fig Ⓐ). This step is repeated rapidly three or four (or more) times until the glass has been stretched so thin that an opening is created or the tweezers can easily poke through it. Once you break on through, you may reheat the lip and procede to open up the piece with the jacks. You may also trim the lip as well, if desired prior to opening the 'cup' all the way.

The lip then may be paddled smooth to even it up and aid in thickening

UP THE LIP AS WELL. (SEE BELOW). AT THE SAME TIME THIS IS HAPPENING TO PIPE #1, PIPE #2 SHOULD BE HAVING THE SAME TREATMENT DONE TO IT, SO THAT THE TWO PIECES MAY BE JOINED WHILE BOTH LIPS ARE HOT AND NOT MUCH TIME IS WASTED.

CALIPERS ARE USED TO MEASURE THE OUTSIDE DIAMETERS OF THE TWO CUPS. ADJUSTMENTS ARE MADE, i.e. PIPE #2 MAY HAVE TO OPEN OR CLOSE-DOWN THE LIP SO AS TO MATCH PIPE #1's DIAMETER. YOU MAY USE THE JACKS TO OPEN IT UP FURTHER OR SOME NEWSPAPER TO SHAPE AND SHRINK THE DIAMETER TO THE RIGHT SIZE. IF YOU DON'T HAVE CALIPERS ON HAND, YOU CAN ALWAYS CHECK THE SIZE BY BRINGING THE TWO LIPS CLOSE TOGETHER AND EYE-BALL IT FROM THERE.

ONCE THE OPENINGS MATCH-UP, YOU CAN JOIN THE TWO. FIRST, FLASH BOTH PIECES AND THEN CONCENTRATE ON HEATING JUST THE LIPS. AS SOON AS THEY HAVE A GLOWING SOFT-NESS, PIPE #1 SITS AT THE BENCH (USUALLY THE GAFFER) AND PIPE #2 IS BROUGHT OVER AS THOUGH YOU WERE PUNTYING-UP. THE GAFFER GRABS PIPE #2 WITH THE DIAMOND SHEARS (fig 152 below), ROTATION OF THE PIPES STOP MOMENTARILY AS THE LIPS ARE JOINED TOGETHER. ONE WAY TO INSURE YOU HIT-THE-MARK AND GET A COMPLETE UNION IS TO BRING PIPE #2 IN AT A SLIGHT ANGLE (THE ASSISTANTS HANDS ARE LOWERED A LITTLE) AND TOUCH-UP FIRST AT THE BOTTOM. THE PIPE IS THEN BROUGHT-UP EVEN AND PARALLEL WITH THE GAFFERS, THERE-BY COMPLETING THE SEAL.

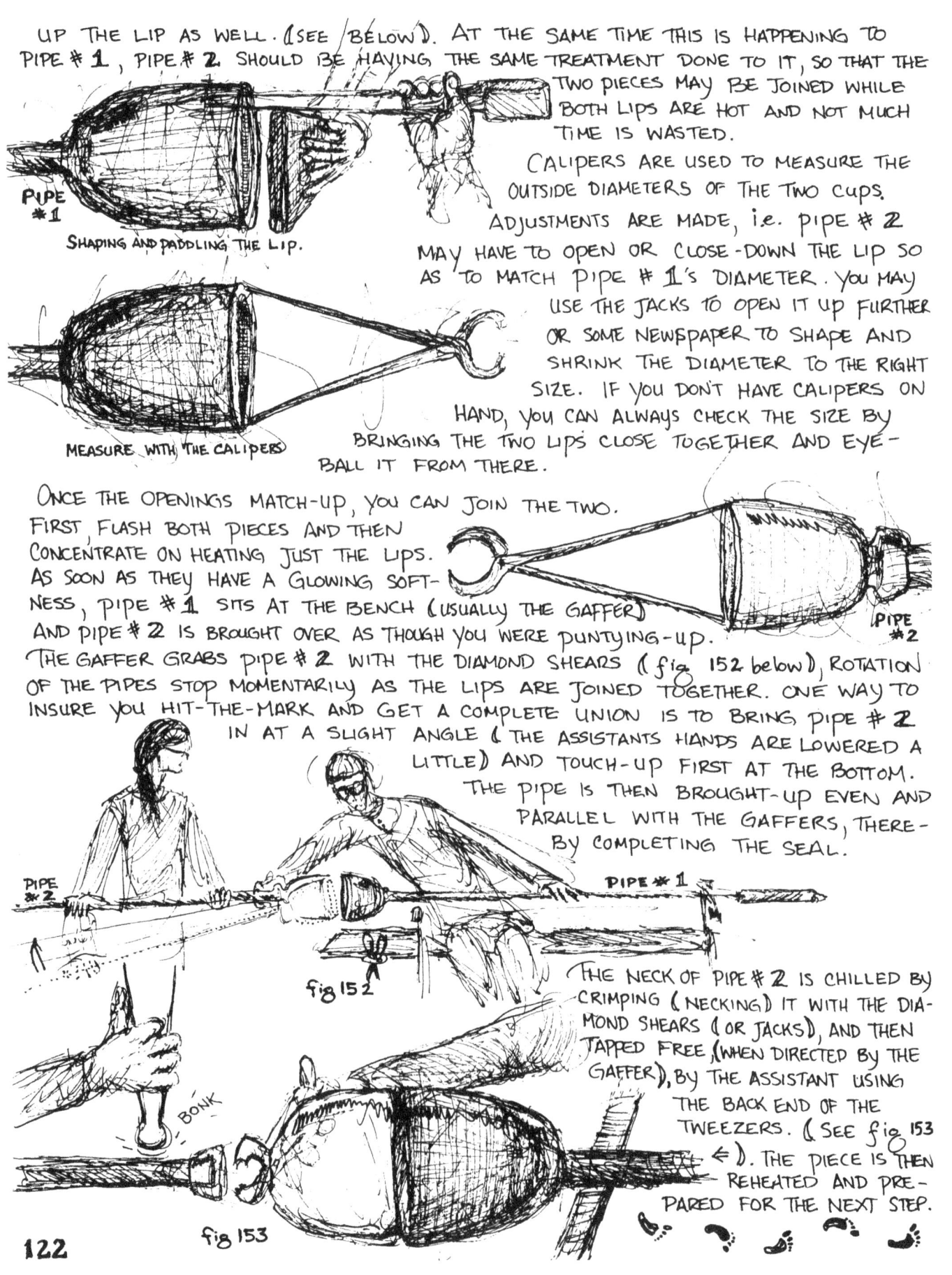

PIPE #1 — Shaping and paddling the lip.
Measure with the calipers
PIPE #2
fig 152
fig 153
BONK

THE NECK OF PIPE #2 IS CHILLED BY CRIMPING (NECKING) IT WITH THE DIA-MOND SHEARS (OR JACKS), AND THEN TAPPED FREE, (WHEN DIRECTED BY THE GAFFER), BY THE ASSISTANT USING THE BACK END OF THE TWEEZERS. (SEE fig 153 ←). THE PIECE IS THEN REHEATED AND PRE-PARED FOR THE NEXT STEP.

The next step is to make certain that you have a complete seal where the bubbles are joined. After the piece is heated, sit back at the bench, have one assistant cap the end of pipe #1 while another assistant blows in the end with a soffietta,

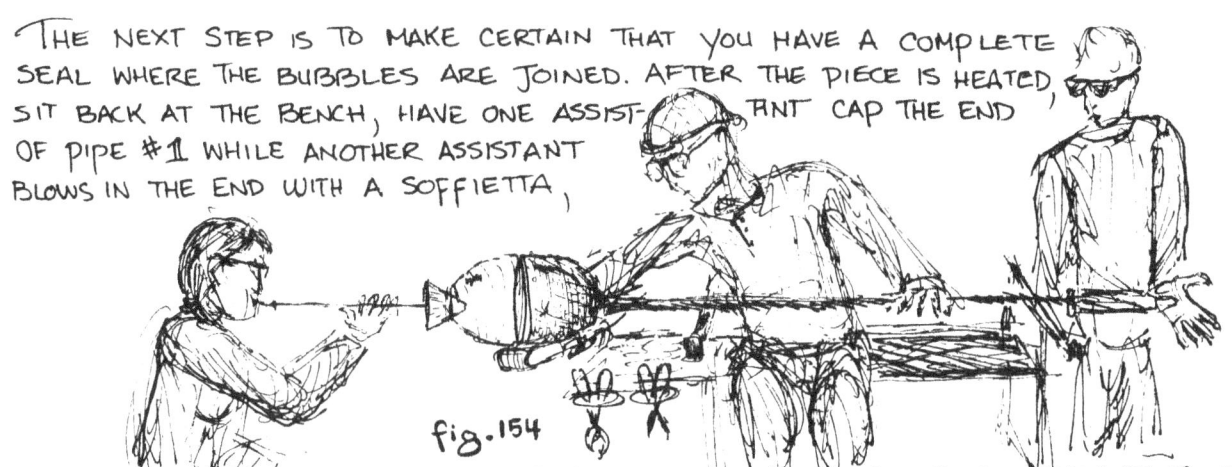

fig. 154

and at the same time the gaffer can smooth the seam with the back of the jacks listening for any escaping air out of a tell tale hole. If you do find a hole, you may try reheating that area again and repeating the previous step, 'marvering' that area smooth and blowing simultaneously with the soffietta while the other end is capped.

Once you have the two bubbles sealed you can either open-up the end and attach another bubble in the same manner, or close it down and blow the piece out. ← The bottom of the piece is reheated and either marvered to a point and closed that way (helpful if your design/form requires a conical-tapered bottom), or the hole may be tweezed, necked and cut-off as shown in fig. 155-157 to the left.

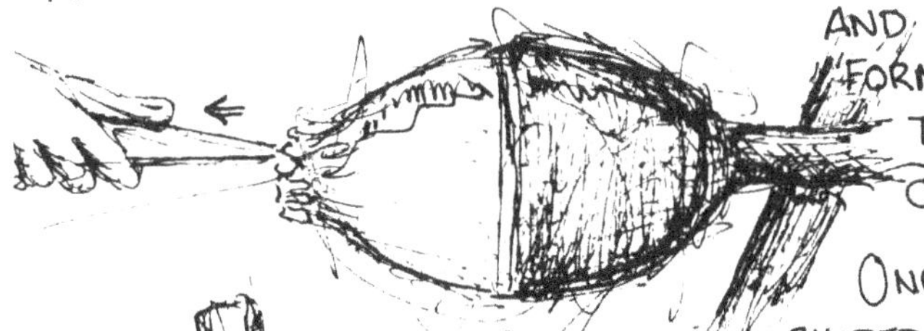

fig. 155

Once the piece is sealed-up, it may be reheated, shaped, necked and blown out to it's final form.

NOTE ☞ When attempting this technique for the first time, it is recommended that you keep the bubbles on the thick side. The added thickness will hold its heat and form better, and the resulting cups are easier to attach together, and get a complete seal.

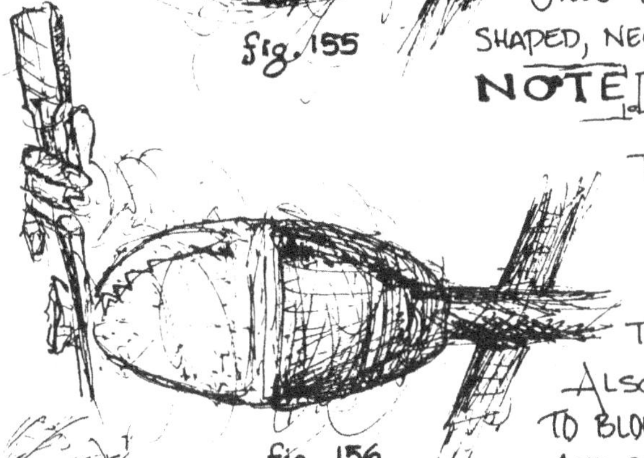

fig. 156

Also, another way to do this technique would be to blow pipe #2's bubble into a cup form, **punty it**, and open it up, matching the opening on pipe #1. This then may be presented to the gaffer and attached in the same fashion (fig. 152). The bonus of this manuver being that the bottom is already shaped and sealed & ready to go, thus saving a little time or allowing for more interesting color or decorative techniques to take place.

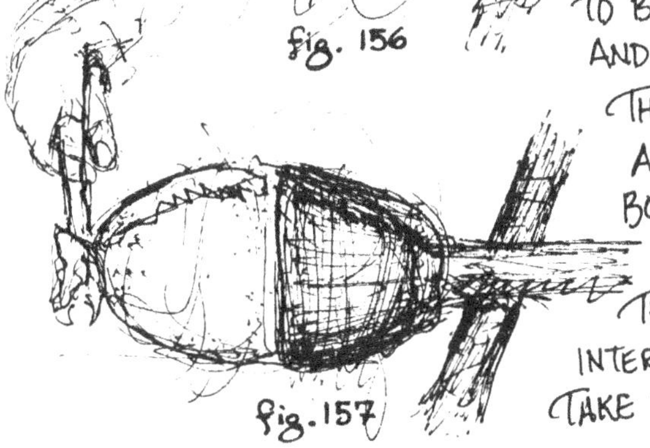

fig. 157

123

AS STATED EARLIER, THERE IS ANOTHER METHOD FOR ACHIEVING A HOLE IN THE END OF YOUR BUBBLE. ONCE YOU HAVE YOUR BUBBLE BLOCKED, BLOWN AND SHAPED-UP, YOU'LL WANT TO HEAT JUST THE VERY TIP - AS SHOWN IN fig. 158. THEN GENTLY PULL A TIP OFF THE END USING YOUR TWEEZERS. NEXT, NECK OFF A KNOB, BEING CAREFUL NOT TO CLOSE-OFF THE INSIDE DIAMETER - fig. 159 - (THIS IS EASIER TO SEE IF YOU'RE USING TRANSPARENT COLORS). A SOFFIETTA MAY BE USED TO CHILL THAT NECKLINE BY BLOWING AIR ON IT AS IT'S BEING NECKED. ONCE IT'S CHILLED SUFFICIENTLY, THE DIAMOND SHEARS MAY CRIMP THE NECKLINE AS THE ASSISTANT TAPS THE END OF THE KNOB OFF WITH THE BACK OF THE TWEEZERS. IF THE KNOB IS STUBBORN AND DOESN'T WISH TO RELEASE IMMEDIATLY ('CAUSE IT'S STILL HOT ON THE INSIDE) YOU MIGHT TRY A FEW DROPS OF WATER ON THE NECKLINE TO CRASH-COOL IT, AND TRY AGAIN.

THE PIECE IS THEN FLASHED, AND THEN THE SMALL HOLE IS HEATED (BEING CAREFUL NOT TO HEAT IT TOO MUCH AS TO CLOSE IT BACK UP AGAIN) TAKEN BACK TO THE BENCH AND OPENED FURTHER WITH THE JACKS.

AGAIN, THE LIP MAY BE PADDLED SMOOTH BY THE ASSISTANT AS THE GAFFER OPENS UP THE LIP. ALSO YOU'LL WANT TO MAKE SURE YOUR JACKS HAVE A GOOD DOSE OF BEESWAX ON THEM TO PREVENT SCRATCHING THE INSIDE OF THE BUBBLE. YOU MAY ALSO WANT TO USE WOODEN JACKS (PACIOFFI'S) TO OPEN THE CUP UP ALL THE WAY TO PREVENT MARKS OR SCARS FROM HAPPENING (AS METAL JACKS ARE PRONE TO DO).

fig. 158 PULL A POINT
fig. 159 NECK & CHILL 
fig. 160 CRIMP & TAP-OFF 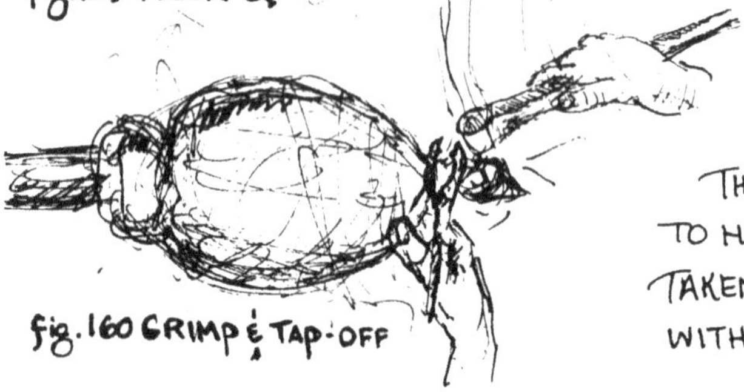
fig. 161 OPEN WITH JACKS... 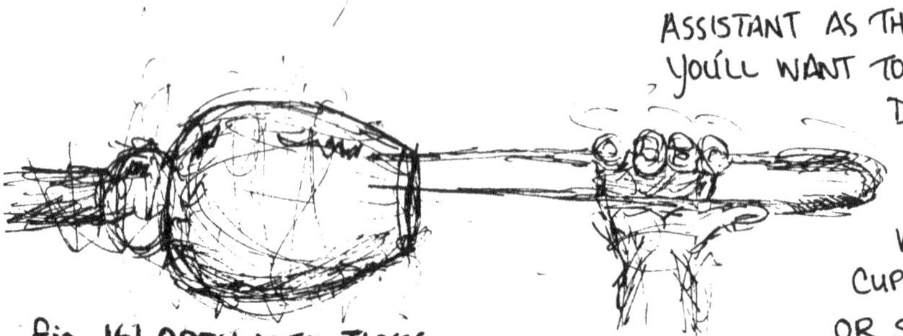
fig. 162 & /OR PACIOFFI'S

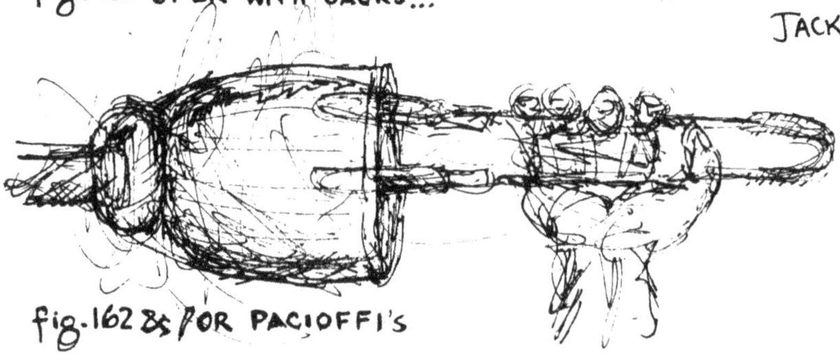

GRAALS

The Graal technique offers the aspiring glass artist an opportunity to obtain specific imagery and/or designs within the blown or solid glass form. A multi-step process whereby a 'blank' of colored (or even colorless) glass is shaped on the pipe, knocked off & annealed and some 'cold' working done to it. The blank may be: engraved cameo-style, sandblasted (or sandcarved), cut, smashed or painted with enamels or specialized glass paints. The blank is then brought-up slowly in annealer, picked-up on a blowing iron, reheated and either shaped and blown out to it's final form or gathered-on and then worked to completion. This technique was first devoloped and perfected by Swedish glassworkers during the 1920's hence the peculiar name GRAAL* (in English - "GRAIL"). * or was it the English that devoloped it first? the debate continues...

Begin first by having a plan. A drawing is a good place to start. Decide what type of imagery or design you'd like on or in your finished piece. Do some preliminary sketches on how it will appear. What effect will blowing it out have on the design? Should you use opaque or transparent colors? What influence will the form have on the overall design? Should the design be on the surface, or get cased? These and other questions should be answered well before you pick up a blowpipe; some you won't know until you try, but the less that's left to guesswork, the better off you'll be.

To create a colored graal blank, you may try the bubble-overlay technique (see pages 104-7). A less traditional method is to roll or sift colored glass powders on the surface of the last gather of your blank. With powders it is a little more challenging to obtain an even colored surface; much less of a clear distinction exists to indicate where one color begins and another ends. Some bleeding or blending of the colors is inevitable - an effect which you may make use of. You can, of course, achieve some interesting color gradations using the powders top to bottom, side-to-side, reversal etc. and/or combine them with other techniques.

Usually graals are made fairly thick. This allows them to be picked-up again on a blowpipe and gathered over. If the walls of the graal are too thin, they may not stand up to the rigors of the gathering process & can collapse while attempting to do so. Also, by having relatively thick walls, the graal may be subjected to more intense coldworking processes - deep carving, cutting etc. It's up to you how big you make the graal blank. Think of it as being your next-to-last gather. Work within your ability. Can you really handle another gather on top of the graal? Better yet, can you effectively pull-off a large scale bubble overlay? To quote an ol' cliche' "SIZE ISN'T EVERYTHING."... Furthermore, the amount to which you wish to blow your blank out has some bearing on the

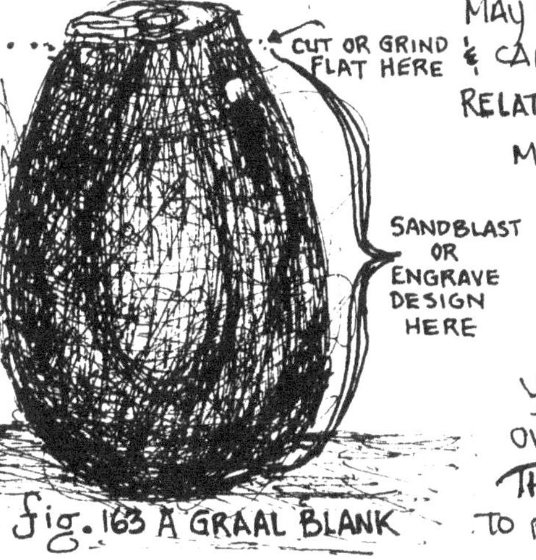

CUT OR GRIND FLAT HERE

SANDBLAST OR ENGRAVE DESIGN HERE

fig. 163 A GRAAL BLANK

125

scale and design of your Graal. The more you blow the piece out, the less crisp and detailed your imagery becomes. Therefore you may need to make your Graal as close to the finished product's size as you can muster, in order to preserve the integrity of your design and hard labor.

As stated earlier, there exists no shortage of methods of what to do with a Graal blank. It is up to you, the artist, to reach within and pull out feeling, soul, VISIONS of Nirvana, or urban overwhelment, — and transfer it to the surface of the glass. Your skills as a coldworker, or your studio's coldworking equipment may also help dictate the depth to which you explore this avenue.

The first step to preparing your blank is to make certain you have a fairly flat surface to re-attach your blowpipe to. This means either cutting or grinding off the top until an uniform surface is present. Of course it's possible even likely that the piece broke off the original blowpipe clean n' even and you won't have to mess with it. It is not necessary to polish this surface, a smooth 220 mesh surface will suffice, because in all probability you'll be necking the piece off below the contact line anyway.

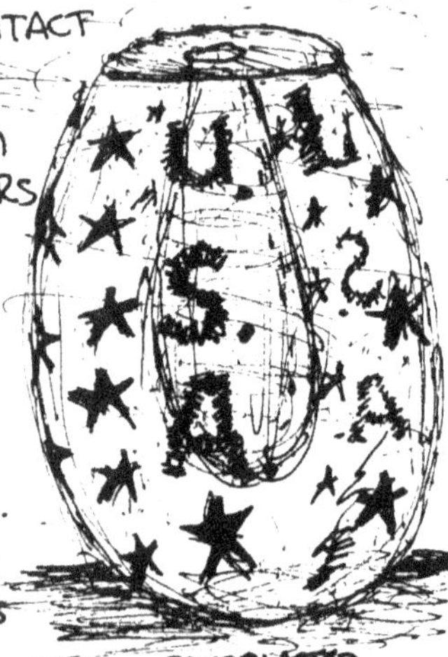

Next, choose your weapon: diamond saw, engraving tools, Merkur lathe, punty wheels, grinders, sandblasters, ball-peen hammer or 22 caliber rifle (really, those impact marks can be quite spectacular blown out → provided of course you don't totally destroy the blank or yourself in the process). It's up to you how far to go with the coldworking. You may choose to just barely scratch the surface, or deep carve through all the color & then some. Take note, however, deep chasms can create air pockets which will trap bubbles during the gathering process. It's an interesting effect in and of itself! → But a real bummer if you don't want them there. ← More on that later...

fig. 164 SANDBLASTED GRAAL.

Let's say for example you've masked-off and sandblasted your Graal with some patriotic theme all over the surface and you're ready to pick the sucker up (fig. 164). Make sure the blank is clean, free-of masking material, grit, and that it is dry. You'll need an annealing oven or pick-up kiln, hopefully one with a digital programmable temperature controller, or you're in for a whole lot of babysitting! If other people in the studio are interested in picking-up Graals at the same time (or after you) you might schedule it so that all the blanks are loaded at the same time — to best conserve energy and space.

If the kiln you're loading the blanks in is a **TOP-LOADER**, you'll want to arrange the blanks so they're close to the top of the lehr for easier access and accuracy during the pick-up. You may have to create a removable shelf system too, if this is the oven you'll be loading finished work in. If your blank has no flat bottom, you may wish to hollow-out a soft-brick to accomodate the Graal so that has some stability and doesn't wobble too much (see page 104). On the other hand, if you have to use a

FRONT-LOADING ANNEALER, YOU'LL WANT TO LAY THE BLANKS WHERE YOU TOO HAVE EASY ACCESS TO THEM, ALSO WITH A BRICK OR SOMETHING SOLID BEHIND THEM SO YOU HAVE SOMETHING FIRM TO PRESS AGAINST WHEN IT COMES TIME TO PICK THEM UP, (SEE fig. 165 to the right).

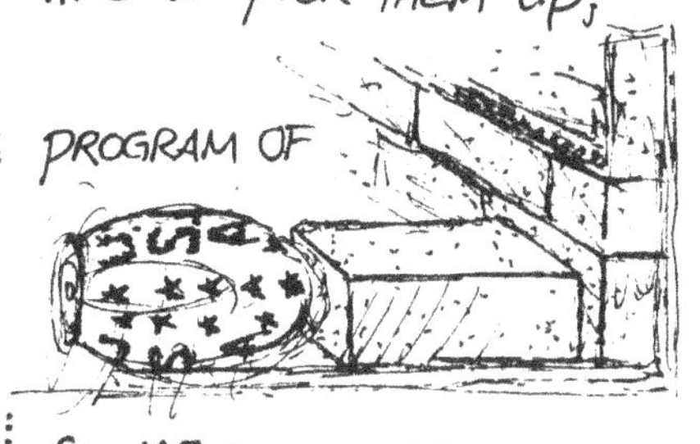

RAMP UP THE ANNEALER USING VIRTUALLY THE REVERSE PROGRAM OF AN ANNEALING CYCLE, i.e. SLOWEST TEMPERATURE CHANGE FIRST (THE SOAK) AND GRADUALLY QUICKER TEMPERATURE INCREASES AS YOU APPROACH THE ACTUAL ANNEALING TEMP. OF THE GLASS YOU'RE USING. (SEE TABLE 166 BELOW FOR A SAMPLE SCHEDULE.)

fig 165 CUT-AWAY VIEW GRAAL IN FRONT LOADER AWAITING PICK-UP

ONCE THE GRAALS ARE READY AND HOLDING AT THE ANNEALING TEMPERATURE, YOU'LL WANT TO BRING THE KILN UP AN ADDITIONAL 50°-100° F FOR THE FEW MINUTES IT TAKES YOU TO MAKE THE (PICK-UP) COLLAR (SEE PAGE 98 FOR INFO ON MAKING A COLLAR). THIS INCREASE IN TEMPERATURE WILL HELP REDUCE THE AMOUNT OF THERMAL SHOCK YOUR GRAAL WILL EXPERIENCE EN ROUTE TO THE GLORY HOLE, AND HOPEFULLY PREVENT IT FROM CRACKING. IF YOU HAVE A PARTICULARLY LARGE GRAAL TO PICK-UP, YOU MAY NEED TO GATHER A LARGER AMOUNT OF GLASS TO MAKE A 'BEEFIER' COLLAR CAPABLE OF HANDLING THE INCREASED WEIGHT AND SIZE.

CUMULATIVE TIME MINUTES	SET TEMPERATURE FAHRENHEIT
0:30-60	250°
1:15	350°
1:45	450°
2:30	550°
3:15	750°
4:00	890°
HOLD	890°
HOLD	950°
HOLD	890°

TABLE 166 SAMPLE SCHEDULE FOR GRAAL PICK-UP ~ USING SPRUCE-PINE BATCH "87" ACTUAL TIMES MAY VARY

ALLOW THE COLLAR TO COOL, THEN REHEAT JUST THE VERY END IN THE GLORY HOLE UNTIL IT'S WARM/HOT (A TRICKY TEMPERATURE TO DESCRIBE). IF THE COLLAR IS TOO HOT, THE BLANK WILL PRETTY MUCH JUST DROP OFF — PULLING A THIN TUBE OUT OF THE GLASS, AND LEAVE YOUR GRAAL TRAILING BEHIND! ON THE OTHER HAND, IF THE COLLAR IS TOO COLD - IT MAY REFUSE TO STICK TO THE GRAAL OR ONLY PARTIALLY ADHERE (A DANGEROUS SITUATION), IN WHICH CASE YOU MAY BREAK-OFF THE ATTEMPT, REHEAT THE COLLAR MORE, AND TRY AGAIN.

YOU'LL REQUIRE STABILITY IN THE COLLAR (therefore don't heat it up too much) WHEN YOU THINK IT'S THE RIGHT TEMP. GRAB YOUR DIAMOND SHEARS, HAVE AN ASSISTANT OPEN THE ANNEALER, AND USING THE SHEARS TO HELP GUIDE THE BLOWPIPE - SET THE COLLAR SMACK-DAB IN THE CENTER OF THE GRAAL (HINT: MOVING YOUR HEAD TO THE RIGHT OR LEFT A TOUCH PRIOR TO CONTACT WILL GIVE A SECOND POINT OF REFERENCE TO DETERMINE 'THE CENTER'). IT'S **VERY IMPORTANT** TO "HIT" THE CENTER AS THE ENTIRE SUCCESS OF BLOWING THE BLANK RELIES ON MAKING THE HOLE IN YOUR COLLAR MATCH THE HOLE IN YOUR BLANK. PRESS FIRMLY, INSURING FULL CONTACT AND REMOVE THE BLANK AND THEN HEAD FOR THE GLORY HOLE (DON'T FORGET

fig. 167 PICKING-UP A GRAAL

to have your assistant reset the annealer control back to annealing temp. (HOLD).

Quickly give your blank a flash and inspect the graal for any dust, DEBRIS or kiln wash that may be sticking there → a quick brush with a damp newspaper or towel (NOT WET → you don't want quench marks happening) should help remove any 'cling-ons'. While you're at it, roll the pipe at the bench to see if your blank's on-center. You may adjust it if necessary by spreading your tweezers and grabbing the graal at the waist lift and push up or down to center it on the pipe. Recheck and realign if necessary. Then return to the glory hole to heat the whole blank up. This reheat will fire-polish all your engraving, sandblasting - designwork, and aid in the next step of blowing out the blank.

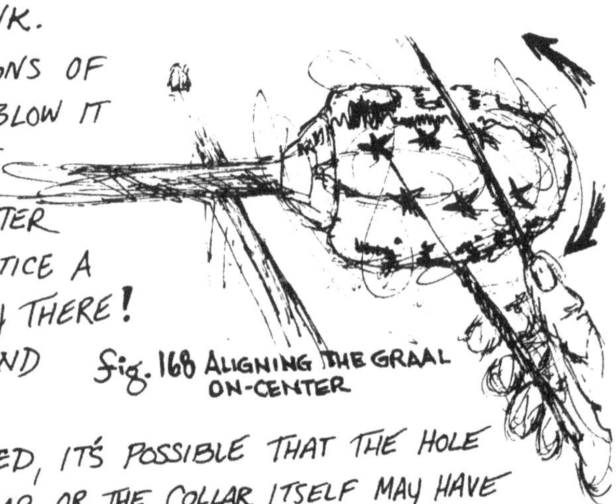

Once the graal is exhibiting signs of heat and 'plasticity', you should attempt to blow it slightly. At the bench, have your assistant blow while you maintain the blank 'on-center' and watch for signs of expansion. If you notice a slight bulge → CONGRATULATIONS! You're halfway there! If not, try reheating the blank some more and attempt to blow again.

fig. 168 ALIGNING THE GRAAL ON-CENTER

If no signs of expansion are observed, it's possible that the hole may have become blocked by glass on the collar, or the collar itself may have closed off. You have four options. The simplest and most heartwrenching is to trash the piece. sorry! ☹ Second, you may chill the collar → tap the blank back off into the annealer → re-coldwork the top (after it's annealed again) and try again to pick up at a later date. Third, just shape (and/or case) the object as is and be happy with it. And lastly, you may punty the blank up → tweeze out or trim-out the opening, have another collar made → and reattach the graal (like you would for a punty at the bench). Considering the amount of time you may have spent on coldworking the blank, this fifteen minute procedure may be a small price to pay to achieve your final form. You're the bus driver...

So, on the brighter side, let's suppose you observe signs of expansion and indications of a match between collar and piece. You may either blow the blank out at this point or gather over it and then blow it to its final form. When gathering over a graal, it's important to have the right temp. — if the collar is too warm, the graal will be difficult to control coming out of the furnace → the neck will be wobbly and the graal may want to just DRIP (or DROP) right off the end. The blank, too, should be stone cold as well, less the imagery become distorted during the gather.

If you don't want air bubbles trapped in every nook n' cranny of your graal, the best method for gathering is to angle the pipe up high → stop rotation and allow your graal to sink slowly into the glass. Once the collar has submerged below the surface you may begin rotating the pipe again and finish out the gather as normal.

For greater stability you'll want to make sure your gather goes up and over your collar. The neck area tends to get hot quick → and may require near immediate attention → by marvering, papering or chilling with compressed air. You may then block, paper, or marver the piece and blow it out as you would for anything else.

fig. 169 Cutaway View Gathering over Graal

You will discover in the course of making graal pieces the limits and dynamics of your color. You'll see what effect(s) form has on your designs and imagery. Exciting things can happen! The behavior of over-laid colors and the resulting linear qualities of the colors as they 'seperate' can be visually stunning. The forces of the pipe turning, blowing and stretching can dramatically alter your intended design. Only practice in making these forms can improve and educate you further.

VARIATIONS ON A THEME:

The are other types of graals you can try: graal cups similar to color overlay cups (page 102) may be blown and then coldworked similar to the aforementioned blanks. These cups are brought-up in an annealer in the same way as ordinary graals. The process differs by dropping a bubble (or solid gather) **INTO** the cup (vs. a collar on the blank) and picking it up like a cup overlay. The Seattle artist **Richard Royal** uses this technique to create his "Royal Cut" vessels.

Nobody says you have to blow your graals. This technique is appropriate for making some intesting solid pieces as well. Virtually the whole process is the same - you just don't have to put a bubble into your piece, and you're free to shape or sculpt it into whatever form you would like.

If coldworking is like fingernails-on-the-chalkboard for you, and the painterly school is more your cup of tea - you may elect the use of **PARADISE PAINTS** via the graal technique. Read on ⇒

PARADISE PAINTS ARE RELATIVELY NEW IN THE HOT GLASS REALM. DEVELOPED BY CALIFORNIA GLASS ARTIST **DAVID HOPPER** DURING THE 1970'S, THESE BRIGHT COLORED ENAMEL PIGMENTS MAY BE PAINTED ONTO THE SURFACE OF A "GRAAL BLANK", INSIDE AND OUTSIDE OF A "GRAAL CUP", OR ON A SOLID-SCULPTED OBJECT. THE RESULTING WORK THEN MAY BE SET IN AN ANNEALER, BROUGHT UP, PICKED-UP AND EITHER FIRED-ON OR GATHERED OVER IN A SIMILAR FASHION TO NORMAL GRAAL WORK.

DIRECTIONS FOR USING PARADISE PAINTS SHOULD COME WITH THE COLORS YOU ORDER (SEE PAGE 313 FOR ADDRESS AND PHONE #), BUT HERE'S SOME TIPS FOR SUCCESS IN CASE YOU ACQUIRE THEM WITHOUT THE INFO:  **FIRST AND FOREMOST** — YOU'LL NOTICE IMMEDIATELY UPON OPENING A CONTAINER OF THIS STUFF A NOXIOUS ODOR COMING FROM WITHIN. THIS **PAINT** IS BAD TO BREATHE, SO DON'T! WORK IN A WELL-VENTILATED AREA e.g. UNDER THE HOOD•NEAR THE FURNACE IS A GOOD SPOT. ALSO, AVOID ANY SKIN CONTACT OR INGESTION OF THIS MATERIAL (DON'T EAT YOUR LUNCH WHILE PAINTING WITH IT!) — AND BE SURE TO WASH-UP WELL AFTER WORKING WITH IT.

THE COLORS CAN BE MIXED LIKE OIL OR ACRYLIC PAINTS WITH SIMILAR TOOLS. THEY MAY BE ALSO USED STRAIGHT OUT OF THE JAR. THESE PAINTS ARE TEMPERATURE-SENSITIVE → THEY ARE EASIER TO APPLY (LESS THICK) WHEN THE COLORS AND GLASS ARE AT ca. 100°F

fig 120 A PAINTED GRAAL CUP

(AGAIN, APPLYING THEM IN AN AREA NEAR THE FURNACE CAN KEEP THEM WARM & AID IN DRYING). PAINT THINNER WORKS BEST FOR THINNING THE COLORS (SHOULD YOU WISH LIGHTER, MORE TRANSPARENT 'WATER-COLORY' EFFECTS), ALTHOUGH ACETONE CAN BE USED AS WELL. THE GLASS SHOULD BE FREE OF GREASE, OILS AND DUSTS BEFORE PAINTING TO PREVENT OFF-GASING DURING THE CASING PROCESS.

IN ADDITION, IT IS BETTER TO PUT ON THINNER COATS OF PAINT THAN ONE THICK ONE. IF THEY'RE APPLIED TOO THICK, THE PAINTS MAY TEND TO CRACK (SOMETIMES FLAKE). ALSO THE COLORS MAY BE PRONE TO 'BLEED' OR MOVE SOMEWHAT DURING THE GATHERING-OVER PROCESS, OR EVEN DRIP AND RUN DURING THE PAINTING SESSION.

IT HELPS TO ALLOW THESE PAINTS TO DRY BEFORE ATTEMPTING TO PICK THEM UP. PLACE THE PIECE(S) IN A WARM, DRY WELL-VENTILATED AREA (YUP, YOU GUESSED IT — NEAR THE FURNACE AGAIN, BUT NOT TOO CLOSE AS TO THERMAL SHOCK 'EM!), OVERNIGHT OR SO UNTIL THE COLORS APPEAR MATTE (NON-GLOSSY). ALSO, BE AWARE THAT THE PAINTS TEND TO SMELL AND GAS-OFF WHEN THEY'RE BEING BROUGHT-UP IN THE ANNEALER PRIOR TO PICK-UP — SO CRACK A WINDOW OR MAKE SURE THERE'S ADEQUATE VENTILATION IN THE STUDIO TO CARRY AWAY THE FUMES.

SOME COLORS SEEM TO FARE BETTER THAN OTHERS. TO INSURE THAT YOUR REDS AND YELLOWS DON'T BURN-OUT FROM OVEREXPOSURE TO EXCESSIVE HEAT, BE CAREFUL IN HOW YOU HANDLE THE GRAAL ONCE YOU PICK IT UP. SAN DIEGO ARTIST **THOR BUENO** (WHO USES THESE PAINTS EXTENSIVELY) RECOMMENDS TURNING DOWN THE gas on your glory hole (or shutting it off completely and use the radiant heat) to prevent reduction &/or the colors from burning out. Also, make sure your furnace isn't too hot, or the colors may be adversely effected as well.

Prior to gathering over, you'll want to make certain your colors are fired-on well first, and get hot enough to bake out the medium.* Like ordinary graals, the pick-up oven should be set 50°F or so above annealing temp. before you pickup your piece. Again, fire-on and 'set' the colors by thoroughly heating the blank first. Then allow it to set-up and get stone cold before attempting to gather over. Procede to gather over as you would for normal graals and finish to completion. Make notes of your results and procedures in the event you hit upon something you really like, and would care to duplicate at a later time. You might also like to do some color tests before embarking on the lengthy graal procedure: take a clear rondel, cut it up into small pieces → mix-up some colors you like → paint the small pieces → allow them to dry then pick 'em up out of a pre-heated kiln → case them and make small paperweights (or whatever) and examine the results upon annealing. This can save you vast amounts of time and resources by giving you quick examples of how these colors behave. And beware – they will look one color as wet paint, and a whole different color after they've been heated, cased and blown out.

* David Hopper also recommends venting the kiln while ramping up to 600°F to allow exhausting gases a chance to escape. This is especially important for reds and yellows.

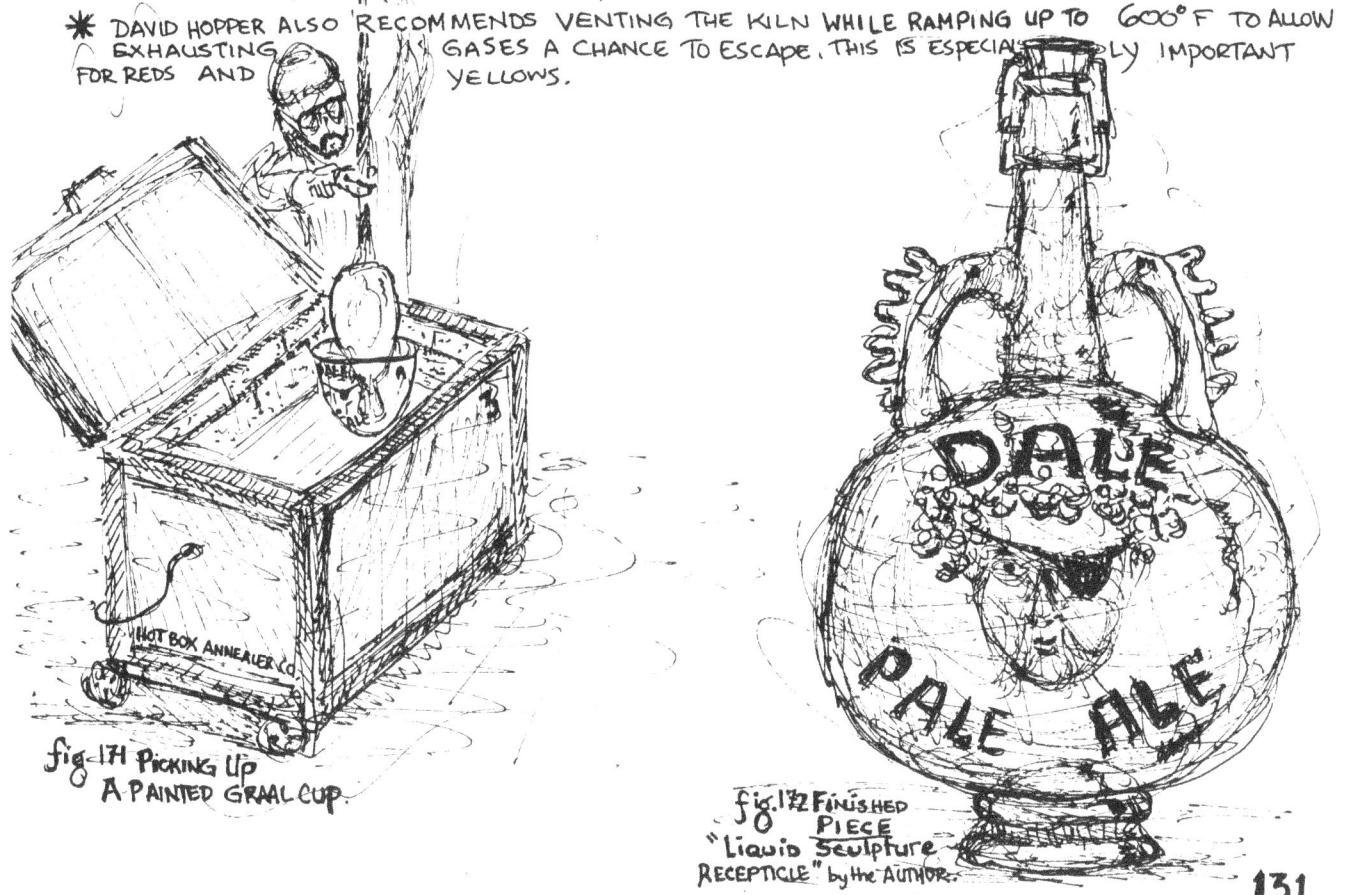

fig. 171 Picking up a painted graal cup.

fig. 172 Finished piece "Liquid Sculpture Recepticle" by the author.

Venetian Style Techniques

- History 134
- Italian Glass Glossary 136
- Avolio 139
- Blown Foot . . . 142
- Goblet Bowls . . 148
- Basic Bowl 150
- Lip Wrap 153
- Optic Mold . . . 154
- Stems 158
- Blown Stem . . . 160
- Solid Stem . . . 161
- Bitwork 162
- The Garage . . . 163
- Cup Assembly I . . 164
- Cup Assembly II . 165
- Cristallo Cup Blues . 166
- Cane . . . 167
- Using Cane . . . 170
- Cane Styles . . 173
- Zanfirico . . . 174
- Intro to Murrine . 176
- Wine Glass Cane Pick-Up on a Bubble . 183
- Champagne Glass Cane Pick-Up on a Collar . 187
- Champagne Glass Pineapple Mold . 193
- Reticello 197
- Simplified Reticello . . 202
- Thin Threads . . . 204
- Chain Wrap . . . 205
- Wine Glass - 3 Bubbles . 206

Venetian Style Techniques

A Little Bit of History:

The term "Venetian" is somewhat a misnomer. When we refer to something in glass as being "Venetian" - it really means 'from the Isle of Murano'. This tiny island across the lagoon from Venice has been the cradle of glassworking techniques since the blowers were exiled there by decree in 1291 A.D. This was done for two main reasons. First and foremost was the concern about fire. Wood-fired furnaces were notorious for getting out-of-hand occasionally - taking every ignitable/combustible substance within it's reach with it. The danger of lighting up Venice got dampened by moving the glassblowers to Murano. This, in turn, helped the Venetians keep tabs on their increasingly popular and profitable craftsmen - (which was the second reason for doing it.) The skills and knowledge the "Venetians" were exhibiting in their handling of this precious material became world-reknown. Much of it came with the advent of **Cristallo**.

Cristallo is an Italian word for "crystal". This was a term first used in Venice in the 14th century to describe glass which looked like the precious rock-crystal. It revolutionized everything within the glassmaking realm. With the discovery of glass "detergents" or decolorizers (such as the addition of maganese), the Italian glassmakers batched a new style of glass that no longer had the characteristic green or blue color from high iron oxides in the formula. For the Venetians it was the greatest thing since sliced bread... uh... maybe that wasn't invented yet... [Another curious ramification which became immeadiately apparent was that their beverages weren't so aesthetically pleasing. It forced the brewers and vinters to clarify their artistic endeavors, which up unto that point were often cloudy and dark.] It also gave rise to new methods of working the glass, in addition to the new styles and designs.

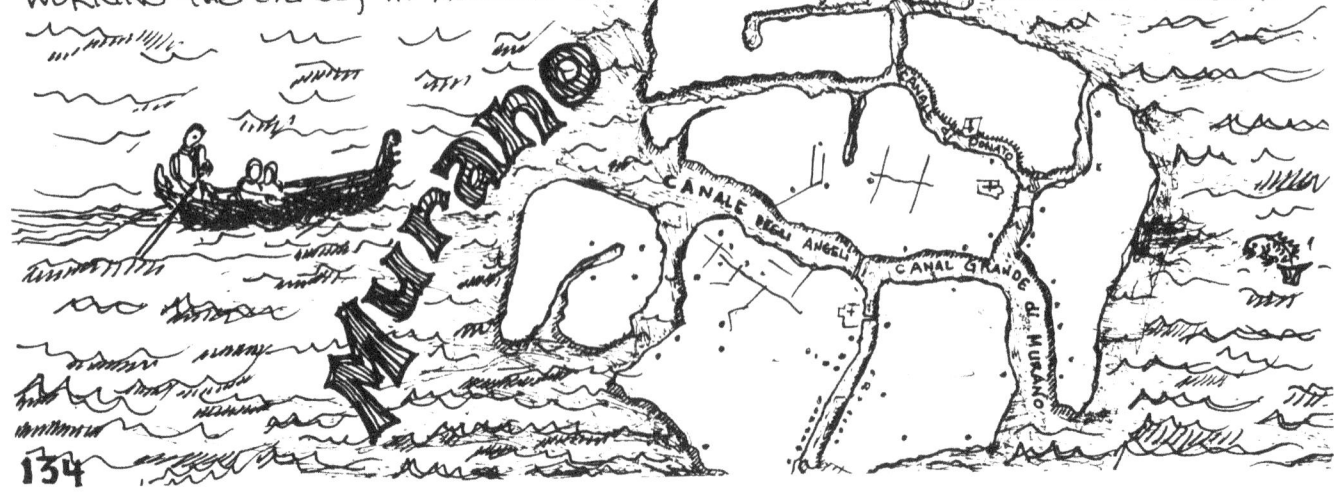

134

The competition amongst the glasshouses became stiff. Each was vying for their fair share of the market with the thinnest, most brilliant glass. Some pieces became incredibly complexed, such as the dragon-stem goblets or elaborate cane-worked pieces. And that was just the vessels. There existed a whole 'nuther world being explored in murrine and bead-making. Even with todays technological advances → work created between the 14th and 16th centuries in Murano remains unparalleled in it's style, finesse, and skill of execution.

Glass was, as it continues to be, a money-making venture. In order to stay on top, the factory had to keep improving their designs. Many techniques and formulas became "top-secret". Oft is told the tale of one factory worker rifling through their neighbor's cullet pile in order to see what new designs they were working on the day before. Once you started working for a factory - you were there until death-do-you-part. No one was permitted to leave the island - although a few did manage to escape and set-up glasshouses in other parts of the continent. The tradition of the family-run factory became firmly rooted and continues today. Fortunately, some of the techniques have been openly shared and become adopted\adapted into modern glass practices. A number of those are illustrated in the following pages.

So... you wanna blow Venetian Style... Just where do you begin? RIGHT HERE!

On paper first. Make some marks. Draw existing cups. Change 'em around to make them more personalized. **Second, watch other glassblowers.** See how they make their pieces. It's a great way to learn. **Third - practice making them.** Repeat steps one through three again & again & again!

Making tissue-thin goblets is just the tip of the iceberg when it comes to Venetian-style techniques. There's a whole host of other methods that the glassmakers in Murano have mastered, and undoubtedly could fill ten volumes as thick as this one. Nevertheless, in the interest of providing you with a broad variety of styles in this context, I am including some of the more popular ways of blowing "traditional" goblets. Many of the techniques addressed can be boosted-up in scale and blown much larger if so desired.

One recommendation is to start from the ground-on-up. Begin by practicing your 'Avolios'. Make a few hundred (to a thousand or so) of 'em first. Then try adding a blown foot to one. Open it up. Attach another Avolio. Then add another blown foot to create a wheel toy deal. These things are great practice pieces. **You don't have to waste so much time blowing the bowls and all the elements right off the bat.** Once you get proficient with the basic foundation(s), you can proceed to more elaborate designs with confidence! But first, let's set the mood & learn **Italian:**

ABRUZZO ITALIAN GLASS GLOSSARY

I would first like to thank **Ferd Thieriot** for supplying me with the following translations. If there any of you who are fluent in Muranese and would care to add or change this compilation - please contact me with the information. (In the front of this book is the address.) -ed.

ANZIPETTO - Heat shield → next to the glory hole or furnace

ANZANELLO - Metal hook attached to the heat shield → old fashioned yoke, before rollers

ASIO - - - Sill of the furnace

AVOLIO - Spool shaped piece of glass which unites bowls-to-stems, stems to feet in goblets

BEVANTE - Bowl of a goblet / drinking cup

BALLOTON - Pineapple mold

BRONZINO - Marver → used to be made of bronze (not marble) hence its name. Marble is used for other purposes

BUFFARIA - Blown glassware for ordinary use

CANNA - Blowpipe

CASSA - Ladle

CASSIOLIN - Small ladle

CONTERIE - Glass beads made from cane

COTIZZO - Cullet

CRISTALLO - Clear glass

CROSIOL - Small crucible 8-10 kg

CROZZOLA - Rake for cleaning the top layer of glass in the furnace - made of glass

FERRO DA BATTER - Flat piece of iron → used to strike the pipe during the transfer process

FILIGRANA - Cane, colored or clear reticello, retortoli etc.

FILO - - - Lip wrap, in variable thickness and colors

GAMBO - Stem of a goblet

GARZONIETTO - The youngest appentice who is given the simplest & most humble tasks

GOBLETTO - Drinking vessels in general

GRANZIOLI - Frit (medium) see MACAE

GRANZIOLONI - Frit (large)

INCALMO - Process of sticking two pieces of hot glass together. Basically a double bubble method to achieve color zones

INCISIONE - Diamond point engraving

INCOSSA - Glass which is not entirely transparent

INFORNARE - Verb referring to the process of throwing batch into the furnace (to charge)

IRIDE - Rainbow effect on the glass achieved by using stanous chloride ☠ Toxic!

LEVAR - The process of gathering → literally - to raise

MAESTRO - The person in charge of a team of glassblowers → responsible for the production area. He who makes the pieces

MAGIOSSO - Wooden block

MAISTRAPA - A glass object of Murano origin → encountered in various inventories but hard to identify

MAISTRO DA CANNA - Name of the person who actually pulls the cane

MARGARITE - Glass beads

MARMORIZZAR - Process of marvering

MARSOR or **MARSORETTO** - A bowl with a foot

MEZZA STAMPALIRA - Half molding ie. to obtain a ribbed effect on ½ of the bowl of a goblet → a small amount of hot glass is added to the lower ½ of the bubble & blown into a mold

MILLEFIORI or **ROSETTA** - What Americans refer to as 'MURRINE' → small cross sections of cane in an infinite variety of patterns

MURRINE - See above

MORISE - Undulating lip-wrap

MORSO - Glass left on the pipe → the moile

NANFA - Crucible holding 30-35 kg

OLDANIO - Archaic term referring to solid glass pieces

ORACANNO - Perfume jar/bottle

ORO GRAFFITO - Gold leaf applied w/ glue

PACIOFA - Wooden jacks

PALATO - Crucible 150 kg "

PADELLA - Crucible 40 kg "

PALETTA - Wooden paddle

PEA - 1st gather before formed with a tool

PIE - Foot of goblet (from "PIEDE")

PONTELLO - Solid iron → a punty

PUNTELLARE - The process of puntying a goblet bowl on the inside in order to finish the lower half

REBOLAR - Process of raking the glass

RAGADIN - The ribbing effect achieved by blowing into a mold

RÙI — RONDELS USED FOR WINDOWS
SCAGNO — BENCH
SCAVO — CORROSIVE GLASS COLORING AGENT POWDERED ON THE EXTERIOR OF THE PIECE - PRODUCING "INSTANT ANTIQUITY"
SERVENTE — THE MAESTRO'S CHIEF ASSISTANT
SERVENTIN — ONE BELOW SERVENTE
STAMPO — MOLD FOR BLOWING, CASTING etc
SUPPIALUME — LAMPWORKING - BUT IN 1600'S PEOPLE HAD TO BLOW (SUPPIA) ON THE FLAME (LUME) UNTIL THE HEAT INCREASED
TAGIAOL — SCULPTING BLADE
TAIÀNTI — SHEARS
 - LISIE → STRAIGHT
 - TONDE → DIAMOND

TEMPARA — ANNEALER / GARAGE
TAPETTO — GOBLETS OR VASES WITH A DOLPHIN OR SWAN STEM
VETRO A FILA — GLASS WITH THREADS - BLOWN PIECES USING CANES LAID OUT IN PARALLEL LINES
VETRO A GHIACCIO — SURFACE DECORATION ACHIEVED BY DIPPING HOT GLASS IN WATER
VETRO A RETICELLO — GLASS BLOWN WITH CANES WHICH FORM A CRISSCROSS PATTERN RESEMBLING A NET - OFTEN WITH SMALL AIR BUBBLES TRAPPED INSIDE
VETRO A RETORTÀ — BLOWN GLASS MADE WITH CANES THAT HAVE BEEN TWISTED TO FORM SPIRALS
VETRERIA — GLASSWORKS
ZANFIRICO — CANE WORK

Quick Reference Chart

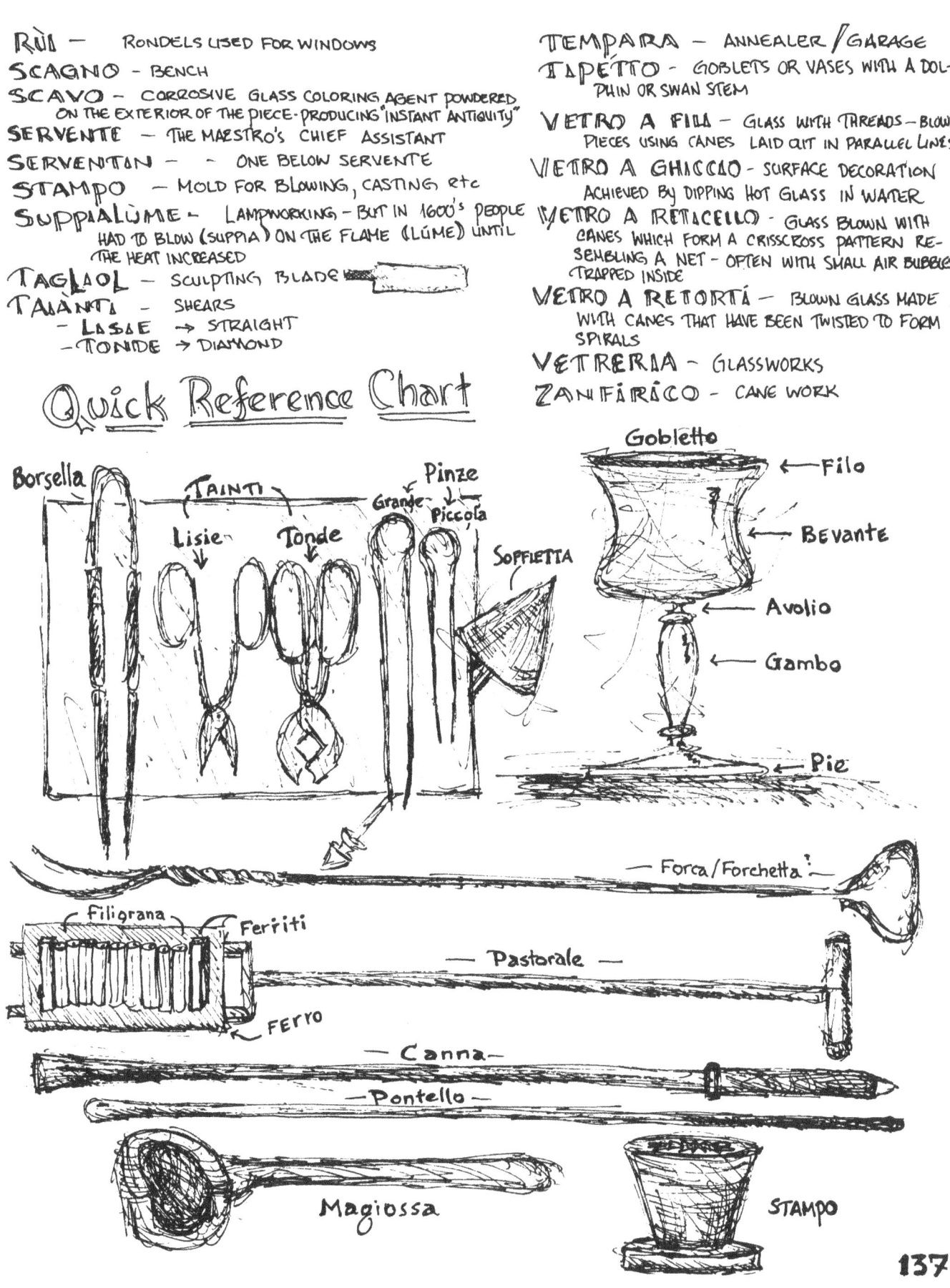

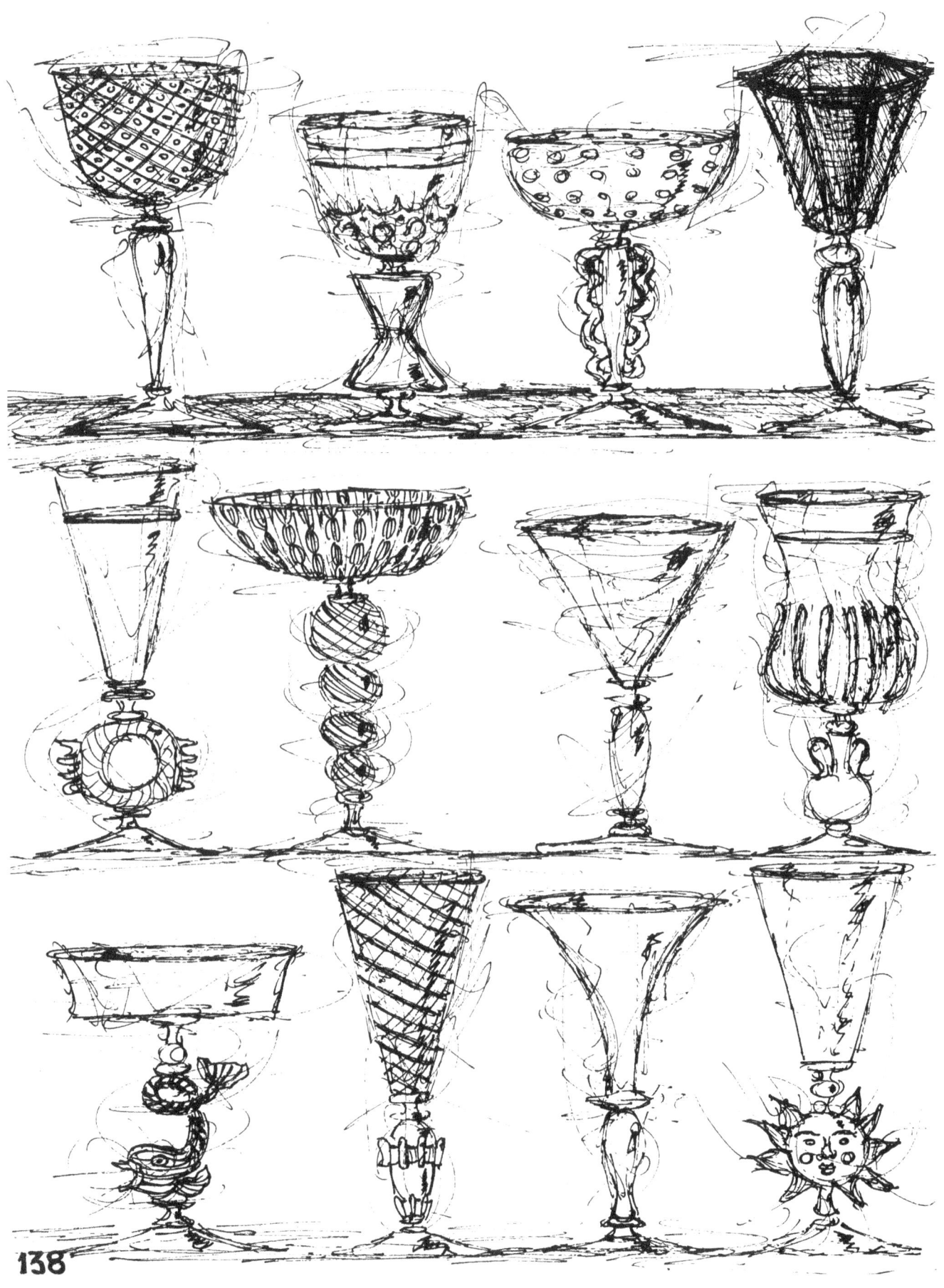

AVOLIO →

In Italian, the word literally translates as "I want... or "I'll take" (a bit of glass). For the purposes of goblet making, the **AVOLIO** is that small hourglass-shaped object which unites the bowl with the stem, and the stem with the foot.

They can be somewhat tricky to make, particularly if you are out of practice – or you haven't fully developed the skill in the first place. In theory they should go on as smooth as winding a thread on a spool and be shaped as easily as cutting-in a nice little neckline on a thimbleful of glass. It is wise to become proficient in making a good solid avolio before proceeding to feet and bowls. It is, afterall, the element which binds them altogether. And one bad avolio can ruin your whole goblet (and I've even seen them ruin some glassblowers whole day! Imagine that!).

So, the word here again is PRACTICE practice **PRACTICE!**

While your assistant is gathering the bit, you should grab the jacks in your hand like you're going to neck the piece. **VISUALIZE** targeting the center of your work, and coiling up a nice even gather there.

FOR THE ASSISTANT ⇒ Gather as much glass as you can on a small punty. Do not marver it! Instead, shape it in the air on your way over to the gaffer. Maintain your punty on a horizontal plane, tilting the punty slightly as you rotate it, to end-up with a uniform floppy finger of glass. **A good percentage of the glass should be off the end of the punty.**

Approach the gaffer like you were going to punty-up the piece. Keep the rod turning until the gaffer indicates to you to stop (she/he may just grip the end of your punty with the jacks → freezing your rotation.) The gaffer then tells you to flip the bit over → 180° – and applies it on-center.

It is essential that you remain loose and allow the gaffer to direct the scene.

Do not attempt to compensate for the gaffers 'mistakes'. They have to learn

...OW TO DO IT RIGHT THEMSELVES.

NOTE: IF THE GLASS IN THE FURNACE IS 'COLD', IT MAY BE NECESSARY TO HEAT THE BIT UP IN THE GLORY HOLE BEFORE ATTEMPTING THE AVOLIO. IT WOULD BE BETTER TO RUN THE FURNACE HOTTER TO BEGIN WITH, AS THE REHEATING PROCESS OFTEN DEVOLOPS INCONSISTENCIES IN HOW THE GLASS BEHAVES.

FOR THE GAFFER ⇒ GRAB THE PUNTY WITH THE JACKS. SET OR POSITION THE HOT BLOB AS CLOSE TO YOUR TARGET AS YOU CAN GET IT. ALLOW THE BIT TO SAG WITH GRAVITY. THEN SAY '**FLIP**', AND, AS THE BIT DROPS BACK TO CENTER, GENTLY ATTACH IT TO YOUR TARGET POINT. IMMEDIATELY LIFT THE PUNTY SLIGHTLY AS YOU ROLL YOUR PUNTY AWAY FROM YOU. THIS INITIATES THE COILING ACTION.

THE GLASS SHOULD WANT TO JUST FALL AND TRAIL ON YOUR TARGET POINT. DO YOUR BEST TO MOVE YOUR JACKS (AND THE PUNTY) WITH THE SAME SPEED AND FLUIDITY THAT YOUR PUNTY IS MOVING AT. WHEN YOU'VE GATHERED ENOUGH GLASS DOWN THERE WHISK THE PUNTY DOWN AND BACKWARDS, AS QUICK AS YOU CAN, TO BREAK THE THREAD OFF CLEAN N' NATURAL-LIKE.

A QUICK TAP WITH THE BACK OF THE JACKS CAN HELP CENTER THE BIT SOMEWHAT. NOW YOU CAN ANGLE THE BACK OF THE JACKS ON TOP OF THE HOT BIT AND RIDE IT THERE TO SHAPE AND 'MARVER' THE BIT INTO A CONE FORM. EVEN THO' THIS OBSCURES YOUR VISION OF HOW THE BIT IS BEING SHAPED, IT IS WHAT YOU MUST DO! (there are exceptions to every rule, but I'm not gonna mention that now...).

AVOID OVERCHILLING THE BIT. IT HAS TO REMAIN HOT IN ORDER FOR YOU TO CUT-IN THE CHARACTERISTIC HOUR-GLASS SHAPE.

YOUR SHAPE SHOULD LOOK SOMEWHAT LIKE THE IMAGE **DRAWN** TO THE LEFT. IT MAY BE THAT YOUR CONTACT POINT DID NOT GO ON AS CLEAN AS YOU HOPED FOR OR YOU ACCIDENTLY SQUASHED IT OFF-CENTER. DON'T WORRY ABOUT IT, AFTER A FEW HUNDRED OF THESE YOU'LL GET THE HANG OF IT!

Ⓗ DETAIL

Now you can begin to cut-in the mini-jack line. Use quick full rotations back n' forth to insure you get full contact with the blades of your jacks. Try to split the cone-shape in half - more or less to taste. If you would like a nice round knob on the bottom - it should come naturally. If you want more of a tight-hourglass or spool shape, you can have your assistant paddle the bottom while you 'neck' with the jacks.

Don't neck it too tightly or you'll end up with a weak spot that's likely to break sometime in the future (if not when you try to transfer the piece, some other time when you set it down too abruptly, or more-than-likely when you attempt to box it [I hate it when that happens..]).

If you angle the jacks outward you can lengthen and stretch your avolio a little bit more. Again, you can overdo it and lose some structural integrity. Just be careful and pay attention to what you're doing.

Some gaffers will make a **TWO-PART AVOLIO**. They will take a small bit and make it into a **MERESE**. Next,

They'll add a second bit and marve/neck it into one uniform avolio → oftentimes with more length and structure than you might obtain from a single bit-style avolio. It's a stylistic option as well.

After you make your first one, go ahead and keep adding more avolios and practicing them.

The more you do, the better you get! Have your assistant use a fresh punty every time. It will help you maintain consistency in your application and you won't have to deal with 'old glass' (mixed in with your fresh bit).

If you absolutely must make something outta your efforts, go ahead and make a 'VERTEBRAE' goblet. It's a fun way to test out the strength of your avolios...

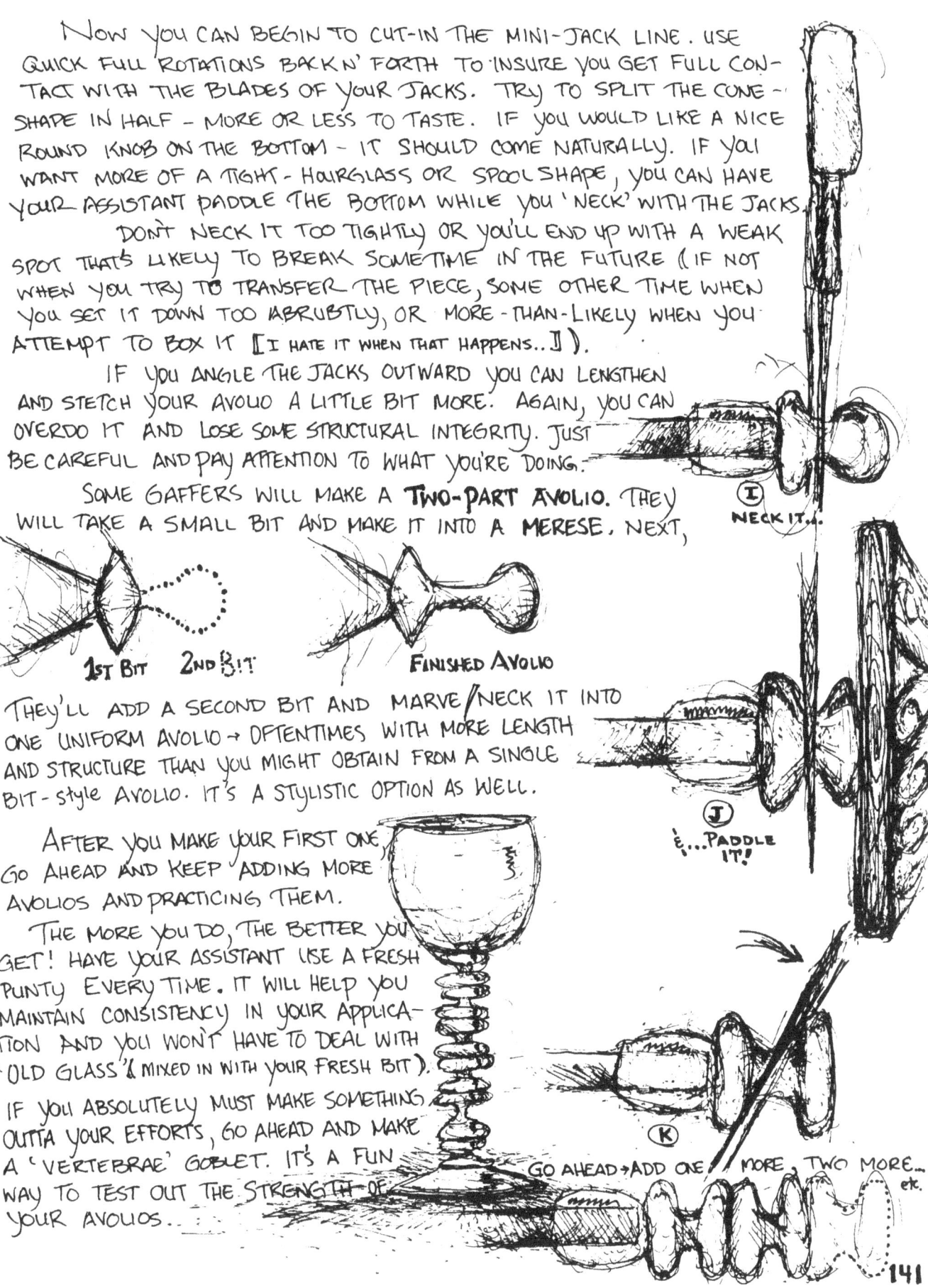

THE BLOWN FOOT

In the following pages, you will see illustrated the steps involved in making blown feet. They do take some practice getting used to, but once you GET the hang of it - they can go on pretty quick with reasonable assurance of success. Teamwork and timing are essential to making it go smoothly. The bubble for the foot has to be blown evenly, necked correctly, reheated just the right amount, and presented to the gaffer in exactly the right manner ⇒ all in under 60 seconds! (or your time is wasted and the gaffer gets 'steamed'...) anyways, here's what it takes:

FOR THE ASSISTANT:

Begin with a nice solid gather of glass, preferrably on a small-goblet-style pipe. Marver the glass off the end → where you can make use of it. Do not marver the tip (it should **NOT** be necessary if you gather correctly & air marver the glass into shape). Once you have a nice compact cylinder of glass to work with - blow and cap the pipe. Immediatly angle the pipe upwards and watch for signs of expansion in the bubble. This little manuver allows you to witness the bubble form, it keeps your bubble compressed, and allows the shoulders to blow out somewhat.

Once you obtain a starter bubble, uncap the pipe! You don't want it too thin! It should appear roughly the size of a golf ball at this point. If the bubble looks

MARVER

BLOW 'N' CAP

SHAPE/CHILL

BLOW

142

A LITTLE BIT WONKY (OR LESS THAN SYMMETRICAL) YOU MAY NEED AN ADDITIONAL PASS OVER THE MARVER TO STRAIGHTEN IT OUT. OR YOU MAY OPT TO BAIL ON IT AND START OVER IF IT LOOKS REALLY MESSED-UP.

ONCE THE STARTER BUBBLE IS ESTABLISHED HEAD OVER TO THE BENCH. YOUR NEXT STEP IS TO BLOW OUT THE BUBBLE AND NECK A LINE IN. IF YOUR BUBBLE IS ON THE THIN SIDE, YOU MAY NEED TO CHILL THE BOTTOM WITH THE BACK OF THE JACKS BEFORE YOU PUFF OUT THE BUBBLE ANY FURTHER. JUST A QUICK PASS OR TWO SHOULD BE ALL THAT'S NECESSARY. THIS IS ALSO A GOOD TECHNIQUE TO HELP CENTER-UP THE BOTTOM OF THE BUBBLE.

EVEN WALL-THICKNESS

A QUICK BLOW SHOULD BE ALL THAT IS NEEDED TO HELP PUFF-OUT THE SHOULDERS. THEN BEGIN NECKING THE BUBBLE. START FIRST IN A STRAIGHT UP AND DOWN FASHION TO ESTABLISH THE NECKLINE AND THEN ANGLE THE JACKS OUTWARD TO STRETCH AND ELONGATE THE BUBBLE.

A FINAL PUFF SHOULD ROUND-OUT THE BUBBLE FORM TO MAKE IT READY FOR THE GAFFER.

CHILL

SOMETIMES IT MAY BE NECESSARY TO REPEAT OR ALTERNATE THE ABOVE TWO STEPS TO ACHIEVE THE DESIRED SHAPE, DO WHATEVER IT TAKES....

THEN IT'S BACK TO THE GLORY HOLE FOR A SPECIALIZED REHEAT. WHAT'S SO SPECIAL ABOUT THIS REHEAT? WELL... IT CAN CHANGE EVERYTHING! IT IS VITAL THAT YOU PAY ATTENTION AT ALL TIMES!

THERE ARE MANY SUBTLE MANUVERS INVOLVED HERE. MOST OF IT OCCURS AS SLIGHT CHANGES IN PIPE ROTATION, ANGLES AT WHICH YOU AIR MARVER AND A POSSIBLE SWING OR SPIN OF THE PIPE (IN ORDER TO STRETCH THE NECK OF THE BUBBLE, FOR INSTANCE). AND **YOU MUST BE FLUID!**

WHEN YOU GO TO REHEAT THE BUBBLE, SLIDE IT JUST INSIDE AND AS CLOSE AS YOU DARE TO THE DOOR. YOU CAN MAKE USE OF THE REFLECTED HEAT THERE TO HELP SPEED UP THE PROCESS.

NECK AND BLOW

ONCE THE BUBBLE IS LOOKING GOOD AND FLOPPY, YOU SHOULD USE THE EYE IN THE BACK OF YOUR HEAD TO KNOW EXACTLY WHERE THE GAFFER IS STANDING. YOU SHOULD ALSO KNOW EXACTLY WHERE YOU'RE GOING TO STAND AND WHERE YOU CAN SAFELY SWING-OUT THE BUBBLE. TARGET THOSE SPOTS AND MOVE IN THAT DIRECTION. JUST BEFORE YOU REACH THE GAFFER, THE BUBBLE IS

GRACEFULLY SWUNG BACKWARDS (ABOUT HALFWAY OR SO BEHIND YOUR BACK) AND THEN SWUNG TOWARDS THE FRONT → IMMEDIATELY FOLLOWING THROUGH WITH THE MANUVER TO LAND SMACK DAB IN THE MIDDLE OF THE ANXIOUSLY AWAITING GAFFER'S SHEARS. THIS LITTLE TRICK STRETCHES THE BUBBLE'S NECK AND MAKES IT EASIER TO CUT.

THE BUBBLE SHOULD BE HOT ENOUGH THAT IT PRACTICALY DRIPS ONTO THE PIECE IN A SMOOTH PREDICTABLE FASHION. IT SHOULD LOOK LIKE A SLIGHTLY BULBOUS TEAR DROP.

AS SOON AS THE GAFFER TAKES CONTROL OF THE PIPE, THE ROTATION IS STOPPED. YOUR HANDS SHOULD REMAIN LOOSE AND ACT AS SUPPORT FOR THE PIPE. ALLOW THE GAFFER TO MAKE THE MOVES. BE READY TO BLOW WHEN INDICATED BY THE GAFFER.

AS GAFFER, THERE ARE A FEW THINGS YOU SHOULD BE LOOKING FOR BEFORE YOU STICK THAT BUBBLE ON. FIRST, YOUR AVOLIO (AND EVERYTHING ELSE) SHOULD BE COOL AND STABLE. MAKE

fig. A — HEAT CLOSE TO THE DOOR

1ST SWING BACK then...

fig. B ATTACH

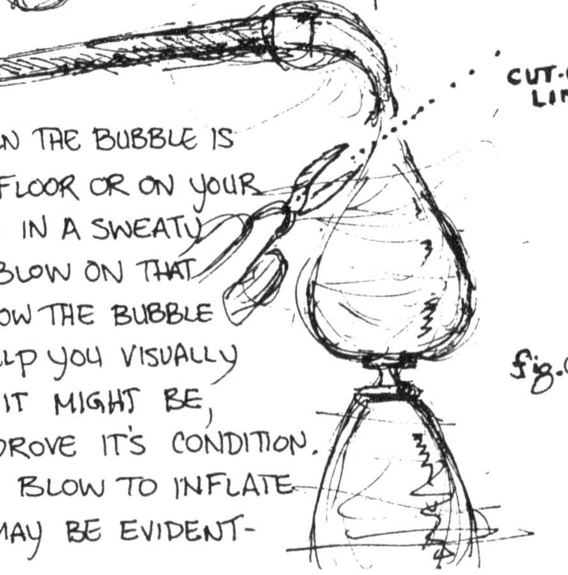

CUT-OFF LINE

SURE THAT IT IS ON-CENTER AS WELL. WHEN THE BUBBLE IS PRESENTED TO YOU → BRACE THE PIPE AGAINST THE FLOOR OR ON YOUR SHOE (AVOID JAMMING IT BETWEEN YOUR TOES IN A SWEATY BIRKENSTOCK SANDAL → SOMEBODY MAY HAVE TO BLOW ON THAT PIPE LATER! yuk!). KEEP AN EYE ON HOW THE BUBBLE IS FALLING (fig B above). THIS WILL HELP YOU VISUALLY GUAGE HOW HOT THE BUBBLE IS, HOW THIN IT MIGHT BE, AND WHAT YOU MIGHT NEED TO DO TO IMPROVE IT'S CONDITION. SOMETIMES YOUR ASSISTANT WILL NEED TO BLOW TO INFLATE IT FURTHER. OTHERTIMES A THIN SPOT MAY BE EVIDENT—

fig. C

in which case you might chill it out with the sides/blades of your shears and have your assistant puff it out at the same time. Or if you're lucky, the bubble may be perfect and you don't have to mess with anything! Many gaffers will gently touch the bubble down on the avolio and rotate their pipe to the right and/or left a bit to make certain it's on center. Then, A SLIGHT pull upwards to stretch the bubble a tad and a quick, deliberate snip with the shears to cut the bubble free. Use an upward motion to cut the bubble. This will help maintain the foot bubble on-center and leave you with a nice little tail (which will help later-on). Use the jaws rather than the tips of your shears to cut with → it's more effective.

fig D
PULL A POINT

OPTIONAL fig E
SQUEEZE 'N' PUFF

fig F
NECK OFF A KNOB

fig G
CHILL IT!

The piece is flashed and then the foot bubble should be heated thoroughly. Return to the bench. Examine your bubble. If it looks good, procede to neck down the bubble → as described below. If on the otherhand the bubble is wonky and off-center ~ you might pull the little tail outwards to straighten things out (fig D). It may be that the bubble got cut short a little. You can expand it slightly by crimping the tail section with the flat part of your tweezers (as in fig E) → this should puff out the shoulders of the bubble and enable you to even things out.

Next, cut a small neckline in on the bottom of your bubble. HOT GOOD!
Use swift full revolutions. Once your neckline is established - continue to squeeze it down while your assistant blows on it (to accelerate the chilling process) - with the small end of the soffietta. Don't neck it so tight as to close off the hole (that would be counterproductive!). Leave enough space that you might be able to slide a pencil through the hole or so. Once you feel some resistance on your jacks from the friction → indicating the glass is sufficiently chilled, have your assistant ready to tap off the little bubble. Crimp the neck with the diamond shears while your assistant

taps the little tail of the bubble in a quick downward motion with the back of their tweezers (or similar tool). The tiny bubble should come free. If not, continue to crimp and chill with the diamond shears (or go back to the jacks) and try it again. Take a reheat.

Keep your eye on the foot. Reheat it just inside the glory hole door until it's good n' hot. Look for signs of movement in the bubble. When the hole looks good and fire-polished, it's probably time to open up the foot. Be careful! Overheating the bubble at this point can cause it to close back up on itself, in which case you have to repeat the previous steps all over again, or cut the bubble off and start a new one.

Return to the bench. Examine the bubble and decide whether you want a folded lip on the foot or not. It's an aesthetic and functional choice, and entirely at your discretion. If you want a folded lip tap the bubble in a bit with the back of your jacks to initiate the process. This will kick the lip in somewhat. If you don't want a folded lip, skip this step.

To open the foot, insert the tips of the jacks just inside the hole and begin to reem and center-up the opening. Again, use quick full revolutions to touch all bases and maintain your foot's integrity. If both blades don't fit, use just one to get it open enough until you can get both in there. If neither

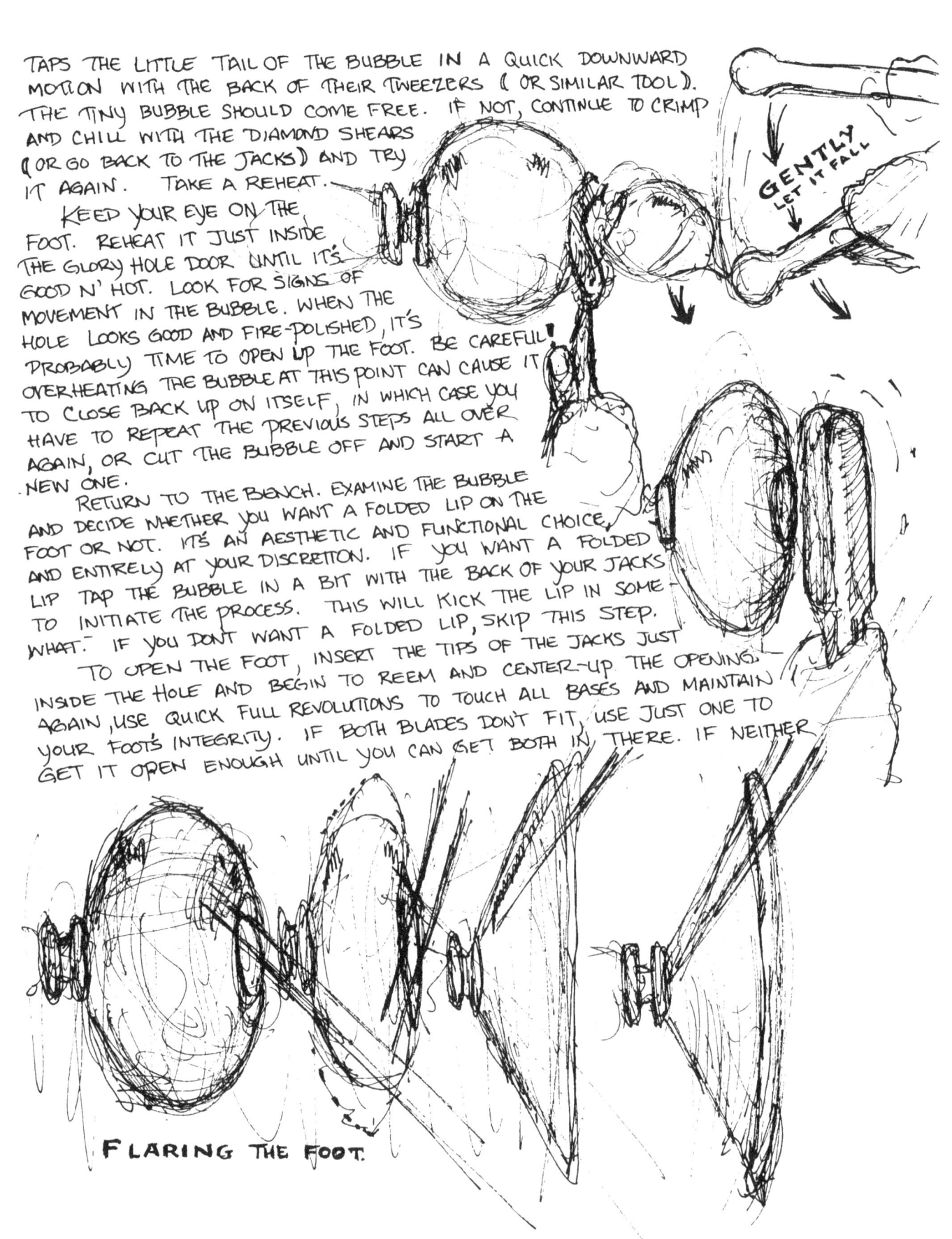

FLARING THE FOOT.

of them fit, you may have to resort to using one blade of your tweezers to get it open. Although it may seem awkward at first, it's best to attack the upper lip of the bubble (vs. the bottom) and try to open it that way. This way you don't have to reach too far to fully open the foot and it allows you to see and respond more quickly to what's happening.

If you heat the bubble correctly - you should be able to open and flare the foot in one fell swoop. Sometimes it may be necessary to take an additional reheat to get the foot fully opened and relatively flat.

Two things which may hamper your efforts are the overheated avolio and the overchilled foot. If your avolio is less-than-stable and flopping around - it will be next-to-impossible to keep your foot on-center and open it up. If that's the case have your assistant blow on the avolio with the soffietta while you freeze it up with the blades of the jacks. As soon as it seems stiff enough → proceed to open up the foot. Now if the bubble isn't heated deep enough you'll probably wind-up with a bell-shaped foot instead of a nice flat or tapered cone-shaped foot. This can be a highly frustrating process until you learn exactly how to heat the glass in exactly the right area for exactly the right amount of time. Other variables can influence your ability to open the foot as well, such as → the workability of the glass → how stiff or soft it is, the temperature of your glory hole and even the shape of your jacks' blades. (Yes, you can ALWAYS blame it on your tools!).

Once you have your foot opened-up, you can have your assistant paddle the foot while you shape the inside surface with the jacks. By angling the jacks outward you can end-up with exactly the size flare you desire. A final reheat and tune-up may be necessary to get everything straight before you're ready to punty up.

PADDLE IT SMOOTH.

GOBLET BOWLS

AFTER THE STEM, THE "CUP" OR "BOWL" IS THE COMPONENT WHICH OFFERS YOU THE MOST AMOUNT OF FREEDOM FOR ARTISTIC INTERPRETATION WITHIN THE "CONFINES" OF THE GOBLET FORM. IT CLEARLY IS THE MOST IMMEDIATE ELEMENT ON DISPLAY ~ THE PART WHICH GETS NOTICED FIRST. SO.... WITH THAT IN MIND → YOU SHOULD CONSIDER AND PLAN/DESIGN CAREFULLY WHEN TRYING TO MAKE THEM.

FIRST, A FEW IDEAS ON <u>FORM & FUNCTION</u>: NOWADAYS, IT SEEMS AS THOUGH YOU COULD DIVIDE THE GOBLET FIELD INTO TWO SEPERATE REALMS: "FUNCTIONAL" AND "SCULPTURAL". THERE ARE THOSE CUPS WHICH ARE MADE TO BE USED (DRANK FROM!) ON A DAILY BASIS (NO, THAT DOESN'T MAKE THEM 'DISHWASHER SAFE' [A DEVICE, WE SUSPECT, DESIGNED BY A DISGRUNTLED FIRST-YEAR GLASSBLOWER, MADE TO DESTROY ALL PIECES OF GLASS except PYREX WITHOUT CONVICTION]). AND, THERE ARE THOSE GOBLETS WHICH ARE BETTER LEFT FOR VIEWING AND COLLECTING (AND DUSTING). NOT MANY OF US CAN AFFORD TO LOSE A LINO CUP TO A SLIP OF THE GRIP DURING A SOCIAL FUNCTION! (ON THAT NOTE - A GOOD 70-80% OF GOBLETS BROKEN HAPPEN DURING ROUTINE CLEANING - what's up with that?).

WHEN YOU BECOME REALLY PROFICIENT AT BLOWING THEM, BOWLS CAN GET TISSUE THIN → TO THE POINT WHERE YOU CAN ACTUALLY SQUEEZE & FLEX THEM! DON'T EVEN THINK OF DROPPING AN ICE CUBE IN ONE! SUCH FEATHERWEIGHT GOBLETS BECOME SCULPTURAL PIECES WHICH USE THE FORMAT OF THE DRINKING VESSEL AS SUBJECT MATTER. WHICHEVER REALM YOU WISH TO SUBSCRIBE TO - **KNOW BEFOREHAND WHAT YOU'RE SHOOTING FOR ~ AND WHY.** [MAKE A DRAWING - please!]

(THERE WAS A TIME WHEN NEARLY EVERY BEVERAGE CONCEIVABLE HAD A SPECIFICALLY DESIGNED GLASS TO COMPLEMENT THE LIQUID BEING SERVED. YOU HAD YOUR SCOTCH GLASS (ON THE ROCKS - WITH SODA; OR 'NEAT') RED WINE, WHITE WINE, PORT AND WATER GLASSES etc. IT'S A FACT, JACK, THAT THE SHAPE, WEIGHT AND VOLUME OF A DRINKING VESSEL CAN AFFECT YOUR DRINKING EXPERIENCE AND PERCEPTION. IN OTHER WORDS, THERE ARE REASONS WHY MANY GLASSES ARE SHAPED THE WAY THEY ARE/WERE. THE SHALLOW, WIDE -RIMMED CHAMPAGNE GOBLETS - ALTHOUGH BEAUTIFUL TO LOOK AT - ARE HORRIBLE TO DRINK FROM. THEY BRING NEW FOUND FRUSTRATION TO THE WORD "TIPSY" AS YOU MAKE EVERY EFFORT NOT TO SPILL A DROP WHILE SIPPING FROM THEM.

UNQUESTIONABLY THERE ARE MANY STYLES AND SHAPES TO CHOOSE FROM OR DEVOLOP ON. DESIGNING AND BLOWING GOBLETS FOR A SPECIFIC FUNCTION OR STYLE OF BEVERAGE IS AN EASY WAY TO NARROW DOWN THE FIELD.

EACH CUP YOU ATTEMPT TO MAKE WILL HAVE IT'S OWN SPECIFIC NEEDS AND TECHNIQUES NECESSARY TO INSURE SUCCESSFUL COMPLETION. HERE ARE A FEW RECOMMENDATIONS ON HOW TO MAKE THE BEST USE OF YOUR TIME WHILE BLOWING THESE CHALLENGING FORMS: **#1. START SIMPLE.** MAKE IT EASY ON YOURSELF. DON'T TRY TO BLOW TISSUE THIN CUPS RIGHT OFF THE BAT. YOU'LL JUST END-UP FRUSTRATING YOU AND YOUR ASSISTANT.

#2. PRACTICE MAKES PERFECT. PICK ONE FORM AND GET SKILLED AT MAKING IT. CUT DOWN ON YOUR VARIABLES. DON'T WORRY ABOUT THE STEMS OR FEET. JUST BLOW THE BOWL, ADD AN AVOLIO, PUNTY IT AND OPEN IT UP — AND BOX 'EM. THROUGH THIS TYPE OF REPETITION YOU WILL BE ABLE TO FOCUS AND CONCENTRATE ON THE ELEMENT AT HAND. LATER ON, YOU CAN SET THE CUPS IN A GARAGE, WARM 'EM UP, BLOW THE REST OF THE PARTS AND PUT IT ALL TOGETHER.

#3. KEEP AT IT! BE CONSISTENT. PRACTICE EVERY DAY IF YOU CAN. DON'T JUST SIT DOWN FOR AN HOUR AND HOPE THAT IT ALL WORKS OUT. YOU NEED TO KNOW HOW THESE THINGS ARE MADE INSIDE AND OUT — IN YOUR SLEEP — IF YOU WANT TO BECOME PROFICIENT AT MAKING THEM.

#4. FIND SOMEONE YOU CAN WORK WITH. HAVING AN ASSISTANT WHO CAN LEARN AND GROW WITH YOU WILL MAKE YOUR EXPERIENCE MUCH MORE ENJOYABLE. YOU CAN SWITCH-OFF POSITIONS FROM TIME-TO-TIME OR DAY-TO-DAY DEPENDING ON YOUR NEEDS OR SCHEDULES, ONE PERSON BEING THE GAFFER AND THE OTHER AS ASSISTANT.

#5. REMEMBER TO RELAX. IT CAN GET PRETTY INTENSE BLOWING THESE DAINTY LITTLE BASTARDS — PARTICULARLY WHEN THEY'RE CRINKLING ON THE RIGHT, JUMPING ON THE LEFT AND LAUGHING AT YOU THE WHOLE WAY DOWN! LIKE THE GAME OF GOLF, SO MUCH OF THIS IS PSYCHOLOGICAL! IT'S EASY FOR ONE MISTAKE TO RUIN YOUR WHOLE DAY. LIGHTEN UP. LET IT GO. TAKE A BREATHER. SMASH SOME OLD GLASS, AND GET BACK ON THE STICK.

#6. GET SET-UP TO MAKE GOBLETS. TURN THE FURNACE UP A NOTCH. THE GLASS HAS TO BE HOT ENOUGH IN THE FIRST PLACE! TRY TO FIND THE RIGHT EQUIPMENT FOR THE TASK AT HAND, OR 'MAKE-DO' WITH WHAT YOU'VE GOT. HAVING "THE RIGHT TOOLS" DOES MAKE A DIFFERENCE WHEN BLOWING GOBLETS — ESPECIALLY WHEN YOU KNOW HOW TO USE THEM. SEE THE SECTION ON TOOLS FOR MORE INFORMATION (PAGE 278)

#7. WORK FROM A DRAWING. BE IT A SKETCH TAPED TO THE HEAT SHIELD BY THE GLORY HOLE, A DESIGN IN YOUR NOTEBOOK OR A CHALK DRAWING ON THE FLOOR, A VISUAL REFERENCE → NO MATTER HOW CRUDELY MADE OR ANATOMICALLY INACCURATE IT IS → CAN HELP CLARIFY IN YOUR MIND'S EYE WHAT YOU'RE TRYING TO MAKE.

#8. WORK QUICK AND FAST. EVEN FRACTIONS OF SECONDS COUNT — SO MAKE THE BEST USE OF YOUR TIME. MOST CLEAR BOWLS SHOULD BE MADE IN THREE MINUTES OR LESS (O.K. MAYBE FIVE — TOPS!). ECONOMY OF MOTION, TOOL PLACEMENT AND TEMPERATURE OF THE GLASS ARE FACTORS WHICH YOU HAVE CONTROL OVER AND SHOULD DO YOUR BEST TO MASTER. IF IT HELPS, MAYBE MOVE THE BENCH CLOSER TO THE GLORY HOLE. YOU WON'T HAVE TO MAKE AS MANY STEPS BACK AND FORTH FOR THE REHEATS.

#9. STUDY WITH A MASTER. IF YOU CAN AFFORD IT, SIGN UP FOR A CLASS WITH SOMEONE HIGHLY SKILLED AT MAKING GOBLETS. THEY CAN SHOW YOU WHAT YOU NEED TO DO TO OVERCOME SOME OF THOSE HURDLES.

#10. IF AT FIRST YOU DON'T SUCCEED — TRY, TRY AGAIN! LEARN FROM YOUR MISTAKES AND KEEP GOING. MOVE FORWARD. NOBODY SAID IT WAS — EASY...

BASIC BOWL

First, begin by selecting a goblet pipe (or the smallest light-weight blowpipe available) - gather as much as you can on one dip. "Air marver" the glass until the glass on the end of your pipe is symmetrical and mostly off the end of the pipe - where you can use it.

Now marver the glass into a cylinder. Keep the pipe horizontal as you make a quick pass or two. Air marver a little more to maintain control and shape of the glass. Blow and cap the pipe to allow the bubble to expand. Tilt the pipe up so you can watch the bubble inflate. As soon as your starter bubble forms, uncap the pipe.

Next, marver your bubble horizontally to chill and shape the sidewalls. An additional puff and you should end up with a uniform bubble.

After a good solid reheat (the whole thing should be moving) sit back at the bench. Use your tweezers to pull a point from the end of your bubble - as close to dead center as you can get it. Tug slightly to elongate the form and tell your assistant to begin blowing. Grab your diamond shears and keep pulling that point while simultaneously blowing (and turning the pipe too!). You can nip more glass further up the bubble to help stretch and thin the bottom of the bubble.

There's a good chance that the bubble will overinflate too rapidly due to really high temperature within the glass - or from the strong lungs of your enthusiastic assistant. Or, the bubble just doesn't seem to be getting much bigger 'cause its too cold and your A-steamed blowing partner is blue-in-the-face from trying. These are things you and your assistant need to work out.

Trouble picking that first point? Do you end-up just pushing it in? Two things may be at fault. Often, the bubble is simply not hot enough on the bottom. Reheat 'til it's almost floppy and try again. Or, there's a strong possibility your tweezers have some wax on them (or they're in bad need of sharpening!) - and you're slippin' instead of gripping. Clean them with some steel wool, heat or both. (See start-up procedures page 12.)

Depending on the style of goblet bowl you're shooting for, you will need to either pull the bottom further out for longer/taller pilsner-style cups, or cut the tip off and begin shaping the bubble with the jacks - for wider or more shallow bowls.

MARVER

BLOW'N'CAP LET EXPAND.

STARTER BUBBLE

PULL A POINT

ELONGATE

Reheat as often as necessary to achieve THE DESIRED SHAPE. Naturally, the thinner the glass is, the less heat/time will be required to get the bubble hot. **PAY ATTENTION** to the behavior of your glass while reheating. It's very easy to overheat and crinkle/collapse the bubble at all stages of goblet making. If you notice that this occurs frequently, you may wish to turn down your glory hole for a kindler gentler flame and a more predictable reheating source/situation.

If you want the shoulders to blow-out thinner, ride the jacks on the lower part of the bubble while your assistant blows at the same time. If you're quick and fortunate enough to retain sufficient heat in the neck of the piece, you may begin cutting in your neckline. HINT: That area closest to the pipe holds the most heat. It's your best bet for a clean and E-Z necking zone.

① CHILL HERE
② PUFF-OUT HERE
③ NECK HERE

Squeeze the jacks slowly at first to cut-in your initial line, then go more aggressively. Be sure to make rapid, full turns/revolutions on the blowpipe. Your assistant may blow slightly to prevent any collapsing of the form. Angle the jacks outward to help stretch the neck. Then reinforce a clean neckline by jacking straight up and down a final time. It may require a quick reheat just to get a well defined neckline, but that's what you need in order for all this to work.

ANGLE THE JACKS

You can, of course, overdo it. You can make such a tight neckline as to close off the hole (oops!)—or one with so little structure that the smallest jarring of the pipe causes your bubble to jump off the pipe into never, never land... (so it goes...) Without some stability there at the neck, your bubble will be very hard to control and keep on center, so → WATCH IT!

After the neck has been cut-in nice-and-clean-like, you may focus your attention to the bottom half of the cup. Reheat, first flashing the whole piece, and then bring it out to concentrate the heat on the lower part. Back at the bench — begin by chilling/shaping the upper part of the bubble (to establish and maintain structural integrity of your bubble/cup), and then move the jacks down the length of the bubble to further shape the bottom. You may have your assistant blow softly to inflate the cup and/or maintain stability within.

If, as stated earlier, you want a longer/taller cup, you can continue to draw out the bottom of the bubble either by pulling it with the diamond shears (at the same time your assistant should be blowing) or by necking a knob down there and drawing it out further.

Use the jacks to shape and chill the bubble. Try to smooth-out any rough spots. Additional reheats and shaping may be necessary to get the form looking right. Avoid the temptation of using newspaper or the marver to get the DESIRED SHAPE — it should be done at the bench with the jacks. And yes! It does take a while to get comfortable using the jacks in this fashion.

Once you obtain the desired shape, go ahead and add your AVOLIO. ... ...

If you're skilled and fortunate enough, your avolio will go on nice and smooth and you'll be ready to punty-up and transfer the cup. If you've succeeded in blowing the bottom of your cup 'wafer' thin → you may notice that part of the avolio got sucked-in mysteriously. It's an aesthetic detail which you may not care for. In the future, there's two ways of dealing with it. The first way is to simply blow your cups with a little more glass down on the bottom so the resulting hot-bit/avolio doesn't create such a heat-sink. Granted, you end-up with a slightly heavier goblet, but it may at least look right.

The second way involves chilling the inside surface of the avolio with the jacks prior to marvering it on into the cone shape. This helps skin-over and center (somewhat) the glass - chilling it enough so it doesn't get absorbed into the bottom of the cup. A quick shaping with the tips of the jacks is all you need - between the cup and your freshly applied bit. And then you can go ahead and mash on the rest of the bit and cut-in the mini-neckline.

The **TRANSFER** is pretty much the same as for most things, except you need more **FINESSE**, less **BRUTE** strength - and **NO WATER!** With a well-defined neckline, you only need to chill the neck with the cooler region of your jacks - with a couple quick revolutions or "crimps", and a quick, gentle tap on the pipe with the back of the jacks. Or you can try it like the pros and just lift the end of the blowpipe off the back rail of the bench a couple of inches and let it fall. With the jacks still crimping the neck, the resulting shock of the pipe hitting the bench should break the cup free n' easy.

DRY TRANSFER METHOD
VENETIAN-STYLE

If your cup doesn't want to come off, try crimping/chilling the neck again and tapping it off. If it still doesn't come free, use just one drop of water as a last result. Oftentimes water can be too much for your cup to handle and will thermal shock your bowl into pieces right before your very own eyes - so be careful with that stuff!

Opening and trimming goblets is pretty much the same as for most things, you just have work faster! In the following pages you will see how several other styles of goblet bowls are made. In some cases, you can make an entire goblet out of one large bubble → cup·stem & foot! A tried n' true time saver, and the only way to ensure your color/design is even and consistent. The best way you can get proficient at blowing cups is by making them, over n' over n' over again. Watching masters work - helps - but it isn't until you get on the stick that all those little, subtle moves begin to make sense.

LIP WRAP   SUITABLE FOR ALL VESSELS

Although this technique was covered in ED's BIG HANDBOOK OF GLASSBLOWING, I'll recap the process once more, in case you've misplaced your copy somewhere, or you never had the opportunity to buy one in the first place.

Begin by smoothing out the lip. Use the jacks, both the back end and the blades to get the hole round and flat. Avoid opening the vessel any more than is absolutely necessary. This is your built-in "fudge factor". In the event that your bit doesn't go on as slick as silk, you have the chance to hide any unsightly blobs by opening the vessel. The more that you open it, the less obvious the flaws become.

SMOOTH IT.

Also, you benefit by having less real estate to cover. If the hole is smaller, the bit can go on faster and hotter, with less distance to travel.

THE BIT. POINT IT!

It's all-important that the bit is shaped and heated correctly. You should have a nice point, with even heat all the way through. This takes some extra time in preparation - particularly for those stiff colors - so try to plan your reheats accordingly. Some gaffers may prefer a blunter tip or more glass on or off the punty. (to each his own.)

APPLY IT.

Most gaffers will take the bit from back behind the bench. You can use the shears to grip and guide the assistants punty - so that if you need to, you can always cut the excess/bit away.

Touch-up lightly at first. Make the marriage of the two a gentle one in the beginning. If you make a big blob at first → you are committing yourself to a fat lip wrap, or one which may go on fat but trail thin towards the end.

PULL IT OFF

If, on the otherhand, you begin with a thin line, you can always BEEF it up anywhere you like it - by turning the rod slower or moving the color closer to the lip. You can also continue to feed more glass on two or three times if you like.

To break the trail off, yank back on the punty, and/or yank the piece away from the color. It should, if it's hot enough, come clean. Sometimes, you might get an excess stringer, which is easily cut clean.

OPEN IT UP!

After a few reheats and some smoothing-out with the jacks, you can open your form to it's final shape.

153

THE OPTIC MOLD

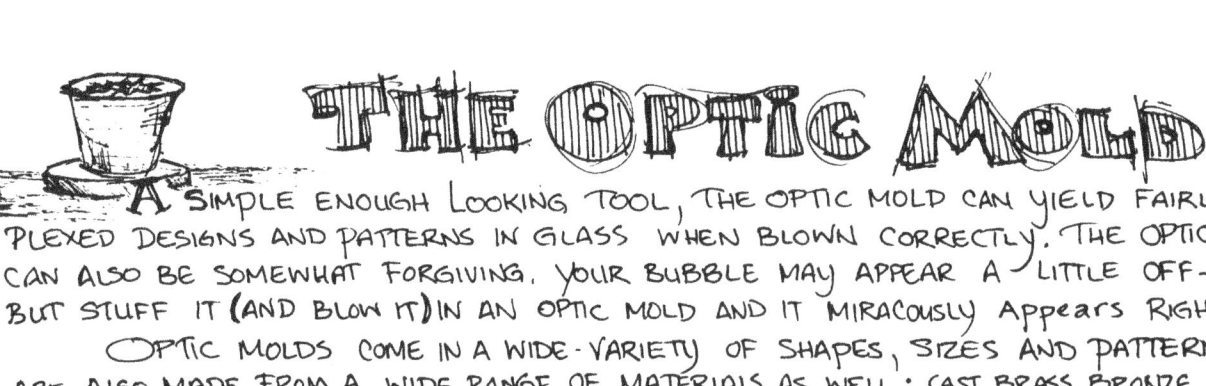

A simple enough looking tool, the optic mold can yield fairly complexed designs and patterns in glass when blown correctly. The optic mold can also be somewhat forgiving. Your bubble may appear a little off-center, but stuff it (and blow it) in an optic mold and it miracously appears right-on!

Optic molds come in a wide variety of shapes, sizes and patterns. They are also made from a wide range of materials as well: cast brass, bronze, aluminum or even iron. Each mold has it's own identity and uniqueness. Some molds you can blow into HARD, whereas others will trap and eat your bubble—if you expand it too large (beware of those Italian "pine-apple molds"), so—sometimes—puff *lightly!*

The key to blowing most optic molds is: **GET YOUR BUBBLE IN THE RIGHT SHAPE ~ First and Foremost**, AND **GET YOUR BUBBLE HOT**. The rest is secondary. As with most forms of moldblowing, you'll want your bubble to look as much like the mold's interior as possible before blowing into it.

For venetian-style cups it's important that your marver and blow your bubble clear down to the bottom before **Stuffin' n' Puffin'**. Doing this will help you retain the optic ribbing effect. NOTE ☞ The more you have to heat and reheat and blow your bubble after you've stuffed it in the optic mold, the LESS CRISP your design will be. So, work fast, blow the mold as hot as you can, and don't monkey with it any more than necessary.

Get your starter bubble marvered and blown into shape. Position your mold near the glory hole (have a step or cinder block handy if you're not tall enough to blow into the pipe/mold). After a good solid reheat, drop the bubble into the mold. As soon as you've made contact with the bottom — puff hard (blow n' cap if you like) blow firm - fill that mold! After a couple of seconds — pull out of the mold and take a quick reheat.

Back at the bench, decide if you want to twist the bubble/design. If you do, neck down a knob at the end with the jacks or crimp a knob down with the diamond shears. By turning the pipe in one direction (vs. back n' forth) you'll initiate a twist in the pattern.

If the knob is cool enough to grab with the diamond shears, you can grip it steady while twisting the pipe (and bubble) with the left hand to gain your optic twist.

If the knob is still soft and hot, you can dip it in water to freeze it up, take a reheat, quench once more and then twist up the whole bubble. Then cut the excess knob off.

From here it's pretty much business as usual. Again, work fast to avoid overheating the optic pattern out. Have your assistant blow while you twist the pattern in. It will help keep your bubble from collapsing. You could decide to do a double stuff and blow the bubble back in the mold a second time to yield another type of optic pattern. You could also add colored powder or do color trails on your bubble prior to blowing it in the mold to achieve interesting color patterns. the possibilities are endless.

Another technique, MEZZO STAMPO, uses the optic mold to pattern the bottom half of the bubble. Oftentimes, a hot gather is dropped on the bubble prior to stuffing it in the mold. The pattern then may be tweeked with to yield several different designs.

DOUBLE STUFFED OPTIC PATTERN

Begin with a starter bubble which has been marvered and blown into a narrow tapered point (see fig. 173). Have your assistant take a gather or two on a punty. Let the glass ball-up off the end of the punty (by air marvering) and then drop it on from overhead. Turn the pipe as the glass makes contact with the starter bubble to make sure the glob is going on even.

DROP IT ON.

COVER 1/2 AND STUFF IT!
fig. 173

When you've covered the bottom 1/3d to 1/2 of your starter bubble - cut the rest off with the diamond shears. Take a quick reheat and stuff the bubble into your optic mold. Blow hard and remove. Take another quick reheat/flash.

If you wish to have a really crisp design on the bottom half of your cup, you'll have to take a few minutes to accentuate each and every rib of the optic pattern. → Use your tweezers and pinch together the tips around the top end of the ribs. Squeeze down the length of each rib. This extra reinforcement really enhances the optic effect — despite being a bit of a chore to do.

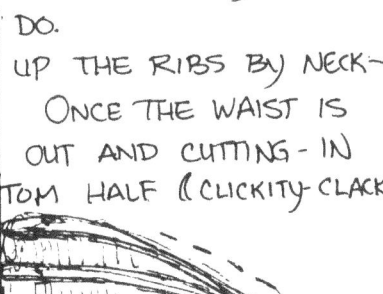
CRIMP EACH RIB

From here, you can use the jacks to centering against them as your partner begins to blow set-up — concentrate on blowing the shoulders up the ribs by necking. Once the waist is out and cutting-in the neckline. You can ride the jacks on the bottom half (clickity-clack) of the piece while your assistant blows.

Once the shoulders are puffed out and you've cut-in your neckline, you can focus on blowing out/stretching the bottom half of the cup. You can use your diamond shears to grip a point, crimp, and begin to draw, pull, and blow out the bottom.

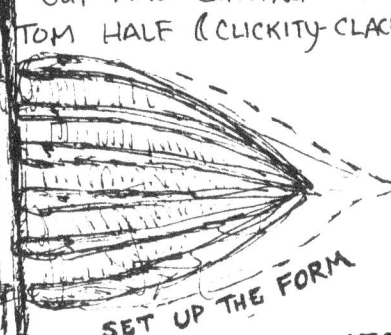
SET UP THE FORM

155

Have your assistant blow as you draw out the length of the bottom with either the diamond shears or the jacks. Do your best not to twist up the ribs by either nipping and pulling or compensating for the twist by UN-TWISTING it with a reverse of direction.

Cut the excess glass off with the diamond shears and neck down the bottom of the cup with the jacks while having your assistant blow.

Shape-up the bottom of your cup with the jacks to your desired form. Add an avolio-punty it up and trim, open-up the top to its final form.

Besides crimping the ribs, you can also try snipping the upper part of each rib to create a small dot or ball above each rib. Use small trimming shears to get in-between each rib and snip as deep as you can get to the base bubble. Additional reheats may be needed to get all the way around the piece.

Once all the ribs have been cut, heat and blow out the cup as you would normally (as described above).

Yet another variation on the mezzo stampo theme is the vertical chain-wrap motif. You can achieve this effect by crimping two of the optic ribs together with the points of your tweezers.

Pick a spot where you want to have the ribs joined. Heat them just enough where you can fairly easily crimp them together.

Avoid heating too deep or too long, you want those ribs to stay fairly crisp.

You can do one, two or three sets of rows depending on your taste. Once all the ribs have been crimped to your satisfaction, you can continue to blow-out the cup as described above.

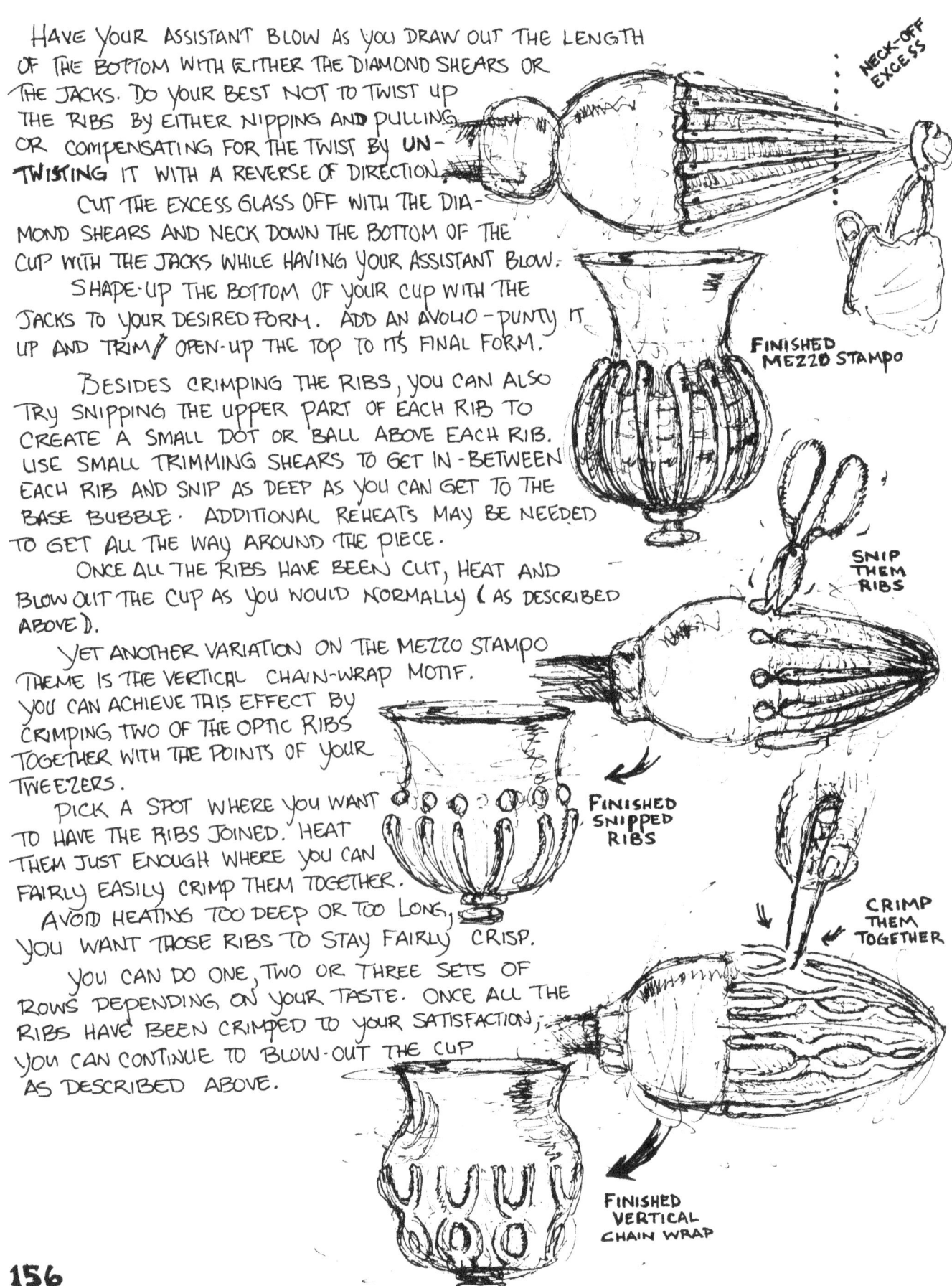

PINEAPPLE MOLDS ARE A SPECIALIZED VERSION OF THE OPTIC MOLD FAMILY. GOOD ONES (USUALLY MADE IN ITALY) ARE EXPENSIVE AND SOMEWHAT HARD TO COME BY. BUT THE EFFECT THEY YIELD MAY BE 'EXACTLY' WHAT YOU'RE LOOKING FOR. SOME OF THE MOLDS YOU'LL USE, WILL BE FOR THE OPTIC EFFECT THAT THEY PRODUCE, WHILE OTHERS MAY BE UTILIZED FOR TRAPPING AIR BUBBLES — WHEN GATHERED OVER.

WHEN USING A PINEAPPLE MOLD — AVOID BLOWING HARD INTO THEM. MANY OF THESE TYPES OF MOLDS HAVE SLIGHT UNDERCUTS TO THEM. IF YOU EXPAND YOUR BUBBLE IN THEM TOO MUCH, YOU MAY N E V E R GET IT OUT! JUST TRY TO GO IN THEM — **HOT N' QUICK** — DON'T HANG-OUT IN THE MOLD TOO LONG EITHER! IF YOU JUST WISH TO USE THE OPTIC RIBBING EFFECT, BLOW THE BUBBLE OUT QUICK AND WITH AS FEW REHEATS AS YOU CAN SO AS TO MAINTAIN THE INTEGRITY OF THE PATTERN.

IF YOU WISH TO USE THE MOLD TO OBTAIN AN INTERESTING BUBBLE PATTERN — AGAIN, GET YOUR STARTER BUBBLE GOOD N' HOT — DROP IT INTO THE MOLD FOR A FEW SECONDS, WITHDRAW IT AND ALLOW IT TO GET "STONE COLD" BEFORE GATHERING OVER. FROM THERE, YOU MAY BLOW THE REST OUT AS NORMAL.

A PINEAPPLE MOLD.

ANOTHER MOLD USED BY VENETIAN-style CUP MAKERS IS THE **FLANGE MOLD**. HERE, A CUP IS BLOWN OUT, TRANSFERRED AND FLARED OPEN. THEN THE CUP IS HEATED A FINAL TIME AND GENTLY SET DOWN ON TOP OF THE MOLD → THE RIBS PUSHING FROM THE INSIDE-OUT. THESE MOLDS ARE AVAILABLE IN VARIETY OF SIZES AND SHAPES — WITH 6, 8, or 12 or MORE RIBS.

THE TRICK TO MAKING THESE WORK IS HITTING THE MOLD RIGHT ON — DEAD CENTER, OTHERWISE YOUR CUP MAY APPEAR LOP-SIDED. GUESS WHAT? IT TAKES PRACTICE! but... YOU CAN YIELD SOME VERY STYLISH CUPS ONCE YOU BECOME PROFICIENT AT USING THEM. plus THEY'RE NOT TOO DIFFICULT TO FABRICATE ON YOUR OWN IF YOU HAVE SOME METAL-WORKING SKILLS AND EQUIPMENT.

FOR A HEXAGONAL MOLD, CUT-OUT 3 EQUAL PIECES OF FLAT STEEL AND NOTCH THEM AS ABOVE. FIT THEM TOGETHER — TAB A → SLOT B etc — SPREAD THEM EQUIDISTANT FROM EACH OTHER AND WELD THEM TO A STEEL BASE ↝ OR IF YOU WANT SOMETHING EASIER TO TRANSPORT, YOU CAN NOTCH-OUT SLOTS IN A WOODEN BASE AND FIT THE STEEL RIBS IN EACH GROOVE.

BASE + MIDDLE + TOP =

STEMS

The central component of the blown glass goblet is the stem. This feature can be the most creative avenue or outlet of artistic interpretation for the goblet maker. It is here where the most traditional of designs may be explored, or perhaps the most unique or bizarre combinations of elements be attempted.... You're the bus driver.

A small kiln (a.k.a. the Garage) or pick-up oven can greatly increase one's ability to boldly blow what's never been blown before. These devices can safely store cups or components at a stabalized temperature until they are needed. They can dramatically serve to expand ones glass vocabulary, in addition to saving valuable time in the creative process.

The introduction of other materials / mixed media may be of interest to you. Nobody (but narrow-minded purists) says you have to do it all "hot" either. With the advancements in the adhesives industry today, there are a wide variety of glues capable of holding your goblets together seemingly indefinately! Have fun. GO WILD!

The stem allows you the greatest arena of self expression in this tradition-dominated form and technique. It can easily set your work apart from other "imitations". Drawing and design are especially helpful in this area. Take some time out to investigate the possibilities confronting you. **THINK BEFORE YOU BLOW.**

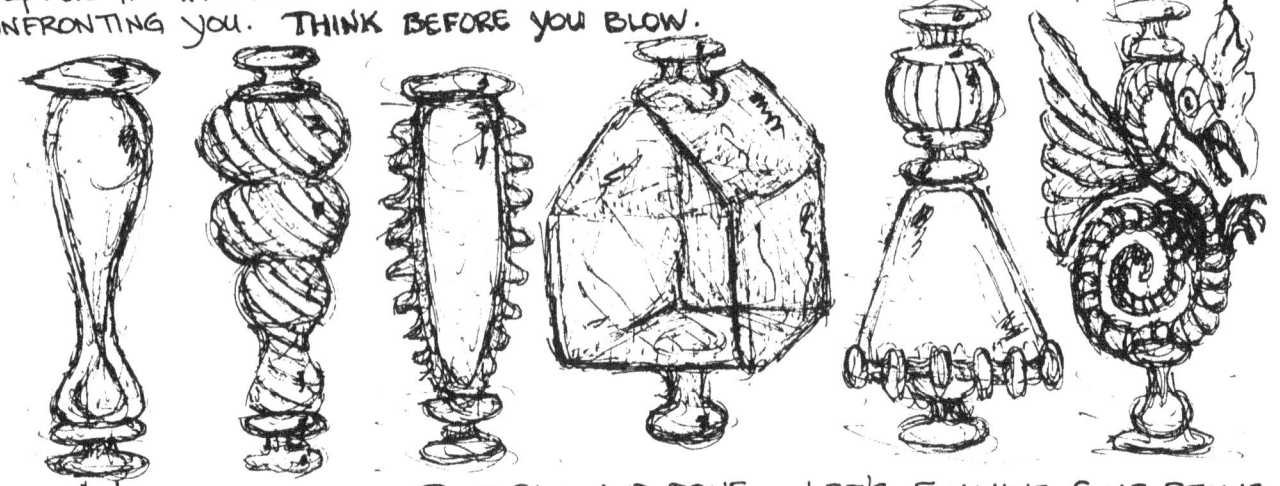

Now, with all of that said and done, - let's examine some stems in order to set a foundation on which to build. There are pro's & cons to all stems. First off, why even bother with a stem? ...Well, maybe you don't want to warm-up the beverage you're drinking by holding the bowl. Or maybe you'd like a taller vessel without the added volume in the cup or foot. Perhaps the stem reflects your personality or cultural backround. Or it might be that you enjoy the simplicity and beauty of the traditional blown goblet.

Whatever the case may be, let's assume you like the idea of a stem. Which style? Should it be blown or solid? The benefits to blown stems are that they're lightweight and visually attractive. The disad-

VANTAGES TO THEM ARE THAT THEY'RE TRICKIER TO MAKE AND TAKE (USUALLY) MORE TIME TO COMPLETE. IT IS ALSO MORE CRITICAL TO KEEP THEM WARM.

SOLID STEMS ON THE OTHERHAND OFFER ENHANCED STRUCTURE, THERMALLY THEY ARE MORE STABLE AND ARE QUICKER TO MAKE. THEY CAN EXHIBIT OPTICAL QUALITIES NOT FOUND IN THEIR BLOWN COUNTERPARTS. THEY ARE, HOWEVER, HEAVIER IN TERMS OF OVERALL WEIGHT - SO THAT MIGHT BE AN ISSUE YOU ARE CONCERNED WITH.

THERE ARE, OF COURSE, EXCEPTIONS TO EVERY RULE. DOLPHIN OR DRAGON-STEMMED GOBLETS, ALTHOUGH MADE UP OF SOLID BITS - ARE FAIRLY LIGHTWEIGHT. THEY DO TAKE QUITE A BIT OF TIME TO MAKE AND REQUIRE CONSTANT REHEATING TO KEEP THEM WARM AND TO PREVENT THE BITS FROM POPPING OFF.

THERE ARE SO MANY WAYS TO MAKE STEMS THAT I COULD SPEND THE REST OF THIS BOOK DESCRIBING THEM. IN AN EFFORT TO MAKE A LONG STORY SHORT, I'LL CONDENSE SOME OF THAT INFORMATION INTO AN ABRIDGED FORM. IN THE FOLLOWING PAGES YOU'LL FIND OUTLINED THE STEPS INVOLVED IN MAKING A BLOWN STEM AND A SOLID ONE. THESE MAY SERVE AS FOUNDATIONS ON WHICH YOU MAY BUILD OR CHANGE.

IN MOST CASES, (I RATHER DISLIKE THIS GENERALIZATION STUFF) VENETIAN-STYLE STEMS ARE BLOWN (RATHER THAN SOLID) WHEREVER POSSIBLE. IN TERMS OF CUP CONSTRUCTION, THERE ARE BASICALLY TWO WAYS TO DO BLOWN STEMS. ONE OPTION IS TO HAVE YOUR ASSISTANT GATHER AND PREPARE A BUBBLE FOR THE STEM. IT'S VIRTUALLY THE SAME TECHNIQUE AS MAKING A BLOWN FOOT → QUICK N' E-Z! YOU CAN DROP THE BUBBLE ON YOUR AVOLIO, NECK, SHAPE AND TRIM ALL IN ONE HEAT. SEE PAGES 208-9 (3 BUBBLE WINE GLASS) FOR MORE INFO. ON THAT STYLE. FOR MORE ELABORATE STEMS, THE PROCESS AND PROCEDURE ARE A LITTLE MORE INVOLVED. IT USUALLY REQUIRES A GARAGE AND/OR EXTRA HANDS.

YOU CAN USE **CANE** TO MAKE YOUR STEM, OR BLOW CHUNKS OF COLOR OUT, OR ANY COMBINATION OF TECHNIQUES. WHATEVER METHOD YOU USE, IT USUALLY BEGIN WITH A STARTER BUBBLE - AS ILLUSTRATED ON THE NEXT PAGE. FROM THERE YOU CAN GOLD-LEAF IT, OPTIC MOLD IT OR BLOW IT INTO ANY OF A B'ZILLION DIFFERENT SHAPES. VARIETY IS THE SPICE OF LIFE!

STEMS WILL GIVE YOU A GOOD RUN FOR YOUR MONEY. THEY'RE BY **NO MEANS** EASY TO MAKE. STEMS, LIKE EVERYTHING ELSE IN GLASS MAKING, TAKE BUTTLOADS OF PRACTICE TO GET 'EM RIGHT. AND THEN THERE'S ADDING THAT PESKY "VOLIO... AND A FOOT... AND A CUP... AND GETTING IT SO IT STANDS UP STRAIGHT... AND OFF THE PUNTY IN ONE PIECE... AND INTO THE BOX... AND...

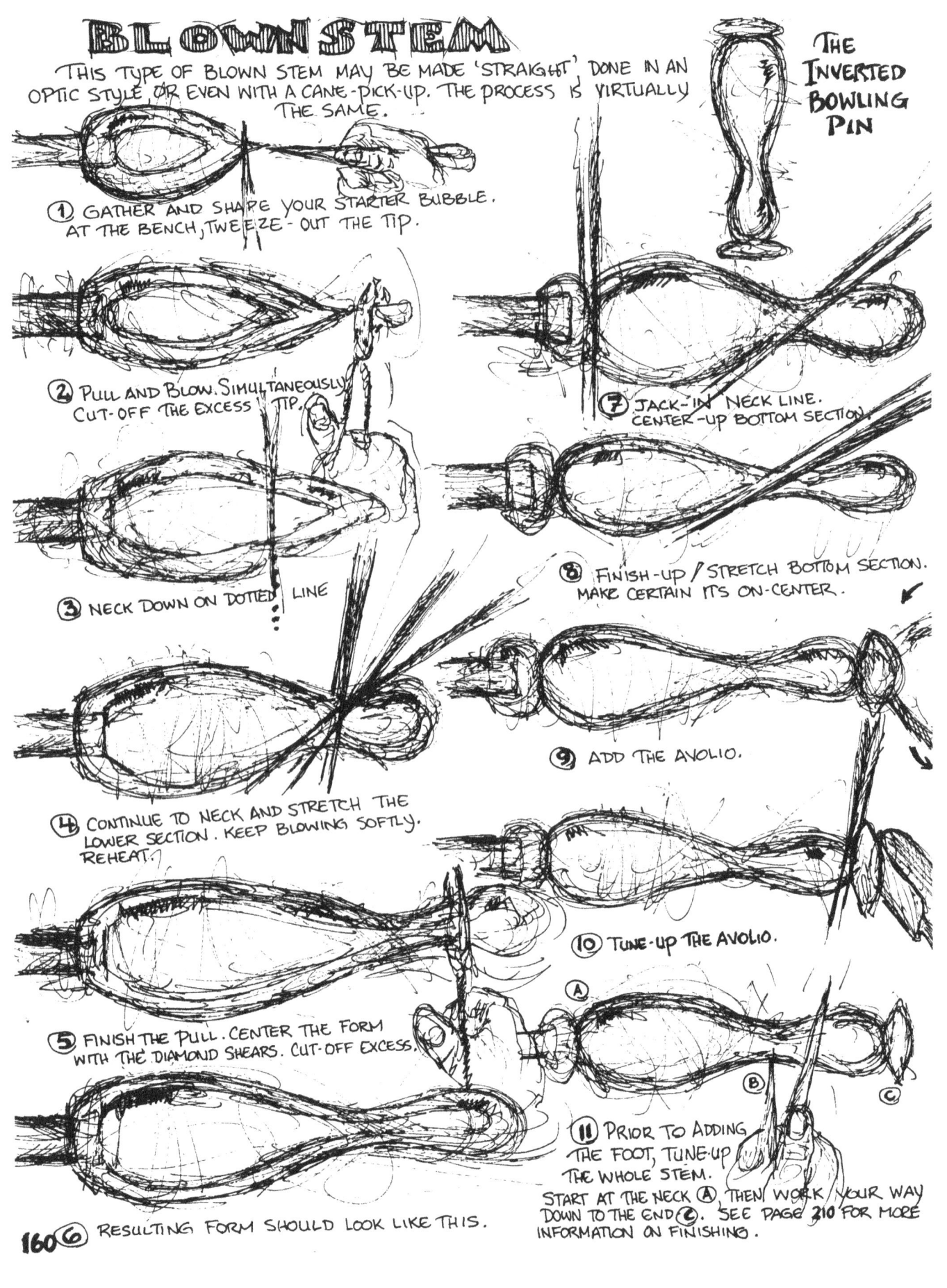

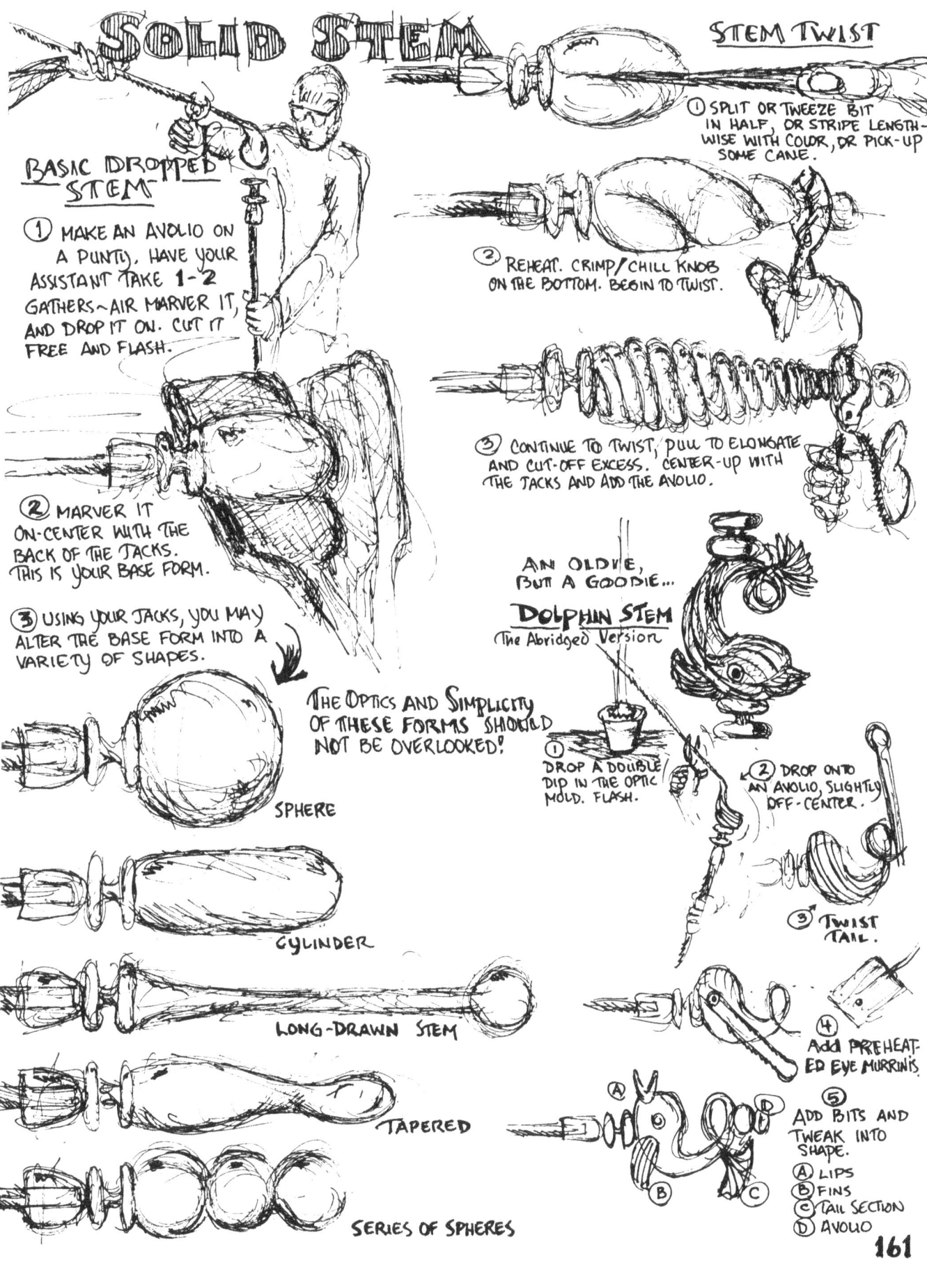

BITWORK

One method by which you can make an ordinary stem (or any piece of glass for that matter) into something EXTRAORDINARY is bitwork. With additive bits applied to your glass you may enhance the beauty and overall presentation/value of your goblet. You can even disguise some mistakes with a properly applied bit!

If you're working on a small scale, e.g. goblet stems - it is imperitive that the bits are brought very hot and in the right shape. If you are making multiples, i.e. identical or matching bits - it is also vital that each bit is as close to it's predecessor as possible. Use a fresh punty each time - if necessary.

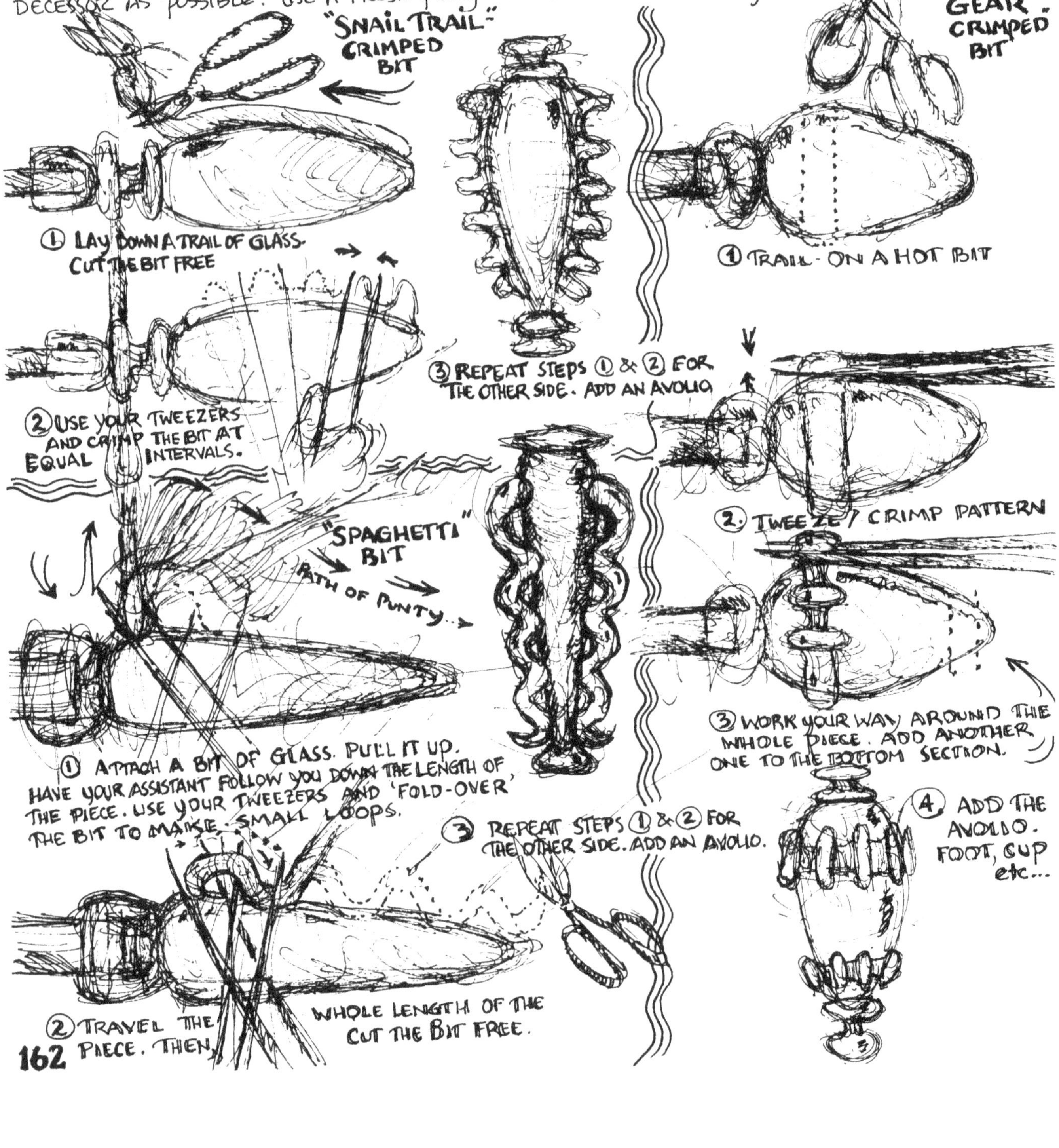

"SNAIL TRAIL" CRIMPED BIT

① Lay down a trail of glass. Cut the bit free.

② Use your tweezers and crimp the bit at equal intervals.

③ Repeat steps ① & ② for the other side. Add an avolio.

"GEAR CRIMPED BIT"

① Trail on a hot bit.

② Tweeze/crimp pattern.

③ Work your way around the whole piece. Add another one to the bottom section.

④ Add the avolio. Foot, cup etc...

"SPAGHETTI" BIT
PATH OF PUNTY

① Attach a bit of glass. Pull it up. Have your assistant follow you down the length of the piece. Use your tweezers and 'fold-over' the bit to make small loops.

② Travel the whole length of the piece. Then, cut the bit free.

③ Repeat steps ① & ② for the other side. Add an avolio.

THE GARAGE

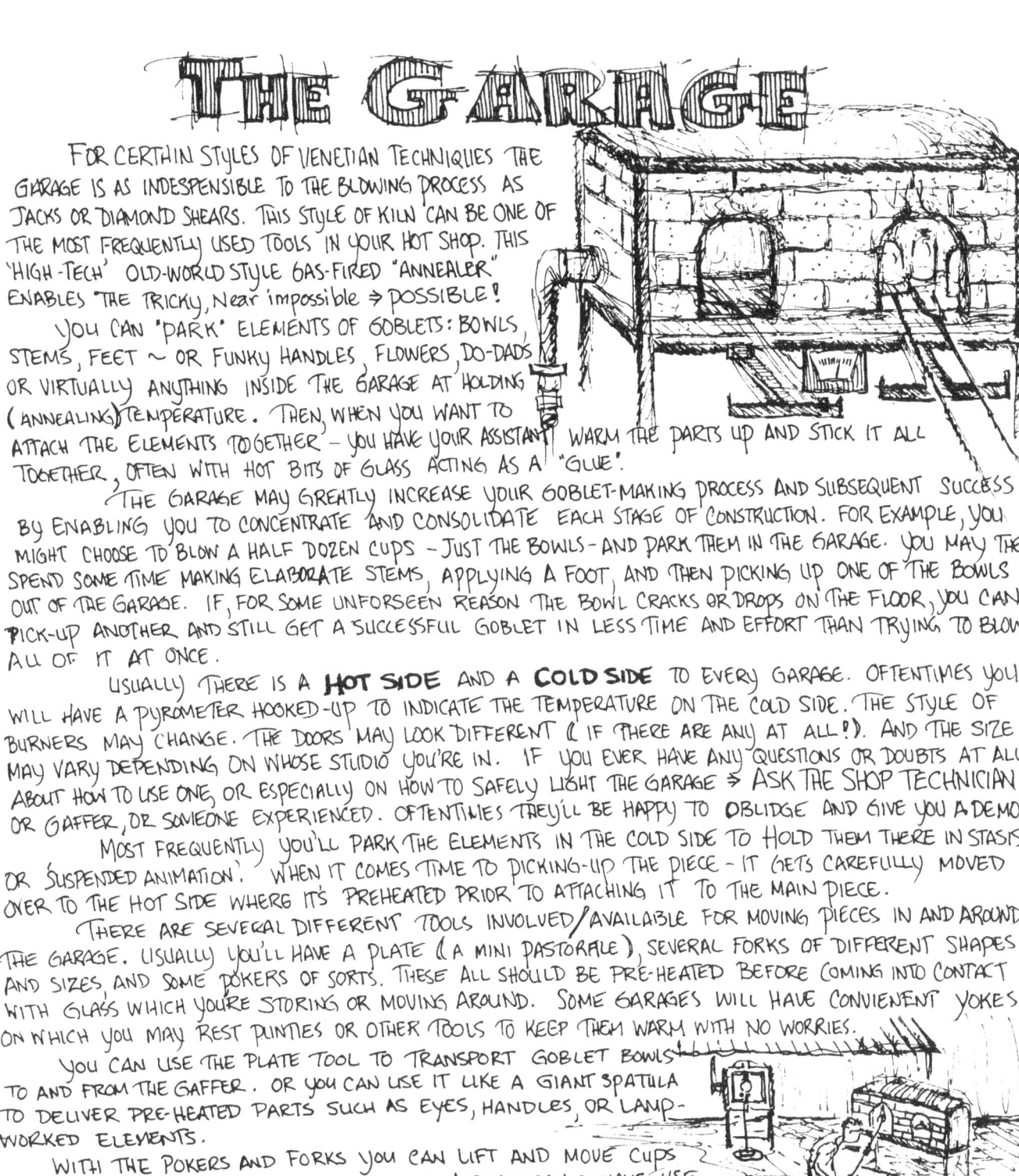

For certain styles of Venetian techniques the garage is as indespensible to the blowing process as jacks or diamond shears. This style of kiln can be one of the most frequently used tools in your hot shop. This 'high-tech' old-world style gas-fired "annealer" enables the tricky, near impossible → POSSIBLE!

You can "PARK" elements of goblets: bowls, stems, feet ~ or funky handles, flowers, do-dads or virtually anything inside the garage at holding (annealing) temperature. Then, when you want to attach the elements together — you have your assistant warm the parts up and stick it all together, often with hot bits of glass acting as a "glue".

The garage may greatly increase your goblet-making process and subsequent success by enabling you to concentrate and consolidate each stage of construction. For example, you might choose to blow a half dozen cups — just the bowls — and park them in the garage. You may then spend some time making elaborate stems, applying a foot, and then picking up one of the bowls out of the garage. If, for some unforseen reason the bowl cracks or drops on the floor, you can pick-up another and still get a successful goblet in less time and effort than trying to blow all of it at once.

Usually, there is a **HOT SIDE** and a **COLD SIDE** to every garage. Oftentimes you will have a pyrometer hooked-up to indicate the temperature on the cold side. The style of burners may change. The doors may look different (if there are any at all?). And the size may vary depending on whose studio you're in. If you ever have any questions or doubts at all about how to use one, or especially on how to safely light the garage → ask the shop technician, or gaffer, or someone experienced. Oftentimes they'll be happy to oblidge and give you a demo.

Most frequently you'll park the elements in the cold side to hold them there in stasis or 'suspended animation'. When it comes time to picking-up the piece — it gets carefully moved over to the hot side where it's preheated prior to attaching it to the main piece.

There are several different tools involved/available for moving pieces in and around the garage. Usually you'll have a plate (a mini pastorale), several forks of different shapes and sizes, and some pokers of sorts. These all should be pre-heated before coming into contact with glass which you're storing or moving around. Some garages will have convienent yokes on which you may rest punties or other tools to keep them warm with no worries.

You can use the plate tool to transport goblet bowls to and from the gaffer. Or you can use it like a giant spatula to deliver pre-heated parts such as eyes, handles, or lamp-worked elements.

With the pokers and forks you can lift and move cups and other elements inside of the garage. And you can always use a punty to pick-up components out of the garage.

Again, remember to preheat any metal that is to come in contact with garaged glass especially the gaffer's tweezers!

If you end up not using all the components in the garage at the end of the day you can either close the whole thing up and shut-off the gas and let 'em coast for the night, or if you're worried about them checking, you can move 'em into an available annealer.

I'LL TAKE THAT CUP NOW PLEASE...

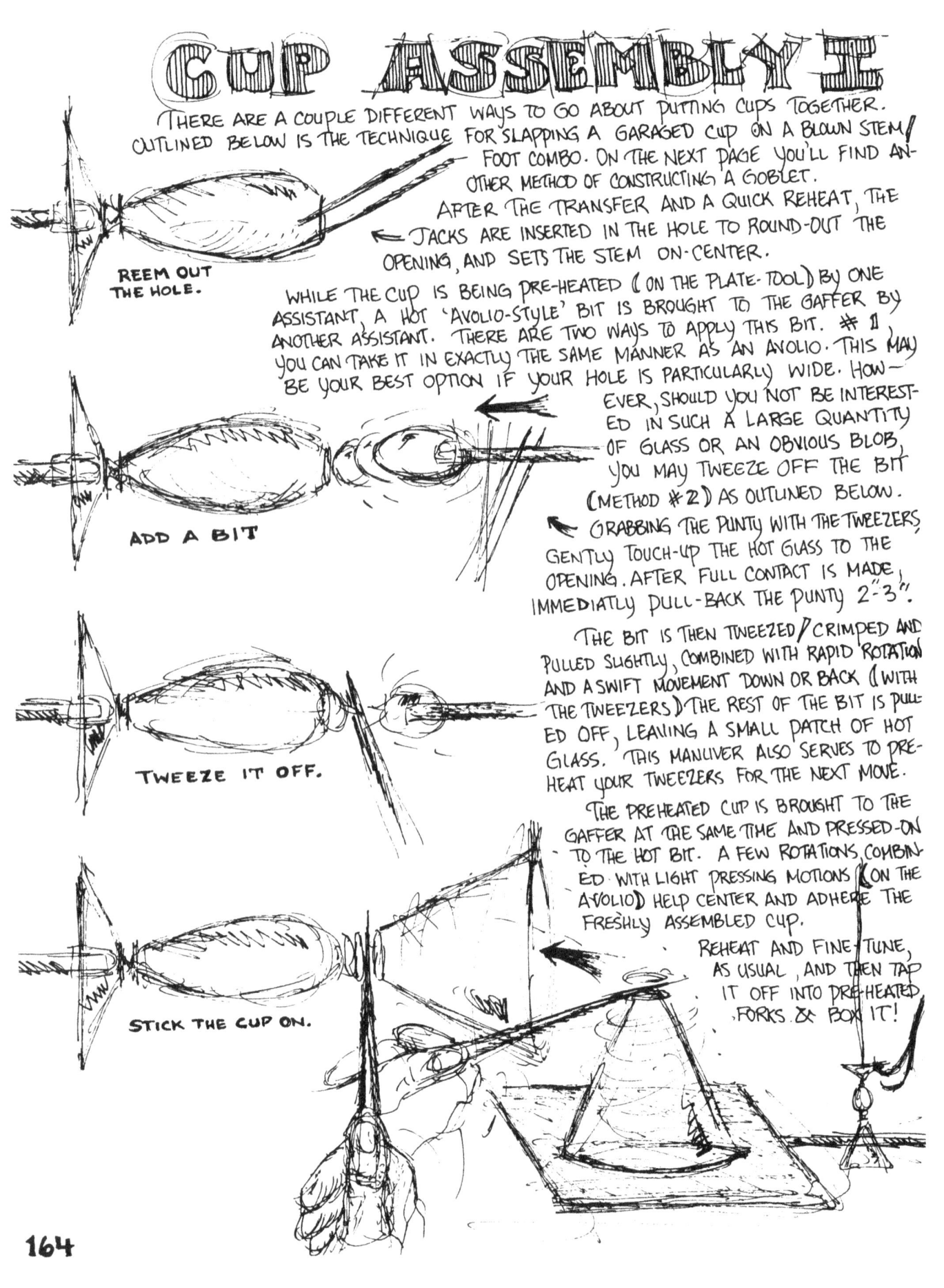

CUP ASSEMBLY II

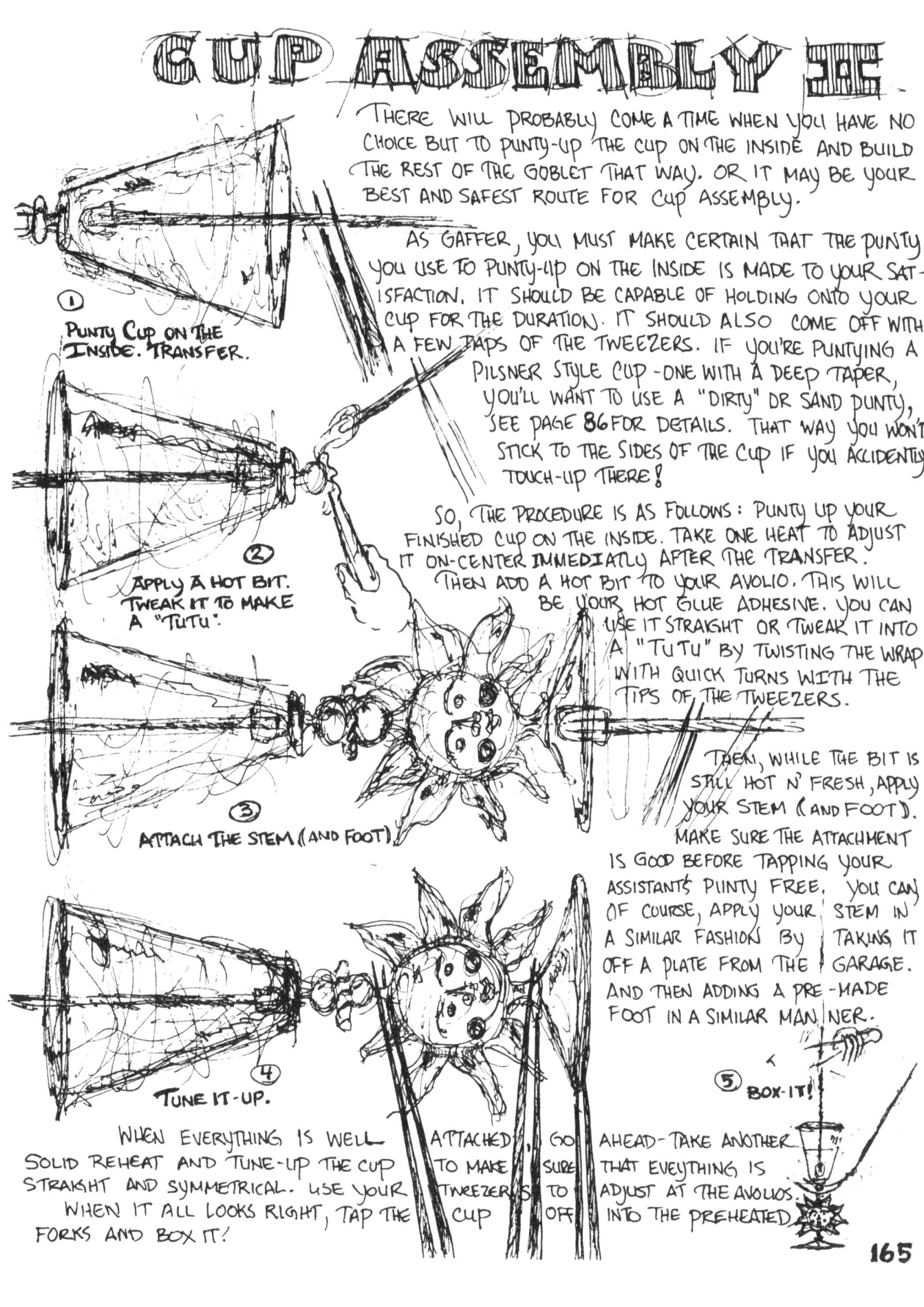

① Punty cup on the inside. Transfer.

② Apply a hot bit. Tweak it to make a "Tutu".

③ Attach the stem (and foot).

④ Tune it up.

⑤ Box it!

There will probably come a time when you have no choice but to punty-up the cup on the inside and build the rest of the goblet that way. Or it may be your best and safest route for cup assembly.

As gaffer, you must make certain that the punty you use to punty-up on the inside is made to your satisfaction. It should be capable of holding onto your cup for the duration. It should also come off with a few taps of the tweezers. If you're puntying a pilsner style cup - one with a deep taper, you'll want to use a "dirty" or sand punty, see page 86 for details. That way you won't stick to the sides of the cup if you accidently touch-up there!

So, the procedure is as follows: punty up your finished cup on the inside. Take one heat to adjust it on-center immediatly after the transfer. Then add a hot bit to your avolio. This will be your hot glue adhesive. You can use it straight or tweak it into a "tutu" by twisting the wrap with quick turns with the tips of the tweezers.

Then, while the bit is still hot n' fresh, apply your stem (and foot). Make sure the attachment is good before tapping your assistant's punty free. You can, of course, apply your stem in a similar fashion by taking it off a plate from the garage. And then adding a pre-made foot in a similar manner.

When everything is well attached, go ahead- take another solid reheat and tune-up the cup to make sure that everything is straight and symmetrical. Use your tweezers to adjust at the avolios. When it all looks right, tap the cup off into the preheated forks and box it!

165

The Cristallo Cup Blues

I tried to blow a goblet,
It didn't look that tough.
I practiced practiced PRACTICED!
But it still wasn't enough.

I tried to make the bowl,
It crinkled in a flash.
I tried to make another,
And it fell in a crash.

I attempted the Avolio –
To coil it like a spool...
It laughed at my vain attempt
And labled me a fool.

The stem should-a been easy,
A simple dropped bubble.
The glass wasn't hot enough,
And became alot of trouble.

Another attempt at the Avolio
Which met with lesser success,
I hear it's summer in New Zealand
I'm beginning to digress....

At last came the foot,
And it had a similar fate.
This goblet-making business
Is something I'm beginning to hate.

I went ahead and puntied,
And tried to open-up the glass.
It didn't reach the annealer
And decided it'd rather smash.

I clutched my head in anger,
And thrust up both my fists.
How could something so simple –
Make me so gosh darn pissed!

Just three basic components:
A foot, a stem, an' a bowl,
I know I can conquer it,
May God have mercy on my soul!

At first you don't succeed,
You may try, try again...
I'll do it if it kills me,
Notify next of kin.

The glass is so seductive –
I was caught under her spell.
Unwillingly and obliginely,
I've created my own hell.

I've got no way outta here,
Since I'm trapped deep within.
Avoid this one-way sink hole
If you value your own skin.

So back to the furnace I go,
To take another dip.
Mother warn your children,
About this hopeless trip.

I could-a been a contender,
My cups would've killed....
Instead I got a 1-way ticket
To this here Pallooka-ville!

Another lost soldier,
In the battle on the pad.
Gravity won that skirmish –
So it don't make me that mad.

'Cause when you finally get good,
And have paid all your dues...
The glass may appear empty & y'know
You've got those Cristallo Cup Blues!

CANE

Take a hot piece of glass on a punty and pull it out to any given length and you have cane. Cane be made in all sizes - lengths and thicknesses. They can be made with any color or combination of colors. Pull it thin and you get **threads**. Pull it thinner still and you get **fibers**. Leave it thick and you have **rod** (or possibly "**marble stock**"). You can case your cane in clear, or use your Kugler "straight" for intense color. You can bundle colored canes together or overlay colors in many different fashions → pull it out into lengths and end-up with **murrine**. You can blow a bubble in your mass of glass → draw it out into lengths and cut it up into hollow-cane pieces or "**beads**".

Cane pulling is a fairly simple process (← NOT to be confused with EASY). It can be an art in itself. The Italians refer to cane itself as "**CANNE**." The Italians have been perfecting and making caneworked pieces for centuries. From the simple process you can get fairly elaborate results. It all depends on how much time you want to invest into making the cane.

Most often, when we refer to cane in the hot shop - we generally mean a rod of glass about the thickness of a pencil. It can be clear, colored or made with any number of designs or patterns.

There are a few things to note when it comes time to making or pulling cane:

1. **GET SET-UP IN THE FIRST PLACE.** Have some wooden paddles (or a cane "ladder" → sections of wood nailed together) laid out on the floor to prevent the cane from becoming thermal shocked from the cold concrete. Also, have a pipe cooler nearby. You need to be able to choke-up on the pipe/punty when starting the pull. Plus - make certain you have enough punties/pipes on hand and in the pipe warmer before starting. If you're pulling colored cane, be sure your color is well pre-heated before beginning.

2. **USING COLOR?** Be sure you have 'ENOUGH'. DON'T SKIMP! When you draw-out color, oftentimes it starts to fade if you: don't have enough, or you end up pulling it further than expected. This is especially important if you're doing multiple pulls or making elaborate "filigrana."

3. **GET THE CORE HOT OR ELSE!** Or else it won't work. It is vital that you get your glass temperature right before you pull or you'll end-up with uneven cane. When the mass is heated correctly - the pull should happen almost effortlessly. Remember, GRAVITY - your friend? The glass should just drop/fall in a nice gentle arc between the pipe and post. It should only require a modest pull to get it even and straight. I might also add that it takes a lot of practice and a keen understanding on how colors/glass behave to get it to that stage!

4. **REMEMBER TO RELAX!** It is, afterall, only cane!

The key to making cane with little or no waste is to have the heat right in the glass that you're hoping to stretch. Essentially you want a compact log form which is HOT throughout. The tip of the glass gets severly chilled by quenching it in water. It usually takes several heats and reheats, with some marvering in between, to get the temperature even. This process of heating and shaping sets up the pull. It is usually performed by the 'maestro' on hand. The assistant in the meantime can, when directed by the gaffer, prepare the **POST** - or landing pad - onto which the cane will be attached to and pulled with.

Let's say you want to make some white cased cane → with which you might make some Zanfirico later on. Begin by getting a stick of white color hot. It's best to do this on a medium-to-large punty (or blowpipe if you're ..in a pinch). Marver the color into a cyliner. Allow to cool (until it's safe to gather over).

Case the color with several layers of clear. Each time you exit the furnace after you gather, hold the glass end up so the clear falls back on the piece, and the bottom doesn't wind up with a big blob of clear there. Marver the piece horizontally so most of the glass stays put - encasing the color evenly. Try to maintain a healthy moile - it will help insulate your color and core.

After you take your last dip (or even before it) have your assistant **prepare the post**. Depending on the size of the pull - they'll need 2-to-3 gathers of clear on a matching punty. Allow the gathers to air cool between successive dips. Then, with the last gather, the glass gets marvered off the end of the punty and then squashed flat (with the punty vertical) on the marver.

Once the post is the right shape, the punty should get cooled at the pipe cooler. **NEVER, EVER** hand-off a post to a gaffer which is hot - they may fry their hand and you may lose your job (or at least get yelled at, or the evil eye)! The glass on the end should be allowed to get stone cold. Now, just hang-out and wait....

As soon as you've obtained the compact cylinder log form - you will do a series of: marvering, heating, and chilling the tip to try and introduce as much heat into the back end of the piece as possible. Squashing the tip works well, and on the very last reheat or just before, you'll want to quench the tip in a bucket of water.

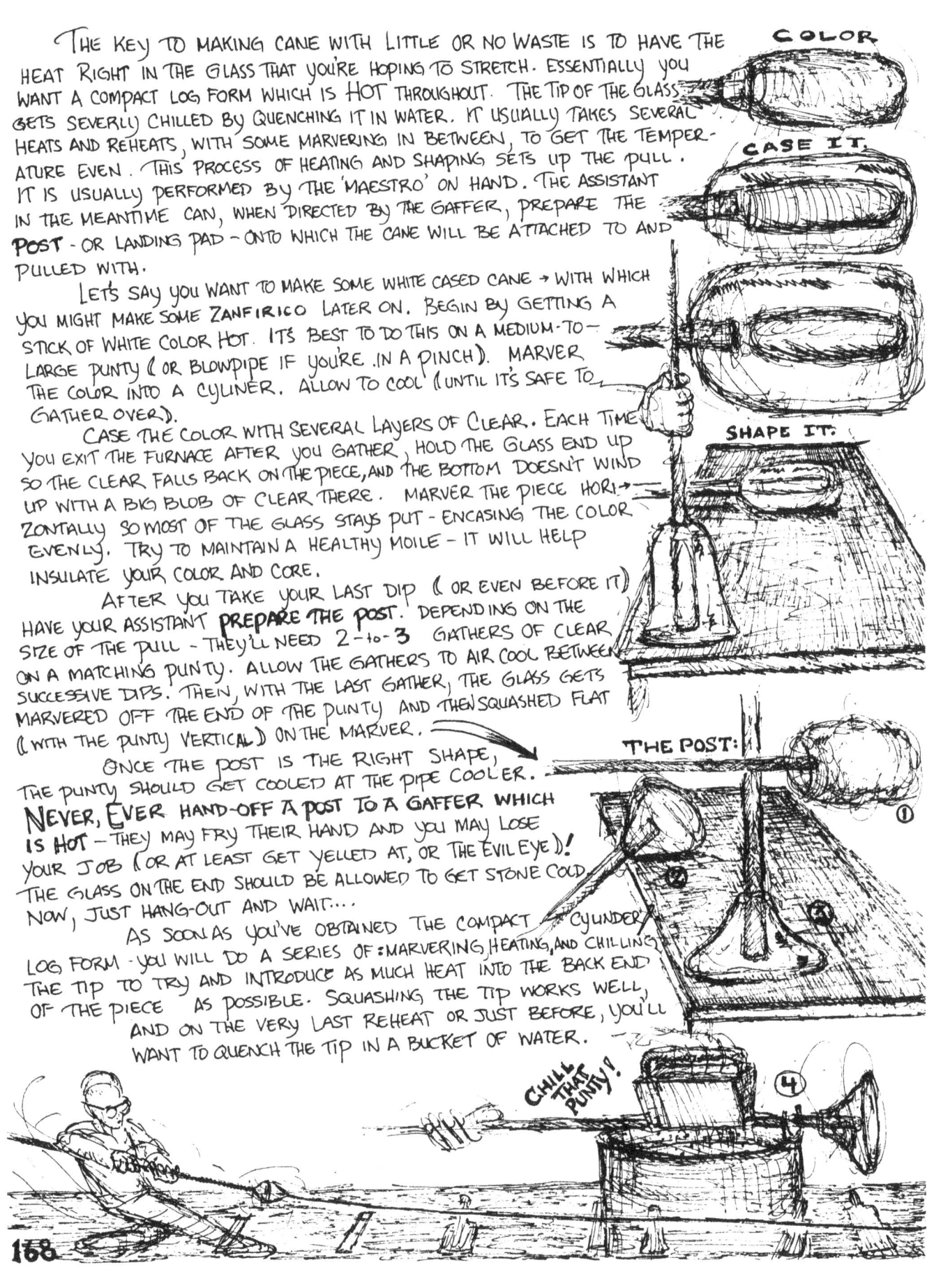

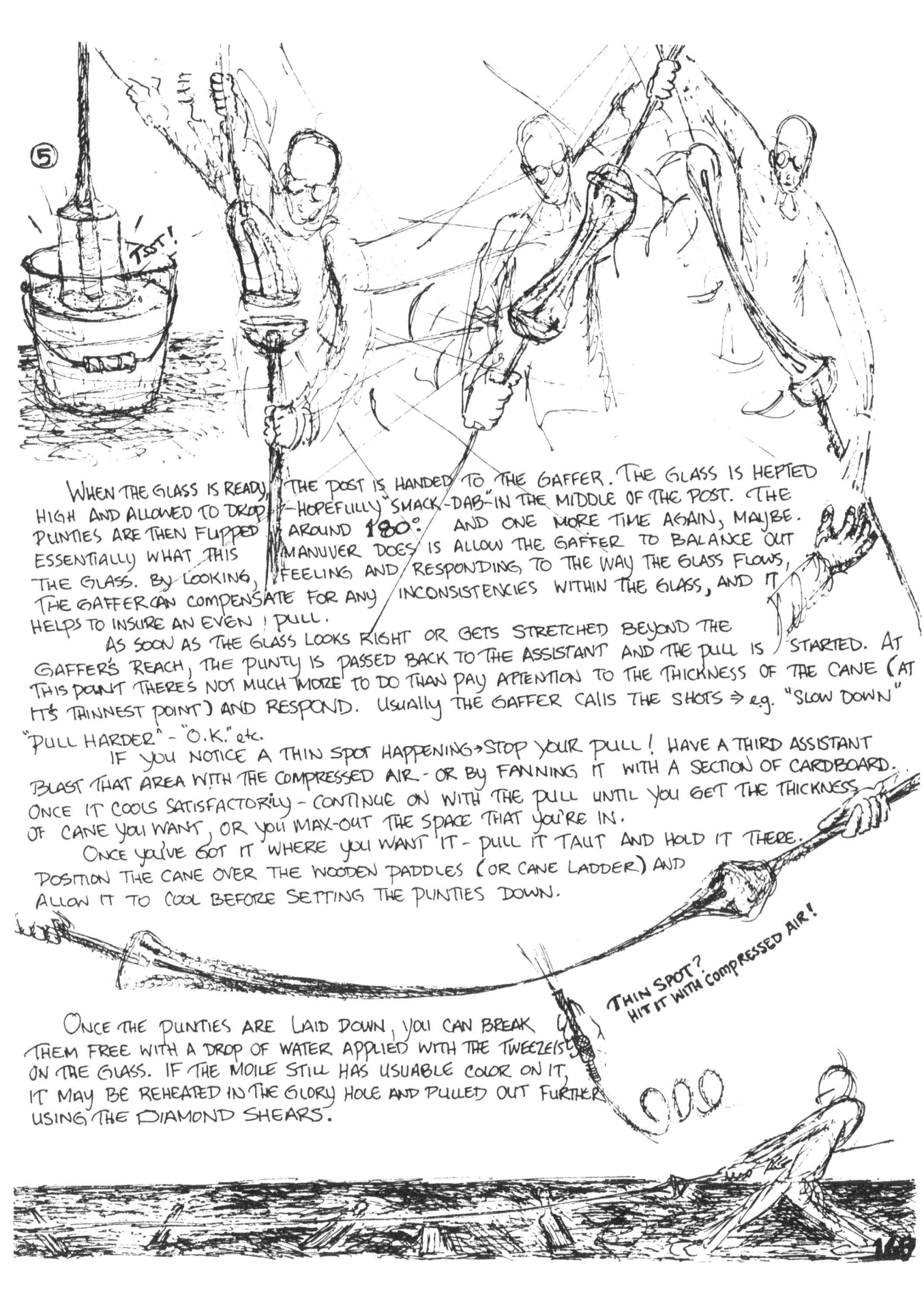

⑤

When the glass is ready, the post is handed to the gaffer. The glass is hefted high and allowed to drop — hopefully "smack-dab" in the middle of the post. The punties are then flipped around 180°. And one more time again, maybe. Essentially what this manuver does is allow the gaffer to balance out the glass. By looking, feeling and responding to the way the glass flows, the gaffer can compensate for any inconsistencies within the glass, and it helps to insure an even pull.

As soon as the glass looks right or gets stretched beyond the gaffer's reach, the punty is passed back to the assistant and the pull is started. At this point there's not much more to do than pay attention to the thickness of the cane (at it's thinnest point) and respond. Usually the gaffer calls the shots ⇒ e.g. "slow down" "pull harder" - "O.K." etc.

If you notice a thin spot happening → stop your pull! Have a third assistant blast that area with the compressed air - or by fanning it with a section of cardboard. Once it cools satisfactorily - continue on with the pull until you get the thickness of cane you want, or you max-out the space that you're in.

Once you've got it where you want it - pull it taut and hold it there. Position the cane over the wooden paddles (or cane ladder) and allow it to cool before setting the punties down.

Thin spot? Hit it with compressed air!

Once the punties are laid down, you can break them free with a drop of water applied with the tweezers on the glass. If the moile still has usuable color on it, it may be reheated in the glory hole and pulled out further using the diamond shears.

USING CANE

O.K. Now that you've pulled some cane — what do you do with it? Well, there is just about a b'izzillion different ways to incorporate cane into blown glass. The most economical way is to make your entire piece out of cane. This is accomplished by picking up the cane on a **COLLAR** (on a blowpipe) off a **PASTORALE**. On the pastorale the cane are laid out next to each other and then preheated in the glory hole. In the glory hole they are tack-fused to each other → not made so hot as to fuse to the pastorale! From there, it's getting the temperatures right and picking-up the cane.

Cane may be rolled-up on a bubble off a preheated **CANE MARVER** and blown out to a final form. Or easier still, you can set small, thinner sections of cane into the ribs of an optic mold and pick them up by stuffing a hot bubble in it.

Of course, you needn't even have a bubble for the above methods. You can make some pretty sophisticated cane by picking-up other cane, then twisting and casing it. With this style of working you can create cane that spirals and twists in double helix patterns or in a vast number of other patterns. It's all in how you lay-out and pick-up the cane. And the Italian glassmakers have a specific name for each style of cane created in this manner.

You can chop your cane into little pieces or cross-sections to wind-up with **MURRINE**. The murrine may then be laid out, pre-heated on a hot plate or pastorale and picked-up on a hot gather or bubble for interesting decoration. Or if you wanna really go all-out, you can do like **DICK MARQUIS** and **DANTE MARIONI** do → make first some rectilinear cane, chop it into cross-sections (murrine), lay it out into a sheet form on a **PASTORALE** → tack fuse 'em together in the glory hole, roll the whole mess up on a collar and then spend an hour or so shaping and blowing the form out.

And then there's **CANEDRAWING** or the possibility of **LAMPWORKING** the cane into imagery or 'botanical poetry' encased in glass. So many choices, so little time!

The first step lies in cutting your cane into a length (and desired thickness) which you can use. This is most easily accomplished when the cane is still fairly hot — right after you pull it. You need only a pair of tweezers and possibly a cup of water. Simply by pulling the whole length of the cane with the tweezers — where you want it to break → you will set-up a thermal shock point. The cane should break free cleanly.

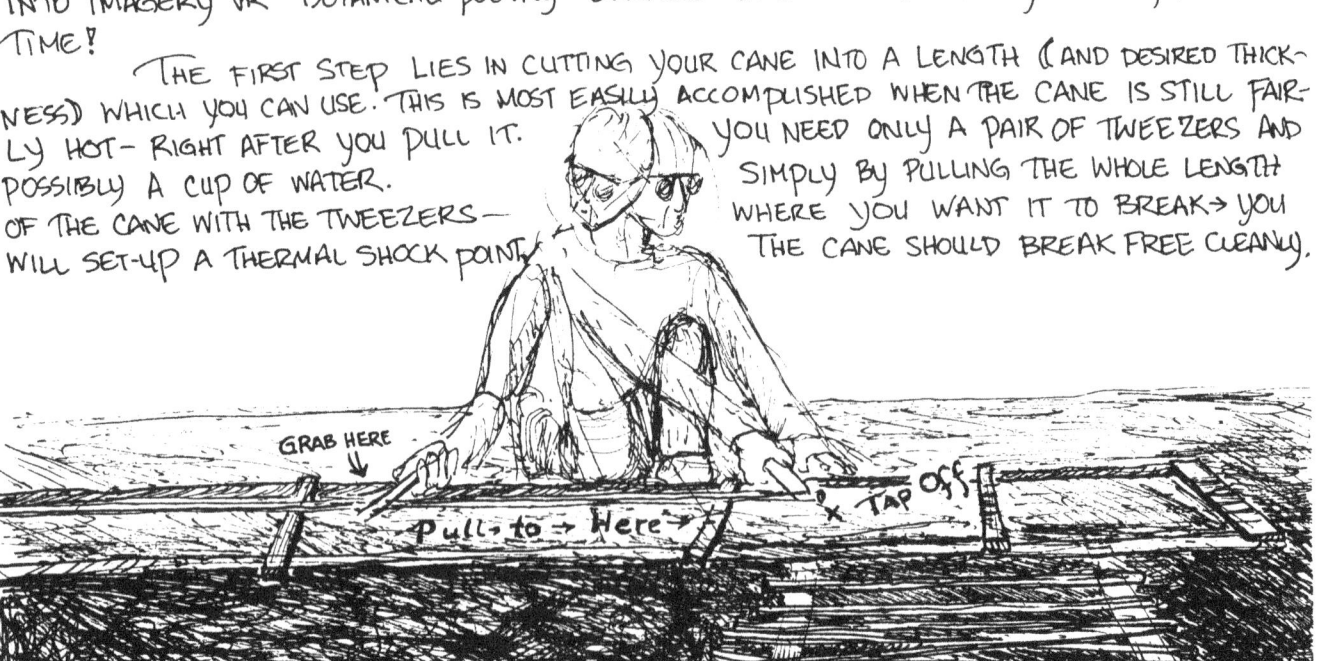

IF IT DOESN'T, YOU MIGHT ADD A DROP OF WATER ON THAT SPOT TO ENCOURAGE IT TO BREAK THERE. A FIRM TAP MIGHT HELP AS WELL.

IF YOUR CANE IS COLD AND YOU WANT TO CUT IT - YOU CAN USE TILE NIPPERS (OR TILE 'PLIERS'- AVAILABLE THROUGH HARDWARE STORES OR TILE CENTERS) OR THE "SCORE AND SNAP" METHOD. TILE CUTTERS ONLY REQUIRE GOOD HAND STRENGTH. SIMPLY SELECT WHERE YOU WANT THE CANE CUT AND SQUEEZE THE PLIERS ON THAT SPOT. UNLESS YOUR NIPPERS ARE DULL, THE CANE SHOULD BREAK FREE.

ANOTHER WAY TO CUT YOUR CANE IS BY SCORING THE GLASS WITH THE EDGE OF A BASTARD FILE (OR EVEN A GLASS CUTTER) WET IT AND SNAP THE PIECE IN TWO. PLACE YOUR THUMBS CLOSE TOGETHER, OPPOSITE THE SCORE, AND PULL OUTWARDS TO BREAK THE PIECE CLEAN.

IF YOUR CANE IS ON THE THICK (OR STUBBORN) SIDE, YOU CAN ALWAYS CHOP IT WITH A KUGLER CUTTER, OR EVEN A DIAMOND SAW.

CANE PICK-UP via THE OPTIC MOLD

THINNER CANE WORKS BETTER FOR THIS TECHNIQUE THAN THICKER. THE REASON BEING THAT THICKER CANE TENDS TO THERMAL SHOCK (AND BREAK) WHEN IT COMES IN CONTACT WITH HOT GLASS. THE THINNER CANE DOESN'T SEEM TO MIND AS MUCH.

TO BEGIN, SIMPLY CUT YOUR LENGTHS OF CANE SO THEY FIT WITHIN THE OPTIC MOLD - AND DON'T STICK OUT TOO MUCH. YOU CAN SET A SECTION OF CANE INTO EACH RIB (OR EVERY OTHER ONE) OF THE OPTIC MOLD.

THE HOTTER YOU CAN GET YOUR GLASS, THE LIKELIER THEY ARE (the CANE) TO STICK TO IT. PERHAPS THE BEST METHOD IS TO SHAPE YOUR GLASS (EITHER BLOWN OR SOLID) EXACTLY TO THE SHAPE OF THE MOLD → ONE GATHER LESS THAN IT WOULD TAKE TO FILL IT. THEN, GATHER UP YOUR LAST DIP, STRIP IT EVEN AND LET IT FALL/DRIP INTO THE MOLD. ALLOW THE HEAT OF THE GLASS TO PENETRATE INTO THE CANE FOR A FEW SECONDS, AND REMOVE FROM THE MOLD. REHEAT. IF THE NECK OF THE PIECE IS OVERSTUFFED - GO AHEAD AND MARVER IT BACK. YOU CAN THEN NECK AND TRIM THE TIP OF THE PIECE TO GET THE CANE EVEN.

FROM HERE YOU CAN EITHER: GO AHEAD AND TWIST UP THE CANE, OR ENCASE IT IN ANOTHER LAYER OF CLEAR, THEN TWIST IT, OR PICK-UP MORE CANE AND TWIST IT. OR IF YOU HAVE A BUBBLE IN YOUR PARISON YOU CAN SHAPE N' BLOW IT OUT TO WHATEVER FORM YOU DESIRE.

NOTE ☞ IF YOU WANT TO KEEP YOUR CANE STRAIGHT AND LINED-UP → TURN THE PIPE IN BOTH DIRECTIONS! IF YOU ONLY TURN IN ONE DIRECTION, THE CANE HAS A TENDENCY TO START TWISTING ON YOU, ESPECIALLY WHILE REHEATING IN THE GLORY HOLE.

THE OPTIC MOLD CANE PICK-UP CAN BE USEFUL IN A VARIETY OF SITUATIONS AND IS ESPECIALLY APPROPRIATE FOR PEOPLE WORKING SOLO. FOR TEAMWORK, THERE'S THE PASTORALE METHOD. Read On......

CANE PICK-UP via THE PASTORALE

A SIMPLE TOOL, THE PASTORALE IS. IT CONSISTS OF A THICK PLATE OF STEEL - ONTO WHICH THE CANE ARE LAID-OUT - AND A HANDLE UNIT. THE HANDLE UNIT FITS UNDER THE PLATE AND IS USED TO HEAT THE PLATE IN THE GLORY HOLE. THE STEEL PLATE HAS TO BE THICK ENOUGH SO THAT IT WON'T WARP WHEN EXPOSED TO THE HEAT (AROUND 1/2" THICKNESS IS GOOD). THE PLATE IS ALSO COATED WITH A THIN LAYER OF TERRACOTTA TO PREVENT THE CANE FROM STICKING TO IT.

TWO **FERRITI** - SMALL SECTIONS OF SQUARE STOCK STEEL - ARE USED TO HOLD/SQUEEZE THE CANE TOGETHER. THEY ALSO PREVENT THE CANE FROM ROLLING AROUND DURING THE PREHEATING STAGES. THEY TOO, ARE COATED WITH TERRACOTTA CLAY (IN MURANO THEY USE MUD OUTTA THE LAGOON - "FANGO.")

BEGIN BY LAYING-OUT YOUR PRECUT SECTIONS OF CANE ON THE PLATE. PIECES ABOUT THE THICKNESS OF A PENCIL AND ABOUT 4 INCHES LONG, SEEM TO HEAT-UP QUICKLY AND ARE FAIRLY EASY TO DEAL WITH. YOU CAN HOLD THE CANE TOGETHER WITH THE FERRITI. USE A **PI DIVIDER** OR OTHER MEASURING TOOL TO ESTIMATE THE DIAMETER YOUR GLASS NEEDS TO BE IN ORDER TO GET COMPLETE COVERAGE IN THE CIRCUMFERANCE. YOUR GLASS MAY BE IN THE FORM OF A COLLAR, A BUBBLE OR A SOLID MASS (OF POSSIBLY PRE-ROLLED CANE FOR AN INTERIOR CORE).

YOUR ASSISTANT MAY PREHEAT THE CANE IN THE FOLLOWING MANNER: PICK-UP THE PLATE OF CANE ON THE HANDLE UNIT. RESIST THE URGE TO TURN THE HANDLE LIKE A BLOWPIPE! MAKE SURE YOU HAVE ENOUGH SPACE TO GET IN THE GLORY HOLE. **VERY SLOWLY** INCH THE PLATE INTO THE GLORY HOLE. DON'T JUST THRUST IT IN THERE OR IT'S LIKELY THE CANE WILL THERMAL SHOCK AND EXPLODE! ONCE YOU'RE ALL THE WAY IN YOU ONLY NEED TO FLASH IT / REHEAT IT FOR SHORT BURSTS - JUST TRYING TO **TACK-FUSE** THE PIECES TOGETHER. ABOUT HALFWAY THROUGH THIS PROCESS YOU'LL WANT TO SET THE PLATE BACK DOWN ON THE MARVER AND TURN THE PLATE AROUND 180° - AND RETURN TO THE HEAT. THIS WAY THE CANE CAN GET EXPOSED TO THE HEAT EVENLY.

DO NOT HEAT THE CANE TOO MUCH !! OR IT MAY FUSE TO THE PLATE. LOOK FOR THE EDGES OF THE CANE TO CURL/SOFTEN SLIGHTLY. THERE'S A FINE BALANCE BETWEEN TOO COOL AND TOO HOT.

JUST PRIOR TO THE PICK-UP SET THE PLATE ON THE MARVER. KICK THE FERRITI OUT OF THE WAY WITH THE TWEEZERS, THEN SQUEEZE THE CANE TOGETHER WITH THE TWEEZERS. THIS HELPS MAKE CERTAIN THE CANE GET STUCK TOGETHER. A FINAL REHEAT (OR TWO) MAY BE WARRANTED FOR THE PICK-UP.

IN THE MEANTIME, THE PIPE IS PREPARED ACCORDING TO THE DESIRES OF THE GAFFER. SOME PEOPLE DO A DIP N' STRIP → THUS INSURING THAT THEIR GLASS IS VERY HOT FOR THE PICK-UP. OTHER GAFFERS JUST GET THEIR PIECE (OR COLLAR) HOT ENOUGH IN THE GLORY HOLE FOR THE PICK-UP. WHATEVER IT TAKES! THE PLATE IS SET ON THE MARVER AND CANE GETS ROLLED-UP LIKE A JELLY ROLL.

SEVERAL EXAMPLES OF THIS TECHNIQUE ARE ILLUSTRATED IN THE FOLLOWING PAGES →......

CANE STYLES

There are two ways you can look at your cane: straight-on and cross-sectionally. Most often when we see canework in pieces, we are viewing them straight-on. They can appear as simple as a single colored line or as complicated as a double helix. The easiest way to understand what is happening in any given piece of cane is to look at it cross-sectionally. In most cases you have something going on in the core and then something casing it. By alternating, exchanging or omitting/adding pieces of cane on the interior and exterior, you can dramatically change the patterns in your resulting cane or zanfirico.

BASIC CANE OR FILIGRANA
Colored core straight pull.

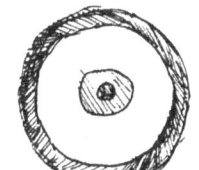

CASED CANE #1
Double overlay core cased in clear. Color overlay on the exterior.

CASED CANE #2
Clear core color overlay on the exterior (or see snorkeling).

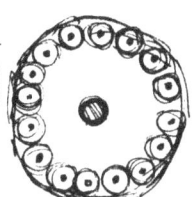

TWISTED CANE
Colored core cased in clear cane pick-up. Exterior & twisted.

You can intensify the patterns by twisting the glass as it is being pulled. The results will vary by how tightly twisted you can get the cane before it sets up.

The cane may be picked-up and constructed in a variety of manners. Change any one method and you'll end-up with a completely different style of cane. Mix or match techniques with colors and you'll get a (nearly) infinite number of possibilities of cane (or swizzle-sticks!).

TIP: Avoid colors which aren't very dense. It's a drag to spend allotta time pulling cane → only to fade by the time it comes to pick 'em up on a piece. Use those colors which are the most saturated (or densest) you can find.

RIBBON
Flattened Kugler (into tongue-shape) cased in clear, then twisted.

SIDE-BY-SIDE RIBBON
Flattened "tongues" of Kugler sandwiched together and cased, then twisted.

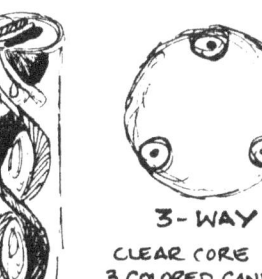

3-WAY
Clear core 3 colored cane picked-up on exterior & twisted.

3-BY
Clear core 3 canes together on the exterior & twisted.

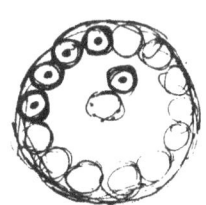

QUAD-WRAPPED SQUIGGLE
Clear core, single cane pick-up (offset) cased. Pick-up four colors on outer layer & twist.

"THE FINGER ONE" aka BALLOTTINI
Five cane as core - cased in clear, then twisted.

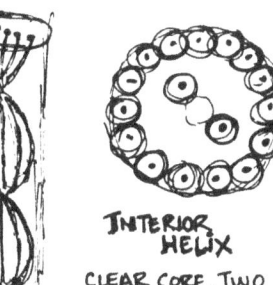

INTERIOR HELIX
Clear core, two canes each side. Case in clear. Cane pick-up on the exterior & twisted.

EXTERIOR WRAPPER
Clear core. Band of color laid on (striped) and sandwiched by two cane, & twisted.

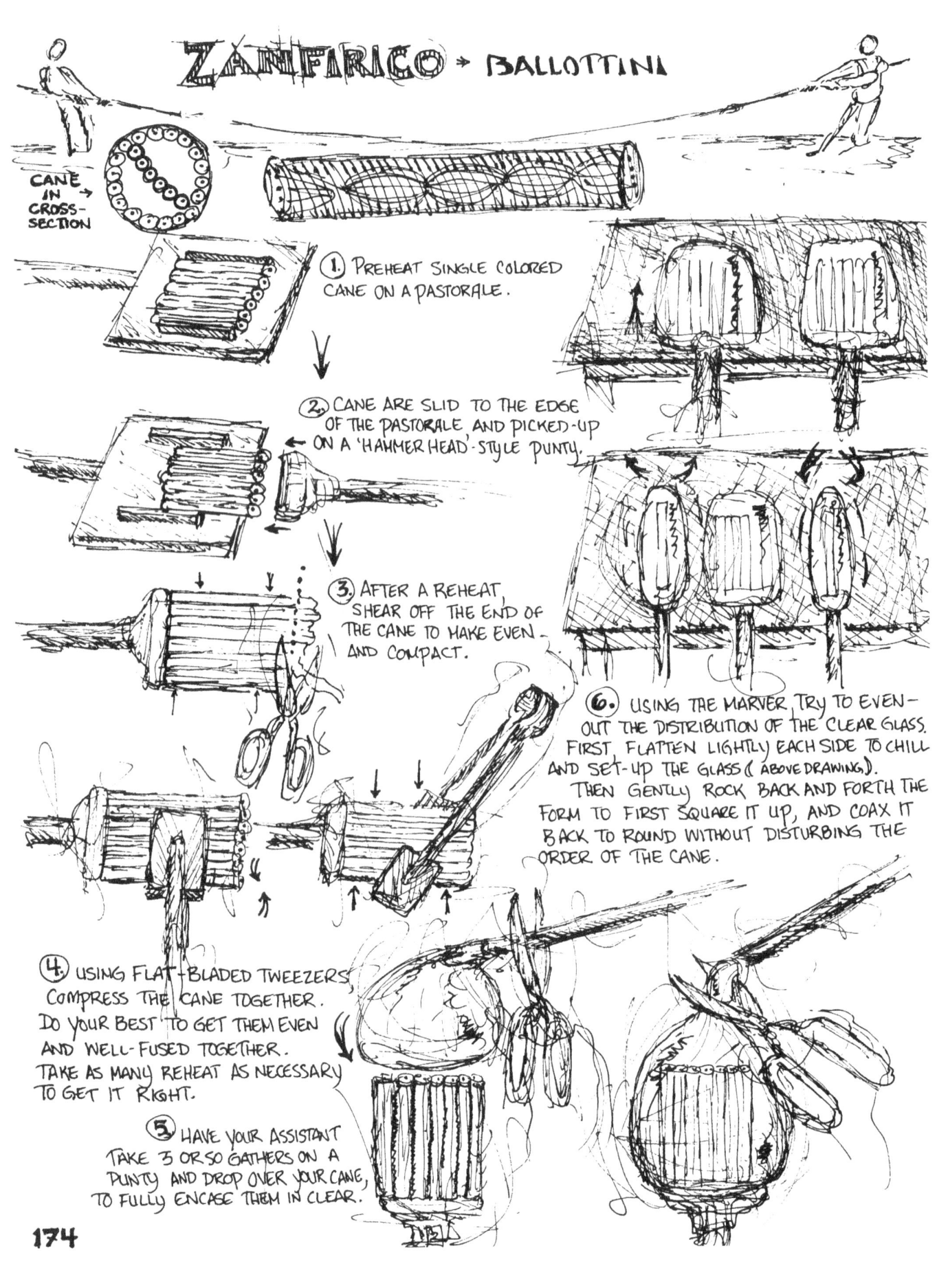

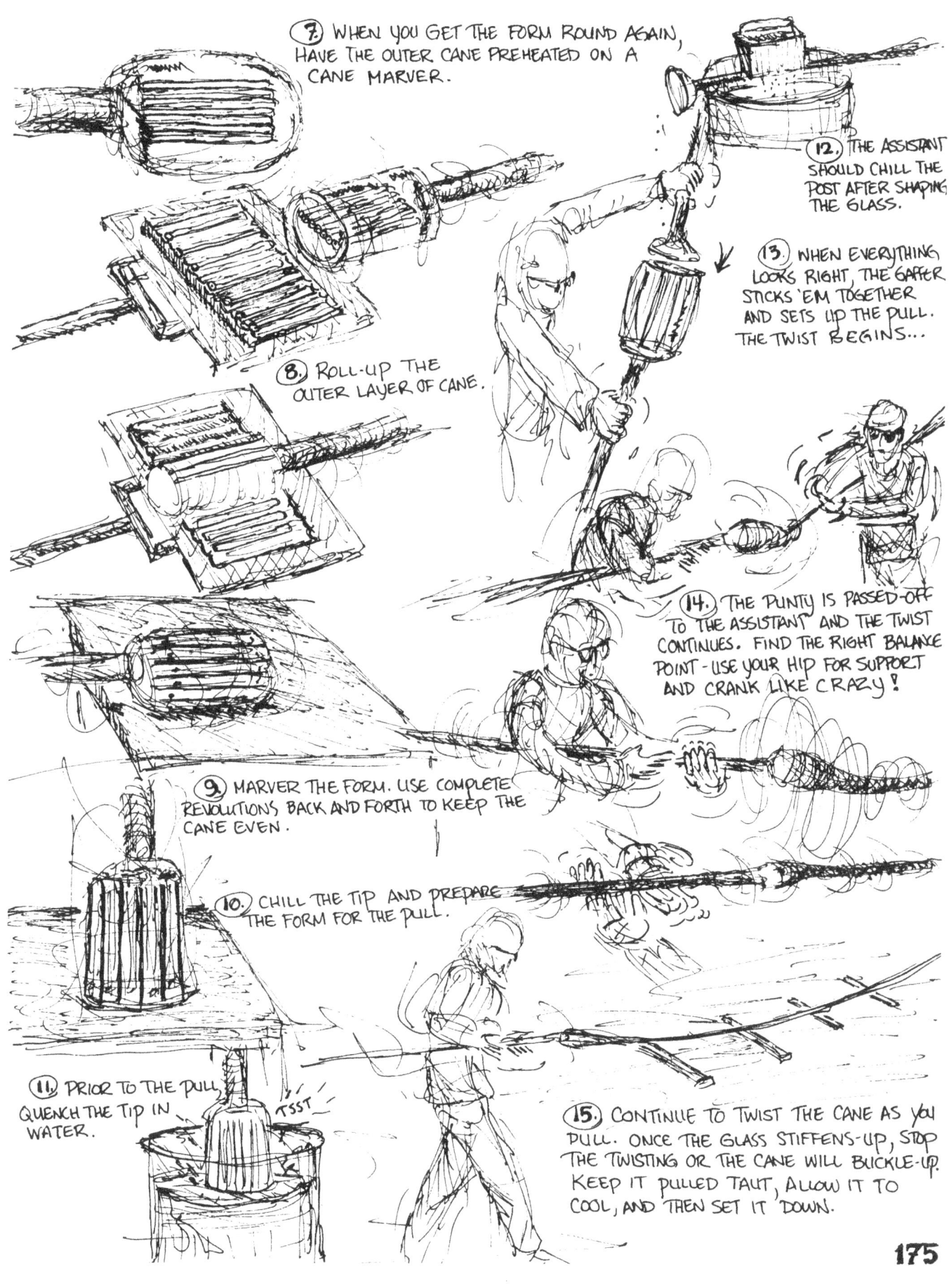

INTRODUCTION TO MURRINE

Unquestionably to give an adequate, in-depth description of the murrine-making process it would easily fill a book of this size, or larger! I'll just attempt to cover some of the basics.

First, let me begin by saying that I have a great deal of respect for those people who have the patience and skill to make murrine. **IT IS NOT A TECHNIQUE FOR EVERYONE!** It takes some non-linear thinking to pull it off. Actually, you have to be thinking cross-sectionally and linear at the same time. The process can be fairly straightforward and simple as is the case with optic molds for example, or it can be extremely complicated, such as making lettering or portrait murrinies.

The long-standing hands-down 'Champeen' of murrine in the United States is **RICHARD MARQUIS**. If you're really wanna learn this technique, take a class from him or read his thesis → it's the Lord's prayer ~ in murrine! Dick also manages to take this traditional technique to the "Nth" degree and make some pretty incredible sculptures out of them.

There are primarily three methods to creating murrine. One method sets your form or image up by using a **MOLD**, or series of molds. Another method uses colored or clear bits, or a combo of both, to **BUILD-UP** your murrine from the inside out. The last method involves **BUNDLING** stringers, sections of cane, or compatible sheet glass together to form a cross-sectional image or pattern. Each method has its own personality and style of result. One method may suit your needs or skills or facility better than another.

Let's say you were stuck in the southwest U.S. somewhere and the local galleries can't sell any work other than those with howlin' coyotes or seguaro cactuses. Having been stung by a cactus at an early age and several "I'LL-NEVER-DRINK-THAT-STUFF-AGAIN" episodes of tequila swilling, you decide the howlin' coyote more palatable and more suitable for your needs. So ya' figure some tumblers with coyote murrines will be your ticket out of the desert to someplace more hospitible to blow glass in... say Seattle. In any case, one of the quickest ways (dependent upon your skills, of course) to make this style of murrine is via the mold process.

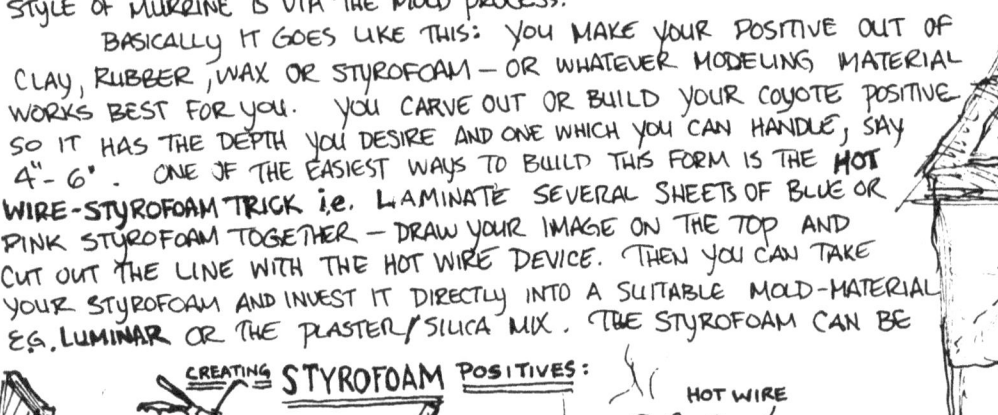

Howlin' Coyote Murrine

Basically it goes like this: you make your positive out of clay, rubber, wax or styrofoam — or whatever modeling material works best for you. You carve out or build your coyote positive so it has the depth you desire and one which you can handle, say 4"- 6". One of the easiest ways to build this form is the **HOT WIRE-STYROFOAM TRICK** i.e. laminate several sheets of blue or pink styrofoam together — draw your image on the top and cut out the line with the hot wire device. Then you can take your styrofoam and invest it directly into a suitable mold-material e.g. **LUMINAR** or the plaster/silica mix. The styrofoam can be

CREATING STYROFOAM POSITIVES:

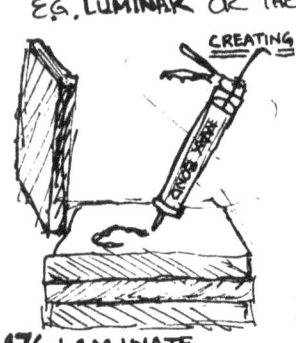

LAMINATE   DRAW DESIGN   CUT IT OUT   THE POSITIVE   MOLD WITH RESERVOIR

HOT WIRE

BURNT OUT USING A TORCH (DON'T BREATHE THE FUMES!). YOU NOW HAVE YOUR NEGATIVE MOLD. YOU CAN CAST OR BUILD A RESEVOIR TO GO ON TOP. THIS WILL HOLD THE GLASS WHICH WILL HELP FILL YOUR MOLD.

O.K. SLAP THE MOLD IN A CASTING KILN, LOAD IT WITH WHATEVER COLOR YOU WANT YOUR COYOTE TO BE (YES, YOU MUST USE A **COMPATIBLE** GLASS TO THAT OF WHICH YOU ARE CASING IT WITH, IN ADDITION TO THE CRYSTAL WHICH YOU ARE BLOWING!). FRIT WORKS FINE FOR THIS PROCESS, AS WELL AS COLOR BAR→BROKEN UP. HEAT UP THE MOLD AND FUSE CAST, AND ANNEAL. UPON COOLING, BREAK OUT THE MOLD, SCRUB OFF OR SANDBLAST AWAY ANY MOLD RESIDUE. BELT-SAND ANY SHARP EDGES OR EXTRANEOUS FLASHING. NOW YOUR POSITIVE SHOULD BE READY-TO-GO.

NOW THERE ARE A BUNCH OF DIFFERENT MOLD METHODS TO CHOOSE FROM THAT'LL GET YOU TO VIRTUALLY THE SAME RESULT. SEEK OUT, PRACTICE AND REFINE THE METHOD YOU LIKE BEST. I JUST CAN'T FIT ALL THAT INFORMATION HERE, NOW......

KEEP YOUR POSITIVES SIMPLE. AVOID LOTS OF SHARP ANGLES — THEY'RE VERY HARD TO FILL. THE SAME GOES FOR UNDERCUTS — CAN'T HAVE 'EM. ALSO, BE AWARE THAT YOU MIGHT NEED TO BEEF-UP SKINNY AREAS LIKE TAILS AND LEGS — THEY TEND TO THIN OUT AND DISAPPEAR (SOMETIMES) DURING THE PULL.

NEXT, PREHEAT YOUR POSITIVE IN A PICK-UP/KUGLER OVEN. PICK-IT UP ON A DECENT SIZED PUNTY, WARM IT UP IN THE GLORY HOLE. DON'T GET IT TOO HOT! OR ELSE YOU'LL LOSE ALL THE DETAIL THAT YOU WORKED SO HARD TO GET. YOUR NEXT ORDER OF BUSINESS IS TO FILL EACH GAP WITH CLEAR OR COLORED GLASS, AND BUILD-UP THE SPACE AROUND THE COYOTE. TAKE FLATTENED OR TAPERED BITS AND LAY THEM IN EACH AND EVERY SPACE YOU CAN FIND. AVOID COVERING THE END IF AT ALL POSSIBLE. YOU MIGHT WANNA SEE WHAT YOU ARE DOING.

NOW'S WHEN YOU NEED TO THINK CROSS-SECTIONALLY AND VISUALIZE HOW MUCH GLASS TO LAY-IN, AND WHERE. WITH CAREFUL PLACEMENT AND THE RIGHT KIND OF TRAIL, YOU COULD EVEN SNEAK A SMALL MOON ABOVE THE COYOTE FOR HIM TO HOWL AT. THAT, TOO, WOULD GET CASED IN WHATEVER GLASS YOU ARE FILLING IN WITH.

WHEN YOU HAVE THE COYOTE FULLY ENCASED AND BUILT-UP YOU CAN: GO STRAIGHT FOR THE PULL, CASE IT IN CLEAR, OR OVERLAY ANOTHER COLOR ON IT IF YOU WISHED. GEE, JUST **WHAT YOU NEED... MORE OPTIONS**. FOR THE SAKE OF ARGUMENT OR AGREEMENT, LET'S CASE THE SUCKER IN CLEAR.

MAKE SURE THE PIECE IS SET-UP BEFORE DIPPING-OVER, OTHERWISE YOU'RE GONNA HAVE ONE HELLUVA HOT WEENIE ON YOUR HANDS AND A WHOLE LOTTA WORK POSSIBLY FLUSHED DOWN-THE-TUBES...

DIP N' STRIP IF NECESSARY. THEN TAKE THE SAME STEPS AS YOU WOULD TO PULL MOST ANY TYPE OF CANE. MARVER, CHILL, MARVER QUENCH REHEAT MARVER SQUASH QUENCH REHEAT etc... MEANWHILE THE POST GETS MADE BY YOUR ASSISTANT, AND YOUR READY FOR THE PULL... OR IF IT'S A SMALL PULL, SKIP THE POST AND PULL USING DIAMOND SHEARS. Drum roll please...

Stick up the glass to the post, do the ol' yin-yang to find the balance of the glass and begin the pull.

This is where the process differs. In order to achieve distortion-free murrine you best do a vertical-style pull vs a normal horizontal pull. Gravity is your friend, & you don't fight with your friends!

So pass off the post to your assistant, and jump up a taller ladder → while paying **close attention** to what's happening on the end of your stick. **Do not be hasty.**

Coordinate with your assistant(s). Loud and clearly direct their motions, and yours as well. They may be standing by with compressed air to chill thin spots or a large torch to heat thick spots. (Watch out that you don't blast the ladder by mistake!).

The more that you pull it, the smaller your murrine will become.

If you pull it thin enough, your cane won't require any annealing. If, on the otherhand, you'd like to have bigger murrine, you should skip the sticks and box the cane.

So, when the pull's over carefully, manuver the cane into the horizontal position and lay 'em out on some small sticks or paddles. Or if you opt for the thicker cane, you can chop and box the cane in the vertical position. Simply position the cane-boxing trough below the cane and thermal shock each section into it. Carry the cane over to the annealer and do your best to load it in the box without destroying it or anything else.

If you end up with still some good imagery on your moile, you can go ahead and reheat it up and try for some more pulls and see what you get.

Second drum roll please.... Now for the exciting part. After your glass cools off (anneals) you can cut the cane with good tile nippers. Or if you discover you really like murrine making, and plan on doing alot of it you can mount your tile cutter on a base, extend one handle of it and save your hands and wrists an unnecessary amount of strain with an ergonomically friendly cutting system. Or you can be inventive like **Chris Funk** and build an automated cane-cutter/guillotine out of old bicycle parts, some scrap metal and gears and a tiny motor.

whatever it takes...

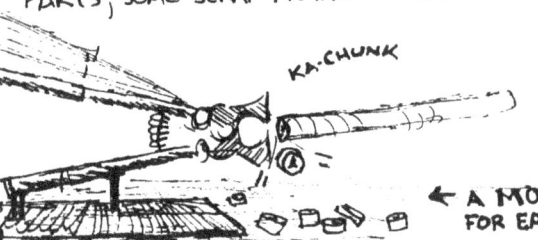

← A MOUNTED TILE-CUTTER FOR EASIER MURRINE CHOPPING

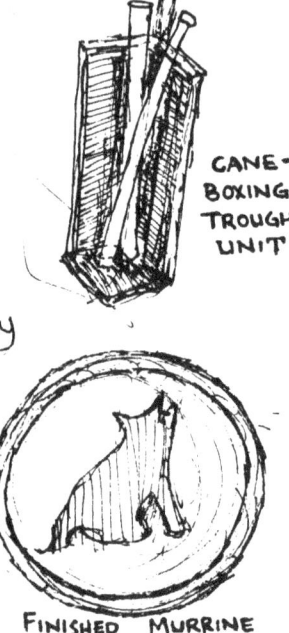

CANE-BOXING TROUGH UNIT

FINISHED MURRINE

THE SECOND METHOD BY WHICH YOU CAN MAKE MURRINE IS BY BUILDING IT UP FROM THE INSIDE-OUT. THIS, TOO, REQUIRES YOU TO THINK LINEARLY AND CROSS-SECTIONALLY AT THE SAME TIME. FUNNY THING IS THAT WE'RE NOT PROGRAMMED TO THINK THAT WAY - USUALLY... SO IT MAY BE A GOOD IDEA TO DRAW OUT **FIRST** → THE MURRINE YOU'D LIKE TO MAKE AND **SECOND** → THE STEPS AND BITS NECESSARY TO GET YOU THERE. THIS FIFTEEN MINUTE EXERCISE CAN SAVE YOU TREMENDOUS AMOUNTS OF TIME AND FRUSTRATION, NOT-TOO-MENTION EXPENSIVE KUGLER!

THIS METHOD OF WORKING IS VERY CONDUSIVE TO MAKING **LETTERS** AND/OR SYMBOLS. LET'S USE THE LETTER "E" FOR EXAMPLE (KEEPING WITH THE POSTULATE - **START SIMPLE**) → IT'S BASICALLY A LETTER COMPRISED OF RECTILINEAR SLABS. SO, LOOKING AT OUR LAY-OUT AND SEQUENCE - WE CAN BEGIN WITH THE CENTRAL COMPONENT.

TAKE A DARK CHUNK OF KUGLER, PICK IT UP ON A PUNTY AND SQUASH IT FLAT → either ON THE MARVER OR WITH SOME FLAT TWEEZERS. SQUARE UP THE SIDES → TO WIND-UP WITH A RECTANGULAR SHAPE. ALLOW IT TO COOL.

NOW ADD YOUR SECOND ELEMENT-IN A LIGHTER/CONTRASTING COLOR. APPLY IT AS HOT AS YOU CAN TO AVOID TRAPPING AIR BUBBLES. SQUARE-UP THE SIDES. ADD YOUR THIRD BIT (MAYBE FROM THE SAME PUNTY ?). AND THEN YOUR FOURTH....

EACH TIME YOU ADD ANOTHER COLOR TAKE THE TIME TO SQUARE IT UP ON THE MARVER. USE A **TAGLIOL** TO KEEP THE SIDES FROM OOZING OUT. FLIP THE PUNTY WITH SWIFT DELIBERATE MOTIONS - LANDING AS CLEAN AS YOU CAN - LEVEL WITH THE MARVER.

FINISH THE LETTER FORM WITH THE REMAINING BITS (No.s 5 & 6). AGAIN, FLATTEN THE WHOLE UNIT INTO A NICE, TIGHT RECTANGULAR MASS, DOING YOUR BEST NOT TO TORQUE IT TOO MUCH.

THE LAST STEP PRIOR TO THE PULL IS TO CASE THE LETTER IN ANOTHER COLOR OR THE SAME COLOR AS THE BACKROUND, IT'S EASIEST TO STAY WITH A RECTANGULAR SHAPE ↝ AND ADD FLAT STRIPES/BITS VESUS TRYING TO FILL-IN EVENLY IN HOPES OF MAKING IT ROUND (BITS Nos 7 to 10).

AT SOME POINT IN THIS PROCESS YOU MAY NEED TO BEEF-UP THE MOILE WITH A GATHER OF CLEAR-TO KEEP CONTROL OVER THE COLOR ON THE END OF THE PUNTY.

ONCE AGAIN, DO YOUR BEST TO AVOID TORQUING THE PIECE DURING THE REHEATING AND SHAPING PROCESS. JUST FLIP THE PUNTY BACK N' FORTH VS. CONTINUALLY TURNING (AS IS COMMON IN MOST FORMS OF GLASSBLOWING.).

WHEN YOU GET THE WHOLE THING SQUARED-UP AND HEATED EVENLY THROUGHOUT, COMPLETE IT BY PULLING OUT VIA THE USUAL MURRINE PULLING TECHNIQUE, ie. IN A **VERTICAL** FASHION!

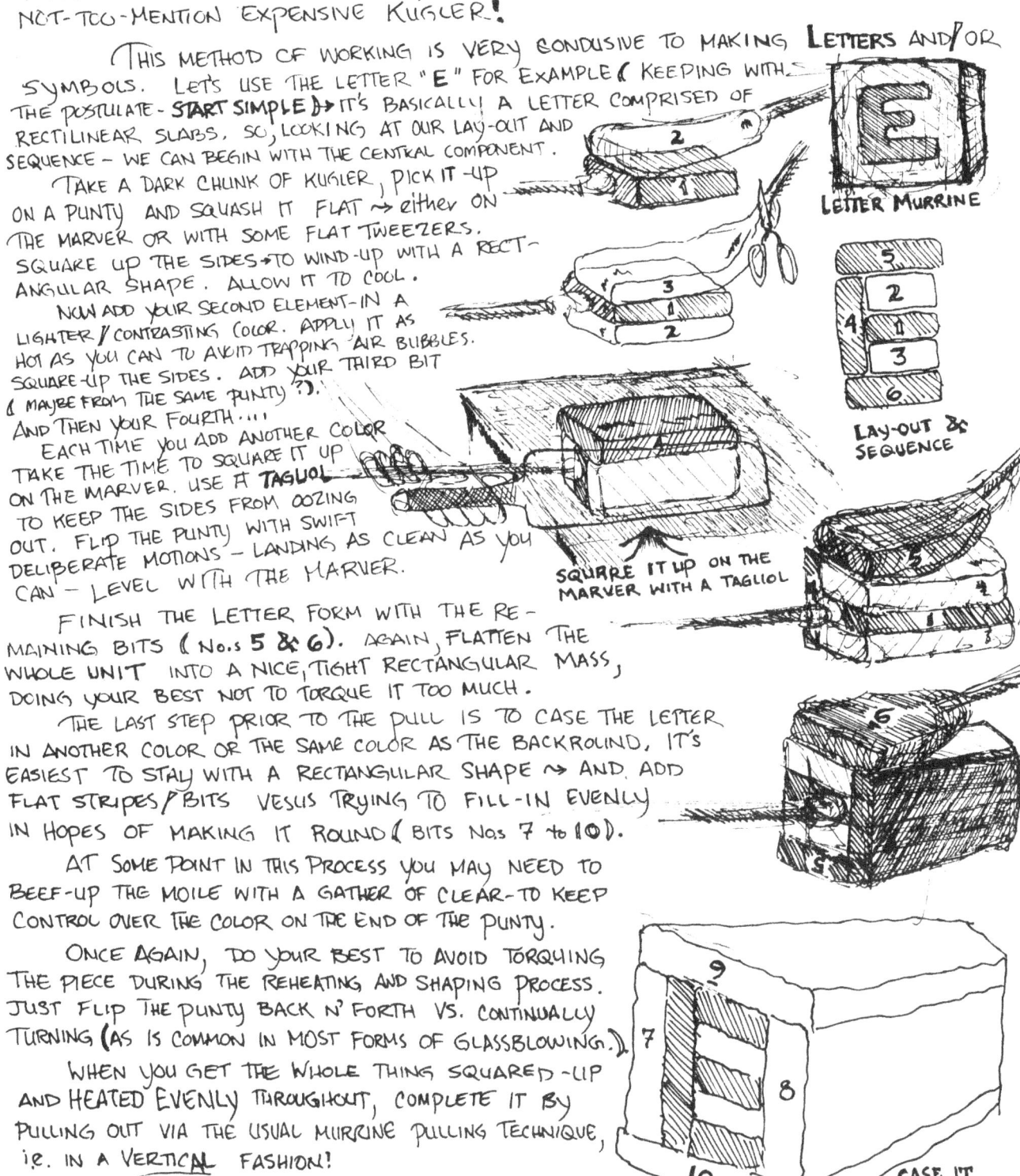

Some letters are easier to make than others. "T" for example is essentially four bits slabbed together to build up the form. Some letters may have dual roles, e.g. "W" & "M" and "N" & "Z". If you make them fairly symmetrical, you can flip them around and use them a second way.

The curvilinear shapes found in certain letters like "C" "D" "R" and "S" for example, are a bit more challenging. One way to make the letter "S" is illustrated below. Letter canes may be made into words or "signature" cane/murrine by bundling and pulling them, as described on the following page.

LETTER "S"

Step 1 Squeeze out color into a tongue shape.

Step 2 Pick-up two rods of color bar.

Step 3 Carefully reheat, curve it with the marver/tagliol into position.

Step 4 Switch axis by puntying up to the other side.

Step 5 Fill in the gaps with bits of the same color, and volume enough to round-out the rest of the letter.

Step 6 Squeeze out any air bubbles with a "double marver" technique.

Step 7 (Not illustrated) Complete the murrine by pulling it as usual.

or...

You can make a small quantity of "Trippy" **Spiral Murrine**:

Step 1 Squeeze together contrasting layers of color into a tongue shape.

Step 2 Carefull reheat just the tip. You can initiate some of the curl at the glory hole and finish it on the marver.

Step 3 Finish the curl. Punty-up to switch the axis.

Step 4 Marver smooth. Squeeze out any bubbles. Heat quench. Heat quench. Get the core hot and...

Step 5 Make the pull.

THE THIRD METHOD BY WHICH YOU CAN MAKE MURRINE IS THE **BUNDLE** METHOD. IN THIS PROCESS YOU CREATE YOUR MURRINE IMAGE BY ASSEMBLING LENGTHS OF CANE, CUT TO THE SAME SIZE, INTO A BUNDLE. THE BUNDLE IS WIRED TOGETHER, PREHEATED IN A KILN, AND PICKED UP ON A **POST** OR **COLLAR**. THE WHOLE THING GETS HEATED IN THE GLORY HOLE, AND ONCE THE ENDS OF THE CANE ARE MELTED (NOT THE WHOLE PIECE) - THE WIRE IS CUT FREE. THEN IT'S A SERIES OF HEATING, MARVERING, QUENCHING AND REHEATING TO EXPEL ANY AIR BUBBLES, AND GETTING THE CORE HOT AS WELL. ONCE EVERTHING'S READY, IT GETS PULLED AS USUAL.

YOU CAN MAKE SOME INCREDIBLY COMPLICATED CANE USING THIS METHOD. WITH REPEATED PULLS AND REARRANGING OF THE RESULTING CANE INTO ANOTHER BUNDLE, PLUS ADDING ADDITIONAL COLORS OR ELEMENTS INTO THE BUNDLE AS YOU GO→YOU CAN OBTAIN SOME HIGHLY DETAILED IMAGERY.

SOME FAIRLY REALISTIC PORTRAIT MURRINE MAY BE CREATED THIS WAY. IT MAY TAKE FIVE-TO-FIFTY PULLS JUST TO GET AN EYE-MURRINE LOOKING GOOD. THEN ANOTHER TWENTY PULLS FOR AN EYE-BROW, NOSE, OR CHEEK PARTS. SHADING AND BLENDING THE COLORS ARE IMPORTANT THINGS TO CONSIDER IN ORDER TO ACHIEVE SOME VOLUME AND DEPTH IN YOUR IMAGERY. IT'S A PAINSTAKING PROCESS BUT THE RESULTS CAN BE PHENOMENAL. ALOT OF WHICH IS DEPENDENT ON YOUR COLOR PALETTE AND KNOWLEDGE ON HOW VARIOUS COLORS BEHAVE NEXT TO EACH OTHER.

BASICALLY IT GOES LIKE THIS: **STEP ONE:** TAKE YOUR PREMADE CANE AND CUT IT INTO EXACTLY THE SAME LENGTHS. ASSEMBLE THEM TOGETHER TO FORM AN IMAGE. IN OUR EXAMPLE WE'VE GOT A CHECKERBOARD PATTERN MADE OUT OF SIXTEEN SQUARE-SHAPED CANE OF CONTRASTING COLORS. THIS THEN GETS BUNDLED TOGETHER WITH NICHROM OR GALVANIZED WIRE.

STEP ONE: ARRANGE THE CANE. YOU CAN SET IT IN CLAY OR BUNDLE W/ RUBBER BANDS. THEN WRAP IT W/ NICHROME WIRE.

STEP TWO: THE BUNDLE GETS PREHEATED IN A PICK-UP OVEN. IF IT SEEMS LIKE THERE ARE A LOT OF GAPS IN YOUR BUNDLE (BETWEEN THE CANE THEMSELVES) YOU MAY ELECT TO PICK-UP THE BUNDLE ON A COLLAR. THIS WAY YOU CAN SQUEEZE OUT ANY AIR BUBBLES THROUGH THE BLOWPIPE. THE COLLAR SHOULD MATCH THE DIAMETER AND SHAPE AS CLOSELY AS POSSIBLE ~ AND SHOULD ALSO GO ON HOT HOT HOT!

ONCE YOU GET THE BUNDLE PICKED-UP AND HEATED/FUSED A BIT TOGETHER, YOU CAN CUT THE BUNDLING WIRE WITH SOME WIRE CUTTERS AND GET RID OF IT.

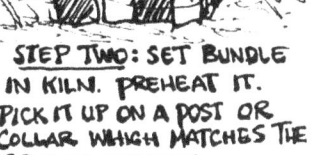

STEP TWO: SET BUNDLE IN KILN. PREHEAT IT. PICK IT UP ON A POST OR COLLAR WHICH MATCHES THE SIZE OF BUNDLE.

STEP THREE: HEAT AND MARVER/SQUEEZE ALL THE AIR BUBBLES OUT OF THE PIECE. YOU CAN USE A PLATE/SQUASHER TOOL TO HELP YOU, OR USE A **MANGLE** (A SECTION OF HALF-PIPE ↙) IF ONE'S AVAILABLE.

SQUEEZING OUT BUBBLES ON A MANGLE

STEP FOUR: REPEATEDLY HEAT AND QUENCH THE TIP, CHILL THE EXTERIOR UNTIL THE CORE GETS HOT. THEN PULL.

A PORTRAIT BUNDLE

Maybe moldmaking isn't your forte. Perhaps something along the lines of a **MILLEFIORI** might interest you. The OPTIC MOLD may be your ticket to beautiful bright murrines without having to get your hands dirty. I'd like to thank **JEFF HOLMWOOD** for his demo on this technique ~ the foundation to his "ELECTRIC KOOL-AID BOWL" series.

This is the process you use when you don't have the luxury of color pots - like they have in the factories. You are usually limited to semi-short pulls unless you have large optic molds and can afford the big bucks to use whole sticks of color bar to case each layer with.

In any event start with a clean punty (STEP ①). Transfer your first chunk of color onto a preheated punty with NO glass on it. This prevents any clear from getting sucked-into the murrine.

OPTIC MURRINE

Once you have the core color centered-up and marvered into a squat rod, add your second color (STEP ②). This can be applied like a **LIP WRAP** - just have your color brought to you as hot as possible - in more of a blunt shape than a point. Wrap it on, and smooth it out with the back of your jacks.

Allow the core to cool and add another layer of color. Do the same thing again. (and again, if you wish.) (STEP ③)

STEP ④ Heat the whole thing up and drop it in the optic mold. The hotter you get it ~ the deeper the optic pattern effect will go.   Remove and cool.

STEP ⑤ Case the optic pattern. You can do this with by dropping some color (or clear) on from overhead fig ⓐ or by filling-in each rib individually with a trail of color, fig ⓑ. Zzzzz...

STEP ⑥ Now you can trail-on a layer of clear glass to create a moile with. Smooth it out with the back of the jacks.

STEP ⑦ Add an avollo - or "post-pad" to the bottom of the color. This conserves your precious color and insures you get the most of your Kugler dollars.

STEP ⑧ (not illustrated) Attach a clear post - after heating the core - to your glass and make the pull in a vertical fashion.

It's the same kind of deal as any murrine pull. Pay attention and try your best to get the heat right. Cross your fingers and make it so...

"ELECTRIC KOOL-AID BOWL" - by JEFF HOLMWOOD
• MURRINE - PICK-UP ON A BUBBLE (OFF A HOT PLATE)

182

WINE GLASS ⇒ CANE PICK-UP → ON A CLEAR BUBBLE

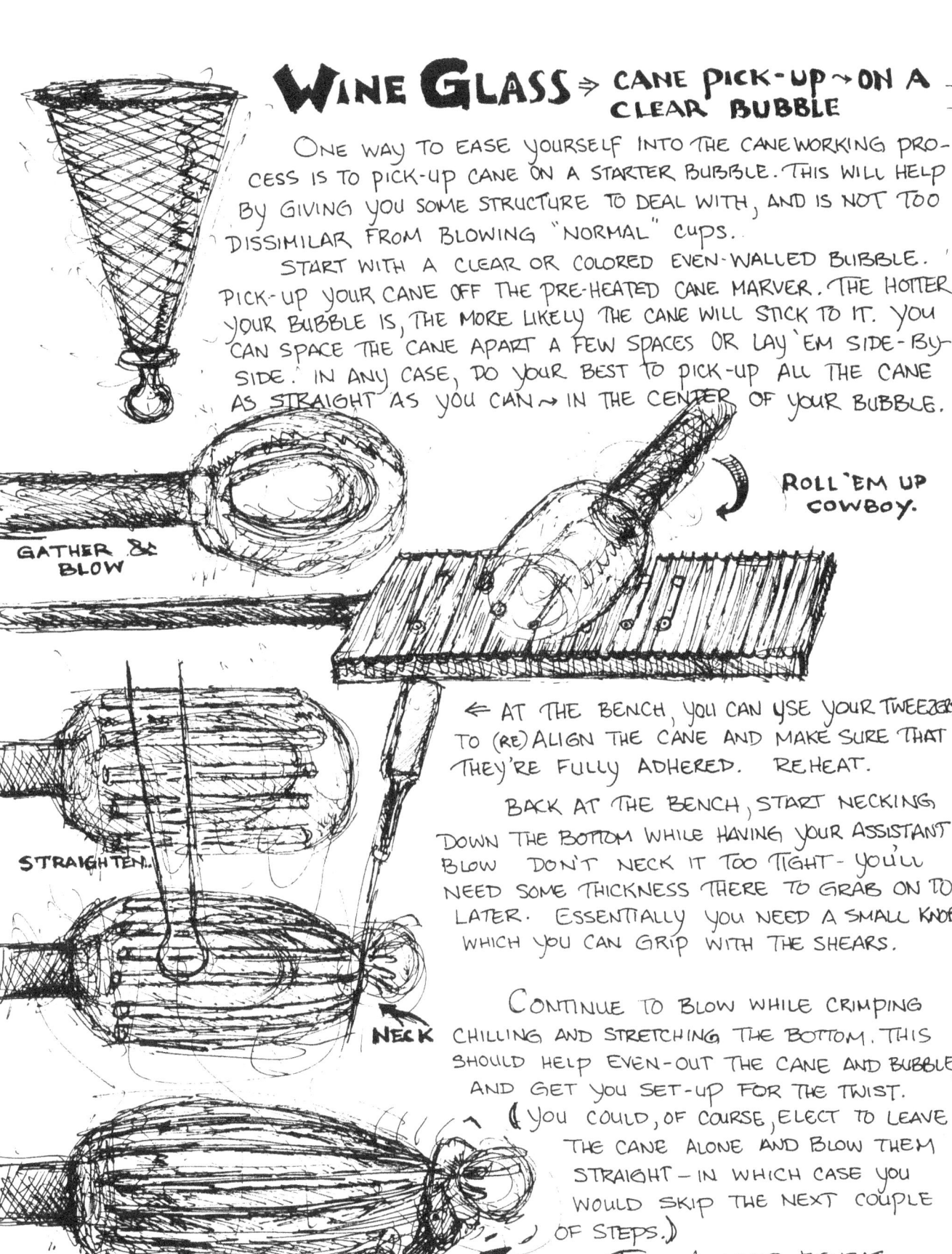

One way to ease yourself into the caneworking process is to pick-up cane on a starter bubble. This will help by giving you some structure to deal with, and is not too dissimilar from blowing "normal" cups.

Start with a clear or colored even-walled bubble. Pick-up your cane off the pre-heated cane marver. The hotter your bubble is, the more likely the cane will stick to it. You can space the cane apart a few spaces or lay 'em side-by-side. In any case, do your best to pick-up all the cane as straight as you can ~ in the center of your bubble.

GATHER & BLOW

ROLL 'EM UP COWBOY.

← At the bench, you can use your tweezers to (re)align the cane and make sure that they're fully adhered. Reheat.

STRAIGHTEN

Back at the bench, start necking down the bottom while having your assistant blow. Don't neck it too tight - you'll need some thickness there to grab on to later. Essentially you need a small knob which you can grip with the shears.

NECK

Continue to blow while crimping chilling and stretching the bottom. This should help even-out the cane and bubble, and get you set-up for the twist.

(You could, of course, elect to leave the cane alone and blow them straight - in which case you would skip the next couple of steps.)

Take another reheat.

BLOW N' PULL

183

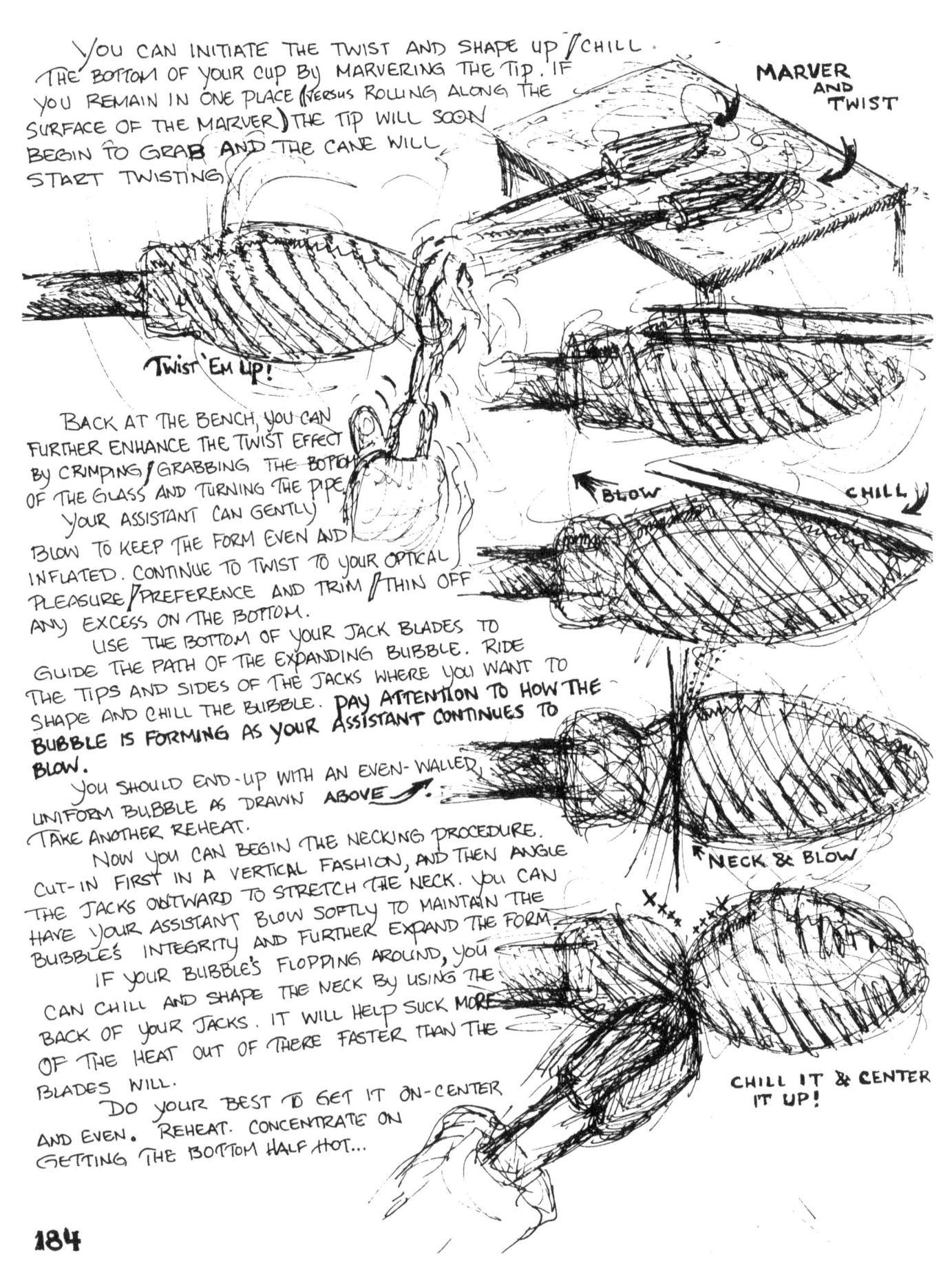

You can initiate the twist and shape up/chill the bottom of your cup by marvering the tip. If you remain in one place (versus rolling along the surface of the marver) the tip will soon begin to grab and the cane will start twisting.

Twist 'em up!

Back at the bench, you can further enhance the twist effect by crimping/grabbing the bottom of the glass and turning the pipe. Your assistant can gently blow to keep the form even and inflated. Continue to twist to your optical pleasure/preference and trim/thin off any excess on the bottom.

Use the bottom of your jack blades to guide the path of the expanding bubble. Ride the tips and sides of the jacks where you want to shape and chill the bubble. Pay attention to how the bubble is forming as your assistant continues to blow.

You should end-up with an even-walled, uniform bubble as drawn above. Take another reheat.

Now you can begin the necking procedure. Cut-in first in a vertical fashion, and then angle the jacks outward to stretch the neck. You can have your assistant blow softly to maintain the bubble's integrity and further expand the form.

If your bubble's flopping around, you can chill and shape the neck by using the back of your jacks. It will help suck more of the heat out of there faster than the blades will.

Do your best to get it on-center and even. Reheat. Concentrate on getting the bottom half hot...

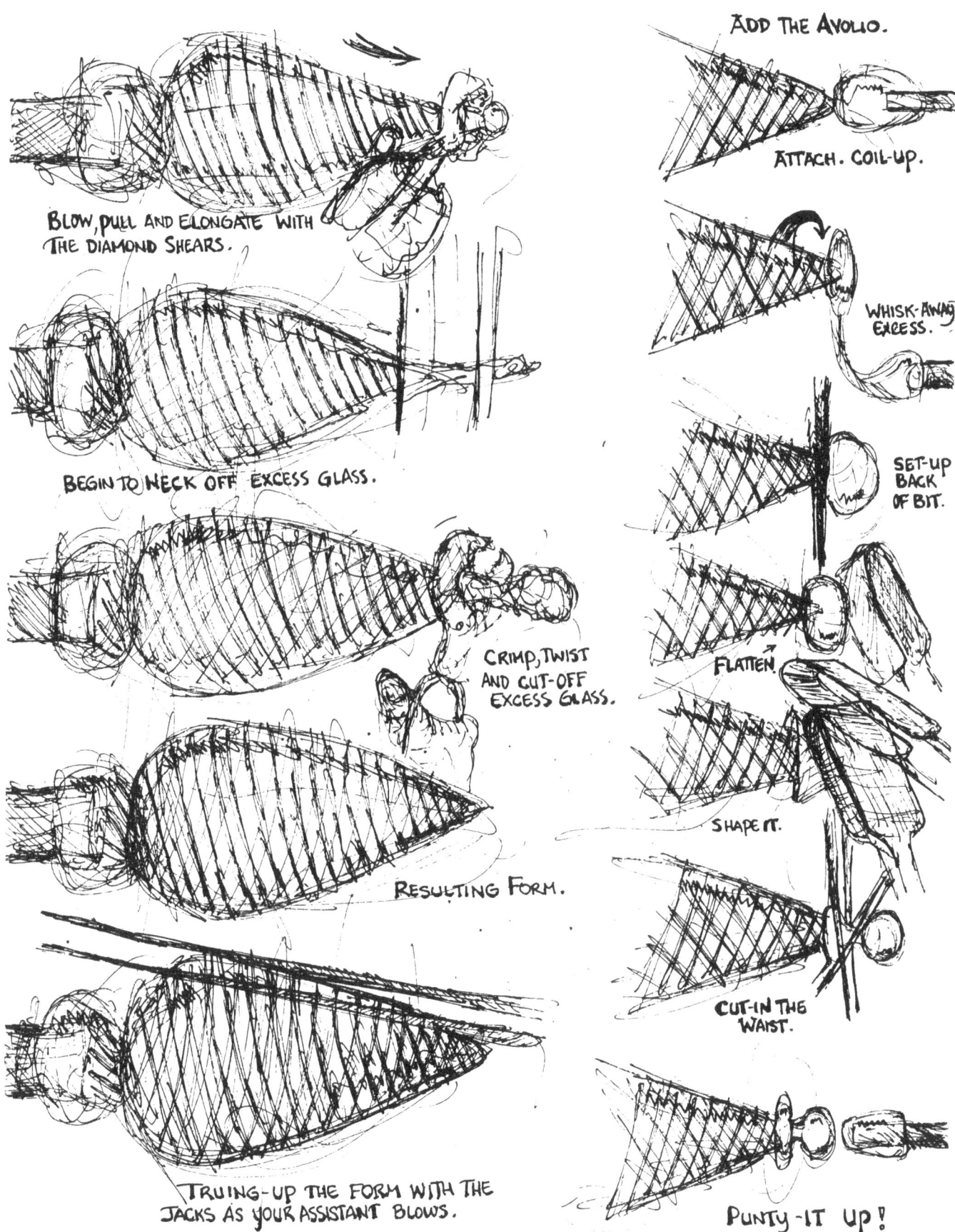

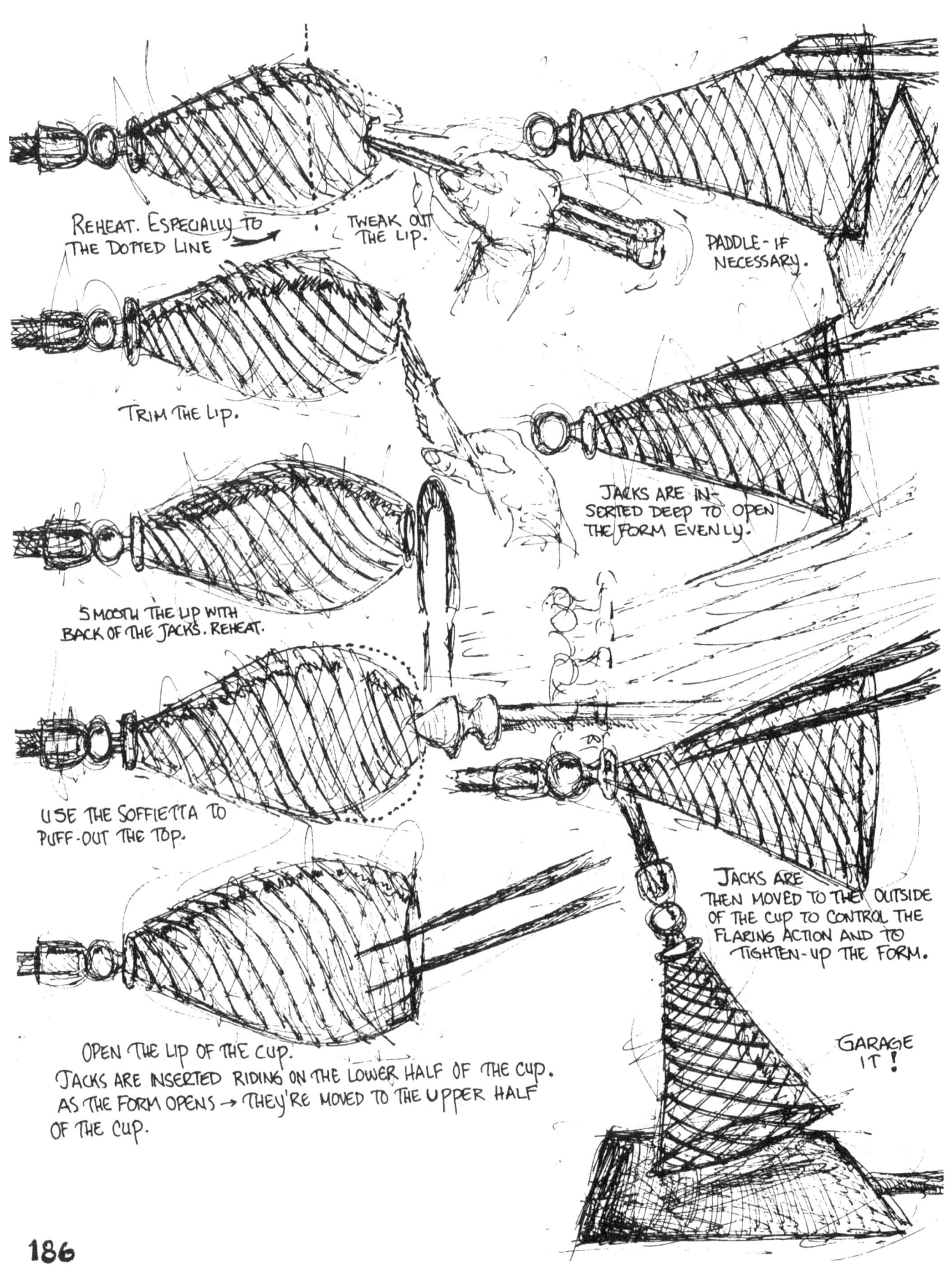

CHAMPAGNE GLASS — CANE PICK-UP ON A COLLAR.

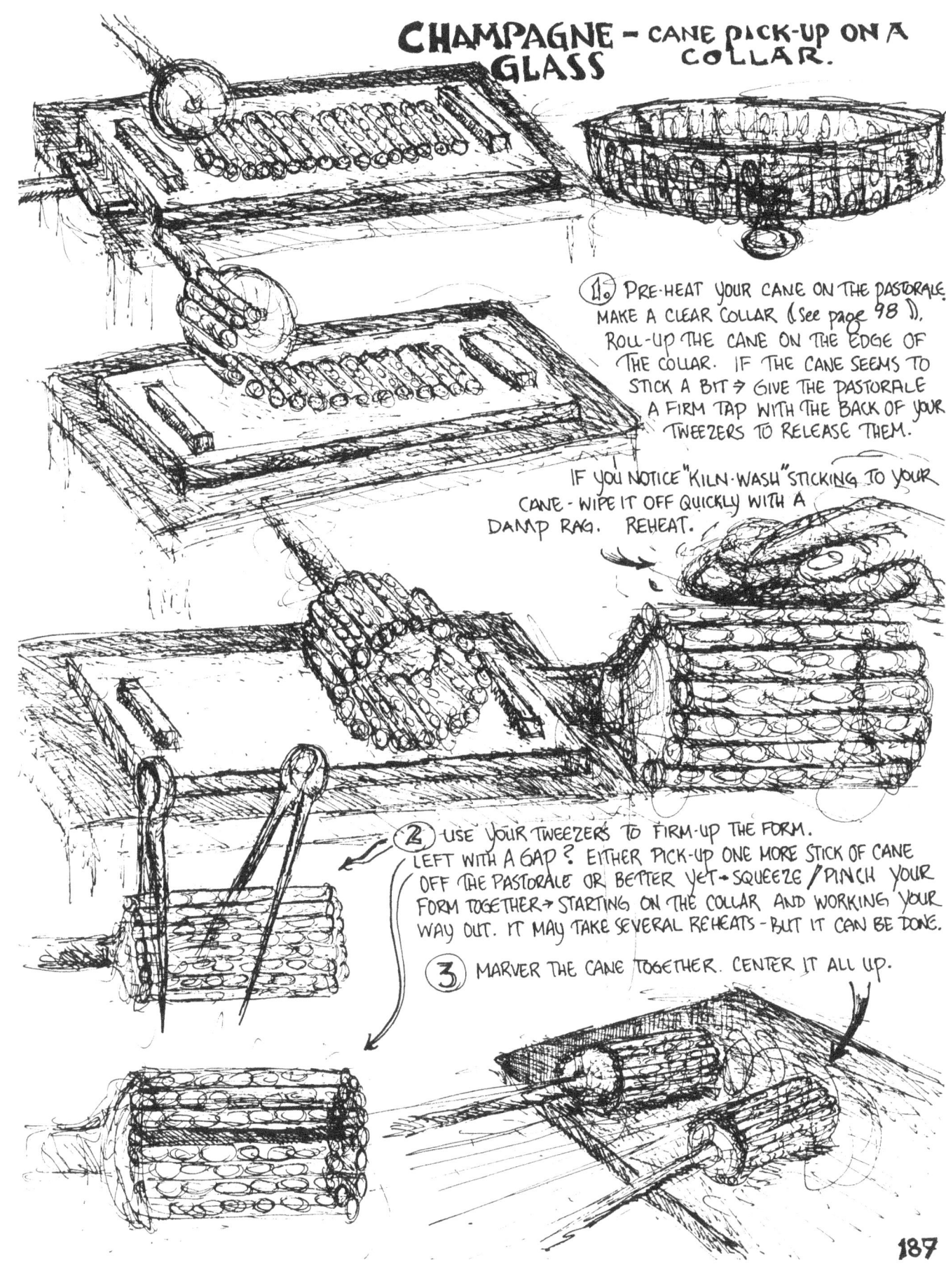

1. PRE-HEAT YOUR CANE ON THE PASTORALE. MAKE A CLEAR COLLAR (see page 98). ROLL-UP THE CANE ON THE EDGE OF THE COLLAR. IF THE CANE SEEMS TO STICK A BIT → GIVE THE PASTORALE A FIRM TAP WITH THE BACK OF YOUR TWEEZERS TO RELEASE THEM.

IF YOU NOTICE "KILN-WASH" STICKING TO YOUR CANE — WIPE IT OFF QUICKLY WITH A DAMP RAG. REHEAT.

2. USE YOUR TWEEZERS TO FIRM-UP THE FORM. LEFT WITH A GAP? EITHER PICK-UP ONE MORE STICK OF CANE OFF THE PASTORALE OR BETTER YET → SQUEEZE / PINCH YOUR FORM TOGETHER → STARTING ON THE COLLAR AND WORKING YOUR WAY OUT. IT MAY TAKE SEVERAL REHEATS — BUT IT CAN BE DONE.

3. MARVER THE CANE TOGETHER. CENTER IT ALL UP.

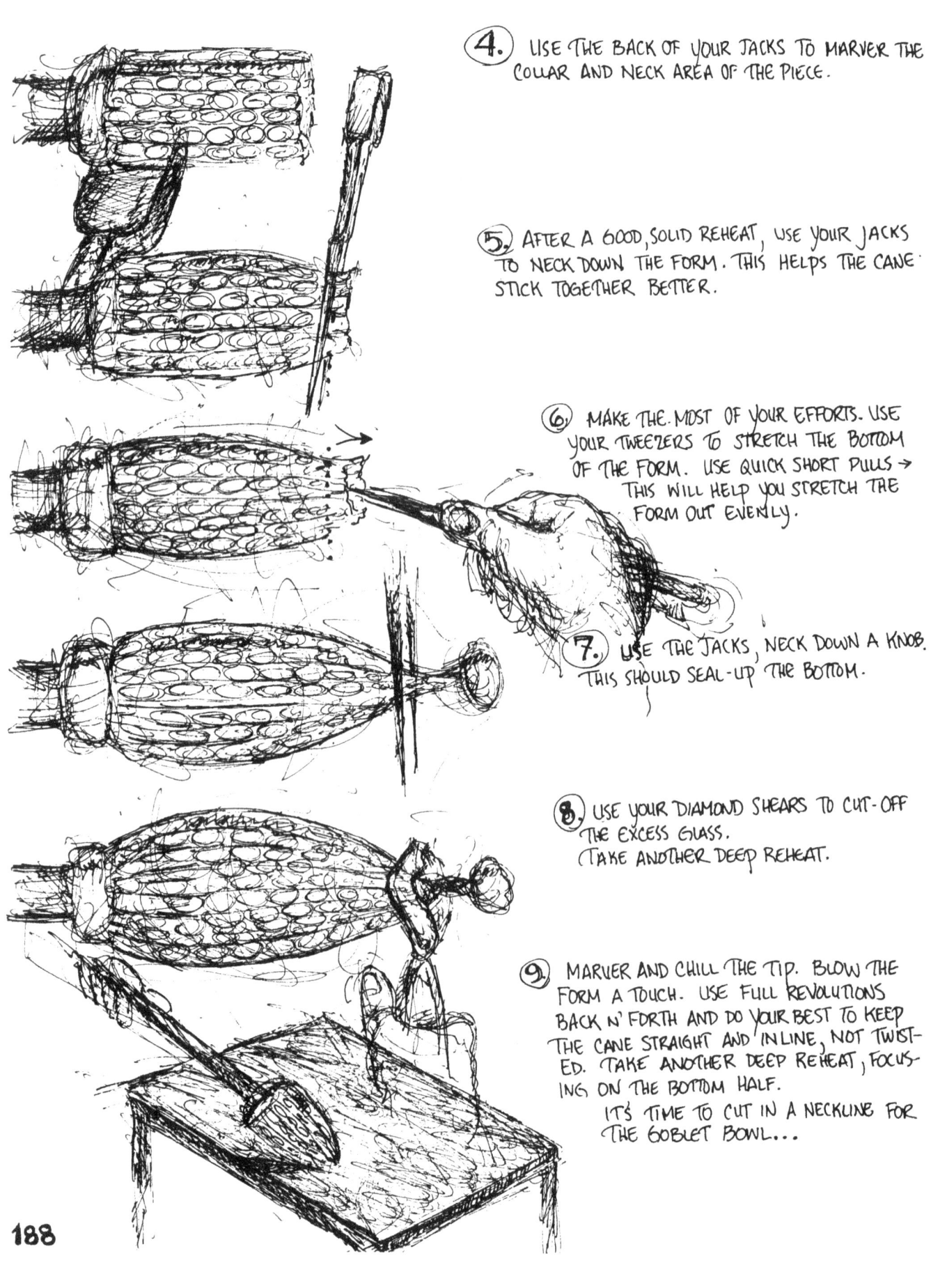

4.) USE THE BACK OF YOUR JACKS TO MARVER THE COLLAR AND NECK AREA OF THE PIECE.

5.) AFTER A GOOD, SOLID REHEAT, USE YOUR JACKS TO NECK DOWN THE FORM. THIS HELPS THE CANE STICK TOGETHER BETTER.

6.) MAKE THE MOST OF YOUR EFFORTS. USE YOUR TWEEZERS TO STRETCH THE BOTTOM OF THE FORM. USE QUICK SHORT PULLS → THIS WILL HELP YOU STRETCH THE FORM OUT EVENLY.

7.) USE THE JACKS, NECK DOWN A KNOB. THIS SHOULD SEAL-UP THE BOTTOM.

8.) USE YOUR DIAMOND SHEARS TO CUT-OFF THE EXCESS GLASS. TAKE ANOTHER DEEP REHEAT.

9.) MARVER AND CHILL THE TIP. BLOW THE FORM A TOUCH. USE FULL REVOLUTIONS BACK N' FORTH AND DO YOUR BEST TO KEEP THE CANE STRAIGHT AND IN LINE, NOT TWISTED. TAKE ANOTHER DEEP REHEAT, FOCUSING ON THE BOTTOM HALF.
IT'S TIME TO CUT IN A NECKLINE FOR THE GOBLET BOWL...

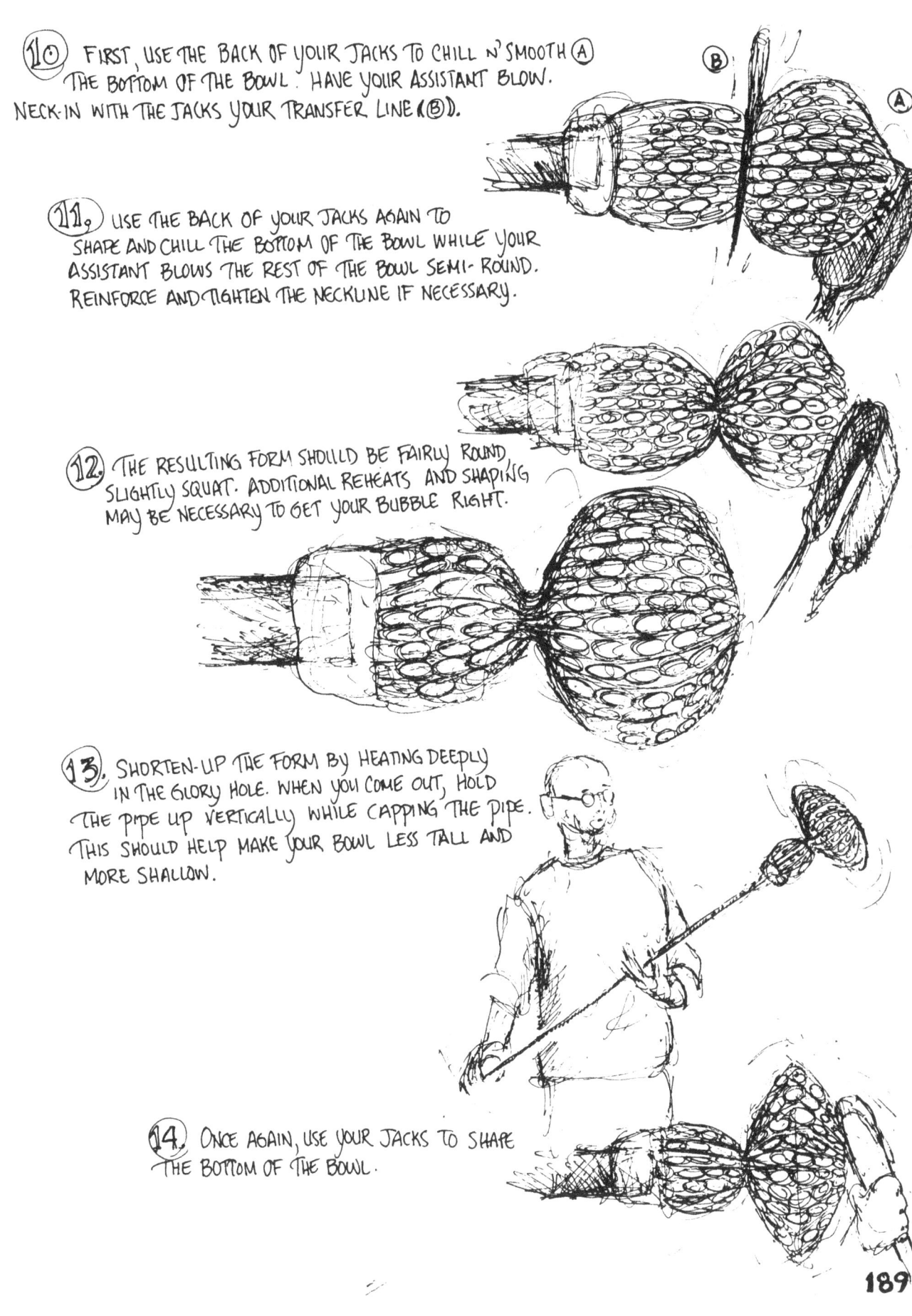

10) First, use the back of your jacks to chill n' smooth Ⓐ the bottom of the bowl. Have your assistant blow. Neck-in with the jacks your transfer line (Ⓑ).

11) Use the back of your jacks again to shape and chill the bottom of the bowl while your assistant blows the rest of the bowl semi-round. Reinforce and tighten the neckline if necessary.

12) The resulting form should be fairly round, slightly squat. Additional reheats and shaping may be necessary to get your bubble right.

13) Shorten-up the form by heating deeply in the glory hole. When you come out, hold the pipe up vertically while capping the pipe. This should help make your bowl less tall and more shallow.

14) Once again, use your jacks to shape the bottom of the bowl.

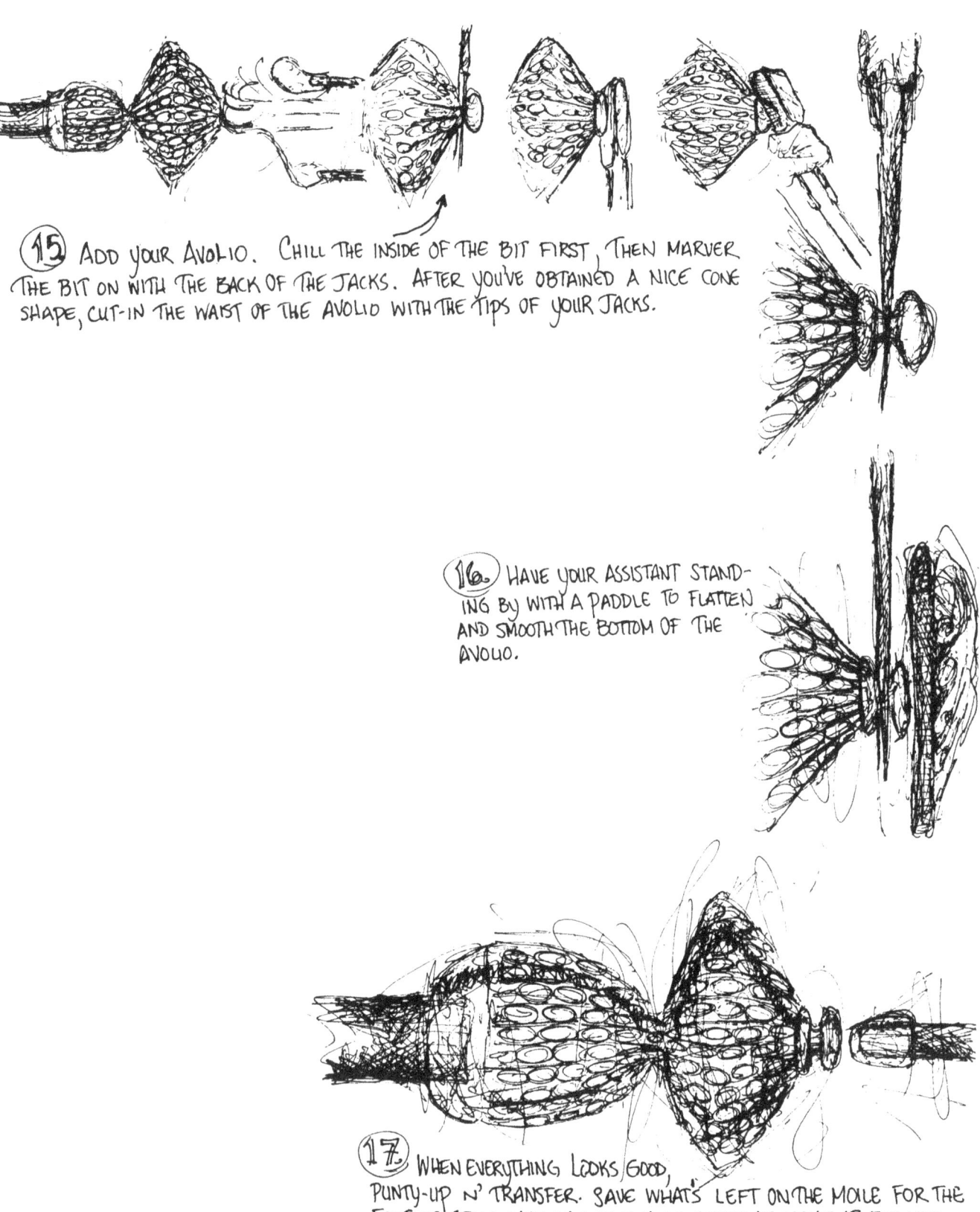

⑮ ADD YOUR AVOLIO. CHILL THE INSIDE OF THE BIT FIRST, THEN MARVER THE BIT ON WITH THE BACK OF THE JACKS. AFTER YOU'VE OBTAINED A NICE CONE SHAPE, CUT-IN THE WAIST OF THE AVOLIO WITH THE TIPS OF YOUR JACKS.

⑯ HAVE YOUR ASSISTANT STANDING BY WITH A PADDLE TO FLATTEN AND SMOOTH THE BOTTOM OF THE AVOLIO.

⑰ WHEN EVERYTHING LOOKS GOOD, PUNTY-UP N' TRANSFER. SAVE WHAT'S LEFT ON THE MOILE FOR THE FOOT OR STEM. YOU CAN HAVE YOUR ASSISTANT MAKE IT FOR YOU, OR YOU CAN HAVE 'EM JUST PARK THE MOILE IN THE GARAGE OR PIPE WARMER FOR LATER WHILE YOU CONCENTRATE ON OPENING UP THE CUP.

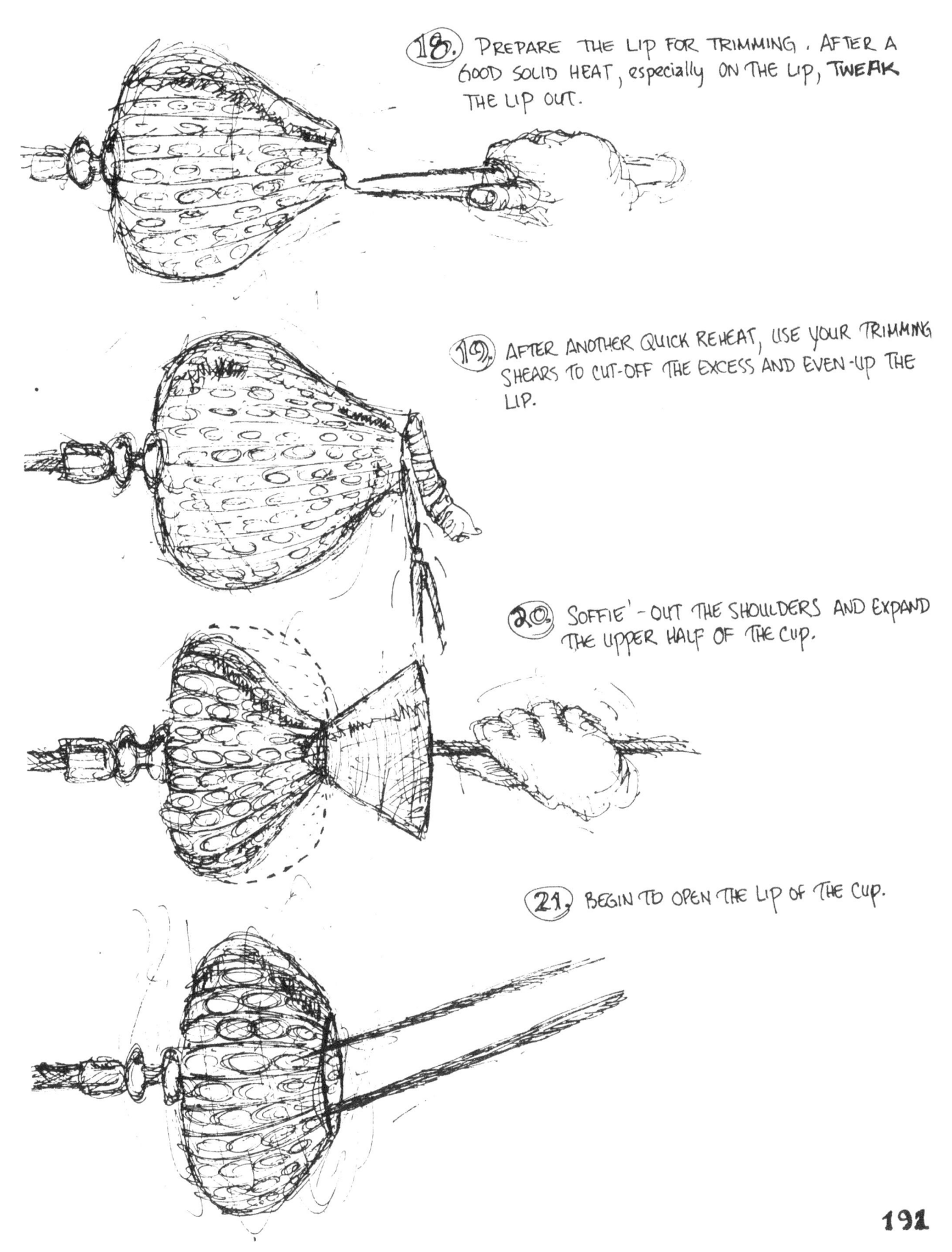

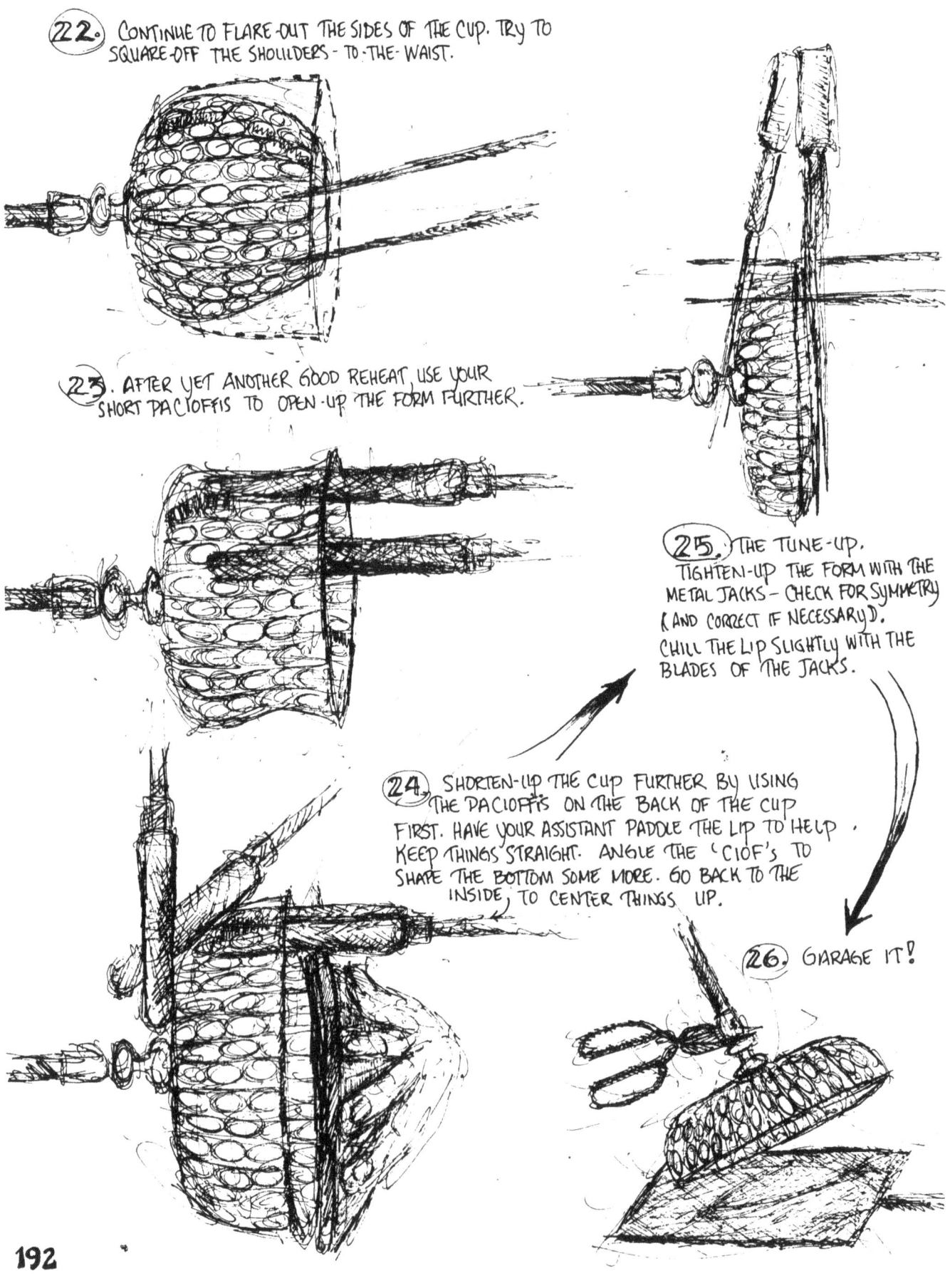

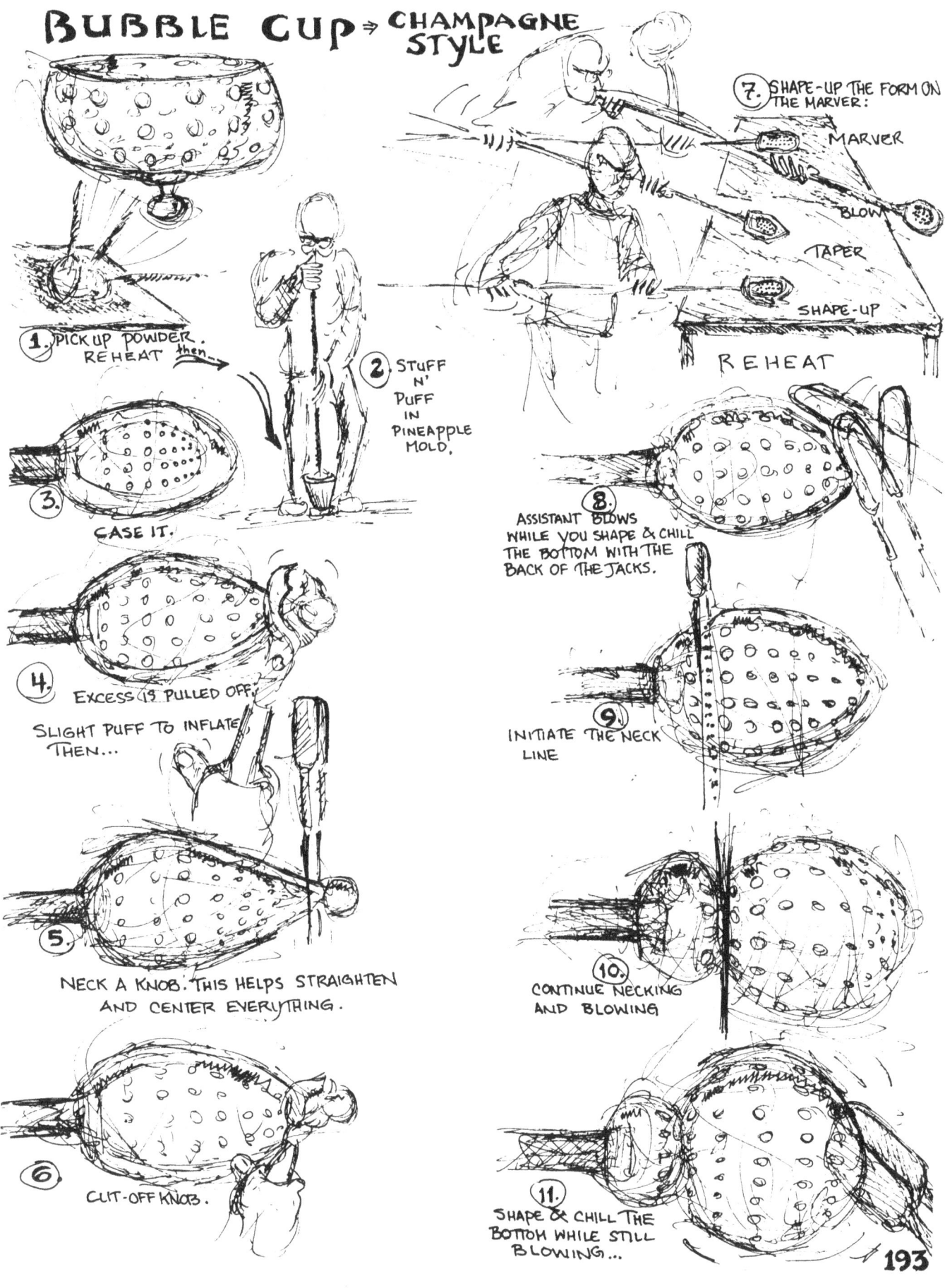

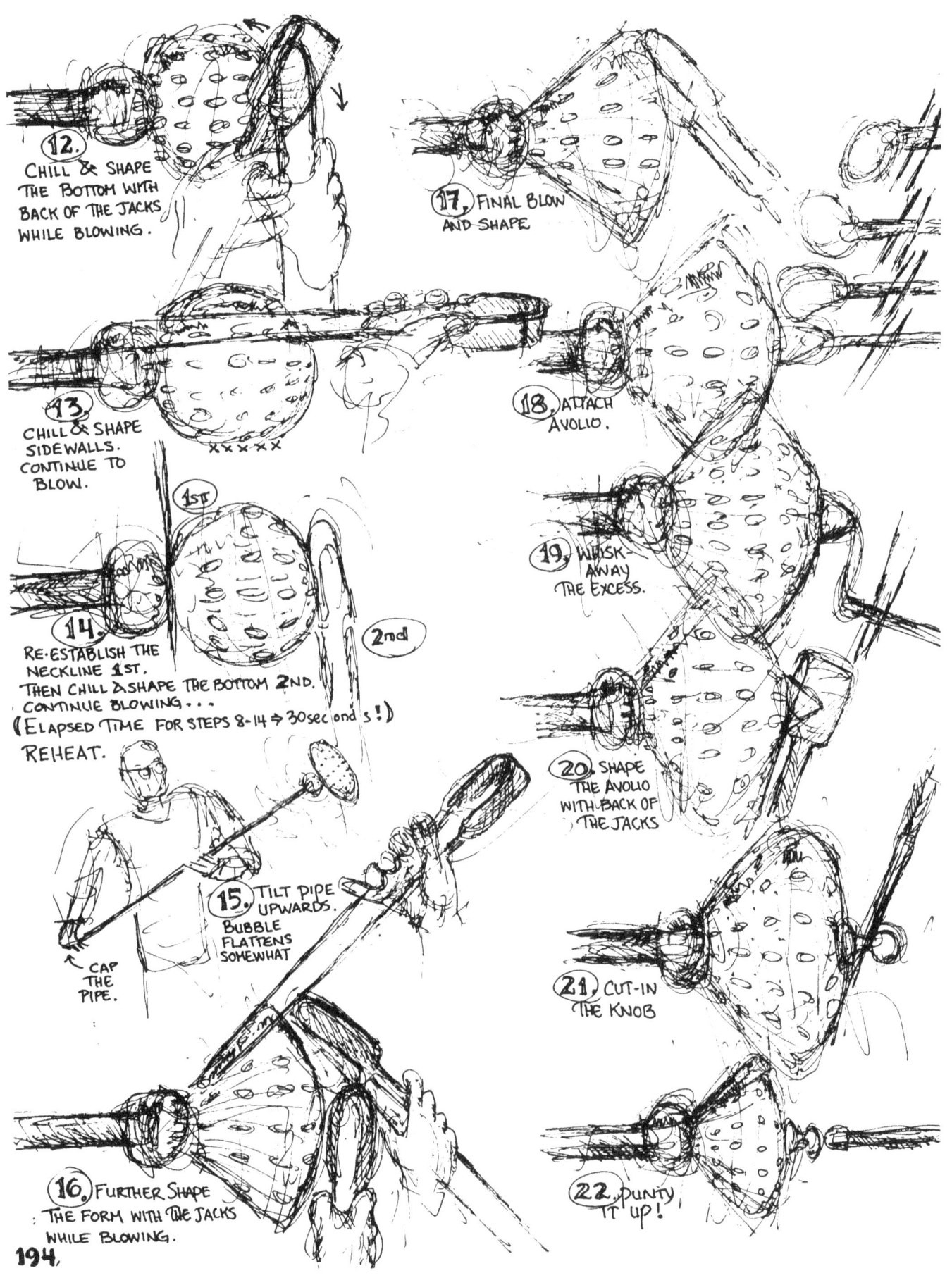

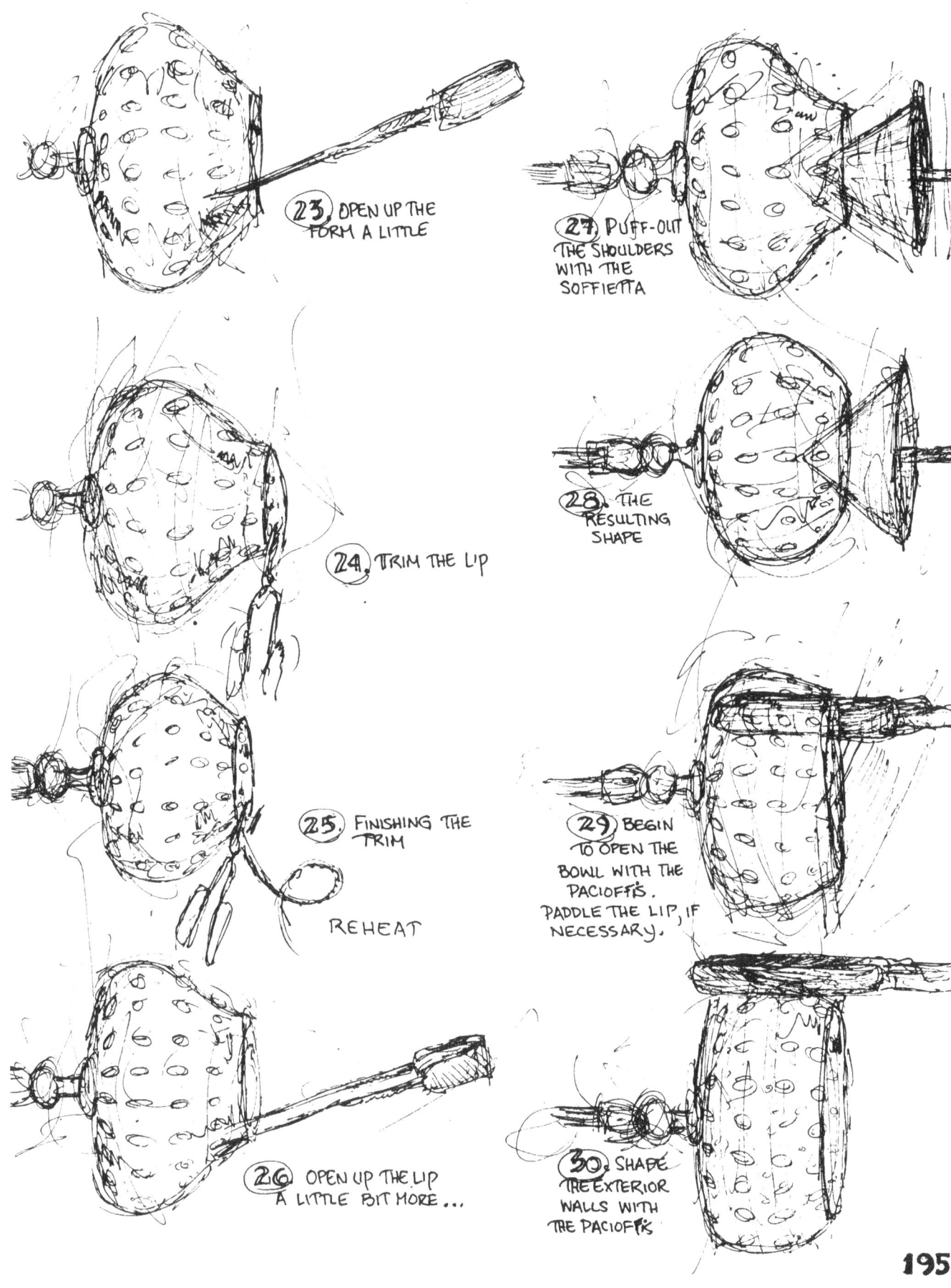

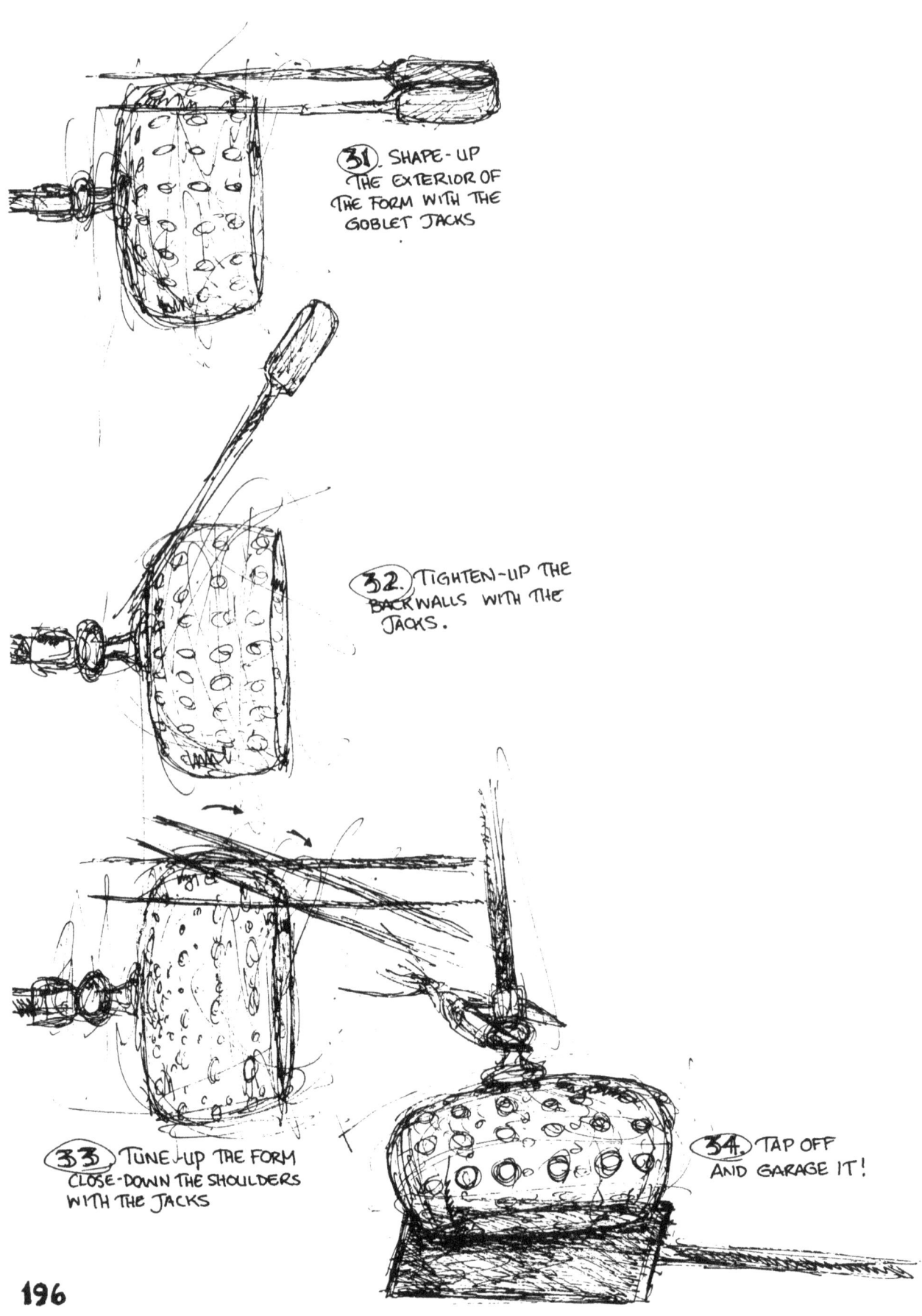

RETICELLO

Reticello is a cane technique which produces one of the most kinetic effects of all hot glass working. It is also one of the trickiest to pull-off correctly. If done right, it will yield a fish net pattern in your piece, often with small air bubbles trapped within each intersecting field. The optic illusions alone may mesmerize you while you blow these things → reason enough to give it a "go".

Essentially reticello is made with two twisted cups-in-one. One cup spirals clockwise and the other counter-clockwise. It is similar to the overlay cup technique, where one bubble is blown-out (and twisted), opened and kept hot while another similar cup (slightly smaller and twisted in the opposite direction) is blown-out into a cone-shaped form. The first cup is tapped off the pipe and set inside a pre-heated optic mold (or similar device). This cup will act as a recepticle for the second bubble.

The second bubble is then immediately brought over and dropped into the first cup. It gets a quick puff to inflate the inner bubble and then taken to the glory hole to be reheated as one unit. From there it can be trimmed, necked and blown-out to its final form.

Suitable for goblets, bowls, vases and platters → whatever — reticello continues to be one of the most challenging and visually exciting of all venetian-styled techniques. Naturally it is labor intensive, risky, and highly habit forming, so — BEWARE!

In the following pages you'll see illustrated the steps involved in making a reticello goblet bowl. The technique is virtually the same for all sizes (and shapes) of work. Most of the reticello I've seen has been made with white cane. Don't let that stop you from trying other colors, or mixing or matching a variety of colors to achieve even wilder patterns. The sky's the limit!

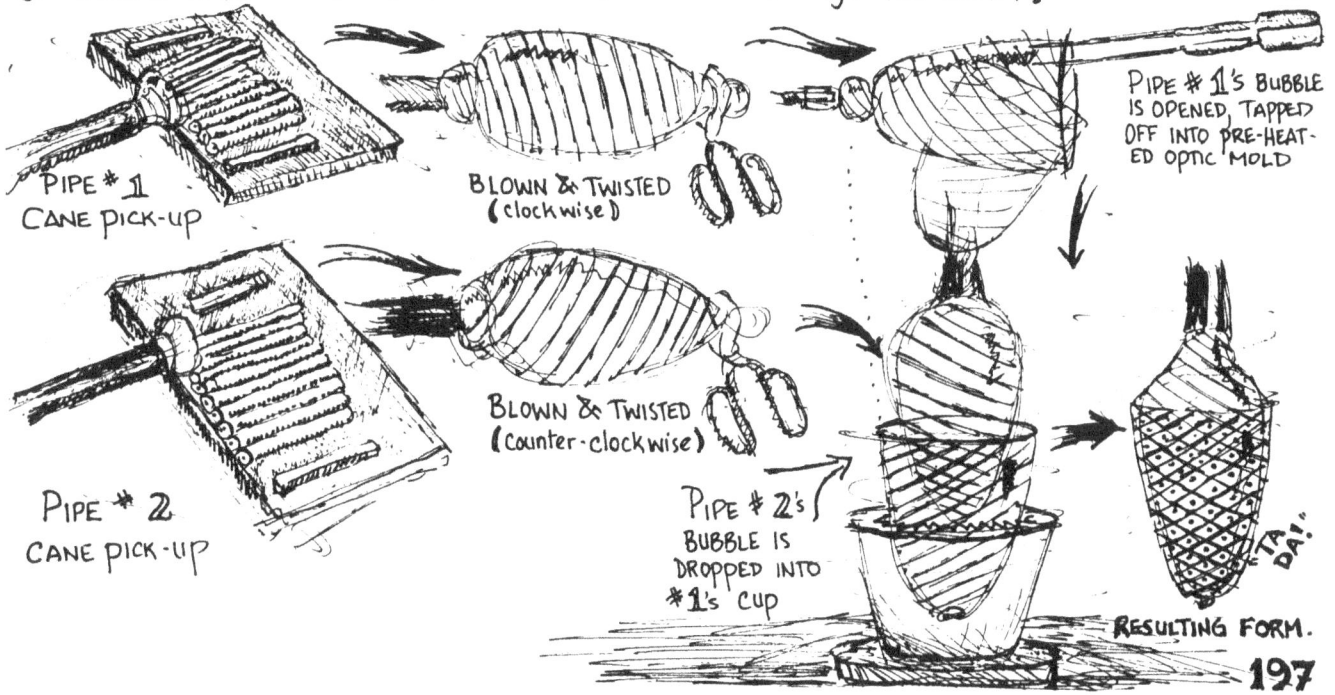

197

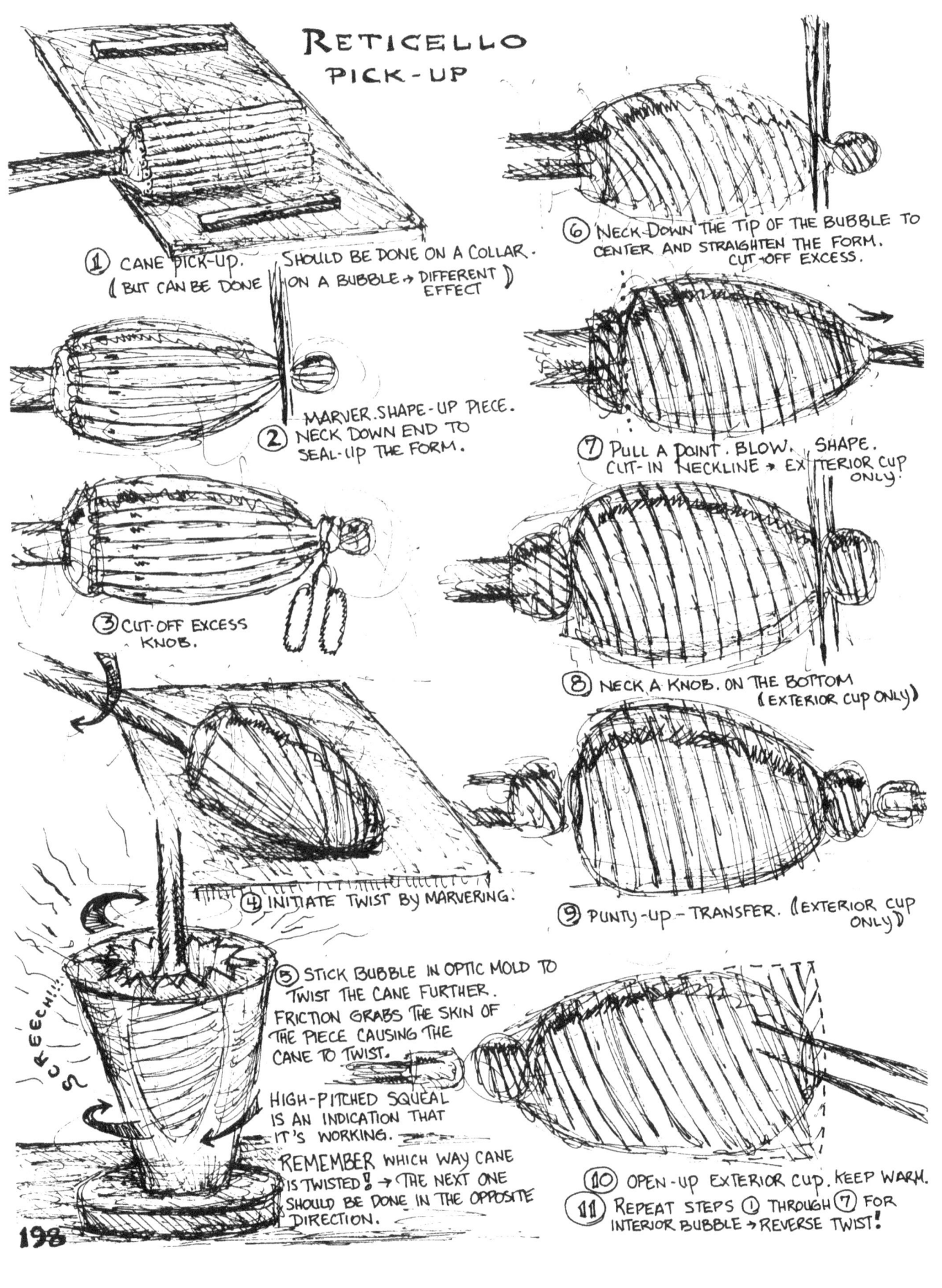

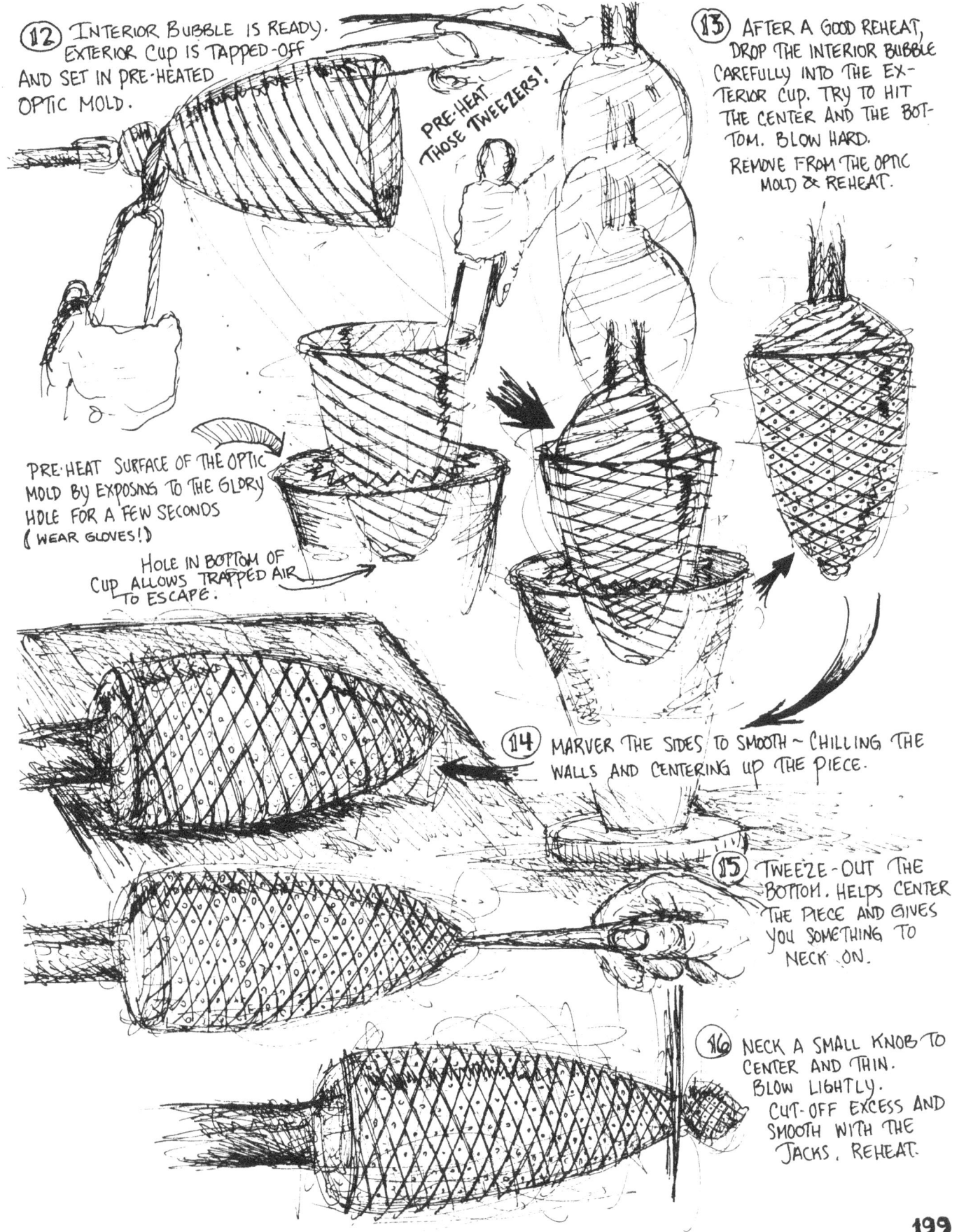

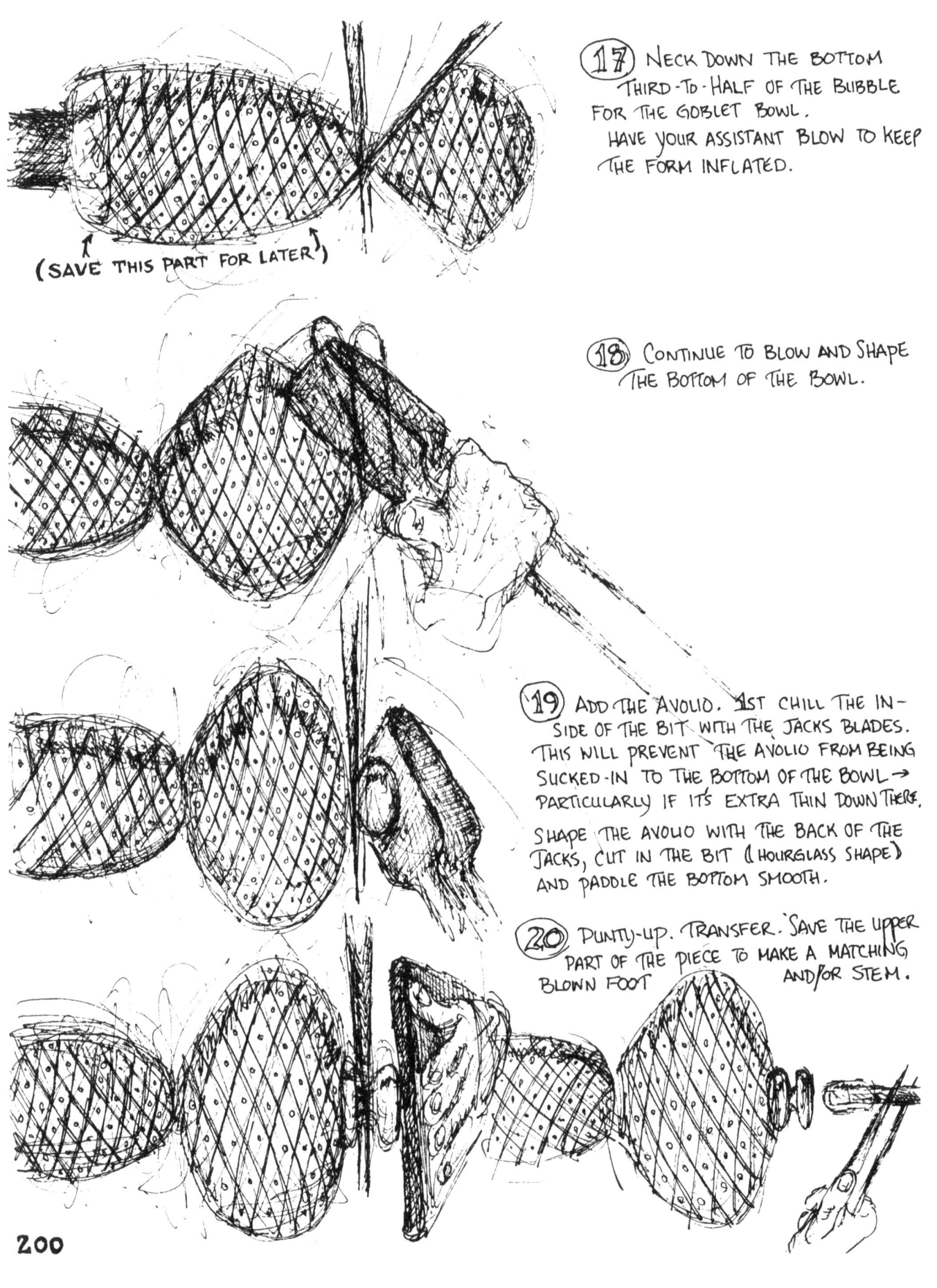

(SAVE THIS PART FOR LATER)

17) NECK DOWN THE BOTTOM THIRD-TO-HALF OF THE BUBBLE FOR THE GOBLET BOWL.
HAVE YOUR ASSISTANT BLOW TO KEEP THE FORM INFLATED.

18) CONTINUE TO BLOW AND SHAPE THE BOTTOM OF THE BOWL.

19) ADD THE AVOLIO. 1ST CHILL THE INSIDE OF THE BIT WITH THE JACKS BLADES. THIS WILL PREVENT THE AVOLIO FROM BEING SUCKED-IN TO THE BOTTOM OF THE BOWL → PARTICULARLY IF IT'S EXTRA THIN DOWN THERE.
SHAPE THE AVOLIO WITH THE BACK OF THE JACKS, CUT IN THE BIT (HOURGLASS SHAPE) AND PADDLE THE BOTTOM SMOOTH.

20) PUNTY-UP. TRANSFER. SAVE THE UPPER PART OF THE PIECE TO MAKE A MATCHING BLOWN FOOT AND/OR STEM.

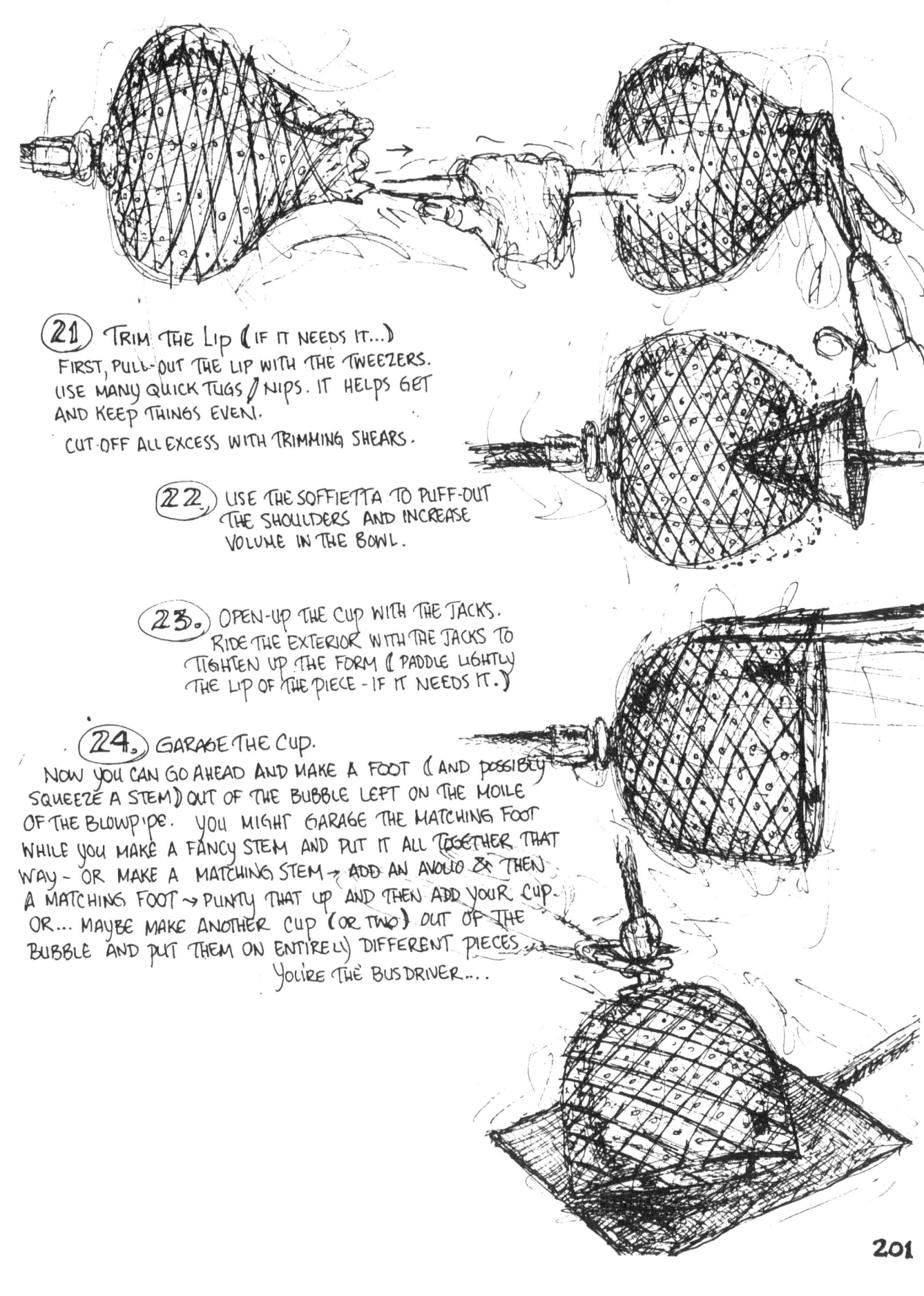

21) TRIM THE LIP (IF IT NEEDS IT...)
FIRST, PULL-OUT THE LIP WITH THE TWEEZERS.
USE MANY QUICK TUGS / NIPS. IT HELPS GET
AND KEEP THINGS EVEN.
CUT-OFF ALL EXCESS WITH TRIMMING SHEARS.

22.) USE THE SOFFIETTA TO PUFF-OUT
THE SHOULDERS AND INCREASE
VOLUME IN THE BOWL.

23.) OPEN-UP THE CUP WITH THE JACKS.
RIDE THE EXTERIOR WITH THE JACKS TO
TIGHTEN UP THE FORM (PADDLE LIGHTLY
THE LIP OF THE PIECE - IF IT NEEDS IT.)

24.) GARAGE THE CUP.
NOW YOU CAN GO AHEAD AND MAKE A FOOT (AND POSSIBLY
SQUEEZE A STEM) OUT OF THE BUBBLE LEFT ON THE MOILE
OF THE BLOWPIPE. YOU MIGHT GARAGE THE MATCHING FOOT
WHILE YOU MAKE A FANCY STEM AND PUT IT ALL TOGETHER THAT
WAY - OR MAKE A MATCHING STEM → ADD AN AVOLIO & THEN
A MATCHING FOOT → PUNTY THAT UP AND THEN ADD YOUR CUP.
OR... MAYBE MAKE ANOTHER CUP (OR TWO) OUT OF THE
BUBBLE AND PUT THEM ON ENTIRELY DIFFERENT PIECES.
YOU'RE THE BUS DRIVER....

SIMPLIFIED RETICELLO

METHOD ONE:

Pick-up cane.

Twist 'em up.

Neck it down.

Fold it over.

Shape it in.

Work it out...

There are a couple other ways to create simulated reticello without having to do the elaborate double-cup process. One way is to take a twisted cane bubble, neck it nearly in half, and open the very end. Then you flare open the end and fold it back over itself to criss-cross the cane pattern. This method can be especially appropriate for making INCALMO-TYPE pieces.

Another technique is more suited for making reticello-styled bowls. In this technique the cane are picked-up on a bubble and twisted. The bubble is then blown-out to a sphere and sucked back in on itself to yield a double walled reticello-styled bowl.

FOR THE FIRST METHOD — You begin by picking-up your cane — either on a collar or a bubble. Neck down a knob and twist-up the cane (very similar to the traditional reticello method). Try to leave the knob on.

OPEN HERE

Then neck the bubble down almost closing off the interior. This should be done about 1/3d to 1/2 way down the bubble (because the lower section will have to be stretched over the top section). The next step involves chilling and tapping off the bottom knob - hopefully leaving you with a hole. If you don't have a hole there, you may have to tweeze one open.

Now, with careful reheats, you flare open and fold-over the bottom section over the top. This is very similar to doing a double-bubble overlay. If you use Paicioppi's they won't suck the heat out of your glass as much as the metal jacks, and you'll get more stretch for your heat.

Once you succeed in folding the glass over, you can use your metal jacks to smooth the glass back down into one uniform section. Now the piece is ready. You can add another section to the bottom (similar to incalmo) or you can close-down the hole and blow the whole thing out or whatever...

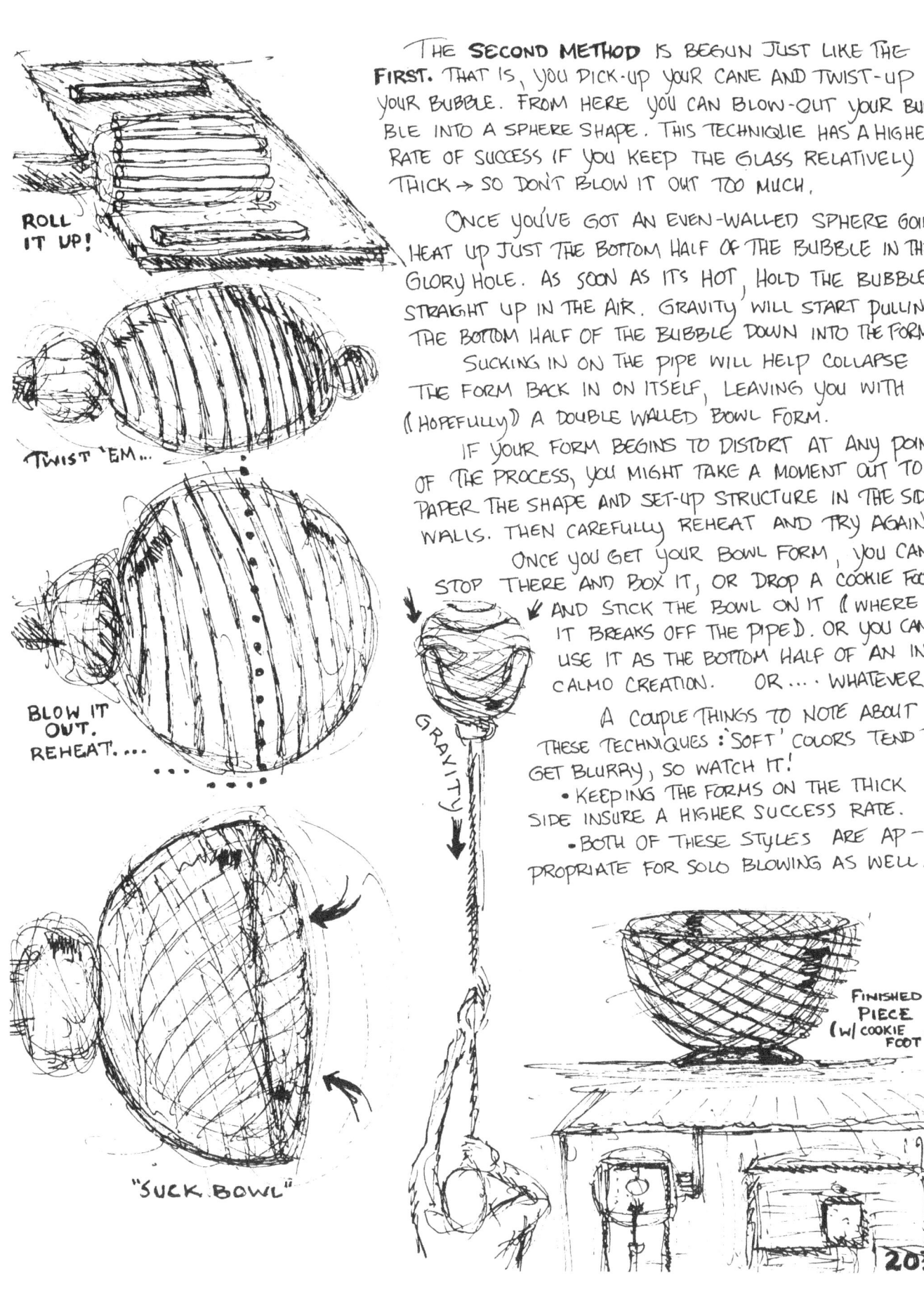

Applying Thin Threads/Wraps

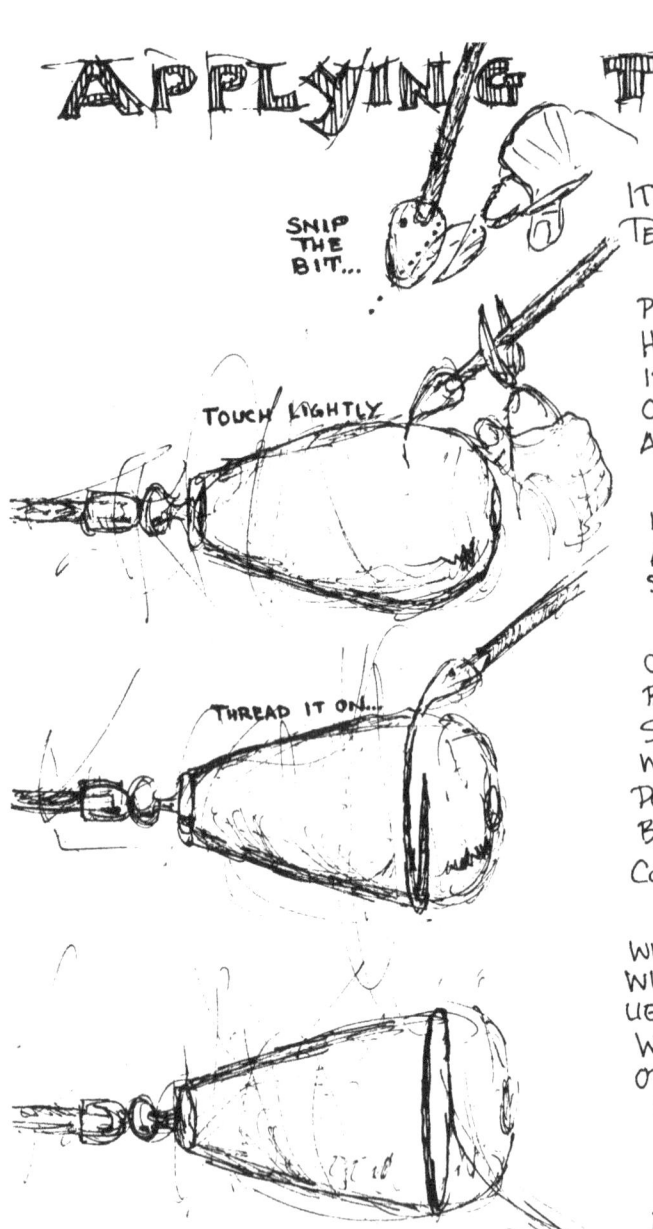

The thin thread serves a dual purpose. It is both a source of decoration and a form of texture offering a no-slip grip.

Usually this type of bit is applied just prior to opening the bowl all the way. I have, however, seen it added just before the piece is boxed. If you add it before you open the cup - the bit has an opportunity to melt in a little and appears more homogeneous.

Most anyone can apply a thread. Making it clean is the tricky part. And making it appear as one uninterrupted line with no starting or finishing bumps is maestro-stuff!

The glass must be hot HOT HOT in order for this technique to work. Take the bit straight outta the furnace - no marver. Snip the bit with a quick, deliberate downward stroke/cut and gently apply the pointed bit where you want it. Cutting the bit in this manner eliminates the obvious contact point → a roundish blob.

Try to hold your shears steady as you wind the trail on so you end up with an even line. When you return to the starting point - continue through it, and just as contact is made with it, whisk the piece (and punty) away (from each other) → drawing the bit into a tiny fiber which breaks free.

Now, if you find that you still wind-up with a bump → there's a slight variation to this technique which you might try: Apply the bit exactly the same. Let it trail all the way around. But this time, when you return to your starting point → wind the trail exactly to the point where you originally made contact.

Stop your rotation for just a split second to make a connection with that point. You may even have to back-up just a touch to make a good connection. Then immediatly whisk the punty away from the piece (or the piece away from the punty) to break the thread free.

Reheat to melt the thread in smooth and finish the cup as usual or go ahead and apply another thread or two.

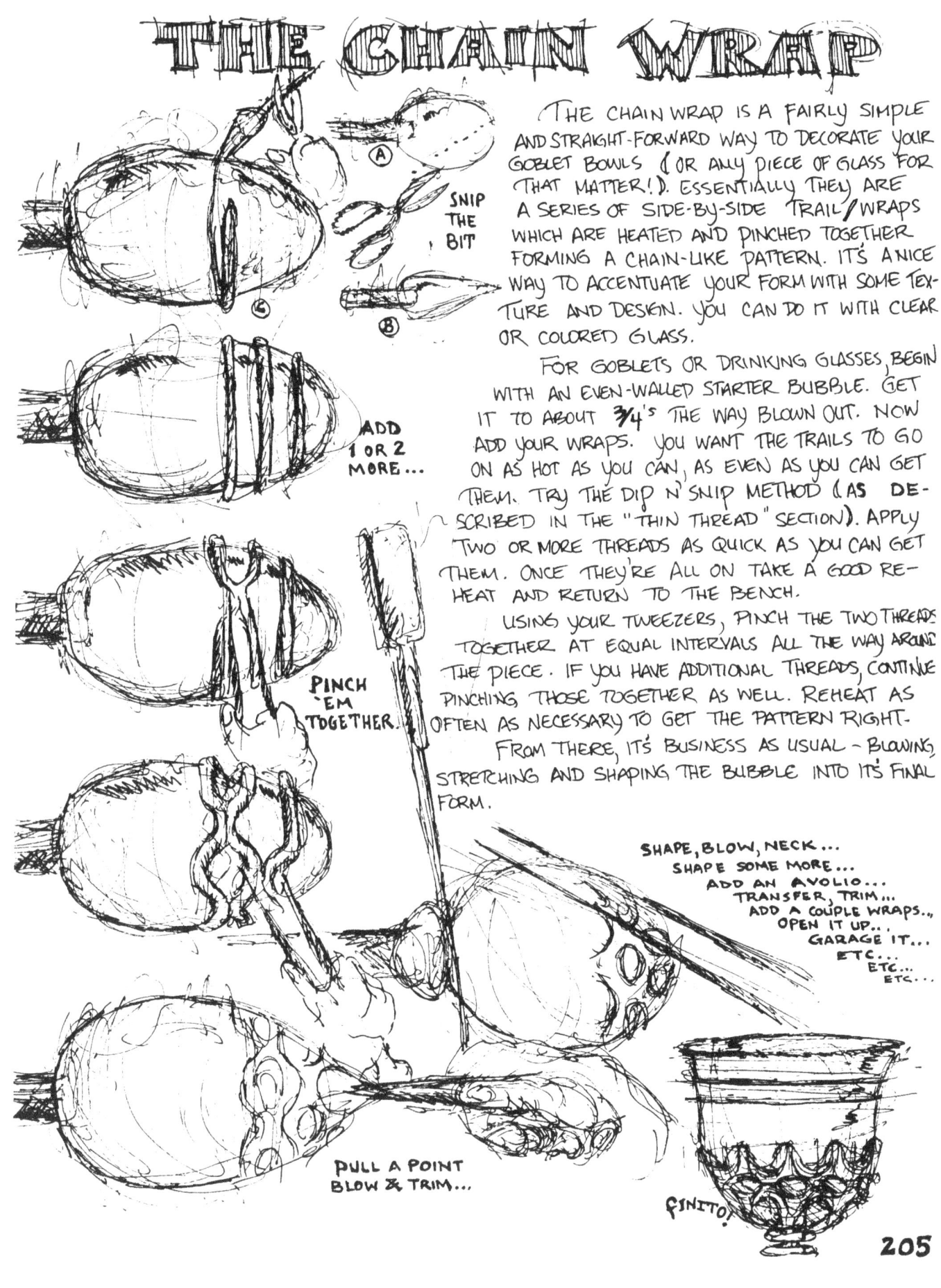

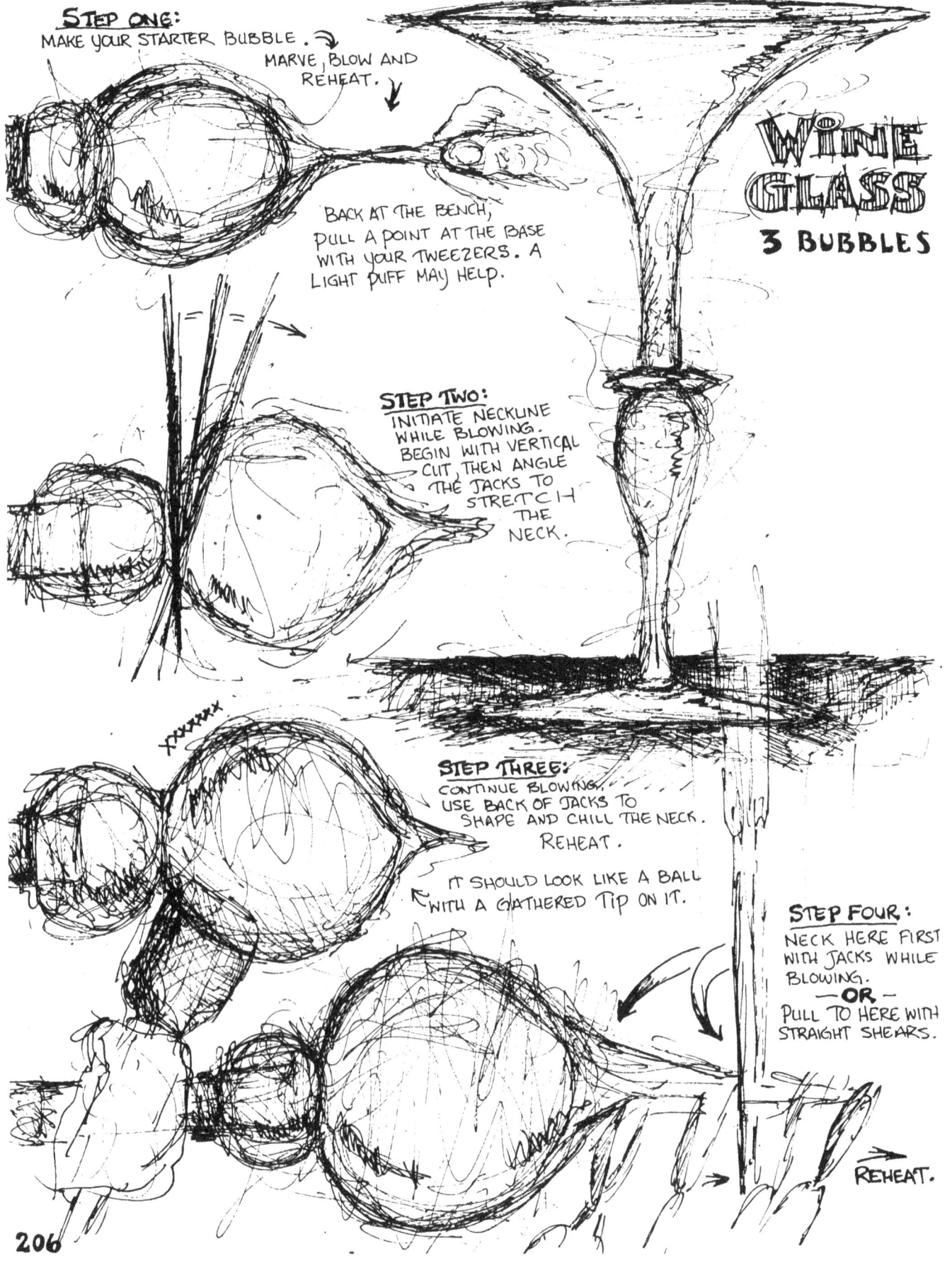

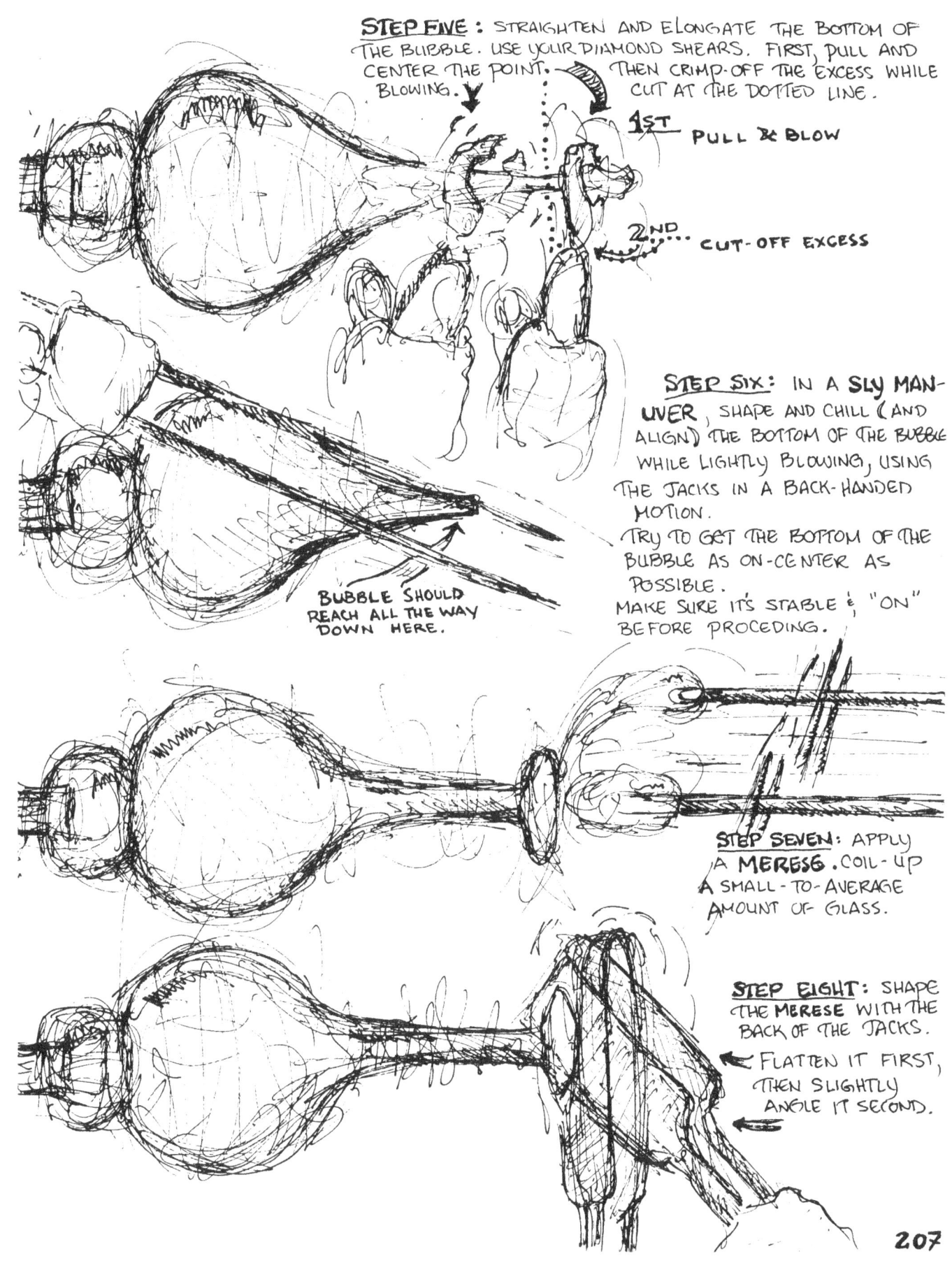

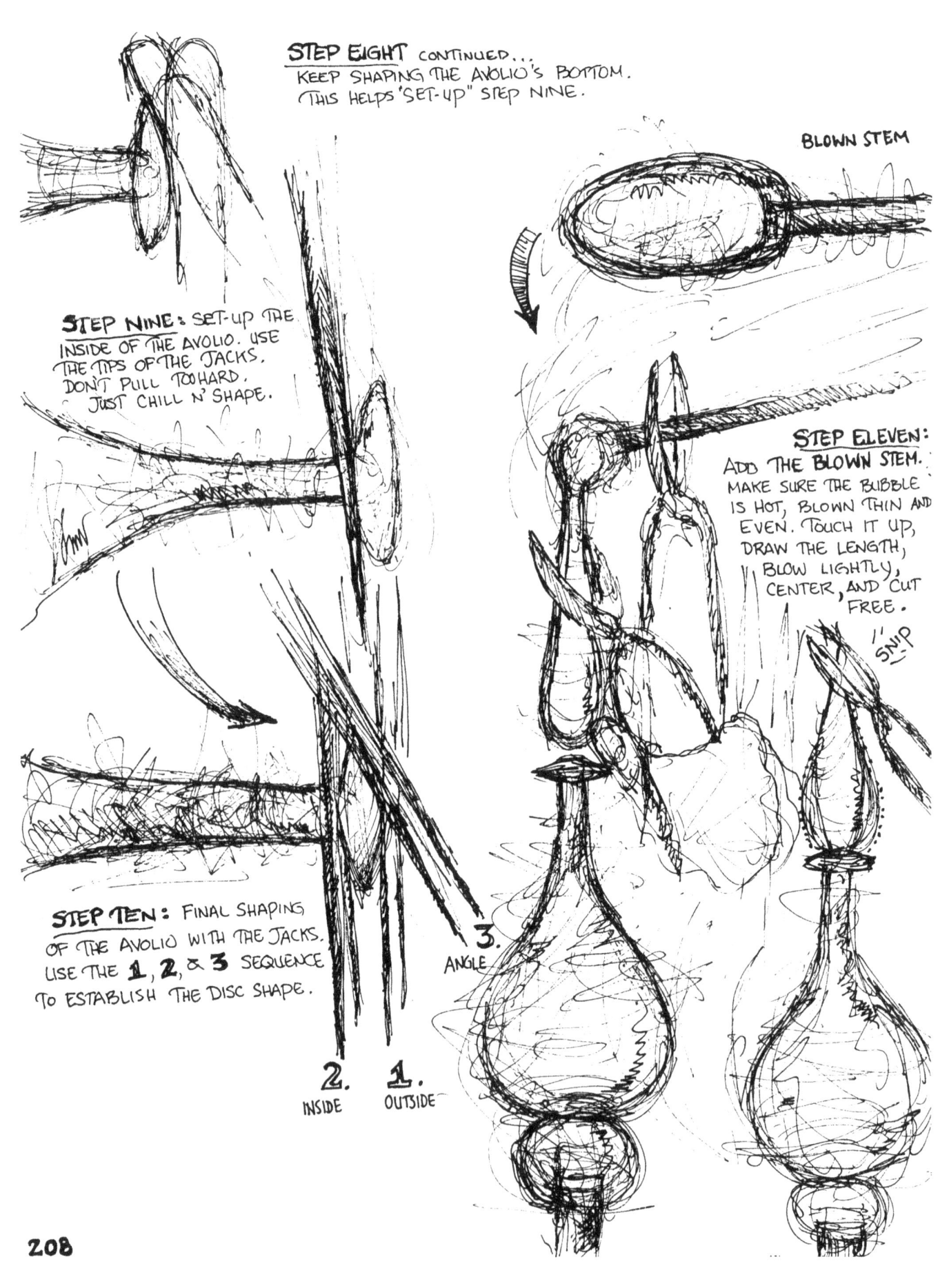

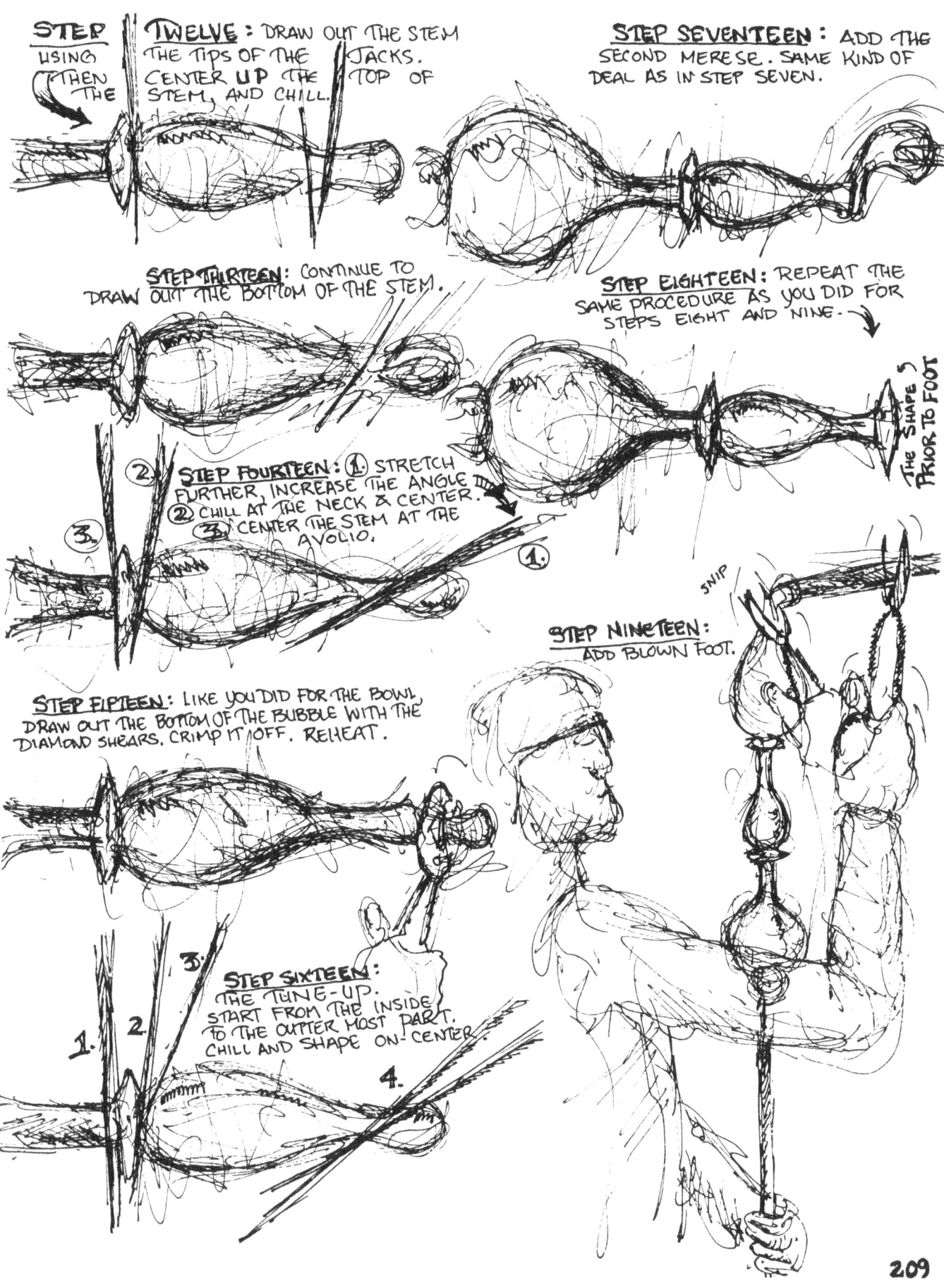

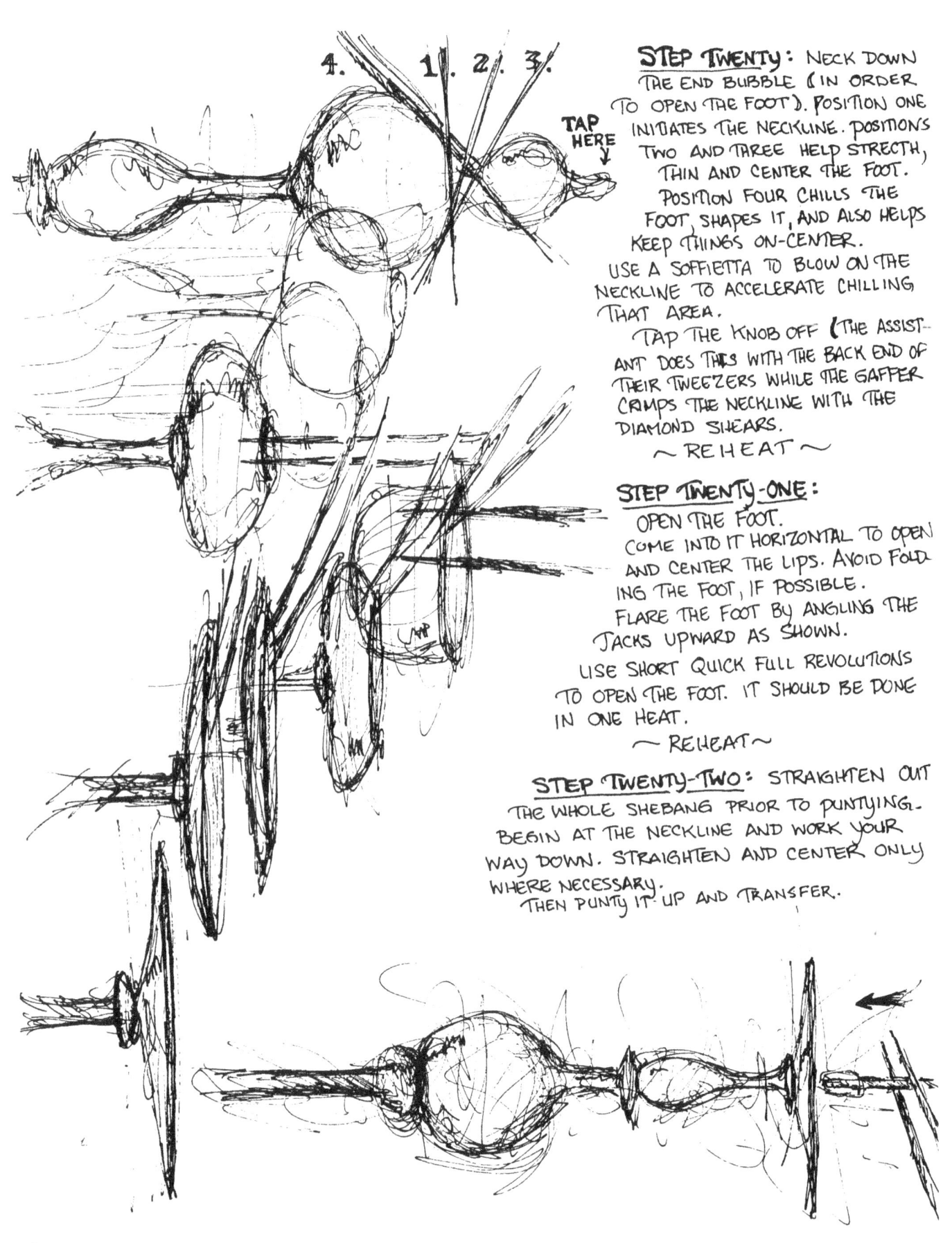

STEP TWENTY: NECK DOWN THE END BUBBLE (IN ORDER TO OPEN THE FOOT). POSITION ONE INITIATES THE NECKLINE. POSITIONS TWO AND THREE HELP STRETCH, THIN AND CENTER THE FOOT. POSITION FOUR CHILLS THE FOOT, SHAPES IT, AND ALSO HELPS KEEP THINGS ON-CENTER.

USE A SOFFIETTA TO BLOW ON THE NECKLINE TO ACCELERATE CHILLING THAT AREA.

TAP THE KNOB OFF (THE ASSISTANT DOES THIS WITH THE BACK END OF THEIR TWEEZERS WHILE THE GAFFER CRIMPS THE NECKLINE WITH THE DIAMOND SHEARS.

~ REHEAT ~

STEP TWENTY-ONE:
OPEN THE FOOT.
COME INTO IT HORIZONTAL TO OPEN AND CENTER THE LIPS. AVOID FOLDING THE FOOT, IF POSSIBLE.
FLARE THE FOOT BY ANGLING THE JACKS UPWARD AS SHOWN.
USE SHORT QUICK FULL REVOLUTIONS TO OPEN THE FOOT. IT SHOULD BE DONE IN ONE HEAT.

~ REHEAT ~

STEP TWENTY-TWO: STRAIGHTEN OUT THE WHOLE SHEBANG PRIOR TO PUNTYING. BEGIN AT THE NECKLINE AND WORK YOUR WAY DOWN. STRAIGHTEN AND CENTER ONLY WHERE NECESSARY.
THEN PUNTY IT UP AND TRANSFER.

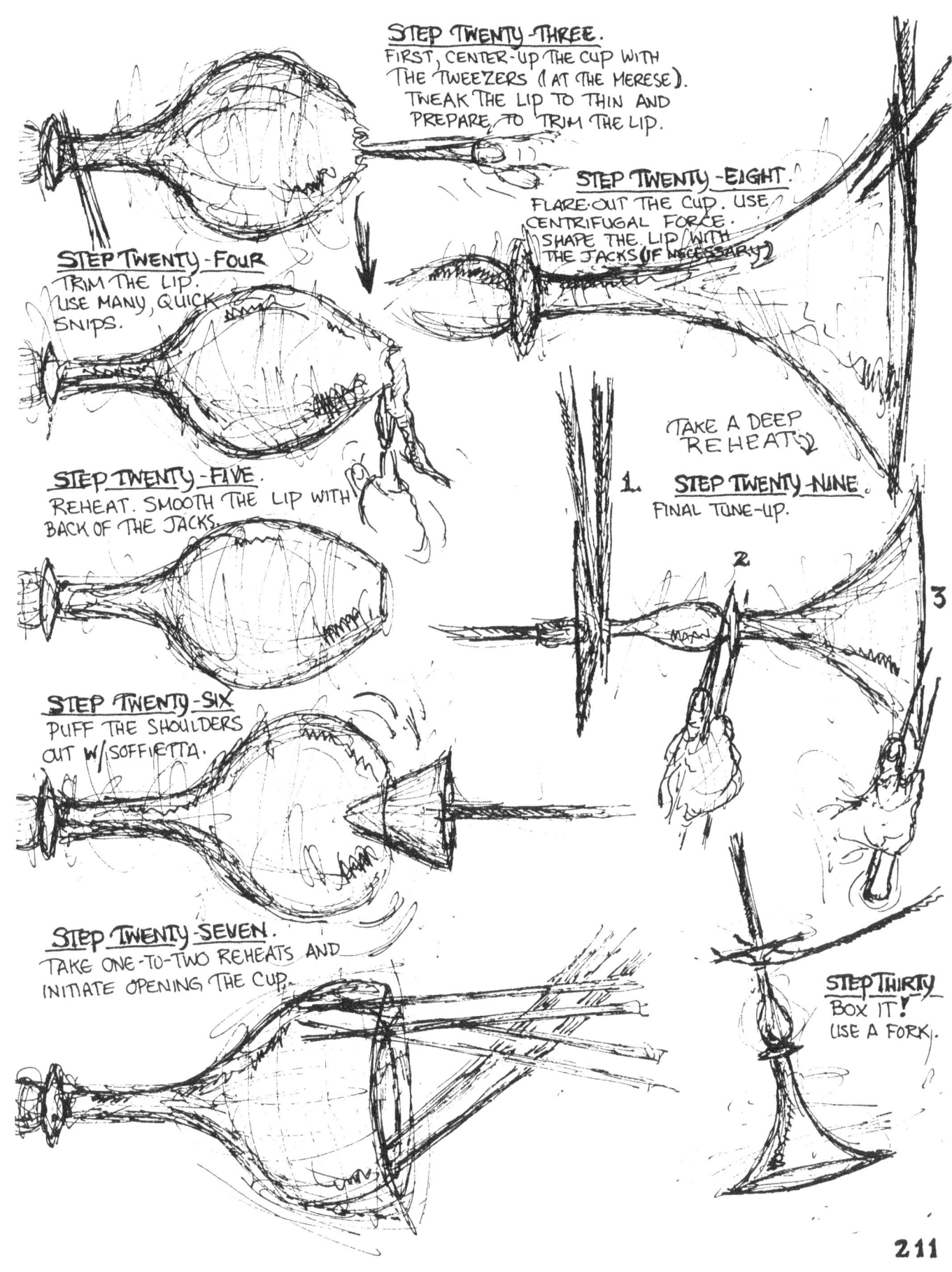

Introduction to Solidworking

- Introduction 213
- Flowers - Iris 214
- Pulling Ponies 218
- Solid Core Sculpting . . 221
- Torso 222
- A Few More Things . . . 226

Introduction to Solidworking

Proof positive that not every piece of hot glass made needs a bubble in it, Solidworking is a whole 'nuther way of working "on the stick". Maybe making a perfect bubble is a struggle for you, or blowing symmetrical objects isn't your bag - then perhaps working solid may be of interest to you. Quite easily this could be a whole book in itself. Because of time and space constraints, I've limited this section to a discussion of three approaches to working with solid glass. This is only the tip of the iceberg. There are infinite possibilities when it comes to hot-core sculpting or additive bit work. It is up to you, the artist, to decide which avenue to take or path you may follow. Give it "a-go". You may find you like this method of working. If it is something that you enjoy, I strongly recommend taking a course or workshop from someone skilled in this area.* Each piece has it's own personality and recipe or itinerary for success. With a quick demo or a couple of pointers a "pro" can often help you overcome certain obstacles and relieve certain stress points. This, in turn, may allow you to open-up and explore more of what you want to say with your glass than to be hung-up on a certain technique.

When it comes down to solidworking, you can pretty much throw away everything you know about blowing glass. There are some things which are the same: **you're working hot glass on a metal rod, gravity is your friend and steel sucks heat.** Some things change e.g. hot is good, cold is good, keep it turning - sometimes, and a blowpipe can be used as a punty - if you need to...

There are pretty much only two ways to approach sculpting hot glass: The **Additive/Build-up Technique** and **Solid Mass/Hot Core Sculpting**.

In the first method you create the form by adding bits of hot glass together. You can sculpt each element individually as they go on. Placement, size of the bits, how you cut them and temperature - not to mention timing - are crucial to success.

In the second method you start with a larger piece of glass - cut it, manipulate it - to literally pull out the form. It is usually necessary to transfer the piece several times in order to achieve the correct proportions and detail desired.

Each method has their own strengths and weaknesses.

Practice, trial & error, and ultimately what comes out of the box will help you decide which method works best for you.

Undoubtedly you'll learn new ways to use your tools, find different ways to make lasting impressions in glass and a whole 'nuther dynamic to working this mysterious material... enjoy.

* See the work of (or if you're lucky - take a class with them) Pino Signoretto, William Morris, Karen Willenbrink, Louis Sclafani, Ferd Thieriot or Scott Darlington.

"Poppy" by Karen Willenbrink

IRISES "Happy Flowers"

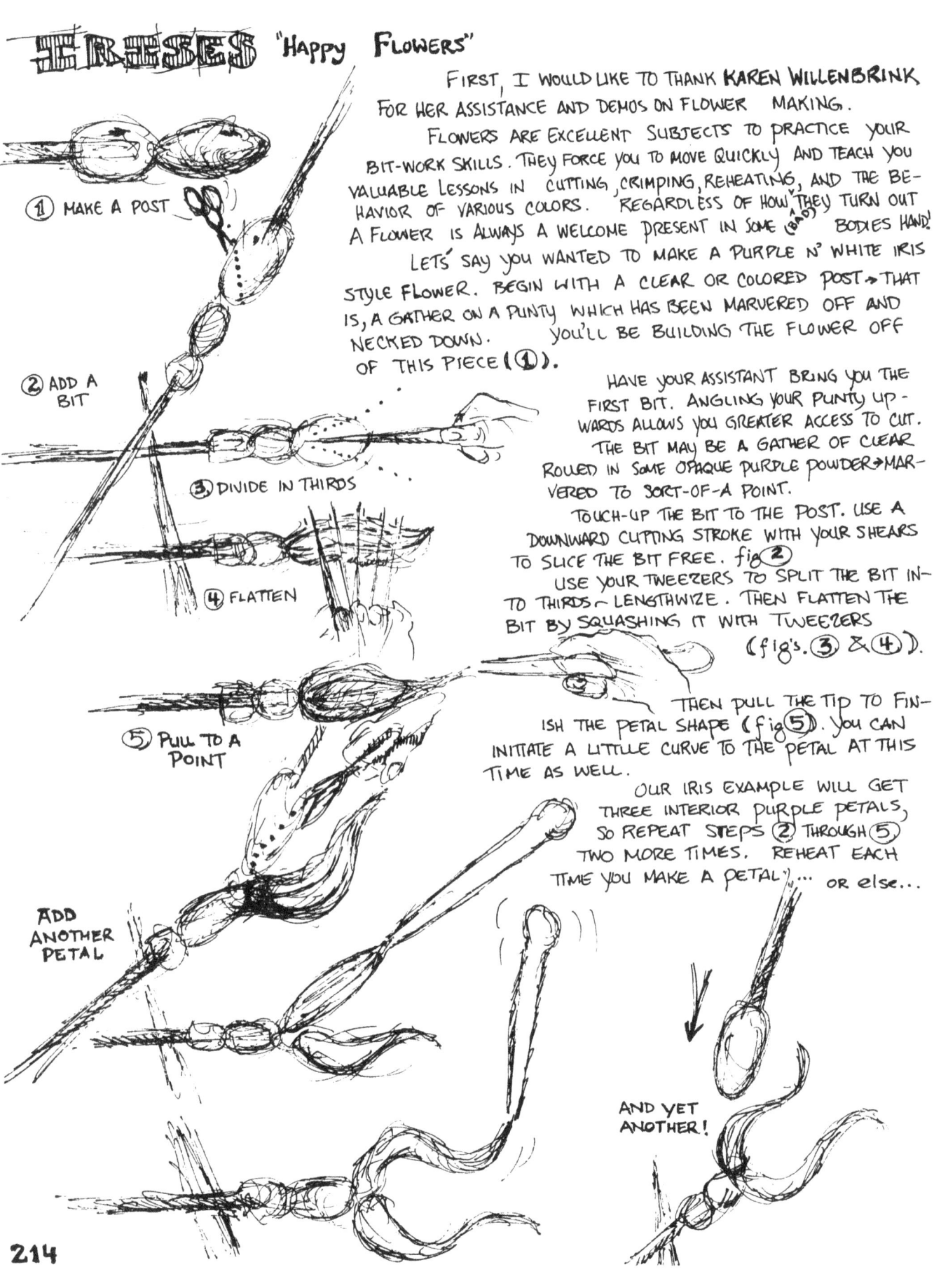

First, I would like to thank **KAREN WILLENBRINK** for her assistance and demos on flower making.

Flowers are excellent subjects to practice your bit-work skills. They force you to move quickly and teach you valuable lessons in cutting, crimping, reheating, and the behavior of various colors. Regardless of how they turn out a flower is always a welcome present in some (BODY) bodies hand!

Lets' say you wanted to make a purple n' white iris style flower. Begin with a clear or colored post → that is, a gather on a punty which has been marvered off and necked down. You'll be building the flower off of this piece (①).

① MAKE A POST

② ADD A BIT

Have your assistant bring you the first bit. Angling your punty upwards allows you greater access to cut. The bit may be a gather of clear rolled in some opaque purple powder → marvered to sort-of-a point.

Touch-up the bit to the post. Use a downward cutting stroke with your shears to slice the bit free. fig ②

③ DIVIDE IN THIRDS

④ FLATTEN

Use your tweezers to split the bit into thirds — lengthwize. Then flatten the bit by squashing it with tweezers (fig's. ③ & ④).

⑤ PULL TO A POINT

Then pull the tip to finish the petal shape (fig ⑤). You can initiate a little curve to the petal at this time as well.

Our iris example will get three interior purple petals, so repeat steps ② through ⑤ two more times. Reheat each time you make a petal... or else...

ADD ANOTHER PETAL

AND YET ANOTHER!

214

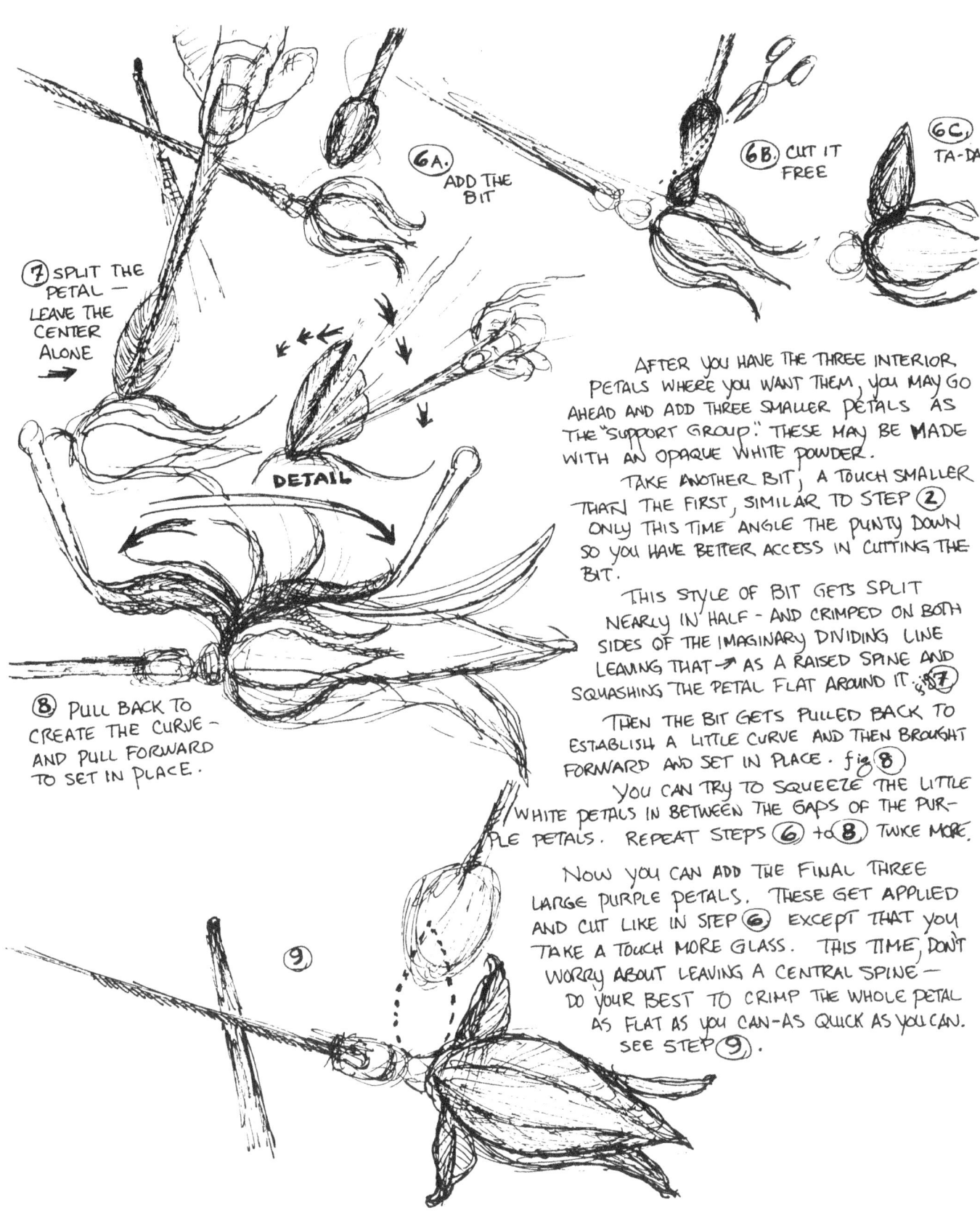

⑥A. ADD THE BIT

⑥B. CUT IT FREE

⑥C. TA-DA

⑦ SPLIT THE PETAL — LEAVE THE CENTER ALONE

DETAIL

⑧ PULL BACK TO CREATE THE CURVE — AND PULL FORWARD TO SET IN PLACE.

⑨

AFTER YOU HAVE THE THREE INTERIOR PETALS WHERE YOU WANT THEM, YOU MAY GO AHEAD AND ADD THREE SMALLER PETALS AS THE "SUPPORT GROUP." THESE MAY BE MADE WITH AN OPAQUE WHITE POWDER.

TAKE ANOTHER BIT, A TOUCH SMALLER THAN THE FIRST, SIMILAR TO STEP ② ONLY THIS TIME ANGLE THE PUNTY DOWN SO YOU HAVE BETTER ACCESS IN CUTTING THE BIT.

THIS STYLE OF BIT GETS SPLIT NEARLY IN HALF — AND CRIMPED ON BOTH SIDES OF THE IMAGINARY DIVIDING LINE LEAVING THAT→ AS A RAISED SPINE AND SQUASHING THE PETAL FLAT AROUND IT. fig ⑦

THEN THE BIT GETS PULLED BACK TO ESTABLISH A LITTLE CURVE AND THEN BROUGHT FORWARD AND SET IN PLACE. fig ⑧

YOU CAN TRY TO SQUEEZE THE LITTLE WHITE PETALS IN BETWEEN THE GAPS OF THE PURPLE PETALS. REPEAT STEPS ⑥ to ⑧ TWICE MORE.

NOW YOU CAN ADD THE FINAL THREE LARGE PURPLE PETALS. THESE GET APPLIED AND CUT LIKE IN STEP ⑥ EXCEPT THAT YOU TAKE A TOUCH MORE GLASS. THIS TIME, DON'T WORRY ABOUT LEAVING A CENTRAL SPINE — DO YOUR BEST TO CRIMP THE WHOLE PETAL AS FLAT AS YOU CAN — AS QUICK AS YOU CAN. SEE STEP ⑨.

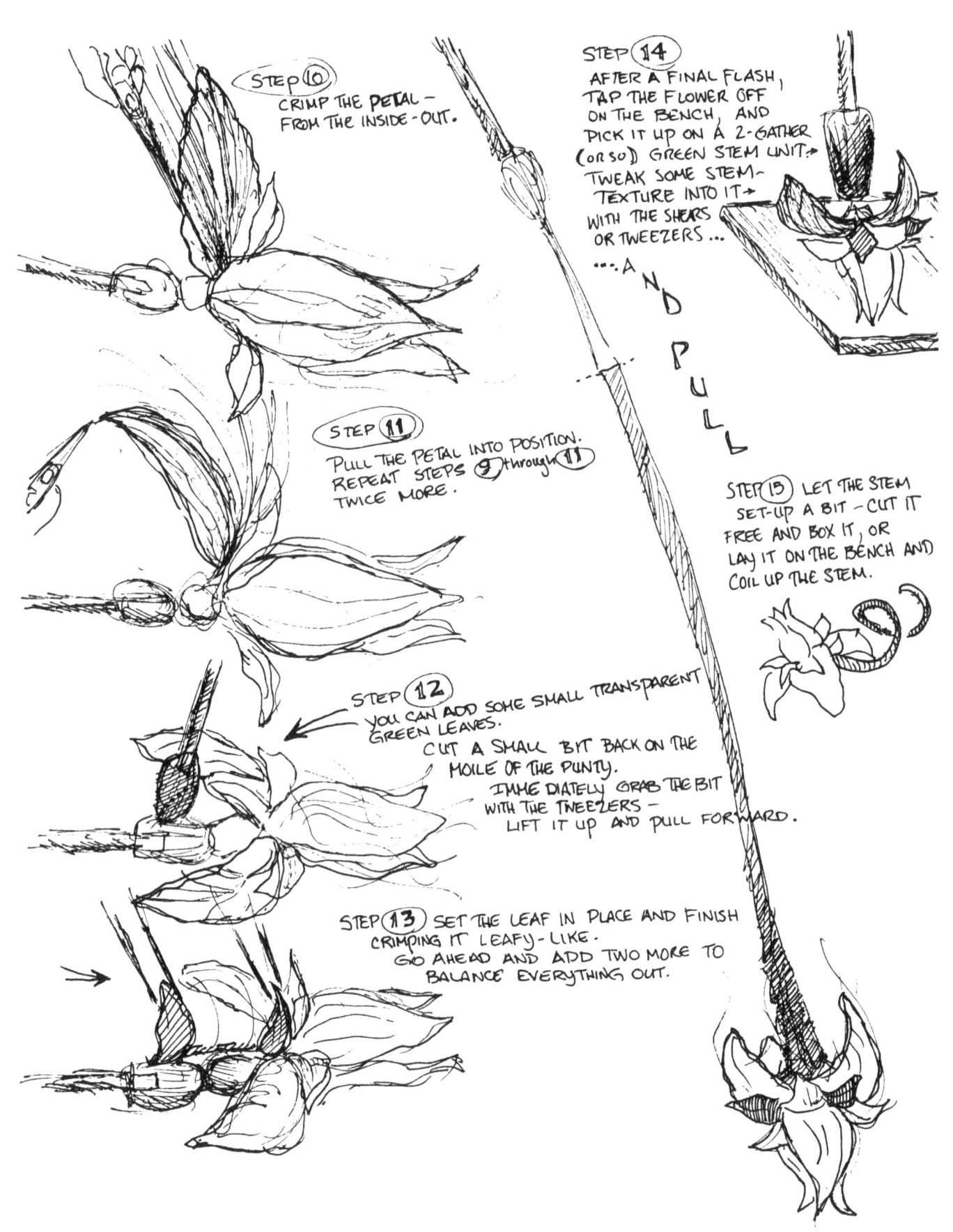

SO MUCH DEPENDS ON THE QUALITY OF BITS YOU RECEIVE FROM YOUR ASSISTANT. THE BETTER SHAPED AND HOTTER THEY ARE, THE EASIER IT IS TO APPLY THEM. BITS WHICH ARE COLD, OR DISFIGURED, ARE A WASTE OF TIME.

TIP: THE **MARVER IS DEATH!** IT SUCKS ALL THE HEAT OUT OF YOUR BIT!
(TO ALL SMALL BITS)

(INSTEAD, TRIM THAT BIT INTO SHAPE! SURE - IT WASTES A LITTLE GLASS, BUT IT INSURES YOU GET A HOT-POINTED BIT WITH COLOR ALL THE WAY TO THE TIP.

ALSO LEARN WHERE THE HOT SPOTS ARE ON OR IN YOUR GLORY HOLE.

HEAT & REHEAT CLOSE TO THE DOOR TO UTILIZE THE REFLECTED HEAT THERE. (POINTS A & B)

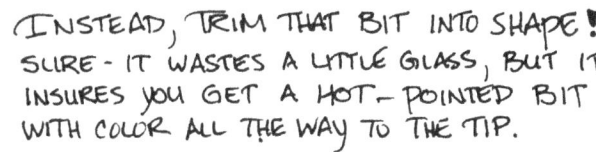

THIS TYPE OF WORK CAN BE TEDIOUS AND TIRESOME FOR YOUR ASSISTANT.

REWARD THEM WELL.

TRY TO ESTABLISH A **RHYTHM** AND **WORKING DIALOG**.

YOU NEED TO PRACTICE THE SAME FORM IN ORDER TO BECOME PROFICIENT, BUT BREAK IT UP ONCE IN A WHILE TO KEEP IT INTERESTING.

TRY MAKING A VARIETY OF FLOWERS IN DIFFERENT COLORS AND SIZES. **LOOK AT NATURE.** REMEMBER: NOT EVERY ONE IS PERFECT, SO... there's no reason to expect that every flower you make need be...

TIP: EXCESSIVE REHEATING KILLS! IF YOU FIND ALL YOUR POINTS GETTING SOFT AND ALL YOUR **DETAIL** IS DISAPPEARING - TURN DOWN YOUR GLORY HOLE OR DON'T REHEAT FOR SUCH A LONG TIME! YOU AND YOUR ASSISTANT MAY NEED TO WORK OUT OF SEPERATE GLORY HOLES IN ORDER TO GET THE HEAT(S) RIGHT.

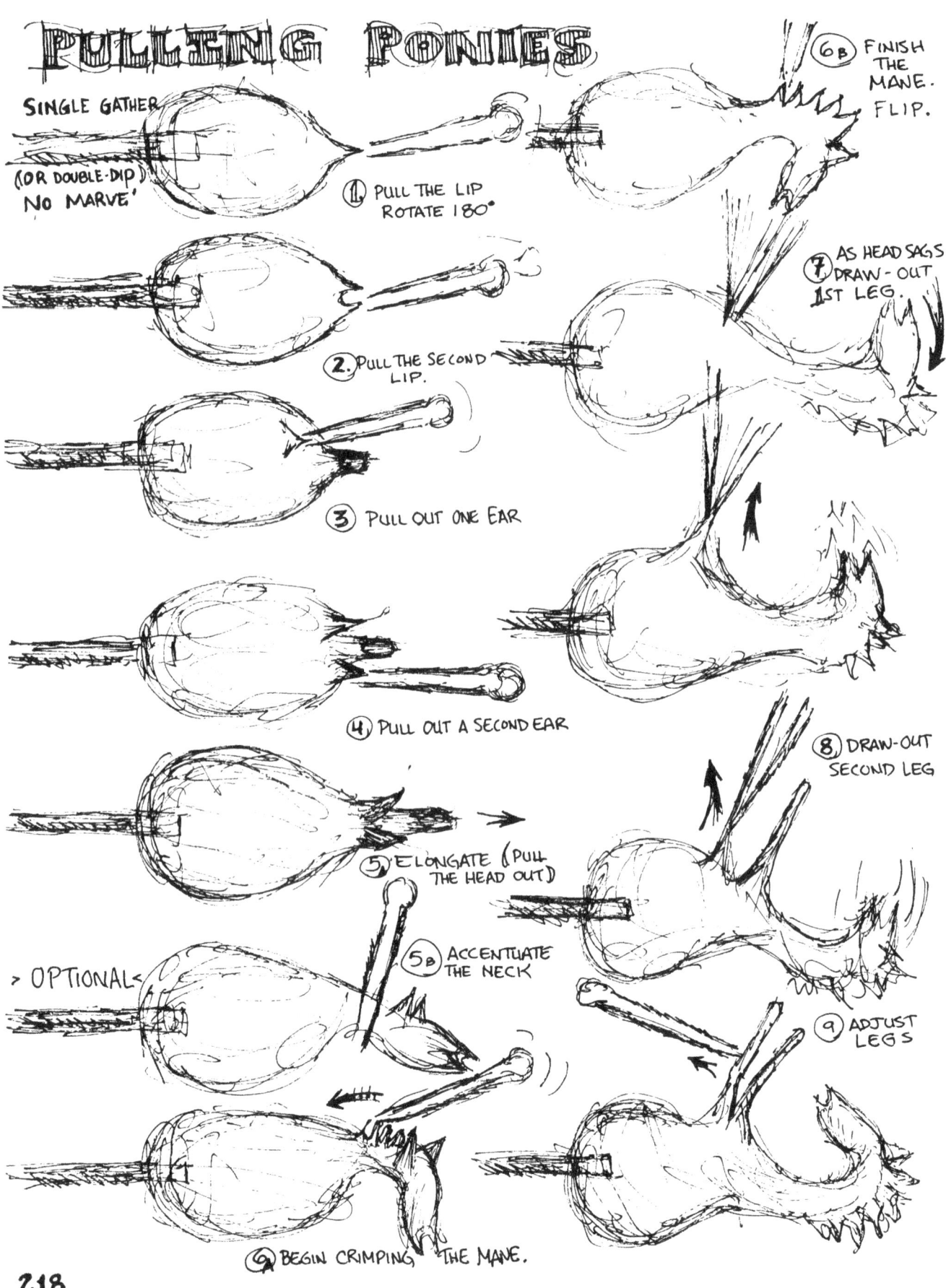

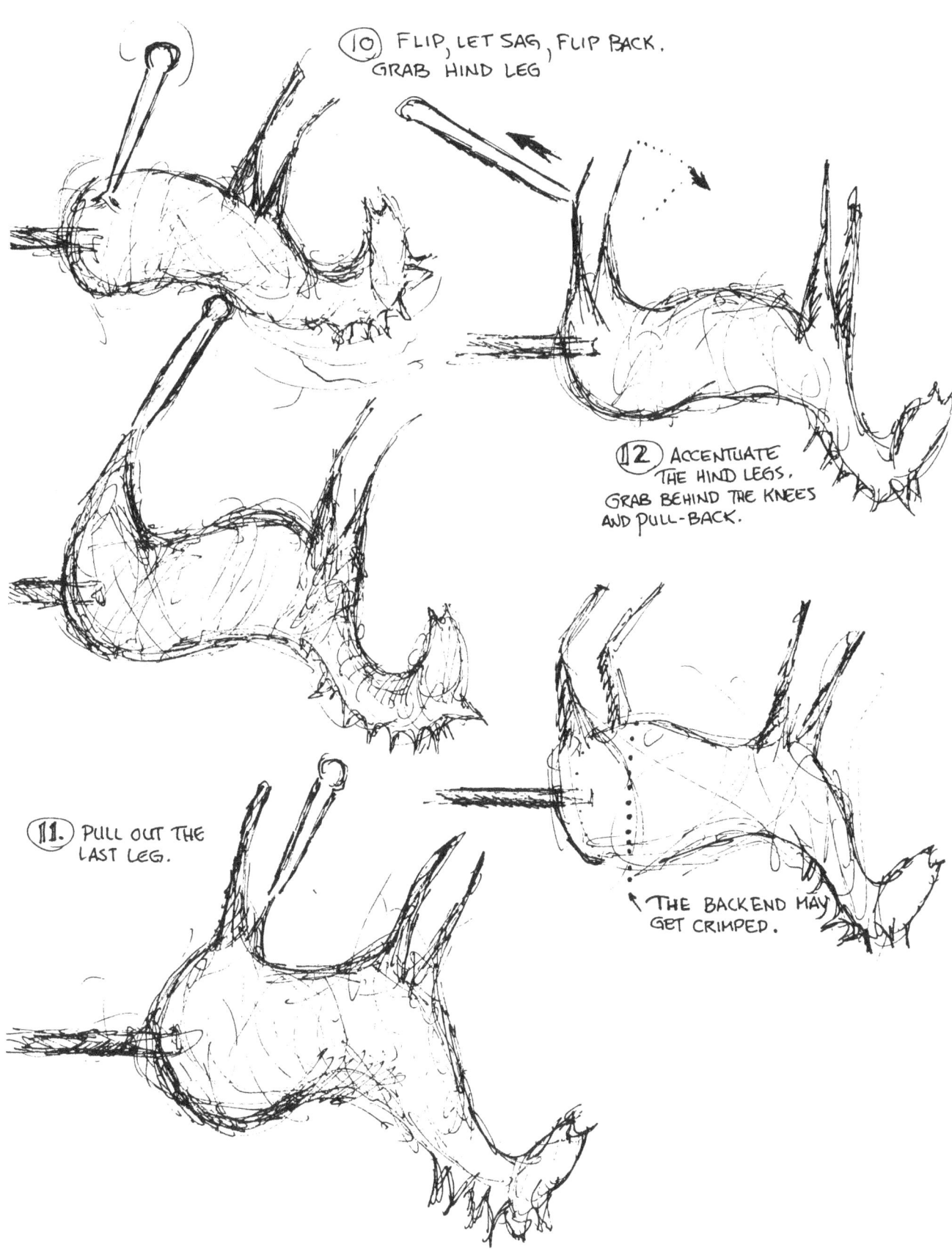

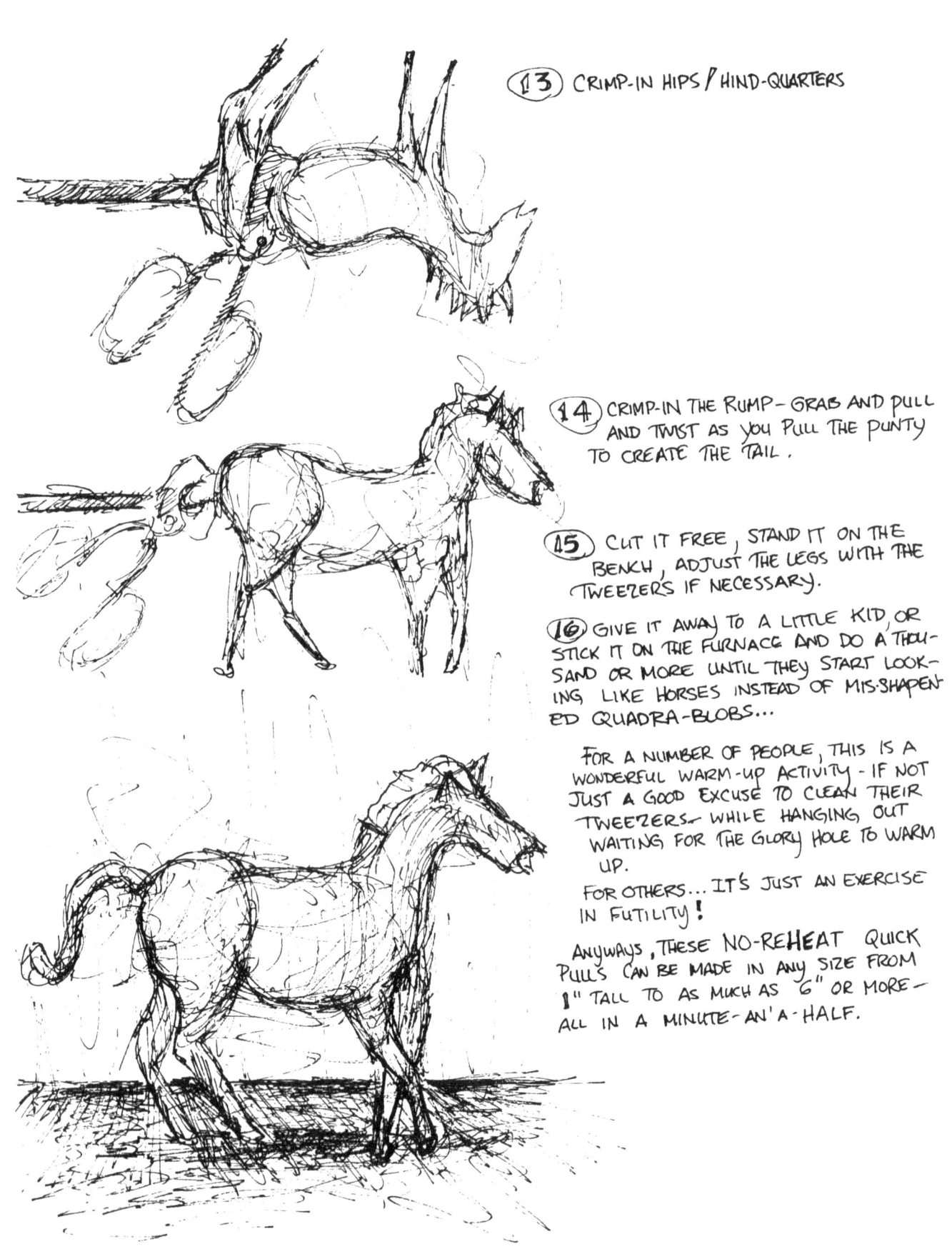

13) CRIMP-IN HIPS/HIND-QUARTERS

14) CRIMP-IN THE RUMP — GRAB AND PULL AND TWIST AS YOU PULL THE PUNTY TO CREATE THE TAIL.

15) CUT IT FREE, STAND IT ON THE BENCH, ADJUST THE LEGS WITH THE TWEEZERS IF NECESSARY.

16) GIVE IT AWAY TO A LITTLE KID, OR STICK IT ON THE FURNACE AND DO A THOUSAND OR MORE UNTIL THEY START LOOKING LIKE HORSES INSTEAD OF MIS-SHAPEN-ED QUADRA-BLOBS...

FOR A NUMBER OF PEOPLE, THIS IS A WONDERFUL WARM-UP ACTIVITY — IF NOT JUST A GOOD EXCUSE TO CLEAN THEIR TWEEZERS — WHILE HANGING OUT WAITING FOR THE GLORY HOLE TO WARM UP.

FOR OTHERS... IT'S JUST AN EXERCISE IN FUTILITY!

ANYWAYS, THESE NO-REHEAT QUICK PULLS CAN BE MADE IN ANY SIZE FROM 1" TALL TO AS MUCH AS 6" OR MORE — ALL IN A MINUTE-AN'-A-HALF.

SOLID-CORE SCULPTING

JUST WHERE DO YOU BEGIN?... A SKETCH IS THE BEST PLACE. EXPLAIN WHAT IT IS THAT YOU WANNA MAKE WITH A RUDIMENTARY SHAPE. THIS IS THE SAME WAY YOU SCULPT THE GLASS → START WITH A BASIC FORM AND THEN FILL-IN THE DETAILS. FOR EXAMPLE, IF YOU WANTED TO SCULPT A FEMALE TORSO - YOU WOULD DRAW A SIMPLE FIGURE-EIGHT SHAPE - SLIGHTLY EXAGGERATED. FROM THERE YOU DIVIDE THE PIECE IN HALF. THIS WILL BE THE WAY YOU WORK THE PIECE.

THERE'S ALOT OF PUNTYING-UP IN THE SOLID SCULPTING PROCESS. IN ORDER TO GET DETAIL IN BOTH HALVES, YOU NEED TO WORK ONE SIDE FIRST ~ GET ALL THE PARTS LOOKING RIGHT ON THE LOWER HALF. PUNTY-UP AND TRANSFER IT. THEN WORK THE UPPER HALF. NOW IT'S POSSIBLE THAT EVERYTHING LOOKS HUNK-DORY, SO - BOX IT... BUT OFTENTIMES BY TRYING TO GET THE TOP HALF LOOKING CORRECTLY, YOU END-UP DISTORTING THE LOWER HALF, OR IT'S POSSIBLE THAT THE PROPORTIONS MAY BE A LITTLE OFF. THEREFORE YOU MAY NEED TO PUNTY-UP ONE MORE TIME IN ORDER TO GET EVERYTHING TO MATCH UP. SURE IT'S A TIME-CONSUMING PROCESS, NOT-TOO-MENTION LABOR INTERSIVE ~ BUT THAT'S THE NATURE OF THE BEAST.

TIPS FOR SUCCESSFUL SOLID-CORE SCULPTING:

- COOL DOWN YOUR PIPE AS OFTEN AS POSSIBLE - THIS ALLOWS YOU IMPROVED HANDLING CAPABILITIES AND GETS YOU CLOSER TO THE GLASS.
- DON'T KILL YOURSELF MAKING PIECES. KNOW YOUR LIMITS AND WORK WITHIN YOUR LEVEL. HIRE AN EXTRA ASSISTANT IF NECESSARY.
- DON'T BITE-OFF MORE THAN YOU CAN CHEW. MAYBE THE PIECE COULD BE MORE EASILY MADE IN SECTIONS AND EITHER ASSEMBLED HOT VIA THE GARAGE, OR COLD VIA GRINDING, AND heavenforbid GLUE.
- SMALLER PIECES REQUIRE THAT YOU WORK FASTER. LARGER ONES, ON THE OTHERHAND, MAY NEED EXTRA TIME TO SET UP. BE PATIENT. IN MANY CASES YOU'LL NEED TO CHILL CERTAIN SPOTS SO YOU CAN WORK ANOTHER.
- LARGER PIECES, TOO, ARE MORE SUSCEPTIBLE TO THE EFFECTS OF GRAVITY, SO YOU NEED TO COMPENSATE FOR IT MORE.
- AVOID THICK-TO-THIN SITUATIONS, WHEREVER POSSIBLE. THEY'RE TRICKY TO SCULPT AND JUST AS HARD TO ANNEAL SUCCESSFULLY.
- DRAW YOUR STEPS. AVOID BAD PLANNING. KNOW WHAT YOUR IN FOR, AND PRACTICE AS MUCH AS YOU CAN. WORK WITH CLEAR GLASS FIRST ⇒ IT RECYCLES NICELY.

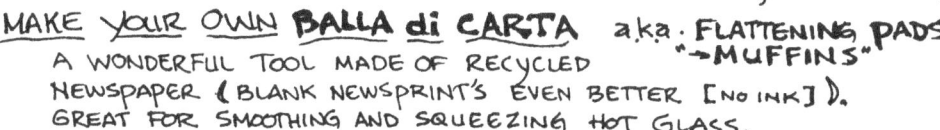

MAKE YOUR OWN BALLA di CARTA a.k.a. FLATTENING PADS → "MUFFINS"

A WONDERFUL TOOL MADE OF RECYCLED NEWSPAPER (BLANK NEWSPRINT'S EVEN BETTER [NO INK]). GREAT FOR SMOOTHING AND SQUEEZING HOT GLASS.

SHRED LOTS OF NEWSPAPER — LET SOAK (2 DAYS - 2 WEEKS)

SQUEEZE OUT THE WATER CHOP IT UP W/ KNIFE ADD 1 OZ OF WOOD GLUE

SQUISH IT TOGETHER FORM DOME-SHAPE W/ HAND HOLES

FINISHED FORMS (BLAST 'EM WITH THE TORCH TO CARBONIZE 'EM FIRST).

FEMALE TORSO

SCULPTING THE HUMAN FORM IS ONE OF THE MOST CHALLENGING OF ALL TASKS IN GLASSMAKING. WHY? I THINK THE MAIN REASON IS THAT WE ALL KNOW THIS FORM SO WELL, AND WE ARE SO FAMALIAR WITH THE PROPORTIONS THAT WHEN IT DOESN'T LOOK RIGHT, IT REALLY DOESN'T LOOK RIGHT. THE SECOND REASON IS THAT SCULPTING SOLID GLASS IS VERY CHALLENGING - AND ELUSIVE. IN ANY CASE HERE'S THE STEPS INVOLVED IN MAKING A FEMALE TORSO, AS RELATED TO ME BY **FERD THIERIOT** (THANKS MAN!)

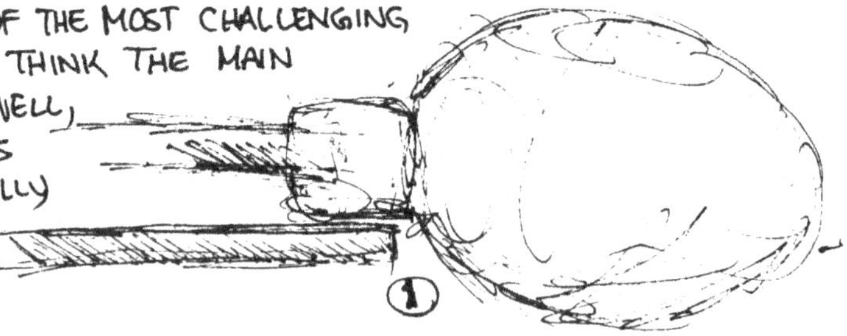

STEP ① MARVER-IN YOUR MOILE AFTER GATHERING AND BLOCKING A SUFFICIENT AMOUNT OF GLASS.

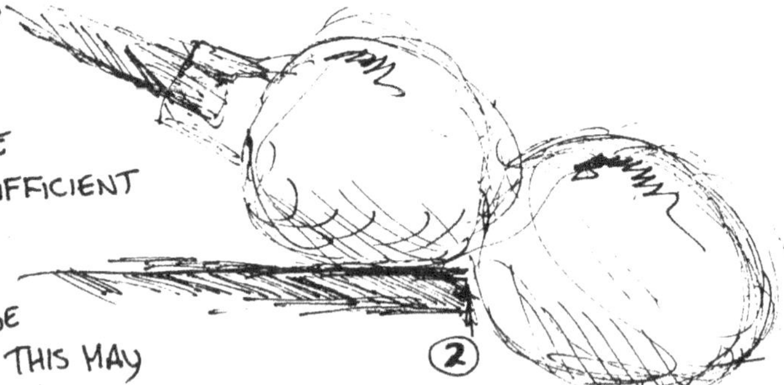

STEP ② DIVIDE THE FORM IN HALF BY CUTTING A LINE-IN ON THE BACK EDGE OF THE MARVER. ON SMALLER PIECES THIS MAY DONE WITH THE JACKS (ANGLE THEM). THIS IS YOUR BASIC FIGURE EIGHT. WORK FAST!

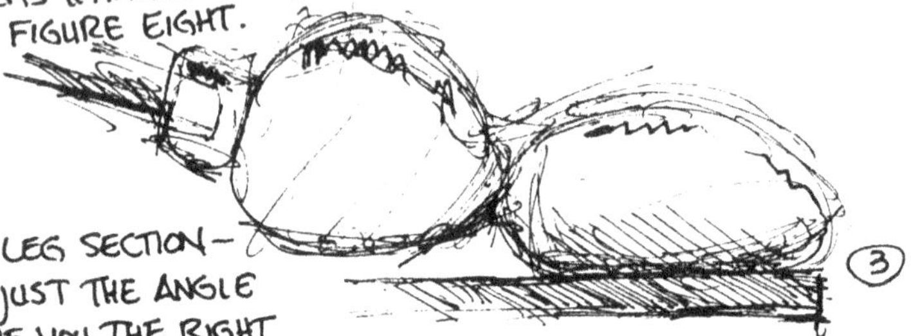

STEP ③ MARVER-UP THE LEG SECTION - VERY QUICKLY. ADJUST THE ANGLE OF THE PIPE TO GIVE YOU THE RIGHT KIND OF TAPER.

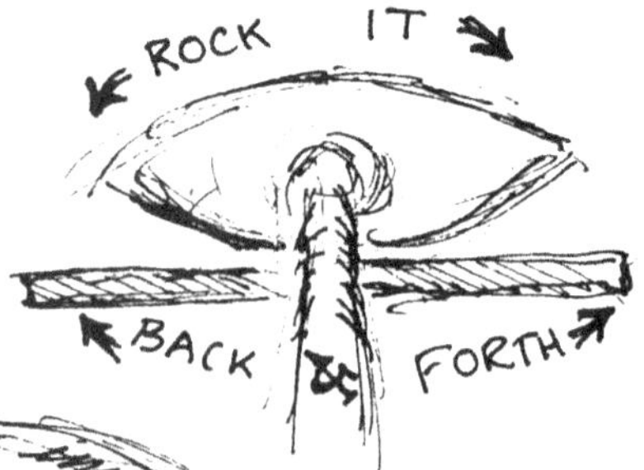

STEP ④ CUT-IN THE BACK, BY MARVERING THE UPPER SECTION IN A ROCKING MOTION. THE LOWER HALF WILL SAG OFF THE BACK OF THE MARVER, THEN...

STEP ⑤ FLIP, ROLL AND SLIDE UP ONTO THE MARVER TO CUT-IN THE CURVE ON THE FRONT OF THE TORSO. ALWAYS KEEP IT ROCKING — (PEOPLE AREN'T FLAT).

222

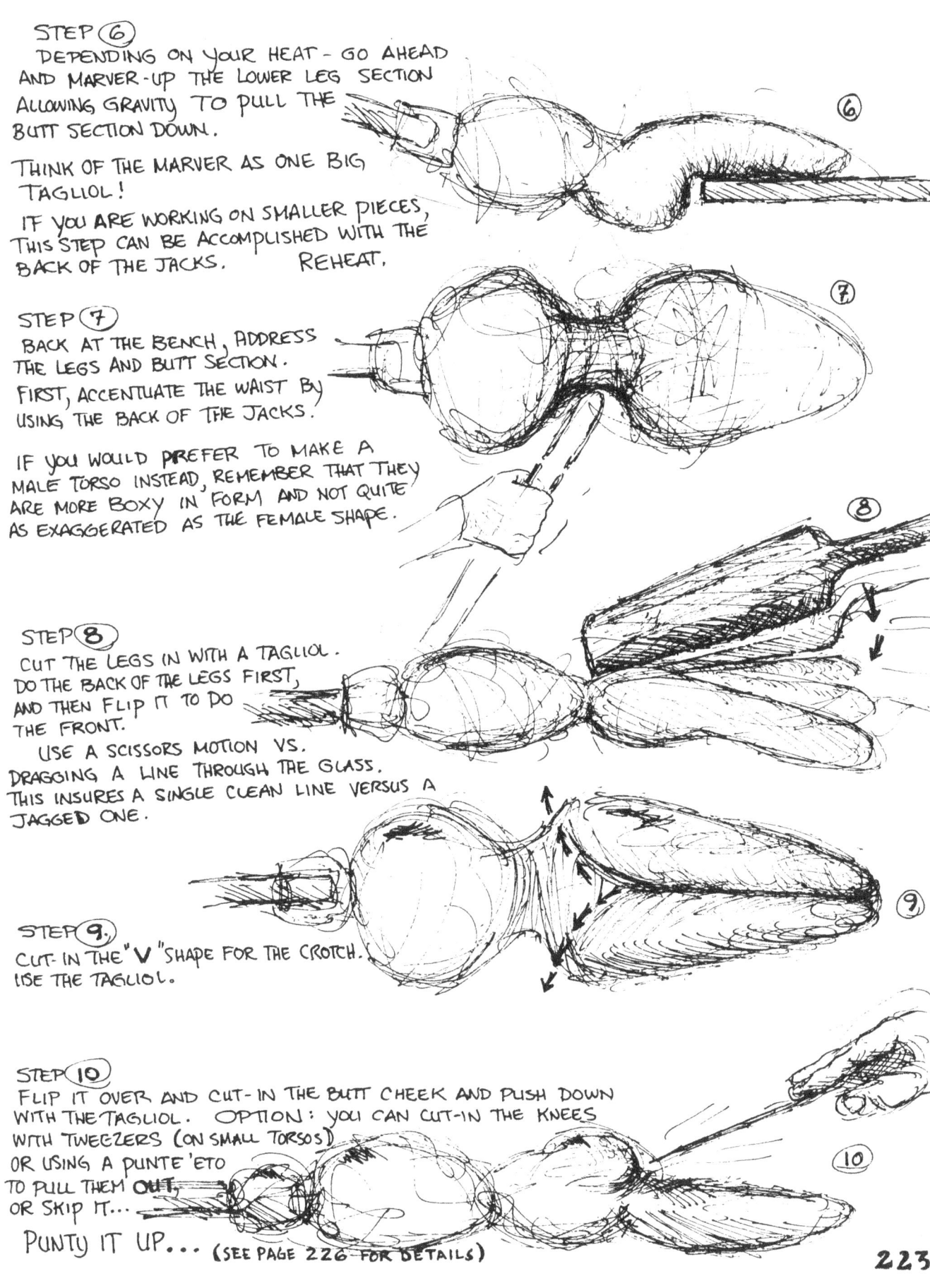

STEP 6
DEPENDING ON YOUR HEAT - GO AHEAD AND MARVER-UP THE LOWER LEG SECTION ALLOWING GRAVITY TO PULL THE BUTT SECTION DOWN.

THINK OF THE MARVER AS ONE BIG TAGLIOL!

IF YOU ARE WORKING ON SMALLER PIECES, THIS STEP CAN BE ACCOMPLISHED WITH THE BACK OF THE JACKS.   REHEAT.

STEP 7
BACK AT THE BENCH, ADDRESS THE LEGS AND BUTT SECTION.
FIRST, ACCENTUATE THE WAIST BY USING THE BACK OF THE JACKS.

IF YOU WOULD PREFER TO MAKE A MALE TORSO INSTEAD, REMEMBER THAT THEY ARE MORE BOXY IN FORM AND NOT QUITE AS EXAGGERATED AS THE FEMALE SHAPE.

STEP 8
CUT THE LEGS IN WITH A TAGLIOL. DO THE BACK OF THE LEGS FIRST, AND THEN FLIP IT TO DO THE FRONT.
USE A SCISSORS MOTION VS. DRAGGING A LINE THROUGH THE GLASS. THIS INSURES A SINGLE CLEAN LINE VERSUS A JAGGED ONE.

STEP 9
CUT-IN THE "V" SHAPE FOR THE CROTCH. USE THE TAGLIOL.

STEP 10
FLIP IT OVER AND CUT-IN THE BUTT CHEEK AND PUSH DOWN WITH THE TAGLIOL. OPTION: YOU CAN CUT-IN THE KNEES WITH TWEEZERS (ON SMALL TORSOS) OR USING A PUNTE'ETO TO PULL THEM OUT, OR SKIP IT...

PUNTY IT UP... (SEE PAGE 226 FOR DETAILS)

STEP 11
AFTER PUNTYING, IT'S TIME TO ADDRESS THE STOMACH/WAIST SECTION. SINCE THE GLASS IS WICKED COLD YOU'LL NEED TO REHEAT IT QUITE A BIT.

ON YOUR **FIRST REHEAT** YOU END-UP JUST HEATING THE SURFACE WHILE THE CORE IS STILL SEMI-SOLID. ANTICIPATE YOUR NEXT MOVE. PUSH THE GLASS WHERE YOU NEED IT.

ON YOUR **SECOND REHEAT** YOU SHOULD BE ABLE TO GET THE CORE HOT. LET THE MASS SAG, FLIP IT - ROCK AND ACCENTUATE THE STOMACH, AND CUT-IN THE CHEST - USE THE TAGLIOL AT A SLIGHT ANGLE TO MAKE IT ROUND.

IF YOU'RE MAKING A MALE TORSO, YOU COULD CUT-IN THE ABS WITH FLAT TWEEZERS (THE EDGE OF 'EM) OR WITH A SCULPTING KNIFE.

STEP 12
GATHER MORE GLASS BY DIPPING EACH SIDE IN THE FURNACE. THIS WILL BE WHAT YOU'LL SCULPT THE SHOULDERS AND BREASTS FROM. IT'S ALSO A QUICK N' EASY METHOD TO REINTRODUCE HEAT BACK INTO THE PIECE, THUS MAKING IT MUCH EASIER TO SCULPT.

USE A TAGLIOL TO KEEP THE GLASS WHERE YOU NEED IT - AROUND THE UPPER CHEST AREA...

STEP 13
USE THE TWEEZERS TO CUT-IN / SQUEEZE THE SHOULDER ZONE. THEN, FLATTEN THE "ARMS" AT THE BOTTOM WITH THE TAGLIOL.

YOU CAN EITHER PULL THE BREASTS OUT WITH A PUNTE'ETO (ON LARGER PIECES) OR ADD THEM AS BITS IN ORDER TO GET THE SIZE AND SHAPE TO MATCH-UP.

IN THE SAME HEAT, YOU CAN GO AHEAD AND PUSH-IN THE BELLY BUTTON WITH THE POINT OF YOUR TWEEZERS.

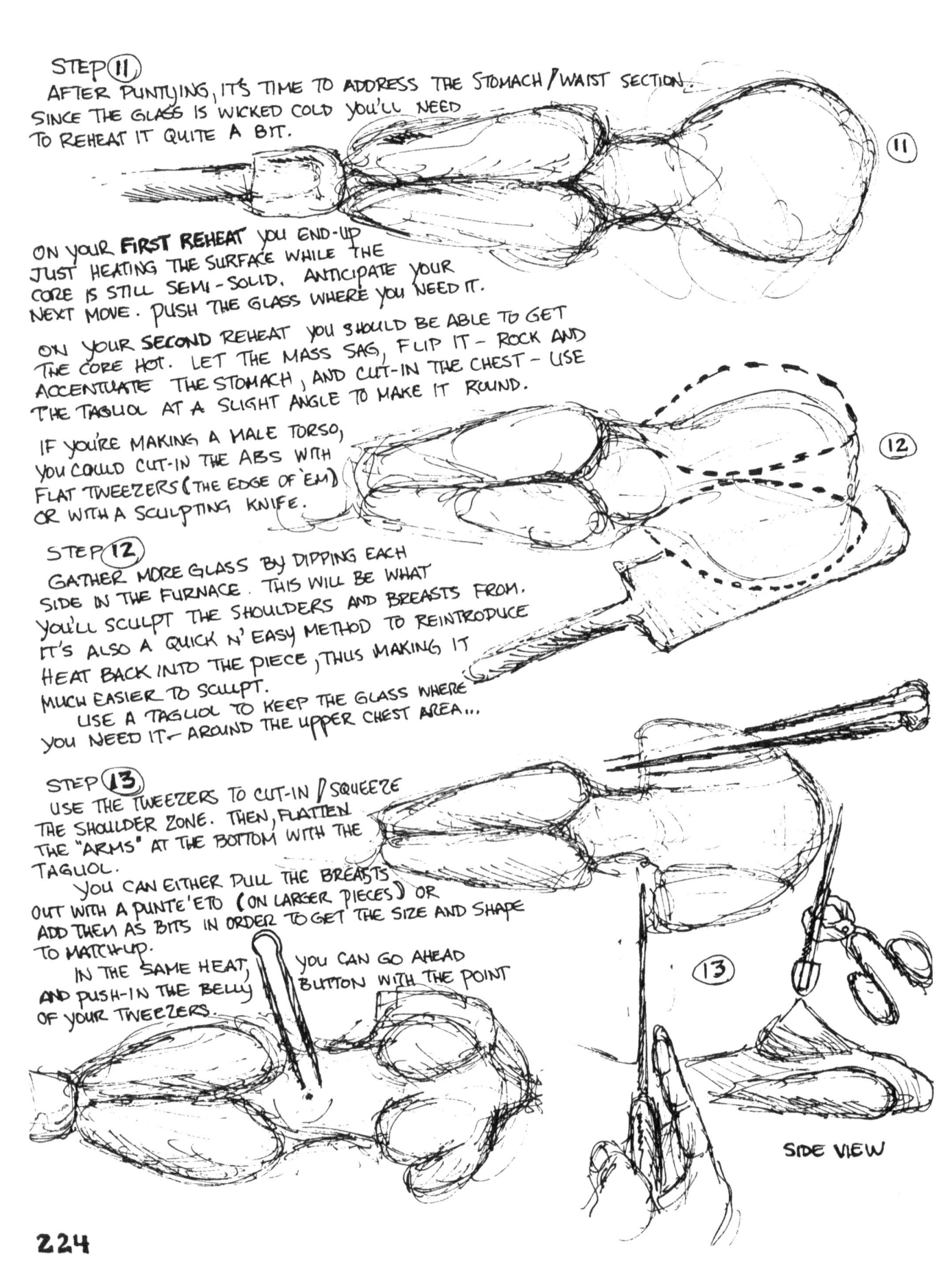

SIDE VIEW

STEP 14

Accentuate the breasts, from the inside-out, with a tagliol or edge of the tweezers. Cut-in the spine in-between (opposite side).

You can also pre-pull the nipples with a punte'eto → they'll melt and shrink into a little ball on the next reheat or you can add a bohemian-prunt bit for a similar affect.

Then reheat just the tip of the piece so you can cut in the shoulder / neck area.

STEP 15

Using your shears, cut-in the shoulders ~ the excess will become the neck of the torso.

A second cut - to trim off excess glass - can reduce the football shoulder-pad look, and is an option you can use to get the proportions right.

Pull the cuttings together to form the neck and reheat.

STEP 16

Snip off the excess on the neck (LINE A) to create a tapered angle and square it off with another cut (LINE B).
Cut the shoulder blades in with the tagliol.

STEP 17

Reheat and tune-up the form with the tagliol.

When everything looks A-OK - take a few extra flashes to equalize the temperature, and **BOX IT!**

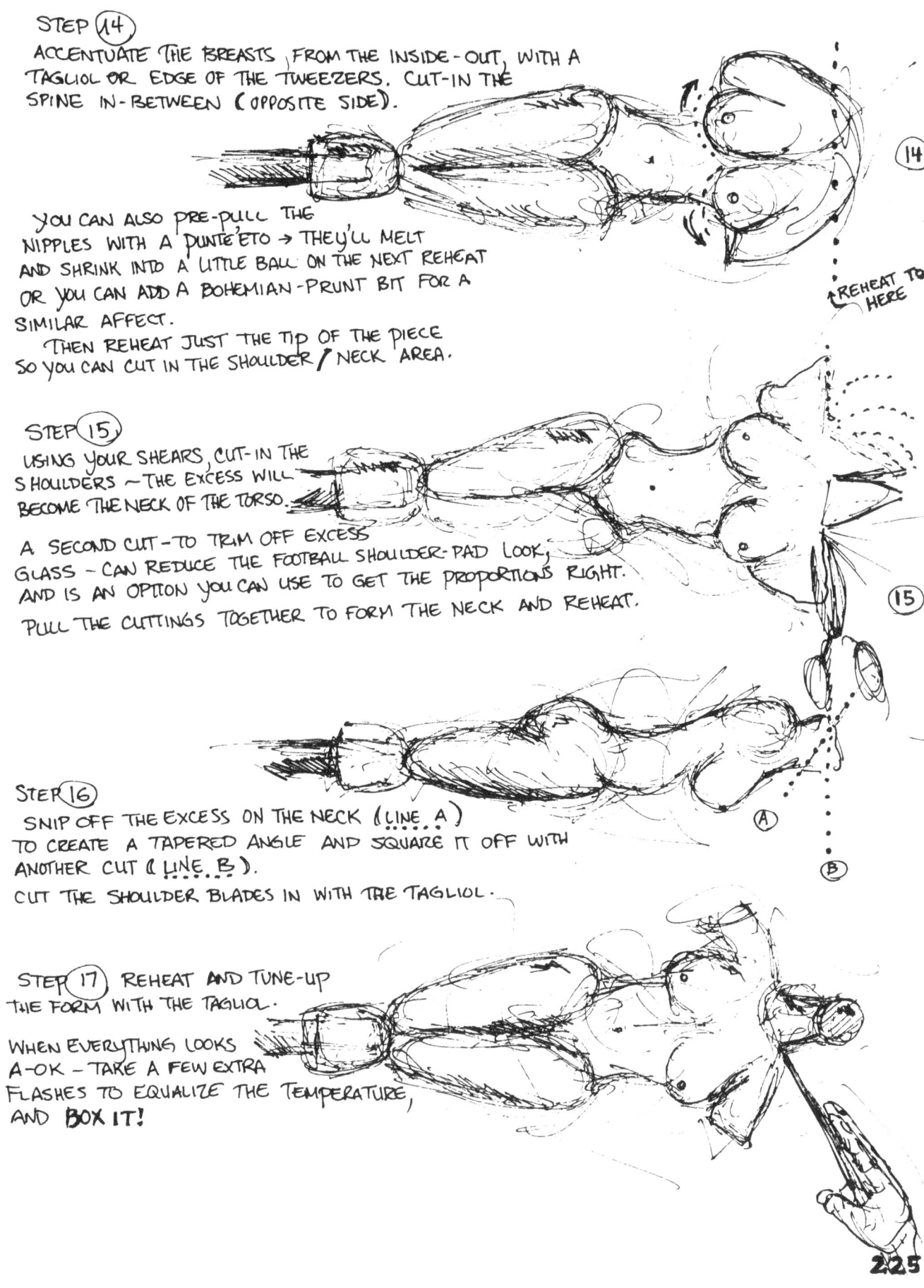

225

A FEW MORE THINGS...

SOLIDWORKING REQUIRES THAT YOU HAVE GOOD SOLID PUNTIES, ESPECIALLY ON LARGER PIECES. YOU NEED A FAIR AMOUNT OF MEAT ON YOUR MOILE - IT HELPS INSULATE THE GLASS AND PREVENTS THE ONSET OF CHECKING PREMATURELY. YOUR FIRST GATHER SHOULD BE MARVERED BACK ON THE PUNTY - NICE N' EVEN, BUT A LITTLE FATTER ON THE TIP. THE SECOND GATHER SHOULD BE DIPPED ABOUT HALFWAY, AND YOU THEN HOLD IT UP (SO IT FALLS BACK ON THE PUNTY) ON THE WAY OVER TO THE MARVER. THEN, MARVER IT BACK. YOU CAN QUENCH THE TIP IN WATER IN BETWEEN GATHERS TO SPEED UP THE PROCESS IF YOU LIKE.

A SCULPTURE PUNTY
1ST GATHER — 2ND GATHER (LET IT GET STONE COLD)

- ALSO, TRY TO MATCH YOUR PUNTY SIZE TO THE SIZE OF THE PIECE WHICH YOU ARE GETTING READY TO TRANSFER. I PREFER THE "BETTER-SAFE-THAN-SORRY" APPROACH AND OFTEN WILL TAKE THAT EXTRA HALF DIP TO MAKE SURE THE PUNTY HOLDS.

- ALSO, THE NO-WATER TRANSFER SEEMS TO WORK SURPRISINGLY WELL. INSTEAD, YOU TAKE A GOOD CHUNK OF IRON (GROUND TO A DULL TAPER) AND WHACK THE TRANSFER LINE THREE TIMES HARD (ROTATING A PARTIAL TURN EACH TIME) AND THE FOURTH TIME ON THE PIPE ITSELF - AND THE PIECE SHOULD BREAK CLEAN. REALLY IT WORKS!

- WHEN **PUNTYING**, THINK ABOUT THE FUTURE... THINK ABOUT HOW THAT PUNTY IS GONNA COME OFF. THINK ABOUT HOW THE PIECE WILL STAND OR SIT (OR HANG). WHAT KIND OF COLDWORKING WILL IT NEED? WHERE YOU PLACE THAT PUNTY CAN HAVE TREMENDOUS INFLUENCE ON HOW YOUR FINISHED PIECE WILL LOOK.

- ALWAYS PUNTY TO AN OUTSIDE CURVE OR EDGE. THAT WAY, YOU HAVE EASY ACCESS TO GRIND OR BELT-SAND THE PUNTY AWAY.

- BE SURE YOUR PIECES GET THE EXTRA ANNEALING TIME THAT THEY MAY NEED. YOU DON'T WANT THEM "GOING OFF" ON YOU WHEN YOU TRY TO GRIND THEM.

- SOLIDWORKING CAN BE ALOT OF FUN. IT CAN ALSO **FRUSTRATE** THE HELL OUT OF YOU WHEN YOUR PIECES GET ALL CONTORTED (TIP: FLIP YOU PIECE BACK N' FORTH DURING REHEATS VS. CONTINUALLY TURNING IT.). IT'S A FINE LINE TO WALK (DANCE). IF YOUR CORE TEMPERATURE IS TOO HOT - YOU'LL DISTORT THE FORM. IF THE SKIN OF THE PIECE GETS TOO HOT, YOU'LL LOSE YOUR DETAIL... TRY TO FIND THE HAPPY MEDIUM.

- ALSO, IF YOU PLAN ON SCULPTING THE FIGURE - DRAW THE FIGURE FROM THE MODEL. IT WILL HELP VISUALLY REINFORCE WHAT IT IS THAT YOU WANT TO MAKE. BE SURE TO COVER ALL ANGLES AND **PRACTICE, PRACTICE, PRACTICE!**

MOLDBLOWING

INTRODUCTION 228
EARTHBLOW 228
BOX O' CLAY 229
WOOD MOLDS 231
METAL & ASSORTED MOLDS . 233
PLASTER 235
POST-GATHERING 240

MOLDBLOWING

Virtually any void may be filled with a hot glass bubble, blown and then removed to produce a mold-blown object. Provided there are no **undercuts** and there exists an opportunity to remove the bubble — nearly any material may serve as a mold. Some materials, however, are more suitable than others.(← more on that in a little bit.)

The most common mold known to glassblowers is the **optic mold**. This simple-looking tapered ribbed cup may yield dozens of patterns and visual effects by altering the bubble before and or after blowing into it (see page 154 for more details on optic molds).

The most common moldblown object utilized by glassblowers is probably the beer bottle...

Anyways, the mold can offer the aspiring artist or entrepreneur an opportunity to reproduce a number of forms with nearly identical results. These molds may be used in a high volume production-line/factory style situation where repetition and speed are desireable. Most often these molds are made of iron/steel, graphite or wet fruit woods such as cherry or apple.

In nearly all molds a releasing agent is used to prevent the glass from sticking to the mold during the blowing process. With steel and iron molds a messy graphite wash or 'Acqua-Dag' is used. In the case of fruit woods → steam is produced, from the water vapor of the **hot glass → wet wood interface**, which acts as a release. Also, after repeated use a layer of carbon is built-up from the charring effects of the extreme temperatures of the hot glass, and helps release as well.

Plaster, clay, sand, the earth, bronze, copper, aluminum, wet newspaper and **luminar** are some other materials which may be utilized in the moldblowing process → especially for the production of more unique limited editions or singular forms.

I personally feel that moldblown glass is the unexplored continent of the art glass world. There are literally infinite possibilities to create intriguing sculptural forms through this process. And so few artists are utilizing it! What's up with that? Too often, it seems, students become entranced by the lure of off-hand glassworking, and thereby confined to the traditions so well-established there, that they miss-out on "the big picture". What is "the big picture"?... It all depends on what station or wavelength you're tuned into — (hint → stay away from those narrow-band frequencies. Visit some galleries, museums — read some books and expose yourself to

EARTH BLOW

DIG A HOLE...

START A BUBBLE...

SLAP THE BUBBLE IN THE HOLE, KICK DIRT ON TOP & BLOW!

← REMOVE TO YIELD COOL ORGANIC FORM.

"THE ARTS" & "KILL YOUR TELEVISION".) THE MOLD CAN EXPAND YOUR VISUAL VOCABULARY LIKE NO OTHER GLASS PROCESS. THINK OF POSITIVE-NEGATIVE SPACES AND FORMS, AND HOW THEY RELATE TO EACH OTHER. TRY ABSTRACTIONS. EXPLORE THE NARRATIVE OBJECT. EXAMINE THE RELATIONSHIP OF THE OBJECT(S) PRODUCED AND THE ACTUAL MOLD ITSELF. presentation is the Key 🗝! GRANTED, MOLD MAKING REQUIRES MORE TIME, EFFORT AND MATERIALS TO FABRICATE, AND MOLDBLOWING TAKES SOME PRACTICE TO BECOME FAMALIAR WITH → BUT THE REWARDS I BELIEVE ARE WORTH IT.

A FEW THINGS ABOUT MOLDBLOWING:
ALMOST ALL TWO-PART MOLDS WILL LEAVE A SEAM LINE ON THE FINAL PRODUCT. THE SEAM LINE IS FROM THE GAP WHERE THE TWO PARTS MEET OR JOIN TOGETHER. THE SMALLER THE GAP, THE LESS VISIBLE THE SEAM WILL APPEAR. THIS MAY HAVE A POSITIVE OR NEGATIVE IMPACT ON YOUR WORK. IT SHOULD BE TAKEN INTO CONSIDERATION WHILE DESIGNING THE OBJECT TO BE MADE. TRY TO INCORPORATE THE SEAM INTO THE WORK BY ACKNOWLEDGING IT'S EXISTENCE OR DISGUISE IT ANOTHER WAY.

FOR SUCCESSFUL MOLDBLOWING:
① TRY TO HAVE YOUR BUBBLE AS CLOSE TO THE SHAPE OF THE MOLD'S INTERIOR THAT YOU ARE GOING INTO → SO THAT IT DOESN'T HAVE TO STRETCH (OR BLOW-OUT) TOO FAR. ② MAKE YOUR BUBBLE ON THE 'THICK-SIDE' → THIS, TOO, WILL PREVENT THE WALLS FROM GETTING TOO THIN OR BLOWING OUT. ③ THE HOTTER YOU GET YOUR BUBBLE, THE MORE DEFINITION YOU'LL OBTAIN FROM BLOWING IT. ④ PRACTICE MAKES PERFECT. IT MAY TAKE SEVERAL ATTEMPTS TO ACHIEVE A SUCCESSFUL PIECE, SO IF AT FIRST YOU DON'T SUCCEED... TRY TRY TRY TRY TRY AGAIN!

MOST **METAL MOLDS** REQUIRE FAIRLY IN-DEPTH FOUNDRY AND/OR FABRICATION PROCESSES WHICH ARE BEYOND THE SCOPE OF THIS BOOK (SORRY!), HOWEVER, SHOULD YOU WISH TO REPRODUCE A PARTICULAR GLASS OBJECT A HUNDRED-FOLD OVER, YOU MAY CONTACT A FOUNDRY OR MACHINIST AND INQUIRE WHAT IT TAKES TO MAKE ONE FOR YOU. (USUALLY LOT$ OF MOOLAH!))

PERHAPS ONE OF THE SIMPLEST AND IMMEDIATE TYPES OF MOLDS (AFTER THE **EARTH-BLOW** MOLD SHOWN ON THE PREVIOUS PAGE) IS THE HINGED-**BOX O' CLAY MOLD**. A TWO-PART BOX CAN BE MADE OF PLYWOOD OR WELDED STEEL WITH EXPANDED METAL WALLS. IT SHOULD BE HINGED TOGETHER TO FORM ONE LARGE BOX, WITH AN ACCESS HOLE IN THE TOP TO ALLOW THE BLOWPIPE TO FIT IN. **HANDLES** CAN BE NAILED, SCREWED, OR IN THE CASE OF THE METAL BOX → WELDED ON. THESE ALLOW EASIER ACCESS IN OPENING AND CLOSING THE MOLDS. THE HANDLES MAY ALSO BE CLAMPED SHUT (WHILE BLOWING) WITH BAR CLAMPS (← LIKE THE ONES USED FOR WOODWORKING.) THE CLAMPS WILL INSURE A TIGHT NON-EXPANDING BOX - AND HELP REDUCE THE NOTICEABLE SEAM VIRTUALLY EVERY 2-PART MOLD BLOWN OBJECT POSSESSES (SEE STEPS BELOW)

TWO PART BOX O' CLAY MOLD

① MAKE A HINGED BOX. DRILL VENT HOLES.
② PACK IT WITH CLAY. CARVE A FORM.
③ MAKE SURE IT CLAMPS SHUT. REEM THE VENT HOLES.

The box is prepared by filling the interior with wet clay, (DO NOT USE PLASTALINE!) in part or entirely. Create a void where the bubble will be blown into. Think and sculpt in reverse to make positive and negative contours. Make sure your access hole is wide enough to accept the blowpipe (or the neck of the bubble) which you'll be blowing into it. Avoid making deep or narrow crevices and sharp angles → there's only so far that your bubble can stretch! Vent holes for escaping steam may be placed in the clay by pushing a 1/4" dowel rod or pencil through the clay to the exterior surface. **IF THE STEAM HAS NO WHERE TO GO — IT WILL FIGHT YOUR BUBBLE FOR ANY UNOCCUPIED SPACE AND PREVENT YOUR BUBBLE FROM BLOWING OUT.**

As with most all mold making, care should be taken to **AVOID UNDERCUTS** where your bubble may get trapped and become impossible to remove without damaging either the glass or mold.

The wet clay requires no additional releasing agent, as the moisture from the clay produces a layer of steam which prevents the glass from sticking. After blowing, some clay residue is likely to adhere to the bubble, and such is the nature of this mold. A spray bottle filled with water may be used to mist the clay just before blowing into it — but avoid collecting water (puddles) in spaces as it may quench or thermal shock the glass while blowing.

If this is the first time for blowing such a mold, you may try a dry run where you coordinate the movements with your assistant. A cinder block or small staircase or pedestal may be set-up behind the mold to provide adequate clearance in accessing the mold. Make sure the clamp is adjusted to the mold so little or no time is wasted fumbling around trying to get it to fit right. Situate your mold where it's close to the glory hole, but not in the pathway to the furnace or where it will interrupt other people working in the studio. Once everything is set-up, and you and your assistant are fully aware of the process, it's time to blow the mold. In keeping with the postulate "HOT IS GOOD, HOTTER IS BETTER" try to heat your bubble as hot and floppy as you can [control]. The bubble should be shaped as close to the space of the mold as possible. You may find it easier to neck the piece prior to going into the mold vs. afterwards. **IT IS ALSO POSSIBLE TO HAVE YOUR ASSISTANT INITIATE A NECKLINE USING THE JACKS WHILE IN THE MOLD AS WELL.**

Once your bubble's screamin' hot, head over to the mold while maintaining the pipe on a horizontal axis (to prevent premature elongation) and drop it into the awaiting mold. Your assistant may close and hold/clamp the mold shut as soon as the bubble stretches and fits inside. Blow as hard as you can, three or four times, capping the end of the pipe as you do so → thus trapping the air inside and causing the bubble to inflate (see image above). If you feel no resistance your bubble may not be fully expanded → so keep blowing. Or it may be because you've blown-through a section where the glass was too thin. *please try again!*...

After 10 – 30 seconds or so – when you feel that the bubble has fully expanded and set-up → tap your foot to indicate to your assistant to open the mold. Some wiggling side-to-side, up and down may be necessary to release the glass from the mold. Proceed to the glory hole to flash the whole piece and equalize its temperature. The piece then may be knocked-off into the annealer as a sculptural form or it may be further blown out, transferred and opened &/or finished as any vessel.

The clay blow mold is usually a one-shot deal, but it is possible to re-mist the interior and reattempt to blow it again. When you are done blowing the mold for the day, the clay may be dug out – remoistened and wedged/stored for another time.

WOOD MOLDS

For the aspiring loggers in the crowd, there's a simple two-part mold that's easy to make, easy to blow, and yields interesting results. Locate a hardwood log of desireable length and girth. Green (wet - freshly cut) wood works better and lasts longer for this purpose. Chainsaw the piece in half - vertically. A space for hinges and handles may also be notched-out at this time as well. Using wood carving tools or the chainsaw, you may chip or carve out the void where your bubble will be blown into. Also, notch out a space for the blowpipe/neck of the bubble to fit in. Be sure to drill vent holes, (should you carve deep canyons in the wood,) to allow escaping gases an easy exit. You may screw some handles onto the sides to aid in opening and closing the mold.

The mold (log) may be pre-soaked in a bucket of water prior to blowing to prevent overcharring of the interior. It can also be blown "dry" - but be ready for some 'fire works' - (big time flames) during the blow. Your assistant should prepare for the worst → wearing gloves and fire resistant clothing, to keep from getting burned.

Blow as normal. The mold should be soaked in water right after to stop it from burning further. This mold may be used repeatedly for interesting generations of pieces, each with its own unique wood grain texture acquired from the charring heat of the hot glass. The mold may be altered at any point, carved further or additional elements (extra pieces of wood) may be inserted/attached to the interior to metamorphose the resulting blown form.

Yet another form of wood mold is the 'adjustable' box mold. This is simply a wooden box or two-part wooden box-mold which may have elements attach-

ED TO THE INTERIOR. THESE ELEMENTS MAY BE SIMPLY SET IN PLACE AND BLOWN TO CREATE UNIQUE FORMS, OR IF YOU HOPE TO REPEAT THE PROCESS TO MAKE MULTIPLES, YOU CAN SCREW OR HOT GLUE THE ELEMENTS WHERE YOU WANT THEM. THE ELEMENTS THEN MAY BE REMOVED AND RECONFIGURED TO CREATE A PLETHORA OF SHAPES INDEFINITELY (WELL... AT LEAST UNTIL THE WOOD BURNS AWAY). NOTE: NOT ALL WOOD IS CREATED EQUAL! DEPENDING ON THE TREES FROM WHICH IT IS HARVESTED FROM, ie. THE SPECIES AND HOW GREEN OR DRY IT IS, IT CAN HAVE A HUGE IMPACT ON THE PERFORMANCE OF YOUR WOOD MOLD. WOOD WILL BURN AT DIFFERENT RATES BECAUSE OF ITS OWN GENETIC MAKE UP → DENSITY OF THE GRAIN, THE PART OF THE TREE FROM WHICH IT IS HARVESTED, ITS OWN NATURAL RESISTANCE TO FIRE, AND ALSO THE METHOD OR MANNER IN WHICH IT IS INCORPORATED INTO A MOLD. IF, FOR EXAMPLE, THE WOOD-GRAIN IS AN AESTHETIC SURFACE WHICH YOU ENJOY → TRY USING 'SOFTER' VARIETIES OF HARDWOOD SUCH AS ALDER, MAPLE OR EVEN BIRCH. THEY WILL, OF COURSE, BURN FASTER AND LIVE SHORTER THAN FRUITWOODS SUCH AS CHERRY OR APPLE. AVOID AT ALL COSTS MAKING MOLDS WITH PLYWOOD ☠, WHERE THE PLYWOOD SURFACE IS EXPOSED TO HOT GLASS! THE FUMES ARE NOT ONLY SMELLY BUT TOXIC AS WELL. IT'S O.K. TO USE IT AS BACKING MATERIAL OR IT MAY SERVE AS STRUCTURAL SUPPORT — BUT DON'T HAVE IT WHERE IT WILL BURN, — AND THE SAME GOES FOR THAT PARTICLE BOARD STUFF TO. THE RESINS AND GLUES USED TO HOLD THEM TOGETHER PRODUCE NOXIOUS GASES WHEN BURNED; SO DO YOUR LUNGS AND STUDIOMATES ((LUNGS)) A FAVOR — GET THE GOOD WOOD TO BEGIN WITH.

THE STUDIO GLASS MOVEMENT PIONEER MARVIN LIPOFSKY HAS BEEN USING WOODEN MOLDS (SUCH AS DRAWN ABOVE) FOR DECADES TO CREATE FORMS FOR HIS SCULPTURES. HE THEN DOES LARGE AMOUNTS OF COLD WORKING AFTER THEY'VE BEEN ANNEALED TO PRODUCE TRULY UNIQUE AND INVITING PIECES.

IF THE ORGANIC THING ISN'T YOUR BAG, AND YOU SEEK A MORE HARD EDGE - CLEAN - CRISP DESIGN APPROACH ↝ THERE ARE A VARIETY OF OTHER MOLDS WHICH MAY SUIT YOUR NEEDS. SYMMETRICAL FORMS MAY BE ACHIEVED USING ROTATIONAL OR 'SPINNING' OR 'TURN-'ROUND' MOLDS, WHERE THE BUBBLE IS BLOWN INTO THE MOLD WHILE SIMULTANEOUSLY TURNING THE PIPE. MOST BOTTLES, VASES AND TABLE N' STEMWARE WERE BLOWN IN SUCH MOLDS PRIOR TO TOTAL AUTOMATION — AND CONTINUE TODAY TO BE MADE THIS WAY IN FACTORIES GLOBALLY. OFTENTIMES, THESE MOLDS ARE BLOWN AS PART OF A MULTI-PERSON TEAM WHERE EACH STEP OF THE PROCESS IS HANDLED BY ONE (OR POSSIBLY TWO) INDIVIDUAL(S) AND PASSED-ON. ANY TIME YOU MIGHT HAVE THE OPPORTUNITY TO VISIT A GLASS FACTORY — FULLY OR PARTIALLY AUTOMATED — TAKE IT! IT'S TRULY FASCINATING TO WATCH THE SPEED AND 'PRECISION' BY

PADDLES OR A HINGED LID (ON TOP)

ADJUSTABLE WOOD MOLD

which glass can be mass produced. Also, if you ever get the chance, check out **NORMAN FAULKNER'S** "**GLASS INDIA**" VIDEO FOR SOME AMAZING FOOTAGE INSIDE A GLASS FACTORY IN INDIA WHERE BLOWPIPES FLY THROUGH THE AIR AND MOLDS ARE OPENED AND CLOSED FASTER THAN YOU CAN SAY "LICKETY-SPLIT". (SEE PAGE 310 FOR DETAILS ON HOW TO OBTAIN YOUR OWN COPY.)

ROTATIONAL MOLDS CAN GREATLY SPEED UP YOUR PRODUCTION IF YOU'RE REPEATEDLY MAKING NEARLY IDENTICAL PIECES TO "FILL ORDERS". THEY MAY ALSO SERVE AS A FOUNDATION STRUCTURE WHICH MAY BE BUILT UPON WITH HANDLES, BITS AND PRUNTS etc. TO YIELD MORE UNIQUE ONE-OF-A-KIND ITEMS.

THE SIMPLEST SPINNING MOLD EXAMPLE IS A STRAIGHT WALLED PIECE OF STEEL PIPE WHICH IS WELDED TO A METAL BASE AND HAS VENT HOLES DRILLED NEAR THE BOTTOM (SEE IMAGE TO THE RIGHT). AN ALCOHOL/GRAPHITE POWDER WASH (OR **COLLOIDAL GRAPHITE** - AVAILABLE THROUGH FOUNDRY SUPPLY HOUSES) MAY BE PAINTED ON THE INSIDE OF THE MOLD TO PREVENT STICKING.

SIMPLE SPINNING MOLD

ANOTHER VERSION OF SPINNING MOLD MAY BE CARVED FROM WOOD (PREFERABLY CHERRY). THESE MOLDS SHOULD BE SOAKED IN WATER PRIOR TO USING. VENT HOLES FOR ESCAPING STEAM SHOULD BE STRATEGICALLY PLACED TO ALLOW THE FORM TO EASILY EXPAND WHILE BLOWING. OR YOU MAY OPT TO LEAVE THE BOTTOM OPEN AND BLOW THE MOLD ON TOP OF A CHERRY PLANK OR PADDLE TO CREATE THE FOOT AND ALLOW THE STEAM AN EASY EXIT.

ROTATIONAL WOOD MOLD
LOCKING PINS

A **STACKABLE MOLD** SYSTEM CAN BE FABRICATED OUT OF WOOD OR GRAPHITE WHERE INTERLOCKING ELEMENTS MAY BE ARRANGED AND RECONFIGURED TO CREATE VARIATIONS ON A THEME. A LOCKING PIN MAY HOLD ALL OF THE ELEMENTS IN LINE DURING THE BLOWING PROCESS AND PERMIT THEM TO BE INTERCHANGED AS NEEDED (SEE DRAWING →). GRAPHITE CAN WITHSTAND TREMENDOUS TEMPERATURES WITH LITTLE OR NO ILL-EFFECT. IT IS PRONE TO BREAKAGE IF DROPPED OR MISHANDLED. GRAPHITE COMES IN VARIOUS DENSITIES OR GRADES AND CAN BE OBTAINED FROM FOUNDRY SUPPLIERS AS WELL. GRAPHITE IS EASILY MACHINED OR MILLED, BUT MUST BE DONE WHERE THE RESULTING DUSTS AND CUTTINGS ARE VACUUMED OR EASILY CLEANED-UP. THIS STUFF CAN FIND IT'S WAY INTO EVERY NOOK AND CRANNY OF YOUR EQUIPMENT AND LEAVE YOU AS BLACK AS A COAL MINER WHEN YOU'RE DONE

STACKABLE WOOD MOLD SYSTEM

WORKING WITH IT! TAKE CARE NOT TO BREATHE GRAPHITE DUST AS WELL → **HINT:** WEAR YOUR RESPIRATOR!

OPEN-FACED MOLDS ARE ANOTHER OPTION. YOU'RE PROBABLY ALREADY FAMALIAR WITH THE MOST COMMON OF THESE: **THE BLOCK**. THEY COME IN EVERY SIZE: FROM TINY, FIRST-GATHER SHAPERS TO HOLLOWED-OUT TREE STUMPS (FOR BLOWING **CARBOYS** OR **DEMI-JOHNS**.) THE IMAGE TO THE RIGHT SHOWS A **TROUGH-MOLD**. SMALL WOOD ELEMENTS OR DOWELS MAY BE SCREWED OR HOT-GLUED TO ONE SIDE OF THE INTERIOR TO AUGMENT THE CYLINDRICAL OBJECT BEING FORMED. ROLLED-UP WET NEWSPAPER MAY ALSO BE SET IN PLACE IN LIEU OF THE WOOD ELEMENTS TO CREATE INTERESTING SIDE WALLS OF THE BLOWN VESSEL. THE PIECE MAY BE BLOWN AT THE SAME TIME AS ROTATING IN THE MOLD OR THE PIPE MAY BE **CAPPED** TO MAINTAIN PRESSURE WITHIN THE BUBBLE AND PREVENT IT FROM COLLAPSING.

TROUGH MOLD

4-WAY OPEN-FACED MOLD

THE NEXT IMAGE SHOWS A VARIATION ON THE OPEN-FACED MOLD WITH **FOUR-CHOICES-IN-ONE**. THE ADVANTAGE TO OPEN FACED MOLDS IS YOU CAN SEE WHAT'S HAPPENING TO YOUR BUBBLE AS YOU SHAPE IT. ALSO, BEING ON A HORIZNTAL PLANE VS. VERTICAL, YOUR PIECE IS NOT SUBJECTED TO THE STRETCHING EFFECTS OF GRAVITY WHICH MAY OR MAY NOT BE BENEFICIAL TO YOU.

MAYBE WELDING STEEL AND FABRICATING METAL TURNS YOUR CRANK. MANY SIMPLE MOLDS CAN BE MADE WITH BITS AND PIECES OF METAL ALREADY HANGIN' AROUND YOUR SHOP. FIGURE **M1** SHOWS A A SIMPLE VERSION OF AN 'OPTIC' MOLD MADE OF STEEL PIPE SECTIONS CUT AND WELDED TO A METAL BASE. ANOTHER VERSION OF THIS USING PIECES OF FLAT STOCK IS DEPICTED IN FIGURE **M2**. MANY VARIATIONS OF THESE MOLDS ARE POSSIBLE, AND ONLY YOUR IMAGINATION IS YOUR LIMITING FACTOR. YOU CAN INCORPORTE FORGED METAL INTO YOUR MOLDS AS WELL. FIGURE **M3.** BELOW ↓ SHOWS A SIMPLE-LOOKING CORKSCREW MOLD, WHICH CAN YIELD SEMI-COMPLEX FORMS WHEN BLOWN INTO. THE RESULTING FORM MUST BE UN-SCREWED FROM THE MOLD TO REMOVE IT!

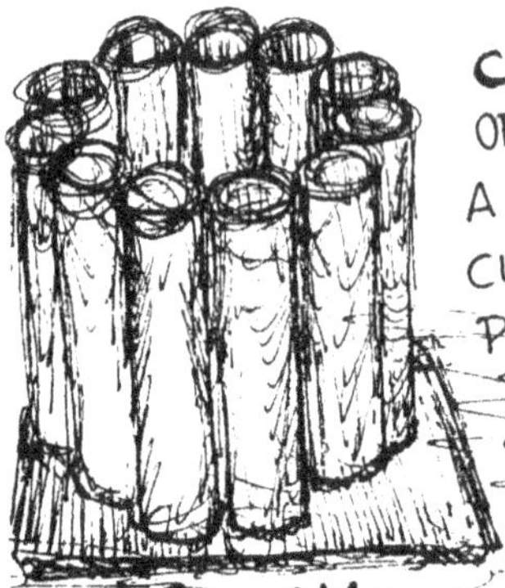

YET ANOTHER POSSIBILITY EXISTS WITH PLATE STEEL MOLDS. THESE MAY BE FABRICATED IN AN INFINITE VARIETY OF SHAPES AND FORMS.

Fig. M1.
fig M2.

BLOW STRAIGHT IN... UNSCREW TO REMOVE

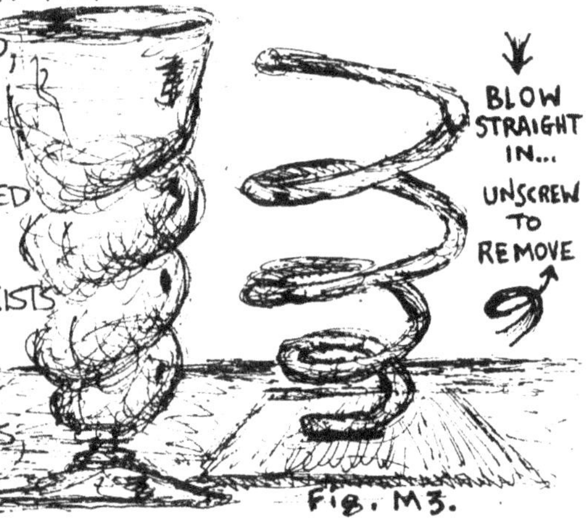

fig. M3.

ELEMENTS MAY BE PLASMA-TORCHED AWAY TO CREATE LETTERING, FIGURES OR DESIGNS WITHIN THE METAL, OR VARIOUS OTHER ELEMENTS ADDED TO THE INTERIOR TO PRODUCE MULTITUDES OF TEXTURES. AS LONG AS YOU HAVE NO UNDERCUTS AND AN EASY WAY TO GET OUT OF THE MOLD, YOU SHOULD HAVE NO PROBLEM BLOWING THIS TYPE OF MOLD A THOUSAND TIMES OVER — WITH LITTLE-TO-NO DEGRADATION OF FORM.

PREHEATING METAL AND GRAPHITE MOLDS IS A GOOD IDEA, SINCE THEY TEND TO SUCK THE HEAT RIGHT OUTTA YOUR GLASS → PARTICULARY IF THE MOLDS HAVE LARGE FLAT AREAS. NOW... DON'T HEAT IT UP TOO MUCH OR YOUR GLASS MAY STICK TO THE METAL! ANOTHER WAY TO DO IT IS TO PRE-BLOW A PIECE IN THE MOLD TO PREHEAT IT, AND THEN BLOW YOUR ACTUAL PIECE MOMENTS LATER. THIS TECHNIQUE WORKS EXCEPTIONALLY WELL IN PRODUCTION-STYLE SITUATIONS.

IF YOU DO NOTICE QUITE A FEW CHILL MARKS OR CHECKING OCCURING, PRE-HEAT THE MOLD MORE. IF IT STARTS STICKING, PREHEAT LESS.

TRIANGULAR METAL MOLD

3-SIDED STOPPERED BOTTLE

PLASTER IS YET ANOTHER MATERIAL SUITABLE FOR THE MOLDBLOWING PROCESS.

PLASTER MOLDS CAN BE EASILY CAST FROM CLAY POSITIVES, (THAT IS IF YOU ALREADY HAVE HAD SOME MOLD-MAKING EXPERIENCE IN SCULPTURE OR CERAMICS...). **FIRST**, MAKE YOUR CLAY POSITIVE EXACTLY THE WAY YOU'D LIKE IT TO LOOK (IN GLASS). **SECOND**, DECIDE WHERE YOUR MOLD LINE/SEAM WILL BE. THIS MAY BE YOUR MOST IMPORTANT DECISION IN MOLDMAKING, AFTER WHAT IT'S GOING TO LOOK LIKE.

TRY TO INCORPORATE THE SEAM INTO THE FORM'S OVERALL DESIGN. HIDE IT WHEREVER YOU CAN. IT IS POSSIBLE THAT YOU HAVE LITTLE-TO-NO CHOICE IN THE MATTER, IF YOUR POSITIVE IS SCULPTED SUCH THAT THE MOLD CAN ONLY PULL APART ONE WAY.

BEWARE OF UNDERCUTS ☠!!
A.K.A. THE VALLEY OF NO RETURN

LET'S SAY YOU'D LIKE TO BLOW SOME HOME BREW BOTTLES BASED ON A HOUSE FORM — SIMILAR TO THE ANTIQUE WHISKEY/BITTERS BOTTLES BLOWN IN NEW JERSEY ALMOST 100 YEARS AGO. THE FIRST STEP IS THE CLAY POSITIVE. USE VIRTUALLY ANY CLAY AVAILABLE. STONEWARE CLAY IS CHEAP, BUT DRIES OUT QUICKLY → SO KEEP IT COVERED WITH PLASTIC. FOR EXCELLENT DETAIL AND MODELING QUALITY → YOU MAY USE PLASTALINE TYPE CLAY (OFTEN USED BY SCULPTORS DOING CASTING OR PRECISION MODELING.)

AGAIN, MAKE SURE THERE ARE NO UNDERCUTS.

THERE ARE SEVERAL WAYS TO TAKE PLASTER MOLDS OFF OF CLAY POSITIVES. THE TRADITIONAL METHOD USED BY SCULPTORS AND CERAMICISTS INVOLVES SHIMMING THE FORM IN HALF AND CASTING THE PLASTER IN PLACE. IT CAN BE A LENGTHY PROCESS. A BIT TOO LONG TO INCLUDE EVERY ASPECT HERE — SO INSTEAD — I'LL OPT FOR A FAIRLY QUICK 'N' EASY BOX RELIEF-STYLE MOLD WHICH IS OUTLINED ON THE FOLLOWING PAGES. FOR MORE SOPHISTICATED FORMS OR TO GAIN MORE EXPERIENCE IN MOLDMAKING — I STRONGLY RECOMMEND TAKING A SCULPTURE (MODELING) CLASS AND/OR LEARN ABOUT SLIP CASTING (CERAMICS).

WIRE TOOL FOR CUTTING CLAY

CLEAN UP YOUR MESS / CLEAN UP YOUR MESS / CLEAN UP YOUR MESS

STEP 1. MAKE YOUR CLAY POSITIVE. HAVE AN AREA WHERE THE NECK OF THE PIECE WILL BE (WHERE YOUR BUBBLE WILL GAIN ACCESS INTO THE MOLD). IN OUR EXAMPLE THIS IS THE CHIMNEY ON THE HOUSE.

2. SPLIT THE POSITIVE IN HALF. USE A WIRE CUTTING TOOL OR LARGE KNIFE. (SEE PREVIOUS PAGE)

3. SET ONE HALF ON A FLAT SMOOTH SURFACE — GLASS, MARBLE, OR FORMICA FOR EXAMPLE.

4. MAKE A "FLASK" (A FRAME/BOX) OUT OF ½" THICK PLYWOOD. MAKE SURE IT'S AT LEAST 2" TALLER THAN YOUR POSITIVE (I USUALLY MAKE IT 10" TALLER OR SO... YOU'LL SEE WHY).

5. SET THE FLASK AROUND THE CLAY POSITIVE. IT MAY BE CLAMPED TOGETHER, OR SCREWED WITH DRYWALL SCREWS. MAKE SURE YOU HAVE AT LEAST 2"-3" ALL THE WAY AROUND YOUR POSITIVE. PRESS THE CLAY FLUSH AGAINST THE WOOD WHERE THE NECK OF THE GLASS WILL BE. (THE CHIMNEY AGAIN.) THIS WILL BE YOUR ACCESS POINT.

6. SEAL THE PERIMETER WITH "WORMS" ROLLED OUT OF CLAY. MAKE SURE IF THERE ARE ANY GAPS IN THE WOOD (AT THE JOINTS) THAT THEY GET PACKED WITH CLAY AS WELL. THERE SHOULD BE NO LIGHT SHINING THROUGH ANYWHERE. **YOU DO NOT WANT YOUR PLASTER TO LEAK OUT ALL OVER THE PLACE!**

7. SET A PENCIL OR DOWEL ROD — WRAPPED IN PLASTIC — INTO THE HIGH POINT OF YOUR CLAY POSITIVE. THIS WILL BE YOUR VENT HOLE. MARK A SPOT 2" ABOVE THE CLAY ON THAT ROD. THIS WILL BE YOUR "FILL-TO-HERE" LINE.

8. PAINT THE CLAY POSITIVE AND THE INTERIOR OF THE MOLD WITH A RELEASING AGENT (e.g. VASELINE OR DILUTED MURPHY'S OIL SOAP WORK WELL). (NOT ILLUSTRATED)

9. GUESSTIMATE YOUR VOLUME. FIGURE OUT HOW MUCH LIQUID IT WILL TAKE TO FILL YOUR MOLD. PUT ABOUT ½ TO ⅔ds THAT MUCH WATER IN A CLEAN PLASTIC BUCKET. IT'S ALWAYS BETTER TO HAVE TOO MUCH THAN TOO LITTLE. ALSO → WARM WATER SETS THE PLASTER FASTER THAN COOL, YOU MAY USE THAT TO YOUR **ADVANTAGE**. NOW YOU'RE READY TO MIX....

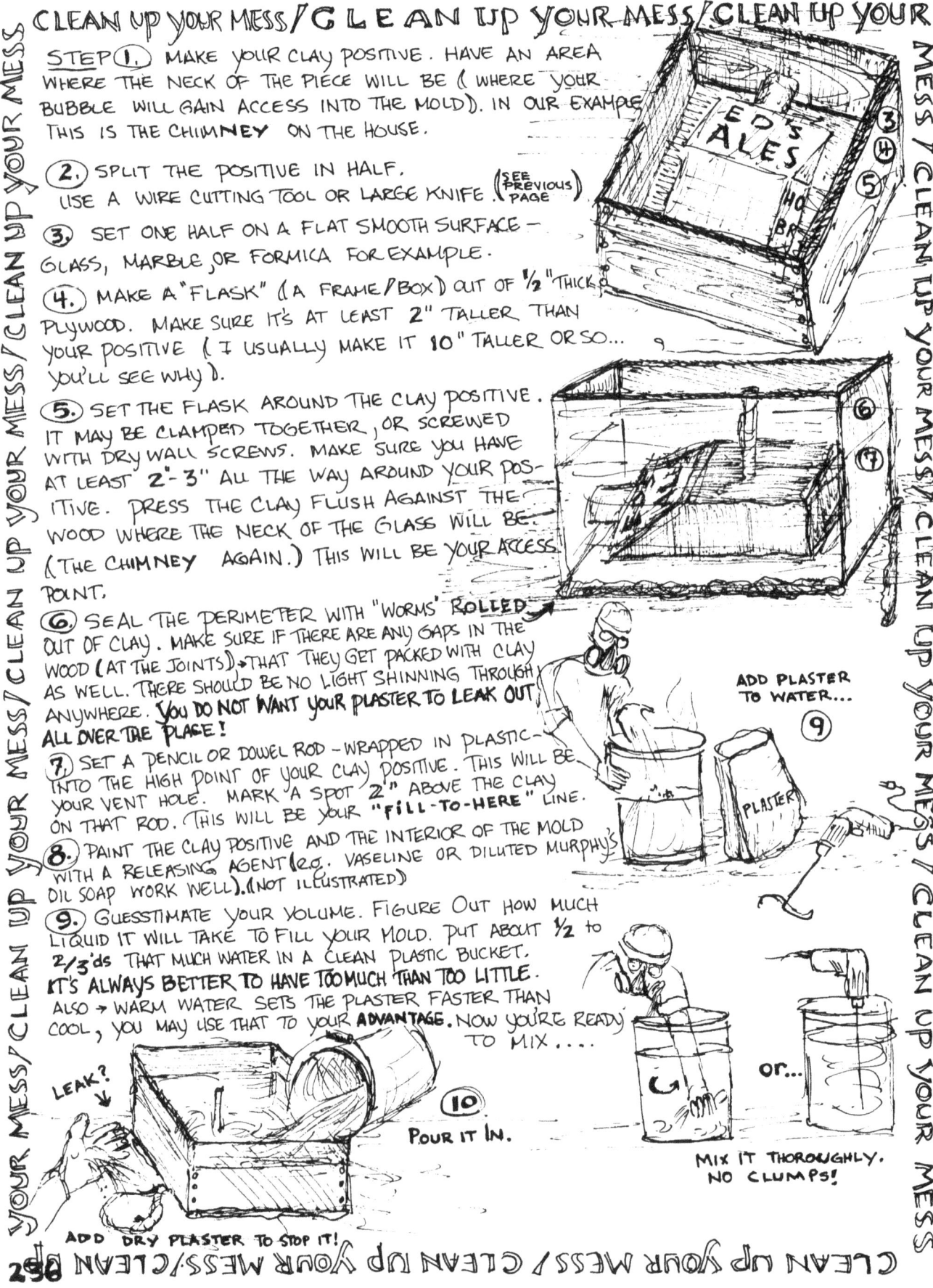

ADD PLASTER TO WATER... 9

10. POUR IT IN.

LEAK?
ADD DRY PLASTER TO STOP IT!

MIX IT THOROUGHLY. NO CLUMPS!

KNOW BEFORE YOU GO MIXING UP THAT PLASTER:...
A. PLASTER IS A MESSY SUBSTANCE.
MIX IT WHERE YOU CAN EASILY CLEAN IT UP.
B. DO NOT BREATHE PLASTER DUST. WEAR A RESPIRATOR (OR AT LEAST A DUST MASK) WHEN MIXING.
C. DO NOT POUR EXTRA PLASTER DOWN THE SINK/DRAIN. USE A GARBAGE CAN. SOMETIMES, IN SOME INSTANCES PLASTER IS EASIER TO CLEAN UP AFTER IT'S SOLIDIFIED.

9. continued... ADD DRY PLASTER TO THE WATER. SIFT IT IN WITH YOUR HAND OR A SCOOP. TRY FOR EVEN DISTRIBUTION. KEEP ON ADDING PLASTER UNTIL SMALL ISLANDS BEGIN TO FORM. OK. THAT'S ENOUGH PLASTER FOR A WET-TO-AVERAGE STYLE OF SLURRY. YOU COULD ADD A BIT MORE PLASTER FOR A THICKER, PASTIER CONSISTENCY - IF YOU NEED SUCH.
  THEN SQUEEZE OUT THE CLUMPS WITH YOUR HANDS AND MIX (OR BLEND IT WITH A HAND DRILL & ATTACHMENT) UNTIL THERE ARE NO CLUMPS AND EVERYTHING'S THOROUGHLY STIRRED.

10. POUR THE PLASTER INTO THE MOLD. FILL UP TO THE LINE. WATCH ALL SIDES OF THE MOLD FOR LEAKS. SHOULD YOU NOTICE ONE, TRY STUFFING A BLOB OF CLAY IN THERE OR ADD DRY PLASTER - IT SHOULD HELP ARREST THE LEAK.
  ONCE FILLED, BANG ON THE TABLE FOR A MINUTE OR TWO. THIS SHOULD RELEASE ANY AIR BUBBLES TRAPPED INSIDE TO RISE TO THE SURFACE. ALLOW THE PLASTER TO "SET" AN HOUR OR SO - OR AFTER IT GETS HOT AND STARTS TO COOL.
  LEAVE ANY REMAINING PLASTER IN YOUR BUCKET. IT WILL SET UP TOO, AND SHOULD EASILY RELEASE NICE N' E·Z AS ONE GIANT HOCKEY PUCK IF YOU SQUEEZE THE BUCKET (AND MAYBE BANG ON IT A FEW TIMES).

11. ONCE THE PLASTER IS SET-UP, UNSCREW (OR UNCLAMP) THE BOARDS (FLASK). PULL THE DOWEL ROD OUT (& VENT HOLE). FLIP THE MOLD OVER.

12. IF ANY PLASTER HAS SEEPED UNDER THE CLAY → CLEAN (BREAK) IT OFF TO FIND THE PERIMETER OF YOUR POSITIVE.
  TAKE A SPOON OR BUTTERKNIFE AND CARVE REGISTRATION MARKS INTO THE FRESH PLASTER. THEY SHOULD BE ABOUT THE DEPTH AND SIZE OF HALF A WALNUT. TWO OR THREE HOLES SHOULD DO THE TRICK.

13. LAY THE OTHER HALF OF THE CLAY POSITIVE ON TOP OF THE ORIGINAL HALF TO COMPLETE THE FORM.

14. REASSEMBLE THE FLASK. SEAL ANY GAPS WITH CLAY, INCLUDING THE NECK SECTION (← IT SHOULD BE FLUSH WITH THE FLASK). SET YOUR PLASTIC-WRAPPED DOWEL ROD INTO THE POSITIVE (AS IN STEP #7). APPLY RELEASING AGENT TO THE CLAY, THE FLASK AND ESPECIALLY THE PLASTER IN THE INTERIOR OF THE MOLD.

15. MIX-UP YOUR PLASTER, AND POUR THE MOLD. ALLOW THE PLASTER TO SET AGAIN.

16. UNDO THE FLASK. PULL THE MOLD APART - BE CAREFUL! TAKE YOUR TIME. IF IT'S A BIT STUBBORN → TRY IT FROM ALL ANGLES AND/OR DIG AT THE SEAM WITH A BUTTER KNIFE OR SIMILAR TOOL. ONCE YOU GET IT APART, REMOVE ALL THE CLAY → STORING IT FOR LATER USE. INSPECT YOUR MOLD. USE A BUTTERKNIFE TO SMOOTH ANY SHARP OR ROUGH EDGES.
  CHECK YOUR VENT HOLES. DRILL EXTRA ONES IF YOU THINK YOU MAY NEED MORE.
WAIT-A-MINUTE... YOU'RE NOT DONE YET! CLEAN-UP YOUR MESS!

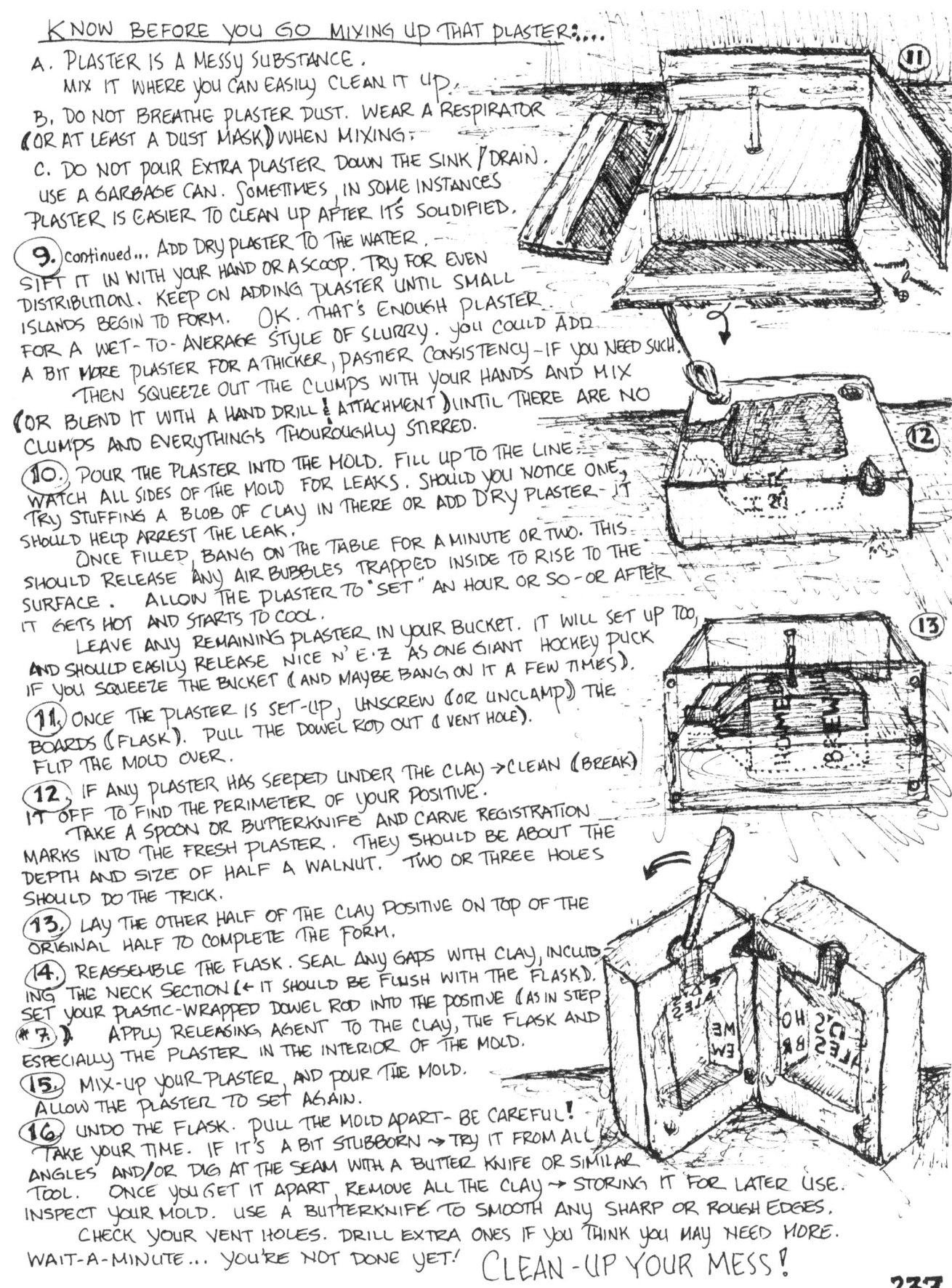

When it comes time to blow the mold - get yourself set up so that the process goes smoothly. Use bar clamps or large "C" clamps to hold the mold tight during the blow. Preadjust them so they can go on in a flash.

Next, soak the whole mold in a bucket of water for 10 to 15 minutes or so → until the little air bubbles stop rising to the surface.

If you want, you can paint a graphite/alcohol wash on the interior of the mold to act as an additional releasing agent - immediatly before you blow it. It may help preserve your mold for a couple extra blows. Or you can line the mold with one sheet of wet newspaper...

PRE-SOAK THE MOLD

Make certain you have easy access to blow the mold. You should have enough height to blow the mold (arrange a step-up if necessary), and your assistant should know how to close and open the mold. Try a dry run first.

Gather what you think might be enough glass to blow n' fill the mold. Shape it as close as you can to the interior of the mold. Make sure your neck on the bubble is skinny enough to fit within the mold.

Get the bubble screamin' hot. Slap it in the mold, clamp it shut and blow hard. Blow until you feel resistance. Blow an' cap a touch-to-alot more. Keep it capped for a few seconds longer. The more pressure you give, the greater detail you'll receive.

Steam should be blasting out of the vent holes. Your assistant should be alerted to all vent holes - so that they're not gonna get accidently burned.

Gloves are good, and can provide adequate protection → so wear 'em!

Your assistant may also initiate a neckline with a pair of jacks while you're in the mold (if so desired).

When you feel the glass has had ample time to fill all the voids and set-up → tap your foot (or shout) to indicate to your assistant to open the clamps and release the mold. You may need to wiggle the pipe a little to get the glass to pop out.

SLAP THE BUBBLE IN THE MOLD...

Flash the glass **IMMEDIATLY** in the glory hole. Take it back to the bench and inspect the glass. If you're lucky, your glass will have even-wall thickness throughout, and crisp detail. Sometimes the distribution of glass may be uneven and you wind up with thin spots or you may actually blow through a spot... please try again.....

If you plan on blowing the mold again - re-soak it in the bucket of water. If not, set it aside to dry and clean up the mess on the floor where you were blowing.

Usually it takes two or three blows to get the hang of any particular mold, and how to shape the bubble and just how hot you need to get it before blowing. So, keep at it!

AND BLOW HARD!

WATCH-OUT FOR VENT HOLES AND ESCAPING STEAM.

FINISHED BLOW.

Auxilary Plaster Mold Blowing Info:

Plaster molds have a finite LIFESPAN~ like most things... They are fragile. Treat them with care. Don't drop them, or they may break. Don't leave 'em in water, or they may break down.

You may get **10** or so good blows before your mold loses definition ~ more or less dependent on how it was made, how much detail there is, and how it is handled and blown. Painting your positive with a face coat or thin slurry of Luminar prior to casting it, may increase the ability of the mold to deal with the extreme temperatures. This may increase it's lifespan.

If your glass sticks, you either have an undercut or a dry spot within the mold. Allow the glass to cool and carefully remove the glass. Either pull it out or chip it free. File down (or carve) the plaster to remove the undercut, or if it has a dry spot ~ soak the mold longer and move it around halfway through the soak to insure all parts get saturated.

If your bubble fails to blow out and fill the mold, you may need to:
1. Drill more vent holes to allow the steam an exit out of the mold
2. Get your glass hotter
3. Stay in the mold longer and/or BLOW HARDER!

It can be really frustrating trying to get all the variables right and manage a successful blow. It's easy to become discouraged an' wanna chuck the whole thing — but **PERSEVERANCE IS THE KEY TO SUCCESS.**

Plaster may stick to your glass too. If this happens frequently — you can use the graphite wash (powdered graphite mixed with denatured alcohol) and paint it in the mold to act as a release. Heavily textured molds can sometimes volunteer-up a chunk of their detail ~ so maybe avoid thin crests and deep caverns in molds which you hope to blow multiple times. Most plaster can be easily washed and scrubbed off your glass after it's been annealed.

Avoid constrictions or places where a bubble will have a hard time trying to fill. Think about how gravity will pull your bubble down. Make it work for you.

The glass artist **JACK WAX** says you CAN blow plaster molds with undercuts. It's a one-shot deal though. You have to preheat your DRY mold in the annealer before you blow it (to prevent thermal shocking your glass). You pull it out - blow it... knock the blowpipe free or cut it off (with a torch and shears) and box the whole kit & caboodle. Once annealed, you can break the plaster away to reveal your masterpiece. Jack has made some pretty sophisticated sculptures via this process. Scope out his artwork.

The sculptural possibilities of the moldblown object are far from being exhausted. Series of pieces may be made highlighting degeneration or some sort of metamorphic change. Or a series based on acknowledging mass production and deviations from the norm. Or the mold blown object may physically be altered with paint or other media to change the overall impact of the piece. Check out the work of **CHARLIE PARRIOTT**. He combines relatively simple looking (hard-to-blow) moldblown forms with paint to create some amazingly beautiful and powerful sculptures.

"FLOWERED SOLDIER" - CHARLES PARRIOTT

POST-GATHERING

Primarily a mold-blowing technique - the post gather can help you gain more glass on the end of your blowpipe without covering over the existing moile. This trick may be necessary to allow you access into tight 2 or 3 part molds with restricted openings. Also, post gathering heats up your parison and makes it more fluid — which may aid in blowing the mold, if not give you an opportunity to pick-up more detail.

Most bubbles which are post-gathered are usually necked beforehand. This eliminates the need to do it later. It also helps keep the moile seperated and insures an easier transfer.

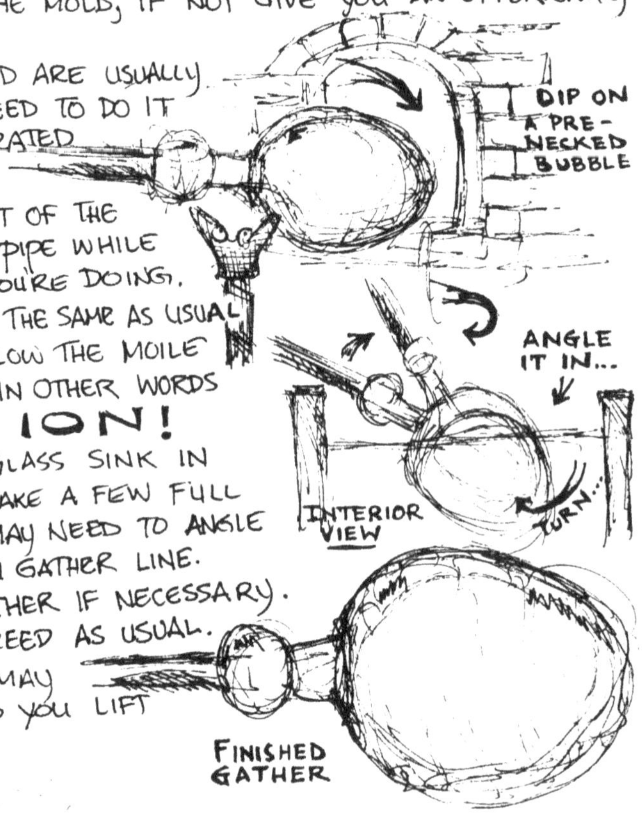

Begin by setting up a yoke in front of the furnace. The yoke can help support your pipe while gathering and allow you to see what you're doing.

Essentially the gathering process is the same as usual except you need to be careful not to allow the moile to go below the surface of the glass. In other words

PAY ATTENTION!

Go slow at first - letting the glass sink in until you reach the level you desire. Make a few full rotations to even out the gather. You may need to angle the pipe up so you wind up with one even gather line.

Exit the furnace, strip the gather if necessary. Chill the pipe - if it needs it and proceed as usual.

For monstrous post-gathers you may need a two-person mobile yoke to help you lift and manuver the pipe around.

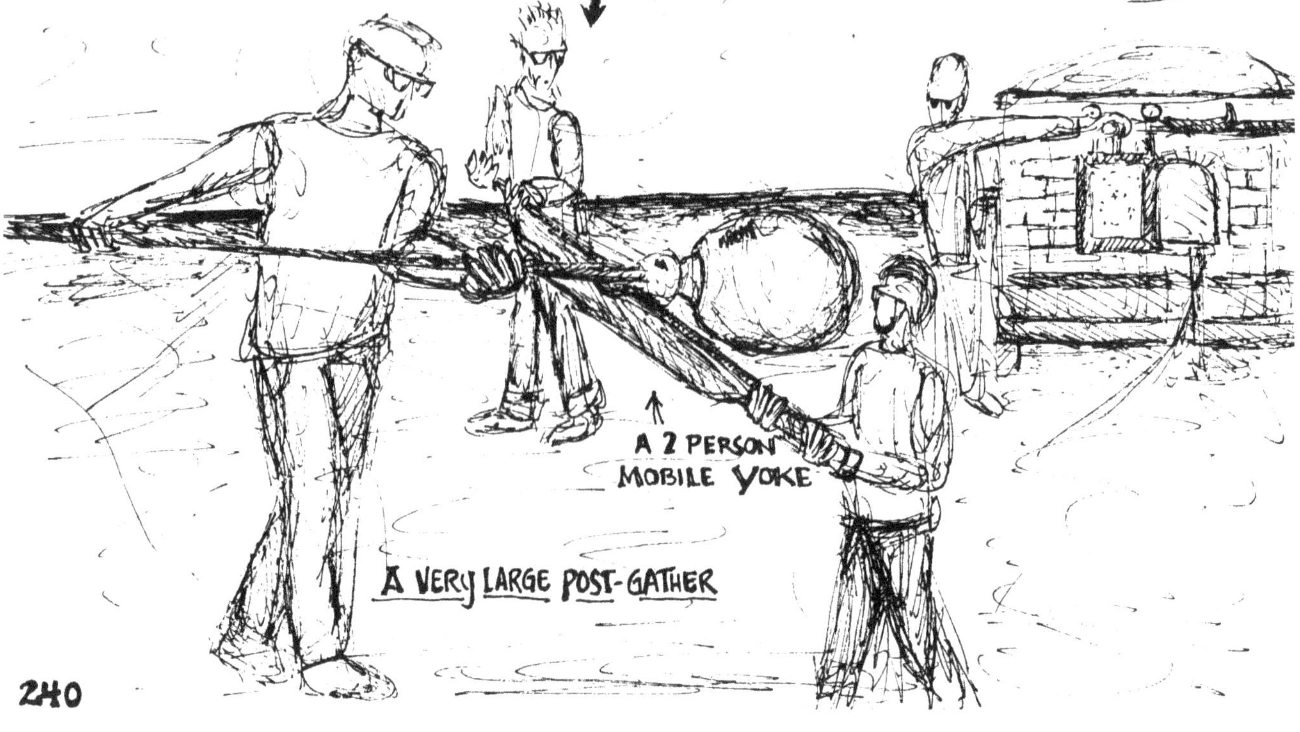

Dip on a pre-necked bubble

Interior view — angle it in... turn...

Finished gather

A 2 person mobile yoke

A very large post-gather

Special Techniques

PAPERWEIGHTS 242
SHIELDING THE GAFFER . . 246
RINGS 248
CREATING HOLES 250
SOLO BLOWING 255
SNORKELING 261
COILS 263
R.I.S.D. RING 264
STEAMSTICK . . . 265
DIP & BLOW . . . 266
FLATTENING 267
ALTERNATE AXES/MONTAGE . 269
SURFACE TECHNIQUES . . 270

PAPERWEIGHTS

In my undergraduate glass courses we were forbidden to utter the "P"-word, much less even consider making one. Paperweights were thought to be the lowest rung on the aesthetic ladder. An easy money maker, no doubt about it; the first step on the "artistic road to ruins" — that of making a quick inexpensive CRAFT object.

I believe my instructor at that time felt that there already were enough paperweights in the world, or this sector of the galaxy, and that our energy was better spent in the pursuit of ART.

Be that as it may, I have since discovered a whole world of incredible glass sculptures within the realm of these small spheres and cubes. Contemporary artists such as Paul Stankard, Daniel and David Salazar, James and Steven Lunberg, Gordon Smith, Barry Sautner — to name a few (and exclude many, my apologies...) have opened-up this century old 'tradition'.

Millefiori weights created during the **Classic Period** ~ ca. 1840-1850's — put paperweights on the map. They became widely produced and widely collected. The glasshouses in France and Southern Germany were the most prolific producers and most skilled. (They set the tone for the next century of glassmakers... yawn... Advances made in glass chemistry and the increase in compatible colors, coupled with a greater demand for paperweights, fueled the fire. Floral designs raged. Inclusions made of lampworked elements and carved/cast sulphides found their way inside of these miniture vitreous worlds.

A CLASSIC WEIGHT

Nowadays virtually any reality may be recreated in a three or four inch diameter weight. All it takes is some special tools, access to glass, a handful of techniques and lots of time (and patience) to practice, perfect, and produce pleasing paperweights.

The **Art of Paperweight Making** could easily be a book by itself. In the interest of making an infinitely long story short, —well, short enough to fit within the confines of the next few pages ~ I'll illustrate some basic paperweight-making concepts. Maybe it'll be enough to whet your appetite. Should you try it and (sorta) like it, but find that you're having a tough time making things "work right" — I suggest doing some research. First, find some artists whose work you like. Check for books, catalogs and assorted galleries. Then, find out if they teach workshops/classes anywhere, or if they have a studio where you might visit, or lo n' behold — be of need of any assistants. Seek these people out. They can probably tell you or show you (if they're willing...), in ten minutes what might take you ten hours, days, or even years to learn. The workshop/class gig is really beneficial in that you gain hands-on experience with little-to-no obligation (except the class fee!). Some artists are more private than others, and may be reluctant to unveil any 'secrets' in which case you may have to learn the old fashion way ~ Trial and Error!

BASIC PAPERWEIGHT: INTRODUCTORY UNIT — #1. FOR ALL AGES

① GATHER. Roll it in frit. Color(s) of your choice. This is the backround, or base color.

② REHEAT. MELT-IN COLOR. BLOCK ROUND AND CHILL.

③ GATHER AGAIN. PICK-UP 2ND COLOR(S). FEEL FREE TO MANIPULATE THE COLOR WITH THE TWEEZERS. REPEAT STEP ②. FOR INTERESTING AIR TRAPS, POKE A HOLE (OR FOUR) WITH AN ICE PICK OR AWL. CHILL.

④ GATHER TRAP AIR YOU POKED. NECKLINE. OCCASIONALLY. AGAIN. THIS SHOULD BUBBLES IN THE HOLE(S) BLOCK ROUND. JACK-IN ALLOW TO COOL, FLASH BOX IT!

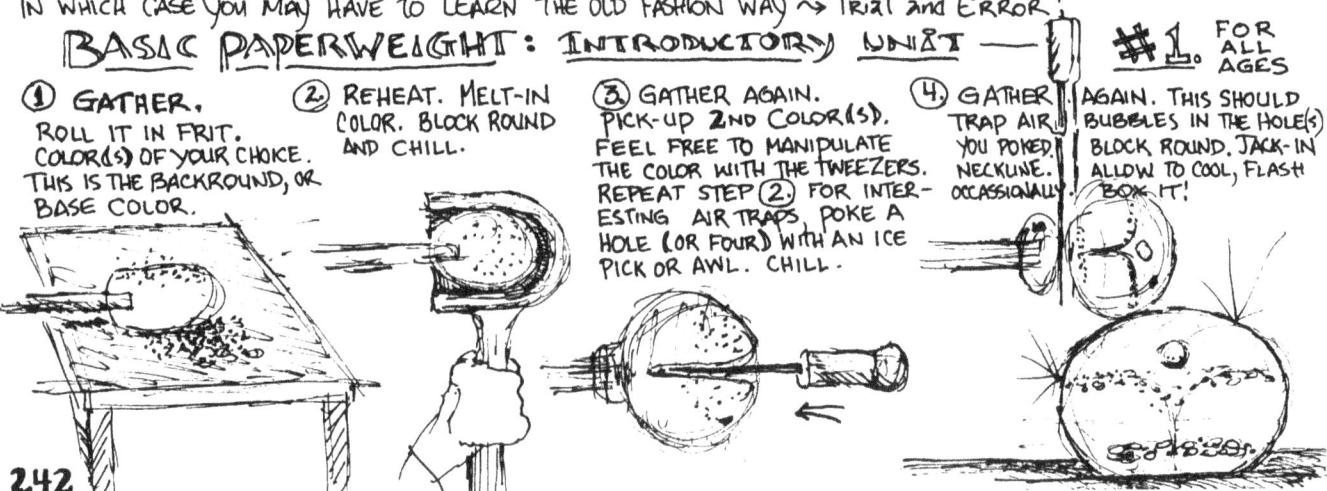

242

There are limitless options available for you at every stage of the paper-weight making process. For instance, you can layer each gather with seperate or matching colors using frit, powder, rod, shards, stringers, cane etc. Or you may selectively decorate any gather, anywhere, at any time for drammatically different results. Or you can skip using color all-together and just trap air bubbles. Check-out the chapter on color for additional ideas and methods in applying color.

If you'd like to make more 3-dimensional style weights, you can do so with some lampworking and or some creative bit work:

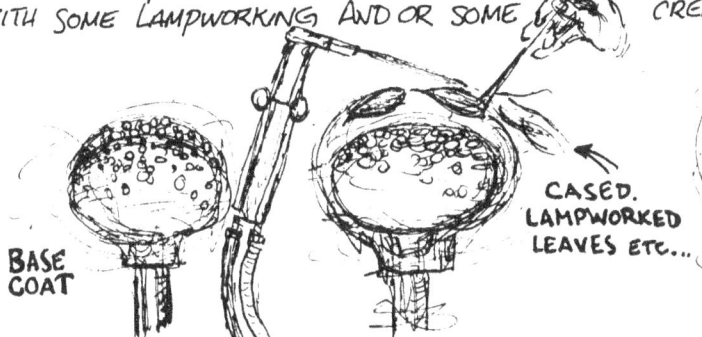

BASE COAT — CASED. LAMPWORKED LEAVES ETC... — CASE WITH CLEAR. — KEEP ON ADDING MORE.

You can build-up your subject matter literally bit-by-bit. Let's say you like flowers. And you want to simulate some botanical situation in glass.

Begin with a gather on a punty. Pick-up or apply some kind of backround or base color. Something down to earth. Case it. Block it.

Now, you're ready to add some leaves. These can be torched-on sections of cane or murrine which are pre-heated and tweezed-on. Or you can just trail-on bits of color directly to the surface of the glass.

Next, you can case each leaf or section of leaves with a small hot gather of clear. Then continue to add another bunch of leaves, another blob of clear. Building up the form as you go. Feel free to add some colorful insects along the way! Finally, add the petals of the flower and any interior designs you desire. Case the whole shebang in clear. Block it. Neck it. Allow it to cool, and box it.

FINISHED WEIGHT.

If you'd rather not do any coldworking you can always flip the piece over and torch n' smooth the punty (with a small graphite paddle) just prior to boxing it.

TAKE HEED: There are a whole host of variables which you undoubtedly will run into. (These include: color compatibility, reducing colors- and those which seem to burn-up mysteriously, colors that react with other colors, colors which run or 'bleed' and those which are as stiff as all-get-out. Well... The **List** just goes on and on... practice! Take a class! Practice some more!

It's vital that your color design looks good before you take that last gather, 'cause it's there to stay and you can't change nuthin' once it has been cased. Casing it in crystal will MAGNIFY all of your detail. Make sure it looks good. Great. FANTASTIC!

Be certain your piece is cold (enough) before loading it into the annealer. Do your best to set it on it's foot or unsightly annealer face (or "facet indicators) may develop. On that note — don't allow the weights to bonk into each other while loading/unloading the box. Otherwise you might get those little white permanent specs or impact marks (a.k.a. facet indicators) on the surface of the glass.

Coldworking? BAH HUMBUG! Torch that punty, anneal it, sign it, box it up & ship it out!

If you want to make round weights, use round blocks. If you have the oval or bullet-shaped blocks → you're gonna have a more challenging time trying to make round things with it. Buy the right blocks and save yourself some frustration. None available? Make your own or trade with a local woodworker. Paperweight blocks can be easily lathe-turned from cherry wood. Green (or wet) wood works best. Make a block for each size gather. Be sure to burn it in well before you start making "keepers".

VACUUM-FORMING

is for the artist determined to make high-quality, extremely detailed, bubble-free paperweights. Most often these weights are typified by lampworked imagery which is cased - under vacuum - with a compatible crystal. The vacuum sucks out all the air (hopefully) and fills any gaps with glass. The results, if done well, can be sheer visual poetry.

Vacuum-forming does however require special equipment. First you need a vacuum pump (although some strong shop-vac's are capable of creating enough vacuum - if you do some creative plumbing). You also need a vacuum plate and collar, both which are designed and made as a set for this process. These parts come in a variety of sizes and shapes to suit everyones needs.

A VACUUM PLATE — A COLLAR

To begin, make sure your whole space is set-up with all the tools you need, and that your assistant knows what is required of her or him.

Place your subject matter in the center of the vacuum plate. A backround of frit &/or powders may be set beneath the subject to provide a visual base - if so desired, just make sure NOT to plug up any of the holes in the vacuum plate. You can also add the base later.

The subject matter can be almost anything. It can be a bunch of lampworked elements attached together. It might be some solid-off-hand sculpture or even a blank painted with paradise paints or some other type of enamel. Hell, it could even be something kiln cast or slumped - or even a heavily coldworked sculpture. Whatever!

A collar is slipped over the plate, fitting snugly within its groove. The whole shebang is carefully preheated with a burner or torch. The heating must be done gently enough so as not to disturb the (often fragile) contents inside - as well as not to cause them to crack, slump or fall apart.

At the same time the subject is being preheated, you or your assistant should be preparing the glass for casing. This may be several gathers out of the furnace or a pre-heated billet made out a compatible glass pick-ed-up outta the annealer (See- you don't even need a furnace to do this!). The main thing to be concerned with is that the temperature, size and shape of the glass is "right". It should be round, on-center, screamin' hot and slightly larger in diameter than the collar.

When the gather is ready and the subject is pre-heated enough - carefully set the gather directly over the subject. Once the glass begins to flow, and as soon as full contact is made with the walls and mouth of the collar, the vacuum is turned on.

THE SUBJECT: SCHEPPS RACING TEAM 9 — TORCH INSIDE TOO!

The glass gets sucked down and settles around the subject. The punty follows the path of the glass down, but care must be given to maintain it's safe distance from the subject. In other words, don't jam your punty down in there too far! Allow the glass to set-up and shut the vacuum off.

Once the glass is set-up – pull the cylindrical blob out and reheat.

The next step is to shape and add the base glass. While the subject half is kept warm, the bottom half can be prepared. It can be as simple as a couple gathers worth of crystal, or as complicated as vacuum-forming another whole unit. In most situations the bottom section is somewhat smaller than the top, but that, too, is up to you to determine. It should be presented to the gaffer nice n' hot. It gets dropped on from above. The excess is cut off with the diamond shears.

The whole weight gets reheated and blocked/shaped to remove any signs of a seam. The foot may be paddled in – if so desired, and then made ready to punty. A standard issue punty should be sufficient.

The piece is transferred as normal. Afterwards, it may be necessary to pick and clean-up the top of the weight to remove any excess or unwanted glass.

Finally the paperweight is heated and shaped into its final form. You may use a block or newspaper – whatever, to get it looking the way you want it for all eternity. Box it when ready.

Remember to adjust your annealing schedules so that the weights get the soak and ramping they require to actually anneal them (and not make 'time-bombs' of self-induced stress).

NOTE: If you choose to use **LEAD CRYSTAL** for your paperweight making, be aware that it can develop a scum on the surface of your glass if your glory hole's combustion is anything more than neutral. Reduction bad! Lead crystal also behaves quite a bit differently than most types of furnace glass. It seems to stay soft for tremendously long working periods, consequently it takes some time getting used to. However, it is the most optically clear of all glasses and offers superior brilliance in cut and polished surfaces and facets. It may be something worth trying out → once you've gained the skills in making decent weights.

Feel fREE to redefine the notion of the paperweight. The parameters of traditional paperweights can be rather confining and restrictive. Tear down the walls! Establish a new set of rules. Be innovative. On that note, remember: Not all paperweights are round (another funny thing ⇒ so few paperweights are ever used to hold down papers!)! Cubes and pyramids and asymetrical weights are becoming more widely produced and collected.

Which brings up another point, **COLDWORKING**. Cutting, grinding and polishing, engraving and sandblasting can save if not totally **SELL** your weight. Consider it when designing and making your pieces. Integrate it to accentuate it's overall presentation.

ADD THE BOTTOM

SHAPE IT.

PUNTY.

BLOCK IT ROUND...

FINISHED WEIGHT

SHIELDING THE GAFFER

THE TRADITIONAL WAY TO LEARN THE ART OF GLASSBLOWING WAS TO APPRENTICE TO A MASTER, IF YOU WERE FORTUNATE ENOUGH TO "GET-IN". YOU WERE TOLD TO WATCH, LISTEN AND LEARN ~ AND THEN MAYBE YOU WERE SHOWN HOW TO CLOSE A MOLD OR EVEN HOW TO MAKE A PUNTY. GLASS EDUCATION HAS CHANGED A GREAT DEAL SINCE THEN. STILL, ONE OF THE EASIEST WAYS OF LEARNING IN ANY HOT SHOP IS BY ASSISTING THE GAFFER. BE IT OPENING DOORS ON THE GLORY HOLE OR SHIELDING THE GAFFER FROM UNPLEASANT HEAT EXPOSURE, YOU CAN PICK UP ALOT BY JUST HELPING OUT.

GATHERING, PAPERING, BLOCKING, NECKING, TWEEZING, TRIMMING, TORCHING, AND EVEN REHEATING ARE ACTIVITIES WHICH HAVE THEIR OWN DEGREE OF POTENTIAL BURN-FACTOR. IT IS YOUR JOB AS A DEDICATED ASSISTANT TO ANTICIPATE, REACT AND PROTECT THE GAFFER FROM GETTING HOT.

THE WHOLE CONCEPT IN A NUTSHELL: DEFLECT HEAT FROM THE SOURCE GETTING TO THE GAFFER. DO THIS WITHOUT OBSTRUCTING THEIR MOVEMENTS OR VISION.

< OPEN FOR ENTRY
< CLOSE WHILE GATHERING >
< RE-OPEN FOR EXIT

GATHERING

HOW YOU ACHIEVE THIS IS STILL UP TO YOU (SEE HINTS BELOW). YOU SHOULD CHOOSE THE METHOD IN WHICH YOU GET FRIED THE LEAST. REMEMBER, COMMONSENSE TELLS US: **DON'T INJURE YOURSELF WHILE PROTECTING THE GAFFER.** (even though there's probably alotta gaffers out there that may disagree with that theory...).

BE CREATIVE. GET INVENTIVE. DEVISE A PADDLE, SHIELD OR METHOD OF PROTECTION WHICH WORKS FOR ALL PARTIES INVOLVED. REMEMBER TO COMMUNICATE! ANNOUNCE CLEARLY, IF YOU'RE THE GAFFER, WHAT TYPE OF PROTECTION YOU NEED — AND WHERE OR HOW IT SHOULD BE GIVEN.

SIDE VIEW

GENERALLY, WHEN WORKING ON SMALL PIECES, LITTLE OR NO PROTECTION IS REQUIRED. THEY DON'T RADIATE ANYWHERE NEAR THE AMOUNT OF HEAT THAT LARGE PIECES DO, AND PADDLES CAN GET IN THE WAY OF DELICATE PROCEDURES WHICH MUST BE MADE WITH SWIFT COMPLICATED MOTIONS.

(SIMULATED COMPUTER-GENERATED DRAWING)

BLOCKING

DURING GATHERS, CLOSE DOWN THE DOOR WHILE THE GAFFER'S TURNING THE PIPE IN THE FURNACE. WATCH THEIR HANDS. AS SOON AS THEY REACH FOR THE PIPE TO PULL IT OUT OF THE FURNACE, OPEN THE DOOR TO LET THEM OUT (SEE ABOVE). THIS HELPS CUT DOWN THE AMOUNT OF KNUCKLE HAIR THE GAFFER CAN LOSE DURING GATHERING. IT IS ESPECIALLY HELPFUL ON THE LARGER GATHERS!

FOR BLOCKING AND NECKING ACTIVITIES, YOU CAN SHIELD THE GAFFER'S HAND WITH A LARGE WOODEN PADDLE. YOU MAY GENTLY REST THE PADDLE ON THE EDGE OF THE NEWSPAPER OR BLOCK, COMPLETELY BLOCKING ANY HEAT RADIATING FOR THE GLASS BEING SHAPED. STATION YOURSELF BEHIND THE BENCH OR AT THE SIDE. DO YOUR BEST TO FOLLOW THE GAFFER'S MOTIONS. STAY AWAKE! THEY MAY MAKE SUDDEN, POSSIBLY UNEXPECTED, MANUVERS WHICH REQUIRE RAPID RESPONSES AND CHANGES IN POSITION. FOR SMALLER PIECES YOU MAY POSITION THE PADDLE HORIZONTALLY — SO THE GAFFER CAN EASILY SEE THE SHAPING OF THE BUBBLE. ON LARGER PIECES, YOU'LL WANT THE PADDLE IN AN UPRIGHT POSITION. THIS OFFERS SOME PROTECTION TO THE GAFFER'S BICEP AND SHOULDER AREA → A SPOT WHICH CAN GET VERY HOT VERY QUICK IF LEFT UNATTENDED.

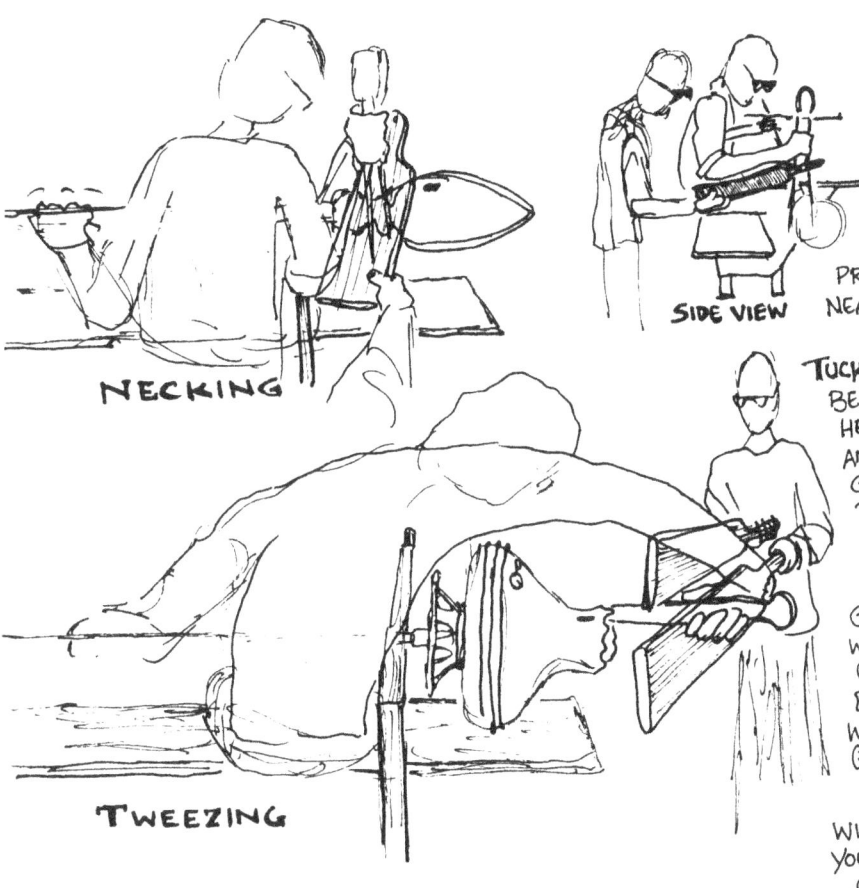

NECKING

TWEEZING

TRIMMING

NECKING—IN TRANSFER LINES AND SUCH IS A CHALLENGING PROCESS IN AND OF ITSELF. WHEN WORKING ON LARGE VESSELS AND THE LIKE, IT CAN BE DOWNRIGHT **PUNISHING!**

SIDE VIEW

THE UNDERSIDE OF THE HAND AND WRIST CAN SIZZLE FROM THE HEAT OF THE GLASS. AN EFFECTIVE WAY TO PROTECT THE HAND IS TO COME FROM UNDERNEATH WITH A PADDLE AND BLOCK THE HEAT.

WORK FROM BEHIND THE BENCH. **TUCK** THE HANDLE END OF THE PADDLE RIGHT BENEATH THE GAFFER'S PINKY FINGER. THIS HELPS SHIELD THE WHOLE ARM AND HAND AND ALLOWS THE GAFFER TO SEE WHAT'S GOING ON. AGAIN, BE SURE TO TRACK THE GAFFER'S MOVEMENTS AS BEST AS YOU CAN.

WHEN **TWEEZING** THE GLASS, YOU CAN GUARD THE GAFFER'S PRECIOUS DIGITS WITH A PAIR OF PADDLES WORKING TOGETHER ON THE TOP AND BOTTOM OF THEIR TWEEZERS. SMALL, LIGHTER-WEIGHT PADDLES WORK BETTER HERE — ALLOWING YOU QUICKER RESPONSE TIME.

TRY YOUR BEST NOT TO INTERFERE WITH THE GAFFER'S MOVEMENTS. CHANGE YOUR ANGLE IF THINGS AREN'T WORKING OR YOU KEEP OBSTRUCTING THE GAFFER'S VIEW. IN THIS CASE, YOU'LL BE WORKING IN FRONT OF THE BENCH FOR EASY ACCESS.

TRIMMING, AS YOU KNOW, CAN BE RATHER BRUTAL. THE THUMB IS ESPECIALLY VULNERABLE TO THE HEAT.

AGAIN, FROM IN FRONT OF THE BENCH, COME FROM UNDERNEATH AND SLIP A PADDLE IN BETWEEN THE GAFFER'S THUMB AND THE PIECE. YOU MAY HAVE TO GET DOWN KINDA LOW—IN A CROUCHED POSITION FOR THIS — AND CAREFULLY MAINTAIN YOUR PROTECTION WITHOUT RUNNING INTO THINGS. HAVE A PAIR OF TWEEZERS HANDY TO DEFLECT THE TRIMMING WASTE AWAY FROM THE PIECE. DO NOT PULL ON THE CUTTINGS OR THE GAFFER MAY KILL YOU (OR WANT TO...).

EACH STUDIO AND GAFFER WILL HAVE THEIR OWN SITUATIONS WHERE ADDITIONAL PROTECTION IS NEEDED. THERE SHOULD ALWAYS BE AN ABUNDANT SUPPLY OF PADDLES IN VARIOUS SIZES AND THICKNESSES. THERE'S NO EXCUSE NOT TO HAVE A PADDLE HANDY WHEN YOU NEED ONE.

AGAIN, COMMUNICATE YOUR IDEAS AND INTENTIONS. DON'T AUTOMATICALLY ASSUME THAT THE GAFFER DOES OR DOES NOT NEED ANY SHIELDING — ASK FIRST! EVERY GLASSBLOWER HAS THEIR OWN THRESHOLD OF PAIN AND TOLERANCE FOR HEAT. SOME GAFFERS CAN GET ANNOYED BY "INVADERS INTO THEIR SPACE" — AND PREFER BURNING OVER 'INTRUSIONS'.

FOR ADDITIONAL SHIELDING PRACTICES, PLEASE REFER TO THE TEAMWORK CHAPTER 2 PAGES 59-82...

RINGS

Making rings out of glass is not too difficult of an affair. Making them with even-thickness and perfectly round is another matter. There are a few different methods for making rings — each dependent on the size of ring desired.

Rings have graced glass objects for centuries. They have been used as accents for vessels (on handles), linked-together to form chain, and as stems for goblets and such. If you find a need, or desire, to try and wing the ring thing → here's a tip or two: If you need only **1 or 2** rings → make **3 or 4** beforehand. That way you can select the best-looking ones to put on your piece and still have an extra one or two for back-up. Also, put the rings on last — if they're to be accents for handles. You don't want to have them flopping all over the place any more than necessary.

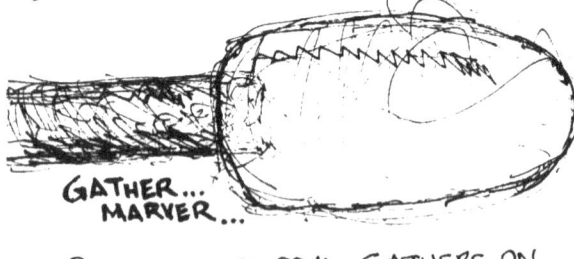

GATHER... MARVER... STRETCH... LOOP.

Begin with several gathers on a medium-to-large punty. Marver the glass into a cylinder. Reheat.

Use the diamond shears to crimp a knob on the end of the glass.

Begin to stretch the glass into an uniform length and thickness — you may have to switch axis to balance the weight out and distribute the glass evenly — similar to setting-up to pull cane (page 169).

Once you have a desired thickness and length, wrap the glass around the bottom of an optic mold or section of pipe. The **optic mold** works nice because it's slightly tapered and 'releases' easily.

Try to make an even connection where the two parts meet. Cut the punty free with the diamond shears. Marver the remaining glass on the punty back up on it, or cut the excess off and marver it smooth. Punty-up the ring on the opposite side of the cut to fire polish the joint/union in the glory hole.

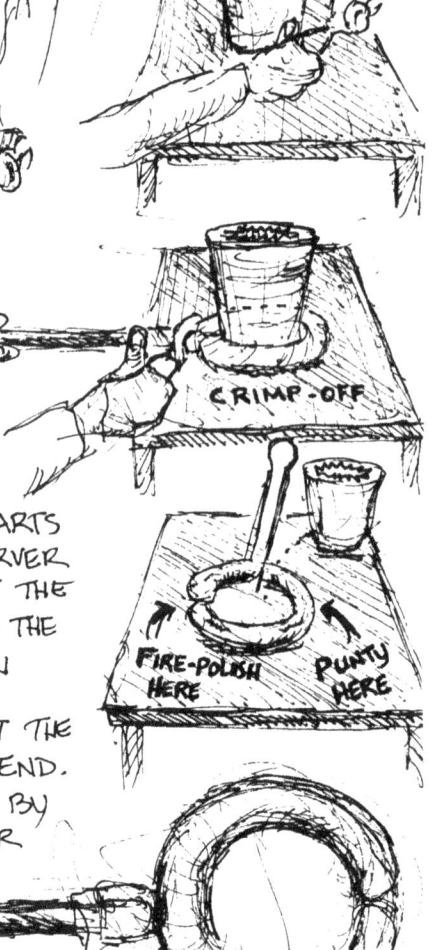

If you have an unsightly amount of excess glass at the joint, you might tweeze it off, and re-fire polish the end. In all likelihood you may have to smooth-out the ring by reaming it gently with the tweezers, graphite rod, or large dowel rod. Then you can garage the ring or simply box it as a finished unit.

Of course, if you want an optic style ring - you can stuff the blob of glass prior to the pull. You can also twist the optic during the stretch to enhance the pattern.

SMALLER RINGS MAY BE MADE IN A SIMILAR FASHION TO THE LARGE ONES - ONLY THIS TIME YOU'LL BE WRAPPING THE GLASS AROUND A PIECE OF COPPER TUBING INSTEAD OF THE OPTIC MOLD.

BEGIN WITH A GATHER OR TWO OF GLASS. MARVER IT INTO A CYLINDER. AGAIN, GRASP A KNOB ON THE END AND STRETCH THE GLASS INTO YOUR DESIRED THICKNESS. NOW YOU'RE READY TO WRAP THE GLASS AROUND THE TUBING.

YOU CAN USE VIRTUALLY ANY DIAMETER OF **COPPER TUBING** (OR IF YOU'RE IN A PINCH - A CHARRED WOODEN DOWEL MAY BE SUBSTITUTED - OR POSSIBLY A GRAPHITE ROD). TRY TO HAVE A LENGTH AT LEAST 12" to 18" LONG. WRAP A PIECE OF DUCT TAPE AROUND ONE END TO INDICATE A HANDLE AREA - YOU DON'T WANT TO BE PICKING UP A "HOT" END ACCIDENTLY.

YOUR ASSISTANT CAN HELP BY PREHEATING THE END (BY THE GLORY HOLE DOOR) FOR A FEW SECONDS. A BIT OF BEESWAX CAN HELP ACT AS A RELEASE FOR YOUR RING, SO HAVE 'EM LUBE IT UP A BIT PRIOR TO WRAPPING.

ALLOW YOUR GLASS TO SAG INTO A BIG "U"-SHAPE AS YOU BRING IT UNDERNEATH THE END OF THE TUBE. WRAP THE GLASS TIGHT AROUND THE CIRCUMFERENCE OF THE TUBE, MEETING TOGETHER AT THE TOP. USE THE DIAMOND SHEARS TO CUT THE PUNTY AND EXCESS FREE. YOUR ASSISTANT CAN JUST HANG OUT WHILE YOU HEAT AND MARVER THE PUNTY SMOOTH. THEN, REATTACH THE PUNTY OPPOSITE OF THE CUT AND SLIP IT OFF THE END OF THE TUBE.

REHEAT JUST THE END TO FIRE POLISH THE CUT AND EITHER BOX THE RINGS OR GARAGE IT, OR USE IT IMMEDIATLY. YOU MAY NEED TO REAM IT A BIT ROUNDER IF NECESSARY PRIOR TO BOXING IT. USE YOUR TWEEZERS TO DO SO.

THE RINGS CAN BE MADE WITH ANY THICKNESS, STYLE OF OPTIC PATTERN, COLOR, OR COMBINATION THAT YOU CAN THINK OF.

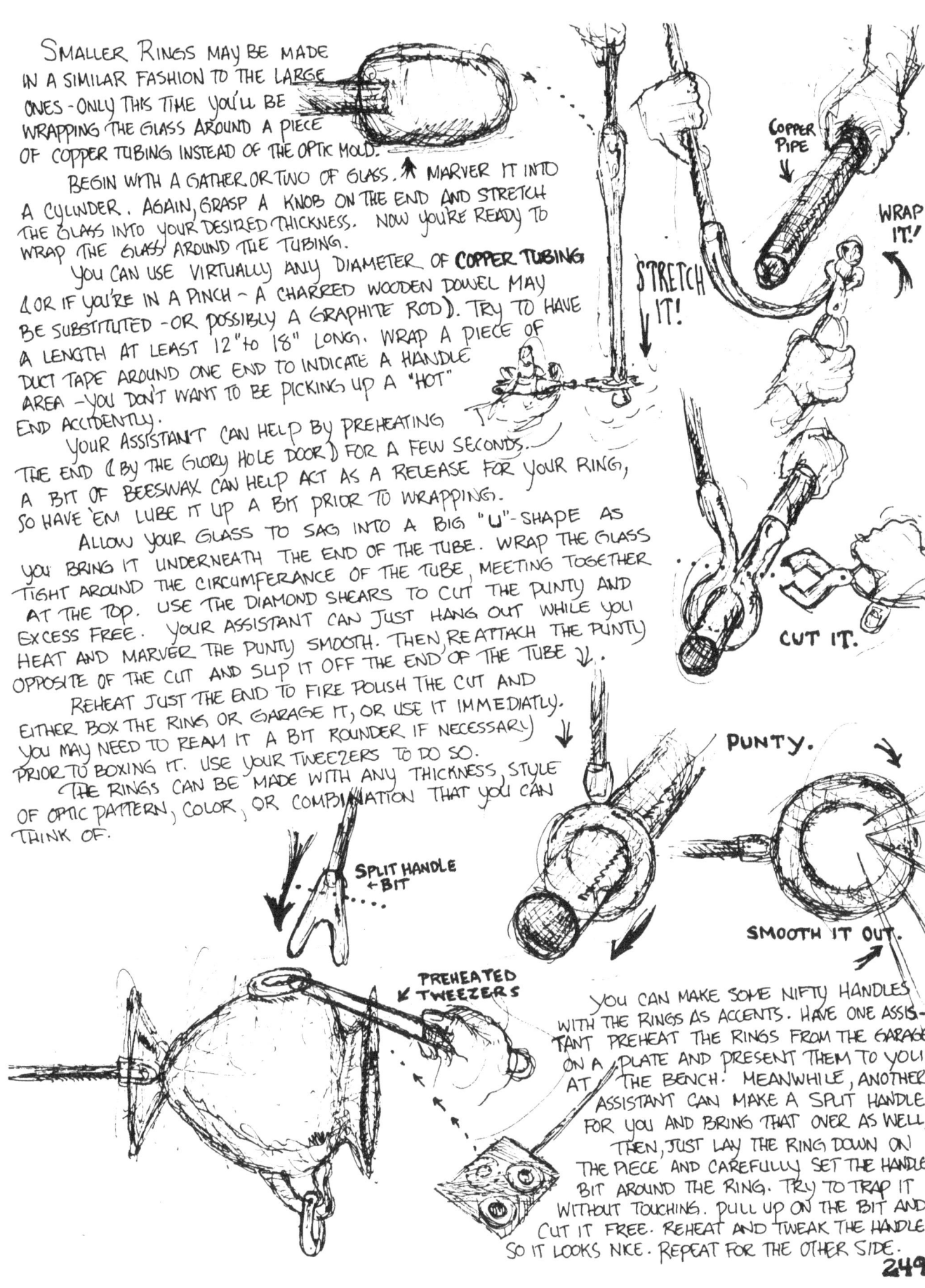

YOU CAN MAKE SOME NIFTY HANDLES WITH THE RINGS AS ACCENTS. HAVE ONE ASSISTANT PREHEAT THE RINGS FROM THE GARAGE ON A PLATE AND PRESENT THEM TO YOU AT THE BENCH. MEANWHILE, ANOTHER ASSISTANT CAN MAKE A SPLIT HANDLE FOR YOU AND BRING THAT OVER AS WELL.

THEN, JUST LAY THE RING DOWN ON THE PIECE AND CAREFULLY SET THE HANDLE BIT AROUND THE RING. TRY TO TRAP IT WITHOUT TOUCHING. PULL UP ON THE BIT AND CUT IT FREE. REHEAT AND TWEAK THE HANDLE SO IT LOOKS NICE. REPEAT FOR THE OTHER SIDE.

CREATING HOLES — VIA HOT TECHNIQUES

The first thing to consider when trying to make holes in blown or possibly solid glass, after why, is HOW. There are several different methods at your disposal. Each technique yields its own 'personality' and likelihood for success.

POKING, TORCHING, BLOWING and **DRILLING** are the methods most commonly used by glassworkers to make holes today. The next question(s) you need to answer is → "How far do I need to go?" → Does the hole go through one side? Both sides? Is it an **IN-NY** or an **OUT-TY**? How big does it need to be? By answering these questions first (via your drawings), you may help determine which route you should take.

POKING A HOLE can be pretty much like it sounds. You may use tweezers, an ice pick, scratch awl, the pointed end of a file, or a piece of metal rod to poke with. Make sure it's clean first, or you may get some unwanted "CRAPOLA" stuck to your glass.

MAKE A BUBBLE

LET IT SAG...

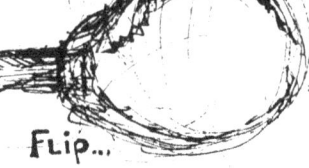

FLIP...

AND POKE...

REAM

Get your bubble blown somewhat thin. Have it nice n' floppy hot. Sitting at the bench, visualize where you want your hole to be. Stop the blowpipe's rotation with your target point facing upwards. This will cause your bubble to fall off-center. Allow it to sag further, then flip the pipe & bubble 180°. Allow it to sag back on-center → This time holding the tweezers right where you want your hole to be.

Have your assistant cap the pipe if you don't want your bubble to get totally distorted or collapse.

If the bubble's too cold, you'll barely make a dent. If the bubble is too hot, you may end up pushing a tube/hole all the way through to the other side!

Reheat if necessary. Ream the potential hole by twisting your poking tool inside the cavity. Then dribble some drops of water to chill and quench the hole. You can try reaming it further or tapping the hole through with a couple of jabs with your poking tool.

FINISHED HOLE:

The biggest drawback to this method is you may end up with a few chunks of broken glass inside your piece.

With a few reheats, particularly if you try to concentrate the heat on the hole, you may be able to fire polish out the jagged edges. NOTE → Once you get all the way through to the inside, you will no longer be able to blow the

PIECE — UNLESS YOU FIND A WAY TO PLUG UP THE HOLE (IN SOME CASES YOU CAN BLOW & OR CAP A SOFFIETTA INTO SUCH AN OPENING). SO, IN OTHER WORDS, MAKE SURE YOUR PIECE IS AS CLOSE TO IT'S FINAL FORM AS YOU CAN GET IT BEFORE YOU BREAK ON THROUGH TO THE OTHER SIDE.

IF YOU HAVE A TORCH CAPABLE OF DELIVERING A PIN-POINT FLAME, YOU CAN ACCELERATE THE PROCESS BY PREHEATING THE AREA WHERE YOU WANT YOUR HOLE TO BE. MORE ON THAT IN A LITTLE BIT...

NOW, IF YOU'D LIKE TO MAKE YOUR HOLE GO ALL THE WAY THROUGH BOTH SIDES OF YOUR OBJECT, THE PROCESS IS PRETTY MUCH THE SAME, EXCEPT THAT YOU NEED TO POKE YOUR HOLE ON BOTH SIDES OF THE OBJECT TO MEET IN THE MIDDLE.

IT HELPS TO FLATTEN THE FORM A LITTLE BEFORE YOU DO THE POKING TREATMENT. THIS WAY YOUR TOOL DOESN'T HAVE AS GREAT A DISTANCE TO TRAVEL AND YOUR FORM IS NOT SUBJECTED TO MASSIVE DISTORTION — SEE BELOW. ONCE YOUR HOLE GOES THROUGH, YOU CAN ALWAYS REINFLATE THE FORM LATER.

THE TRICK HERE IS TO GET BOTH POINTS TO MEET AT THE SAME PLACE. THE SECOND PART OF THE TRICK IS DRIPPING SOME WATER IN THE HOLE TO ACCELERATE THE CHILLING PROCESS AND TAPPING THROUGH. SINCE JABBING THE POINTS OF YOUR TWEEZERS INTO COLD GLASS IS A TOOL UNFRIENDLY PROCESS (YOU'LL DULL THE TIPS) — YOU MIGHT USE A DIFFERENT TOOL FOR BREAKING THE HOLE THROUGH. YOU ONLY NEED A FEW DROPS OF WATER THERE. ALLOW IT TO SIZZLE IN THE HOLE A LITTLE BIT BEFORE TRYING TO BREAK THROUGH. DON'T USE TOO MUCH WATER OR YOU MAY THERMAL SHOCK YOUR PIECE AND END UP WITH A HOLE MUCH LARGER THAN YOU ANTICIPATED — OR A PILE OF BROKEN GLASS ON THE FLOOR.

ONCE YOUR HOLE GOES THROUGH YOU CAN SUCCESSIVELY REHEAT AND REAM IT LARGER (IF DESIRED) WITH THE TWEEZERS. THIS CAN HELP SMOOTH-OUT THE ROUGH SPOTS. YOU CAN ALSO RE-INFLATE YOUR FORM TO WHATEVER SIZE YOU DESIRE, AND FINISH THE PIECE THE WAY YOU LIKE IT.

POKING A HOLE THROUGH A BUBBLE:

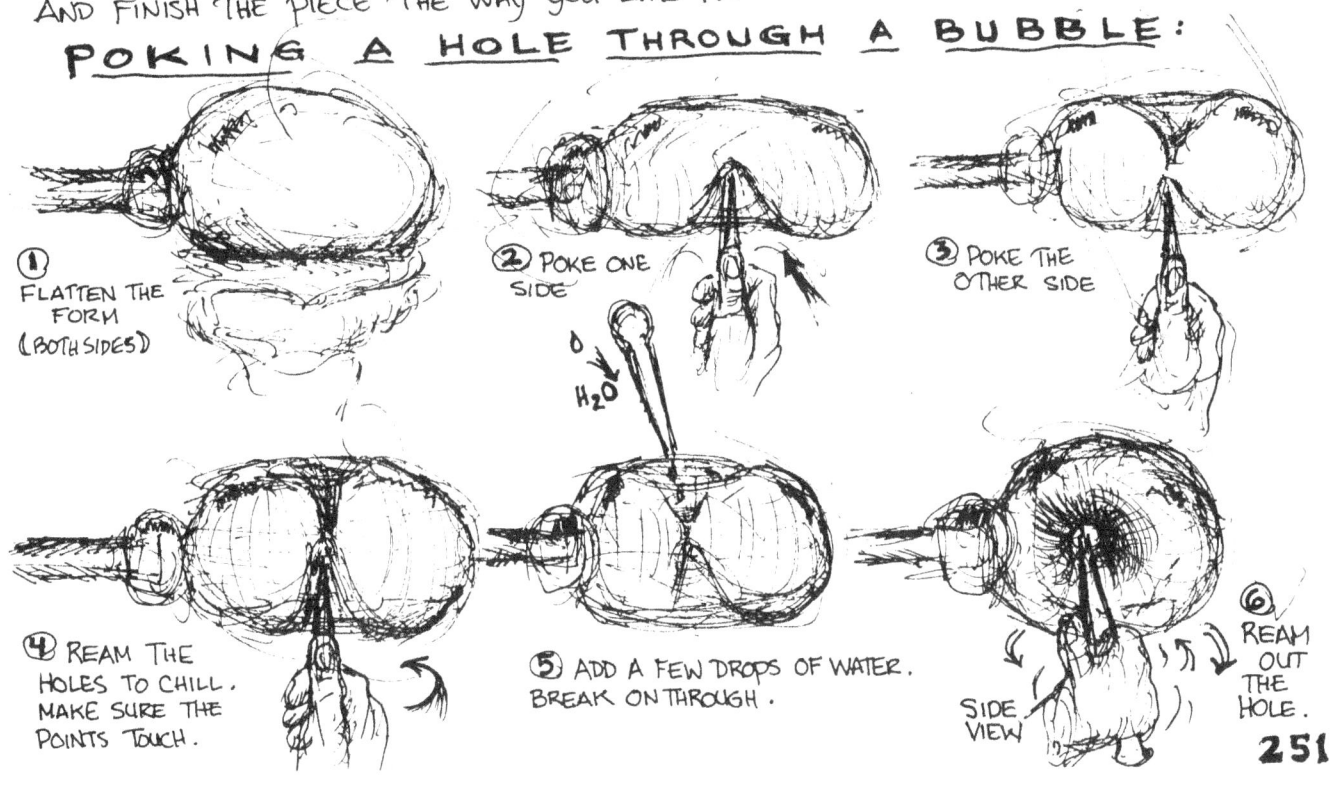

① FLATTEN THE FORM (BOTH SIDES)

② POKE ONE SIDE

③ POKE THE OTHER SIDE

④ REAM THE HOLES TO CHILL. MAKE SURE THE POINTS TOUCH.

⑤ ADD A FEW DROPS OF WATER. BREAK ON THROUGH.

⑥ REAM OUT THE HOLE. SIDE VIEW

Another method utilizes a hot bit to accelerate your poking potential. It definately helps to have your piece blown semi-thin (in order for the heat from the bit to penetrate the wall-thickness). Allow your piece to get stone cold. Apply a screaming hot bit → straight from the furnace with little or no marvering → right where you want your hole to be. Let the bit set up a touch and cut it free. Use your diamond shears. Allow the bit to "soak in" somewhat before proceeding. You may even take a flash while waiting. Be sure to blast that spot by the burner, if you do so. It will increase your heat potential.

You can, at this point, either ream through to the other side - as described on the previous two pages - (and shown on the right →) or blow the bit out by puffing and capping the pipe with a good hard blast from your lungs. Keep your thumb on the pipe and allow the heat from the bit and air pressure to do the work.

Keep your eye on that spot! Once you see a bulge beginning to appear, get ready to pull your thumb off. If you let it keep going, it's possible that the bit will blow completely out - showering you (and the studio) with hazardous glass cellophane. The hole then may be much larger and 'uglier' than you planned.

The glass will be much thinner at that spot. It's just a matter of pulling a point, with the tweezers or a punteto, - 'necking' a knob with the diamond shears (fig ④) and tapping that knob off to open up the hole. You may need to add a couple drops of water on that knob to ice it down enough so that it breaks free.

You can then flash and fire polish the hole. You might also want to ream the hole open further with your tweezers.

If you'd like a larger hole, use a bigger bit of glass. You can make spouts for vessels in a similar fashion. You just need to draw the bit-blob out further. Have your assistant blow softly while you gently pull the bit out to elongate it.

Tap the knob off to open the hole and Voila! - a spout!

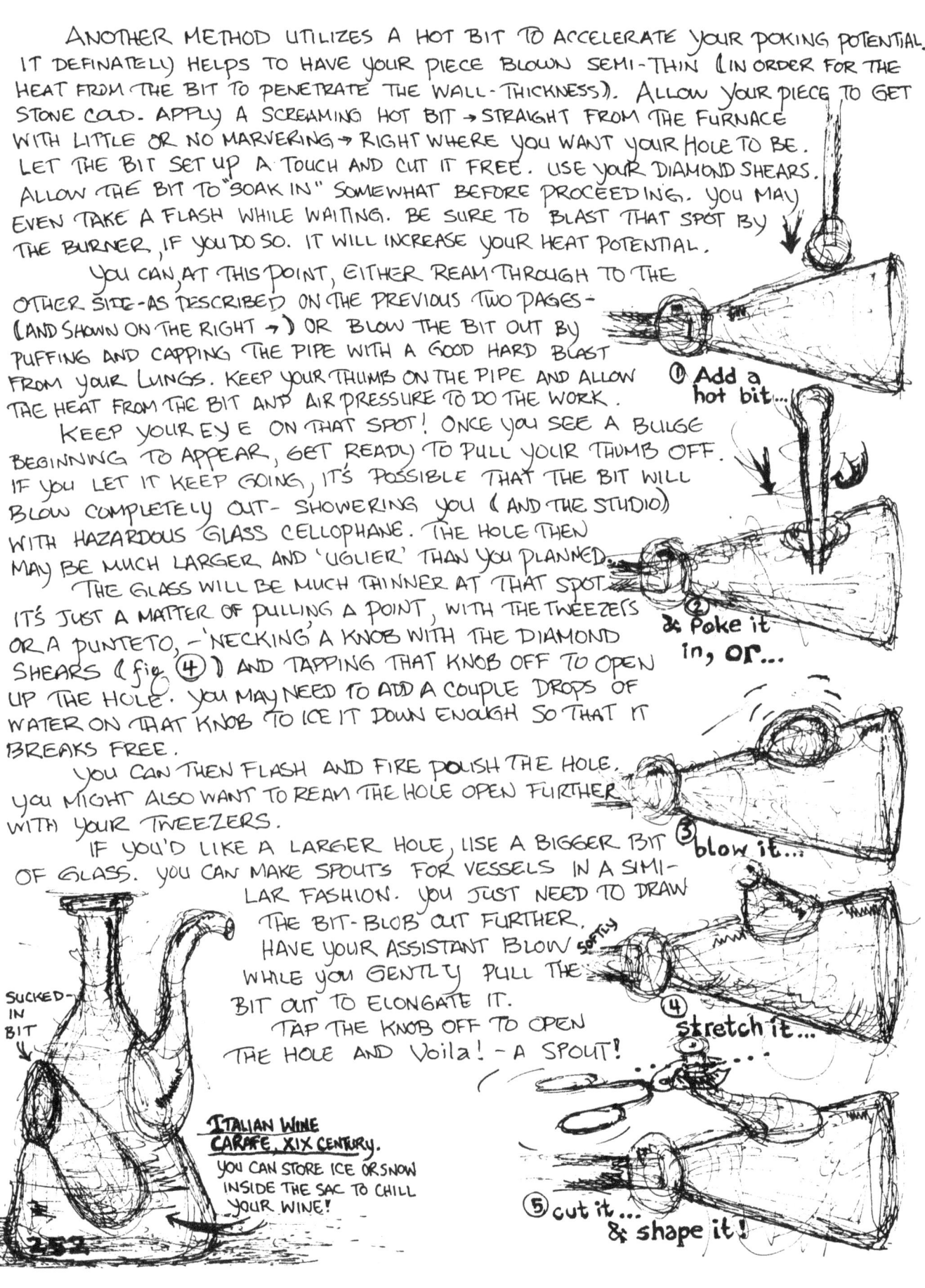

① Add a hot bit...
② & Poke it in, or...
③ blow it...
④ stretch it...
⑤ cut it... & shape it!

SUCKED-IN BIT

ITALIAN WINE CARAFE, XIX CENTURY. You can store ice or snow inside the sac to chill your wine!

You can use a torch to help you put holes in your pieces. An oxy-pro or oxy-acetylene set-up will get you there faster than the hand-held plumbers torch, **plus** offer you pin-point accuracy. Please see "Tips on Torching" (pages 76-78) for additional information concerning the safe operation of these devices.

Simply select a spot in your bubble (or anywhere on the object) where you want your hole to be. Blast that spot with the torch. The wider your flame, the larger area you'll be heating up, and possibly the larger your hole can be.

The intensity of the flame is contingent upon the style of torch you're using. If your flame is white hot you may blister or burn your glass — so watch out! If you just get the area orange-to-red hot, it should be plastic enough to either blow a hole out or ream a hole in. Of course, it is dependent upon how thick and hot your glass is. The thicker and colder it is, the longer you'll have to heat it to get it to do what you want it to do. Sometimes you may have to reheat and retorch that spot several times to get through.

Once you succeed in getting through, you can spot-heat and fire-polish the hole to make it nice and clean looking. You can also ream the hole larger by further heating and twisting your tweezers inside.

BE CAREFUL WHEN REHEATING! Holes have a tendency to widen and grow larger, as if they have a will of their own.

If you're interested in creating small holes in your glass you can try the **TUNGSTEN-STEEL WIRE TRICK**. Take a piece of tungsten wire (thin rod) [available from welders supply] and mount it in a wooden dowel/handle. Your glass piece needs to be hot — but not moving. There should be a 'skin' on the outside and the interior should be still plastic. Now preheat the tungsten wire.* It's very important that you get the heat right. The wire should be **GLOWING RED**. Do not get it white hot → it will stick to your glass! Begin rotating the wire as you push it in where you want the hole to be. If you don't rotate the wire, it will stick too! It's the heat of the wire which melts the glass. Once you succeed in getting through you can continue to ream it a little wider (if desired) and withdraw the wire — Ta Da!

TORCH...

AND REAM!

USING TUNGSTEN WIRE TO REAM A HOLE...

TWIST IT!

* Use a torch to do this. Your assistant can help you out with this part.

The final method by which you can make holes is by drilling them. **Yup! DRILLING!** Use a ½" paddle drill bit (or so → it can be larger or smaller depending on your preference) — the style bit used to drill holes in wood. Cordless drills work well for this process.

First, flatten your piece as much as you can. You can do this process to both blown and solid work. If it's a blown piece you're trying to drill through — be sure to cap the pipe while drilling or your bubble can (and will!) collapse. Next, get your glass as hot as you can. Slap it on a cheap piece of wood (one which you wouldn't mind a few holes in). Have your assistant standing by armed with the drill. As soon as the piece is laid down, they should drill through — **FAST AND WITH CONVICTION** — where indicated. Once the bit breaks through to the other side, remove it and reheat the glass. You can then drill more holes if desired, or just fire-polish or ream further the hole you created. **NOTE:** This method can produce fragments and chips of possibly unwanted glass. Be aware! Also, the hotter the glass is, the better and easier it is to drill.

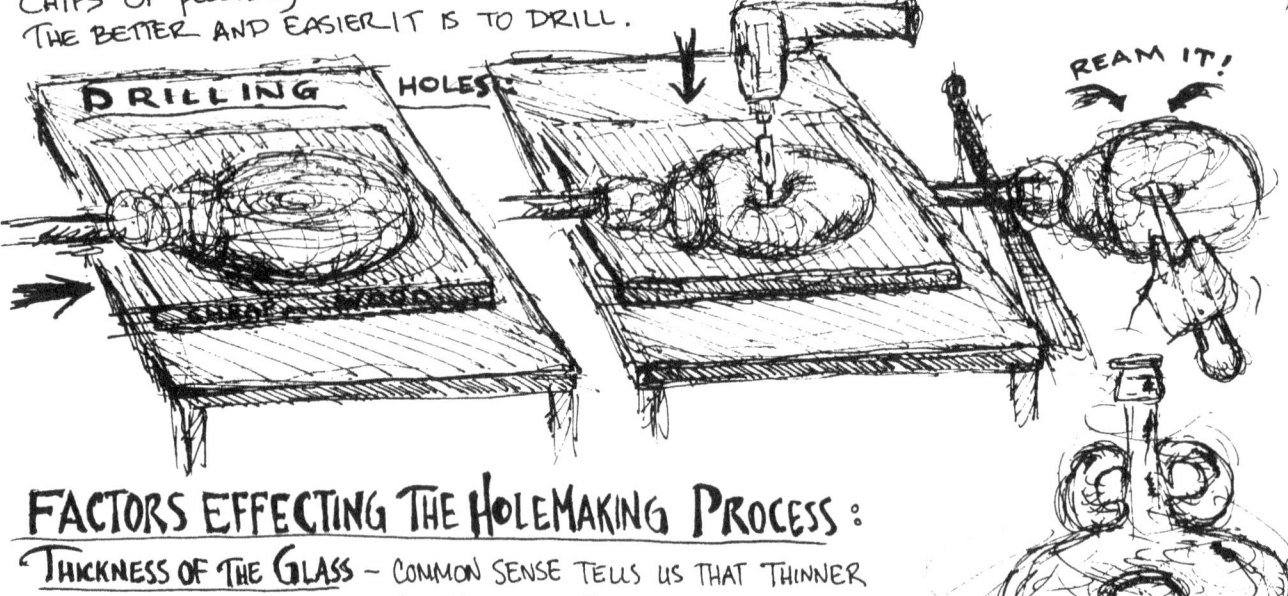

Holy Homebrew Bottle by the Author

Factors Effecting The Holemaking Process:

Thickness of the Glass — Common sense tells us that thinner glass is much easier to make holes in than thicker glass. You simply have less material to try and penetrate. The downside (to the thin stuff) is that it cools more rapidly than the thicker pieces — so move faster!

Temperature — That ol' saying, "Hot good, cold bad" holds especially true here. It takes much less effort to get through glass when it's smokin' hot than when it's barely warm. You do, however, run the risk of distorting your form fairly radically when pushing it to the edge, but you can do your best to compensate for it after you get your hole(s) in.

Size of the Piece — Small pieces can be somewhat tricky to get nice clean holes in, but they won't cook your hands quite as much as large pieces will. The physics change a little when working larger (e.g. more effort to turn the pipe) — but the holes seem to be easier to deal with.

Tools and Experience — Having the right kind of torch can be a real asset. Coupled with skilled hands — holemaking can be done with accuracy and predictable results. So, if one route doesn't quite cut the mustard for you, go ahead and try another. And of course practice, practice, **PRACTICE!**

SOLO BLOWING

One of the hardest ways to learn and blow glass is to lock the doors to the studio and work by yourself. Yet there are people who insist on blowing solo, or they have little or no choice in the matter. Whatever the case may be, there are a few things to keep in mind when you're going to be working alone: **#1. GET SET-UP 'RIGHT' IN THE FIRST PLACE** and **#2. KNOW WHERE EVERYTHING IS.** It is akin to the Boy Scout motto → "BE PREPARED!". **#3. DON'T BITE OFF MORE THAN YOU CAN CHEW** or in other words, ease into those complicated techniques. Build up your skills to match your designs, otherwise you may end-up just frustrating yourself. **#4.** As with all types of glassworking → **KNOW (BEFOREHAND) WHAT YOU'RE GOING TO MAKE.** We will cover all of these and more in this section. Read on...

The **MAIN KEY** to success in blowing solo is getting yourself set-up right to begin with. Every tool and piece of equipment should be situated and ready-to-go BEFORE you get started. You'll save yourself time and energy not having to fumble around for things — 'cause there's a good chance that nobody will be around to help you.

Even though I spent my first several years in glassworking blowing primarily by myself → learning the hard way (through countless floor models) → I don't recommend it. For one, it's much more difficult. And two, it's not as much fun. Also, solo blowing is potentially dangerous. I once received a very serious cut while blowing alone late at night, and fortunately a person happened to be nearby, answered my cry for help and took me to the hospital (thanks Mary Fox!). You never know what can happen. It's not too different from skin/scuba diving and sensible swimming → practice the buddy system! It works.

Nevertheless — many glassblowers, for whatever their reasons, do blow solo and enjoy it very much. They prefer it that way. Some are very good at it as well. Imagine making a dragon-stemmed goblet → all by yourself. The N.Y. based artist **BILL GUDENRATH** proves that it's possible.

THE SET-UP: If the conditions in your studio allow it, move the pipe buckets within an arm's reach of the bench and/or glory hole. This way you needn't move too far to trash a pipe or punty after you're done with it. Also, you can easily grab a 'clean' one and "put-it-up" to preheat without any extra running around. Efficiency of movement is vital.

Having some method of keeping your piece in stasis while you gather a punty, handle or some other type of bit can be a big help. For many years the hanging yoke was my only assistant. I would 'park' the pipe there making sure the piece wasn't too hot (or else it would be subjected to unwanted stretching) — run — gather n' blow a foot — attempt to reheat both of them without getting them stuck together (or to the side of the glory hole!) and attach them without losing the piece.

Some artists skilled in equipment building have invented clever devices enabling them to blow solo easier. One such unit is the **HANGING YOKE GARAGE.** Here, a top-loading annealer has an access port in the top of it and a pipe may be set inside and 'held' at annealing temperature indefinitely. It works great for small-to-medium sized pieces.

A CONVERTED TOP-LOADER

KERKVLIET MFG. CO.

REMOVABLE TONGUE-SHAPED BRICK (FOR WHEN NOT IN USE)

THE HANGING YOKE

255

The California based artist SONNY CRESSWELL has devised a slightly different way to park his pieces. He has an automated horizontal yoke which turns his pieces at a pre-set speed. A seperate burner mounted on the end of the unit keeps the piece warm while he gathers the next bit. He can also increase the rotation in order to thread-on colors in a machine-like fashion. I have also seen similar motorized turning mechanisms mounted on pipe-warmers in order to maintain lip wraps and punties (and the like) warm and on-center. Depending on your skills, you might also find or create similar devices which can help you become a better-equipped solo blower. Plus, you can always swear or yell at the equipment 'til you're blue-in-the-face when things go wrong — and their feelings won't be too hurt... I guess......

AUTOMATED YOKE / PIECE WARMER

Anyways, the MAIN THING is being prepared for the whole solo experience. This means anticipating your every move → from the first dip to boxing the piece. That's why having a drawing of WHAT you're going to make helps BIG TIME! You can then see if you'll need additional punties up for bits, wraps, handles etc. Plus you can plan the sequence of events so you avoid floundering and always know what's coming up next.

YOUR EQUIPMENT SHOULD FUNCTION AND BE CONTROLLED EASILY WITH ONE HAND. This allows your other hand to turn the pipe while you do other things. The furnace door should be easy to open and close with one hand. Place a yoke or similar tool near the furnace so you can free-up one hand to do that. Your glory hole doors must open easily. They, too, should be able to open and close without fumbling around for a door hanger or whatever.

Many shops have incorporated pneumatic door systems which open and close with a press of the foot! Oftentimes, I'll just leave the door open during certain maneuvers so I don't waste precious seconds trying to gain access. I'll gladly sacrifice a little heat for the sake of a piece! (And peace of mind.)

Your annealer should also be easy to access. Have a break-off table adjacent to the box so you can tap your piece off in it and glove it into the annealer.

Make sure your tools are set out where you can find them at a glance. Have your newspaper made and ready before you start because, in all likelihood, you'll not have any time to do it later!

THE SOLO GLASSBLOWER'S STUDIO

Most of the techniques used in team blowing will carry over into the solo blowing realm. There are a few exceptions where you have to play gaffer and assistant all at the same time. Most notably when it comes time to do the punty and/or adding bits or additional elements, things can get a bit "sticky".

GATHERING single handed takes practice. Use the sill on the furnace or place a yoke in front of the door to have something stationary to roll against while taking a gather. Keep both eyes on what you're doing and your third eye watching what's happening in your other hand. (Just a glance back n' forth will do).

If you're in a hurry to make a punty or something don't worry about closing the door - take care of it later! Go ahead and deal with the matter at hand.

When your gathers become excessively large on either pipe, you'll need to find a way to 'park' the extra pipe to free up your other hand. You can allow the piece to get stone cold and just leave it at the end of the bench. Usually, you'll get some sag in the piece → which can easily be corrected with a good solid reheat. The hanging yoke is a slight improvement over this → your piece will likely stretch → hanging in the vertical position - but at least it will be on-center!

GATHERING A BIT... (SINGLEHANDED)

BLOCKING and **PAPERING** are pretty much the same activities as in teamwork blowing. The only difference is that you don't have anyone helping you turn the pipe or shielding you from the heat. When I'm blowing large pieces solo - I usually wear long-sleeved shirts to protect me from the excessive heat. I also use really wide sections of newspaper to shape the glass with. The extra bit of newspaper shields my wrist from the heat. I like to use really large jacks for necking procedures - which helps keep me away from the heat.

MARVERING bits and punties with one hand can be fairly challenging. You just have to learn to find the balancing point in the pipe and turn from there. In addition, you need to allow the glass to roll under it's own weight while you marver.

MARVERING... (SINGLEHANDED)

Attempting to force the glass to do something inevitably leads to lop-sided pieces - which in turn usually takes both hands to correct. Air marvering is very effective in solo blowing. It's a great way to shape your glass without sucking out the heat.

BLOWING or inflating your bubble can be accomplished with an optional device called a **BLOW HOSE**. Extensively used in the neon and scientific glass industries - the blow hose enables a person to blow without the need of an assistant. It frees up your hands so you can manipulate the bubble while you simultaneously inflate it.

It requires a bit of juggling to manuver the hose on and off → and keep it out of the way of your hot blowpipe, so practice a few dry runs first to become familiar with it. Loop the hose around your neck. Keep the mouthpiece handy and accessible. A swivel mounted on the other end allows the pipe to be rotated without bunching-up the hose into a horrible knot. The rubber

Cone-shaped fitting slips over the mouthpiece on the blowpipe — enabling you to blow whenever you need air. In time, with practice, you can become quite accustomed to using the blowhose. You will find you have even more control over how your bubble inflates than you could ever get in team blowing.

Need to 'cap' the pipe? Just stick your tongue over the mouthpiece!

The blowhose is indispensible in making witches balls (a.k.a Christmas ornaments) and other thin delicate pieces — by yourself. The main thing is to keep a close eye on your work as you inflate it!

USING A BLOWHOSE.

The **TRANSFER** can be done in two different ways. One way is to hang the pipe up (or leave it on the bench) while you gather and shape your punty. And the other way is to keep the piece in your one hand while gathering the punty with the other. There are advantages (and disadvantages, of course!) to both. If you hang the piece up or leave it on the bench, it's likely that your piece may sag or stretch if it's the least bit hot. However, you do have both hands free to deal with making your punty, and it is possible to correct the sagging or stretching (up to a point) once you've got your piece puntied-up. On the otherhand you can eliminate unwanted elongation or off-centerness by gathering the punty with one hand while keeping the pipe turning in the other. It's a little awkward juggling the pipes around (and potentially dangerous) and a bit of a challenge making the perfect punty, but it can be done. Use the method you're most comfortable with, or the one which is most appropriate for the style of work you are making.

THE TRANSFER

FOR HEAVY PIECES, USE A BUCKET OF SAND

Watch those shirt tails if you're leaning over the punty to get water to break-off with. They have a nasty habit of catching on fire! It's best to place a small bucket of water within easy reach for puntying purposes. Also, if you find your piece is too heavy and wants to fall on the floor instead of staying put on the bench, you can counterweight the handle end with a bucket of sand or similar object.

One way to **PULL CANE SOLO** is to lock or jam the punty into a position where it won't move when you start the draw. The closer you can get to the floor, the less distance the cane can drop, droop and/or crash. All you need to do is get your blob or cylinder of color hot — set the punty in the "V" (or crotch) of the bench — wedge it inside some cinder blocks — whatever ~ grab your diamond shears and pull away! Of course you might not be able to get as long of pulls as you would with an assistant, but it is at least one way to pull it off by yourself.

SOLO CANE PULLING

You can pick-up the cane out of the optic mold (as described on page 171) or out of an annealing oven or pick-up kiln (page 114). So, complex cane-worked pieces are possible with a little bit of experimenting and creative problem solving.

You can also use your Kugler oven or an extra annealer as an electric garage (sounds like a '60's band → the Electric Garage!?). You can park bowls and feet, and/or stems in the box & hold them at annealing temperature, while you work on other parts. When it comes time to pick-up a part, ramp the kiln up an extra 50°-100° F for a minute or five, to give it a extra bit of heat, and prevent it from cracking. You can gather up or apply a hot bit of glass to 'glue' the pieces together and pick them up right out of the kiln. After flashing the piece, you may have a second or two to reset the elements straight, and on-center, before proceeding to the next step. Oh, and don't forget to ramp the kiln back down to annealing temperature or you might slump whatever else is in the kiln!

SOLO AVOLIO

Adding Bits, trails, decoration or avolios may be something you're interested in. If you are planning on using color you might premake some bits and set them in the pipe warmer to keep them warm. Then, when you want to add the color, you simply heat the bit up in the glory hole - flash the main piece briefly, and sit back down at the bench and apply the color. If you tuck the punty under your arm, you can help stabilize it enough to become pretty accurate with how the color gets put on. Avolio's can be applied in a similar fashion. You might place a pipe bucket behind the bench so you have a place to trash the punty when you get done with it.

Another way to apply bits and blobs is in a vertical fashion - using gravity (your friend) to your advantage. You can lean the pipe against the bench, but it has a tendency to slide around. One way to stabilize your pipe is to set it in a piece of **PVC** tubing (or similar section of pipe) clamped to the side of the bench. Another device - the flag pole holder (available from hardware stores) can be fastened to the arm of the bench and your pipe can be easily snapped into place. This will then allow you to have both hands free to add bits, drop color on, or even blown stems!

Of course, blowing 3-to-5 part **Goblets** solo borders on the insane - or might fall under the "biting-off-more-than-you-can-chew" category. It looks and sounds alot easier than it actually is. If you enjoy self-inflicted pain, then by all means → go for it!

ADDING A BLOWN ELEMENT.

A flag-pole clip holder or section of **PVC** may help stabilize your pipe while adding bits.

Should you be interested in putting on some **HANDLES** by yourself, (why not, the sky's the limit) you may do so. It just takes impeccable timing and a good understanding of how your glass behaves.

Usually you get your piece nearly, if not totally, **COMPLETED** before you add the handle(s). Allow the piece to set-up and become stone cold. Hang the piece up after a quick flash or just lay it on the bench while you gather up your handle. If it's a particularly large handle, such as might be found on a pitcher — you'll need to do the one-handed reheat/flash while maintaining the gathers for the handle in the other hand.

ADD THE BIT...

Set the piece on the bench snug-up against the rail-stop so the friction braces the pipe there without rolling away. Apply the freshly marvered bit as you would for most handles — the exception being that you're working on the outside of the bench.

AVOID drawing out the bit to it's full length. If you do, the bit may continue to stretch on you or it may slump over and attach itself where you don't want it.

CUT & FLIP 180°

HEAT WITH CARE!

Once you cut the bit free, it is likely that the piece will rotate 180° with the gravitational force and the weight of the bit pulling it down. This is why you want a short squat bit.

Trash the punty and head for a quick flash/reheat. Keep your eye on the handle-bit at all times. Control the handle's elongation by rotating the piece very slowly or by flipping the piece back and forth while in the glory hole. Or, if you don't want the bit to stretch at all — hold the punty stationary while reheating, with the bit pointing up (image above).

DRAW IT OUT & ATTACH.

Return to the bench, have a seat, grab your diamond shears, draw and cut your handle to your desired length and attach it where you want it. Take another quick reheat and adjust (if necessary) the handle so it looks and works good.

All of this takes split-second timing, adequate preparation, total concentration and a fair amount of P-R-A-C-T-I-C-E! No doubt you'll lose some work in the process of LEARNING... but that comes with the territory.

Solo Blowing is...

A. Highly challenging
B. Very frustrating (potentially)
C. Incredibly rewarding (with a modest degree of satisfaction)
D. All of the above
E. Other: _____

SNORKELING

A GREAT WAY TO CLOG YOUR PIPES!

Well, you don't have to fly to Hawaii, the Great Barrier Reef or even the Grand Caymens to enjoy 'snorkeling'. You can try this technique in the privacy of your own hot shop. This might go down as 'Cool Trick 66' because it's pretty impressive the first time you see it being done. I have no idea who first came up with this bizzare method. It kinda goes against what you know and have learned about glassblowing, but I saw an italian master teaching at Pilchuck do it, so perhaps it's an italian invention.

In any case - the idea here is to make a tube out of a colored bubble and suck hot glass up inside the tube. You then end-up with a very hot weenie of glass which then may be ① pulled into cane ② sculpted into another form ③ shaped whatever way you like ④ or puddled into an uncontrollable mess on the floor.

METHOD #1:

Begin by getting some color in a bubble on your blowpipe. This may be some color rod on a collar, an overlay of color(s) on a clear or colored starter bubble, some frit or powder on the outside ~ whatever works with your aesthetic.

Then blow and marver the bubble into an uniform tube/cylinder shape — making sure that interior bubble reaches all the way down to the very end.

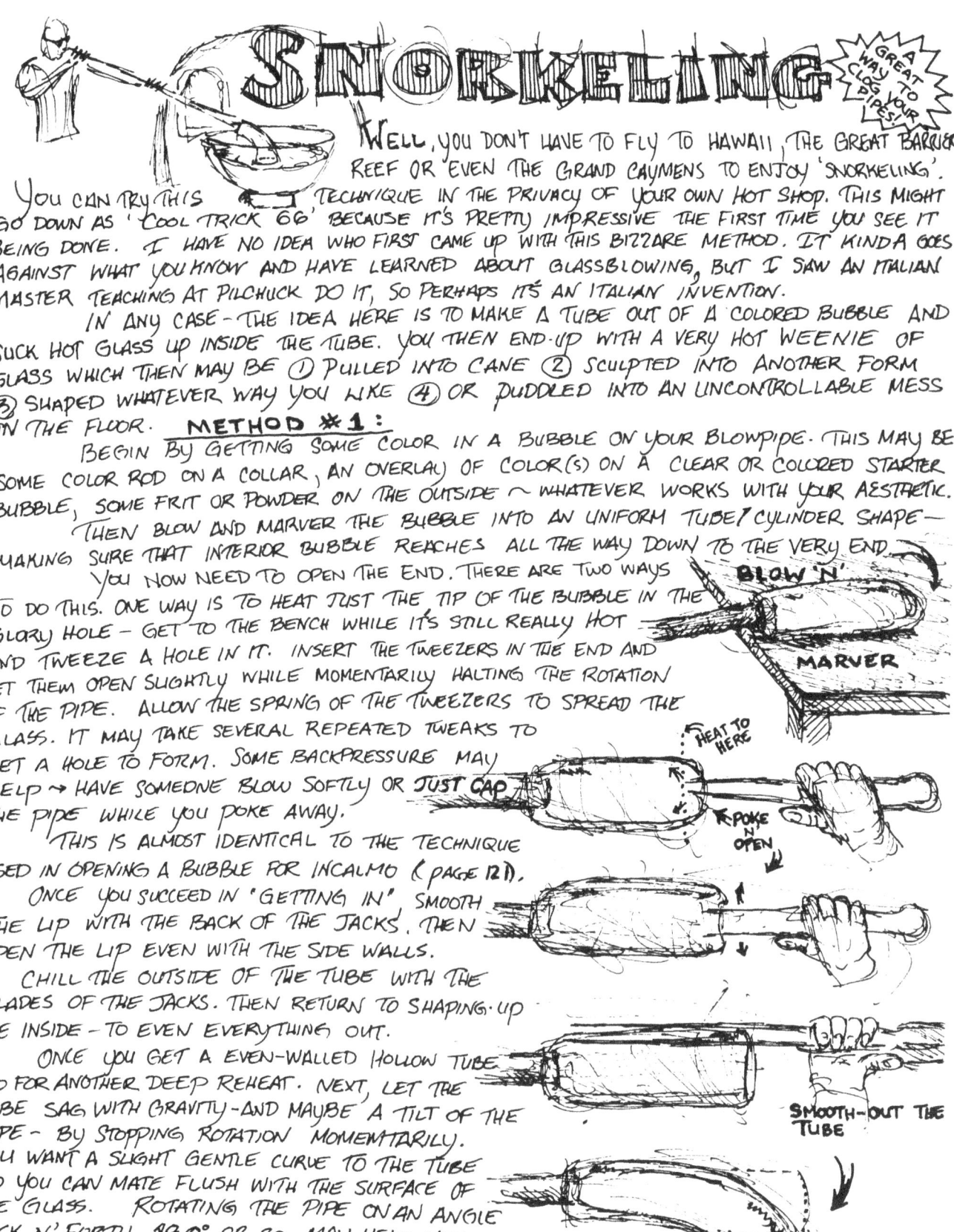

BLOW 'N' MARVER

You now need to open the end. There are two ways to do this. One way is to heat just the tip of the bubble in the glory hole - get to the bench while it's still really hot and tweeze a hole in it. Insert the tweezers in the end and let them open slightly while momentarily halting the rotation of the pipe. Allow the spring of the tweezers to spread the glass. It may take several repeated tweaks to get a hole to form. Some backpressure may help ~ have someone blow softly or JUST CAP the pipe while you poke away.

HEAT TO HERE

POKE 'N' OPEN

This is almost identical to the technique used in opening a bubble for incalmo (page 121).

Once you succeed in 'getting in', smooth the lip with the back of the jacks. Then open the lip even with the side walls.

Chill the outside of the tube with the blades of the jacks. Then return to shaping-up the inside - to even everything out.

Once you get a even-walled hollow tube go for another deep reheat. Next, let the tube sag with gravity-and maybe a tilt of the pipe - by stopping rotation momentarily. You want a slight gentle curve to the tube so you can mate flush with the surface of the glass. Rotating the pipe on an angle back n' forth 180° or so may help you achieve the form.

SMOOTH-OUT THE TUBE

ALLOW IT TO SAG. THEN COOL...

As soon you as you have the correct curve, allow your glass to get stone cold.

261

NOW, FOR THE FUN PART: OPEN THE DOOR TO THE FURNACE AND SET THE BLOWPIPE ON THE SILL. HAVE THE CURVE POINTING DOWN AND SLIDE THE PIPE IN FURTHER. ENTER AT A HIGH ENOUGH ANGLE TO MATCH THE LIP OF THE TUBE TO THE SURFACE OF THE HOT GLASS. ALLOW THE LIP TO TOUCH AND SLIGHTLY SUBMERGE INTO THE GLASS. THEN GIVE A QUICK SUCK ON THE BLOWPIPE TO DRAW THE GLASS INTO THE TUBE → LIKE YOU WERE ENJOYING A MILKSHAKE THROUGH A STRAW. ☠ CAUTION: YOU MUST MAKE FULL CONTACT WITH THE LIP AND SURFACE OF THE GLASS! ☠ OTHERWISE, IF YOU HAVE A "LEAK" - YOU MAY GET A LUNGFULL OF HOT AND DEADLY AIR. IF YOU FEEL NO RESISTANCE WHEN YOU'RE SUCKING-IN, **STOP IMMEDIATLY** AND EITHER PLUNGE THE PIPE DEEPER OR REMOVE IT FROM THE FURNACE AND ATTEMPT IT A LITTLE LATER. IF YOU CAN'T SEE WHATS GOING ON, DON'T EVEN BOTHER. TRY **METHOD #2**.

A QUICK SUCK SHOULD BE ALL THAT YOU NEED. IF THE GLASS IS HOT ENOUGH, IT SHOULD FILL THE WHOLE TUBE IN A FLASH. REMOVE THE GLASS FROM THE FURNACE AND DO YOUR BEST TO GET IT UNDER CONTROL. THE INTERIOR OF THE TUBE (FRESH HOT GLASS) WILL RAPIDLY HEAT-UP YOUR WHOLE PIECE. TRY AIR MARVERING IT BACK ON CENTER FIRST. THEN TAKE A PASS OR TWO OVER THE MARVER TO EVEN THINGS OUT.

FROM THERE, IT'S UP TO YOU WHAT TO DO WITH IT. YOU CAN MAKE SOME INTERESTING CANE/MURRINE OUT OF IT OR SCULPT IT INTO SOMETHING ELSE. OR WHATEVER... More food for thought...

THE OTHER WAY TO OPEN YOUR TUBE, IF THE POKE N' TWEEZE METHOD ISN'T HAPPENING FOR YOU, IS TO NECK DOWN A HOLLOW KNOB ON THE END OF THE TUBE. YOU THEN CHILL AND TAP THE KNOB OFF REVEALING A SMALL HOLE. THE HOLE THEN MAY BE REHEATED AND OPENED-UP WITH THE JACKS TO GET THE DESIRED TUBE SHAPE. THIS IS PRETTY MUCH THE SAME AS OPENING A HOLE IN THE INCALMO TECHNIQUE (PAGE 124)

ONCE YOU GET THE TUBE EVENED-OUT, YOU CAN GO AHEAD AND HEAT N' SLUMP IT TO GET THE DESIRED CURVE AND SUCK THE GLASS UP AS DESCRIBED ABOVE, OR TRY METHOD #2.

METHOD #2. A 'SAFER' METHOD WITH VIRTUALLY THE SAME RESULTS. INSTEAD OF CURVING THE TUBE TO SUCK GLASS UP WITH, YOU FLARE THE ENDS SLIGHTLY AND DROP A HOT GATHER OF GLASS INTO THE INTERIOR. THIS METHOD SUCCEEDS IN CLOGGING YOUR PIPES AS WELL, SO BE AWARE.

ONCE YOU HAVE THE TUBE OPENED AND SLIGHTLY FLARED, HAVE YOUR ASSISTANT BRING OVER A COUPLE OF GATHERS AS HOT AS THEY CAN BRING IT. CENTER THE GATHERS OVER THE OPENING OF THE TUBE AND ALLOW THEM TO DRIP AND FILL THE TUBE. HOPEFULLY IT'S ENOUGH TO FILL THE TUBE COMPLETELY. TRIM OFF ANY EXCESS WITH THE DIAMOND SHEARS, AND AWAY YOU GO.

THIS TECHNIQUE IS APPROPRIATE FOR MAKING CLEAR CORED CANE IN A HURRY - PARTICULARLY IF YOU DON'T NEED ALOT OF IT. YOU OF COURSE CAN COMBINE IT WITH A HOST OF OTHER GLASS TECHNIQUES DEPENDING ON YOUR NEEDS OR DESIGNS.

NOTE: IF YOU DO USE THIS TECHNIQUE, BE CONSIDERATE OF OTHERS AND TAKE A FEW MINUTES OUT TO UNCLOG YOUR PIPE(S) AFTERWARDS. IT'S JUST A COMMON COURTESY, AND MAY SAVE ONE OF YOUR STUDIOMATES ALOT OF FRUSTRATION.

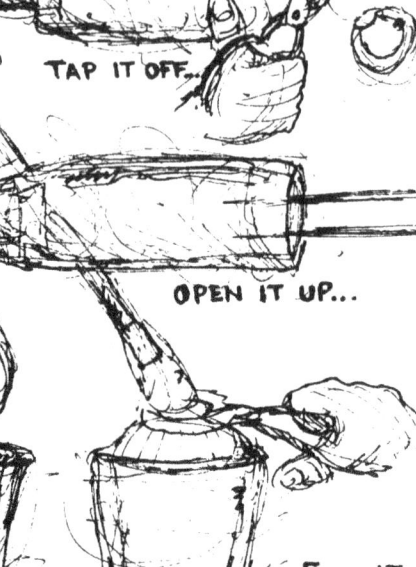

INSERT INTO THE FURNACE AND SUCK-UP THE GLASS.

NECK A KNOB...

TAP IT OFF...

OPEN IT UP...

FILL IT WITH GLASS.

Coils

Coils or springs? Whatever you wanna call them, it's fine by me. These spiraling rods of cane can be used to introduce a feeling of movement within a sculptural form. Or in a slightly smaller format, they make interesting goblet stems or can be twisted-up to make the body of a dragon/serpent stem. Or they make fun little novelty items for the 'easily impressed'. In any case, they're pretty easy to make.

Essentially coils are hot bits wrapped around a rod of sorts. You can use a cold punty, or wooden dowel or even a old broomstick. Just as long as they are straight and have a slight taper to them or won't get caught when you're trying to remove the coil.

You can make them in any length, thickness or color you desire. You can wrap them as tight or as loose as you like.

Begin by gathering as much glass as you'll need to create the thickness and length of coil you want. Practice and trial n' error will help you guage this amount. You may also introduce the color at this point if you like.

Marver the glass into a cylinder. Grab a knob on the bottom of the glass with the diamond shears and begin to draw it out into a thick section of cane.

Have your assistant hold the rod stable against the bench or other firm surface. Set the knob of glass down against the rod - and continue to hold it there stationary. At the same time, with the punty in your other hand, begin to wrap and wind the glass around the rod or 'mandrel'.

Wrap it fast. The glass/cane tends to cool rapidly. Continue to wind it on until you have a sufficient amount of coil-age to suit your needs.

Then slide the coil off the end off the rod. It may take a little jiggling to get the whole thing off, but take it easy → the coils are fragile - and can't put up with much lateral tension. You can lop the starter knob off before or after you slide the coil free.

You can also reheat and trim or fire-polish the end at this point. Or heat the whole thing up and twist it into something else. Or punty it up and work the other end. Or just box it and cold-work it into something else later.

DRAGON STEM GOBLET
IMAGINARY WORK BY THE AUTHOR.

THE R.I.S.D. RING   A.K.A. The Roman Ring

The R.I.S.D. Ring (pronounced "RIZ-DEE") may already be familiar to you. It was at the Rhode Island School of Design in the '70's that some young glassblowers (re)discovered this technique and made it nationally famous. In any case, it's an interesting and relatively simple technique to learn.

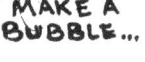
MAKE A BUBBLE...

Essentially it is a necking procedure which will leave you with a thick ring or rim within the structure of your bubble. This ring has optical qualities which you may find desirable in your design. It is not too dissimilar from the union line created during the Incalmo process (pages 121-4).

Begin by necking your hot bubble down in the area where you wish the ring to be. This may be done either before or after you neck-in the transfer/break-off line. Less distortion to the ring will occur if you do it after you've initiated your neckline.

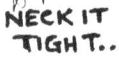
NECK IT TIGHT...

The hotter the piece is, **naturally**, the easier it is to cut this line in. It is up to you how far you want to cut it in. The deeper the cut, the smaller the interior hole will be. Basically you're shooting for an hourglass shape. The form is then reheated (if necessary) and papered or possibly marvered back together ~ creating a crease or 'ring' in the glass.

Always keep the pipe level/horizontal during this procedure. It will prevent the piece from stretching out all wonky-like, and aid in maintaining a nice symmetrical form. It's pretty easy to accidentally bump or jar the pipe - causing your hourglass shape to prematurely touch down (usually NOT where or when you want it to!) This may result in a lop-sided ring or a trapped air bubble. (An unwanted one at that!) To prevent it from occurring:

PAPER IT BACK TOGETHER...

① Keep your eye on the bubble at all times!
② Be smooth with your pipe rotations.
③ Avoid tilting the pipe up or down - maintain it on a horizontal plane
④ Work hot!

With wet newspaper in hand, concentrate on papering the bottom half section back into the top half of the piece. Try using your thumb (underneath the paper) to coax the bottom half inwards toward the pipe by pushing upwards on the glass slightly, while your palm craddles the seam area of the bubble.

Once the bubble is compressed back together, the resulting constriction creates an obvious line. The piece may then be further reheated, marvered or papered smooth. You may wish to further blow out the form. (The more you blow it, the less noticeable the ring will appear.

Try making multiple rings, or mix n' match with other techniques. For added visual bonus, try this technique with transparent color rod or incorporate it into a cane-worked pieces. The resulting rings can optically accentuate your form and add to its overall design and presentation.

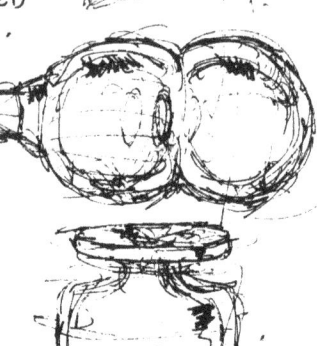

FINISHED PIECES BY NO ONE IN PARTICULAR

STEAMSTICK

A natural way to soffietta work, the Steamstick is a simple tool popular with glassblowers who work solo. You can puff-out the shoulders and lip area of your piece with little effort. Hell, there's some folks in Denver Colorado that blow their entire pieces this way!

Steamsticks are often made of cherry wood, simple lathe turned cones mounted on some type of handle. They are usually kept wet - way down in the bottom of your block bucket. When placed in contact with hot glass, the moisture in the soaked wood vaporizes into steam.

Provided an adequate seal between the glass and the steamstick is established and maintained - the expanding gas escaping from the steamstick has nowhere to go but inflate into the glass. This causes the glass to expand and stretch.

The hotter the glass, the faster the effect occurs. The expansion can easily be stopped by simply pulling the plug, i.e. removing the steamstick. **IT'S THAT EASY!**

Just make sure you have a complete seal and that your **GLASS IS HOT HOT HOT!** Sometimes it takes a few seconds for the expansion to 'kick-in', so be patient and stick with it.

The same effect can, of course, be achieved with compressed air if your studio is so equipped. You just need the cone-shaped adapter unit for your air line and you're ready to go.

Be careful with these types of "puffers" - a little blast can go a long way!

A STEAMSTICK

STICK IT IN AND SEAL...

COMPRESSED AIR-PUFFER UNIT

Another sizzling HOT TIP FROM DR. GLASS*
He's not a real doctor... "I have a Masters Degree in... GLASS!"

CLIP ○ AND ○ SAVE

HEY KIDS MAKE YOUR OWN **STEAMSTICK** FROM **RECYCLED MATERIALS!**

In a pinch? Can't find that wooden steamstick that sunk long ago in the Davy Jones Locker of your blockbucket? Have we got the solution for you!?! Ya sure ya betcha! Make your own disposable Steamstick from RECYCLED STUFF! Here's how:

FIRST: Find a wooden dowel ~ even a big pencil might work... Next, get a section of newspaper ~ a page or two should do the trick. And you need a small amount of wire ~ ask your dad or mom for some, or link several twist ties together.

SECOND: Fold your newspaper into triangles. Next, wrap the newspaper tightly around your wooden dowel. Do it so you make a skinny end and a fat end - with maybe a piece of the dowel showing through - like a handle. It should look like a **FUNNY CARROT** ⇒. Then, use your section of wire to secure the newspaper, NICE AND TIGHT - like, so it doesn't go **KA-SPLOO-EY** everywhere! WOW! You now have a raw steamstick!

○ **To make it work** ⇒ Soak the steamstick in water for 10-15 minutes and "Voila" it is ready to go! Use just like a normal steamstick and puff-away like the pro's!

○ **WARNING:** Do not leave your steamstick in the blockbucket or it will turn into paper maché, or even worse ⇒ dissolve into tiny pieces and end up deep down in Davy Jones Locker.

① Fold newspaper into triangles
WOW! IT'S NEAT!

② Wrap newspaper around dowel rod

③ Tie it up with wire.

④ soak n' puff!

Dip and Blow

This technique is probably as old as glassblowing itself. Even though the process is simple and straightforward, the results may vary a great deal. It offers tremendous potential for sculptural forms. This method of blowing exemplifies the plasticity of this medium. Introducing color and combining it with some creative coldworking, you can produce some very sophisticated and immaginative pieces. So, if the **ORGANIC THING** is your bag, then this technique could be for you!

The idea is to take a **2 or 3** (or more, perhaps even less) gathered bubble and dip it part way into the furnace. This coats an area on your bubble with a layer of hot glass. Air is then blown into or sucked out of the blowpipe to produce an auxiliary bubble or cavity. The piece may be dipped again to create additional **bulges** or **pockets**. It can be also hot-sculpted into other shapes, transferred and finished-off into whatever shape you like.

DIP IT.

Begin with a bubble. A bubble with even wall thickness and which is symmetrical (on-center) helps, but isn't completely necessary. **RELAX**. It's just *Sculpture!*... Allow it to cool. Return to the furnace. Dip the bubble back into the glass, perhaps ⅓ d to ½ (or possibly more) of the way in. It's up to you! The more surface area you cover, the larger of an area you have to play with. BE QUICK! or you'll fry yourself from the heat of the furnace. If you can't exactly see what you're doing, or you don't want to get your blowpipe excruciatingly hot, you might set up a yoke in front of the door. You can then gain some leverage while 'dipping', without having to roll on the sill.

ROCK IT.

To avoid the long thin trails of glass which can result from this technique, and mess up your studio (especially your furnace door), rock the blowpipe back n' forth - almost 180° to drip off in the furnace. As soon as the glass peels off, exit the furnace.

Keep your eye on the bubble at all times! It may require immediate attention. As that freshly dipped area begins to soften-up, it will either start to sag inward or droop outward, depending on which way you're turning it, flipping it back and forth, or stopping it still.

You can work standing up with the pipe in a yoke, or hanging over the back of the marver, or seated back at the bench. You can gently blow the bubble out and cap it, or softly suck it back in. Combined with how your blowpipe is angled you can 'air sculpt' the glass with a fair amount of accuracy. Continuous pressure, either out or in, is more desirable than short blasts. It allows you some reaction time to halt the swelling or shrinking of your glass.

BLOW IT OUT OR...

SUCK IT IN..

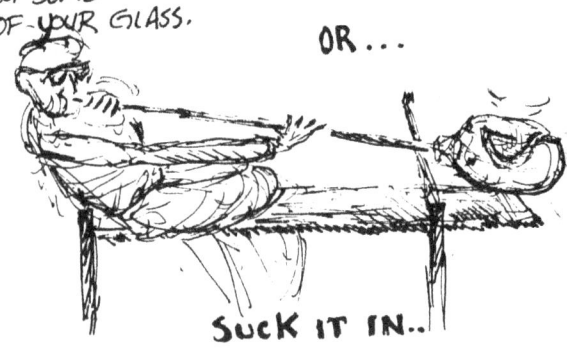

"THE INTRO & OUTRO."

MORE IMAGINARY GLASS BY THE AUTHOR.

FLATTENING

There are a few different methods by which you may flatten blown or solid glass objects. Each method yields it's own style of results. The easiest method is to flatten the piece on the marver. Simply get the piece hot (where you want it flattened), and keep the pipe turning until you have it over the marver. Then, just lay the piece down, stopping the rotation as you do so. Lift off and flip the piece over to do the other side.

Several things might happen. If it's blown and the piece is really hot - the walls may collapse inward → even touch together in the center of the piece. To prevent the touchdown from happening → **CAP THE PIPE AS YOU FLATTEN TO MAINTAIN INTERNAL PRESSURE**. Or if it's a really big piece you may have an extra assistant do that for you.

If the glass isn't quite hot enough, you may not get it as flat as you like. You may have to repeat the procedure several times until you do get it flat.

You may also notice chill marks from the steel marver. Regardless of how hot or large the piece is, you cannot change the surface texture that the marver will contribute.

Maybe the chill marks are an aesthetic choice you like. If it isn't, try using a marble marver (if one's available). It will impart fewer marks. Marble doesn't suck the heat out of the glass nearly as fast as steel. Or, for even fewer marks, and if your piece is small enough, you can use your wet newspaper at the bench. You can get your piece screaming hot and just lay it on there to gently flatten it, or accelerate the process by squashing it on the paper with a paddle.

If you anticipate making a series of flattened pieces, you may want to construct some flattening boards. They should be made of cherry wood or similar hardfruitwood. There should be no nails or screws exposed (which might catch the glass).

Flattening boards are best used dry. Wet boards will leave chill and/or quench marks. The larger of the two can lay flat on the marver (or similar stable table). The smaller - squasher - board should have handles on the backside.

When the glass is good n' hot, it's brought over to the boards and laid down. The squasher board is pressed down on top momentarily - to squeeze the piece flat. The gaffer pulls the piece out, swings it back (to stretch the piece slightly and flip it over) - and slaps it back on the boards for another pressing. This process is repeated as often as necessary until the desired flatness is obtained. Again, if you don't want the center of the piece to collapse (for blown work), have a thumb or palm handy to cap the pipe to maintain some internal pressure.

Another quick, inexpensive alternative to cherry wood flattening boards is to use a (damp) **PAPER MARVER** and a large wooden paddle. See page 70 for information on paper marvers. It can be used in exactly the same manner as the boards described above.

Most often you'll wanna flatten your piece before putting a bottom on it, as this technique dramatically distorts the bubble. Just get your object as flat as you want or need it and spend the extra few reheats to get your bottom looking the way you want it. If the shoulders need to be flattened more, you can take care of that when the piece is on the punty. Keep a paddle handy to insert inside the lips to prevent them from touching.

267

Maybe you'd like to make a flattened vessel by blowing the bottom and sidewalls simultaneously. You may try "The Poor Man's Mold". Just set-up a couple of boards with the desired gap. Find some way to keep the boards from moving with the expanding bubble. You can line the boards with a few sheets of wet newspaper if you don't want any wood texture or chill marks.

During the blow, you'll have to watch the bubble's expansion on the sides of the piece - as there's nothing to restrict its movement there. To keep the sides in check, you can slap some boards there too - essentially making a box mold. See the section on moldblowing for additional hints on this process (pages 227-40).

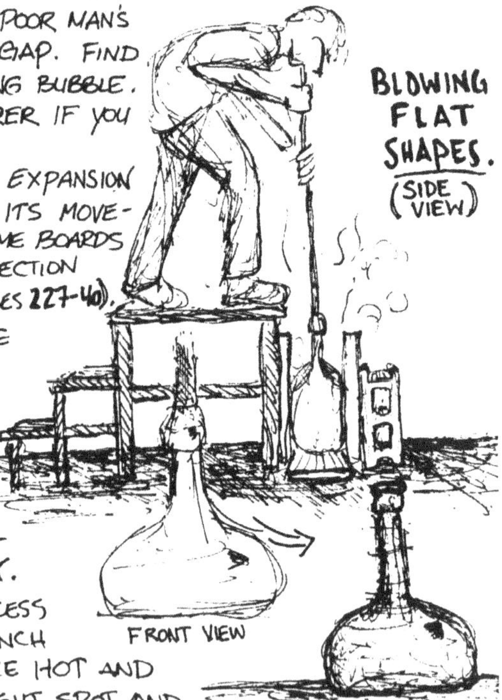

Yet another method for flattening work may be accomplished at the bench using cork or newspaper paddles. If you're fortunate enough to have a source of large chunks of **CORK** nearby, you can saw/carve them up into rectangular blocks. Then glue some smaller pieces on the backs of them for handles and PRESTO! CORK PADDLES! Or you can make your own newspaper paddles for next-to-nothing → see page 221 for information on how-to D.I.Y.

Whichever set of paddles you end up using, the process is the same. The gaffer stands off the edge of the bench and works from there. The assistant gets the whole piece hot and sets it down on the bench. The gaffer selects the right spot and tells the assistant to stop (rotation). Both paddles are pressed together against the glass - working in unison - to squeeze the glass. Moving the paddles in a circular motion seems to yield a more uniform surface.

The assistant should flip the piece (when indicated by the gaffer) to compensate for the sagging. The flattening may continue, with additional reheats - if necessary, until the desired shape is obtained. If the piece is blown rather than solid, the assistant should be standing by to cap the pipe as well to maintain the internal pressure and prevent the form from collapsing.

NOTE: Be aware that the flattening process can greatly expand the width of your work - consequently requiring more space within the glory hole. Be careful that you don't flatten your piece beyond the width of your glory hole or you'll be S.O.L.

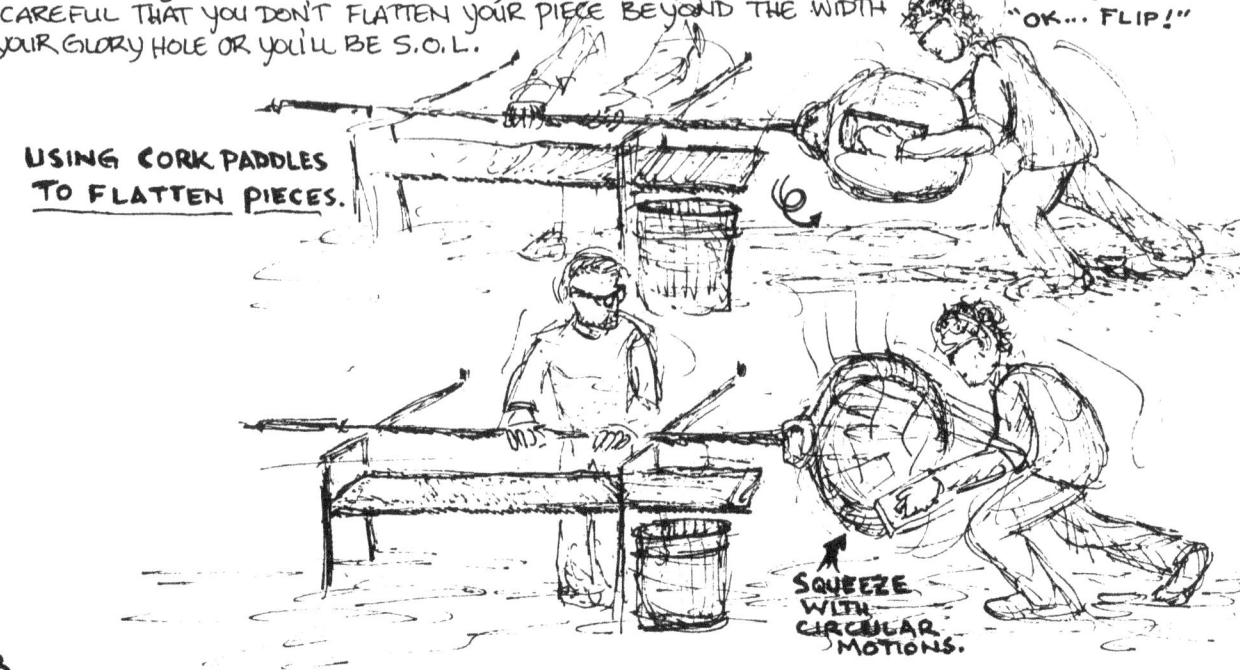

BLOWING FLAT SHAPES. (SIDE VIEW)

FRONT VIEW

THE SADDLE "FLASK". POPULAR WITH EQUESTRIANS ca. NINETEENTH C.

"OK... FLIP!"

USING CORK PADDLES TO FLATTEN PIECES.

SQUEEZE WITH CIRCULAR MOTIONS.

268

ALTERNATE AXES/MONTAGE

THIS IS A TECHNIQUE FOR THOSE OF YOU WHO FIND TRADITIONAL GLASSBLOWING BORING AND PREDICTABLE, AND ARE LOOKING FOR SOMETHING NEW, SOMETHING DIFFERENT, SOMETHING INCREDIBLY LABOR INTENSIVE!... THE RESULTS, HOWEVER, CAN MAKE EVERY MINUTE OF TIME INVESTED WORTHWHILE. IMAGINE IF YOU WILL... YOU THREAD A BUBBLE WITH COLOR. YOU THEN POP

A HOLE IN THE MIDDLE OF THE BUBBLE. THEN YOU ATTACH ANOTHER BLOWPIPE TO THAT HOLE AND TRANSFER THE BUBBLE TO THAT SECOND PIPE. YOU HAVE JUST ALTERNATED THE AXIS OF THE BUBBLE SO THAT THE SPIRAL WRAP IS NOW IN A VERTICAL ORIENTATION INSTEAD OF A HORIZONTAL ONE.

YOU CAN HEAT UP THE HOLE (LEFT-OVER FROM THE ORIGINAL PIPE), TWEEZE AND CLOSE IT UP AND BLOW THE PIECE OUT. THAT'S ESSENTIALLY WHAT TRANSFERRING THE BUBBLE TO AN ALTERNATE AXIS IS ALL ABOUT. BUT WHY STOP THERE? YOU CAN GO THE EXTRA STEP AND CREATE A **MONTAGE** PIECE BY COMBINING THE AFOREMENTIONED BUBBLE WITH OTHER BUBBLES OF A DIFFERENT SORT-VIA THE INCALMO PROCESS. THIS MAY THEN YIELD A HIGHLY COMPLICATED WORK THAT CAN KEEP PEOPLE GUESSING... "HOW'D THEY DO DAT?"

SO FOR THE MONTAGE, YOU MAY TAKE THE SPIRAL WRAPPED BUBBLE FROM ABOVE, POKE A HOLE IN THE BOTTOM AND OPEN IT UP. THEN YOU CAN TAKE A SECOND BLOWN BUBBLE OF A DIFFERENT COLOR OR DESIGN, POKE A HOLE IN THE BOTTOM OF THAT ONE AND OPEN IT UP. (SEE PAGES 121-4 FOR MORE INFO. ON HOW TO DO THIS IF YOU'RE NOT SURE). NEXT ATTACH THE TWO BUBBLES TOGETHER IN AN INCALMO STYLE AND TRANSFER TO PIPE NUMBER TWO.

FROM THERE YOU CAN OPEN UP THE BOTTOM SECTION (THE TRIPPY SPIRAL-WRAPPED GUY) AND ATTACH A THIRD BUBBLE TO THE BOTTOM. IT CAN BE A MATCHING SECTION TO THE TOP OR ONE OF A COMPLETELY DIFFERENT NATURE OR DESIGN. ONCE THE THIRD SECTION IS ADDED, YOU CAN GO AHEAD AND BLOW IT OUT TO IT'S FINAL FORM, OR CONTINUE ADDING MORE BUBBLES TO REALLY PUSH THE ENVELOPE. (THE SKY'S THE LIMIT - (OR MAYBE THE LENGTH OF YOUR BLOWSLOT IS...)!

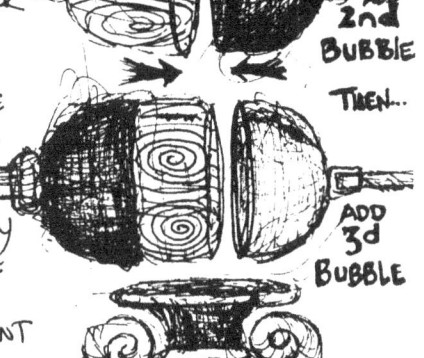

DUE TO THE COMPLEXITY OF ALL THE STAGES OF DEVOLOPMENT INVOLVED IN THESE TYPES OF PIECES, I STRONGLY RECOMMEND SERIOUS PLANNING BEFORE YOU GET STARTED. THIS MEANS HAVING WORKING DRAWINGS AND ASSEMBLING TWO TEAMS CAPABLE OF HANDLING THE GLASS WITH THE SKILLS AND TIMING YOU REQUIRE. USING TWO TEAMS (VS. ONE) WILL SAVE YOU TIME DURING THE FABRICATION (INCALMO) PROCESS - WHICH, IN TURN, CAN HELP YOU MAKE MORE PIECES IN A DAY. AND THE WORKING DRAWINGS WILL ENABLE THE TEAMS TO HAVE A REFERENCE POINT AND KNOW WHAT IS EXPECTED OF THEM.

Surface Techniques

The slick, smooth surface resulting from most hot glass processes is probably the easiest one to achieve. It occurs naturally and requires no extra effort. Many other proven techniques exist which exemplify various qualities of molten glass, and may be of interest to you. Humans by nature are tactile creatures. Our sense of touch has tremendous influence on our perceptions and memory. Therefore, the role of texture should not be overlooked when designing and making hot glass objects. It could be the element which sets your work apart from all the rest.

One of my favorite hot glass textures is out of this world! Well, it just looks and feels that way... It is achieved by rolling a hot gather straight outta the furnace into some large chunks of frit or small chunks of cullet. I learned this from Willie Dexter teaching at Pilchuck ten years ago. The hot glass sticks remarkably well to the cold glass. You can then immediately blow your bubble out into whatever form you like. The more you heat and reheat the piece, the more the surface softens up. The texture is very organic. It can be left very sharp or softened nearly smooth.

You can use a wide variety of other materials to roll your hot glass in. **Sand, dirt, copper, silver, gold,** — you name it. Some things adhere to the glass better than others. Some materials will merely stain or deposit a residue on the glass.

Quenching your hot glass in a bucket of cold water is a quick and easy method which produces a fractured surface texture. See pages 110-111.

Naturally, glass sticks best to itself and countless methods exist by which you may introduce texture to your pieces. **Threads**, barely melted-in, can offer some nice texture. So can **shards, prunts, stringers** and even sections of **cane** or **murrine**. **Frit** (as mentioned above), **chips and powders** — not too mention **scavo** — produce their own quality of surface enhancement.

Most every type of **mold** will imprint a texture upon the glass which is blown into it. The material of which they're made of can contribute a lot or a little to the surface of the glass. Optic molds may be used nearly indefinately with little or no degradation to the mold. The rib design is very structured and predictable. It nevertheless has pronounced tactile qualities in addition to visual optics. A wood mold on the other hand has a more limited lifespan. As the wood burns up, more texture is revealed and less detail becomes apparent. See the chapter on moldblowing for more information.

There are of course many options available in the **coldworking** realm. You can use **paint** in a painterly fashion; enamels seem to adhere the best. There are a wide variety of **adhesives** more than willing to stick to your glass — given the opportunity. You might even try **mosaics** and cover your blown glass with other bits and chunks of stuff.

You can try to increase the value of your glass by leafing it with **silver** or **gold**. Or devalue it perhaps by casing it in lead. Wrapping it with **copper** (or any metal) wire can accentuate your form. Or if you have access to **electro-plating** equipment ~ you can try to electro-form the surface of your glass.

Then there's **sandblasting/** sandcarving, diamond and acid **etching** and **engraving** which can enhance the surface and design of your glass.

And finally one of the nicest and most natural surfaces may be achieved by burying your glass in the backyard and waiting for a few thousand years to dig it back up.

"Lavaware"

Resourceful Info

Health & Safety 272
Tools 278
Common Misconceptions . 290
Teach Your Children . . 291
Instruction 292
The Business 293
Scrapbook 296
Special Ed Section . . . 300
Glossary 301
Source Directory . . . 310
Index 314
Backword 318
About the Author . . . 318
The Last Word . . . 320

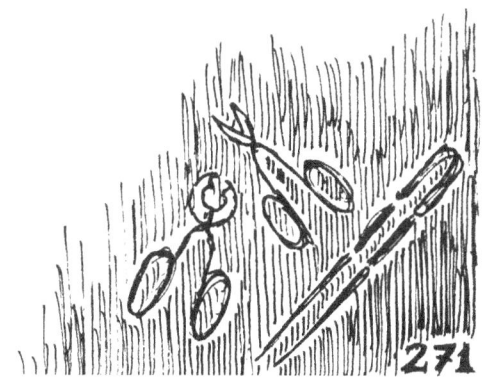

Health + Safety

"D'ya ever get cut?" "D'ya ever get burned?" (Do you ever get tired of hearing people ask those silly questions?) "Nope." → "Never been cut or burned — what's it like?" ... Of course you get cut and burned, scraped, gouged, sliced and diced. I know after extensive amounts of hot and cold glassworking, I resemble 'Edward Hamburgerhands' — just the nature of the beast. However, after multitudes of cuts and burns (one severe enough to cause permanent impairment of my right ringfinger) — I've become aware of first-aid practices which may reduce **shock, further tissue damage, blood loss, infection** etc. These techniques should be as familiar to you as blocking, marvering, and blowing.

RULE NUMERO UNO: SAFETY FIRST! Know exactly where your first aid kit is and check that it is stocked with adequate supplies. Know also where the closest phone is → dialing **9·1·1** in an emergency situation may be your best and wisest move. And above all, you should use common sense while working in a glass studio. Avoid those situations and practices which put you and/or your studio-mates at risk. Outlined below are some of the factors you may encounter while in a glass shop and how to deal with them accordingly.

CUTS, PUNCTURES AND ABRASIONS where the surface of the skin is broken will require **direct pressure** to stop the bleeding. Use a fresh sterile gauze or bandage and apply pressure to the wound. If it is deep, long, or continues bleeding after several minutes → seek professional medical attention. Notify the shop supervisor and make them aware of the situation. Wash any wound thoroughly as well → with a disinfectant soap — to prevent the risk of infection. Keeping the wound clean and dry will aid in the healing process.

BURNS result (usually) from exposure to heat, electricity, radiation or caustic chemicals. Most frequently, it'll happen to you in the hot shop (or in my case → the kitchen.)

FIRST DEGREE BURNS appear as reddening of the skin.
SECOND DEGREE BURNS appear as the formation of blisters — usually from close or direct contact with heat. Do not "pop" the blister — it's your body's natural process of healing itself and you run the risk of infection by doing so.   Seek medical attention.
THIRD DEGREE BURNS destroy both upper and lower layers of your skin, and are the most serious of burns. You must seek medical attention to reduce pain, shock and infection.

TREATMENT: If you get burned, put the glass piece down and deal with the burn **IMMEDIATELY!** Immerse the injured area in a bath of clean ice water. This will prevent oxygen from "feeding" the "fire". Your skin continues to burn up to 20 minutes after exposure, given the oxygen to do so. The pain can be excruciating! A couple aspirin or ibuprofen may be taken for temporary relief until you see a doctor. Silvadene, a prescribed ointment, may be applied to relieve the pain, and aids in healing. Aloe vera and Vitamin E work wonders as well.

HEAT EXPOSURE\HEAT STRESS. Imagine if you will... you're blowing in the hot humid summer: feeling a little light-headed in your puddles of sweat? Tired? Weak? These may be the symptoms of heat stress/exposure. It's very easy to become dizzy and pass-out from too much heat. Your body shuts down when it can no longer cope with prolonged exposure to heat; its natural cooling system → sweating is ineffective. "If you can't stand the heat then stay out of the kitchen!" — so the ol' cliche goes. As with many of our colorful idioms such as this, there is a ring of truth to them. If you're feeling dizzy, get away from the heat source. Or reschedule your blowslot to the nightime, when it's cooler. Or reduce the time in which you are exposed to the heat. It takes time to acclimate yourself to working in front of a furnace and glory hole. There are warning signs of heat illness and methods to treat it.

Heat Fatigue

is recognized by loss in motor skills, impaired performance — mental or physical — when exposed to heat. Oftentimes it's from lack of acclimazation, compounded by the fact that you're tired. Instead of working straight through your blowslot, break it up a little bit. Trade off with your partner, allow them to gaff a piece while you kick-back for a bit. Take a break once in a while. Be sure to have some food in your system and drink plenty of fluids.

Heat Rash

a.k.a. prickly heat comes from sweating continuously in humid heat. Your sweat glands get plugged, and turn red. Mild drying lotions and cleaning your skin should help as well as relaxing in cooler enviornments.

Heat Cramps

are painful muscle spasms which can occur from working long and hard in the heat — sweating alot and drinking only water. This in turn depletes your body of salt. It's important to consume some salt in your diet if you anticipate working and sweating in hot enviornments. Or drink those thirst quenchers popular with athletes.

Heat Exhaustion

may be felt as nausea, fatigue, or headaches. Your skin may be clammy and moist, pale or possibly flush complexion. Often it's from working too long in front of the heat, not being used to it, and most likely a result of dehydration. Usually, too, your urine volume is small and highly concentrated. TREATMENT → Move to a cooler enviornment (outside, downstairs to a basement, Seattle or Iceland), lie down & chill out! Drink plenty of fluids to maintain an equilibrium, and take it easy.

Heat Stroke

is recognizable by hot, dry red skin, confusion and loss of consciousness. Contributing factors include: sustained exhertion in heat, lack of physical fitness and obesity, recent alcohal intake, dehydration, individual susceptibility, and chronic cardiovaslular disease. It's best treated by rapid cooling → immersion in chilled water or wrapping up in a wet sheet & fanning with cool dry air, and treating for shock if necessary).

Prevention

is the key to avoiding these situations. People typically don't recognize heat stress for what it is. They're too engaged in concentrating on keeping their bubble on-center and completion of their masterpiece to worry about being 'hot'. Remember to take breaks, drink plenty of fluids and minimize your exposure to the heat, i.e. stand back from the furnaces and glory holes, use heat shields, and keep a good flow of air going through the studio.

Noise

is often overlooked as a potential health risk, yet prolonged exposure will contribute to reduced hearing and even deafness. Industrial hygenists will tell you that this is a serious hazard and steps should be taken to reduce the level of exposure in the workplace — either directly or locally. Use of sound shields/barriers around noisy equipment: blowers, burners, grinders etc. will help contain sound from reaching you. You may opt to wearing earphones or earplugs should there be no way, physically or financially to deal with the situation. These simple devices can drastically reduce the decibel level and still allow you to hear directions or people talk. Cranking up the stereo is not a solution — it only compounds your level of noise exposure. Personal stereos (Walkman's & the like) can make you deaf to the world, and thereby potentially hazardous as well.

Air Quality

in the glass studio is vitally important. There are a number of factors, agents and situations which directly effect the air you breathe. There are also a number of steps which may be taken to insure that it is the cleanest and freshest available.

First, IF YOU SMOKE → QUIT!! This can greatly reduce numerous health risks. The smoker has little in the way of protective tissues which

The body provides as natural filtration systems. In addition, the tar & resin from the things you smoke act as glue for nasties to stick to your lungs, thus increasing your susceptibility to respitory hazards & illness. Also, it stinks!

Like noise, **AIR POLLUTION** can be dealt with directly or locally. **VENTILATION** is the key to clearing and cleaning up the overall picture in any shop. The exhaust of burning gases from furnaces and glory holes contains carbon monoxide. Overexposure to carbon monoxide can cause headache, nausea, weakness, dizziness, confusion, hallucinations and fainting. Smokers are even more susceptible to its effects. A ventilation hood over the furnace and glory holes are strongly recommended. An adequate supply of fresh air should be present as well. Those pieces of equipment which combust gases are competing for the same air you breathe. An open window, door or vent should allow air to get in.

NUISANCES such as **DUST, AIRBORNS, PARTICULATES** and **OFF-GASES** must also be addressed. Some of these may never have an odor, such as asbestos or silica dust, while others may bring tears to your eyes. (y'know, that cool flourine smell you get from white powdered glass that reel-y cleans out the ol' sinuses?!). **PREVENTION**, once again, is the best deterrent in combating this problem.

V IS FOR VENTILATION. If you're using powdered glass or scavo to color your pieces, do it in a powdering booth, or at least under the hood. Wear an approved respirator. A 'neckerchief' don't cut it pal! The chemicals in those pretty colors are very easy and very bad to breathe. The vapors given off when they make contact with hot glass are toxic as well.

SILICA, the main ingredient in glass, is akin to asbestos. It is a hooked-shaped particle which enters the lungs and attaches to the cilia there, **PERMANENTLY**. After prolonged exposure, enough of these particles bunch-up and form nodules, contributing to their own form of lung cancer known as **SILICOSIS**. Again, **PREVENTION** is the key in limiting your exposure to this nasty, but necessary, element.

Powdered glass contains a large percentage of free (unmelted) silica. Batched glass, powdered or pelletized, contains silica and must be handled with care. A seperate room, well-ventilated and dry is recommended for mixing and storing & bagging batch that is to be charged. All surfaces and floors should go through periodic cleaning to cut down on hazardous dusts which tend to accumulate with time. Use floor sweeping compounds or wet clean-up methods to keep those dusts down, and **WEAR A RESPIRATOR**.

A WORD OR TWO ON RESPIRATORS: It's important to use the correct respirator for the task which you are performing. Many dust masks will protect against dusts, mists and welding fumes; but not against gases and vapors. For gas and vapor, a cartridge respirator may be required. For a proper fit, a user can **NOT** have facial growth (beards) — any break in the seal of the mask negates the effectiveness of the respirator. Tighten the straps and blow out to see if the mask pushes away from the face, then suck in to see if the mask gets tighter on the face. A change in size may be necessary to achieve a complete seal. Keep your respirator stored in a sealed plastic bag to prevent contamination. Change the filters as needed — this depends on how often you use it. Clogged cartridges can in some cases, be more harmful than helpful, giving you false confidence in something which doesn't work.

CHARGING GLASS exposes you to a double-dose of health hazards: heat and particulates. A face shield, protective safety glasses, gloves (kevlar are recommended) proper clothing (long sleeved cotton shirts) and a respirator should cut down on most problems you may encounter. "Get in & get out as quick as you can" is my motto. Especially with powdered/sandy batch — alot of airborn material is kicked-up during the charging process. Simply moving the batch from the barrel or mixing recepticle — to the charging scoop/shovel — to the furnace produces a fair amount of airborns. And that's just clear glass! Colored glass batch has a whole host of nasties in it that should be avoided at all costs. It's a funny trick of nature and chemistry that the prettiest colors are also the most toxic.

BAGGING YOUR BATCH is a simple and effective method for cutting down on superfluous dusts common to the charging process. Batch may be transferred to paper lunch bags, sealed and chucked-in to the awaiting hungry furnace. The bags burn up without a trace so you can breathe easy.

"Keep the scene clean." "Pack it in, pack it out." "Cleanliness is next to Godliness." Whichever cliché you may subscribe to, keeping your studio clean is important for many reasons. First, it's easier to find things. Second, it looks better. Third, it's healthier for all people using the facilities. Most studios I've worked in require that you clean up your mess when you're done working. This includes the area around your bench, the glory hole and furnace and any other equipment you've been using. Use floor sweeping compounds to keep the hazardous dusts down, and if possible, hose and squeegee the floor afterwards. Avoid leaving standing water / puddles in the blowing area where it may be slippery and dangerous for blowers working after you.

Be careful when sweeping and disposing of floor models. They are most likely sharp and hot. Not only will it burn your broom (or skin → don't touch!), it may ignite your trash barrel on fire! Place all potentially hot trash in a metal waste barrel dedicated to this specific purpose.

As a visual artist your eyes may be your most coveted organs. They too are susceptible to their own set of hazards while blowing glass.

Heat, first and foremost, will effect your eyes. Any pair of glasses will protect you from excessive heat radiation and from them drying out (your eyes).

Infarred and ultra-violet radiation are two other by-products of melting glass chambers and glory holes (& most torches as well). **Didymium glasses**, popular with most lampworkers, are **not** completely sufficient in filtering all harmful wavelengths of light experienced in furnace-style glassworking. Welders lenses with a 3.0 rating or better can help filter most harmful radiation you'll encounter. There are some businesses which specialize in making lenses designed specifically for furnace glassblowers. They claim to filter all the harmful wavelengths of U/V and IR without leaving you in the dark (like some welding glasses can.) Although they're expensive, they may be your best bet for protection regarding your eyes, and they may be made to your perscription if you already wear glasses.

Another recommendation for wearing glasses is the safety they provide in protecting your eyes from flying objects. Frequently, glass pops off the end of cooling pipes, or from ones being pre-heated. **Glass breaks.** Flying hazards occur. An unnecessary accident may only take a split-second and no amount of "I should da..." or "If only I'd..." will reverse potentially permanent damage. Again, safety glasses with side-shields are your best form of protection. And they only work if they're on your face, not just hanging around your neck!

Ergonomics is another matter to be aware of. Glassblowing is, as you are probably aware of, a very physically demanding process. It is easy to overdo it! Problems such as **tendonitis, carpul tunnel syndrom** and **back strain** are common ailments experienced by glassblowers who overextend and repeat the same motions frequently. This is often seen in production-style situations which require repition. The key to avoiding these forms of overexertion is to recognize them beforehand and adapt. This may mean adjusting your body english (language) i.e. how you sit or stand, how you turn the pipe and work with your tools. Changing your position slightly may make a dramatic difference on the negative impacts of the process. If you perform repitious tasks — break it up by performing other jobs which use other muscle groups.

Anti-Fatigue Mats, although pretty smelly when you drop hot glass on 'em, can reduce back strain and foot injury. A backrest at the bench may help too.

If your glory hole and gathering ports are high, you may risk overexerting your back, shoulder and arm muscles by constantly lifting up your glass pieces, particularly with thick or large objects. Try lowering, if possible, the glory hole to a height closer to your waist. The less up-and-down lifting/lowering you have to do, the better!

Your **pipe diameter** also plays a role in the ergonomic outlook. Small goblet pipes are not advised to make large bowls or platters from. You simply are forced to turn these small diameter pipes more frequently and subsequently over-work your wrists. Use the largest diameter pipe you can — appropriate for the piece at hand — to reduce over-exertion on your wrists. Many glassblowers also **wear wristbands** when working large and heavy pieces to limit overextension while turning/lifting the blowpipe. A **pipe cooler** can make your life easier as well. Being able to grip and turn the pipe closer to the piece will make better use of your energy, give you better balance, more control, and make you closer friends with your artwork!

Get help when lifting heavy objects. Don't allow pipe buckets to become full before you need to empty them. Make a practice of dumping them safely every day, or before they're a third full. Be careful of hot glass, sharp glass and glass dust within! Wear gloves, protective glasses, a dust mask, and lift with your legs, not your back!

FIRE!

They say that if you play with fire, you're gonna get burned. Well, with glassblowing that's practically a given. Working with molten glass carries with it the risk of fire. **1st, – Do you know where your fire extinguisher(s) are?** Is it charged? Has it been inspected regularly? Is it the right type of fire extinguisher? Do you know how to use it? Hopefully, you've answered 'yes' to all of the previous questions. If not, take some time out and check on it. A little time spent in famaliarizing yourself with the techniques and practices of fighting fires may be what saves your studio, your life or someone elses. Local fire departments often are happy to instruct people in the use of fire extinguishers, and also conduct first-aid and safety classes as well.

In most cases, if it's a small 'contained' fire, you may deal with it by yanking the extinguisher off the wall, pulling the safety pin/ring, squeezing the handle while aiming at the base of the fire (not just the flames) — until it's extinguished. If the fire is more than you can deal with and getting out of control ⇒ alert all people in the building (pull a fire alarm, if it's available) to get out, if you can locate the gas main safely ⇒ shut it off and get out of the building yourself. As in any emergency situation or first aid crisis, call **9·1·1** and get help. Stay on the phone and be sure to provide the dispatcher with all of the necessary information.

IF THE VALVE IS PERPENDICULAR TO THE GAS LINE IT IS "OFF"

IF THE VALVE'S 'IN-LINE' THEN IT'S "ON".

A GAS VALVE

Planet Awareness

If the environment is of any concern to you, (as it should be) you might think before you act. There is a tremendous amount of waste in many of the studio situations I've seen. Poorly insulated glass furnaces and glory holes consume unnecessary amounts of fuel to run. Inefficient combustion systems also lead to high gas bills and waste our natural resources.

Well-crafted and carefully designed furnaces will "pay-for-themselves" in a year's time. The use of recuperation systems can reduce your fuel intake by making use of the hot off-gases / exhaust of your furnace.

When designing your studio, think of the short term as well as the long term impact that you'll be encountering. Granted - more efficient systems generally cost more to install, but the time, money, and effort will benefit you (and others) in years to come.

Glassmaking has a long-standing history of enviornmentally unfriendly practices. In the pre-industrial age, trees were stripped from every available hillside to fuel the glass and iron furnaces of yesteryear. It literally changed the landscape of many countries in a geologically short period of time.

Now instead of burning wood or coal, [for the most of us], we burn some form of fossil fuel - either propane or natural gas. Depending on where you live, this can be cheaper and easier to run than an electric-melt furnace. However, in some instances, it is more efficient and enviornmentally safer to melt with electricity. Using a hydro-electric system would be ideal, and is an avenue I think more studios should consider.

It's not just melting glass that you should be enviornmentally aware of. Where you store your batch, chemicals and colorants ~ not too mention HOW you handle them and dispose of the excess ~ should be dealt with with as much care and thought as goes into making a Venetian-style goblet.

We're all in this together.... Consider this fact: You spend **100%** of your life on this planet (unless of course you're an astronaut or in aviation). What part of that **100%** of the time do you commit to it's benefit (the planet that is)? Usually it's TAKE TAKE TAKE with very little, or no, give give give. What's up with that? Sooner or later the planet's gonna get fed-up with that equation and call it quits. The warning signs are becoming more obvious every day.....

<u>A Call For "Enteries"</u>: I invite all participants in the glass making community an opportunity to further their medium of choice into the future: → Devise ways of melting glass in enviornmentally-friendly fashions. Or dedicate a percentage of your time or profit to cleaning-up the "scene". Create works of art which address enviornmental issues and present it to the public.

Educate everyone you know what's good for them, or what's good for Mother Earth is good for her children, and her childrens children and keep the spirit alive.

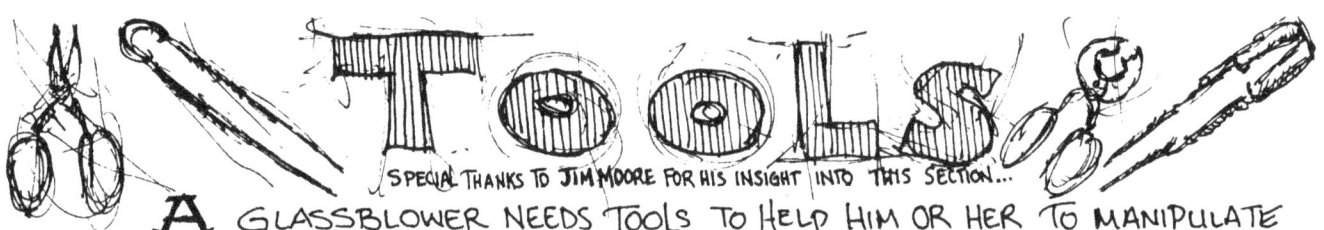
Tools

Special thanks to Jim Moore for his insight into this section...

A glassblower needs tools to help him or her to manipulate hot glass. **Tools should not be mistaken for skills.** A great glassblower with crummy tools can still make great glass, perhaps not as easily. Conversely, an inexperienced glassblower with great tools will still wind up struggling with the glass, but not have the convenient excuse of blaming their tools for their mistakes.

You'd be surprised at how often I've heard: "If only I had a good pair of Dino's..." Good tools will enable you to move the glass the way you want to — without a struggle, if and only if you understand HOW to move the glass in the first place. Instead of spending thousands of dollars on a new set of hand tools and pipes (which you're not sure how they work,) you're probably better off investing in a summer course at Pilchuck, Penland Haystack, Corning or any other fine schools. In the long run you'll thank yourself.

There are a wide variety of tools available for the glass artist today. Many different companies manufacture tools worldwide. Price may be a deciding factor when you choose to purchase a particular tool. Name or reputation may be another. Unfortunately, availability may be yet another. Usually, you get what you pay for. A well made set of tools should last you years IF YOU TAKE CARE OF THEM. Tools will wear out. Some faster than others. Most of it depends not so much on the time or frequency the tool is used, rather how the tool is used. Ever wonder why the shears in most school situations are dull and seemingly ineffective? It's because they get abused by people who think that the tool's responsible for the work, and not the glassblower. They cut glass which is too cold and consequently dull the edge on the tool. Also, because there's usually no one who wishes to claim responsibility to maintain them. **Tools require T.L.C.** to keep them working properly and you happy. (yes... Tender Loving Care!)

Remember these basic recommendations when handling tools in the hot shop:

- **Shears are not hammers.** • **Shears are not saws.** → In other words → don't bang on the glass to make it do something it doesn't want to do. Never cut cold glass with your shears. period. Hot good. Cold bad.

- **Never, ever, borrow a tool without asking first!** Stealing someone else's tools is a crime worse than... well, you can imagine. May the curse of checked glass befall any individual who stoops so low......

- **Rust is a common ailment of glass tools.** Usually it's from dropping them accidently in the blockbucket or water from your wet newspaper. Rust is easily removed by buffing the tool with a light grade of steel wool.* Lightly coating the tool with oil (any kind) will protect it from further rust. (*Or, those Scotchbrite pads work nicely for cleaning too.)

- **Store your tools in a warm, dry place** when not in use. Don't use gun bluing to "protect" your tools. That stuff contains selenium → toxic stuff you don't need to handle.

- **Shears are easily damaged.** Most often it's from dropping them on the floor. You can ruin them by using them when they are too loose. Keep your shears snug.

- Metallic oxides stick to glass, not clean metal. Another reason to keep your tools clean.
- Avoid melting wax off your tools with hot glass. It's a myth. It takes longer than using steel wool, is more abusive to the metal and a waste of glass you're better off blowing. Clean them first with steel wool. It should remove most of the wax. Then, warm up the tools and wipe them with a rag. Then, as a last resort you can use hot glass. Read on....

PIPES AND PUNTIES

Pipes and punties are as indispensible to blowing hot glass as the molten vitreous material itself. They're available in all lengths, diameters and weights. USE THE RIGHT ONE FOR THE JOB AT HAND. **Bent pipes got you down?** Don't bend 'em in the first place!!!

If you want your pipes to last → Don't quench them in water. Let them air cool in a pipe bucket to get the glass to pop off. **Tip→** Buy enough pipes in the first place so you're not forced to quench them all the time. **Safety Tip→** If you have to quench a blowpipe for whatever reason, put your thumb on the end of the pipe before sticking it in the water. Otherwise you'll end up shooting steam out the end in a highly hazardous fashion.

Sometimes you may pick up a pipe, (or more likely a hollow punty,) which is screamin' hot-to-touch-out of the pipewarmer. Chances are, water is trapped on the inside (and turned to steam). Oftentimes with the punties a small pin hole has occurred near the weld and water has entered there. Set it aside, mark it, and get it fixed (tig weld or send it back to the manufacturer.).

Avoid heating too deeply in the furnace or glory hole. This will put unnecessary stress on your pipe. Don't heat it too quickly - if you can help it - for the same reason. If, by chance, you forget your pipe's heating-up in the glory hole and it's screamin' hot - pull it out and stand it in the corner to air cool naturally. DO NOT QUENCH IT! ouch!

CLEANING PIPES

If your pipe gets clogged — heat up the tip and blow out the junk with a blast of compressed air (watch where you're aiming that pipe - you don't wanna nail someone accidently!) or a big puff from your lungs & cap the pipe. Use your tweezers to pull the rest of the **SCHMUTZ** out. Avoid jamming your shears or tweezers inside your pipes. It may end up pushing the glass further up the pipe, and is tool unfriendly.

For glass which is stuck on the pipe head, either leave it and gather over it. Or allow it to **FULLY COOL** to see if it will pop-off naturally. Don't use a hammer (or your shears!) to smash the glass off! You could try blasting it with a torch to thermally shock the glass to make it pop off. Don't try this in the pipe warmer or glory hole. Sure, it's an effective technique, but it's bad for the equipment. And don't get the pipe screaming hot and cut the glass off with the trimming shears. It's harsh on the shears and the pipe. And, as stated earlier, quenching the blowpipe shortens the lifespan of the tool however it does do the trick if you're in a big hurry, and have money to burn.

SCALE

ALL STEEL IS PRONE TO SCALE. IT'S THE NATURE OF THE BEAST. IT'S THE BLOWPIPE (TUBE) - NOT THE HEAD WHICH IS MOST LIKELY TO SCALE. IT'S A SIGN THAT THE PIPE HAS BEEN ABUSED. THERE'S NOT MUCH YOU CAN DO FOR IT. YOU CAN SEND IT BACK FOR REPAIR. OR RETIRE IT BY THE WAYSIDE (PIPES MAKE NICE WALL ORNAMENTATION). OR YOU CAN GIVE IT AWAY TO A BEGINNER WHO IS FOND OF THE MIXED MEDIA APPROACH TO GLASSMAKING. THOSE MYSTERIOUS BLACK METAL "INCLUSIONS" MIGHT JUST BE THEIR TICKET TO SUCCESS.

PITS AND FRACTURES

NEARLY EVERY STUDIO HAS AT LEAST ONE PIPE THAT LOOKS LIKE IT WAS USED TO STOKE THE COALS FOR WORLD WAR III. THE END OR HEAD APPEARS HEAVILY PITTED, EVEN FRACTURED. THE POOR PIPE HAS BEEN SUBJECTED TO LIFE-SHORTENING ABUSE. GRANTED, MOLTEN GLASS IS A CORROSIVE, BUT IT IS COMPOUNDED BY DRAMATIC CHANGES IN TEMPERATURE → FROM QUENCHING, WHICH LEADS TO IT'S ULTIMATE DEMISE. IF THE PITS AND FRACTURES ARE NOT TOO DEEP, YOU CAN TRY BENCH GRINDING THE METAL TO SMOOTH THINGS OUT. OR IF THEY'RE REALLY DEEP, YOU MAY WANT TO SEND THE PIPE OUT TO GET A NEW HEAD WELDED ON IT. ALL THOSE PITS ARE LIKELY TO TRAP AIR BUBBLES - WHICH CAN BE DISENCHANTING FOR PEOPLE WANTING NICE CLEAN GATHERS.

STRAIGHTENING PIPES

THE FIRST THING TO SAY ABOUT STRAIGHTENING PIPES AND PUNTIES ⇒ **DON'T BEND THEM TO BEGIN WITH!** rule #1.

HEY..!!! IF YOU EVEN SUSPECT THAT YOU'RE GOING TO NEED OR USE EXTRA GATHERS OF GLASS - GET A PIPE (OR PUNTY) WHICH IS DESIGNED AND BUILT TO HANDLE THE WEIGHT OF THE GLASS WHICH YOU ARE WORKING. SEEING YOUR PIPE BOW UNDER THE WEIGHT AND STRAIN OF BIG GATHERS MAY MAKE YOU FEEL MACHO - BUT INEVITABLY LEADS TO BENT PIPES.

PIPES AND PUNTIES ARE PARTICULARLY PRONE TO BENDING WHEN THEY ARE HEATED TOO DEEPLY IN THE FURNACE AND GLORY HOLE. THIS CAUSES YOU TO GRIP THE PIPE FURTHER AWAY AND SHIFTS YOUR POINT OF BALANCE. THAT, IN TURN, MAKES IT MUCH MORE DIFFICULT TO MANUVER THE PIPE, AND MAY FORCE YOU TO LET THE PIPE SLAM DOWN ON THE YOKE OR MARVER OR BENCH CAUSING IT TO BEND. OOPS!

DAMN! GUESS I SHOULD'VE USED A HEAVYWEIGHT PIPE THIS TIME!

BITING OFF MORE THAN YOU CAN CHEW. (I ACTUALLY SAW THIS HAPPEN TO A STUDENT AT PILCHUCK™ IN 1987!)

WELL, THE EASIEST WAY TO STRAIGHTEN YOUR PIPES IS TO SEND THEM BACK TO THE MANUFACTURER AND HAVE THEM FIX IT. MOST OF US CAN'T WAIT THAT LONG OR AFFORD IT. THEY ARE, HOWEVER, BETTER EQUIPPED FOR DEALING WITH IT AND IT MAY TEACH YOU THE FIRST RULE OF BENT PIPES MORE EFFECTIVELY (THAT IS, THROUGH YOUR WALLET!)

ONE OF THE WORST WAYS TO TRY N' STRAIGHTEN YOUR PIPES IS TO HEAT THEM DEEPLY IN THE GLORY HOLE AND SLAM THEM DOWN ON THE BENCH. EVEN THOUGH YOU MAY HAVE SEEN SOME 'EXPERIENCED' GLASSBLOWERS DO IT THAT WAY - AND IT SEEMS TO WORK - IT'S VERY TOUGH ON THE WELD THAT JOINS THE PIPE TO THE HEAD. IT'S ALSO **VERY EASY** TO SCREW THINGS UP WORSE AND COMPOUND THE BENDS IN YOUR PIPE - FORCING YOU TO HAVE TO SEND THE THING BACK ANYWAY. HERE'S WHAT YOU CAN TRY TO GET YOUR PIPE BACK ON-CENTER.

FIRST, YOU HAVE TO LOCATE WHERE THE PIPE IS BENT. A SET OF ROLLERS CLAMPED TO THE MARVER CAN HELP. TURN THE PIPE TO FIND THE HIGH SPOT. SIGHT DOWN THE LENGTH OF THE PIPE AND DOUBLE CHECK BY LOOKING AT IT FACE-ON → PERPENDICULAR TO THE AXIS. MARK THE HIGHSPOT WITH CHALK OR A CHINA MARKER. SET THE PIPE (OR PUNTY) BETWEEN TWO 2"x4"'s AND GIVE IT A GOOD WHACK WITH ANOTHER 2"x4".

CAUTION: GO SLOW! DON'T WAIL ON IT SO HARD THAT YOU BEND IT TOO FAR! TAKE SMALL STEPS. CHECK AND RE-CHECK THE ROLL AND REALLY STUDY THE NATURE OF THE BEND. IT'S SIMILAR TO THE CARPENTERS ADAGE → **MEASURE TWICE, CUT ONCE**. OR WHAT KNITTERS SWEAR BY: "A STITCH IN TIME SAVES NINE."

ANOTHER WAY YOU CAN STRAIGHTEN THEM IS BY USING THE JAWS OF A VISE TO TRY AND UNBEND YOUR PIPE. LOCATE THE HIGH SPOT AND SET IT GENTLY IN THE VISE WITH

THE HIGH SPOT RIGHT ON THE OUTER EDGE OF THE JAWS. YOU'LL BE TORQUING AGAINST THAT SPOT TO TRY AND UNBEND IT THERE BY PULLING OR HITTING THE PIPE IN THE OPPOSITE DIRECTION OF THE BEND. **DO NOT PULL ON THE HANDLE** → EVEN THOUGH IT MAY GIVE YOU TREMENDOUS LEVERAGE - IT CAN LIKELY BOW YOUR PIPE IN THE MIDDLE AND COMPLICATE EVERYTHING FURTHER. FIND A SPOT ABOUT MIDWAY FROM THE BEND AND THE END OF THE PIPE TO PULL OR HIT AGAINST. AGAIN, GO SLOW - CHECK AND RECHECK AND TRY YOUR BEST TO GET IT REALIGNED.

BUYING PIPES: GET AS MANY PIPES AS YOU CAN AFFORD. THEY'RE WORTH THE INVESTMENT! PURCHASE THE ONES YOU NEED. IF YOU PLAN ON MAKING VENETIAN-STYLE CUPS, FIND A SOURCE FOR LIGHTWEIGHT PIPES AND PUNTIES. ASK OTHER GAFFERS. ATTEND A G.A.S. CONFERENCE AND SEE FOR YOURSELF WHAT NEW WARES ARE AVAILABLE.

IF YOU'RE BLOWING LARGE GLASS OR SOLID WORKING HEFTY PIECES - YOU'LL WANT LARGE DIAMETER PIPES WITH PUNTIES OF EQUAL DIAMETER. IT MAKES THE TRANSFER PROCESS EASIER TO DEAL WITH. COUNTERWEIGHTED PUNTIES ARE NICE. THEY HELP YOU MAINTAIN AN EVEN BALANCE AND WON'T TORQUE YOUR WRISTS AS BAD. STEP-DOWN PUNTIES ARE CONVENIENT - IN SOME CASES. THEY ALLOW YOU MORE GRIPPING AREA WITH LESS SURFACE CONTACT ON THE TIP. IT MAY BE WHAT YOU NEED.

USUAGE TAKE CARE OF YOUR PIPES AND PUNTIES. ENGRAVE YOUR NAME ON THEM. MARK THEM ALSO WITH COLORED TAPE NEAR THE HANDLE. THIS WILL HELP MAKE YOUR PIPES EASY TO IDENTIFY — AND HOPEFULLY NO ONE WILL TAKE THEM BY MISTAKE.

ADJUST YOUR PIPE WARMER SO THE PIPE TIPS GLOW A NICE SOFT ORANGE, NOT BRILLIANT RED. IT'S A GOOD IDEA TO STATION A SMALL BUCKET OF WATER ON THE FLOOR IN FRONT OF THE FURNACE. YOU CAN DIP YOUR PIPE 2"- 3" (Remember to cap the pipe!) IN IT PRIOR TO YOUR FIRST GATHER. THIS MICRO-QUENCH WILL HELP CLEAN OFF ANY CARBON THAT MIGHT GET DEPOSITED THERE FROM THE PIPE WARMER. IT SEEMS TO KEEP THE PIPES FROM OFF-GASING AND CREATING SMALL AIR BUBBLES. ALSO, IT SEEMS TO ALLOW THE GLASS TO STICK BETTER TO THE PIPE.

BLOCKS

These fundamental tools can make your life as a glassblower much easier. They require little-to-no maintenance. Just keep them wet so they don't dry and crack. As stated earlier in this book, they may require a little burning-in period. A hot gather with continuous blocking and occasional quenches in the water should carbonize the interior of the block sufficiently.

You can purchase blocks in all sizes and shapes. Or you can carve or lathe-turn your own out of apple, or preferably, cherry wood. The wood should be green and you should know your way around a woodshop to get what you want. It does take time, but there's nothing quite like using a tool that you made yourself — especially one which works!

JACKS

The shape of this tool hasn't changed much in the last two thousand years of glassblowing. They come in all sizes and shapes. Some are designed for very specific purposes, while others do a good job as all-around jacks. Each pair of jacks has their own personality — from the spring in the handle to the shape of its blades. Jacks should not require much in the way of maintenance. Keep them well-lubricated with beeswax or carnauba wax. Avoid dropping them on the floor! **NEVER NECK PIECES WHICH ARE COLD.** You'll end up grinding off the metal and shortening the lifespan of the tool. → Ever wonder why you have to trim off that black shit on the lips of your pieces?... Get a clue → HOT GOOD, COLD BAD!

When buying jacks for the first time, select a pair which you can afford and works best for the style of glass which you intend on working.

"**You should not buy $300 cup jacks unless you're selling cups for $300!**" - Jim Moore. Simple economics. Unless, of course, you have oodles of cash to burn and/or you like to collect tools.

Know your regions of your jacks. Periodically check the blades for wear and tear. It's possible to have new ones put on if you're particularly tough on them (lighten-up dude!).

Preheated jacks will cut better than cold ones (some gaffers blast the blades with a torch prior to necking), but usually after coming in contact with the hot glass the jacks will get plenty hot! When they're hot, it's a good time to continue to wax 'em, especially if you feel extra resistance, or they start squeaking on you.

You can straighten your jacks, if, for whatever reason, they get bent. Like blowing glass you start from the back and work your way forward. First, locate the bend by sighting where it occurs. Look down the lengths of the blades. Examine it sideways. If the handles are not in-line with each other — you'll have to retorque them back into position. You grip a handle in each hand. Depending on which side you think needs to be realigned — set that handle in the torquing hand (your dominant hand). Use the other hand as a brace — in fact you can actually

Labels on jacks diagram: MINI MARVER, HANDLE (BOTTLE OPENER), COOLER REGION FOR CHILLING, NECKING AND GRIPPING AREA, REGIONS OF THE JACKS

Brace it against your body for additional support. Give a short deliberate pull and check it. Hopefully you've done just enough to get it back in-line. Take it in small steps. Repull/retorque if necessary. Or if you've gone too far, bend it back in the other direction. Once you have the handles matched-up and in line, it's time to pay attention to the blades.

Start from this end - down →

If bend is here

Grip here and tug lightly ↓

Using a vise: straightening the jacks.

Oftentimes one blade might be outta whack, and the other may be straight. If that's the case, you only have to get that first blade straight, and can use the other as a guide. Again, sight down the length of the blade to find where the kink or bend is. Mark that spot by setting your thumb and forefinger there. Place the blade into the vise - you don't have to clamp it down, you only need a gap in which you can bend against. Set that point where your thumb or forefinger are at the edge of the vise and tug slightly in the opposite direction of the bend to straighten it. Lift the jacks out of the vise and check what you did. Continue your way down the length of the blade(s) to get the whole thing straight and inline.

Once your blades are straight, recheck the handle. It's possible that it may need to be realigned after all that bending. If you fail miserably to re-straighten your jacks, you can always send 'em in to be re-tuned...

CUP JACKS

These tools are specially designed for working on goblets. You can take one blade from normal jacks and make two blades for cup jacks out of them. In other words, the blades are thinner and lighter. They consequently won't chill the glass quite as quickly as the regular jacks will.

The blades are also specially shaped to allow you to open up feet (on goblets) uniformly. There's a slight angle in the jacks to accommodate this. When the jacks are slightly opened, the blades become parallel, allowing you to flare feet and bowls in a straight line, whereas the normal jacks have a curve to them ↝ which makes it very difficult to get the right shape to occur.

The **tips** of **cup jacks** are also **domed**. This feature allows you to ride on the inside of your cups (and flares) without fear of scratching, or jabbing, or sticking the interior.

If you spend the money on these puppy's, take good care of 'em. Use them only for goblets and delicate work. Do not attempt to use them to neck gargantuan pieces, (or open paint cans with!).

PACIOFFI'S

Also known as wooden jacks, **PACIOFFIS** are hybrids. They have very specific uses, such as for overlay work, opening certain styles of goblets and accentuating various forms and curves. The fact that the tips are made of wood allow this tool to do it's work without chilling or marring the surface of your glass.

Normally these tools are made from spring steel. That means that they will rust away to nothing given the moisture or water to do so. What that means is: **DON'T STORE THEM IN A BUCKET OF WATER!**

THE TRICK TO MAINTAINING YOUR PACIOFFIS IS TO STORE THE HANDLES IN A DRY WARM PLACE AND THE WOODEN DOWELS ('BLADES') IN A BUCKET OF WATER. BE SURE TO DRY OFF YOUR METAL AFTER YOUR DONE USING THEM.

YOU CAN USE SEVERAL DIFFERENT LENGTHS AND SHAPES OF STICKS IN THE SAME HANDLE - INCREASING THE VERSATILITY OF THIS TOOL. OFTEN THE STICKS ARE MADE OF CHERRY WOOD.

PACIOFFIS

YOU CAN ALSO USE GRAPHITE RODS - WHICH WILL ALSO LEAVE YOUR GLASS SCAR-FREE. GRAPHITE, HOWEVER, TENDS TO SUCK THE HEAT OUT OF YOUR HOT GLASS, SO THEIR PERFORMANCE IS SLIGHTLY DIFFERENT. THEY CAN ALSO BE CARVED FOR SPECIFIC USES, SUCH AS FOR CREATING A CERTAIN DIAMETER NECKLINE IN THE MAKING OF LAMPSHADES OR SOME OTHER PRODUCTION-LINE ITEM. THE ONLY OTHER DRAWBACK TO GRAPHITE IS THAT IT IS VERY BRITTLE. DO NOT DROP THEM! THEY CAN, AND WILL BREAK!

THE FINISHING TOOL

ANOTHER STYLE OF JACKS WHICH IS DESIGNED AND BUILT FOR ONE SPECIFIC PURPOSE - TO CREATE AN EXACT NECK AND/OR LIP ON YOUR BLOWN GLASS. I HAVE ONE WHICH ALLOWS ME TO CREATE THE BOTTLE NECK AND MOUTH WHICH ACCEPTS THE CROWN CAPS FOR MY HANDBLOWN HOMEBREW BOTTLES. PRIOR TO AUTOMATION, TOOLS LIKE THESE WERE USED TO FINISH ALL SORTS OF CAPPABLE BOTTLES. THEY ARE STILL FOUND IN THE LAMPWORKING/SCIENTIFIC GLASS INDUSTRY AND USED TO CREATE SEALS AND JOINTS IN BOROSILICATE TUBING.

TO USE THEM, FIRST YOU HAVE TO FIND A PAIR. OR YOU CAN HAVE A MACHINIST MAKE A PAIR FOR YOU - EXACTLY TO THE DIMENSIONS YOU NEED. THESE TOOLS WORK BEST WHEN PREHEATED. YOU MAY USE BEESWAX, CARNAUBA WAX, "MILTON MUD", OR A GRAPHITE WASH AS A LUBRICANT TO KEEP THE TOOL FROM STICKING TO THE GLASS, AND PROLONG THE LIFE OF THE BLADES.

THE PIECE YOU'RE WORKING ON SHOULD BE GOOD N' HOT TOO. AS WITH ANY MOLD-BLOWING/FORMING PROCESS, THE CLOSER YOU CAN GET YOUR GLASS TO THE SIZE AND SHAPE OF THE MOLD - THE BETTER. YOU DON'T WANT TO FORCE THE GLASS TO DO SOMETHING IT DOESN'T WANT TO DO. YOU'LL NEED SOME STABILITY IN THE NECK OR IT WILL CRINKLE WHILE ATTEMPTING TO FORM THE LIP. USE COMPRESSED AIR OR A PUFF FROM THE SOFFIETTA TO CHILL IT UP, OR JUST BE CAREFUL ON HOW YOU HEAT IT.

INSERT THE TOOL UP INSIDE THE NECK AND SLOWLY CLAMP DOWN, MAKING FULL REVOLUTIONS AS YOU DO SO. ALLOW THE COMPLETE ROTATIONS AND CONTACT WITH THE TOOL TO DO THE WORK. DON'T FORCE IT! LOOK CLOSELY AS YOU DO SO TO MAKE SURE YOU HAVE COMPLETE CONTACT.

IT SHOULD ONLY TAKE A PASS OR TWO DOWN THE RAILS TO GET THE LIP FULLY FORMED. BOX THE PIECE WHEN COMPLETED.

A FINISHING TOOL & BOTTLE.

THESE TOOLS SHOULD NOT REQUIRE TOO MUCH IN THE WAY OF MAINTENANCE. BE SURE TO USE SOME FORM OF LUBRICANT ON THE BLADES. YOU MAY END UP HAVING TO REPLACE THE BLADES OR CENTER POST AFTER THEY NO LONGER FUNCTION CORRECTLY, BUT IT'LL TAKE ALOT OF USE (OR ABUSE) TO GET THEM THAT WORN.

TWEEZERS THESE TOOLS ARE THE CLOSEST YOU CAN COME TO TOUCHING HOT GLASS WITHOUT BURNING YOUR FINGERS. THEY ARE AVAILABLE IN SEVERAL DIFFERENT SIZES AND A COUPLE OF DIFFERENT SHAPES. FOR MOST GLASS ARTISTS, A PAIR OF TWEEZERS ARE ONLY AS GOOD AS THEIR POINTS ARE SHARP. THE REST IS SECONDARY. WELL... ALMOST. THE SPRING ACTION IN THE HANDLE IS IMPORTANT. YOU DON'T WANT TO HAVE TO APPLY TREMENDOUS AMOUNTS OF PRESSURE JUST TO GET THE TIPS TO MEET, AND LIKEWISE YOU DON'T WANT A PAIR THAT FEELS MUSHY OR IS SLOW TO OPEN, OR DOESN'T OPEN UP FAR ENOUGH. ALSO, IN ORDER FOR THIS TOOL TO WORK WELL FOR YOU, IT'S HELPFUL IF THE POINTS MEET WHEN YOU CLOSE THEM!

STRAIGHT, POINTED, TWEEZERS DO REQUIRE SOME ATTENTION PERIODICALLY TO KEEP THEM IN SHAPE. FIRST, TRY TO KEEP THEM FROM RUSTING. DON'T STORE THEM IN YOUR BLOCK BUCKET! IF THEY GET WET, DRY THEM OFF, ESPECIALLY AT THE END OF YOUR BLOWING PERIOD.

AVOID DROPPING YOUR TWEEZERS! THE TIPS ARE LIKELY TO GET DULLED BY SUCH ABUSE. THESE TOOLS ARE NOT INDESTRUCTIBLE. IF YOUR POINTS DO GET DULL, YOU CAN FILE THEM DOWN UNTIL THEY ARE SHARP AGAIN. USE A STRAIGHT, FINE TOOTHED FILE (FOR METAL), CLAMP THEM IN A VISE AND FILE UNTIL THE POINTS ARE HOW YOU LIKE THEM.

NOT ALL TWEEZERS ARE CREATED EQUAL. NOT ALL TWEEZERS ARE MADE TO WORK WITH HOT GLASS. THE TEMPERATURES THAT TWEEZERS COME IN CONTACT WITH ARE MORE THAN ENOUGH TO MELT AND DESTROY "ORDINARY TWEEZERS". IF YOU LOOK CLOSELY AT A PAIR OF STANDARD TWEEZERS (DESIGNED FOR HOT GLASS USE) YOU'LL NOTICE AN EXTRA BIT OF METAL THERE RIGHT BEHIND THE POINTS. THIS IS DONE SO YOUR TIPS CAN WITHSTAND EXTREME TEMPERATURES WITHOUT MELTING OR BENDING THE METAL, AND SO YOUR TWEEZERS WILL LAST LONGER. AS TEMPTING AS IT IS - DON'T GRIND OR FILE AWAY THIS METAL. YOU CAN'T PUT IT BACK! INSTEAD - IF YOU WANT A PAIR OF REALLY POINTY TWEEZERS - BUY THEM! MANY TOOL MAKERS HAVE AVAILABLE A SMALLER, MORE DELICATE STYLE OF TWEEZERS WITH WHICH YOU CAN REMOVE SPLINTERS, PULL PONIES, AND YANK NOSE HAIRS. DO NOT, HOWEVER, GO DIGGING BUBBLES OR STONES OUTTA BIG GATHERS OF HOT GLASS WITH THEM IF YOU EXPECT THEM TO LAST YOU ANY LENGTH OF TIME. THE METAL CAN'T TAKE THAT KIND OF ABUSE.

IF YOUR POINTS DON'T LINE-UP AND MEET WHEN YOU CLOSE THEM, YOU CAN TRY TORQUING THE HANDLES A LITTLE UNTIL THEY DO. YOU CAN CURVE THE TIPS SLIGHTLY BY COLD FORGING THEM WITH A HAMMER. SET THE TIPS CLOSELY TO THE END OF A METAL TABLE OR NEAR THE END OF A VISE AND TAP LIGHTLY UNTIL YOU ACHIEVE THE CURVE YOU DESIRE. OR YOU CAN ATTEMPT TO BEND THEM IN A NEARLY CLOSED VISE BY TORQUING THE TIPS THERE. GO SLOWLY SO AS NOT TO OVERDO IT! **CHECK AND RECHECK** YOUR PROGRESS EVERY STEP OF THE WAY.

TRY TO KEEP YOUR TWEEZERS AWAY FROM THE WAX. IT'S SO FRUSTRATING WHEN YOU GET TO A CRITICAL POINT IN YOUR BLOWING PROCESS AND YOUR TWEEZERS SLIP OF THE GLASS INSTEAD OF GRABBING HOLD. IF YOU DO GET WAX ON THEM, WARM-UP THE TWEEZERS BY A HEAT SOURCE AND WIPE THEM OFF ON A RAG, PANTLEG OR SOME NEWSPAPER. YOU CAN ALSO USE A LIGHTWEIGHT (00) STEEL WOOL OR "SCRUBBIE" TO CLEAN YOUR TOOLS WITH. THE HOT GLASS METHOD OF CLEANING TOOLS, ALTHOUGH EFFECTIVE (SOMEWHAT) ISN'T THE FASTEST OR BEST WAY TO GO ABOUT REMOVING WAX. IT JUST PUTS UNNECESSARY STRESS ON THE METAL, IT CAN EASILY BURN YOU AND CAN SHORTEN THE LIFE OF YOUR TOOL. THE BEST TIP TO OFFER CONCERNING UNWANTED WAX ON YOUR TOOLS IS → DON'T GET WAX ON THEM IN THE FIRST PLACE! PLACE THOSE TOOLS AWAY FROM YOUR JACKS AND THE WAX. HANG THEM UP ON A HOOK OR SET THEM ON THE SEAT OF THE BENCH - WHERE YOU CAN EASILY REACH THEM - AND RETURN them to that spot when you are finished. MARK GIBEAU, a Canadian glass artist and equipment builder came up with an innovative solution to the problem. He welds rings on the edge of the bench (about the diameter of a beer can). The rings will universally accept any size of shears, make them easy to see and grab, and are a simple target to hit when you're done using them. They're great to hang tweezers on too! Another benifit is they wont jab you in the leg like nails or pegs will if you bump-up against them accidently.

If you enjoy doing bitwork and adding **ACCENTS** to your glasswork, you might consider investing in a pair of **FLAT-BLADED TWEEZERS** AND/OR **LEAF CRIMPS**. These tools are made in several different sizes, widths and styles. Before you lay out the bucks to buy a pair, ask around first. Maybe borrow a friends tool (asking first, of course) and try them out. Understand how they work, and if they'll do the job you want them to. There may be a time you want to squash some glass without lines (like are produced from leaf crimps) — and other times you do. Maybe you should buy both pairs... It all depends on what you're making and how vital a particular tool is to the process. Maybe you can get by or make do with another tool or method.

WAX ON YOUR TOOLS? HANG 'EM UP!

The nice thing about flat-bladed tweezers and crimps is that they require little-to-no maintenance. Just do your best to keep them warm and dry — rust free, and they should offer you years of obedient service.

SHEARS
Most glass tools are designed to withstand a fair amount of use and abuse. Shears are no exception to the rule. They will, however, get dull and fail to cut glass properly if they are used incorrectly ~ i.e. if you attempt to cut glass when it's too cold. I've said it once, I'll say it again, **SHEARS ARE NOT HAMMERS! SHEARS ARE NOT SAWS!** It's not so much how often you use 'em, it's HOW you use them.

DIAMOND SHEARS, TRIMMING SHEARS, CUP SHEARS, AND CASTING SHEARS come in all sorts of sizes and shapes. They're manufactured in many different countries. Selecting a pair or three can be something of a challenge. There are pro's and con's to virtually every pair. Meniconi-Putsch make great shears, yet their blades will break if you drop them too hard. So be careful. Some shears are easier to sharpen than others. Alot of it has to do with their individual design and manu- facture. If you're in the market for shears, ask around first. See and feel as many styles as you can. Some shears will fit better in your hand than others. Some shears seem to cut better than others. Some of that may be on how sharp the tool is, how hot or thick the glass is, or even how you go about cutting the glass itself.

MOST SHEARS CAN BE TAKEN APART AND SHARPENED. The easiest way to do this is to put 'em in a box and send them back to the manufacturer to get **RE-TUNED**. You can, however, sharpen them yourself. That is, of course, if you have the right tools and <u>SKILL</u> to do so. Now, you don't have to be a rocket-scientist to do this, but you should be famaliar with metal working tools and techniques. It's possible that you can ruin them in the process of trying to fix 'em, in which case you put the pieces in a box and send them back to the manufacturer to get it done the right way, or if you're too embarrassed by your mistake — just buy another pair and keep your mouth shut, and the tool locked-up (or donate it to a glass school.)

Anyways, following the seven-step program outlined on the next page or two, you should be able to put a nice edge on your shears in around 30 minutes or so.

SHARPENING SHEARS:

STEP ONE: Perhaps the most important one of them all. Look closely at your shears BEFORE you take them apart. You cannot properly sharpen your tool if it's bolted together. Examine how they are made. The biggest problem people encounter when they take their tools apart, is how to reassemble them correctly. Most shears only go together one way, otherwise they just won't work. Either lay the tool out in a specific pattern or lable everything, so you know exactly how to put them back together. Use a box-style wrench to loosen the nut.

STEP TWO: Look again closely at your shears. See if there are signs of wear. Look at the gap between the blades by holding them up to the light, for diamond shears. If there's alot of wear, you may have to send them back to get worked on. It takes some special equipment to deal with that problem. Some shears, however, will show a gap because their blades have a slight curve built into them e.g. Menicuni-Putsch. Don't worry about it then. Once you have your tool taken apart, lay it out in a safe place, mark each piece if that helps, and deal with each blade individually.

Look between the blades for a gap showing wear.

Check for wear here

Inside surface

STEP THREE: Most glass shears have two bevels ground into them. There's a **MACRO BEVEL** and a **MICRO BEVEL**. The macro bevel is the large obvious angle to the cutting surface. It's designed to hold the cutting edge. The micro bevel is the actual cutting edge and is (as it sounds) very small. Ordinary kitchen knives ONLY HAVE A MICRO BEVEL, for example. There exists a balance between the two bevels which makes them work and suitable for cutting hot glass. It's a balance of heat contact and the work it's suppose to do. If the micro bevel is too large — the metal will be very thin there, consequently it will heat up too quickly and wear away faster. If the micro bevel is worn or absent ALTOGETHER — you'll only have a macro bevel to cut with → and you may end up just pushing the glass around instead of cutting it.

MACRO BEVEL
MICRO BEVEL
CROSS-SECTION OF A GLASS SHEAR CUTTING EDGE.

Your task here is to determine which bevel you need to grind. Most of the time your only concern is to tune-up the micro bevel. But if it has been worn out of existence, you may need to take the macro bevel down a little to make room for the micro-bevel.

STEP FOUR: Grinding your bevels. Usually you only need to regrind the micro bevel. Begin by wearing the correct safety equipment → protective goggles or safety glasses, gloves, hearing protection and a respirator. Since most shears are constructed of metal harder than most files — you're going to have to use a disc sander → hand held angle grinder style → to do the job. You could use a diamond hone (available through industrial supply houses and cutlery suppliers) to grind or sand the metal with — but most glass shops will have an angle grinder handy.

A used 60-grit or fresh semi-80 grit disc works best. Don't use one right out of the box — if they're too sharp they have a tendency to take away too much metal too fast! **GO SLOW!** Once it's gone, it's gone. You can't put the metal back. Slap your tool in the vise and clamp it so you can easily see and grind the angle you need without being in an awkward position. Feel free to reposition the tool in the vise for every angle you're grinding. Try to use the established lines as your guide. Check to be certain the angle of your grinder is match-

ING THAT OF THE MICRO BEVEL. MAKE A PASS OR TWO. LOOK AT WHAT YOU DID. ADJUST IF NECESSARY, THE ANGLE AT WHICH YOU'RE GRINDING.

ALWAYS WEAR PROPER SAFETY EQUIPMENT WHEN GRINDING!

CONTINUE TO GRIND UNTIL THE BEVEL IS EVEN AND PARALLEL TO THE OTHER (MACRO BEVEL). EVERYTHING SHOULD APPEAR SYMMETRICAL.

SAND THE MACRO BEVEL IF NECESSARY. START AT THE BACK END OF THE BLADE FIRST. GET IT SO THE BEVEL IS UNIFORM. THEN RE-ESTABLISH YOUR MICRO BEVEL. IT'S A 15° ANGLE - ALMOST PERPENDICULAR TO THE CUTTING BLADE, BUT WITH A SLIGHT TILT. ← MAKE SURE THAT SLIGHT TILT GOES THE RIGHT WAY (SAME DIRECTION AS THE MACRO BEVEL!), OR THE SHEARS WON'T CUT FOR YOU.

MOST DIAMOND SHEARS WILL EITHER HAVE A 90° CUT IN THEM OR SPORT A RADIUS CURVE ON THEIR INSIDE CUTTING EDGE. WHICH-EVER YOUR SHEAR HAS, DO YOUR BEST TO MIMIC THAT LINE. DON'T LEAVE "BOOGERS" OF METAL THERE WHEN GRINDING, IT WILL SCREW UP YOUR CUTTING POTENTIAL. AGAIN, DO YOUR BEST TO MAINTAIN THE ESTABLISHED LINES. ONCE YOU FINISH THE FIRST BLADE DO THE SECOND IN THE SAME MANNER.

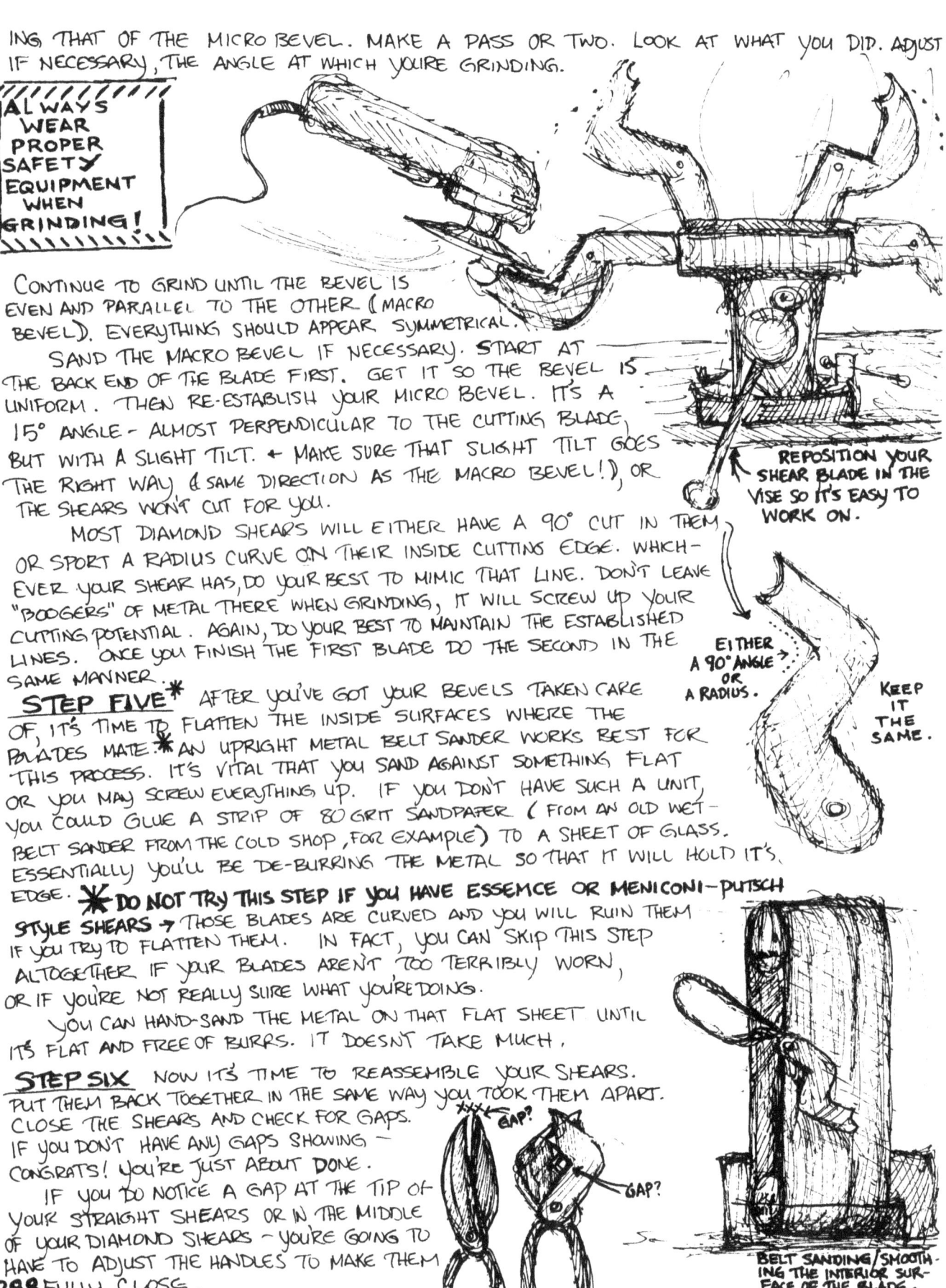

REPOSITION YOUR SHEAR BLADE IN THE VISE SO IT'S EASY TO WORK ON.

EITHER A 90° ANGLE OR A RADIUS. KEEP IT THE SAME.

STEP FIVE*
AFTER YOU'VE GOT YOUR BEVELS TAKEN CARE OF, IT'S TIME TO FLATTEN THE INSIDE SURFACES WHERE THE BLADES MATE. * AN UPRIGHT METAL BELT SANDER WORKS BEST FOR THIS PROCESS. IT'S VITAL THAT YOU SAND AGAINST SOMETHING FLAT OR YOU MAY SCREW EVERYTHING UP. IF YOU DON'T HAVE SUCH A UNIT, YOU COULD GLUE A STRIP OF 80 GRIT SANDPAPER (FROM AN OLD WET-BELT SANDER FROM THE COLD SHOP, FOR EXAMPLE) TO A SHEET OF GLASS. ESSENTIALLY, YOU'LL BE DE-BURRING THE METAL SO THAT IT WILL HOLD IT'S EDGE. * **DO NOT TRY THIS STEP IF YOU HAVE ESSEMCE OR MENICONI-PUTSCH STYLE SHEARS** → THOSE BLADES ARE CURVED AND YOU WILL RUIN THEM IF YOU TRY TO FLATTEN THEM. IN FACT, YOU CAN SKIP THIS STEP ALTOGETHER IF YOUR BLADES AREN'T TOO TERRIBLY WORN, OR IF YOU'RE NOT REALLY SURE WHAT YOU'RE DOING.

YOU CAN HAND-SAND THE METAL ON THAT FLAT SHEET UNTIL IT'S FLAT AND FREE OF BURRS. IT DOESN'T TAKE MUCH.

STEP SIX
NOW IT'S TIME TO REASSEMBLE YOUR SHEARS. PUT THEM BACK TOGETHER IN THE SAME WAY YOU TOOK THEM APART. CLOSE THE SHEARS AND CHECK FOR GAPS. IF YOU DON'T HAVE ANY GAPS SHOWING - CONGRATS! YOU'RE JUST ABOUT DONE.

IF YOU DO NOTICE A GAP AT THE TIP OF YOUR STRAIGHT SHEARS OR IN THE MIDDLE OF YOUR DIAMOND SHEARS - YOU'RE GOING TO HAVE TO ADJUST THE HANDLES TO MAKE THEM FULLY CLOSE.

GAP? GAP?

BELT SANDING/SMOOTH-ING THE INTERIOR SUR-FACE OF THE BLADE.

HERE, YOU HAVE TO SET THE HANDLE METAL (ROD) IN THE VISE. **DO NOT CHUCK UP THE BLADE IN THE VISE!** YOU'RE LIABLE TO BREAK IT, ESPECIALLY THE MENICONI-RUTSCH STYLE OF SHEARS. BONK THE INSIDE EDGE OF THE HANDLE OUTWARDS WITH A MALLET. DO IT ONCE. REPEAT THIS TECHNIQUE WITH THE OTHER HALF. ONCE. REASSEMBLE YOUR SHEARS AGAIN AND CHECK FOR GAPS. REPEAT AND ADJUST AGAIN IF NECESSARY UNTIL YOU GET IT RIGHT.

BONK OUTWARDS

GRIP THE HANDLE, NOT THE BLADE IN THE VISE.

STEP SEVEN: REASSEMBLE YOUR SHEARS, CHECK AGAIN FOR GAPS IN THE BLADES AND BETWEEN THE BLADES. IF THERE'S ALOT OF LIGHT SHOWING THROUGH WHEN YOU LOOK AT THEM SIDEWAYS - YOU MAY HAVE TO SEND THEM IN TO GET READJUSTED. IT IS POSSIBLE WITH **MOORE AND TOENSING** STYLE SHEARS TO BONK THE BLADES - AT JUST THE RIGHT SPOT - TO CLOSE THAT GAP, BUT IF YOU DO IT IN THE WRONG SPOT, YOU'LL END UP BREAKING THE BLADE.

NOW IT'S TIME TO FINE-TUNE YOUR SHEARS. THERE'S SOME DEBATE AMONGST GLASSBLOWERS AS TO EXACTLY HOW TIGHT OR HOW LOOSE YOU SHOULD HAVE YOUR SHEARS. IT'S TRULY A MATTER OF PERSONAL PREFERENCE. IF THE SHEARS ARE SOMEWHAT SNUG, THEY SEEM TO CLOSE AND CUT BETTER. **PINO SIGNORETTO**, HOWEVER, PREFERS HIS SHEARS LOOSE, AND HIS HANDS SQUEEZE THE BLADES TOGETHER AS HE CUTS WITH THEM. TO EACH HIS OWN.

YOU MAY ADD A DROP OF OIL TO HELP GET THE NUT AND BOLT ASSEMBLY TO GO ON EASILY. FIRST, MAKE IT ALL FINGER TIGHT. USE A BOX WRENCH TO HELP TIGHTEN EVERYTHING JUST SNUG. A PROPERLY ADJUSTED PAIR OF SHEARS WON'T FALL OR SLAM SHUT BY THEMSELVES. THEY SHOULD HAVE A SLIGHT AMOUNT OF TENSION IN THEM. YOU CAN BACK THE BOLT OUT $1/8$th A TURN AND RECHECK. YOU THEN MAY HAVE TO TIGHTEN THE NUT UP A TOUCH TO SNUG THINGS A LITTLE FURTHER. RECHECK AND READJUST. ESSENTIALLY YOU'RE ADJUSTING THE TENSIONAL FORCE WITHIN THAT BOLT-NUT-THREADED SHEAR ASSEMBLY. THIS IS WHY THE SHEARS ARE ONLY GOING TO WORK IF THEY'RE PUT BACK TOGETHER THE WAY IN WHICH THEY'RE MADE. SO IF IT SEEMS LIKE YOU CAN'T GET THEM TO WORK NO MATTER WHAT YOU DO, YOU MAY HAVE PUT THEM TOGETHER WRONG. TRY IT ANOTHER WAY.

YOUR SKETCHBOOK: LAST BUT MOST CERTAINLY NOT THE LEAST...

YOUR SKETCHBOOK MAY BE THE CHEAPEST GLASS TOOL YOU CAN BUY, AND THE MOST VALUABLE ONE YOU HAVE. IT'S AMAZING HOW OVERLOOKED THIS "TOOL" IS. MY GUESS IS THAT MOST GLASSWORKERS CAN'T FIGURE OUT HOW IT WORKS, OR WHAT A TREMENDOUS TIME-SAVER IT CAN BE. SO USUALLY IT GETS SHELVED AWAY AND FORGOTTEN ABOUT. WHAT A SHAME...

"I CAN'T DRAW" IS THE LAMEST EXCUSE I'VE HEARD FROM MOST OF MY COLLEAGUES. BULLSHIT. ANYONE WITH AT LEAST ONE EYE, AN APPENDEGE AND A TOOL WHICH MARKS CAN DRAW!

YOU SIMPLY HAVE TO TRY IT! PRACTICE. DEVOLOP THE SKILLS NECESSARY TO SIMULATE WHAT IT IS YOU'RE TRYING TO RENDER. WHEN YOU FINALLY REALIZE THAT A DRAWING IS A **LIE - A BIG ILLUSION** - AND NOTHING MORE THAN MARKS ON A PIECE OF PAPER - THEN, YOU CAN GO ABOUT MAKING THAT ILLUSION MORE REAL. LIKE GLASSBLOWING, CERTAIN TECHNIQUES CAN HELP YOU GET TO THE FINAL RESULT EASIER AND FASTER. LOOK AT THE DRAWINGS IN THIS BOOK, FOR EXAMPLE, COPY THEM OR TRACE 'EM IF YOU HAVE TO. THEY'RE JUST A BUNCH OF SQUIGGLES! TAKE A DRAWING/DESIGN COURSE AND LEARN "THE WAY (or several of them) & uh oh... PRACTICE PRACTICE **PRACTICE!**

Common Misconceptions The World Has About Glassblowers

(or Statements / Questions which we get tired of hearing......)

1. "Oh, you make those cute little animals" or... "I saw it at the carnival" or... "Can you make me a carousel" or "Wedding cake top?"
2. "Do you ever get burned?" "Do you ever get cut?" } Only when people ask me that stupid question...
3. "Don't suck in..." (wish I had a dollar for everytime I've heard that one)
4. "Do you know Dale Gilhooly?"
5. "Can you make a bong?"
6. "Do you have this in blue? Teal? or Mauve?"
7. "How come it's so expensive?" or... "I saw it cheaper at K-Mart..."
8. "How long does it take to dry?" (Actual question asked by a spectator. Here's one more...)
9. "So, you make 'em in orange. How do you get other colors in the glass?"
10. "Aren't you hot?"
11. "I can do that... it looks easy!"
12. "Can you make a living at that?"
13. "Where's the sand?"
14. "It's like throwing pots!"

...And...

Common Misconceptions Glassblowers Have About The World...

1. "Everything can (and should) be made in glass."
2. "It ALL must be made hot."
3. "Ceramics are for losers who can't blow glass, or stand the heat."
4. "Pilchuck™ will make me famous!"
5. "If only I had good tools (or assistants) I'd be able to blow better."
6. "It's true 'cause Lino says so..."
7. "I'll have it made if I could only get in the **New Glass Review**."
8. "Nobody's buying my art... I must suck..." ☹
9. "Everyone's buying my work... I must be a good artist!" ☺
10. "Paperweight-making is for losers who can't blow."
11. "If I move to Seattle, I'm bound to become successful" or at least get a show at the Bubba Mavis gallery.

o o ☆ o o ✶ o o ☆ o o ✶ o o ☆ o o ✶ o o ☆ o o ✶ o o ☆ o o ✶ o o ☆ o o ✶ o o ☆ o o

These were some of the most popular of misconceptions. Perhaps you have some of your own favorites. Please SEND THEM IN! (address in front of book.) If they get published in the next edition - you get it free!

TEACH YOUR CHILDREN WELL

At some time or another someone along the way will ask you what all this glassblowing business is about. They may even ask you to show them how it's done or actually teach them how to do it! DON'T PANIC! Remember, someone once showed you the ropes — was patient to stand by an' watch you burn n' learn, crash n' cry. Consider it part of the fun, an opportunity to pass on useful information of what this medium is about.

IT'S SHOW N' TELL TIME...

#1. KNOW YOUR AUDIENCE. Put yourself in their shoes (the viewers). Have they ever seen glassblowing before? If they're young-uns more than likely they've never experienced the incredible magic of molten glass. Just about anything you do will amaze them. The following exercises may captivate and educate a group of school kids for a good chunk of time:

- <u>PULLING "CANE"</u>. → Run with a marble sized gather and stretch it to the limit. Practical application: this is sorta how fiber-optics are made.

- <u>BLOWING JUMBO BUBBLES</u> → Take a gather, no marver. Allow some student to blow as hard as they can to make it as large as they can. It demonstrates the plasticity of the material, and the fact you don't have to blow very hard to inflate a bubble.

- <u>ALLOW GLASS TO DRIP OFF YOUR PIPE</u> → It demonstrates the viscosity of molten glass and the effects of gravity.

- <u>KNOCK OFF A PIECE AND DON'T ANNEAL IT.</u> → In a safe location tap off a piece to demonstrate what happens to glass which doesn't get annealed. Continue with another demo and wait for it to crack.

- <u>DEMONSTRATE COLOR USUAGE</u> — use some frit or color bar — blow it out and show them the changes in color as it cools.

KEEP IT INTERESTING!
Be enthusiastic! This is, afterall, what your life is about. And who knows what effect it will have on your audience. You may recruit some future glassblowers in the crowd.

SLIDE SHOWS are another avenue by which you may inform the public about what you do and who you are. Having sat through hundreds of slide presentations, I know there are certain techniques which can lead to a successful showing:

DO: Keep it interesting. Show slides you like and ones which will appeal to your audience
- Project your voice
- Show a funny slide once in a while. Humor helps break the ice.
- Mix it up. Show process shots and finished works.
- Show your influences — other artwork, shots of nature etc.

DON'T:
- MUMBLE! → Project your voice. SCREAM
- Talk in a monotone. → A sure way to have everyone in the audience wish you were dead.
- Repeat the word "um"..."um" → It makes it seem as though you're uncertain about what you're trying to describe.
- Show 35 slides of virtually the same object → It's boring. Variety is the spice of life!
- Show the same slide SHOW over n' over. It's boring for you & the audience knows!

INSTRUCTION

Teaching can be one of the most rewarding activities, or the most harrowing experience, for any glass artist. Your approach and attitude are what can make or break the quality time spent with students.

There is nothing quite like that teaching feeling you get when you observe that look in a students eye of "I GET IT"! – as some concept or technique is (finally) understood.

Teaching is a great way to learn as well. You will learn about yourself. You will learn about someone else and their approach to life and working. You will learn about communication. → Just because you said it one way, doesn't mean it can't be interpeted another way. You will learn (if you don't already know...) the value of making mistakes. And reluctantly you will discover that people don't always listen, or can't remember a damn thing you've told them. So it goes...

A FEW RECOMMENDATIONS ON TEACHING BEGINNERS (FOR BEGINNING TEACHERS).

#1. Get them a copy of "ED'S BIG HANDBOOK OF GLASSBLOWING". I have it on good authority that this book works and explains most aspects of beginning glassblowing. It can save you alotta breath. Or better yet give them a copy of this book too!

#2. Get used to saying the following phrases – or get a T-shirt with it printed on the front and back "KEEP IT TURNING" & "HOT GOOD – COLD BAD!"

#3. Start out with a studio tour. Inform them about health and safety – first and foremost. Make sure they know where the first aid kit is and what to do in case of an emergency.

#4. Introduce yourself and everyone in the class. This will help everyone get familiar with each other.

#5. Do some basic demos. Put yourself in their shoes and explain everything you can think of. Introduce them to the heat of the furnace and glory holes – show 'em where to stand etc. Have them open doors and act as assistants. This is good training for them and allows them to become involved immediately.

#6. Practice gathering. Have them crimp-off a "flower" with the tweezers. This will help them get comfortable sitting at the bench and using tools.

#7. Practice necking spheres off with the jacks. It's tricky, but good to start them early on this challenging task.

#8. Blow some bubbles, solo and as a team. Don't bother to punty. They should learn how easy it is if the glass is hot!

#9. Paperweights are good practice for blocking and necking techniques. You can't go wrong with this one!

#10. 1st Tumbler. After a demo or two – let 'em rip! Have 'em work in teams of two or three – with one as gaffer, and the other assisting. After the piece, the roles are switched.

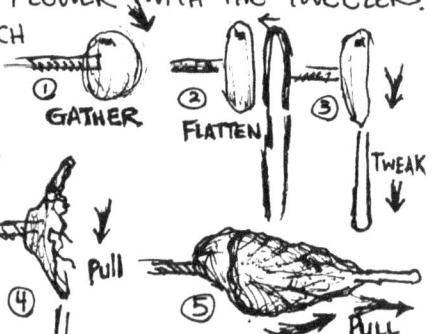

THE BUSINESS

So... you can take a dip... make a product... and sell it for big bucks... Just what makes you think you can make a living off this bewildering stuff? — Cause a few galleries sold some pieces? ...

Most everyone bitten by the glass bug dreams of having their own studio. A place where they can make whatever-the-hell they want, and they don't have to listen to anyone else telling 'em what to do. Well... there's a price that comes with that territory. And it ain't cheap! Listed below is an accumulation of observations and philosophies I have gathered over the years — primarily as a result of having worked for, & in, a number of "artists" studios.

Glass is Cheap. Melting it on the other hand isn't. The equipment you need, the fuel you burn, and the operating capital you consume — even for a small studio — can cost you in the tens of thousands of dollars!

Once you're Hot - you're Hot! Once you turn that furnace on, there's no going back. Forget about vacations. Forget about "free time". And forget about "a good nights sleep". That hungry little furnace requires fuel and glass to work. Both of which cost money.

The realization that your furnace has to run 24 hours-a-day, 365 days-a-year can be quite intimidating. The equation **Time = Money** gnaws at the back of your brain. The catch-22 / viscious circle eats away at your soul: **"To make money I need hot glass..."** **"To get hot glass, I need money..."**

Suddenly your focus changes... "Art? Who needs art? I need money!"... with thoughts like that, you know you're on the path to the point of no return.

Production is production. period. Reproducing a piece of glass time and time again in blue, purple and green should not be confused with art making. Even tho' each piece may be slightly different in shape or appearance — the reason and intent behind it's creation is to MAKE MONEY.

Making money is not what art is about. If you want to build a "factory" (a.k.a. production studio) to make money so you can fund your art habit — GOOD LUCK! Rare is the bird that can make it fly. Oftentimes you end-up 'selling your soul' just to make the bucks to survive. You discover that you no longer have the time to make the art that got you started blowing glass in the first place... unless, of course, you can stick to your plan and budget your time accordingly.

It's a Hard Road Ahead. ... Especially if you plan on doing it all by yourself. Nobody ever said it was gonna be easy. There are so many (hidden) steps involved in operating a glass studio that you damn-well better have a plan worked-out BEFORE you start shelling-out the bucks for the bricks, plumbing and building. Here's a few pointers I can come up with that may help you along the way:

Take a Few Business Courses. Or hire someone else to run the business end of things and maintain your sanity. A word of caution here — that "someone" may end-up telling you what to make in order to keep your business alive. In all likelihood - it's probably something you don't wanna hear (or especially wanna make) therefore taking that business course might be your best course of action - so, YOU can call the shots.

Have a Plan. Conduct a feasibility study. Write down what you'd like to make, how you plan to market it, what costs are involved in producing it versus the profit you stand to make off it, and what kind of demand there is for it. Sound alot like business? Congratulations... you're catching on. Much of this may depend on where you locate your studio and how you envision it operating. Are you keen to live in the

293

mountains or some rural setting, away from "civilization" — hoping to ship everything out? Or perhaps working in an urban enviornment is more to your liking. There's less power outages, cheaper utilities and more traffic flow...

Will your studio have it's own gallery? — Be open to the public or closed-up tight? You can make alot of money if you have a situation where people can watch someone working the lava (see Common Misconceptions page 290). When some people see glassblowing for the first time ~ they're usually so bedazzled that they don't think twice about coughing up the bucks for a 'souvenir' to take home with them. "**Sold-Before-It's-Cold**" is the way to go... Of course, working with the public can be very taxing (besides highly profitable). Answering the same (ignorant) questions day-in & day-out can suck the life force out of you — so beware of these types of 'gold mines.' There's not much worse than dreading having to go to work everyday ~ especially if you feel like you're a performing monkey on a stage. It all boils down to attitude. Some people thrive on the attention while others shy away from it. In this type of situation you are providing a service, an education, and creating a product all at the same time. Usually you only get paid for one of those activities, but in the long run it may pay off in the end — with repeat customers and referrels.

Consider Hiring Employees. It's very, very hard to run a hot glass business all by yourself. You need tremendous amounts of energy and enthusiasm to charge the glass, melt the glass, blow the glass, anneal the glass, coldwork the glass, market the glass, pack and ship the glass, and then deal with getting paid for the glass. By having employees or assistants, you can unload some of the less favorable of those tasks on them. Of course you're opening a whole 'nuther can of worms once you hire someone on. There's a whole list of responsibilities you need to be aware of, especially in the sue-happy society we live in. In order for you to be happy and safe, and your employee(s) as well — here's a few things to consider:

✳ 1 **Know what you want!** After that it's easy. Well, almost... Take the guess out of guesswork. That way you can delegate the needs of the business accordingly.

✳ 2. **Beware of the empty promise.** Never offer anything you can't deliver on. Your employee(s) have a remarkably clear memory when it comes to 'bene's' and activities that you entice them with. It's one of the quickest ways to lose the respect of your workers ~ to propose something (good) and not follow up on it.

✳ 3 **Be clear and honest with your employees.** Or you'll lose them.

✳ 4 **Remember the "Trickle-Down Theory".** If you're not F✱@kin' excited about your work/studio — no one else will be! Your behavior, philosophy appearance and modis operendi rubs off on the people around you.

✳ 5 **Understand the needs and wants of your employees.** Listen to them. Encourage them to make suggestions. Offer them the opportunity to use the studio in the off hours. These types of benefits, although potentially costly, will pay off in the long run, and help garner respect from your employees. Hell, they may even **LIKE** working for you then.

✳ 6 **Make certain you have a safe enviornment to work in.** With the proliferation of sue-happy lawyers today, you cannot afford to take the risk of short term or long-term injury. Buy that respirator. Invest in anti-fatigue mats. Build a powdering booth. Get some hearing protection. Have a well-stocked first-aid kit. etc.

✳ 7. **Get insurance.** Accidents happen.

✳ 8. **Take a management course.** This may help if you seem to be having problems with your workers, or if you are uncertain of your legal responsibilities and rights. Or possibly hire someone you can trust for that position.

#9. Make good use of your employees. Don't assign them tasks which are so remedial that any high school kid could do. Use them to their fullest potential to get your money's worth. And last, but definately the least...

#10 Never, ever bounce a paycheck to your employees! It's the last message you want to send to them. Always pay your workers before you 'pay' yourself. Your staff may be your most valuable resource and they should always come first. Y'know, you don't have to be their friend, but it helps!

There are a few things you can do to help yourself keep fresh and on top of the ball. I have been to too many studios where everyone is bored out of their minds.

Remember to draw! Keep your ideas flowing. Draw the pieces you make and then do five variations on them. Hopefully you can generate new forms or decorations etc. and continually evolve instead of repeating the same ol'-same ol'... Even your customers will tire of your work if it looks the same year after year (there are, of course, exceptions to every rule).

THE SAME OL' SAME OLD...

Take a class once in a while. If saving for a course at Corning, Penland, or Pilchuck (or even something completely different at a university or community college) isn't in your **budget** yet → it should be! Get refreshed, learn something new. Find a new approach and avoid becoming stale.

Go on a vacation once in a while. See the world, open your eyes. It's a great way to forget about business and an opportunity to get inspired.

Don't forget to laugh. There's W A Y too many people that take life too seriously and cease to have fun. Nobody says you can't have fun & work too!

Becoming a "glass artist" doesn't require much thought. It just seems to happen to people. Mostly it takes guts to abonden other (well paying) careers or academic pursuits.

Now, becoming a SUCCESSFUL glass artist or running your own studio is a much different thing. It takes serious planning and budgeting. To build your own equipment or just buy some package deal? There are pro's and con's to that whole scene. My own personal feeling is that only a fool would have a studio and not know how it runs or what to do if something goes wrong. 'Course, if you've got a-lotta money to burn - you can hire a technician and leave your worries behind.

Selling your glass can be easy or a huge chore. It depends on what it is, where you market it, and how much it costs. Or possibly what name gets engraved on the bottom. The sad thing is — it's not what you make, it's how good the SLIDE is. In other words, get the best possible slides of your work that you can afford. It'll get you into shows and galleries and will pay for itself in the long run.

Finally... **Work with the Community.** Both the glass art world and your local community can benefit by your participation and interaction. You'll reap rewards you never even thought of. Communication is so vital to surviving in this rapidly evolving information age. Don't be left behind.

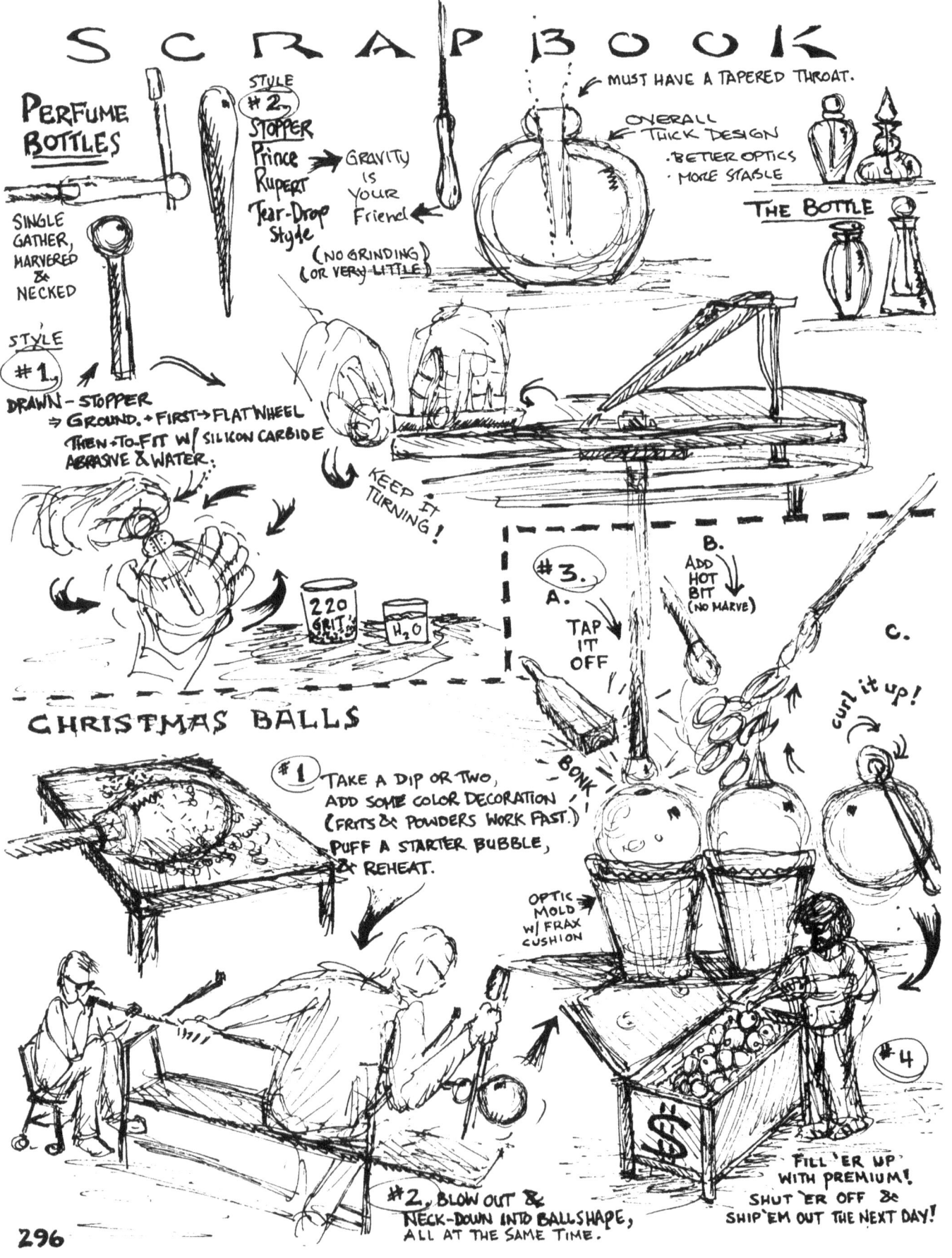

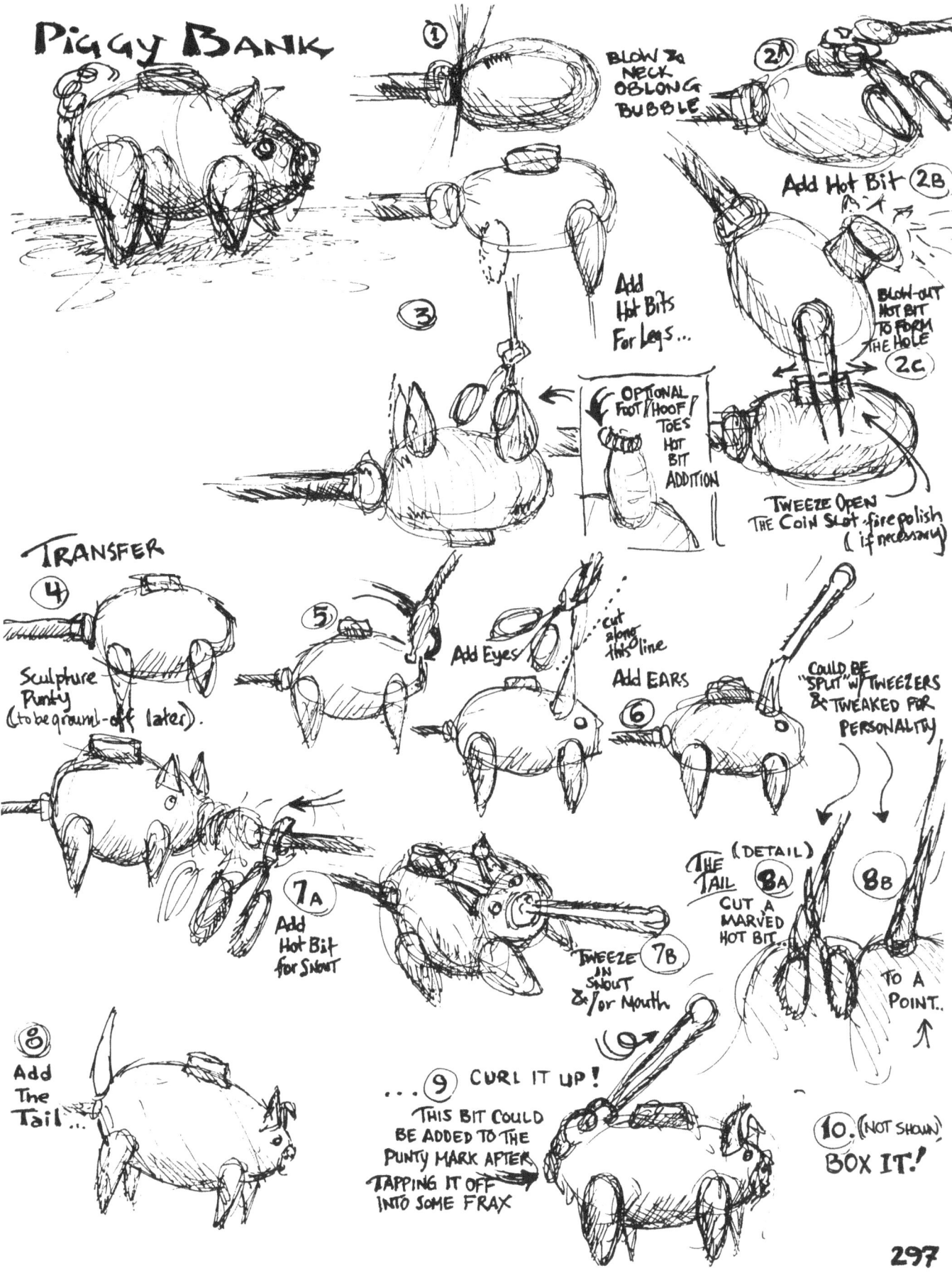

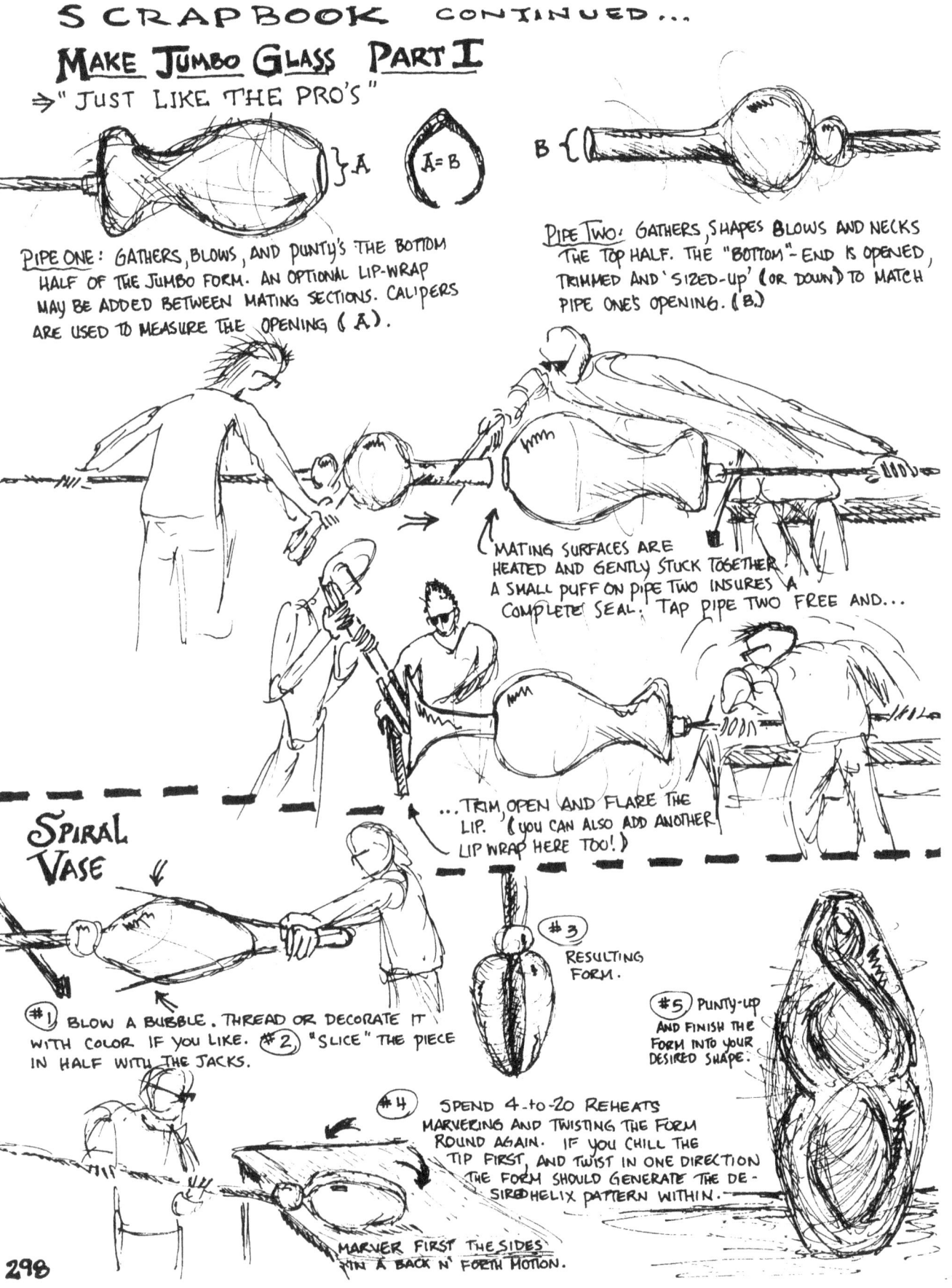

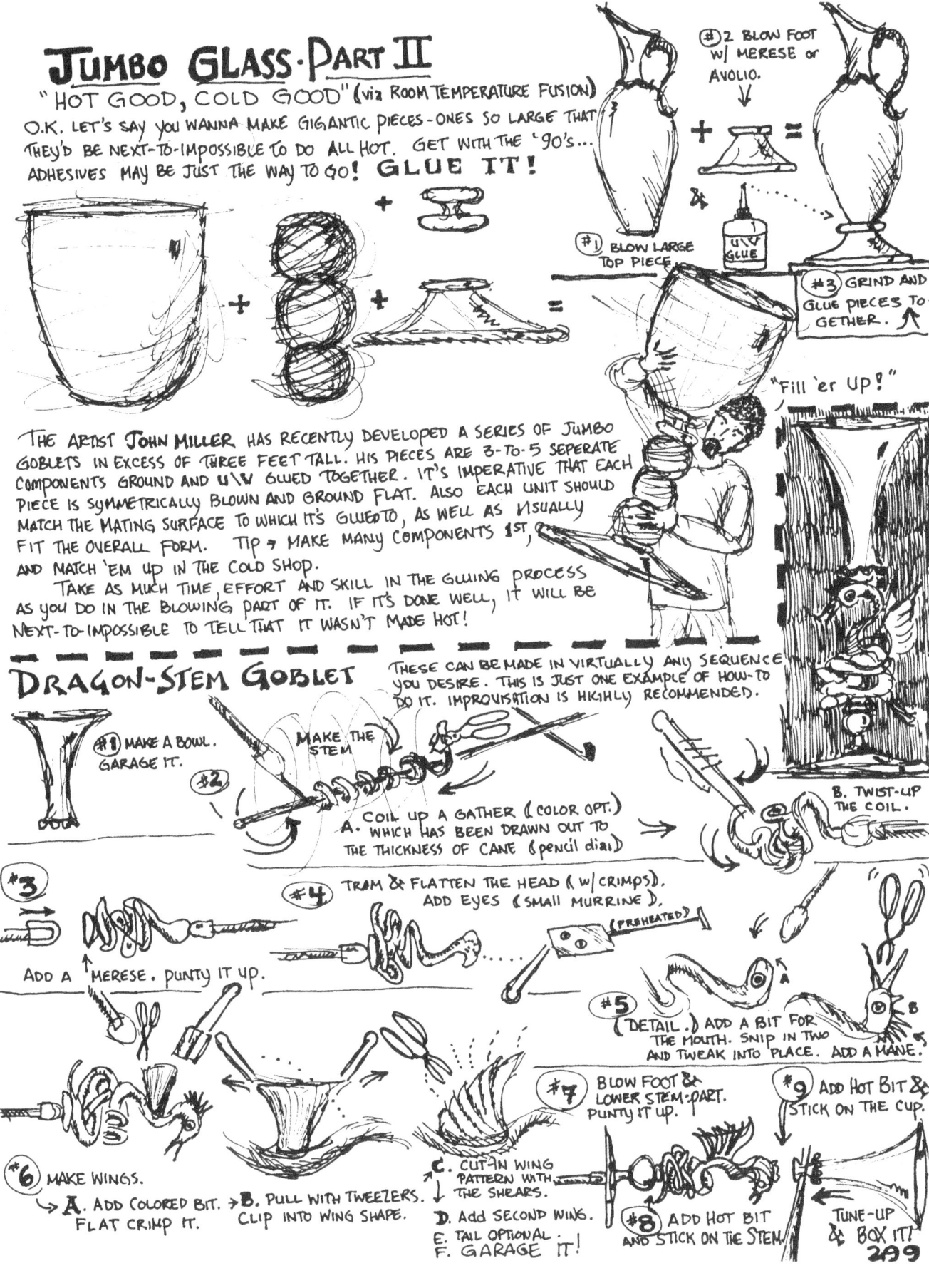

SPECIAL ED SECTION
How to make your very own "Good-for-Life" Homebrew Bottles.

STEP

① LEARN HOW TO BLOW GLASS. SHOW SOME ENTHUSIASM AND PROMISE.

② LEARN HOW-TO HOMEBREW. GIVE IT A WHIRL. DO IT FOR A FEW YEARS. ENTER A FEW COMPETITIONS, WIN SOME RIBBONS. MAYBE WORK IN A MICROBREWERY TO GAIN EXPERIENCE. AVOID BOIL-OVERS AT ALL COSTS!

③ REMEMBER TO RELAX, DON'T WORRY, AND HAVE A HOMEBREW.

④ BLOW SOME COOL BOTTLES, IN ORDER TO GET THEM TO SEAL, HIRE SOMEONE TO MAKE YOU A NIFTY **FINISHING TOOL** SO YOU CAN CAP THE BOTTLES, (OR JUST EYEBALL IT AND DRILL TWO HOLES AND USE A CONVENTIONAL SWING-TOP TYPE CLOSURE.) YOU ALSO BLOW YOUR OWN CARBOYS AND DRINKING VESSELS AS WELL!

⑤ AFTER THE BOTTLES ARE ANNEALED FILL THEM WITH YOUR BEST BREWS/ELIXAR. CAP 'EM AND WAIT AT LEAST TWO WEEKS TO BOTTLE CONDITION. (DO NOT OVERPRIME YOUR BOTTLES → THEY CAN EXPLODE!)

⑥ SHARE A BOTTLE WITH A FRIEND OR BARTER WITH THEM FOR ARTWORK, OR USE 'EM FOR BIRTHDAYS, WEDDINGS, ETC. SAVOR THE FLAVOR AND ENJOY THE BENEFITS OF HOMEBREW.

WHEN THE BOTTLE'S EMPTY, REFILL IT REPEATING STEPS 5 to 6 AD INFINIUM, OR UNTIL YOU STOP MAKING BEER, WINE, OR MEAD, OR UNTIL YOU DIE...

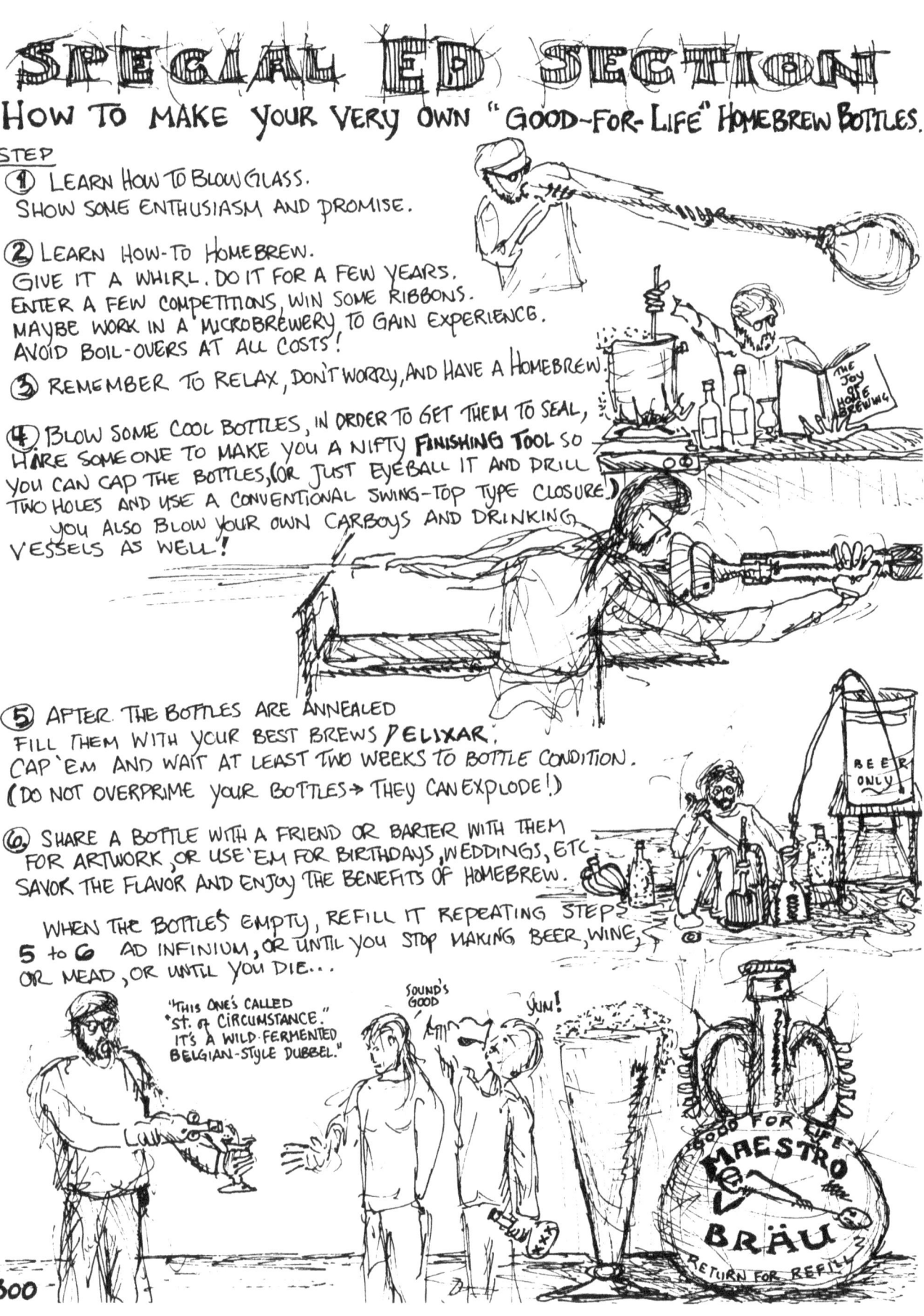

GLOSSARY

A.K.A. – ALSO KNOWN AS...

AIR MARVER SHAPING GLASS ON A PIPE OR PUNTY USING ONLY GRAVITY AND ROTATION.

AMPHORA CLASSIC VESSEL SHAPE WITH NARROW NECK & TAPERED BOTTOM, RANGES IN A VARIETY OF SHAPES AND SIZES.

ANNEAL THE PROCESS OF COOLING GLASS & RELIEVING STRESS CAUSED BY THERMAL INBALANCES FROM THE INSIDE OF THE GLASS TO IT'S EXTERIOR.

ANNEALER A.K.A. "THE **BOX**," INSULATED CHAMBER DESIGNED TO **ANNEAL** GLASS. OFTEN HEATED BY ELECTRICAL ELEMENTS AND COMPUTER CONTROLLED. OLD-STYLE ANNEALERS WERE GAS FIRED, OR RUN OFF WASTE HEAT FROM THE FURNACE.

AVOLIO HOUR GLASS SHAPED BIT WHICH UNITES THE BOWL OF A GOBLET WITH THE STEM AND THE STEM WITH THE FOOT.

AVENTURINE MANUFACTURED GLASS WITH PARTICALS OF COPPER THROUGHOUT. SIMULATES GOLD. VERY POPULAR WITH VENETIAN GLASSMAKERS. COMPATIBILITY IS QUESTIONABLE. The stuff reminds me of that fiberglass you see bumber cars and motorcycle helmets made of.

BAR 1. KUGLER OR CONCENTRATED COLORED GLASS ROLLED INTO A ROD SHAPE. 2. ESTABLISHMENT FREQUENTED BY THIRSTY AND/OR FRUSTRATED GLASSBLOWERS.

BATCH TERM FOR MIXTURE OF RAW CHEMICALS WHICH MAKE UP THE GLASS FORMULA. WHEN HEATED TO IT'S MELTING POINT IT TURNS INTO GLASS

BENCHBLOW PROCESS OFF BLOWING INTO THE PIPE. DONE BY AN ASSISTANT WHILE THE GAFFER WORKS SEATED AT THE BENCH.

BIG GUN(s) TOP O' THE HEAP. THOSE ARTISTS MOST FAMOUS FOR EXCELLENCE IN GLASS MAKING.

BIT A BLOB OF HOT GLASS OFTEN GATHERED ON A PUNTY. USED TO DECORATE AND/OR ATTACH PIECES OF GLASS TOGETHER.

BLANK 1. USUALLY SIMPLE GLASS FORM USED AS A BASE UPON WHICH OTHER GLASS TECHNIQUES MAY OCCUR: e.g. PAINTING/ENAMELING, SANDBLASTING OR GRAAL TECHNIQUE. 2. **MARTIN** SEATTLE-BASED GLASSBLOWER/INSTRUCTOR/SCULPTOR EXTRAORDINAIRE.

BONK TO STRIKE A PIPE OR PUNTY INTENTIONALLY IN ORDER TO RELEASE THE OBJECT ON IT'S END.

BONKER A LENGTH OF DENSE WOOD USED TO BONK WITH.

BOWL 1. A SHALLOW-TO-DEEP & WIDE VESSEL. 2. TERM FOR THE CUP PART OF A GOBLET. 3. RECREATIONAL ACTIVITY TO PARTAKE IN WHEN NOT BLOWING GLASS.

BOX n.v. 1. ANNEALER 2. PROCESS OF PUTTING A PIECE IN THE ANNEALER.

BUENO, THOR SAN DIEGO-BASED GLASS ARTIST/INSTRUCTOR & SURF DUDE. SEE **PARADISE PAINTS** page 130.

BULLSEYE 1. ARCHAIC TERM REFERRING TO THE PUNTY MARK LEFT ON BLOWN GLASSWARE esp. RONDELS USED BY STAINED GLASS ARTISTS. 2. GLASS MANUFACTURER BASED IN PORTLAND, OREGON– AWESOME COMPANY SPECIALIZING IN COMPATIBLE GLASSES IN A VARIETY OF COLORS AND FORMS.

BUS DRIVER THE ONE WHO DECIDES WHERE TO GO... AND WHEN TO STOP. **NOTE:** They don't necessarily follow schedules either!

BUTTON A SMALL **BIT** OF GLASS APPLIED TO THE BOTTOM OF BLOWN OBJECTS (PARTICULARLY THIN PIECES). HELPS INSURE THAT THE PUNTY WON'T BREAK THROUGH OR OUT DURING THE COMPLETION OF THE OBJECT.

CAMEO TECHNIQUE OF CUTTING/ENGRAVING OVERLAYS OF GLASS IN RELIEF TO REVEAL COLORS UNDERNEATH, AND TO ACCENT VISUAL IMAGERY. see **GRAAL**.

CANE GLASS WHICH HAS BEEN DRAWN OUT INTO A ROD. see **FILIGRANA**.

CANE MARVER A SLAB OF STEEL WITH GROOVES IN IT – ON WHICH PIECES OF CANE ARE LAID-OUT & PREHEATED & PICKED-UP ON A PIPE OR PUNTY.

CAP PROCESS OF PLUGGING THE COLD END OF A BLOWPIPE – WITH THE PALM, FINGER, OR THUMB – SO THAT THE BLOWN FORM (ON THE HOT END) DOESN'T COLLAPSE.

CARBOY A LARGE GLASS VESSEL USUALLY USED TO STORE LIQUIDS esp. TO FERMENT HOME-BREW IN. See **DEMI-JOHN**.

CASE HOT PROCESS OF COVERING A LAYER OF GLASS (OFTEN COLORED) WITH A GATHER OF CLEAR GLASS OR ANOTHER COLOR.

CHARGE PROCESS OF ADDING BATCH OR CULLET INTO A FURNACE TO MELT GLASS.

CHECK 1. TERM FOR A VISIBLE CRACKLINE IN GLASS DUE TO STRESS & IMPROPER ANNEALING OR HANDLING. 2. THAT WHICH YOU HOPE IS "IN THE MAIL"

CHIHULY, DALE A FOUNDER OF THE PILCHUCK GLASS SCHOOL. DECLARED A NATIONAL LIVING TREASURE BY THE U.S. GOVERNMENT. PERHAPS THE MOST FAMOUS LIVING AMERICAN GLASS ARTIST → RESPONSIBLE IN PART FOR PUTTING BLOWN GLASS BACK "ON THE MAP". (AND TACOMA)

CHILL MARKS VISIBLE INDENTATIONS OR CRACKS IN (OR ON) BLOWN/SOLID GLASS—LEFT BY COLD TOOLS, OR GLOVES (WHEN BOXING PIECES), OR EVEN FROM DROPS OF WATER OR SWEAT FALLING ON PIECES PRIOR TO ANNEALING.

CIOFS pronounced "CHOFES" see **PACIOFFIS**

COLDWORK PROCESS OF MANIPULATING GLASS WHEN IT'S IN A SOLID STATE → e.g. GRINDING, POLISHING, CUTTING, ENGRAVING, etc.

COLLAR A TRANSITIONAL ELEMENT OF GLASS BETWEEN THE BLOWPIPE AND ANOTHER PIECE OF GLASS (MOST OFTEN MADE OF CLEAR GLASS)

COLOR A.K.A. ROD, FRIT, POWDER, KUGLER REFERS TO GLASS WHICH IS FLAVORED WITH METALLIC OXIDES—A WHOLE PALETTE OF HUES. IT MAY BE TRANSPARENT OR OPAQUE—COMPATIBLE OR NOT.

COMPATIBILITY A.K.A. "FIT" (EACH OTHER) DESCRIBES TWO DIFFERENT GLASSES WITH RELATIVELY THE SAME THERMAL COEFFICIENT OF EXPANSION i.e. THEY WILL EXPAND AND CONTRACT AT NEARLY THE SAME RATES. **INCOMPATIBLE** GLASSES WILL SHOW SIGNS OF STRESS UNDER A POLARISCOPE (OR IN PIECES IN THE BOTTOM OF THE ANNEALER). THE ARE PRONE TO **CHECK**, CRACK, OR, EVEN EXPLODE.

CONTINUOUS A FURNACE DESIGN WHICH CONSTANTLY MELTS GLASS BY **CHARGING** IN ONE SIDE (THE DOG HOUSE) AND WORKING/GATHERING OUT THE OTHER. USUALLY THE CAPACITY EXCEEDS 600 lbs OF MOLTEN GLASS.

CORDS VISIBLE STRIATIONS FOUND IN MOLTEN GLASS (WHICH HAS BEEN ANNEALED). DUE TO INCONSISTENT **BATCHING** AND/OR MELTING PRACTICES. OFTEN FOUND CLOSER TO THE BOTTOM OF THE FURNACE WHERE THE STALE GLASS HANGS OUT.

CORNING A TOWN IN EASTERN NEW YORK STATE. SITE OF THE **CORNING GLASS WORKS** → LARGE MANUFACTURER OF SCIENTIFIC (BOROSILICATE) GLASS AND DOMESTIC WARES. ALSO HOME TO THE LARGEST GLASS **MUSEUM** IN THE UNITED STATES, **STEUBEN GLASSWORKS** AND NEWLY ESTABLISHED SCHOOL "The Studio of the Corning Museum of Glass."

CRACKLE _ see **QUENCH**

CRIMPS A FORM OF **TWEEZERS**. SOMETIMES REFERRED TO AS LEAF TOOLS → FLAT BLADED OR GROOVED THEY ARE USED TO SQUEEZE GLASS BITS.

CRISTALLO ITALIAN TERM FOR CLEAR GLASS. MADE FAMOUS BY THE VENETIAN (MURANO) GLASSBLOWERS DURING THE XV th CENTURY WHEN THEY DISCOVERED DECOLORANTS → THUS ENABLING THEM TO PRODUCE NEAR-PERFECT "CLEAR" GLASS.

CRUCIBLE AKA "POT" A SPECIALLY FORMULATED CLAY BODY CAST OR THROWN INTO A LARGE BOWL SHAPE → WHICH WHEN FIRED TO HIGH TEMPERATURES CAN WITHSTAND THE RIGORS OF HOLDING MOLTEN GLASS.

CRYSTAL 1. CLEAR GLASS 2. LEAD CRYSTAL—A SPECIAL BATCH FORMULATED WITH A PERCENTAGE OF LEAD TO INCREASE OPTIC CLEARITY AND CUTTING BRILLIANCE.

CULLET SOLID GLASS WHICH HAS BEEN PREVIOUSLY MELTED — OFTEN BROKEN UP INTO SMALLER PIECES OR CHUNKS. THIS GETS **CHARGED** INTO A FURNACE AND IS EASIER THAN **BATCH** TO MELT, LESS CORROSIVE ON THE FURNACE, AND LESS TOXIC TO DEAL WITH.

CUP A GLASS FOR DRINKING OR A **GOBLET** IN WHOLE, OR ONLY THE BOWL SECTION.

DALE SEE **CHIHULY**

DAY TANK A BRICK STYLE FURNACE WHERE GLASS IS CHARGED, MELTED AND USED — IDEALLY WITHIN 24 HOURS. USUALLY LARGER IN SIZE THAN MOST **POT FURNACES**, THE DAY TANK MAY TOLERATE MORE ABUSE AND COST MORE TO BUILD, AND RUN.

DEMI JOHN A LARGE **CARBOY**

DEVITRIFY PROCESS OF GLASS CHEMICALLY CHANGING → THROUGH THERMAL ACTIVITY → FROM AN AMORPHOUS SOLID INTO A CRYSTALLINE STRUCTURE. THIS ALSO WEAKENS THE GLASS. IT APPEARS AS A DULL AND HAZY FOG ON YOUR GLASS — MOST COMMONLY FOUND ON SLUMPED, FUSED, OR CAST GLASS.

DIAMOND SHEARS JAW-LIKE "SCISSORS" DESIGNED TO CUT GLASS (HOT) GRIP PIPES, PUNTIES AND OTHER HOT OBJECTS. ONE OF THE MOST COMMONLY USED TOOLS BY GLASS BLOWERS. ALSO REFERRED TO AS "COMBINATION SHEARS."

DICHROIC A TYPE OF MANUFACTURED GLASS WHICH EXHIBITS TWO COLORS OF LIGHT — ONE WHICH IS REFLECTED AND THE OTHER TRANSMITTED. IT'S SPARKLY STUFF! VERY EXPENSIVE, BUT IT SELLS LIKE HOT CAKES — IF YOU PUT IT IN YOUR WORK!

DIDYMIUM A SPECIAL GLASS MANUFACTURED TO FILTER OUT MUCH OF THE HARMFUL INFARED AN U/V RADIATION FROM HOT GLASS BURNERS AND COMBUSTION. OFTEN USED FOR LENSES IN SAFETY GLASSES FOR GLASSWORKERS.

DINO'S TOOLS MADE BY DINO TEDESCHI — AN ITALIAN TOOLMAKER REKNOWN FOR HIGH QUALITY JACKS, TWEEZERS etc.

DIP see **GATHER**

DIP N' STRIP PROCESS OF GATHERING FROM THE FURNACE AND HOLDING THE PIPE VERTICAL, SO AS TO ALLOW THE 'EXCESS' GLASS TO DRIP OFF INTO A STRIPPING BUCKET (OR APPROPRIATE

RECEPTICLE) IN ORDER TO ACHIEVE AN EVEN GATHER OF DESIRED MASS.

DUCKBILL SHEARS
SPECIAL "SCISSORS" → SHORT BLADES, SLIGHTLY BLUNT TIPS, MOST OFTEN USED FOR TRIMMING HOT GLASS

ED. 1. FIRST NAME OF THE AUTHOR OF THIS BOOK. 2. SHORT FOR EDITOR → SAME PERSON.

ELEMENTS
ELECTRICAL WIRING FOUND IN ANNEALERS WHICH GENERATE THE HEAT NECESSARY TO GET THEM HOT AND HOLD THEM AT ANNEALING TEMPERATURE.

AVOID TOUCHING METAL OBJECTS SUCH AS PIPES AND PUNTIES AGAINST THEM ~ THEY MAY BE "LIVE" AND YOU RISK ELECTROCUTION

ENAMEL N.V. PIGMENT USED TO PAINT/DECORATE GLASSWORK. CAN BE PAINTED ON COLD OR FIRED-ON.

ESSEMCE SWEDISH MANUFACTURER OF FINE GLASSWORKING TOOLS.

FEATHERING
DECORATIVE TECHNIQUE OF PULLING/COMBINING A THREADED PATTERN ON HOT GLASS, RESULTING IN A FEATHER PATTERN.

FROM ANCIENT CORE-FORMED VESSELS TO TIFFANY AND THE ART NOUVEAU DESIGNERS/CRAFTSMAN TO PRESENT DAY ARTISTS, THIS TECHNIQUE IS A TIMELESS BEST-SELLER MOVE.

FIBERFRAX A.K.A. "FRAX"
WHITE FIBEROUS MATERIAL - SIMILAR TO FIBERGLASS INSULATION (IT ACTUALLY IS) USED IN GLASS EQUIPMENT. HAZARDOUS TO HANDLE AND INHALE, USE PROPER SAFETY PRECAUTIONS WHENEVER WORKING WITH IT.

FILIGRANA
A TYPE OF CANE - USUALLY A COLOR WHICH IS CASED IN CLEAR - WHICH MAY BE MADE INTO FANCY CANE LIKE ZANFIRICO e.g. RETE, OR BALLOTTINI OR SETTEFILI.

FINE PROCESS OF ALLOWING MELTING GLASS AMPLE TIME TO SIT, AND LET AIR BUBBLES (TRAPPED FROM THE CHARGING PROCESS) FLOAT TO THE SURFACE AND DISAPPEAR (BURST). THE LONGER THE FINING PERIOD THE LESS SEEDS THERE ARE, AND THE CLEANER THE GLASS APPEARS.

FLAMEWORKING see **LAMPWORKING**

FLASH TO EXPOSE A PIECE OF GLASS TO HEAT FOR A SHORT TIME (e.g. 5 SECONDS) EITHER IN A GLORY HOLE OR THE FURNACE

FLASK 1. A FRAME USED IN FOUNDRY WORK FOR CREATING MOLDS. 2. A STYLE OF FLATTENED BOTTLES, esp. FOR SPIRITS

FLOOR MODEL THE UNWANTED RESULT OF A LEARNING PROCESS IN ACTION. USUALLY GRAVITY AND THE CONCRETE FLOOR WIN, AND YOU BECOME BETTER EDUCATED IN "WHAT NOT TO DO" IN THE FUTURE.

FRAX see **FIBERFRAX**

FRIGGER A.K.A. **END OF THE DAY PIECE**
HISTORICALLY A FUN ITEM MADE BY FACTORY WORKERS DURING THEIR LUNCHBREAKS AND AFTER WORK, THESE 'KNOCKOFFS' INCLUDED PAPERWEIGHTS, WALKING CANES, MUSICAL INSTRUMENTS AND FIGURINES, AND MADE AS GIFTS, NOT SOLD.

FRIT CRUSHED GLASS, OFTEN COLORED. IT MAY BE SIFTED INTO SPECIFIC MESH SIZES. RESEMBLES FISH TANK GRAVEL. IT CAN BE INCORPORATED IN MANY WAYS TO COLOR HOT GLASS.

FRONT LOADER
A TYPE OF ANNEALER → ONE WHICH HAS THE DOORS HINGED IN THE FRONT (LIKE A REFRIGERATOR) VS. ON TOP.

FUME PROCESS OF SPRAYING STANNOUS CHLORIDE OR SIMILAR METALLIC OXIDE ON THE SURFACE OF HOT GLASS TO PRODUCE AN IRIDIZED SURFACE. HIGHLY TOXIC & DANGEROUS TO WORK WITH—USE ONLY WITH PROPER EQUIPMENT AND TRAINING.

GABBERT NAME OF A DISTRIBUTOR OF GLASS CULLET IN WEST VIRGINIA

GAFFER ARCHAIC FORM OF "GRANDFATHER". THE ORCHESTRATOR. TOP DOG. HEAD HONCHO. THE PERSON WHO DIRECTS THE ASSISTANTS IN A GLASS BLOWING TEAM. HE/SHE USUALLY REMAINS SEATED AT THE BENCH.

GARAGE A HEATED, INSULATED SPACE WHERE GLASS PIECES MAY BE "PARKED" AT ANNEALING TEMP. AND USED AT A LATER TIME. NEARLY ESSENTIAL FOR VENETIAN TECHNIQUES AND WORKS WHERE MULTIPLE PARTS ARE PIECED TOGETHER.

GAS 1. COMBUSTIBLE FUEL SUCH AS PROPANE, OXYGEN AND NATURAL GAS. 2. ACRONYMN FOR THE **G**LASS **A**RT **S**OCIETY.

GATHER THE METHOD OF REMOVING MOLTEN GLASS FROM THE FURNACE BY DIPPING A PIPE OR PUNTY IN IT, AND TURNING. THE GLASS MAY BE ACCUMULATED WITH SUCCESSIVE LAYERS OR GATHERS TO A DESIRED SIZE. A.K.A. A "DIP"

GENIUS THE GUY THAT DEVELOPED A SIMPLE IDEA "FIRST" (USUALLY APPROPRIATED FROM SOMEWHERE ELSE), MILKED IT, AND MADE A MILLION. see **CHIHULY**. Mt. St. Helens Ash.

303

GLASS 1. An amorphous solid. 2. A seductive and unforgiving mistress who will corrupt your world view and cause you to focus all of your energy into her little world.

GLASS BUG Once bitten, this parasite invades the body and forces the host to want to do nothing but make more glass, living, breathing, and eating it for breakfast.

Thought to be introduced by direct contact — handling handmade glass for example, we now know the mere sight of the glassblowing process is enough for a person to be "bitten" and thus infected... There exists NO known cure.

GLORY HOLE — Insulated horizontal drum which is heated with gas and forced air. It's a reheating chamber used by glassblowers to make cold glass hot & "good". They range in sizes and designs.

GOBLET Generally a 3-part drinking vessel consisting of a bowl, stem and foot. Avolios may join each element. Highly challenging form to blow.
- Bowl
- Stem
- Foot

GRAAL Swedish term for "Grail". A glass technique where a BLANK is blown annealed, coldworked, reheated & picked-up on a blowpipe and made into its final form. It may be blown out straight, or CASED.

It's an excellent method for obtaining specific imagery within blown and solid glass forms.

GRAVITY 1. Your friend 2. Second only to heat as the most influential force affecting the behavior of molten glass. Learn to understand it & it may do wonders for you.

HOPPER, DAVID A founding father of Orient & Flume and originator and distributor of Paradise Paints. See COLOR section page 130.

HOT HEAD A person who is thermally disadvantaged and short tempered A.K.A. a jerk.

INCALMO Technique of joining two or more bubbles together to form one larger piece.

INCLUSION An element of glass or metal which is encased within another form of glass.

INCOMPATIBLE Not COMPATIBLE.

IRIDIZE A shiny, metallic looking finish on the surface of glass → frequently achieved by reducing the atmosphere in the GLORY HOLE, thus exposing the colors to that environment.

JACKS Tong-like tool. Used by the GAFFER to neck and shape molten glass. They exist in a variety sizes & configurations e.g. GOBLET, small, med. lg. See PACIOFFIS.

JIMMIES Another form of FRIT. Usually the larger chunks, which resemble ice-cream toppings.

KEVLAR Super fabric used in bullet-proof vests and fire-proof gloves & protective wear.

KILN A.K.A. "BOX" See ANNEALER

KUGLER One German manufacturer of condensed colored glass available to glassblowers. Used in nearly every hot shop today. See REICHENBACH, ZIMMERMAN.

KUGLER OVEN A small annealer designed to preheat pieces of glass esp. KUGLER & the like. You can use 'em as pick-up kilns too!

LAMPWORKING Process of heating up glass over a torch. Often incorporating the use of rods and tubing to create works of art. Often (although not limited to) smaller scaled pieces of incredible detail and complexity.

"LATTICINO" From Italian: LATTE = MILK. "A style of cane using only white glass color, often twisted creating a lattice effect," or so we thought... It's FICTION!

For a long time, most Americans referred to all cane worked pieces incorrectly as "Latticino". FILIGRANA is really what we're talking about. The only thing close to "Latticino" is LATTIMO → a style of white glass.

LINO See TAGLIAPIETRA

LIP 1. Unwanted advice from a smart ass 2. Top of a vessel A.K.A. RIM 3. LIPOFSKY, MARVIN — famous BIG GUN.

LIP WRAP A thread of glass applied to the mouth of a vessel, often colored. Usually done prior to opening the vessel.

MAESTRO Italian term for MASTER. Only the best of the best earn this distinction — usually from decades of hard work and tremendous skill. He/she heads the glass team/production

MARQUIS, RICHARD "DICK" An American MURRINE genius and all-around

PHENOMENAL GLASSWORKER/SCULPTOR.

MARVER FROM FRENCH – MEANS "MARBLE" LARGE FLAT TABLE-LIKE SURFACE ON WHICH GLASS IS SHAPED. NORMALLY MADE OF STEEL, THE ORIGINAL ONES WERE MADE OF MARBLE.

MERESE FROM FRENCH "TO MARRY" ONE HALF OF AN **AVOLIO**. A SINGLE DISC SHAPED OBJECT USED TO JOIN ELEMENTS TOGETHER ESP. VENETIAN-STYLE GOBLETS

MILLEFIORE FROM ITALIAN "THOUSAND FLOWERS" SPECIALIZED **CANE** OR **MURRINE** WITH FLORAL MOTIF. MADE POPULAR BY PAPERWEIGHT MAKERS DURING THE LATE 19th CENTURY

MOILE GLASS THAT IS GATHERED ON THE BLOWPIPE (OR PUNTY). IT PROVIDES STRUCTURAL SUPPORT FOR THE GLASS 'OFF-THE-END'. OFTEN WE REFER TO THE MOILE AS THE GLASS ABOVE THE NECKLINE.

MOLD A CAVITY WHICH IS MADE TO BE FILLED WITH ANOTHER MATERIAL (GLASS) TO CREATE AN OBJECT WITH A PREDETERMINED SHAPE. CAN BE CAST OR BLOWN INTO. MAY ALSO BE MADE OF A VARIETY OF MATERIALS.

MONTAGE A METHOD OF REJOINING BUBBLES IN A VARIETY OF CONFIGURATIONS TO CREATE INTERESTING COLOR PATTERNS

MOORE (S) JIM SEATTLE-BASED MANUFACTURER OF FINE GLASSWORKING TOOLS AND A SUPER-NICE BLOKE TO BOOT!

Mt. ST. HELENS ASH, centralia Washington ONE OF THE BEST MARKETING SCHEMES IN DECADES. THEIR BATCH INCLUDES SOME (UNDETERMINED) AMOUNT OF THIS VOLCANO'S ASH. INVENTED (AND PATENTED) by HANK CLAYCAMP

MURANO, ITALY A SMALL ISLAND ACROSS THE LAGOON FROM VENICE, WITH A LONG-STANDING TRADITION OF EXCELLENCE IN GLASSMAKING. HOME TO "Gli Maestri" – SOME OF THE WORLD'S GREATEST GLASSMAKERS.

MURRINE (see **DICK MARQUIS**) CROSS-SECTIONAL PIECES OF CANE. AN AGE-OLD VENETIAN TECHNIQUE BY WHICH BUNDLES OF CANE ARE ASSEMBLED, HEATED AND STRETCHED SO AS TO CREATE SPECIFIC IMAGERY WITHIN THE RESULTING CANE (CROSS-SECTIONALLY AGAIN)

NECK 1. THE CONSTRICTED AREA ON A VESSEL CLOSEST TO THE LIP. 2. PROCESS OF CUTTING-IN A TRANSFER POINT/LINE BY ROTATING HOT GLASS AND GENTLY SQUEEZING THE JACKS AT THE DESIRED POINT – USUALLY CLOSE TO, BUT BELOW, THE **MOILE**.

NECK WRAP A.K.A. **MOILE WRAP** A METHOD OF MAINTAINING HEAT ON THE NECK/MOILE AREA WITHOUT THE NEED FOR DEEP REHEATS IN THE **GLORY HOLE**. USUALLY APPLIED WHEN THE **MOILE** SHOWS SIGNS OF THERMAL STRESS OR CRACKING.

NERD OUT-DATED AMERICAN TERM FOR **AVOLIO**.

ONE-TRICK-PONY LABEL WHICH APPLIES TO (OFTEN FAMOUS) ARTISTS WHO DO ONLY ONE STYLE OF GLASSWORK – USUALLY FOR DECADES... BECAUSE IT SELLS WELL AND REQUIRES LITTLE OR NO CREATIVE THOUGHT OR EFFORT.

OPTIC (MOLD) AN INVERTED CONE-SHAPED UNIT WITH SYMMETRICAL RIBS ON IT'S INTERIOR. OFTEN CAST METAL EG. ALUMINUM OR BRONZE/BRASS. THEY COME IN COUNTLESS SIZES AND CONFIGURATIONS. CAN BE USED TO SIMULATE OPTIC PATTERNS OF CUT CRYSTAL IN BLOWN GLASS.

OVERLAY TECHNIQUE OF LAYERING ONE COLOR OVER ANOTHER

PACIOFFI'S WOODEN TIPPED – JACKS USED TO OPEN PIECES WITHOUT LEAVING TOOL MARKS ON THE GLASS.

PAD THE AREA OR ARENA WHERE GLASS-MAKING TAKES PLACE.

PADDLE A WOODEN BOARD USED TO FLATTEN HOT GLASS. CAN BE USED TO SHIELD THE GAFFER FROM EXCESSIVE HEAT.

PAPER MARVER SEVERAL SHEETS OF WET NEWSPAPER LAID OUT ON A BOARD – USED AS A MARVER BUT ONE WHICH LEAVES LITTLE-TO-NO CHILL MARKS.

PARADISE PAINTS ENAMEL GLASS PIGMENTS DESIGNED ESPECIALLY FOR BLOWN AND SOLID WORKED PIECES. DEVELOPED AND SOLD BY **DAVID HOPPER** IN PARADISE, CALIFORNIA.

PARISON THE MASS OF GLASS OFF THE END OF THE BLOWPIPE – USUALLY ROUNDISH-SHAPE AND MOST OFTEN IS A BUBBLE.

PASTORALE AN ITALIAN TERM FOR THE METAL TOOL ON WHICH PIECES OF CANE GET PREHEATED IN THE GLORY HOLE OR FURNACE. USED IN VENETIAN-STYLE WORK.

PENLAND "CRAFT" SCHOOL LOCATED IN (OF ALL PLACES) PENLAND, NORTH CAROLINA. YOU CAN STUDY GLASSWORKING OR NUMEROUS OTHER ART DISCIPLINES THERE. PRIMARILY A SUMMER SCHOOL, THEY DO OFFER LIMITED RESIDENCIES AND INTENSIVES YEAR-LONG.

PI DIVIDER A CALIPER STYLE TOOL USED TO GUAGE THE DIAMETER OF A BUBBLE OR PIECE OF GLASS IN ORDER TO DETERMINE IT'S CIRCUM-FERANCE FOR AN EVEN COATING OF A PREDE-TERMINED AMOUNT OF MATERIAL e.g. CANE, MURRINES, OR POWDERED DESIGN.

PICK-UP TECHNIQUE OF ADHERING PIECES OF GLASS OR OTHER MATERIAL TO THE SURFACE OR INTERIOR OF HOT GLASS. USUALLY, IT'S BEST TO PREHEAT THE ITEM BEFOREHAND TO INSURE SUCCESSFUL COHESION.

PILCHUCK GLASS SCHOOL LOCATED IN STANWOOD WASHINGTON, FOUNDED BY JOHN HAUBERG, AND ANNE GOULD HAUBERG AND DALE CHIHULY IN 1971. GREAT PLACE TO STUDY GLASSMAKING IN TRULY INSPIRATIONAL SURROUNDINGS. IT'S EXPENSIVE, INTENSIVE AND GOING ON EVERY SUMMER.
"IT CHANGED MY LIFE."

PINO see **SIGNORETTO**

PIPE COOLER MANUAL OR AUTOMATIC TOOL USED TO CHILL HOT PIPES/PUNTIES ~ USUALLY AFTER GATHERING ~ BY RUNNING COLD WATER OVER IT.

PIPE WARMER CHAMBER WHICH PREHEATS THE TIPS OF PIPES AND PUNTIES

PONTIL C'mon, nobody calls it that anymore... It's a **PUNTY**!

POSITIVE TERM IN MOLDMAKING USED TO DESCRIBE THE ORIGINAL FORM FROM WHICH A MOLD MAY BE TAKEN FROM.

POST A CLEAR GLASS LANDING PAD MADE ON A PUNTY - USED TO STRETCH CANE WITH.

POST GATHER A TYPE OF GATHERING WHERE THE PIECE IS SUBMERGED IN THE FURNACE UP TO, BUT NOT OVER, THE MOILE. MOST COMMON IN MOLDBLOWING.

POT 1. A CRUCIBLE 2. AN EXPERIMENTAL RECREATIONAL LUBRICANT WHICH IS REPUTED TO MAKE BAD GLASS LOOK GOOD, OR PRODUC-TION WORK TOLERABLE.

POT FURNACE A FREE STANDING OR IN-VESTED CRUCIBLE FURNACE USED FOR MELTING GLASS. MOST PRIVATE STUDIOS USE THIS TYPE OF FURNACE FOR ITS LOW COST OF CONSTRUCTION AND OPERATION.

POWDER COLORED GLASS WHICH HAS BEEN PUL-VERIZED INTO A FLOUR CONSISTENCY. MAY BE DUSTED ON OR ROLLED INTO HOT GLASS, AMONG OTHER THINGS.

PRODUCTION 1. MAKING GLASS FOR BUCKS. 2. USUALLY A FACTORY-STYLE SITUATION WHERE MULTIPLES OF A LIKE-DESIGN (CLONES) ARE EXECUTED. 3. death.

PROTECTION PROVIDING A HEAT SHIELD FOR SOMEONE BEING EXPOSED TO HOT GLASS RADI-ATION.

PRUNT A DECORATIVE BIT APPLIED TO BLOWN OR SOLID GLASS. POPULAR WITH THE WALDGLAS BLOWERS IN BOHEMIA DURING THE DARK AGES. IT KEPT THEIR GLASSWARE FROM SLIPPING OUT OF THEIR MUTTON-ENCRUSTED GREASY FINGERS!

PUFFER see **SOFFIETTA**

PUNTETTO A SMALL GATHER MARVERED BACK ON A PUNTY, POINTED UP AND ALLOWED TO GET STONE COLD. IT IS USED TO PULL POINTS OUT OF HOT GLASS BY STICKING IT ON AND YANKING IT OUT.

PUNTY A METAL ROD OR TUBE USED TO TRANSFER ONE PIECE OF HOT GLASS TO ANOTHER.

PUNTY WRAP SAME AS A **NECK WRAP** BUT DONE ON A PUNTY. PREVENTS FLOOR MODELS (HOPEFULLY) FROM HAPPENING WHEN THE PUNTY SHOWS SIGNS OF FATIGUE (CHECKING).

PUTSCH ANOTHER MANUFACTURER OF GLASS WORKING TOOLS.

PYREX A BRAND NAME OF BOROSILICATE GLASS, USED PRIMARILY IN **LAMPWORKING**, (AND YOUR KITCHEN.)

PYROMETER A SPECIAL THERMOMETER USED TO GAUGE HIGH TEMPERATURES COMMON-LY FOUND IN THE FIRE ARTS (e.g. GLASSBLOW-ING), ESPECIALLY FOR READING KILN AND FURN-ACE TEMPERATURES

QUENCH A HOT GLASS TECHNIQUE WHERE THE BUBBLE OR BIT IS PLUNGED IN AND OUT OF COLD WATER ~ THUS CRACKING THE EXTERIOR SURFACE (THROUGH THERMAL SHOCK) WHILE THE INTERIOR REMAINS HOT AND INTACT.

RAKE SIMPLE TOOL USED TO PUSH BUBBLES OR SURFACE SCUM BACK AGAINST THE

FAR WALL OF THE FURNACE TO INSURE A HEALTHY CLEAN GATHER.

REDUCE, REDUCTION
TO CHANGE THE COMBUSTION IN THE GLORY HOLE (OR FURNACE) BY TURNING UP THE GAS OR CUTTING BACK ON THE AIR UNTIL FLAMES APPEAR. THIS CAN CHANGE THE COLOR OF YOUR GLASS IF IT'S CHEMISTRY IS SUSCEPTIBLE TO A REDUCING ATMOSPHERE e.g. CERTAIN FORMS OF KUGLER WILL GET REAL SHINY WHEN REDUCED.

REHEAT PROCESS OF EXPOSING GLASS TO HEAT IN THE FURNACE OR GLORY HOLE TO REGAIN PLASTICITY AND MAKE IT EASIER TO BLOW OR MANIPULATE.

REICHENBACH
ANOTHER GERMAN MANUFACTURER OF COLORED GLASS PRODUCTS.

RETICELLO
ITALIAN TERM → "FISH NET"
DESCRIBES A CANE-WORKED PIECE WHICH EXHIBITS A FISH-NET PATTERN. MADE BY SANDWICHING TWO OPPOSITELY TWISTED BUBBLES TOGETHER.

ROD see **BAR, COLOR**

RONDEL A LARGE FLAT PLATTER MADE BY OPENING A BOWL IN THE HEAT AND SPINNING IT LIKE CRAZY (AT EXACTLY THE RIGHT MOMENT). THESE WERE THE PREDECESSORS TO MANUFACTURED WINDOW OR SHEET GLASS – USED PRIMARILY BY THE STAINED GLASS INDUSTRY & ARTISTS

ROYAL, RICHARD
SEATTLE-BASED GLASSBLOWER, AN EXCELLENT DESIGNER/EDUCATOR WHO DOES INNOVATIVE WORKS WITH CANE AND GRAAL TECHNIQUES AMONGST OTHER THINGS. AN AMERICAN **MAESTRO** WITH A KEEN UNDERSTANDING OF MOLTEN GLASS.

SCUDGE SLIME, SCUM, SNOT, UNDESIRABLE STUFF WHICH MYSTERIOUSLY APPEARS ON YOUR GLASS. ACCIDENTS HAPPEN. DOORS GET TAGGED, MARVERS GET DIRTY, PEOPLE FORGET TO CLEAN CULLET etc.

SEED A SMALL AIR BUBBLE FOUND IN MOLTEN GLASS. MOST FREQUENTLY DUE TO SHORT FINING PERIODS DURING THE CHARGING/MELTING PROCESS.

SERIES A "HIGH ART" CODE WORD FOR **PRODUCTION**. IT HAPPENS WHEN AN ARTIST DISCOVERS A FORM WHICH THEY LIKE (OR CAN EASILY SELL) AND THEY CONTINUE → SOMETIMES SPANNING UP TO SEVERAL THOUSAND PIECES – OVER SEVERAL DECADES.

SHARDS PIECES OF BROKEN GLASS → OFTEN COLORED, WHICH MAY BE PICKED-UP AND USED FOR DECORATION OR INCLUSIONS.

SHIELD TO OFFER PROTECTION USUALLY DONE WITH A PADDLE.

SIGNORETTO, PINO
AN ITALIAN SOLIDWORKING **MAESTRO** WHO HAS INSPIRED A WHOLE BUNCH OF GLASS THIRSTY AMERICANS THROUGH WORKSHOPS AND CLASSES. PINO CAN MAKE JUST ABOUT ANYTHING AND MAKE IT WELL!

SLUMP 1. TO HEAT A PIECE OF GLASS ABOVE IT'S **ANNEALING POINT** SO THAT IT BEGINS TO SOFTEN AND MOVE. MAY BE DONE INTENTIONALLY, OR MIGHT OCCUR ACCIDENTLY (ESP. IF THE ANNEALER IS SET TOO HIGH). 2. THE DOLDRUMS OF EXISTENCE OBSERVED IN UNINSPIRED PRODUCTION WORKERS.

SOAK AN **ANNEALING** TERM → TO ALLOW YOUR GLASS TO REMAIN AT ANNEALING TEMP. (OR ANOTHER SETPOINT) TO LET THE WORK EQUALIZE IT'S INTERNAL TEMPERATURE TO THAT OF IT'S EXTERIOR, THUS RELIEVING THE STRESS AND LIKELIHOOD OF CHECKING.

SOFFIETTA
A.K.A. PUFFER
A METAL TUBE WITH A CONE SHAPE ON IT'S END – THROUGH WHICH ITEMS MAY BE BLOWN OR PUFFED ON. USED FREQUENTLY IN GOBLET MAKING.

SOFT A TERM WHICH DESCRIBES THE WORKING PROPERTY OF MOLTEN GLASS. LITHIUM AND LEAD FLUXED GLASSES TEND TO HAVE A LONGER WORKING TIME AND SEEM SOFTER THAN OTHER SODA-LIME BATCHES WITHOUT. CERTAIN COLORS WILL EXHIBIT A SOFT-WORKING CHARACTERISTIC AS WELL.

SOLD-BEFORE-IT'S-COLD AN IDEAL SITUATION WHERE A WEALTHY SPECTATOR BUYS THE PIECE YOU ARE WORKING ON EVEN BEFORE YOU'VE BOXED IT.

S.O.L. MILITARY TERM / ACRONYMN FOR SHIT-OUTTA-LUCK. (LIKE WHEN YOU RUN OUTTA COLOR OR BATCH...)

STEAMSTICK THE SOLO-WORKERS **SOFFIETTA**. OFTEN SOAKED IN WATER (IN SMELLY **BLOCKBUCKETS**) THIS DEVICE GETS INSERTED INTO HOT GLASS ORAFICES IN AN ATTEMPT TO PUFF IT OUT.

STEINERT MANUFACTURER OF GLASS **BLOW**PIPES AND PUNTIES, OPTIC MOLDS AND A HOST OF OTHER GLASS WORKING TOOLS.

STIFF A TERM WHICH REFERS TO WORKING PROPERTY OF MOLTEN GLASS. SOME FORMS OF RECYCLED GLASS ARE SAID TO BE STIFF → IN THAT THEY SEEM TO SET-UP REALLY FAST.

COLORS CAN BE **STIFF TOO** IN THAT THEY RESIST BEING BLOWN OUT. JUST THE OPPOSITE OF **SOFT**.

STONE COLD THE TEMPERATURE OF A HOT GLASS PIECE WHERE LITTLE-TO-NO MOVEMENT IS OBSERVED WHEN PIPE ROTATION IS HALTED. USUALLY THE TELL-TALE ORANGE GLOW OF HOT GLASS HAS FADED AT THIS POINT AND THE GLASS APPEARS CLEAR.

STONES 1. SMALL, ROCK-LIKE LOOKING PARTICALS (THEY CAN EVEN BE QUITE LARGE!) - WHICH CONTAMINATE MOLTEN GLASS. IT MAY BE FROM THE CHARGING PROCESS, OR A SIGN THAT YOUR CRUCIBLE OR TANK HAS CORRODED INTO PIECES AND A SURE SIGN OF OLD AGE AND TIME FOR A NEW ONE.... AW..... 2. FAVORABLE GLASSBLOWING MUSIC

STRIKE, STRIKING TERM WHICH DESCRIBES THE BEHAVIOR OF CERTAIN COLORS WHICH WHEN HEATED TO A CERTAIN TEMPERATURE CHANGE COLORS. e.g. SOME STICKS OF **KUGLER** MAY APPEAR CLEAR WHEN YOU BUY THEM, BUT BECOME INTENSELY RED OR ORANGE WHEN YOU HEAT THEM UP.

STRINGER A SMALL THREAD OF GLASS — OFTEN COLORED. CAN BE USED AS A DECORATIVE ELEMENT (OR CLEANED OFF THE BOTTOM OF THE GATHERING PORT!)

SURFACE MIX A TYPE OF TORCH WHERE THE GASES MIX AND BURN RIGHT AT THE TIP OF THE TORCH (VS. PREMIXED). USUALLY, THEY ARE QUIETER, MORE VERSATILE AND CONSEQUENTLY MORE EXPENSIVE.

TAGLIAPIETRA, LINO
A **MAESTRO** FROM MURANO WHO HAS TAUGHT HUNDREDS OF GLASSBLOWERS WORLD-WIDE THE FASCINATING WIZARDRY OF VENETIAN-STYLE TECHNIQUES. HE'S A PHENOMENAL CHEF AS WELL!

THERMAL SHOCK A TEMPERATURE DIFFERENTIATION WITHIN A PIECE OF GLASS WHICH CAUSES IT TO **CHECK**, CRACK OR POSSIBLY EXPLODE. USUALLY OCCURS WHEN THE EXTERIOR OF A PIECE IS COOLED MORE RAPIDLY THAN THE INTERIOR.

THREAD
THE TECHNIQUE OF APPLYING A HOT BIT OF GLASS TO A ROTATING PARISON TO CREATE A LINEAR PATTERN OR SURFACE DECORATION BY WINDING ITSELF OVER THE SURFACE.

TOP LOADER A TYPE OF ANNEALER; ONE IN WHICH THE DOOR IS ON TOP OF THE KILN (VS THE FRONT). PIECES ARE LOADED DOWN INTO IT.

TRANSFER TO PUNTY-UP. USUALLY ADHERING ONE PIECE OF GLASS TO ANOTHER PUNTY AND BREAKING FREE FROM IT'S ORIGINAL PIPE OR PUNTY.

TUMBLER 1. A SIMPLE STRAIGHTFORWARD VESSEL OF INDETERMINATE SIZES.
2. A GYMNAST → OF NO GREAT CONSEQUENCE OR IMPORTANCE TO GLASSWORKING.

TWEEZERS A.K.A. "PINCERS"
TOOL USED TO GRAB OR MANIPULATE HOT GLASS OR OTHER HOT TOOLS/OBJECTS.

U\V ULTRA-VIOLET
1. A POTENTIALLY HARMFUL WAVELENGTH OF LIGHT, IT IS PRODUCED FROM THE COMBUSTION OF GASES COMMON TO GLORY HOLES AND FURNACES. PROLONGED EXPOSURE CAN HARM UNPROTECTED EYES. ADEQUATE FILTERS (AS FOUND IN SPECIALIZED EYEGLASSES) ARE RECOMMENDED. 2. A TYPE OF ADHESIVE USED FOR GLASS - ACTIVATED BY CERTAIN TYPES OF **U/V**.

UNDERCUT AN INDENTATION IN A MOLD (USUALLY) WHERE YOU CANNOT REMOVE AN OBJECT BY SIMPLY PULLING IT OUT AFTER FILLING IT. SOMETHING TO AVOID WHEN MAKING MOST TYPES OF MOLDS.

UNDERLAY THE COLOR WHICH LIES CLOSEST TO THE INSIDE OF THE BUBBLE, OFTEN COVERED BY AN OVERLAY

VENETIAN-STYLE 1. INACCURATE REFERENCE TO GLASS WORK AND TECHNIQUES LIKELY ORIGINATING FROM **MURANO**. TYPIFIED BY THINLY BLOWN OR EXPERTLY CRAFTED GLASS. 2. AN UNCOMMON COITAL POSITION WHICH IS BETTER LEFT TO YOUR IMAGINATION THAN DESCRIBED HERE.

VENETIAN-VIRUS
1. A SUB-GENUS OF THE **GLASS BUG**. IT CAUSES THE HOST TO WANT FOR NOTHING OTHER THAN TO MAKE PERFECT **CRISTALLO** RECREATIONS DAY IN & DAY-OUT. OFTEN TERMINAL... THERE IS NO KNOWN CURE. 2. S.T.D. CONTRACTED BY ENGAGING IN THE **VENETIAN-STYLE**.

VESSEL 1. A HOLLOW OBJECT CAPABLE OF CONTAINING STUFF. e.g. GOBLETS, BOWLS, AND VASES. 2. THAT WHICH YOU MAY "POP" WHEN YOU DISCOVER HOW EXPENSIVE GLASSMAKING CAN BE.

WRAP PROCESS OF ADDING A HOT BLOB OF GLASS AROUND ANOTHER PIECE OF GLASS. CAN

BE ORNAMENTAL - SUCH AS IN THE CASE OF THREADING OR AS A PRECAUTIONARY METHOD SUCH AS FOR **NECK OR PUNTY WRAPS**.

YOKE A PLACE TO SET YOUR PIPE OR PUNTY DURING REHEATS AT THE GLORY HOLE. OFTEN CONSTRUCTED OF A SET OF BEARINGS (ALLOWING YOU TO TURN THE ROD WITHOUT MUCH RESISTANCE) WHICH ARE MOUNTED ON SOME SORT OF FIXED STAND, OR MOBILIZED UNIT.

ZANFIRICO FANCY CANE.

ZIMMERMAN 1. MANUFACTURER OF COLORED GLASS - LOCATED IN GERMANY. 2. JEFF. AN AMERICAN GLOBE-TROTTIN' GLASSBLOWER WHO MAKES COOL OBJECTS - AND THE LAST NAME IN THIS GLOSSARY.

BALLAD OF THE UNSUNG HEREOS

AN ODE TO THE GLASSBLOWERS HANDS.

O' THESE HANDS OF MINE
CALLOUSED, WORN, BEATEN AND USED.
IF THEY COULD TALK, THEY WOULD SCREAM!
THE MILES OF STEEL THEY'VE ROLLED,
THE HEAT AND BURNS - PAINFUL MEMORIES LOST
TO THE COUNTLESS SCARS, CUTS, AND ABRASIONS
THAT LOG TIME LIKE RINGS OF A TREE.
ONE RED MARK WANES AS ANOTHER WAXES...
WHERE DO THEY COME FROM?
WHERE DO THEY GO?...

I DON'T HAVE TIME FOR INFECTION SKIP THE STITCHES... FETCH ME A BUTTERFLY N' SOME DUCT-TAPE AND BACK ON THE STICK.

SILENT SERVANTS. OBEYING UNHEARD COMMANDS. SURE THEY COMPLAIN FROM TIME-TO-TIME AND SOMETIMES DON'T DO WHAT THEY ARE TOLD.

BUT...THEY'RE FINE, O' THESE HANDS OF MINE...

Source Directory

Listed below are some of the more popular goods and outlets for glassblowing-related activities. This is by no means complete. If you'd like your product or school mentioned, please contact me (at the address on page 2), and I'll do my best to include it in the next book.

📚 Books => For the best selection, make a pilgrimage... → GO TO THE RAKOW LIBRARY! at the Corning Museum of Glass (in Corning New York)

Beginning Glassblowing   by Edward T. Schmid   120 pages
$24.95   Glass Mountain Press.   927 Yew St. Bellingham, WA 98226   www.glassmtn.com

This is the second edition of "Ed's Big Handbook of Glassblowing" - bigger and better than ever! It has been revised, updated, and now sports an index making it easier to find what you need. Great for teaching and training assistants, it covers all of the info you need to know to start blowing glass.

Glass Notes   by Henry Halem   290 pages
ph. 330·673·8632   fax. 330·677·2488
$30.00   Franklin Mills Press   P.O. Box 906   Kent, OH   44240   www.glassnotes.com

Information on building glass equipment, technical sections dealing with glass chemistry, annealing, casting and assorted glassmaking methods. Henry's latest edition is the best yet and easily worth every penny.

A Glassblower's Companion   by Dudley F. Giberson, Jr.   136 pages
ph. 603·456·3569   fax. 603·456·2138
$35.00   Joppa Press   P.O. Box 202   Warner, NH 03278   www.joppaglass.com

Information on building and maintaining various glassmaking equipment such as furnaces, glory holes and annealers, with interesting historical footnotes.

Contemporary Lampworking   by Bandhu Scott Dunham   500+ pages
ph. 800·515·7281   fax 928·541·9670
$49.95   Salusa Glassworks   P.O. Box 2354 Prescott, AZ 86302   www.salusaglassworks.com
(two volume set)

Bandhu's book is the most comprehensive lampworking book to date. There's a lot of information which will carry-over into furnace working as well. It's got everything you need to know about working on a torch, plus some inspirational quotes to boot. Now in it's 3rd edition.

Firing Schedules for Glass   The Kiln Companion   by Graham Stone   224 pages
fax (613) or (03) 9598 0176   e-mail: stoneg@melbpc.org.au
Approx. $59.00   Graham Stone   20 Sydenham St Highett Vic 3190, Australia

Another 'must-have' book for any studio using hot or "warm" glass processes. It fully covers all aspects of annealing glass, in addition to giving you specific examples and schedules for many types of glass. Take the mystery and guesswork out of annealing and produce glasswork free of stress.

📖 Book Dealers

Whitehouse-Books.com   ph. 800·935·8536   e-mail: julia@whitehouse-books.com
PO Box 16   fax 607·936·2465
Corning, NY 14830

They carry one of the best selections of current and out-of-print books on glass and ceramics in the country. Videos, such as the must see "Glass India" by Norman Faulkner are also available amongst a host of other titles. Give Julia a call, she may have what you're looking for.

Lightwriters
834 Bach Street   ph 847·291·4160   www.lightwriters.com
Northbrook, IL 60062   fax 847·291·6865

ORGANIZATIONS

The Glass Art Society - G.A.S.

1305 Fourth Avenue Suite 711
Seattle, WA 98101-2401
ph 206·382·1305
fax 206·382·2630   www.glassart.org

This international organization is dedicated to bringing glass artists together and sharing information. Their annual conferences are always fun and informative, their membership truly global. If you haven't done so already, consider joining: G.A.S. can connect you with tons of glass shops, schools, galleries, collectors and more.

Glass Art Association of Canada - G.A.A.C.

Box 475
Saltspring Island, BC V8K 2W1
CANADA
www.glassartcanada.ca

SCHOOLS

The Studio at the Corning Museum of Glass

One Museum Way
Corning, New York 14830
ph 607·974·6467
fax 607·974·6370   www.thestudio@cmog.org

New renovations to the hot shop and lampworking facalities make this school bigger and better-than-ever! Access to the museum and the Rakow Library truly make this a unique and informative glass learning enviornment.

Pilchuck Glass School

430 Yale Avenue North ← (main office)   or →   1201 316th St. N.W. ← (summer campus)
Seattle, WA 98109-5431   Stanwood, WA 98292
ph 206·621·8422   ph 360-445-3111
fax 206·621·0713   fax 360-445-5515
www.pilchuck.com

Thirty summers and still smokin'! Pilchuck is an amazing enviornment to study glassmaking and connect with other glass artists. It's expensive, but worth attending at least one session to understand what everyone's talking about, who knows?... It may change your life...
— It did mine.

Penland School of Crafts

P.O. Box 37
Penland, NC 28765
ph 828·765·2359
fax 828·765·7389
www.penland.org

This school has been around for "ages & ages". Not just for the study of glass, but for many art disciplines. Check 'em out.

Haystack Mountain School of Crafts

PO Box 518
Deer Isle, ME 04627
ph 207·348·2306
fax 207·348·2307   www.haystack-mtn.org

Since 1950 this school has been attracting professional artists and students to work and study in beautiful coastal Maine. They too, offer courses in many different media.

SCHOOLS CONTINUED

Pratt Fine Arts Center
1902 South Main Street
Seattle, WA 98144
ph 206.328.2200
fax 206.328.1260
www.pratt.org

Bullseye Connection
1308 N.W. Everett
Portland, OR 97209
ph 503.227.2797
fax 503.227.2993
www.bullseye-glass.com

Gossamer Glass Inspiration Farm
617 East Laurel Road
Bellingham, WA 98226
ph 360-398.7061
fax 360.398.2142
www.inspirationfarm.com

Eugene Glass School
575 Wilson Street
Eugene OR 97403
ph 541.342.2959
fax 541.342.2924
www.eugeneglassschool.org

Urban Glass
647 Fulton Street
Brooklyn, NY 11217-1112
ph 718.625.3685
fax 718.625.3889
www.urbanglass.org

Hands-On Glass
Corning, NY 14830
ph/fax 607.962.3044
www.handsonglass.com

Steinert Glass School at Plum Creek
1393 Mogadore Road
Kent OH 44240
ph 330.677.0729
fax 330.677.1731
www.steinertindustries.com

Glass Impact
1611 2nd Avenue
Rock Island IL 61201
ph 309.793.1611
fax 309.732.4030
www.glassimpact.com

Bildwerk Frauenau
Frauenau D-94258
Germany
ph/fax (49) 9926.18.92.47
www.bild-werk-frauenau.de

Glass Mountain Studios
927 Yew Street
Bellingham, WA 98226
ph/fax 360.733.3497
www.glassmtn.com

Firehouse No. 12
518 Main Street
Vancouver WA 98660
ph 360.695.2660
fax 360.695.2684
www.firehouseno12.com

Public Glass
1750 Armstrong Avenue
San Francisco CA 94124
ph 415-671.4916
fax 415-671.4917
www.publicglass.org

Red Deer College
Contact: Anne Brodie
P.O. Box 5005
Red Deer AB
T4N 5H5
Canada
ph 403.542.3130
or: 888.886.2787
e-mail: anne.brodie@rdc.ab.ca

This small school/studio has been around for years and just seems to get better and better. It's less expensive to study there than most programs and offers a wide variety of classes throughout the summer. Give Anne a call, and tell her Ed sent you.

Many of the schools listed above offer scholarships and/or fellowships. Some have internships as well. Be sure to inquire about them when contacting each institution.

One of the best fellowship programs exists at C.G.C.A. Call or write them for details. It was one of the most productive three months of my life when I (finally) received a fellowship there.

The Creative Glass Center of America - C.G.C.A.
1501 Glasstown Road
Millville, NJ 08332
ph 856.825.6800 ext. 2733
fax 856.825.2410
www.creativeglasscenter.com

If at first you don't succeed... keep on applying! It's free! (It took me 6 years of trying before I got "in" to C.G.C.A.) Perseverance pays off. Just keep on making better work and getting the best possible slides of it as you can.

Color, Batch, & Such...

Spruce-Pine Batch
P.O. Box 159
Spruce Pine, NC 28777
ph 828.765.9876
www.sprucepinebatch.com

popular source of batch, color and adhesives

C&R Loo Inc.
1085 Essex Avenue
Richmond, CA 94801
ph 800.227.1780
fax 800.932.7810
www.crloo.com

large supplier of color and glass products

Spectrum Glass Co. Inc.
P.O. Box 646
Woodinville, WA 98072-0646
ph 425.483.6699
fax 425.483.9007
www.SpectrumGlass.com

Nice cullet with a wide variety of compatible colors also available.

Olympic Color Rods
818 John Street
Seattle, WA 98109
ph 800.445.7742
fax 888.880.RODS
www.glasscolor.com

Mountains of color and accessories for all your glassblowing needs.

Bullseye Glass Co.
3722 S.E. 21st Avenue
Portland, OR 97202
ph 503.232.8887
fax 503.238.9963

A popular stained glass producer with many additional forms of glass for warm and hot processes.

Uroboros Glass
2139 N Kerby Avenue
Portland, OR 97227
ph 503.284.4900
fax 503.284.7584
www.uroboros.com

Supplier of fusible glass colors in many shapes and forms

East Bay Batch & Color
169 South First Street
Richmond, CA 94804
ph 800.322.6567
fax 888.442.3337
www.eastbaycolor.com
Specialty batch, color & more!

Gabbert Cullet Co.
P.O. Box 63
Williamstown, WV 26187
ph 304.375.6435

Long time favorite for cullet.

Safety Glasses
Aura Lens Products
Robert Aurellus
51 - 8th Street North
Sauk Rapids, MN 56379
ph 800.281.2872
fax 320.253.1239
www.auralens.com

Bob's glasses aren't "cheap", (neither are replacements for your eyes...) - but they are some of the best at what they do. I own two pair, one for furnace working and another for lampworking.

Hand Tools, Pipes, & More

Jim Moore Tools for Glass
PO Box 1151
Port Townsend, WA 98368
ph 360.379.2936

Steinert Industries Inc.
1507 Franklin Avenue
Kent, OH 44240
ph 800.727.7473
fax 330.678.8238
www.steinertindustries.com

Spiral Arts
430 South 96th St #5
Seattle, WA 98108
ph 206.768.9765
fax 206.768.9766
e-mail fmetz@spiralarts.com

For Burners, Elements & A Host of Other Stuff:
Dudley F. Giberson Jr.
JoppaGlassworks.com
Box 202
Warner NH 03278
ph 603.456.3569
fax 603.456.2138

Carlo Doná
Calle Berovier, I/A
30141 Murano, Venice Italy
ph/fax 041-739257

Putsch
PO Box 5128
Asheville, NC 28813
ph 800.847.8427

Palmer Tools
10506 Crestridge Dr
Minnetonka, MN 55305-1610
ph 952.546.6025

Hub Consolidated, Inc.
P.O. Box 175
Weston, VT 05161
ph 802.824.4255
fax 802.824.4209
www.hubglass.com

Wet Dog Glass
New Orleans LA 70122
ph 504.286.9529
fax 504.283.9324
www.wetdogglass.com

Cutting Edge Products
P.O. Box 3809
Chico, CA 95927
ph 530.342.1970
fax 530.342.0771
www.cuttingedgeprdx.com

Wale Apparatus Co. Inc.
PO Box D
Hellertown, PA 18055
ph 800.334.9253
fax 610.838.7440
www.waleapparatus.com

Paradise Paints
David Hopper
2902 Neal Road
Paradise, CA 95969
ph 530.872.5020
fax 530.872.5052
www.paradise-co.com

INDEX

A
AIR MARVER 16, 17
   QUALITY 273
AMPHORA 75-81, 301
ANNEALER 10, 301, 33
   see also TOP LOADER, FRONT-LOADER, pick-up
AVENTURINE 301
AVOLIO 139-41, 301

B
BALLAD OF THE UNSUNG HEREOS 309
BALLOTTINI 173, 174-5
BALLS, CHRISTMAS 296
BAR see COLOR
BATCH 274, 301
BENCHBLOW 301
BIT 301
BITWORK 51, 162
BLANK
   see GRAALS
BLOCKING 19-21
   LARGE GLASS 66
   SOLO 254
BLOCKS 282
BLOMDAHL, SONJA 121
BLOW 'N' CAP explained 18
BLOWN FOOT 142-7
   SIMPLE 39
BLOWPIPES 279
   CLEANING 279
   STRAIGHTENING 280-1
   BUYING 280
BOOKS 310
BOTTLES
   FOR HOMEBREW 235, 300
   PERFUME 296
BOTTOM see also FEET
   FLATTENING 71
BOWLS 36-7, 301
BOX 301 see also ANNEALER
BOX IT! see above, 74, 33

C
BUENO, THOR 130, 301
BULLSEYE 42, 301
   GLASS CO. 312, 313
BURNS 272
BUSINESS 293-5
BUTTON 71, 301

CAMEO 104, 125, 301
CANE 167-9, 301
   PICK-UP, COLLAR 187
   , BUBBLE 183
   , VIA OPTIC MOLD 171
   , CANE MARVER 183
   , PASTORALE 172
   STYLES OF: 173
   USING 170
   DRAWING 120
CASE 55, 102, 125, 301
CAP 18, 301, 54, 68
C.G.C.A. 312
CHAMPAGNE GLASS
   BUBBLE-STYLE 193
   CANE 187-192
CHARGE 120, 301
CHIHULY, DALE 116, 301
CHILL MARKS 70
CIOF' see PACIOFFIS
COILS 263
COLLAR 98
COLOR 94-129
   BUBBLE OVERLAY 104
   CUP OVERLAY 102
   FRITS 112
   GRADATION 102, 110
   MAKING A COLLAR FOR 98
   PREHEATING 96
   POWDERS 108
   SHARDS 113
   THREADING 116
   SUPPLIERS 313
COMBING 118
CONE 8
CORD(S) 302
CORNING 44, 295, 302
   STUDIO AT 311

CRACKLE see QUENCH
CRESSWELL, SONNY 256
CRISTALLO 134
   -CUP BLUES 166
CRIMPS 302 see also TWEEZERS
CRUCIBLE 302
CULLET 302
CUP ASSEMBLY - PART I 164
                 PART II 165
CUTS 272
CYLINDER 8
   LARGE 63-74

D
DAY TANK 302
DESIGN 13, 135, 289
DEVITRIFY 302
DIAMOND SHEARS 285, 302
DICHROIC 302
DIDYNIUM 275, 302
DIP 14
DIP 'N' BLOW 266
DIP 'N' STRIP 64, 302
DRAGON-STEM GOBLET 299
DUCK-BILL SHEARS 303

E
EARTH BLOW 228
ELEMENTS (electrical) 303
ELECTRIC KOOL-AID BOWL 182
ENAMEL 270, 308
ENVIRONMENTAL CONCERNS 277
ERGONOMICS 65, 275-6
EYE SAFETY 275

F
FEATHERING 118
FEET
   BLOWN - SIMPLE 39
   VENETIAN-STYLE 142-7
   COOKIE 38
   VARIATIONS OF: 138-41
FILE - ASSORTED THOUGHTS... 88

FILIGRANA 173, 303
FINING 303
FINISHING TOOL 284, 300
FIRE 276
FLASH 303
FLASK 268
   FOR MOLDMAKING 236, 303
FLATTEN(ING)
   THE BOTTOM 71
   BUBBLES 267-8
FLOOR MODEL 303
FLOWERS 214-7
FOOT - see FEET
FRIGGER 303
FRIT 112
FRONT LOADER 127, 303
FUME 303, 62

G
GAFFER 60-1, 303
GALLE 118
GARAGE 183, 303
G.A.S. 303, 312
GATHERING 14-5, 18-9, 303
   POST 240
GIBERSON, DUDLEY F. 313
GIBEAU, MARK 286
GLASS 304
   BLIG 304
      THE GAME 132
   INDIA 233, 310
   NOTES 310
GOBLET, 304
   BOWLS 148-9
   BASIC 150-2
   STYLES 138
   see also VENETIAN TECHNIQUES
GOSSAMER GLASS 312
GRAAL 125-9, 304
GRAVITY 16, 304
GUDENRATH, BILL 255

H
HANDLES 44-58
   BLOWN 54-5
   COLORED 55
   FACTORS AFFECTING 57
   FLAT 52
   GARAGED 55
   MULTIPLE 50

HANDLES cont.
   OPTIC 51
   PRO'S & CONS 56
   ROMAN/SPLIT 53
HANDS-ON-GLASS 312
HAYSTACK 62, 311
HEALTH & SAFETY 272-7
HEAT EXPOSURE 272-3
HEAVY GLASS 65, 275-6
HOLES 250-4
HOLMWOOD, JEFF 182
HOPPER, DAVID 130, 304

I
INCALMO 121-4, 304
INCLUSION 304
INSTRUCTION 292
IRIDIZE 110, 304

J
JACKS & MISC. 282-3
   see also NECK(ING)
JUMBO GLASS 298-9

K
KILN see ANNEALER, PICK-UP
KIRKPATRICK, JOEY 120
KUGLER 95-101, 304
   OVEN 10, 96, 304

L
LABINO, DOMINICK 102
LAMPWORKING 114, 304, 310
LARGE GLASS 63
   BLOCKING 66
   HANDLING 64
   MARVERING 68
   NECKING 67
   VASE - AMPHORA 75
"LATTICINO" 304 - see CANE INSTEAD.
LINO see TAGLIAPIETRA
LIP 304
   WRAP 153, 304
LIPOFSKY, MARVIN 232
LITTLETON, HARVEY 102

M
MACE, FLORA 120
MAESTRO 314
MARIONI, DANTE 60, 170
   , PAUL 116

MARQUIS, RICHARD 92, 170, 176, 304
MARVER(ING) 21-3, 68-9, 305
   CANE 183
   PAPER 70
   SOLO 257
MERESE 207, 209, 305, 141
MEYERS, JOEL PHILIP 116
MEZZO STAMPO 155
MILLEFIORE(I) 182
MISCONCEPTIONS 290
MT. ST. HELENS ASH 305
MOILE / PUNTY WRAP 80
MOLDBLOW(ING) 227-40, 305
   METAL 234-5
   OPTIC 154-7
   PLASTER 235
   SPINNING 233
   WOOD 231-4
MONTAGE 269, 305
MOORE, BEN 116
   JIM 278, 305, 313 282
MURANO 134-5, 305
MURRINE 176-82, 305
   CHECKERBOARD 181
   FIGURES 176-8
   LETTERS 179-80
   OPTIC 182
   PORTRAIT 181
   SPIRAL 180

N
NECK(ING) 25-6, 305
   LARGE GLASS 67
   ON THE MARVER 69
   WRAP 305, 80
NEWSPAPER 12
   see PAPER(ING)
NOISE 273

O
OPTIC 305
   MOLD 154-7, 228
   MURRINE 182
OVERLAY 305
   BUBBLE 104-7
   COLOR 99-101
   CUP 102-3

P
PACIOFFIS 283, 305, 79
PAD 305
PADDLE 305, 71, 79

PAINTS – see PARADISE
PAPER(ING) 23, 305
    MARVER 70
    TEAM STYLE 66, 78
PAPER WEIGHTS 242-5
PARADISE PAINTS 130-1, 305, 313
PARISON 305
PARRIOTT, CHARLES 239
PASTORALE 137, 170, 172, 305
PENLAND 62, 306, 310
PERFUME BOTTLES 296
PICK-UP(S) 114-6, 306
PI DIVIDER 172, 306, 109
PIGGY BANK 297
PILCHUCK 62, 306, 310
PINEAPPLE MOLD 157
PIPE(S)
    BUYING 281
    COOLER 306, 65
    MAINTENANCE 279
    PASSING 82
    STRAIGHTENING 280-1
    UNCLOGGING 279
    WARMER 306
PONY – pulling one 218-20
POST GATHERING 240
POWDER(S) 108, 306
    BOOTH 110
    SIFTING 109
PRATT 312
PRODUCTION 293, 306
PRUNT 306, 56
PUFFER – see SOFFIETTA
PUNTETTO 306, 84
PUNTIES 83-93
    GOBLET 84
    BLOWPIPE-AS A – 92-3
    CROWN 89
    DOME 85
    DOUGHNUT 87
    2-3 PRONG 91
    SAND 86
    SCULPTURE 90, 226
    WRAP 80
PYROMETER 306

Q
QUENCH 110-11

R
RAKE 307
RED DEER COLLEGE 311
REDUCTION 110, 307
REHEAT 307
REICHENBACH 307
RETICELLO 197-201, 307
    SIMPLIFIED 202-3
RHODE ISLAND SCHOOL OF DESIGN 264
RINGS 248-9
RISD RING 264
ROMAN RING 264
RONDELS 42-3, 307
ROYAL, RICHARD 129, 307

S
SCALE
SCAVO 111
SCUDGE 307, 101
SCULPTING 221
SEED(S) 307
SET-UP 11
SHARDS 113-6, 307
SHEARS 286-9
    CLEANING 12
    SHARPENING 286-9
SHIELD 246-7, 307
SIGNORETTO, PINO 213, 307
SKETCHBOOK 289
SLUMP 307, 114
SNORKELING 261-2
SOAK 307
SOFFIETTA 73, 123, 191, 307
SOLO BLOWING 255-60
SOLID CORE SCULPTING 221
SOLIDWORKING, intro to 212
    FLOWER 214-7
    PONY 218-20
    TORSO 222-5
SPECIAL ED SECTION 300
SPHERE 8
SPRINGS see COILS 263
SPOUTS 252
SQUAT (form) 9
START 11, the 16
STEAMSTICK 265, 307
STEINERT 307, 313
STEMS 158-9
    BLOWN 160
    DRAGON 299
    SOLID 161

STIFF 307, 55
STONE(S) 308
STONE COLD 15, 128, 308
STRIKE(ING) 308
STUDIO BASIC LAYOUT 10
    @ CORNING MUSEUM 311
SURFACE-MIX 77, 308
    -TECHNIQUES 270

T
TAGLIAPIETRA, LINO 62, 121, 308
TEACHING 291
TEAMWORK 59-82
    HISTORY OF, 61
    LARGE GLASS 63
THERMAL SHOCK 28, 308, 88
THREAD(ING) 116-9, 308
TIFFANY 116, 117
TOOLS 278-89
TOP LOADER 126, 308
TORCHING 72, 75-8
    TIPS ON- 76-8
    TYPES OF 76-8
TRANSFER 27, 308, 88
    LARGE GLASS 72
    SOLO 258
    VENETIAN-STYLE 152
TRIMMING 30-3, 191, 195
TUMBLER 308
TWEEZERS 285-6, 308
    CLEANING 12

U
U/V 230, 135, 308
UNDERCUT 230, 308
URBAN GLASS 312

V
VACUUM-FORMING 244-5
VASES 34-5
VENETIAN-STYLE 308
    -TECHNIQUES 133-211
    -VIRUS 308, 62
VENTILATION 274
VESSEL 308

W
WAX
    BEES 11, 12, 282
    JACK 239

Willenbrink, Karen 213, 214
Wineglass 183-6
Wrap 308
  Neck/Moile 80

Y

Yoke 309
  Mobile 10, 63

Z

Zanfirico 174-5, 309
Zimmerman 309

BACKWORD

Well, ... there it is. I hope that there's enough stuff to keep you busy and your wheels spinning. If, however, I've managed to leave out the techniques you're really interested in, let me know. I'll do my best to look into it, and if enough people wanna see it (or if it's really cool...) I'll try to include it in the next edition. Feel free to write me with your comments and suggestions.

All the best with the glass!
Ed Schmid

GLASS MOUNTAIN PRESS
927 YEW STREET
BELLINGHAM, WA 98226

ABOUT THE AUTHOR

Ed Schmid has been working with hot glass (more or less) since 1984. He received his M.F.A. from the Ohio State University in 1990. He wrote "Ed's Big Handbook of Glassblowing" as a precursor to the book that's in your hands, in 1993. He has taught numerous workshops and courses accross the United States, and most recently Canada. His work may be found in several museums, collections, and refrigerators globally. (Ed is also an award-winning brewer of meads and beers.)

For the past ten years he has participated in summer sessions at the Pilchuck Glass School - in many different capacities.

Together with Elena Enos he owns and operates Glass Mountain Studios in Bellingham, Washington.

NOTES

THE LAST WORD

persevere.